87249

UG
1242
.D7
D755
2016

Drones /

W9-CHP-622

DATE DUE

			PRINTED IN U.S.A.

Current
CONTROVERSIES

| Drones

Other Books in the Current Controversies Series

Current
CONTROVERSIES

Drones

Tamara Thompson, Book Editor

GREENHAVEN PRESS
A part of Gale, Cengage Learning

GALE
CENGAGE Learning®

Farmington Hills, Mich • San Francisco • New York • Waterville, Maine
Meriden, Conn • Mason, Ohio • Chicago

Judy Galens, *Manager, Frontlist Acquisitions*

© 2016 Greenhaven Press, a part of Gale, Cengage Learning

Gale and Greenhaven Press are registered trademarks used herein under license.

For more information, contact:
Greenhaven Press
27500 Drake Rd.
Farmington Hills, MI 48331-3535
Or you can visit our Internet site at gale.cengage.com

For product information and technology assistance, contact us at

Gale Customer Support, 1-800-877-4253
For permission to use material from this text or product, submit all requests online at www.cengage.com/permissions

Further permissions questions can be emailed to permissionrequest@cengage.com

Articles in Greenhaven Press anthologies are often edited for length to meet page requirements. In addition, original titles of these works are changed to clearly present the main thesis and to explicitly indicate the author's opinion. Every effort is made to ensure that Greenhaven Press accurately reflects the original intent of the authors. Every effort has been made to trace the owners of copyrighted material.

Cover image © Alexander Kolomietz/Shutterstock.com.

LIBRARY OF CONGRESS CATALOGING-IN-PUBLICATION DATA

Drones / Tamara Thompson, book editor.
    pages cm. -- (Current controversies)
    Includes bibliographical references and index.
    ISBN 978-0-7377-7422-1 (hardcover) -- ISBN 978-0-7377-7423-8 (pbk.)
    1. Drone aircraft--United States. 2. Drone aircraft--Moral and ethical aspects--United States. 3. Drone aircraft--Government policy--United States. I. Thompson, Tamara.
    UG1242.D7D755 2015
    358.4'183--dc23
                                2015026925

Printed in Mexico
1 2 3 4 5 6 7 20 19 18 17 16

Contents

Chapter 2: Should the Military Be Allowed to Use Drones?

Because drones can monitor targeted individuals over time and establish patterns of behavior, they are more likely to correctly identify their targets and can be more selective about the time of engagement, hence reducing civilian casualties. The argument that drones kill too many innocent civilians is not supported by recent facts.

No: The Military Should Not Be Allowed to Use Drones

Chapter 3: Should Domestic Law Enforcement Agencies Be Allowed to Use Drones?

Yes: Domestic Law Enforcement Agencies Should Be Allowed to Use Drones

Chapter 4: Should Commercial Drone Use Be Allowed?

No: Commercial Drone Use Should Not Be Allowed

Foreword

B y definition, controversies are "discussions of questions in which opposing opinions clash" (*Webster's Twentieth Century Dictionary Unabridged*). Few would deny that controversies are a pervasive part of the human condition and exist on virtually every level of human enterprise. Controversies transpire between individuals and among groups, within nations and between nations. Controversies supply the grist necessary for progress by providing challenges and challengers to the status quo. They also create atmospheres where strife and warfare can flourish. A world without controversies would be a peaceful world; but it also would be, by and large, static and prosaic.

The Series' Purpose

The purpose of the Current Controversies series is to explore many of the social, political, and economic controversies dominating the national and international scenes today. Titles selected for inclusion in the series are highly focused and specific. For example, from the larger category of criminal justice, Current Controversies deals with specific topics such as police brutality, gun control, white collar crime, and others. The debates in Current Controversies also are presented in a useful, timeless fashion. Articles and book excerpts included in each title are selected if they contribute valuable, long-range ideas to the overall debate. And wherever possible, current information is enhanced with historical documents and other relevant materials. Thus, while individual titles are current in focus, every effort is made to ensure that they will not become quickly outdated. Books in the Current Controversies series will remain important resources for librarians, teachers, and students for many years.

In addition to keeping the titles focused and specific, great care is taken in the editorial format of each book in the series. Book introductions and chapter prefaces are offered to provide background material for readers. Chapters are organized around several key questions that are answered with diverse opinions representing all points on the political spectrum. Materials in each chapter include opinions in which authors clearly disagree as well as alternative opinions in which authors may agree on a broader issue but disagree on the possible solutions. In this way, the content of each volume in Current Controversies mirrors the mosaic of opinions encountered in society. Readers will quickly realize that there are many viable answers to these complex issues. By questioning each author's conclusions, students and casual readers can begin to develop the critical thinking skills so important to evaluating opinionated material.

Current Controversies is also ideal for controlled research. Each anthology in the series is composed of primary sources taken from a wide gamut of informational categories including periodicals, newspapers, books, US and foreign government documents, and the publications of private and public organizations. Readers will find factual support for reports, debates, and research papers covering all areas of important issues. In addition, an annotated table of contents, an index, a book and periodical bibliography, and a list of organizations to contact are included in each book to expedite further research.

Perhaps more than ever before in history, people are confronted with diverse and contradictory information. During the Persian Gulf War, for example, the public was not only treated to minute-to-minute coverage of the war, it was also inundated with critiques of the coverage and countless analyses of the factors motivating US involvement. Being able to sort through the plethora of opinions accompanying today's major issues, and to draw one's own conclusions, can be a

complicated and frustrating struggle. It is the editors' hope
that Current Controversies will help readers with this struggle.

Introduction

> *"There are as many potential uses for drones as there are types of them, so whether drone technology should be considered a positive thing or a dangerous thing depends very much on who one asks."*

Even when technology has the power to dramatically reshape the world—like atomic energy or the Internet—it is still frequently regarded as being neutral, meaning the technology itself is considered neither inherently good nor bad and its impact depends entirely on how it is used.

Such is certainly the case for drones, a catch-all term that represents a wide array of remotely controlled, unmanned aerial vehicles—typically outfitted with cameras—that range greatly in shape and size. Some drones are as small as an insect or shaped like a flying saucer, while others are as big as a standard airplane and look like one as well.

There are as many potential uses for drones as there are types of them, so whether drone technology should be considered a positive thing or a dangerous thing depends very much on who one asks. Each type of drone use comes with its own set of potential benefits and problems, and as with other emerging technologies, unforeseen consequences may reveal themselves as the technology is further developed and more widely adopted.

To the military, drones are an important modern weapon that allows the United States to conduct essential surveillance and carry out targeted killings of terrorists in faraway lands without risking the lives of US service members. The military credits the US drone strike program with eliminating thousands of suspected Islamic militants and believes drones are a vital element of national security that could one day replace manned aircraft entirely.

To human rights advocates and antiwar activists, however, military drones are killing machines that indiscriminately terrorize indigenous communities and kill people who present little or no risk to the United States, including countless civilians. The ease and anonymity of using drones, they say, allows the military to take lives without the due process of law or a congressional declaration of war and without sufficient transparency, accountability, or oversight.

To domestic law enforcement agencies, drones are a new and powerful tool for finding missing persons in rugged terrain, providing aerial views of hostage standoffs, tracking fleeing crime suspects, and searching for survivors following natural disasters. Drones are especially attractive to law enforcement because they cost a fraction of what helicopters or planes cost to operate and they keep officers out of harm's way.

To many Americans, however, the use of drones by police raises serious questions about their potential for invasions of privacy, illegal searches, mass surveillance, and even weaponization. Critics fear law-enforcement drones will eventually be used to conduct routine warrantless surveillance, monitor lawful activity, and be used to troll for evidence of crimes in incidental video and images gathered during drone flights for other purposes.

Public backlash on the issue prompted the Seattle Police Department to abandon its nascent drone program in 2013—one of the few selectively permitted by the Federal Aviation Administration (FAA)—and many state and local governments have preemptively banned or significantly restricted the use of law-enforcement drones since then.

Similarly, the use of military-style spy drones by the US Customs and Border Protection agency to conduct surveillance for illegal immigration, drug smuggling, and border security has generated backlash about their potential use and misuse against American citizens, to the extent that some states and local governments have enacted laws banning government drones in their airspace.

That such strong negative sentiment has taken hold even before drones have been widely adopted by American law enforcement—indeed, even before the FAA has enacted guidelines for their use—is quite telling of the mixed feelings Americans have about drone technology. Because while the public is clearly wary of drones in the hands of law enforcement and government entities, consumers are going crazy for small, inexpensive hobby drones, and interest in using them for commercial purposes is massive.

To consumers, cheap and easy-to-fly quadcopter drones are a popular and fun way to shoot photos or video and play with technology, so much so that in 2015 global sales of consumer drones hit 4.3 million units worth about $1.7 billion—a 167 percent sales spike in just two years. But those same hobby drones can be put to endless commercial uses, which have traditionally been prohibited by the FAA.

The market for commercial drones is poised to explode, however, pending the expected September 2015 enactment of new FAA regulations that for the first time specify how and when commercial drones may be used. The FAA estimates that one hundred thousand commercial drones could take to the skies by 2017 under its new rules, which won't be broad enough to allow for the delivery of goods in most cases. (See chapter 4 for more on commercial drone use.) The FAA's regulations can't come a moment too soon for many.

To businesses, industries, and entrepreneurs nationwide, drones represent a giant leap forward in efficiency, economy, and ability. The Hollywood film industry has been clamoring to use drones for years, as have commercial photographers of all stripes. Journalists want them for live traffic reports and other newsgathering tasks, while real estate agents are eager to give their clients a drone-eye-view of listed properties. Fire departments are eyeing drones to map wildfires, monitor the position of fire crews, and assess the safety of burning buildings. Wildlife groups favor drones to prevent poaching and count animals, and the agriculture industry wants drones to keep an eye on crops and livestock and to monitor water and soil conditions. Topographical mapping, geographic surveys, and oil and gas exploration are just a few of the many other important roles that drones are expected to play in this new growth industry that will soon become an economic powerhouse. The Association for Unmanned Vehicle Systems International (AUVSI), a pro-drone industry group, estimates that drones will create more than one hundred thousand new jobs by 2025 and generate some $82.1 billion in economic benefit between 2015 and 2025.[1]

To others, though, a sky filled with drones means a sky filled with risk and danger.

When drones malfunction and fall, they can badly injure people, and drone operators can make dangerous piloting mistakes that jeopardize safety as well. There have already been cases of athletes being hit by drones filming their sporting events, drones crashing into buildings, and a variety of other incidents in which individuals' hair or hands got caught in drone rotors. Of special concern is that, despite being prohibited near airports, hobby drones have already been involved in dozens of documented near misses with commercial aircraft, a potentially deadly interaction.

To sexual predators and other criminals, drones are an easy way to watch children, case houses, peep in windows, deal drugs, and keep lookout for the police during a crime. Officials also worry that consumer drones could be turned

1. Darryl Jenkins and Bijan Vasigh, "The Economic Impact of Unmanned Aircraft Systems Integration in the United States," Association for Unmanned Vehicle Systems International, March 2013. https://higherlogicdownload.s3.amazonaws.com/AUVSI /958c920a-7f9b-4ad2-9807-f9a4e95d1ef1/UploadedImages/New_Economic%20Report %202013%20Full.pdf.

into weapons or that terrorists could use them to gather intelligence and deliver explosives to targets within the United States.

Nevertheless, with the demand for domestic drones so strong and the FAA set to release rules for their operation, their widespread use is all but inevitable for law enforcement, government agencies, commercial enterprises, and consumers alike. Regardless of how drones are ultimately used, they clearly represent a revolutionary technology that is destined to reshape the world.

The authors in *Current Controversies: Drones* present a wide variety of viewpoints about the promises and perils of drones and explore the questions of whether their use by law enforcement, consumers, businesses, and the military should be permitted.

CHAPTER 1

Why Are Drones Controversial?

Overview: Do Drones Promise Protection or Peril?

Margaret Steen

Margaret Steen is a contributing writer for Emergency Management *magazine.*

Imagine giving firefighters the ability to identify hot spots in a wildfire, through real-time images, without risking the lives of staff members—or helping search and rescue teams scan a large area quickly for survivors after a disaster.

The technology to do this exists and is being used by some public safety agencies already with unmanned aerial vehicles. But UAVs (unmanned aerial vehicles) have drawbacks, as well. Some agencies are adopting them, but concerns about safety, regulation and privacy are slowing the process.

UAVs are the vehicles flown by unmanned aircraft systems, or UASes, which include the aircraft and all the equipment required to control it. Both terms are used by those in the field. A more common name for them, drones, is not considered accurate by those who work most closely with the technology.

"Drones were remote-controlled aircraft that were targets for missiles," said Todd Sedlak, director of sales and flight operations and small UAS subject matter expert for Detroit Aircraft. The public sees them as "a mindless thing that does one thing." He said UAVs have the capacity "to save lives, to help people and to prevent damage to equipment, property and people."

UAVs come in all sizes: Some fit in the palm of a hand, while others are as large as full-size aircraft. There are two main types of UAVs: fixed-wing, which resemble airplanes and need runways, and vertical takeoff and landing, which can hover.

The U.S. Forest Service has been exploring potential uses of UAVs and UASes for several years, said Jennifer Jones, public affairs specialist with the agency's Washington office.

UAVs could help monitor the condition of forests, determine the effectiveness of reforestation efforts or assess damage from events such as fires, landslides or floods.

"We're very interested in this technology, and we've identified a lot of potential missions they could be used for," Jones said. "And we have used them in a few cases very successfully."

Some Examples of Use

The Forest Service used unmanned aircraft in a partnership with the California Air National Guard to fight the 2013 Rim Fire. In the response to the fire, the UAVs allowed the incident team "to view events while they were happening," said Jones. The equipment was used, for example, to verify new hot spots and detect the perimeter of the fire.

"It provided live, real-time images that could supplement those traditional nighttime infrared flights," Jones said.

The Forest Service's mission extends beyond fighting fires. There are several other ways UAVs could be used:

- Forest protection and management: UAVs could help monitor the condition of forests, determine the effectiveness of reforestation efforts or assess damage from events such as fires, landslides or floods. They could also help detect and map damage from insects, diseases and invasive plant species.

- Watershed management: UAVs could monitor the condition and boundaries of watersheds and sample air quality at various altitudes.

- Fish, wildlife and plant management: UAVs could help map habitats and survey fish and wildlife populations. They could also monitor the populations of threatened and endangered fish, wildlife and plant species.

- Law enforcement: Authorities could use UAVs to help detect activities like narcotics production and timber theft.

- Post-fire response: UAVs could help map burn severity, evaluate debris flow and monitor vegetation recovery and ongoing flooding threats to downstream communities.

The Forest Service does not have a formal program in place for using UAVs, but it does have a working group looking at how it could use the systems. There could be advantages in terms of cost, safety and flying in locations and under conditions where manned aircraft couldn't be used.

An aircraft will search every square inch that you tell it to. . . . It will never get tired; it will never get bored.

The Forest Service is not the only agency that's moving slowly on the use of UAVs. The California Department of Forestry and Fire Protection (Cal Fire) has tested them in partnership with other agencies to see if they give commanders better real-time information about fires. But Cal Fire has no plans to use unmanned aircraft regularly, though it continues to evaluate them. "We're constantly looking at new technology," said Lynne Tolmachoff, a spokesperson for Cal Fire.

One agency that has been using UAVs for several years is the Mesa County Sheriff's Office in Colorado. The program has flown more than 55 missions, totaling more than 225 flight hours.

A Multitude of Uses

Unmanned aerial vehicles (UAVs) have a number of potential uses for emergency response and public safety:

Search and rescue A UAV "can search a very large area very accurately and quickly," said Todd Sedlak, director of sales and flight operations and small UAS subject matter expert for Detroit Aircraft. This can be particularly helpful for water rescue, since a warm body in cold water shows up quickly on thermal cameras. In the mountains after an avalanche, a UAV can search in conditions where it's too dangerous to send a manned aircraft. "An aircraft will search every square inch that you tell it to," he said. "It will never get tired; it will never get bored."

Situational awareness for first responders "Let's say a SWAT team has to serve a high-risk warrant—they have the ability to have a good view of the neighborhood, and if a suspect were to flee, where they're going," Sedlak said.

Traffic control UAVs can help authorities see where traffic is backing up during a major event like a football game, or to get an aerial view of the aftermath of a traffic accident. A UAV is "a low-cost, safe and easy-to-use alternative to anything that police are already using helicopters for," Sedlak said.

There are several uncertainties and concerns regarding [UAV] use, and these have slowed some agencies' efforts.

Firefighting A UAV with a thermal camera can show whether the roof of a building has fire underneath it—a faster and safer way to make this determination than having a firefighter climb on the roof and use a hammer to find soft spots. It also can help determine what other buildings are at risk based on the wind speed and direction. In a forest fire, a

UAV's camera can see through the forest canopy to show where fire is spreading below. "This is already being done with manned aircraft," said Sedlak. "This is cheaper, faster and safer."

A Cost-Effective Answer

The sheriff's office first acquired an unmanned helicopter in 2009 and worked with the FAA to get a certificate of authorization that would allow the department to fly it. By the fall of 2010, the sheriff's office had FAA permission to use the system anywhere in the county during the day, and it expanded its tests and started using the UAV to help other agencies with aerial photos during the response to events like fires and fatal traffic accidents.

In 2012, the department tested a fixed-wing UAV, which has a longer flight time than the helicopter and could be used for more searches or fire monitoring over larger areas. Now the department is beginning to use the systems for day-to-day operations.

One of the advantages UAVs offer public safety and emergency management officials is that they can see areas that are otherwise inaccessible because of the danger to human pilots. Another big advantage is cost.

Mesa County officials estimate that the UAVs they use would cost between $25,000 and $50,000 each. (They have spent much less because they have partnerships with the manufacturers to help test the systems.) Larger systems would cost even more.

However, the costs are still much less than for flying manned aircraft. Mesa County officials project that the long-term operating costs of their UAVs is about $25 per hour. Planes and helicopters with pilots can cost between $400 and $1,200 per hour to operate.

Safety in the Spotlight

If UAVs provide such great help to public safety agencies at such a low cost, why aren't they being more quickly adopted? There are several uncertainties and concerns regarding their use, and these have slowed some agencies' efforts.

One issue is safety. UAVs are considered aircraft, and some can be quite large. This is one issue that the Forest Service's advisory group is looking at, Jones said. "Our top priority in the Forest Service is safety," she said. That includes the safety of firefighters and other agency employees, as well as the safety of the public.

"They can pose a risk to people on the ground if one of those is flying overhead and a communications link is lost," said Jones. "We've got to make sure that we can fly them safely, given the other aircraft that are often flying in fire environments."

There are other details to be worked out, as well, Jones said. "We're trying to define the mission requirements." A lot of missions can also be performed by manned aircraft, and the agency wants to determine when officials would turn to UAVs and who would operate them.

There's also some uncertainty about how UAVs will ultimately be regulated. Private citizens can buy and operate their own UAVs as a hobby, with few restrictions from the FAA as long as they are not flown too high or too close to an airport. The FAA hasn't issued specific regulations about when UAVs can be used by people who are being paid to operate them, however. The FAA is working on rules that would allow commercial use of certain UAVs in some circumstances.

Public agencies are able to get a certificate of authorization from the FAA to use unmanned aircraft under certain circumstances. But these can take a long time to receive, so most agencies can't simply buy a UAV and start using it.

Privacy Concerns

Another big concern is privacy. The Seattle Police Department last year [2013] abandoned a program to use UAVs while it was still in the planning and testing phase because of public concerns about privacy. It ended up giving the UAVs to the Los Angeles Police Department, which has said it won't use them until the city decides on terms for their implementation into operations.

A number of states have passed or are considering laws that would limit the ways law enforcement could use UAVs, such as requiring a warrant for many uses.

A final hurdle for some agencies is the rapid development of the technology, which can make decisions difficult.

Although UAVs may be sent to photograph wildfires and storms in situations where sending a manned aircraft is too dangerous, in urban settings most of what they are documenting could also be photographed by manned aircraft. The concerns raised by privacy advocates stem from their low cost and ease of use: If UAVs can be operated cheaply and easily, what is to prevent law enforcement from conducting constant surveillance?

"Commonsense Checks and Balances"

"Our main concern is the suspicion-less use for mass surveillance," said Jay Stanley, a privacy expert with the Speech, Privacy and Technology Program of the American Civil Liberties Union [ACLU]. He said the ACLU is not opposed to all uses of UAVs. "I don't think anybody objects to the use of a drone to find a lost child in the woods. Or if the police are raiding a crime kingpin's home and want some aerial support and have a warrant to raid the home, we wouldn't object to that. We just want to put in place some commonsense checks and balances."

There are also questions about what secondary uses of the video are acceptable, Stanley said. For example, what if authorities collect video of a large area to assess damage after an earthquake but later decide to examine the footage to look for evidence of people growing marijuana? That could provide evidence that in other situations they would have needed a warrant to collect.

A final hurdle for some agencies is the rapid development of the technology, which can make decisions difficult.

"Every year something new and better is coming out," said Tolmachoff of Cal Fire. "We're looking at all avenues. We're still researching and trying to figure out which one will work best for our department."

Military Use Gives Peaceful Drones a Bad Reputation

Ben Acheson

Ben Acheson is a policy adviser at the European Parliament in Brussels, Belgium.

Drones kill innocent civilians. What else is there to say?

This is the go-to argument for many opponents of 're-motely piloted air systems' (RPAS) or unmanned aerial vehicles (UAVs). Even when drones eliminate 'legitimate' targets, their use sparks fervent public outrage. The recent media frenzy over the killing of [Islamic militant] Hakimullah Mehsud confirmed as much.

Mehsud's four-year reign as head of Pakistan's most barbaric militant group was characterised by brutal attacks on soldiers, government officials and civilians, but his death still caused widespread consternation. The government of Pakistan described the attack as a "violation of Pakistan's sovereignty and territorial integrity" and bemoaned that it derailed efforts at peaceful dialogue. Predictably, eristic peace activists relished the media coverage as a platform to condemn US forces.

Even before Mehsud's death, a UN human rights investigator called for a moratorium on the testing and use of 'lethal autonomous robots' due to the lack of legal accountability. The 'War Child' charity echoed concerns and suggested that drones will lead to increased child casualties in future wars.

So if we condemn drone attacks when they don't get the bad guys, but we also denounce them when they do, should we just ban the technology altogether?

No. The public debate on drones is too focused on targeted killings. The very mention of the word 'drone' conjures images of Islamic militants scarpering across a dusty desert whilst unmanned, emotionless killing machines whirl ominously in the skies above. Consequently, the use of drones in more peaceful settings, such as agricultural pest control and high resolution imagery, is routinely overlooked.

Drone Debate Demands Reason, Not Reaction

To brand the entire technology as 'immoral' is unfair. The drone debate must be approached with reason, not hijacked by the same type of short-sighted, hysterical activists whose blind, misguided ideology focuses more on banning every type of human development which, with refinements, could actually aid some of their own overarching aims.

Many drones are designed purely to save lives, rather than take them.

Most people partner drones with the 'War on Terror' in Afghanistan, Pakistan and Yemen, but the technology actually dates back to 1917 when the Hewitt-Sperry Automatic Airplane made its maiden flight in the United States. The first armed drones were not used until the Iran-Iraq war in the 1980s.

Two decades later, the US employed weaponised drones in Pakistan's tribal areas. Since 2004, nearly 400 strikes have hit the region, killing many al-Qaeda leaders and Taliban militants. However, civilian fatalities have overshadowed the efficacy of these strikes because groups of men are often targeted based on behaviour patterns rather than known identities.

The backlash is not wholly unwarranted. Around 2,200 people have been killed and at least 400 of those were civilians. A recent UN investigation identified 33 drone strikes that resulted in civilian casualties and violated international humanitarian law. The criticism has mainly been levied at the US due to its reluctance to declassify information about CIA operations. A senior UN official even commented that the CIA's intransigence caused "an almost insurmountable obstacle to transparency".

Some Drones Save Lives

The oft-overlooked fact is that the military is not the only user of remotely piloted aircraft. Many drones are designed purely to save lives, rather than take them. RPAS technology helps air traffic controllers and those who create high resolution imagery. It is also being developed in conjunction with science, agriculture, environmental protection, transport and border security.

Drones are already used for whale spotting, academic research, rescue missions, sports and filming. They help prevent elephants from trampling on crops and deter poachers in Kenya. The 'Defikopter' is a defibrillator-carrying drone which can be on-hand to administer first aid within minutes. It can fly up to 43 miles an hour and isn't affected by a paramedic's worst enemy—traffic.

In the future, drones will fight forest fires. There are also plans to use unmanned drones to battle mosquitos. The insects are becoming such a problem in Florida that Florida Keys Mosquito Control is using drones with shortwave infrared cameras to locate pools where larvae are most likely being hatched.

Even Domino's is getting in on the action. The pizza-making giant is testing delivery by Domicopter; a robotic remote-controlled helicopter. This is surely nothing more than a clever marketing ploy, but it is not unprecedented. GPS-operated drones have also been used to deliver beer to revellers at the South African OppiKoppi music festival.

Moving the Conversation Forward

Pizza and beer aside, the legal moral, ethical and human rights implications of the targeted killing programmes undoubtedly deserve the highest levels of attention, but the drone debate needs to move beyond the confines of the current discussion.

Drones are not just emotionless killing machines. Yes, some targeted killings go wrong. Yes, civilian casualties are *intolerable.* Yet it is up to the law of armed conflict to set limits on the military use of RPAS and provide guidance on military necessity, proportionality, surrender and the treatment of combatants.

Drone technology is ultimately a useful tool. It brings a competitive advantage to the battlefield. It will continue to be used by the military. We must not forget that UAVs may alter how some military tasks are conducted but they do not change what the military must accomplish. Beyond the battlefield, drones will soon assume a more prominent, and important, role in peaceful activities.

Campaigning for a ban on the technology is not only disproportionate; it is ridiculous. The inarguable fact is that, whether we like it or not, drone technology is the future.

No-Fly Zone: How "Drone" Safety Rules Can Also Help Protect Privacy

John Villasenor

John Villasenor is a nonresident senior fellow in governance studies at the Center for Technology Innovation at the Brookings Institution.

For most of the 20th century, obtaining overhead images was difficult and expensive. Now, thanks to advances in unmanned aircraft systems (UAS)—people in the aviation field tend to dislike the word *drone*—it has become easy and inexpensive, raising new and important privacy issues. These issues need to be addressed primarily through legal frameworks: The Constitution, existing and new federal and state laws, and legal precedents regarding invasion of privacy will all play key roles in determining the bounds of acceptable information-gathering from UAS. But safety regulations will have an important and less widely appreciated secondary privacy role.

Why? Because safety regulations, which aim to ensure that aircraft do not pose a danger in the airspace or to people and property on the ground, obviously place restrictions on where and in what manner aircraft can be operated. Those same restrictions can also affect privacy from overhead observations from both government and nongovernment UAS. FAA [Federal Aviation Administration] regulations make it unlawful, for example, to operate any aircraft (whether manned or unmanned) "in a careless or reckless manner so as to endanger the life or property of another." Aircraft must also be operated at a sufficiently high altitude to allow "an emergency landing without undue hazard to persons or property on the surface" in the event of an engine failure. Flying a UAS around someone else's backyard can be a bad idea for lots of reasons, including the possibility of violating these rules.

"Line of Sight" Rules

UAS safety (and other) regulations are in the midst of an overhaul. Last year [2012], President [Barack] Obama signed an FAA reauthorization bill that provides for the integration of UAS into the national airspace by late 2015. Under this new law, since May 2012 law enforcement agencies have been able to apply for expedited authorizations to use certain types of small UAS, which must be operated during daylight, less than 400 feet above the ground, and within "line of sight" of the operator. This means that the operator can see a UAS with his or her own eyes as it is being flown. (The phrase "visual line of sight" is sometimes distinguished from "line of sight," which can refer to operation in which a radio signal can be transmitted directly from an operator to a UAS that may be beyond visual line of sight. However, in the 2012 FAA reauthorization bill, "line of sight" is almost certainly intended to mean "visual line of sight.")

An individual, company, or other organization that runs afoul of FAA rules could face fines or other legal consequences and find its authorization to operate unmanned aircraft suspended or revoked.

Visual line of sight operation is also required under a definition provided for "model aircraft" in the 2012 law. However, that definition is specific to that section of the law and may not apply to all hobbyist unmanned aircraft. The FAA's Advisory Circular on "model aircraft operating standards" does not mention line of sight, though model aircraft operation beyond the line of sight would risk being viewed by the FAA as careless or reckless. The FAA is also very likely to require visual line of sight operation in new rules for most (but not all) commercial, research, and other uses of UAS.

FAA Rules Are Disincentive to Abuse Drones

From the FAA's standpoint, line-of-sight rules are aimed solely at ensuring safety, since an operator who can't see the aircraft he or she is flying can find it harder to "see and avoid" other aircraft in the vicinity. But line-of-sight operation also provides some measure of privacy protection by excluding some of the most egregious potential abuses. It is very hard for an operator in front of a house to maintain visual line of sight while lowering an unmanned aircraft into the fenced-in backyard to obtain eye-level images through the back windows of the house.

While there is nothing physically preventing an unmanned aircraft from being flown in violation of these and other FAA rules, the potential consequences of doing so can provide a strong set of disincentives. An individual, company, or other organization that runs afoul of FAA rules could face fines or other legal consequences and find its authorization to operate unmanned aircraft suspended or revoked. That may not stop the most determined paparazzi from snapping overhead pictures of sunbathing movie stars, but it should help dissuade many would-be UAS voyeurs.

And what would happen if a law enforcement agency violated FAA rules while using a UAS to get images of a suspect's backyard? Would acquiring those images be a Fourth Amendment "search," and therefore be unconstitutional without a warrant?

Prior Case Law

While the Supreme Court has never specifically ruled on UAS privacy, it considered warrantless observations from manned government aircraft on three occasions in the 1980s. In the 1986 *California v. Ciraolo* decision, for instance, the court ruled that police observations from an airplane flying at 1,000 feet of marijuana growing in a backyard were constitutional. Noting that the "observations . . . took place within public navigable airspace . . . in a physically nonintrusive manner," the court held that the "Fourth Amendment simply does not require the police traveling in the public airways at this altitude to obtain a warrant in order to observe what is visible to the naked eye." In two other decisions involving observations of private property from aircraft—*Dow Chemical Co. v. United States* in 1986 and *Florida v. Riley* in 1989—the justices also viewed the fact that the aircraft were lawfully operated as a factor, although far from the only one, in finding no Fourth Amendment violation. In light of these precedents, a court might well find gathering images from government aircraft operated in violation of FAA regulations to be unconstitutional.

It's still far too early to know exactly how FAA rules designed to provide safety and efficiency will affect unmanned aircraft privacy. Commercial UAS operation in the United States is not yet permitted, and the number of law enforcement organizations that have received FAA authorizations for operational (as opposed to training) UAS use is still very limited. And while there is a large and growing community of "drone" hobbyists, the overwhelming majority of them fly safely and in a manner respecting privacy.

However, as unmanned aircraft use increases there will inevitably be instances in which UAS are operated by private individuals, paparazzi, companies, and law enforcement agencies in ways that raise privacy concerns. Determining whether those uses violate reasonable expectations of privacy will

sometimes start—though certainly not end—with an inquiry
into whether the UAS was operated in compliance with FAA
regulations.

Drone Use Takes Off Despite Safety Concerns, Restrictions

Joan Lowy

Joan Lowy is a staff writer for the Associated Press, a news wire service.

The government is getting near-daily reports—and sometimes two or three a day—of drones flying near airplanes and helicopters or close to airports without permission, federal and industry officials told The Associated Press. It's a sharp increase from just two years ago when such reports were still unusual.

Many of the reports are filed with the Federal Aviation Administration by airline pilots. But other pilots, airport officials and local authorities often file reports as well, said the officials, who agreed to discuss the matter only on the condition that they not be named because they weren't authorized to speak publicly.

Michael Toscano, president of a drone industry trade group, said FAA officials also have verified the increase to him.

While many of the reports are unconfirmed, raising the possibility that pilots may have mistaken a bird or another plane in the distance for a drone, the officials said other reports appear to be credible.

The FAA tightly restricts the use of drones, which could cause a crash if one collided with a plane or was sucked into an engine. Small drones usually aren't visible on radar to air traffic controllers, particularly if they're made of plastic or other composites.

"It should not be a matter of luck that keeps an airplane and a drone apart," said Rory Kay, a training captain at a major airline and a former Air Line Pilots Association safety committee chairman. "So far we've been lucky because if these things are operating in the sky unregulated, unmonitored and uncontrolled, the possibility of a close proximity event or even a collision has to be of huge concern."

In some cases the FAA has "identified unsafe and unauthorized (drone) operations and contacted the individual operators to educate them about how they can operate safely under current regulations and laws."

The FAA requires that all drone operators receive permission from the agency, called a certificate of authorization, before they can fly their unmanned aircraft. Most certificates limit drones to 400 feet in altitude and require that they remain within sight of the operator and at least 5 miles away from an airport. Exceptions are made for some government drones. The military flies drones in great swaths of airspace in remote areas designated for military use. Customs and Border Protection flies high-altitude drones along the U.S. borders with Mexico and Canada.

Jim Williams, who heads the FAA drone office, caused a stir earlier this year when he told a drone industry conference that an airliner nearly collided with a drone over Tallahassee, Florida, in March. The pilot of the 50-seat Canadair Regional Jet reported the camouflage-painted drone was at an altitude of about 2,300 feet, 5 miles northeast of the airport. The FAA hasn't been able to find the drone or identify its operator.

Some other recent incidents:

- The pilots of a regional airliner flying at about 10,000 feet reported seeing at least one drone pass less than 500 feet above the plane moving slowly to the south toward Allegheny County Airport near Pittsburgh. The drone was described as black and gray with a thin body, about 5 feet to 6 feet long.

- Air traffic controllers in Burbank, California, received a report from a helicopter pilot of a camera-equipped drone flying near the giant Hollywood sign.

- Controllers at central Florida's approach control facility received a report from the pilots of an Airbus A319 airliner that they had sighted a drone below the plane at about 11,000 feet and 15 miles west of Orlando. The drone was described as having a red vertical stabilizer and blue body. It wasn't picked up on radar.

- The pilots of a regional airliner reported spotting a drone 500 feet to 1,000 feet off the plane's right side during a landing approach to runway 4 of the Greenville-Spartanburg International Airport in South Carolina. The drone was described as the size of a large bird.

- A 5-foot-long drone with an attached camera crashed near Dallas Love Field in Texas. The wreckage was discovered by a worker at a factory near the airport. Police said they were looking for the operator.

In some cases the FAA has "identified unsafe and unauthorized (drone) operations and contacted the individual operators to educate them about how they can operate safely under current regulations and laws," the agency said in a statement. The FAA also said rogue operators have been threatened with fines.

Aviation safety expert John Goglia, a former National Transportation Safety Board member, said he's skeptical of some of the reports because most of the small drones currently being sold can't reach the altitudes cited by pilots. Still, "it needs to be run to ground. That means a real investigation, real work done to determine just what these reports mean," he said.

More than 1 million small drones have been sold worldwide in the past few years, said Toscano, the official with the drone industry group. It is inevitable that some will misuse them because they don't understand the safety risks or simply don't care, he said.

"This technology has a phenomenal upside that people are still just trying to understand," he said. "As unfortunate as it would be that we have an incident, it's not going to shut down the industry."

The FAA is expected to propose regulations before the end of the year that would allow broader commercial use of drones weighing less than 55 pounds. The FAA prohibits nearly all commercial use of drones, although that ban is being challenged. So far, the only commercial permits the agency has granted have been to two oil companies operating in Alaska and seven aerial photography companies associated with movie and television production.

But the ban has been ignored by many other drone operators, from real estate agents to urban planners to farmers who use them to monitor crops.

Safely Adding Drones to US Airspace Is a Formidable Challenge

US Department of Transportation Office of Inspector General

The Office of Inspector General at the US Department of Transportation (DOT) provides Congress with independent, objective reviews of the efficiency and effectiveness of DOT operations and programs and works to detect and prevent fraud, waste, and abuse.

The Federal Aviation Administration (FAA) forecasts there will be roughly 7,500 active Unmanned Aircraft Systems (UAS) in the United States in 5 years, with over $89 billion invested in UAS worldwide over the next 10 years. Unmanned aircraft range in size from those smaller than a radio-controlled model airplane to those with a wingspan as large as a Boeing 737. These aircraft can serve diverse purposes, such as enhancing border security, monitoring forest fires, and aiding law enforcement, as well as potential commercial use, such as food and package delivery. Due in part to the safety risks associated with integrating UAS into the National Airspace System (NAS), FAA authorizes UAS operations only on a limited, case-by-case basis. While the capabilities of unmanned aircraft have significantly improved, they have a limited ability to detect, sense, and avoid other air traffic.

Concerned with the progress of integrating UAS into the NAS, Congress established specific UAS provisions and deadlines for FAA in the FAA Modernization and Reform Act of 2012. These actions include publishing a 5-year roadmap, es-

US Department of Transportation, "FAA Faces Significant Barriers to Safely Integrate Unmanned Aircraft Systems into the National Airspace System," Office of Inspector General Audit Report, June 26, 2014.

tablishing six test ranges, and completing the safe integration of UAS into the NAS by September 2015. The Chairmen and Ranking Members of the Senate Commerce Committee and the House Committee on Transportation and Infrastructure, and those Committees' Aviation Subcommittees, requested that we assess FAA's progress in these efforts. Accordingly, our audit objectives were to assess (1) FAA's efforts to mitigate safety risks for integrating UAS into the NAS, and (2) FAA's progress and challenges in meeting the UAS requirements cited in the act.

While it is certain that FAA will accommodate UAS operations at limited locations, it is uncertain when and if full integration of UAS into the NAS will occur.

We conducted this review in accordance with generally accepted Government auditing standards.

FAA Faces a Variety of Barriers

Significant technological, regulatory, and management barriers exist to safely integrate UAS into the NAS. First, following many years of working with industry, FAA has not reached consensus on standards for technology that would enable UAS to detect and avoid other aircraft and ensure reliable data links between ground stations and the unmanned aircraft they control. Second, FAA has not established a regulatory framework for UAS integration, such as aircraft certification requirements, standard air traffic procedures for safely managing UAS with manned aircraft, or an adequate controller training program for managing UAS. Third, FAA is not effectively collecting and analyzing UAS safety data to identify risks. This is because FAA has not developed procedures for ensuring that all UAS safety incidents are reported and tracked or a process for sharing UAS safety data with the U.S. Department of Defense (DoD), the largest user of UAS. Finally, FAA is not effectively managing its oversight of UAS operations. Although FAA established a UAS Integration Office, it has not clarified lines of reporting or established clear guidance for UAS regional inspectors on authorizing and overseeing UAS operations. Until FAA addresses these barriers, UAS integration will continue to move at a slow pace, and safety risks will remain.

FAA's efforts to integrate UAS depend on ensuring that UAS technology is advanced and robust enough to operate safely in the same airspace as manned aircraft.

Behind Schedule

FAA is making some progress in meeting UAS-related provisions of the FAA Modernization and Reform Act of 2012, but the Agency is significantly behind schedule in meeting most of them, including the goal of achieving safe integration by September 2015. FAA has completed 9 of the act's 17 UAS provisions, such as selecting 6 test sites, publishing a UAS Roadmap, and developing a comprehensive plan outlining FAA's UAS plans in the near- and long-term. However, the Agency missed the statutory milestones for most of these provisions, and much work remains to fully implement them. FAA is also behind schedule in implementing the remaining eight UAS provisions. For example, FAA will not meet the August 2014 milestone for issuing a final rule on small UAS operations. FAA's delays are due to unresolved technological, regulatory, and privacy issues, which will prevent FAA from meeting Congress' September 30, 2015, deadline for achieving safe UAS integration. As a result, while it is certain that FAA will accommodate UAS operations at limited locations, it is uncertain when and if full integration of UAS into the NAS will occur.

We are making recommendations to enhance the effectiveness of FAA's efforts to safely integrate UAS into the NAS. . . .

Airspace Integration Has Been Stalled

Although FAA is taking steps to advance UAS operations, significant technological barriers remain, limiting FAA's progress in achieving safe integration. In addition, FAA has not yet achieved consensus on regulatory standards for integrating UAS into the NAS, including defining minimum performance and design certification standards. FAA faces further challenges because the Agency has yet to develop standardized air traffic control (ATC) procedures specific to the unique characteristics of UAS, and the Agency has not established a sufficient framework for sharing and analyzing safety data from UAS operators. Finally, organizational barriers—such as a lack of clear lines of reporting for UAS staff—are further impeding FAA's progress in integrating and overseeing UAS operations.

FAA's efforts to integrate UAS depend on ensuring that UAS technology is advanced and robust enough to operate safely in the same airspace as manned aircraft. However, two technological barriers that pose significant UAS safety risks are delaying FAA's goals. First, because there are no pilots on board, a UAS cannot comply with the "see and avoid" requirements that underpin operational safety in the NAS. However, there is currently a lack of a mature UAS technology capable of automatically detecting other aircraft operating in nearby airspace and successfully maneuvering to avoid them. Experts we interviewed stated that "detect and avoid" is the most pressing technical challenge to integration.

Second, UAS must maintain an adequate link to ground control commands to ensure that pilots never lose control of their aircraft. However, UAS still lack the adequate technology to prevent "lost link" scenarios—disruptions between the ground based operator and the aircraft—which creates significant safety challenges for both controllers and operators. . . .

No Consensus on Regulatory Standards or Training

FAA has not established a regulatory framework for integrating UAS into the NAS. This includes defining minimum performance and design certification standards and issuing rules describing when and how UAS are authorized to operate in U.S. airspace. Instead, FAA currently allows UAS operations only on a case-by-case basis, either under COA procedures with restrictions, or Special Airworthiness Certificates in the experimental or restricted category. In both cases, the applicant submits a standardized application to FAA. FAA reviews each application to ensure that the prospective operator has mitigated safety risks to an acceptable degree. However, to move beyond case-by-case authorizations, FAA will need to establish [performance and certification] standards and guidance. . . .

In addition, FAA has not resolved many other critical issues related to regulatory requirements and standards, including UAS pilot and crew qualifications, ground control stations, and command and control reliability. . . .

Currently, although FAA has authorized some UAS to operate in the NAS at select locations, such as along the Nation's borders, the Agency has not developed the procedures, training, and tools for controllers to effectively manage UAS in the same airspace as other aircraft. . . .

As the number of UAS operating in domestic airspace increases, safety risks will persist until FAA establishes performance, air traffic control, and certification standards to regulate UAS use.

Furthermore, FAA has not provided adequate automated tools for managing UAS traffic, largely because FAA's air traffic control equipment was not developed with UAS operations in mind. . . .

FAA's efforts to integrate UAS are further limited because the Agency has not obtained comprehensive data on UAS operations. Because integrating UAS into the NAS is in the early stages, any and all data regarding the safety of UAS operations are paramount to understanding and mitigating hazards that may arise. FAA routinely collects safety data from current public use UAS operators as required by the agreements with each operator. However, the Agency does not know whether it is receiving a sufficient amount of data from UAS operators because it has not established a process to ensure that operators report all incidents as required. . . .

FAA Must Step Up

FAA's primary mission remains ensuring the safety of the NAS. As such, the FAA Modernization and Reform Act's goal of integrating unmanned aircraft into the NAS by 2015 presents unique and complex safety challenges for the Agency. Now is the time, while UAS operations are currently still limited, for FAA to build critical knowledge by collecting and analyzing UAS safety data and better managing its oversight through the UAS integration office. However, as the number of UAS operating in domestic airspace increases, safety risks will persist until FAA establishes performance, air traffic control, and certification standards to regulate UAS use. Until FAA is successful in establishing these standards and adhering to a comprehensive integration plan with other public and private stakeholders, it will remain unclear when, and if, FAA can meet its goals to safely integrate UAS.

CHAPTER 2

Should the Military Be Allowed to Use Drones?

Overview:
The Global Proliferation
of Military Drones

Patrick Tucker

Patrick Tucker is technology editor for Defense One, *an online publication for national security professionals and others interested in US defense issues.*

Virtually every country on Earth will be able to build or acquire drones capable of firing missiles within the next ten years. Armed aerial drones will be used for targeted killings, terrorism and the government suppression of civil unrest. What's worse, say experts, it's too late for the United States to do anything about it.

After the past decade's explosive growth, it may seem that the U.S. is the only country with missile-carrying drones. In fact, the U.S. is losing interest in further developing armed drone technology. The military plans to spend $2.4 billion on unmanned aerial vehicles, or UAVs, in 2015. That's down considerably from the $5.7 billion that the military requested in the 2013 budget. Other countries, conversely, have shown growing interest in making unmanned robot technology as deadly as possible. Only a handful of countries have armed flying drones today, including the U.S., United Kingdom, Israel, China and (possibly) Iran, Pakistan and Russia. Other countries want them, including South Africa and India. So far, 23 countries have developed or are developing armed drones, according to a recent report from the RAND organization. It's only a matter of time before the lethal technology spreads, several experts say.

"Once countries like China start exporting these, they're going to be everywhere really quickly. Within the next 10 years, every country will have these," Noel Sharkey, a robotics and artificial intelligence professor from the University of Sheffield, told *Defense One*. "There's nothing illegal about these unless you use them to attack other countries. Anything you can [legally] do with a fighter jet, you can do with a drone."

Drones Are Spreading Fast

Sam Brannen, who analyzes drones as a senior fellow at the Center for Strategic and International Studies' International Security Program, agreed with the timeline with some caveats. Within five years, he said, every country could have access to the equivalent of an armed UAV, like General Atomics' Predator, which fires Hellfire missiles. He suggested five to 10 years as a more appropriate date for the global spread of heavier, longer range "hunter-killer" aircraft, like the MQ-9 Reaper. "It's fair to say that the U.S. is leading now in the state of the art on the high end [UAVs]" such as the RQ-170.

While the U.S. may be trying to wean itself off of armed UAV technology, many more countries are quickly becoming hooked.

"Any country that has weaponized any aircraft will be able to weaponize a UAV," said Mary Cummings, Duke University professor and former Navy fighter pilot, in a note of cautious agreement. "While I agree that within 10 years weaponized drones could be part of the inventory of most countries, I think it is premature to say that they will. . . . Such endeavors are expensive [and] require larger UAVs with the payload and range capable of carrying the additional weight, which means they require substantial sophistication in terms of the ground control station."

Not every country needs to develop an armed UAV program to acquire weaponized drones within a decade. China recently announced that it would be exporting to Saudi Arabia its Wing Loong, a Predator knock-off, a development that heralds the further roboticization of conflict in the Middle East, according to Peter Singer, Brookings fellow and author of *Wired for War: The Robotics Revolution and Conflict in the 21st Century*. "You could soon have U.S. and Chinese made drones striking in the same region," he noted.

From Science Fiction to Science Fact

Singer cautions that while the U.S. may be trying to wean itself off of armed UAV technology, many more countries are quickly becoming hooked. "What was once viewed as science fiction, and abnormal, is now normal. . . . Nations in NATO that said they would never buy drones, and then said they would never use armed drones, are now saying, 'Actually, we're going to buy them.' We've seen the U.K., France, and Italy go down that pathway. The other NATO states are right behind," Singer told *Defense One*.

Virtually any country, organization or individual could employ low-tech tactics to "weaponize" drones right now. "Not everything is going to be Predator class," said Singer. "You've got a fuzzy line between cruise missiles and drones moving forward. There will be high-end expensive ones and low-end cheaper ones." The recent use of drone surveillance and even the reported deployment of booby-trapped drones by Hezbollah, Singer said, are examples of do-it-yourself killer UAVs that will permeate the skies in the decade ahead—though more likely in the skies local to their host nation and not over American cities. "Not every nation is going to be able to carry out global strikes," he said.

Weaponized Drones Are Inevitable

So, what option does that leave U.S. policy makers wanting to govern the spread of this technology? Virtually none, say experts. "You're too late," said Sharkey, matter-of-factly.

Continued indecision by the United States regarding export of this technology will not prevent the spread of these systems.

Other experts suggest that its time the U.S. embrace the inevitable and put weaponized drone technology into the hands of additional allies. The U.S. has been relatively constrained in its willingness to sell armed drones, exporting weaponized UAV technology only to the United Kingdom, according to a recent white paper, by Brannen for CSIS. In July 2013, Congress approved the sale of up to 16 MQ-Q Reaper UAVs to France, but these would be unarmed.

"If France had possessed and used armed UAVs ... when it intervened in Mali to fight the jihadist insurgency Ansar Dine—or if the United States had operated them in support or otherwise passed on its capabilities—France would have been helped considerably. Ansar Dine has no air defenses to counter such a UAV threat," note the authors of the RAND report.

In his paper, Brennan makes the same point more forcefully. "In the midst of this growing global interest, the United States has chosen to indefinitely put on hold sales of its most capable [unmanned aerial system] to many of its allies and partners, which has led these countries to seek other suppliers or to begin efforts to indigenously produce the systems," he writes. "Continued indecision by the United States regarding export of this technology will not prevent the spread of these systems."

The Missile Technology Control Regime, or MTCR, is probably the most important piece of international policy that limits the exchange of drones and is a big reason why more countries don't have weaponized drone technology. But China never signed onto it. The best way to insure that U.S. armed drones and those of our allies can operate together is to reconsider the way MTCR should apply to drones, Brannen writes.

"U.S. export is unlikely to undermine the MTCR, which faces a larger set of challenges in preventing the proliferation of ballistic and cruise missiles, as well as addressing more problematic [unmanned]-cruise missile hybrids such as so-called loitering munitions (e.g., the Israeli-made Harop)," he writes.

Is Full Autonomy Possible?

The biggest technology challenge in drone development also promises the biggest reward in terms cost savings and functionality: full autonomy. The military is interested in drones that can do more taking off, landing and shooting on their own. UAVs have limited ability to guide themselves and the development of fully autonomous drones is years away. But some recent breakthroughs are beginning to bear fruit. The experimental X-47B, a sizable drone that can fly off of aircraft carriers, "demonstrated that some discrete tasks that are considered extremely difficult when performed by humans can be mastered by machines with relative ease," Brannen notes.

Less impressed, Sharkey said the U.S. still has time to rethink its drone future. "Don't go to the next step. Don't make them fully autonomous. That will proliferate just as quickly and then you are really going to be sunk."

Others, including Singer, disagreed. "As you talk about this moving forward, the drones that are sold and used are remotely piloted to be more and more autonomous. As the technology becomes more advanced it becomes easier for people to use. To fly a Predator, you used to need to be a pilot," he said.

"The field of autonomy is going to continue to advance regardless of what happens in the military side."

Military Drones Help Keep American Troops Safe

Keith C. Burris

Keith C. Burris is editorial page editor of the Journal Inquirer *newspaper in Manchester, Connecticut.*

Drones carry smart missiles that can be used to target enemies and encampments with incredible precision and without risking the life of a U.S. pilot.

They are unmanned, programmed, and piloted remotely—almost like a video game. And their targets are intelligence targets.

That blurs spying and war.

Drones have been used in the war on terrorists by presidents George W. Bush and Barack Obama.

Some key terrorist leaders in Iraq and Afghanistan were taken out with drones.

Drones have also been used where the USA does not have troops, or, ostensibly, a war—in Pakistan and parts of Africa. And they have been used against American citizens fighting in behalf of the Taliban.

Now some members of Congress are raising questions, saying they want more accountability regarding the government's use of drones. That's not unreasonable, though there is a generous amount of disingenuousness and posturing going on here.

There should be strict oversight of the use of drones. It's just too bad only Congress, which is generally far more irresponsible and undisciplined than the executive branch, is the only branch to do it. (Occasionally the courts do get involved, but so far this has not hampered the military or the CIA [Central Intelligence Agency].)

Yes, drones are scary.

Yes, there is potential for abuse.

Yes, there are constitutional balancing questions.

Yes, Congress is entitled to ask about civilian casualties.

[Drones] have eliminated many dangerous enemies of the United States.

And yes, the Senate is entitled to advise and consent regarding the use of drones. (Again, given the modern Senate, that's a shame.)

Yes, drones also blur assassination and war.

But the bottom line on drones is:

They have eliminated many dangerous enemies of the United States. People who wanted to kill us—a lot of us. You may not like the idea of a war on terror, but there are a lot of terrorists out there, and the USA is Target No. 1.

Drones have been more successful than the conventional wars in Iran and Afghanistan. That is startlingly true. Their results have been better, with many fewer casualties. There were tens of thousands of civilian casualties of the conventional wars in Iraq and Afghanistan.

There has been no case that we know of of someone being killed by a drone because the CIA or the Defense Department thought he was a terrorist and he wasn't. No charge of an innocent terrorist. Most of our targets bragged about their plans to kill Americans. There has been no case of: "We got the wrong bunker and hit a bunch of innocents and the bad guys got away."

So, on the record, our government seems to have used drones fairly judiciously. Again, have the recent wars been more productive, rational, or humane? Have they been less bloody than drones?

On the contrary.

Drones Spare American Soldiers

Every time a drone takes out a terrorist leader, and maybe a few of his henchmen, that is a firefight saved. That is precious young American life saved. And that's a very good thing.

We will always need conventional soldiers. But the last two wars have shown us that conventional warfare has limited potential for success in today's world.

Drones are a tool in a new kind of warfare.

No form of war is decent or moral.

But the aim, in warfare, is to kill as many bad guys as possible and save as many of our guys as possible. Drones further that aim.

A world without war would be a better world. But in war drones are preferable to the massive bombing of Baghdad during the "shock-and-awe" phase of the 10-year war on Iraq; the bombing of hospitals in North Vietnam during that war; the firebombing of Dresden during World War II.

Remember the plot to assassinate Hitler? Suppose it had worked.

Imagine getting Hitler or [Iraqi President] Saddam [Hussein] with a drone.

Many, many American lives and many civilian lives would have been spared.

US Drone Strikes: Beneficial to US Security

Aaron Badway and Cloe Bilodeau

Aaron Badway and Cloe Bilodeau wrote this viewpoint as an assignment while graduate students at the Paul H. Nitze School of Advanced International Studies (SAIS), a division of Johns Hopkins University. Because they were assigned a position to argue, it does not necessarily represent their personal views on the subject.

Since the beginning of the war on terror, drone strikes have presented the most effective way to combat terror. US drone strikes against Islamic militants have the tacit support of the Pakistani and Yemeni governments and are vital to the national security of the US and its allies. While the drone strike program is rightly criticized whenever it leads to civilian casualties, the program is the US' best option to ensure security in the region for five key reasons.

First, drone strikes are necessary. The US faces a real threat from terrorist groups like al-Qaida, which actively recruit individuals in remote areas to attack US citizens. These groups currently kill civilians whom they perceive to be threats to their ideology, while promoting the notion that the US is an enemy of Islam. Further, while the US funds development and capacity building programs in both Pakistan and Yemen, drone strikes ensure these programs can be implemented. They are therefore necessary to US security and complementary to development initiatives aiming to stem terrorism.

Second, drone strikes are effective. Drone attacks in Afghanistan, Pakistan, Yemen and Somalia have killed approximately 3500 militants, including top leaders, and reduced these groups' communication networks and recruitment mechanism. Bin Laden himself stated that al-Qaida would not be able to fight repeated drone strikes against their leadership. In Pakistan, strikes have disrupted threats to the US and reduced the violence of the Pakistani Taliban and al-Qaida. There is no evidence that drone strikes create more terrorism against the US, but a lot of data suggests that drone strikes dismantle militant networks.

The drone program is young, and there is certainly room for reform. Still, drone strikes remain the best option.

Additionally, drone strikes are cost-efficient. The US can now sustain a longer-term presence in remote areas than was not possible using conventional warfare tactics. This poses a blow to terrorists' long-term strategy. The drone program costs around one percent of the US military budget, compared to ground troops or manned aerial vehicles which can cost between six to 42 times more.

Drone strikes also reduce civilian deaths. Drones kill fewer foreign civilians as a percentage of total fatalities than any other military weapon. The New America Foundation estimates civilian casualties caused by drones are around six to 17 percent. This low number has decreased as drones become more precise. Further, drones have reduced terrorist groups' ability to kill civilians in their home countries. Drone strikes are also more humane than relying on the Pakistani or Yemeni militaries, which have a history of unprofessionalism and of human rights violations. Civilians do not flee from drones en masse, but whenever the Yemeni military launches an offensive against terrorist strongholds, civilians leave by the thousands.

For all the strategic and moral benefits of drones, there needs to be greater transparency in their use. The greatest threat is criticism of impunity for the use of drones, and classifying information regarding the program prevents true accountability. The drone program is young, and there is certainly room for reform. Still, drone strikes remain the best option.

Military Drones Reduce Civilian Casualties

Michael W. Lewis

Michael W. Lewis is a law professor at Ohio Northern University.

Mark Bowden's cover story in this month's *The Atlantic* magazine is one of the best things I've seen written on drones in the past several years. The *Black Hawk Down* author's descriptions and takeaways on most aspects of the drone program are consistent with my own experience in military aviation and the information I have gathered from human rights organizations, drone operators, military lawyers, senior military, and CIA personnel who have run the drone programs, as well as from senior military policy advisors who were involved in changing the way drones are used.

Perhaps most importantly, his description of the drone operator's reaction—one of shock and uncertainty—to performing a specific mission clearly undermines the widely circulated but exceptionally irresponsible criticism that drones have created a "Playstation mentality" among their operators. An additional fact that the article did not include, but that has been understood (although not widely reported) for several years now, is that drone operators suffer from PTSD [post-traumatic stress disorder]-like symptoms at rates similar to— and sometimes greater than—those experienced by combat forces on the ground. It turns out that even from 8,000 miles away, taking human life and graphically observing your handiwork is nothing like playing a video game.

Focus on Civilian Casualties

Another highlight is his treatment of the question of civilian casualties. All armed conflicts cause civilian casualties, and most modern conflicts have done so in large numbers, in part due to the fact that insurgents often hide among the civilian population. The 2006 Israeli conflict with Hezbollah and its 2009 and 2012 battles with Hamas in Gaza, the 1999 Russian war with Chechen rebels, and the final stages of the struggle between Sri Lanka and the LTTE (Tamil Tigers) all killed more civilians than combatants, in some cases substantially more. Although the U.S. has not caused civilian casualties at rates that high, there have been memorable examples of civilian casualties in each of the recent conflicts in which we have been involved, and those casualties were caused by all kinds of weapons systems. The 1991 Gulf War had the Al-Firdos bunker airstrike that killed up to 400 civilians. The Kosovo campaign included airstrikes that hit the Chinese Embassy in Belgrade and struck a civilian train in the Grdelica gorge. The 2003 Iraq War included civilian casualties caused by Marine ground troops in Haditha and military contractors in Nisoor Square, while a cruise missile strike in 2009 killed approximately 35 civilians at al-Majalah in Yemen.

[The] potential of drones to vastly reduce civilian casualties was not fully realized at first, but it has been dramatically attained in the past few years.

Better Intelligence, Better Results

Like any other weapon, drones have caused civilian casualties. But they also have the potential to dramatically reduce civilian casualties in armed conflicts, and particularly in counterinsurgencies. Their ability to follow targets for days or weeks accomplishes two things that contribute to saving the lives of innocents: First, it confirms that the target is engaged in the behavior that put them on the target list, reducing the likelihood of striking someone based on faulty intelligence. Second, by establishing a "pattern of life" for the intended target, it allows operators to predict when the target will be sufficiently isolated to allow a strike that is unlikely to harm civilians.

Another feature that reduces civilian casualties is that drones are controlled remotely, so the decision to employ a weapon can be reviewed in real time by lawyers, intelligence analysts, and senior commanders without any concern (in most cases) that a hesitation to act may cost lives. Even more importantly, the operators themselves are not concerned for their own safety, eliminating the possibility that the combination of tension, an unexpected occurrence, and a concern for personal safety leads to weapons being fired when they shouldn't be.

This potential of drones to vastly reduce civilian casualties was not fully realized at first, but it has been dramatically attained in the past few years.

In 2007, the U.S. Army and Marine Corps began disseminating the COIN Manual that emphasized the need for soldiers to be involved in nation-building and bolstering local civil-society institutions, in addition to defeating insurgents militarily. Part of implementing this strategy involved minimizing civilian casualties. When Gen. Stanley McChrystal took command of ISAF in Afghanistan in 2009, he emphasized the need to continue reducing civilian casualties in all phases of operations. He assigned teams of civilians and military officers to conduct root-cause analysis of every civilian casualty in theater and tasked them with developing protocols to eliminate such deaths.

Targeting Vehicles, Not Compounds, Reduces Collateral Damage

These teams produced a number of recommendations for drones. One of the most significant was switching the preferred method of targeting from compounds to vehicles. While targeting compounds improved the likelihood that the right individual was being targeted, it also greatly increased the chances that members of the target's family and the families of his bodyguards and close associates would be harmed. Although vehicle strikes ran a greater risk of target misidentification, increasing surveillance and pattern-of-life analysis mitigated that risk. Because it is easier to determine who is in a vehicle than to keep track of everyone who enters and leaves a compound, vehicle strikes reduced the likelihood that family members and friends would be collateral damage. Also, because vehicle strikes can be conducted on isolated roads, the likelihood of other civilian bystanders being harmed was minimized.

There can be no question that drones as they are currently operated are the ideal counterinsurgency weapon.

How do we know that this has succeeded? Bowden mentions studies done by several independent organizations that have assessed civilian casualties caused by drones in Pakistan. The three most well respected and independent sources on this issue are the *Long War Journal*, the New America Foundation and The Bureau of Investigative Journalism (TBIJ). Among these, the U.K.-based TBIJ has consistently produced the highest estimates of civilian casualties for drone strikes. According to TBIJ, between January 2012 and July 2013, there were approximately 65 drone strikes in Pakistan, which they estimate to have killed a minimum of 308 people. Yet of these casualties, even TBIJ estimates that only 4 were civilians (that number has been revised down from 7 in the past month or so). This would amount to a civilian casualty rate of less than 1.5 percent, meaning that only 1 in 65 casualties caused by drones over that 19-month period was a civilian. This speaks to drone-effective discrimination between civilian and military targets that no other weapons system can possibly match.

Critics Have Faulty Arguments

In spite of this success, there are many critics that continue to claim that drones are illegal, immoral and/or ineffective, largely because they cause too many civilian casualties and thereby create more enemies than they eliminate. Most such claims are backed by references to the total aggregate TBIJ numbers to demonstrate how many total civilians have been killed by drones since 2007, but the drones' performance over the last year and a half is always ignored. Others are backed by anecdotal evidence like the Senate testimony of a Yemeni activist, Farea al-Muslimi who claimed that his personal research indicates that the vast majority of those killed by drones in Yemen were civilians. However his methodology, asking friends and family members of the victims if the dead were AQAP [al Qaeda in the Arabian Peninsula], leaves much to be desired in terms of rigor.

There may be questions about whether the armed conflict approach is the right one to take against insurgent groups like core al Qaeda, AQAP or AQIM [al Qaeda in the Islamic Maghreb] (and given their success when not opposed by substantial military force, those questions should answer themselves), but there can be no question that drones as they are currently operated are the ideal counterinsurgency weapon. Any argument that drones cause too many civilian casualties to be effective in counterinsurgency operations, essentially concludes that counterinsurgency operations cannot succeed.

Military Drones Can Help Protect Human Rights

Kristin Bergtora Sandvik and Kjersti Lohne

Kristin Bergtora Sandvik is a senior researcher at the Peace Research Institute Oslo and director of the Norwegian Centre for Humanitarian Studies. Her research focuses on the relationships between international law, humanitarianism, technology, and violence. Kjersti Lohne is an academic visitor at Oxford and a PhD research fellow at the University of Oslo.

This article explores and attempts to define the emerging concept of the humanitarian drone by critically examining actual and anticipated transfers of unmanned aerial vehicles (UAVs), or drones, from the global battlespace to the humanitarian emergency zone. . . .

In recent years, the humanitarian cost of the drone wars has become the focus of international attention. Much less visibly, terms such as *humanitarian drones, drone humanitarianism, drones for human rights* and *humanitarian missiles* have been migrating from the far corners of the blogosphere into mainstream discussions of humanitarian action and humanitarian policy. As the 'humanitarian drone' gains currency as a political concept, it is important to disentangle the ideas from which that concept has emerged, and to think about the implications for humanitarian action. In this article, we do so by considering a range of actual and projected transfers of unmanned aerial vehicles (UAVs, hereinafter also *drones*) from the global battlefield to the humanitarian emergency zone.

Under a well-established definition, the term *humanitarian assistance* refers to aid and action designed to save lives, alleviate suffering, and maintain and protect human dignity during and in the aftermath of emergencies. As an analytical starting point, the concept of the humanitarian drone can be understood as a set of contested representations of technology, and technological functions, intended to meet some of these assistance needs.

Just as drones have rapidly become intrinsic to modern warfare, it appears that they will increasingly find their place as part of the humanitarian governance apparatus.

Over the past decade, the close relationship between military action and humanitarian aid during international engagements in Afghanistan, Iraq, Haiti and Libya has led to debates about the nature and ends of the humanitarian enterprise. Although the geographies of war and humanitarian aid have always overlapped—at least since the battle of Solferino in 1859, which ultimately led to the founding of the International Red Cross—what has changed are the ways in which armed conflict, humanitarian interventions and humanitarian aid operations intersect as fields of global governance, spanning both war and disaster zones.

The Global Battlefield

The concept of the 'global battlefield' or the 'global battlespace', which originated in US military doctrine and refers to the multidimensional nature of modern warfare, is gaining increasing currency. As a conceptual and material project, war is now 'everywhere', woven into the matrix of contemporary social life. Within the global battlespace, Predators (General Atomics, United States), Herons (IAI, Israel) and Watchkeepers (Thales, France) provide intelligence for armed attacks or occupation, while MQ-9 Reapers (also General Atomics) and

Hermes 450s (Elbit Systems, Israel) are deployed to eliminate individuals identified as insurgents or terrorists. The cargo drone Kaman K-Max (Lockheed Martin and Kaman Aerospace, US) supplies troops to remote outposts in Afghanistan. Interconnecting with the global battlespace is a humanitarian emergency zone, where a global system of international organisations, donor and troop-contributing nations, and non-governmental organisations (NGOs) operate in parallel with and across domestic state structures to respond to and administer a permanent condition of crisis.

Just as drones have rapidly become intrinsic to modern warfare, it appears that they will increasingly find their place as part of the humanitarian governance apparatus. What opportunities do drones offer for humanitarian governance? How will drones change humanitarian practices and, by extension, the humanitarian profession? We consider the notion of the humanitarian drone as it has recently surfaced in two different types of discourse: (1) as a way of labelling technical and logistical humanitarian functions a drone might potentially fulfill, such as providing better data on unfolding crises or ongoing human rights violations, delivering aid to victims in hard-to-get locations, or supporting a responsibility-to-protect (R2P) mandate; and (2) as a way of describing ethically desirable uses to which drones might be put, such as enhancing the understanding of assistance needs, making aid more effective, and ending human rights violations.

We expect that the use of drones will permeate the humanitarian field, and that the drones will be operated not only by states or intergovernmental actors, but also by [nongovernmental organizations].

Our goal is to analyse these two types of discourse and their broader implications for humanitarian action. Although we recognise the potent force of humanitarianism as a discourse in global governance, and as a popular 'transnational concern to help persons in exceptional distress', humanitarian action is here conceived broadly as material, political and military responses—by the humanitarian arms of the United Nations (UN), international NGOs, and states—to particular invocations of humanitarian suffering. Significantly, as used here, this form of 'humanitarian reason' is claimed as the prerogative of liberal democracies. We situate our discussion of the rise of the humanitarian drone in the context of two observations regarding current thinking on technology and crisis, both of which we address critically in the course of the article: (1) optimism about the possibility of using technology to improve humanitarian action (including mitigating the increasing insecurity of humanitarian workers), and (2) the idea that more precise weapons technology is 'humanising' warfare.

The Military-to-Civilian Transfer

Many of the technological innovations in question are the outcomes of military-civilian transfer—thus, they are so-called dual-use technologies, which can be used for both peaceful and military aims. While there is a dearth of scholarly focus on the 'turn to technology' in humanitarian action, the rich literature on technological transformations and politics can help bridge the gap. Our argument is based on two assumptions about drones as a purported form of humanitarian technology: first, technology is not neutral, that is, instead of society passively adopting technology, technology and society engage in a mutually constitutive relationship. Thus, the construction of technology is subject to political contestation and to the realities of professionalism, finance and politics; nevertheless, in keeping with Daniel R. McCarthy's reflections on technological determinism, the diffusion of non-human objects 'generates new political settlements', which, in themselves, constitute a form of institutional power. As evidenced by the ongoing drone wars, UAV technology enables a specific set of political and military rationales and projects that must be examined—not for their oft-cited 'newness' but for the power they represent.

Our second assumption is as follows: although UAV technology may still be relatively primitive, it will evolve and proliferate as a technological paradigm. Consequently, we expect that the use of drones will permeate the humanitarian field, and that the drones will be operated not only by states or intergovernmental actors, but also by NGOs. So far, however, the implications of this proliferation and use for humanitarian action have barely begun to be recognised, and no critical attention has been given to how the humanitarian use of drones is framed and discussed—or by whom. . . .

The humanitarian drone should be understood, at least in part, as a war dividend flowing from military spending on the war on terror.

We argue that this process should be understood not merely as a mechanical transfer of hardware, but also as the transfer of social, cultural and political practices. In our account of the humanitarian drone, the military and the humanitarian fields are enmeshed—politically, materially and socially. Hence, any humanitarian use of drones must be read in the context of their origin as military technologies. . . .

Making Sense of the Humanitarian Drone

This article attempts to make sense of the emergence of the humanitarian drone as a political concept by subjecting UAV technology, and the ideas that have formed around it, to some much-needed scrutiny. We are particularly concerned about the potential consequences for humanitarian discourse and the humanitarian enterprise. In our view, a focus on weaponised drones fails to capture the transformative potential of

71

humanitarian drones and their possible impact on humanitarian action, and the associated pitfalls.

The starting point for our investigation is the emerging assumption that drones will change the humanitarian enterprise for the better. To explain the rise of the concept of the humanitarian drone, we note that the humanitarian enterprise embraces the idea of improving humanitarian action through technology. We further suggest that the humanitarian drone should be understood, at least in part, as a war dividend flowing from military spending on the war on terror. Importantly, just as the humanitarian enterprise has been identified as a significant market for UAVs, the humanitarian ethos has become an important commodity for drone manufacturers. Hence, it is important to attend to the strong commercial logic underpinning the promotion of the humanitarian drone. It is equally important to be aware of the ways in which drone use may shift humanitarian agendas and the political and financial priorities of governments (who tend to be protective of domestic defence contractors), international organisations and NGOs. Also of note is the industry's attempt to forge a moral economy based on a shared humanitarian logic that is, in part, embraced by a humanitarian enterprise that holds firm to the belief that adding technology automatically generates progress.

In addition to predicting that military rationales and practices will travel with drones used for humanitarian purposes, we propose that existing tensions between the military and the humanitarian fields will shape how the humanitarian drone is used to mediate and respond to human suffering. . . .

Many Questions Left to Ask

We would like to conclude by indicating where we think more research is needed. First, we encourage international relations scholars to follow the money: what is the political economy of humanitarian drones? How do the development and marketing of new prototypes correspond to regulatory efforts, and with the ways in which UAV procurements are processed, labelled and legitimated by governments and international organisations? Second, given the increasing use of drone technology in civilian airspace, it is essential to examine the political meanings surrounding representations of all categories and uses of drones—from human rights drones, to eco drones, anti-poaching drones, agro drones, and so forth. How do other types of drones, and the work they do, compare with the idea of the humanitarian drone? Third, returning to our argument that practices travel with hardware, sound empirical research is needed to explore not only how humanitarian drone practices are enacted, and by whom, but also how this novel form of humanitarian praxis is experienced and interpreted by those at the receiving end.

Military Drone Use Makes War More Likely

Lauren McCauley

Lauren McCauley is a staff writer for Common Dreams, a news and opinion website for the progressive community.

The embrace of killer drones by the United States government is likely to increase anti-U.S. sentiment, erode national sovereignty and trigger a "slippery slope" into endless war, a prominent military and intelligence panel warned in a new report published Thursday [June 26, 2014].

Recommendations and Report of the Task Force on United States Drone Policy is the result of a year-long study by a high-level task force of military, intelligence and foreign policy experts assembled by the nonpartisan Stimson Center.

In the report, the panel warns that the proliferation of killer drones as a "pillar of U.S. counterterrorism strategy" has enabled policies that "likely would not have been adopted in the absence of UAVs [Unmanned Aerial Vehicles]," particularly the "extraordinarily broad" interpretation of the Authorization for Use of Military Force, or AUMF.

Echoing the concerns of many anti-war groups, the panel notes that the increasing use of lethal drones "may create a slippery slope leading to continual or wider wars."

The report continues:

> The seemingly low-risk and low-cost missions enabled by UAV technologies may encourage the United States to fly such missions more often, pursuing targets with UAVs that would be deemed not worth pursuing if manned aircraft or special operation forces had to be put at risk.

UAVs also create an escalation risk insofar as they may lower the bar to enter a conflict, without increasing the likelihood of a satisfactory outcome.

The panel says that the United States' unilateral targeting of individuals in foreign sovereign states "may encourage other states to follow suit with their own military platforms or commercial entities."

The report argues that the use of drones in an "unprecedented and expanding way" raises significant strategic, legal and ethical questions.

Risks Are Many, Benefits Few

Among the strategic risks, the group argues that "blowback" from civilian casualties may "increase anti-U.S. sentiment and become a potent recruiting tool for terrorist organizations."

Further, the panel says that the United States' unilateral targeting of individuals in foreign sovereign states "may encourage other states to follow suit with their own military platforms or commercial entities."

Citing the failure on the part of the American government to carry out a thorough analysis weighing the costs and benefits of continuing their drone war, the report concedes: "There is no indication that a U.S. strategy to destroy Al Qaeda has curbed the rise of Sunni Islamic extremism, deterred the establishment of Shia Islamic extremist groups or advanced long-term U.S. security interests."

Despite this, and the panel's criticisms regarding the U.S. government's lack of transparency and the risks inherent in the use of drones, the report concludes on the assumption that killer drones will continue to be a fundamental tool in military operations.

Thus, the panel issued the below list of recommendations, quoted from the report, to shape and guide U.S. drone policy:

1. Conduct a strategic review of the role of lethal UAVs in targeted counterterrorism strikes;

2. Improve transparency in targeted UAV strikes;

3. Transfer general responsibility for carrying out lethal UAV strikes from the CIA to the military;

4. Develop more robust oversight and accountability mechanisms for targeted strikes outside of hot battle-fields;

5. Foster the development of appropriate international norms for the use of lethal force outside traditional battlefields;

6. Assess UAV-related technological developments and likely future trends, and create an interagency research and development strategy geared toward advancing US national security interests in a manner consistent with US values;

7. Review and reform UAV-related export control rules and FAA rules, with a view to minimizing unnecessary regulatory burdens on the development of the US UAV industry, while still safeguarding US national security interests and ensuring responsible UAV development and use; and

8. Accelerate the FAA's efforts to meet the requirements of the 2012 FAA Reauthorization Bill.

Responding to the report's release, Steve Vladeck, co-editor in chief of the *Just Security* blog, who was part of one of the "working groups" that gave informal advice to the task force, wrote: "Folks won't necessarily agree with all of its recommendations (or believe that they go far enough), but given the Task Force's bipartisan, high-level composition, its recommendations will be ignored at its readers' peril."

Military Drone Strikes Violate Human Rights

Deborah Dupre

Deborah Dupre has been a human rights, environmental, and peace activist for more than thirty years.

As other nations are having popular revolutions to strengthen human rights, former US president Jimmy Carter says the United States government counterterrorism policies are clearly violating at least 10 of the 30 articles of the Universal Declaration of Human Rights and that drone strikes and targeted assassinations see the nation violating rights in a way that "abets our enemies and alienates our friends."

"Revelations that top officials are targeting people to be assassinated abroad, including American citizens, are only the most recent, disturbing proof of how far our nation's violation of human rights has extended," writes the 39th president in the *New York Times* on Monday, June 25, 2012. Carter's critical Op Ed, *A Cruel and Unusual Record*, states that "with all the revolution sweeping around the world, America should 'make the world safer.' Instead, however, 'America's violaton of international human rights abets our enemies and alienates our friends.'"

In 1948, with US leadership, the Universal Declaration of Human Rights was adopted as "the foundation of freedom, justice and peace in the world." It was a clear commitment that power would no longer serve as a cover to oppress or injure people. The core principle behind each of the 30 articles of the declaration is equal rights. The articles detail the

Declaration's equal rights of all people to life, liberty, security, protection of law and freedom from torture, arbitrary detention and forced exile.

"US's government counterterrrorism policies are now clearly violating at least 10 of the 30 articles written in the Universal Declaration of Human Rights," Carter wrote. "As a result, our country can no longer speak with moral authority on these critical issues."

Investigations indicate that a large part of the drone casualties were civilian and that numbers have increased dramatically since Barack Obama assumed the presidency.

War Crimes "un-American"

Carter's Op Ed regarding the US abandoning its role as the global champion of human rights appeared less than a week after the UN released a report on US drone strikes to "combat terrorism." On June, 21, 2012, UN rapporteur on extrajudicial killings, summary or arabitrary executions, Christof Heyns asserted that the US needs to be held legally accountable for using armed drones, possibly involving war crimes. If it is true, he said, that "there have been secondary drone strikes on rescuers who are helping (the injured) after an initial drone attack, those further attacks are a war crime."

A second UN rapporteur, Ben Emmerson QC, who monitors counter-terrorism, stated that protection of the ultimate human right, the right to life, required countries to establish independent inquiries into each US drone killing. While the US is not a signatory to the International Criminal Court (ICC) nor many other international legal forums where legal action could begin, it is part of the International Court of Justice (ICJ) where one nation state can initiate a case against another.

While a definitive number of drone victims remains publicly unknown, the American Civil Liberties Union (ACLU) estimated that approximately 4,000 people fell victim to US drone raids between 2002 and 2011 in Yemen, Pakistan and Somalia alone. (Drone strikes threaten 50 years of international law, says UN, Owen Bowcott, *The Guardian*, 21 June 2012.) Most drone casualties were civilian and those murders increased dramatically after Barack Obama became president, according to independent investigations. Threatening 50 years of international law, Obama has stated drones are his "weapon of choice," according to a now deleted *Washington Post* article quoted by this author. (CIA drones intolerable says Pakistan, despite Obama's 'weapon of choice', Examiner.com, 10 Oct. 2011.) The *Washington Post* later referred to drones being Obama's "go-to weapon" in Eugene Robinson's OpEd, President Obama's immoral drone war (2 Dec. 2012). US drone attacks "are killing innocent civilians in a way that is obscene and immoral," Robinson opined. Concurring with human rights defenders globally, he stated, "I'm afraid that ignoring this ugly fact makes Americans complicit in murder."

Human rights group Reprieve brought to light that the official Pentagon term for a drone victim is "Bugsplat." (Rare photos of CIA drone "Bugsplat" bodies in secret blackhole battle released, D. Dupré, *Examiner*, 14 Dec. 2011.) North Waziristan resident Noor Behram worked with Reprieve charity organization's founding director Stafford Smith. Behram spent years photographing drone strike aftermaths, often at personal risk.

"I want to show taxpayers in the Western world what their tax money is doing to people in another part of the world: killing civilians, innocent victims, children," Behram said. (Rare photos of CIA drone "Bugsplat" bodies in secret blackhole battle released.)

In 2014, using Bureau of Investigative Journalism reports, Reprieve examined cases in which specific people were targeted by drones multiple times. Those data raised questions about accuracy of US intelligence "guiding strikes" that American officials describe with words such as "clinical" and "precise." Reporting on Reprieve's findings, *The Guardian* stated that "even when operators target specific individuals—the most focused effort of what Barack Obama calls 'targeted killing'—they kill vastly more people than their targets, often needing to strike multiple times." Attempts to assassinate 41 men resulted in killing an estimated 1,147 people. (*The Guardian*, 24 Nov. 2014.) While it is unknown precisely how many hundreds of innocent civilians US drone attacks have killed, each strike and death was approved by Washington's highest authorities, unthinkable before the Obama regime.

Three days before Carter's harsh criticism of Obama's drone human rights abuses, in a Huffington Post Blog, former US Senator Fritz Hollings of South Carolina declared killing by drone "un-American":

> "I've been an American for 90 years and drone killing is un-American. It's an excellent weapon to use in a war, but not to declare war. Article I, Section 8 of the Constitution reserves the declaration of war for the Congress—not the President, not the CIA, not the Defense Department. Already we have a dispute in Pakistan where the Ambassador has the authority of the US but the authority is now being used by the CIA. I know about the authority of Congress a week after 9/11 to hunt down and capture or eliminate terrorists. I voted for it. But having worked on the Defense Budget for 38 years, I didn't contemplate drone killing. We had never heard of drones. We were looking for Osama bin Laden and the crew that devastated the World Trade Towers. The majority of this crew was from Saudi Arabia. We have never used drones in Saudi Arabia, but are now drone killing in Yemen and Somalia that are no threat to the US. In America we are able to face our accuser and defend ourselves." (Sen. Fritz Hollings, Former US senator [D-SC], *Un-American*, 22 June 2012)

"Targeted Individuals" Claim Surveillance and Attacks

Media and rights advocates' attention to drone abuse is welcomed by thousands of innocent individuals in the US struggling to survive government-sponsored covert assaults that escalated under the Obama administration with the president's "Targeted Killings," his political lingo for assassinations. In the US, a cohort of thousands of innocent victims known as Targeted Individuals (TIs), including many reputable professionals and other credible victims, consistently allege being kept under constant surveillance and covertly attacked, some by unmanned aerial technologies and most by cyber-terrorism—Internet hacking. Many of these TIs provide evidence that law enforcement refuses to protect them from these attacks. [The American Civil Liberties Union] ACLU investigations later found that police involved in spying on and targeting Americans are called rakers. (*Are You a Targeted Individual? Foolproof Research Criteria Secrets*, D. Dupré, Before It's News, 28 July 2015.)

> This law violates the right to freedom of expression and to be presumed innocent until proved guilty, two other rights enshrined in the declaration.

Recent laws allow "unprecedented violations of our rights to privacy through warrantless wiretapping and government mining of our electronic communications," Carter stated. He called for Washington to "reverse course and regain moral leadership."

"While the country has made mistakes in the past, the widespread abuse of human rights over the last decade has been a dramatic change from the past."

The Universal Declaration of Human Rights "has been invoked by human rights activists and the international community to replace most of the world's dictatorships with democracies and to promote the rule of law in domestic and global affairs," Carter stated. "It is disturbing that, instead of strengthening these principles, our government's counter-terrorism policies are now clearly violating at least 10 of the declaration's 30 articles, including the prohibition against 'cruel, inhuman or degrading treatment or punishment.'"

Expanded Presidential Powers

Beginning with the George W. Bush regime's USA PATRIOT ACT, during the Barack Obama regime, legislation legalized the president's right to detain a person indefinitely on suspicion of affiliation with terrorist organizations or "associated forces," Carter reminded the public, referring to the National Defense Authorization Act (NDAA 2012). "This law violates the right to freedom of expression and to be presumed innocent until proved guilty, two other rights enshrined in the declaration," Carter wrote.

Terrorism and Counterterrorism Program senior counsel for Human Rights Watch, Andrea Prasow had previously asserted that "mandatory military detention is what martial-law states do, not democracies," as the *New York Times* reported just before Obama signed the NDAA into law, codifying martial law. Prasow called the mandatory detention provision an "outrageous" undermining of prosecutorial discretion. (Martial law provision secretly passed in Congress Committee, Deborah Dupré, Examiner.com, June 25, 2011.)

There are "unprecedented violations of our rights to privacy through warrantless wiretapping and government mining of our electronic communications," Carter continued. "Popular state laws permit detaining individuals because of their appearance, where they worship or with whom they associate."

Instead of making the world safer, "America's violation of international human rights abets our enemies and alienates our friends," Carter said. . . .

Human Rights Remain a Concern

Instead of fostering human rights, the US is rapidly changing from "One nation under God," as stated in the US Pledge of Allegiance, to One nation under drones. Congress passed legislation for what the Federal Aviation Authority (FAA) predicted approximately 30,000 drones in operation in US skies by 2020 and the targeting of human rights defenders is predicted to increase. Spy drones, commercially available for less than $1,000, are barely different from those police departments use to spy on the public. In August 2015, North Dakota has become the first state to authorize weaponized drones in the US.

In Africa, then Secretary of State and at the time of this writing [September 2015], presidential hopeful Hillary Clinton spoke openly about the US's need to improve drone capabilities. Clinton was in Uganda speaking to president Yoweri Museveni and surveying US drones used by the Ugandan military in Somalia to reportedly fight al-Qaeda-linked militants.

"Now we have to figure out how we can see through thick vegetation to find [Ugandan guerilla leader] Joseph Kony," she said, referring to the controversial "Kony 2012" documentary propaganda film that had over 92 million views about capturing fabled enemy Joseph Kony. Analysts say that the film was created to spur widespread outrage and manipulate support for the US to invade Africa. It depicted Kony as a ruthless African warlord who would kidnap children, butcher victims, and take women as sex slaves. . . .

In her memoir, *Hard Choices*, Clinton defends the Obama regime's drone targeted assassinations. In chapter 9, Clinton says drone strikes quickly became "one of the most effective and controversial elements of the Obama Administration's strategy against al Qaeda and like-minded terrorists." She defends the careful planning of drone strikes. Hundreds of dead babies and children drone victims alone have proven Clinton's statements to be unfounded or untrue. Drone propaganda and censorship, however, continue. . . .

While not legally binding, the June 2012 UN report on drones "escalates the volume of international concerns" over "the Obama administration's weapon of choice against Al Qaeda and its allies," the *New York Times* reported. Jim Galloway, political insider of the *Atlanta Journal Constitution* summarized Carter's stinging *New York Times* Op Ed piece: "Jimmy Carter isn't too thrilled with the idea of President Barack Obama . . . picking individual winners and losers in the war on terror."

A 2014 report, "Testing Theories of American Politics: Elites, Interest Groups, and Average Citizens," showed findings of a peer-reviewed study at Princeton and Northwestern Universities that the US is not a democracy based on human rights. It is, according to the major report, an "oligarchy" in which the US government meets demands of the wealthy, whereas desires and rights of everyone else are ignored. Drones are indeed an "effective tool" for this end.

America's Foreign Drone Strike Program Lacks Transparency

Matthew Spurlock

Matthew Spurlock is a legal fellow at the American Civil Liberties Union's National Security Project.

Targeted killings have been a central part of U.S. national security strategy for more than a decade, but the American public still knows scandalously little about who the government kills, and why. Today we're filing a new lawsuit in our continuing fight to fix that.

The CIA and the military use drones to target suspected "militants," "insurgents," and "terrorists" in at least half a dozen countries. American drone strikes have killed thousands of people abroad, many of them children. The program has engendered pervasive fear and anger against the United States in countries where the attacks frequently occur.

Our government's deliberative and premeditated killings—and the many more civilian deaths from the strikes—raise profound legal and ethical questions that ought to be the subject of public debate. The Obama administration has made numerous promises of greater transparency and oversight on drones. In his 2013 State of the Union address, President Obama pledged to make lethal targeting "more transparent to the American people and the world" because "in our democracy, no one should just take my word for it that we're doing things the right way."

But the administration has failed to follow through on these commitments to openness, and it is continuing to withhold basic information. When it has released anything—or been compelled to by lawsuits—discussion of crucial aspects of the program have been omitted or redacted. This lack of transparency makes the public reliant on the government's self-serving and sometimes false representations about the targeted-killing program.

That's why today the ACLU filed a new lawsuit to enforce a Freedom of Information Act request asking for basic information on the program, including records on how the government picks targets, before-the-fact assessments of potential civilian casualties, and "after-action" investigations into who was actually killed.

[The US government] chooses to keep nearly all the details about how the [drone] program works hidden from view.

The ACLU has made some headway for transparency. We are litigating two other FOIA lawsuits seeking information about targeted killings. One of them is about the strikes that killed three Americans in Yemen: Anwar al-Aulaqi, his 16-year old son Abdulrahman, and Samir Khan. Despite the public promises of openness, the government has continued to fight tooth-and-nail against releasing documents in those cases—or in some instances, even admitting that it has any documents at all.

In both cases we have won important rulings in federal appeals courts, forcing the government to release some documents, including a 41-page Justice Department Office of Legal Counsel memo addressing the legal theories that were the basis for the extrajudicial killing of Anwar al-Aualqi. The belated publication of the memo was an important victory for transparency, which led to a broad and long-overdue debate about the lawfulness of the government's targeted-killing program and, in particular, of the lawfulness of the government's deliberate and pre-meditated killing of a U.S. citizen. But the memo—almost a third of which was redacted—leaves many questions unanswered.

For example, the memo doesn't explain the government's definition of imminence, the circumstances that would make "capture infeasible" (and therefore, according to the government, lethal targeting permissible), or the reasons for the government's targeting decisions. Worse, it point(s) to a whole body of secret law that the administration continues to shield from the American public.

The administration's subsequent gestures towards transparency are just as scant. The public summary of the secret *Presidential Policy Guidance*—which sets new standards for lethal targeting—relies on the same conclusory definitions as the Office of Legal Counsel memo. In a major speech at the National Defense University in 2013, the president asserted that "before any strike is taken, there must be near-certainty that no civilians will be killed or injured—the highest standard we can set." But multiple investigative reports contradict this assurance. The government could dispute these findings, but instead it chooses to keep nearly all the details about how the program works hidden from view.

We aren't giving up. One of the most important aspects of our new lawsuit is that it covers more recent documents, including the Presidential Policy Guidance under which the targeted killing program likely now operates.

The government's drone program lives far too deep in the shadows. As long as the government continues its campaign of secret, unacknowledged lethal strikes across the globe, we will fight to subject this policy to the scrutiny and debate it deserves.

The Dangerous Seduction of Drones

Medea Benjamin

Medea Benjamin is the founder of the international human rights organization Global Exchange and the antiwar group Code Pink. She is the author of the recent book Drone Warfare: Killing by Remote Control.

Senior [President Barack] Obama administration officials say our government is sharply scaling back its drone strikes in Pakistan. That's a step in the right direction. It would be even better if the entire U.S. program of targeted killings in Pakistan, Yemen, and Somalia were scrapped.

By embracing drones as a primary foreign policy tool, President Barack Obama has taken on the role of prosecutor, judge, jury, and executioner.

Without declaring a war there, U.S. forces have hit Pakistan with more than 350 drones strikes since 2004. These U.S.-engineered operations have left a death toll of somewhere between 2,500 and 3,500 people, including almost 200 children.

Despite being billed as a weapon of precision, only 2 percent of those killed in these drone strikes have been high-level Taliban or al-Qaeda operatives. Most have been either innocent people or low-level militants.

Simply put, our drones have killed young men with scant ability—or intent—to attack Americans. And drones don't just kill people, they terrorize entire communities with their constant buzzing and hovering overhead.

A Stanford/NYU Law School study called *Living Under Drones* shows how the mere presence of drones disrupts community life. Parents grow too afraid to send their children to school or remain in their own homes. They're afraid—with good reason—to attend community gatherings, or go to weddings or funerals.

With every drone strike, more and more join the ranks of al-Qaeda to seek revenge.

"Your government is terrifying 250,000 people in my province to get one or two individuals, who could easily be captured," a young woman leader named Entisar Ali told me in Yemen during my trip there last year. "In your fight against terrorism, you are terrorizing us."

A Powerful Recruiting Tool

By fueling anti-U.S. sentiment, drones also act as a recruiting tool for extremists. In Yemen, when the Obama administration started drone attacks in 2009, there were perhaps 200 people who identified as members of extremist groups. Today, there are over 1,000.

With every drone strike, more and more join the ranks of al-Qaeda to seek revenge. Worldwide, a decade of drone strikes hasn't wiped out al-Qaeda. In fact, al-Qaeda has grown. It now has a larger presence in Syria and Iraq, as well as in several countries in North and West Africa.

If other states were to claim this broad-based authority to kill people anywhere, anytime, using drones "the result would be chaos," explained Philip Alston, a former UN Special Rapporteur on Extrajudicial Executions.

Former Director of National Intelligence Dennis Blair has called drones "dangerously seductive" because they make the government feel it has a strategy for combating terrorism yet really only move the focal point from one place to another and guarantee a perpetual state of war.

A New Arms Race

Finally, drones are dangerous because they are fueling a new arms race. As of today, only the United States, the UK, and Israel have used weaponized drones, but there is already a multibillion-dollar arms race going on. Israel is the No. 1 drones exporter, followed by the United States and China. Over 80 nations possess some form of drones, mostly for surveillance purposes. Between 10 and 15 nations are working on weaponizing their drones.

Another factor fueling the proliferation of armed drones is a global push to make smaller weapons that can be tailored to fit smaller aircraft. This will make it easier for non-state actors like al-Qaeda to get their hands on these types of weapons.

After 10 years of an unsuccessful policy of remote-control killing, it's time to seek effective solutions that adhere to international law and promote democratic ideals. These include peace talks, alliance-building, treating terrorists as criminals who are arrested and tried, targeted development aid, and empowering women. The drone wars are making us less safe by simply creating new enemies abroad.

CHAPTER 3

Should Domestic Law Enforcement Agencies Be Allowed to Use Drones?

Overview: Drones over America—Public Safety Benefit or "Creepy" Privacy Threat?

Anna Mulrine

Anna Mulrine is a staff writer for the Christian Science Monitor.

Shortly after Alan Frazier became a part-time deputy sheriff in Grand Forks, N.D., the police began looking into the possibility of buying some aircraft to boost their law enforcement capabilities. They wanted some help doing things like finding missing people or carrying out rescues in a region dotted by farmsteads threatened by flooding that wipes out access to roads.

Buying a turbine engine helicopter, however, would cost $25 million, a prohibitive price tag even with 11 law enforcement agencies—eight from North Dakota and three in western Minnesota—willing to share the cost.

So Mr. Frazier, also an assistant professor of aviation at the University of North Dakota (UND), began looking into unmanned aerial vehicles (UAVs) as a possible alternative.

But what appears, on one level, to be a sensible, practical, and affordable solution for local law enforcement—the price tag for a small UAV is about the cost of a tricked-out new police cruiser at $50,000—has run smack into public concerns about yet another high-tech invasion of privacy and the popular image of drones as stealthy weapons used against terrorists.

Nonetheless, the technology's potential benefits in pursuing a raft of public safety measures at relatively low cost have enormous appeal for law enforcement agencies across the country, since President Obama signed a bill last year directing the Federal Aviation Administration (FAA) to further open US airspace to drones for both public and private use.

Even before that, the number of permits, known as certificates of authorization (COAs), that the FAA issued to organizations to fly UAVs more than doubled from 146 in 2009 to 313 in 2011. As of February 2013 there were 327 active COAs.

The growth in drones is big business. Some 50 companies are developing roughly 150 systems . . . ranging from miniature flying mechanical bugs to "Battlestar Galactica"-type hovering unmanned airplanes.

The bulk of these permits go to the US military for training, and the Pentagon expects their numbers to grow considerably in the years to come. According to a March 2011 Pentagon estimate, the Department of Defense will have 197 drones at 105 US bases by 2015.

The US Border Patrol has the country's largest fleet of UAVs for domestic surveillance, including nine Predator drones that patrol regions like the Rio Grande, searching for illegal immigrants and drug smugglers. Unlike the missile-firing Predators used by the Central Intelligence Agency to hunt Al Qaeda operatives and their allies, the domestic version of the aircraft—say, those used by the border patrol—is more typically equipped with night-vision technology and long-range cameras that can read license plates. Groups like the American Civil Liberties Union (ACLU) also complain that these drones have see-through imaging technology similar to those used in airports, as well as facial recognition software tied to federal databases.

The growth in drones is big business. Some 50 companies are developing roughly 150 systems, according to *The Wall Street Journal*, ranging from miniature flying mechanical bugs to "Battlestar Galactica"-type hovering unmanned airplanes. It's an industry expected to reach some $6 billion in US sales by 2016.

Those forecasts notwithstanding, neither the FAA nor the association of UAV operators says it knows how many non-military drones are operating in the United States. The ACLU is seeking that information.

The growth in the development of UAVs by both private companies and the US government has not gone unnoticed, creating a backlash in some communities.

In Seattle last month, community members quashed their city's drone program before it even got started. The program was being considered for search-and-rescue operations and some criminal investigations, but was referred to by protesters as "flying government robots watching their every move."

The president says you can take out American citizens in foreign countries. . . . Well, if you can do that, you can take out somebody here as well.

Mayor Mike McGinn spoke with Police Chief John Diaz, "and we agreed that it was time to end the unmanned aerial vehicle program," the mayor wrote in a statement. The drones were returned to the manufacturer.

Just days earlier, Charlottesville, Va., had become the first city in the country to pass a "no-drone zone" resolution, putting in place a two-year moratorium on the use of drones within Charlottesville limits.

"The big concern for us is that they're going to be everywhere," says John Whitehead, an attorney and president of

The Rutherford Institute, a civil liberties organization in Charlottesville, which launched a preemptive fight against drones before the city council.

The move followed an Obama administration memo justifying the use of drones overseas to kill US citizens suspected of taking part in terrorist activities. "The president says you can take out American citizens in foreign countries," Mr. Whitehead says. "Well, if you can do that, you can take out somebody here as well."

On March 6, Attorney General Eric Holder may have reinforced such fears in testimony before the Senate Judiciary Committee when he refused to rule out the use of armed drones on US soil in an emergency "to protect the homeland."

If it all has an air of hysteria about it—Mr. Holder said there are no plans for the domestic use of armed drones and called the scenario "entirely hypothetical" and unlikely—privacy groups point to California's Alameda County, where officials insisted they wanted drones for search-and-rescue missions. An internal memo that surfaced from the sheriff's department, however, noted the drones could be used for "investigative and tactical surveillance, intelligence gathering, suspicious persons, and large crowd-control disturbances." The county dropped its plans.

The first and only known use of a drone in the arrest of a US citizen occurred in December 2011 in North Dakota, when the Nelson County Sheriff's Department asked to borrow one of the US Customs and Border Protection UAVs. The drone provided a good view of the three sons of the owner of a 3,000-acre farm who were involved in a standoff with law enforcement officers. As a result, police were able to tell that the brothers were unarmed, allowing them to enter the farm and arrest the brothers without the confrontation turning into a shootout.

Whitehead imagines a day when drones equipped with sound cannons, which release painful high-decibel sound waves that cause crowds to disperse, could be dispatched by the government to political protests and used as well to "effectively stifle free speech."

The concern that such technologies can be misused to invade privacy and suppress free speech "is a legitimate fear," says UND's Frazier. "Anytime we increase the technological capabilities of the government there's a justifiable concern there. But I think these fears can be offset by the fact that the drones we're using have very limited capabilities."

FAA regulations stipulate that weaponized drones cannot fly in unrestricted US airspace.

Nevertheless, privacy concerns are what have prompted groups including the nonprofit Electronic Frontier Foundation (EFF) to use the Freedom of Information Act to obtain hundreds of documents from the FAA outlining who has been requesting to use drones in America's skies, and why.

Roughly 40 percent of the drone flight requests submitted to the FAA are from the US military. "They are flying drones pretty regularly—eight hours a day, five days a week—to train pilots so that they will be able to fly drones," says Jessica Lynch, a staff attorney for EFF.

These drones are equipped with infrared scanning capabilities and other surveillance gadgets. "Drones have quite a number of technologies on board, including thermal cameras and the ability to intercept communications," Ms. Lynch says. "If they are training pilots, they are training them in these surveillance tools."

FAA regulations stipulate that weaponized drones cannot fly in unrestricted US airspace. The agency also has specific parameters for law enforcement drones. Law enforcement groups, for example, must maintain visual contact with the drone at all times and must also fly at relatively low altitudes.

These are regulations with which the Grand Forks Sheriff's Department has become familiar in the three years since it began looking into using drones, first establishing an Unmanned Aerial Systems unit as part of the department and then applying for COAs to use the drones. The unit, which went fully operational Feb. 1, has conducted 250 simulated missions, but has yet to use a drone in an operation.

Certification tends to be a lengthy and arduous process, Frazier says, adding that there are also some parameters for usage that are meant to promote safety, but can make it tricky for law enforcement to do its jobs.

One provision, for example, is that the drones can fly only by day. Another early rule was that the police had to give 48 hours' notice if they were going to use the drones.

"It's tough to predict if there is going to be a fire tomorrow, or a bank robbery the day after tomorrow," he says. The department was able to convince the FAA to let it fly the drones on one-hour notice instead.

That said, Frazier understands the public's concerns about the use of drones. For that reason, Grand Forks established a 15-member committee—made up of one-third public safety officials, one-third UND faculty, and one-third community residents—to evaluate the use of drones and to troubleshoot questions and concerns of the public. Every law enforcement action involving the drones is to be reviewed by the committee.

Frazier told committee members that the department did not intend to ask for the ability to use the drones for covert surveillance. "We will not use them to, quote, spy on people," Frazier says. Even if that were the intention, he adds, "These small drones are not particularly robust platforms for covert surveillance. I think the public can't understand that my little UAV can only fly for 15 minutes, can't fly out of my line of sight, and can't fly in greater than 15-knot winds."

Out of concern that average citizens could be filmed by sensors on the aircraft, one of the committee's first acts was to instruct police to post road signs warning the public when UAVs are in use.

As technology becomes cheaper and easier to use, it's tempting to use it all the time.

Yet some of the conversations EFF's Lynch has had with other law enforcement agencies haven't been as reassuring about privacy, she says. "We've talked to police about this, and they've said, 'Well, we're going to fly the drones in public airspace, and if you walk around in public you don't have an expectation of privacy in your movements.'"

"While that might be true for a police officer following you down the street, I don't know if that applies when a drone can fly over and surveil everybody walking down that street for an extended period of time," Lynch says.

"You can make the case that drones are helping law enforcement better do their jobs for less [cost] and we should incorporate it," she adds. "As technology becomes cheaper and easier to use, it's tempting to use it all the time."

That is the fear of Texas state lawmaker Lance Gooden, who in February proposed some of the toughest anti-drone legislation in the country. It would prevent drone operators from collecting images, sounds, and smells—or hovering over any home—without permission.

"Two to four years from now, it'll be impossible to get legislation passed because every law enforcement agency will want drones," says Mr. Gooden. While the drone lobby is growing, it is not as powerful as it will become, he adds.

Currently, his bill has the support of 101 of the 150 members of the state Legislature. But some longtime drone experts say such laws are overkill and could impede growth of technology that is useful and relatively inexpensive.

"The ordinances that have been passed are absolutely absurd," says retired Lt. Gen. David Deptula, the first deputy chief of staff for Intelligence, Reconnaissance, and Surveillance for the US Air Force. "And what's precluded are the very valuable civilian applications in terms of traffic control, firefighting, disaster response, border security, the monitoring of power lines—the list goes on and on."

As for privacy concerns, "I can't think of another way of saying it, but that they are unfounded," Deptula adds. "All you have to do is look up in any major metropolitan city and see the cameras all around. And have they ever heard of satellites? Where do they think Google maps come from?"

Frazier concurs. People with a good zoom lens have better cameras than do his small drones, he adds, pointing out that one of the Grand Forks Sheriff's Department's drones has a simple off-the-shelf Panasonic.

The average GPS-enabled cellphone can now track people and their movements to within a few feet, he notes.

That said, "I understand what people mean when they say it's 'creepy,'" Frazier says. "I value my privacy as much as anyone does—it's very sacred in this country." Even if they could do it legally, law enforcement agencies would be making a big mistake using drones for covert surveillance—for the time being, he adds.

"It would be a fatal mistake at this point. We really need to take a crawl, walk, run approach. To go to covert surveillance brings us to a run," Frazier says of the law enforcement community. "If that means we're not Buck Rogers in the 21st century, we're comfortable with that."

Drones Are Essential Tools for Modern Law Enforcement

Eli Richman

Eli Richman was an editorial intern at Governing *magazine when he wrote this viewpoint.*

When an inmate escaped from jail in Montgomery County, Texas, a few years back, police took to the skies. Montgomery County sits just north of Houston, but the inmate fled into a nearby wooded area, making it harder for law enforcement officers to track him down. Fortunately, the sheriff's department was able to secure a helicopter from the Texas Department of Public Safety. Officers located the inmate using an infrared camera, and they directed deputies to the location.

Today, they'd just use a drone.

Unmanned aerial vehicles, better known as UAVs or drones, are beginning to be embraced by local law enforcement agencies across the United States. Unmanned drones have, of course, made headlines in recent years for their use in foreign military operations. Drone surveillance helped target Osama bin Laden's compound, and a CIA Predator drone fired the missile that killed Anwar al-Awlaki, another high-profile Al Qaeda figure. Now, the vehicles are likely moving into domestic airspace as well. In an effort to push for drone use in police and fire departments, the U.S. Department of Homeland Security (DHS) has reportedly awarded more than $3 million in grants to at least 13 local law enforcement agencies to purchase small drones—including Montgomery County, which last year became one of the first local agencies in the country to acquire its own aerial drone. The county

Eli Richman, "The Rise (and Fall) of Drones," governing.com, December 2012. Governing.com. Copyright © 2012 Governing. All rights reserved. Reproduced with permission.

purchased a ShadowHawk MK-II drone last year for about $300,000, using a $220,000 DHS grant.

It's not just police departments that see big potential in unmanned drones. Fire departments and other emergency response teams could use them [as well].

Drones Are a Natural Fit for Police

Drones could revolutionize police work. Helicopters are expensive to fuel and maintain, and flying them takes specialized piloting skills. Because they're in relatively short supply, using a helicopter often requires interdepartmental coordination, as was the case in Montgomery County's manhunt. By comparison, drones are easy. They cost about 100 times less than a helicopter, and operating a drone costs significantly less per hour. They're extremely light: Montgomery's gas-powered ShadowHawk weighs just 49 pounds. At six feet long, it can fit in the back of an SUV, and piloting it requires nothing more than a laptop computer and a remote control. It's a nimble crime-fighting tool that will be an essential asset in the future, says Montgomery Chief Deputy Randy McDaniel. When McDaniel's office acquired the drone last year, he issued a statement saying, "I absolutely believe it will become a critical component on all SWAT callouts and narcotics raids and emergency management operations."

"Having eyes in the air above an incident will enhance the awareness of the commander on the ground, to ensure his officers' safety and the public's safety," McDaniel says today. "You can't literally surround a building or a house every time. Having that drone up in the air above it can enhance safety for law enforcement." The device would also help in non-crime situations, McDaniel says, such as tracking down hikers who have lost their way in nearby Sam Houston National Forest. "People get lost in that forest every year," McDaniel says.

"It would certainly be more effective to put that UAV up as opposed to sending 30 or 40 search-and-rescue personnel to walk it."

Many First Responders Could Benefit

It's not just police departments that see big potential in unmanned drones. Fire departments and other emergency response teams could use them to help pinpoint the source of a building fire or, say, map a hazmat spill. The federal Department of Agriculture uses a drone to monitor experimental crops in Georgia and Alabama; state agriculture departments could no doubt find plenty of similar uses. Documents disclosed by a Freedom of Information Act request this summer from the Electronic Frontier Foundation showed that the federal government had approved drones for 18 public entities around the country, including police departments in Seattle, Miami-Dade, Fla., and North Little Rock, Ark., as well as places like Ohio University and the city of Herington, Kan. Thanks to anticipated changes in federal aviation regulations, thousands of private and commercial drones could also take to the air by 2015. According to FAA estimates, more than 30,000 drones could fill the American skies by 2020. As University of Texas assistant professor Todd Humphreys, who has investigated the use of domestic drones, testified to Congress earlier this year, "The UAV revolution is coming."

Needless to say, privacy concerns are huge. Nothing says "Big Brother police state" quite like the idea of faceless surveillance drones flitting through the sky, tracking and videotaping civilians' every move. According to one recent national poll, while 44 percent of Americans support the use of drones by police forces, a large minority—36 percent—were opposed because of the potential for privacy invasion. Those fears are further stoked by comments like a recent statement from Alameda County, Calif., Sheriff Gregory Ahern, who said his department, which has filed for drone clearance from the

FAA, would use the vehicles to troll for marijuana farms and other forms of "proactive policing."

Surveillance Suspicions

"Our ultimate concern is that drones become a tool for pervasive, routine, suspicionless surveillance," says Jay Stanley, a senior policy analyst for the American Civil Liberties Union's (ACLU) Speech, Privacy and Technology Project. "We don't want to see them used for 24/7 tracking of vehicles or individuals, and over towns or cities or neighborhoods. We don't want to see them used for individual suspicion. We don't want them to be used in ways that are invasive."

At the federal level, the ACLU has recommended that government use of drones be banned except in very specific cases.

Law enforcement officials say that's not their intention, and they couldn't use drones that way even if they wanted to. "We did not obtain this for the purpose of surveillance," says McDaniel. "Our ShadowHawk's maximum aloft time is only two hours and 20 minutes, and you would never fly it for that length of time to begin with." FAA regulations prohibit drones from flying higher than 400 feet, and they require that drones remain in line of sight of the user. In other words, says McDaniel, if a drone's around, you'll know it. "It's not like its 30,000 feet up in the air and you can't see it and you can't hear it. It's going to be visible to the naked eye, and you're certainly going to hear it."

Laws Should Preempt Problems

Current drone technology may not lend itself to stealth surveillance, but that's why privacy legislation should be passed now, before it becomes a problem, say advocates. "While drones are new and novel and everybody's worried about the privacy issue," says Stanley, "we need to put in place some far-seeing rules and protections that will cover every possible evolution of this technology." . . .

In August, the International Association of Chiefs of Police adopted guidelines for the use of unmanned aircraft. The guidelines call for transparency in how the vehicles are used, and say that any images captured by aerial drones and retained by police should be open to the public. In cases where drones might collect evidence of criminal wrongdoing, or if they will intrude on reasonable expectations of privacy, guidelines suggest police should obtain a prior search warrant. Those instructions aren't binding, but they're a good start, privacy advocates say.

At the federal level, the ACLU has recommended that government use of drones be banned except in very specific cases. One piece of legislation has been introduced in Congress by Republican Sen. Rand Paul of Kentucky, which would ban domestic governmental drone use except in patrolling the border or in high-risk security situations. The bill currently lacks bipartisan support. While the ACLU says the bill isn't perfect, its legislative counsel Chris Calabrese says the bill is "starting in the right place, and we're going to work with him as he moves forward."

Drone Spoofing and Hacking

In addition to questions about privacy, another concern is drones' security. First, there's the immediate worry that comes from allowing individually operated aircraft in domestic airspace, particularly in a post-9/11 world. That concern was borne out last year, when a man in Massachusetts was thwarted after attempting to equip several drones with C4 explosives and fly them into the Capitol and Pentagon. Second, civilian drones can be hacked, or "spoofed," by a counterfeit GPS signal. (Unlike military GPS signals, civilian signals are not encrypted.) The spoofed drone thinks it's in a different place, allowing the hacker to take rudimentary control of it. In a demonstration in June, the University of Texas' Humphreys led a team of researchers who successfully hacked into one drone's navigation system.

There's no question that unmanned aerial vehicles could forever change crime fighting, disaster response and a host of other functions.

Regulating this type of vehicle typically would fall under the purview of Homeland Security, but that department has so far declined to regulate the UAV industry. That's a major problem, says Texas Rep. Michael McCaul, who chairs the House Subcommittee on Oversight, Investigations and Management. "I find this to be a bit of a 'nobody's minding the store' type scenario," McCaul says. "No federal agency's willing to step up to the plate, and when you have the [Government Accountability Office] saying the DHS needs to do it, I tend to agree with them." Without regulation at the federal level, security oversight could fall to individual states.

For his part, Humphreys says he's not overly worried about drone security. Spoofing a UAV requires a high level of expertise and very expensive software. But as with the privacy issues, it's an issue that almost certainly will be exacerbated as technology advances. "What my nightmare scenario would be," he says, "is looking forward three or four years, where we have now adopted the UAVs into the national airspace without addressing this problem. Now the problem is scaling up, so that we have more heavy UAVs, more capable UAVs and yet this particular vulnerability isn't addressed."

There's no question that unmanned aerial vehicles could forever change crime fighting, disaster response and a host of other functions. Given the push from the federal government, it seems inevitable that drones will increasingly be a part of police assets around the country. But it's important to address concerns over privacy and security now, says Humphreys. "Let's let it go ahead," he says. "But let's be vigilant."

Drones Can Help Improve Public Safety

Colin Wood

Colin Wood has been writing for Government Technology *and* Emergency Management *magazines since 2010.*

While drones have been deployed in many military actions, domestic drone deployment in the United States faces opposition on several fronts. Many in the public view drones as overly invasive or machines of war, as demonstrated by the legislative acts of many states, capped off by Seattle's recent decision to scrap the police department's drone program.

But hobbyists and many in the public safety community argue that privacy concerns over drones may be keeping the public from seeing the true potential the unmanned aircraft could offer, especially in emergency management and response.

Law enforcement could use drones to gain better situational awareness and keep officers and civilians safe during dangerous operations like drug busts or hostage situations. Firefighters could use them to scout wildfires, or identify hidden hot spots in structure fires. Rescue teams could save trapped or missing people in areas that helicopters can't reach. In the right hands, drones could make the public safer.

For hobbyists, there are virtually no obstacles to flying a small, unmanned aircraft. A beginner drone costs a few hundred dollars, and the Federal Aviation Administration (FAA) allows toy drones to go essentially unregulated. But if a drone is used as a tool, whether for fire scouting or to bring water to a stranded hiker, then the drone is no longer a toy and requires a certificate of authorization. There's a lot of paperwork and months of waiting in store for any public safety agency seeking to use a drone legally. But this will soon change, according to Don Shinnamon, a former police chief who sat on the first rule-making committee for drones.

If a public safety agency has between $40,000 and $100,000 to spend on drone technology, they can get a turn-key system that works well.

"As a pilot of manned aircraft," Shinnamon said, "I don't necessarily want to be dodging a hundred unmanned aircraft that are flying around. So I support the notion that the integration of unmanned aircraft has to go slowly so we can guarantee the safety of the national airspace." While Shinnamon supports conservative drone legislation for safety purposes, he is also a major proponent of increased domestic drone use. He drafted a provision of the FAA Modernization and Reform Act of 2012 that will make it simpler for public safety agencies to get authorized.

Law Enforcement Looks to Cut Costs

With fewer regulations keeping law enforcement agencies from using drones, Shinnamon expects the technology will become a more viable option, especially given their potential to enhance public safety. "We are a tradition-bound profession," Shinnamon said, referring to those in law enforcement who don't support the use of drones, "but the economy has forced us to look for better ways to provide the same levels of service or more economical ways of providing a higher level of service. The technology has proven it can save the lives of troops on the ground in combat zones. And that same technology can provide a much higher level of safety for police officers and firefighters doing dangerous things here in our country."

But even those public safety leaders interested in reaping the benefits of drones don't necessarily have the knowledge, funding or time to research the technology. That's where hobbyists come in.

Hobbyists Help Sell Drone Idea

If a public safety agency has between $40,000 and $100,000 to spend on drone technology, they can get a turn-key system that works well, according to Oregon-based hobbyists Patrick Sherman and Brian Zvaigzne. Calling themselves the Roswell Flight Test Crew, the two are showing agencies in their region what drones can accomplish at a modest cost.

The team has worked with fire and rescue agencies in Portland, Ore.; Tualatin Valley, Ore.; Clackamas, Ore.; and Longview, Wash. Sherman reports that their level of involvement has ranged from preliminary talks to field demonstrations, and they've encountered wide variations in officials' openness to the potential of drones.

Commercial drones on the market today are much easier to control than those available just a few years ago.

"We've had some firefighters who've been just enthralled with the idea of this technology," he explained, but others staunchly defend their agency's current operations, questioning what value the unmanned craft would bring. "I'm not saying there's anything wrong with the way they do things. I think this can be an enhancement," Sherman said.

According to Sherman, drones made by hobbyists like the Roswell Flight Test Crew work as well as the big-name turn-key drone systems sold by commercial vendors, but cost about 95 percent less. But drones require maintenance, system integration and someone has to know how to fly them.

Unmanned Civil Air Patrol

Just as the Civil Air Patrol employs volunteer pilots to support operations of the U.S. Air Force, there are drone hobbyists around the country who might consider joining an unmanned civil air patrol, he suggests. "There's a long tradition of amateur radio operators helping out in emergencies," Sherman said, adding that until drone technology becomes more broadly used, drone hobbyists, similarly, could fill this vital role.

Commercial drones on the market today are much easier to control than those available just a few years ago. If a drone pilot takes his hands off the controls, GPS and altitude positioning allow the aircraft to simply hover in place until the pilot is ready to continue. This technological progress is thanks to engineers and researchers like Mary "Missy" Cummings, an associate professor at MIT who focuses much of her research on drone control architectures.

According to Cummings, a major reason drones have gotten cheaper in the last few years is that manufacturers have cut corners on things like user interface. "Unfortunately the big barrier to UAVs [Unmanned Aerial Vehicles] being successful in the commercial marketplace is that they're going to have to be as safe as commercial aircraft," she said. "Companies are going to have to start taking safety, efficiency, well designed interfaces, the reduction of human error, they're going to have to start taking that stuff seriously."

Cummings said although she liked the idea of an unmanned civil air patrol, she noted that there are several major barriers to implementation, including collision avoidance, command and control support and coordination.

Asset Management

Consider, she said, a major earthquake in California. "Like in a lot of cases where you have a community grass-roots effort, you need somebody who can actually manage this and now we're not talking about just managing people and rescuers, we're managing all the data that's going out to support rescuers." So while it's a good idea, she said, the program would need structure to make it work.

Regardless of whether a grass-roots effort can impact public safety in an emergency, drones can augment operations in ways that no other technology can, Cummings said. "These automated systems can exceed human abilities and take over in the times when we can't do something because of our physical limitations, and I think that is what we're going to start seeing in the future," she said. "You don't want to send a manned helicopter into a burning area to pick up, let's say, some firefighters that were pinned in by some out of control fire. You wouldn't want to risk a human life to do that, but you would easily send in a helicopter to do that."

Cummings thinks that it is just these kinds of emergency response scenarios that might help change public perceptions about drone use. "We're going to have the next Hurricane Katrina, the next Hurricane Sandy," she explained. "We're going to start seeing unmanned vehicles bringing in badly needed supplies and . . . I think as soon as we do that, it's going to be amazing the change we see in people. People just see UAVs as bad. I think there's a change coming."

Drones Are Vital for
US Border Security

Perla Trevizo

Perla Trevizo is a staff writer for the Arizona Daily Star *newspaper.*

B order security is the first step of the proposed immigration reform bill—and some lawmakers see 24/7 surveillance as a key to stopping illegal crossers.

Ten drones already fly along the U.S. southern and northern borders. But U.S. Customs and Border Protection [CBP] has not been able to fully use them, partly because of Federal Aviation Administration restrictions and partly because of a lack of money to operate them, said Randolph Alles, assistant commander of the Office of Air and Marine, which supervises the drones.

After nearly eight years of operating drones along the border, Alles said the agency is now reaping the benefits, but the program is still not where he wants it to be.

"Looking backward, it probably would have been better if we were able to bring them on slower," he said.

The most commonly used drone, the Predator B, can fly about 20 hours without having to refuel, compared with a helicopter's average flight time of just over two hours. With new technology such as VADER, Alles said the agency is getting more use out of the aircraft than before.

VADER, which stands for Vehicle and Dismount Exploitation Radar, was developed for the war in Afghanistan. It lets agents track activity in real time and distinguishes humans from animals from an altitude of 25,000 feet. Last year, CBP borrowed the radar from the military to test it in Arizona.

U.S. Sen. John McCain is among VADER's supporters.

A total of 10 drones fly now [for border control]—five days a week, 16 hours a day out of Sierra Vista [Arizona] and five days a week, 10 hours a day out of the locations in Texas, Florida and North Dakota.

"It seems to me that's an incredible technology tool," McCain told Alles during a congressional hearing in April [2013]. "Don't you believe that VADER plus drones could be absolute vital tools in attaining effective control of our border?"

As lawmakers started to debate the immigration bill last week [June 2013], McCain said the government needed to use more technology such as drones and VADER to increase border security.

Boosting Drone Effectiveness

Alles would not comment on possible requirements of the immigration bill, saying his immediate goal is to get better use out of the drones he has by training more personnel, flying the dones longer and attaching better surveillance equipment to the aircraft.

A total of 10 drones fly now—five days a week, 16 hours a day out of Sierra Vista and five days a week, 10 hours a day out of the locations in Texas, Florida and North Dakota.

Alles' long-term goal is to fly drones seven days a week, 16 hours a day—"we are not there yet," he said.

CBP's original plan was to purchase 24 unmanned aircraft, but Alles said he doesn't have the money to buy more—and even if he did, he doesn't have enough money to operate them all.

The agency spends $32 million to $34 million to operate and maintain the 10 aircraft a year. That includes expenses related to ground-control stations, repairs, satellite communication and engineering support. The total cost of the program has been estimated at several hundred million dollars.

In fiscal year 2010, CBP had to transfer $25 million from other programs to address operations and maintenance funding shortfalls.

Since the program's inception, critics have questioned if the $18 million cost for each fully equipped aircraft is the best use of taxpayer money.

"Desired Capability"

If CBP were flying seven drones—the number the agency had at the time of a 2012 report by Homeland Security's inspector general—it would need to fly them 13,328 flight hours annually to reach its "desired capability."

At a per-hour flight cost of $3,234, that would require nearly $62 million per year—about 12 percent of the entire operations, maintenance, and procurement budget for CBP's Air and Marine branch.

Given the operational cost of the Predator B, the amount of drugs and people the drones help seize is not impressive, said Adam Isacson, a regional security policy expert for the Washington Office on Latin America, an organization that studies the effects of U.S. policies on Latin America.

Nationwide, drones have helped seize more than $650 million worth of drugs.

The four drones based in Sierra Vista—which fly mostly along the Southwest border but can be shifted to other areas as needed—have flown nearly 12,000 hours and helped seize 82,000 pounds of marijuana since fiscal 2006. CBP didn't provide the number of apprehensions.

From fiscal years 2008 through last month, Border Patrol agents along the Southwest border seized more than 13 million pounds of marijuana.

Nationwide, drones have helped seize more than $650 million worth of drugs, "which basically pays for the program by itself," Alles said.

The unmanned aircraft are also used during floods and hurricanes, he said, although 95 percent of their missions are along the borders.

VADER Sees All

VADER is helping, too. The radar can detect about 11 people an hour, Alles said, more than any other detection tools in the system, including fixed towers or other aircraft.

Isacson said drones and radars like VADER, though expensive, will help CBP see more of what's going on at the border, which is good.

But he questions if the agency will have the personnel needed to catch everything detected on the nearly 2,000-mile stretch of the southern border.

The Center for Investigative Reporting and the *Los Angeles Times* reported that Border Patrol agents last year apprehended fewer than half of the people VADER spotted crossing into a stretch of Southern Arizona.

Among the limitations, the internal reports revealed that Border Patrol agents often are not available to respond because of rugged terrain or other assignments, the Center for Investigative Reporting found.

Alles said the internal report was misused and doesn't reflect apprehensions in the zone where the radar was used. CBP is getting two of the $5 million VADER systems and plans to deploy at least one in Arizona in about a year. At the recent Congressional hearing he told McCain the goal was to have six radars.

Whatever shape comprehensive immigration reform takes in the end, Isacson said, it's not likely to pass without requiring the use of more drones.

"Putting more drones and technology on the border is an easy way to convince more conservative members of Congress to vote for this," he said. "It feels it's inevitable."

Law Enforcement Drones Pose Multiple Dangers

Glenn Greenwald

Glenn Greenwald is an American journalist and lawyer best known for exposing the National Security Agency's (NSA) mass surveillance programs based on classified information leaked by former intelligence contractor Edward Snowden.

The use of drones by domestic US law enforcement agencies is growing rapidly, both in terms of numbers and types of usage. As a result, civil liberties and privacy groups led by the ACLU [American Civil Liberties Union]—while accepting that domestic drones are inevitable—have been devoting increasing efforts to publicizing their unique dangers and agitating for statutory limits. These efforts are being impeded by those who mock the idea that domestic drones pose unique dangers (often the same people who mock concern over their usage on foreign soil). This dismissive posture is grounded not only in soft authoritarianism (a religious-type faith in the Goodness of US political leaders and state power generally) but also ignorance over current drone capabilities, the ways drones are now being developed and marketed for domestic use, and the activities of the increasingly powerful domestic drone lobby. So it's quite worthwhile to lay out the key under-discussed facts shaping this issue.

I'm going to focus here most on domestic surveillance drones, but I want to say a few words about weaponized drones. The belief that weaponized drones won't be used on US soil is patently irrational. Of course they will be. It's not just likely but inevitable. Police departments are already speaking openly about how their drones "could be equipped to carry nonlethal weapons such as Tasers or a bean-bag gun." The drone industry has already developed and is now aggressively marketing precisely such weaponized drones for domestic law enforcement use. It likely won't be in the form that has received the most media attention: the type of large Predator or Reaper drones that shoot Hellfire missiles which destroy homes and cars in Pakistan, Yemen, Somalia, Afghanistan and multiple other countries aimed at Muslims (although US law enforcement agencies already possess Predator drones and have used them over US soil for surveillance).

The handful of genuinely positive uses from drones will be endlessly touted to distract attention away from the dangers they pose.

Cheap and Agile Weaponized Drones

Instead, as I detailed in a 2012 examination of the drone industry's own promotional materials and reports to their shareholders, domestic weaponized drones will be much smaller and cheaper, as well as more agile—but just as lethal. The nation's leading manufacturer of small "unmanned aircraft systems" (UAS), used both for surveillance and attack purposes, is AeroVironment, Inc. (AV). Its 2011 Annual Report filed with the SEC [Securities Exchange Commission] repeatedly emphasizes that its business strategy depends upon expanding its market from foreign wars to domestic usage including law enforcement:

> "As we explore opportunities to develop new markets for our small UAS, such as border surveillance, law enforcement, first response and infrastructure monitoring, we expect further growth through the introduction of UAS technology to non-military applications once rules are established for their safe and effective operation in each country's national airspace."

AV's annual report added: "Initial likely non-military users of small UAS include public safety organizations such as law enforcement agencies. . . ." These domestic marketing efforts are intensifying with the perception that US spending on foreign wars will decrease. As a February, 2013 CBS News report noted, focusing on AV's surveillance drones:

> "Now, drones are headed off the battlefield. They're already coming your way."

> "AeroVironment (AV), the California company that sells the military something like 85 percent of its fleet, is marketing them now to public safety agencies."

Like many drone manufacturers, AV is now focused on drone products—such as the "Qube"—that are so small that they can be "transported in the trunk of a police vehicle or carried in a backpack" and assembled and deployed within a matter of minutes. One news report AV touts is headlined "Drone technology could be coming to a Police Department near you," which focuses on the Qube.

"The Ultimate Assassin Bug"

But another article prominently touted on AV's website describes the tiny UAS product dubbed the "Switchblade," which, says the article, is "the leading edge of what is likely to be the broader, even wholesale, weaponization of unmanned systems." The article creepily hails the Switchblade drone as *the ultimate assassin bug.*" That's because, as I wrote back in 2011, "it is controlled by the operator at the scene, and it worms its way around buildings and into small areas, sending its surveillance imagery to an i-Pad held by the operator, who can then direct the Switchblade to lunge toward and kill the target (hence the name) by exploding in his face." AV's website right now proudly touts a February, 2013 *Defense News* article describing how much the US Army loves the "Switchblade" and how it is preparing to purchase more. *Time* magazine heralded this tiny drone weapon as "one of the best inventions of 2012," gushing: "the Switchblade drone can be carried into battle in a backpack. It's a kamikaze: the person controlling it uses a real-time video feed from the drone to crash it into a precise target—say, a sniper. Its tiny warhead detonates on impact."

What possible reason could someone identify as to why these small, portable weaponized UAS products will not imminently be used by federal, state and local law enforcement agencies in the US? They're designed to protect their users in dangerous situations and to enable a target to be more easily killed. Police agencies and the increasingly powerful drone industry will tout their utility in capturing and killing dangerous criminals and their ability to keep officers safe, and media reports will do the same. The handful of genuinely positive uses from drones will be endlessly touted to distract attention away from the dangers they pose.

Unmanned aircraft carrying cameras raise the prospect of a significant new avenue for the surveillance of American life.

The Militarization of Law Enforcement

One has to be incredibly naïve to think that these "assassin bugs" and other lethal drone products will not be widely used on US soil by an already para-militarized domestic police force. As Radley Balko's forthcoming book *Rise of the Warrior Cop* details, the primary trend in US law enforcement is what its title describes as "The Militarization of America's Police Forces." The history of domestic law enforcement particularly after 9/11 has been the importation of military techniques and weapons into domestic policing. It would be shocking if these weapons were not imminently used by domestic law enforcement agencies.

In contrast to weaponized drones, even the most naïve among us do not doubt the imminent proliferation of domestic surveillance drones. With little debate, they have already arrived. As the ACLU put it in their recent report: "US law enforcement is greatly expanding its use of domestic drones for surveillance." An *LA Times* article from last month [February 2013] reported that "federal authorities have stepped up efforts to license surveillance drones for law enforcement and other uses in US airspace" and that "the Federal Aviation Administration said Friday it had issued 1,428 permits to domestic drone operators since 2007, far more than were previously known." Moreover, the agency "has estimated 10,000 drones could be aloft five years later" and "local and state law enforcement agencies are expected to be among the largest customers."

"The Gorgon Stare"

Concerns about the proliferation of domestic surveillance drones are typically dismissed with the claim that they do nothing more than police helicopters and satellites already do. Such claims are completely misinformed. As the ACLU's 2011 comprehensive report on domestic drones explained: "Unmanned aircraft carrying cameras raise the prospect of a significant new avenue for the surveillance of American life."

Multiple attributes of surveillance drones make them uniquely threatening. Because they are so cheap and getting cheaper, huge numbers of them can be deployed to create ubiquitous surveillance in a way that helicopters or satellites never could. How this works can already been seen in Afghanistan, where the US military has dubbed its drone surveillance system "the Gorgon Stare," named after the "mythical Greek creature whose unblinking eyes turned to stone those who beheld them." That drone surveillance system is "able to scan an area the size of a small town" and "the most sophisticated robotics use artificial intelligence that [can] seek out and record certain kinds of suspicious activity." Boasted one US General: "Gorgon Stare will be looking at a whole city, so there will be no way for the adversary to know what we're looking at, and *we can see everything."*

In sum, surveillance drones enable a pervasive, stealth and constantly hovering Surveillance State that is now well beyond the technological and financial abilities of law enforcement agencies.

Drones and the Surveillance State

The NSA [National Security Agency] already maintains ubiquitous surveillance of electronic communications, but the Surveillance State faces serious limits on its ability to replicate that for physical surveillance. Drones easily overcome those barriers. As the ACLU report put it:

> "But manned aircraft are expensive to purchase, operate and maintain, and this expense has always imposed a natural limit on the government's aerial surveillance capability. Now that surveillance can be carried out by unmanned aircraft, this natural limit is eroding. The prospect of cheap, small, portable flying video surveillance machines threatens to eradicate existing practical limits on aerial monitoring and allow for pervasive surveillance, police fishing expeditions, and abusive use of these tools in a way that could eventually eliminate the privacy Americans have traditionally enjoyed in their movements and activities."

I've spoken previously about why a ubiquitous Surveillance State ushers in unique and deeply harmful effects on human behavior and a nation's political culture and won't repeat that here. ... Suffice to say, as the ACLU explains in its domestic drone report: "routine aerial surveillance would profoundly change the character of public life in America" because *only* drone technology enables such omnipresent physical surveillance.

Beyond that, the tiny size of surveillance drones enables them to reach places that helicopters obviously cannot, and to do so without detection. They can remain in the sky, hovering over a single place, for up to 20 hours, a duration that is always increasing—obviously far more than manned helicopters can achieve. As AV's own report put it, their hovering capability also means they can surveil a single spot for much longer than many military satellites, most of which move with the earth's rotation (the few satellites that remain fixed "operate nearly 25,000 miles from the surface of the earth, therefore limiting the bandwidth they can provide and requiring relatively larger, higher power ground stations"). In sum, surveillance drones enable a pervasive, stealth and constantly hovering Surveillance State that is now well beyond the technological and financial abilities of law enforcement agencies.

Only the most authoritarian among us will be incapable of understanding the multiple dangers posed by a domestic drone regime.

The Drone Lobby Is Powerful

One significant reason why this proliferation of domestic drones has become so likely is the emergence of a powerful drone lobby. I detailed some of how that lobby is functioning here, so will simply note this passage from a recent report from the ACLU of Iowa on its attempts to persuade legislators to enact statutory limits on the use of domestic drones:

> "Drones have their own trade group, the Association for Unmanned Aerial Systems International, which includes some of the nation's leading aerospace companies. And Congress now has 'drone caucuses' in both the Senate and House."

[Progressive blogger] Howie Klein has been one of the few people focusing on the massive amounts of money from the drone industry now flowing into the coffers of key Congressional members from both parties in this "drone caucus." Suffice to say, there is an enormous profit to be made from exploiting the domestic drone market, and as usual, that factor is thus far driving the (basically nonexistent) political response to these threats.

What is most often ignored by drone proponents, or those who scoff at anti-drone activism, are the unique features of drones: the way they enable more warfare, more aggression, and more surveillance. Drones make war more likely precisely because they entail so little risk to the war-making country. Similarly, while the propensity of drones to kill innocent people receives the bulk of media attention, the way in which drones psychologically terrorize the population—simply by constantly hovering over them: unseen but heard—is usually ignored, because it's not happening in the US, so few people care. It remains to be seen how Americans will react to drones constantly hovering over their homes and their childrens' schools, though by that point, their presence will be so institutionalized that it will likely be too late to stop.

The Dangers of a Domestic Drone Regime

Notably, this may be one area where an actual bipartisan/trans-partisan alliance can meaningfully emerge, as most advocates working on these issues with whom I've spoken say that libertarian-minded GOP state legislators have been as responsive as more left-wing Democratic ones in working to impose some limits. One bill now pending in Congress would prohibit the use of surveillance drones on US soil in the absence of a specific search warrant, and has bipartisan support.

Only the most authoritarian among us will be incapable of understanding the multiple dangers posed by a domestic drone regime (particularly when their party is in control of the government and they are incapable of perceiving threats from increased state police power). But the proliferation of domestic drones affords a real opportunity to forge an enduring coalition in defense of core privacy and other rights that transcends partisan allegiance, by working toward meaningful limits on their use. Making people aware of exactly what these unique threats are from a domestic drone regime is the key first step in constructing that coalition.

Law Enforcement Drones Spur Public Backlash

Nadia Prupis

Nadia Prupis is a staff writer for Common Dreams, *a news and analysis website for the progressive community.*

Police departments in the U.S. are increasingly considering the use of drones as a law enforcement tool, even as civil rights groups and media turn up scrutiny of police militarization in the wake of brutal crackdowns on anti-brutality protesters in Ferguson, Missouri and other cities.

The *Baltimore Sun* reported on Sunday [August 24, 2014] that agencies in several Maryland counties are considering testing drones, or unmanned aerial vehicles (UAVs), for intelligence gathering and "high-risk tactical raids." That news comes less than a week after anti-war activists in California protested against "mission creep" by the Los Angeles Police Department (LAPD) which recently acquired several of their own drones. Indiana police departments also recently announced their plan to pursue adding drones to their weapons arsenal. In a letter to LA Mayor Eric Garcetti, Drone-Free LA spokesperson Hamid Kahn expressed "deep concerns about the recent 'gifting' of two Draganflyer X Drones" by the Seattle Police Department [SPD] to the LAPD. "We believe the acquisition of drones signifies a giant step forward in the militarization of local law enforcement that is normalizing continued surveillance and violations of human rights of our communities," Kahn wrote.

The SPD originally purchased the unmanned aerial vehicles using a federal grant called the Urban Areas Security

Initiative—a common example of the effects of the government's pervasive, $34-billion militarization program that enables domestic police departments to acquire and trade tools and weapons intended for warfare. In a June press conference, LAPD chief Charlie Beck said drones would be useful in "standoffs, perimeters, suspects hiding," and defended the department's acquisition of the UAVs by stating, "When retailers start talking about using them to deliver packages, we would be silly not to at least have a discussion of whether we want to use them in law enforcement."

A lot of what can be done with this equipment is very much questionable, as far as adherence to the Fourth Amendment.

Critics Sound the Alarm

But while many police departments claim that they would use the vehicles strictly for high-risk scenarios, critics have sounded the alarm over the risks of drone use, particularly by entities they say are as historically oppressive as American law enforcement agencies.

Tara Tabassi, national organizer with the War Resisters League, told *Common Dreams* that with the "current nationwide public outcry against police militarization, it is the many invisible methods of domestic warfare, such as the use of drones by police departments, that must be a major focus. . . . Warfare indeed knows no borders, nor does the US government's lack of transparency and accountability as they choose to protect the identities and crimes of drone operators over the civil liberties and human rights of unarmed populations across the globe."

Police militarization and violent police responses to peaceful protests have faced increased scrutiny in recent weeks after activists and reporters in Ferguson were tear gassed and shot at while demanding justice for Michael Brown, the unarmed teenager who was shot to death by a police officer earlier this month. "A lot of what can be done with this equipment is very much questionable, as far as adherence to the Fourth Amendment," Nathan Sheard, a campaign organizer with anti-war group CodePink, told *Common Dreams*. "The fact that it's being paid for by Department of Homeland Security shows a very obvious connection with militarization. When police departments start to be armed . . . as military forces, rather than protecting and serving, they start occupying and oppressing."

Fourth Amendment Worries

In California, Kahn pointed to the LAPD's history of "lies, brutality, and violence against communities," and said that the department is "incapable of creating any policy that would protect our human and civil rights."

Sheard also noted "the very real possibility of installing infrared cameras" on UAVs, models of which have already appeared in the U.S.

The risks are "beyond what's just visible to the eye," Sheard said. "These are cameras that would pick up heat signals rather than video. How does that play into the Fourth Amendment protections against search and seizure?"

David Rocah, senior staff attorney with the ACLU of Maryland, told *WJZ* that drones pose an inherent risk to the right to privacy. "That is completely incompatible with a free society and I think poses real dangers and is a real possibility unless we act to prevent it," Rocah said.

Regulation of drone technology is a concern as well. Claims from police departments that the UAVs would be used transparently and "would not sacrifice public trust," as LAPD spokesperson Bruce Borhian told *KNX*, are not enough, Sheard said.

The Fox Guarding the Henhouse?

"Who is monitoring [the police]?" Sheard told *Common Dreams*. "Who's holding them accountable? What ability do citizens have to view that information? Where do those recordings go? There are just too many questions." He noted a successful CodePink campaign to end the use of drones by a department in Washington state that simply resulted in the vehicles being traded to an agency in California. "The equipment just changed hands," Sheard said.

"Now is the time to stop the engine of surveillance technology and state repression," Tabassi told *Common Dreams*. "By continuing to build across all communities mobilizing against police militarization, we can effectively resist the solidifying relationship between the Pentagon and police departments, demanding an end to all drones, and militarization more broadly."

Pending Senate approval, the presence of drones in US airspace is projected to increase by 10,000 in 2015, Tabassi said. Although the use of drones by police departments is still in relative infancy, waiting on testing and Federal Aviation Administration rules, more than 500 agencies were approved to use them in the last year alone.

Drones Are Ineffective for Border Patrol

Brian Bennett

Brian Bennett covers homeland security and immigration for the Los Angeles Times *newspaper.*

Drones patrolling the U.S. border are poorly managed and ineffective at stopping illegal immigration, and the government should abandon a $400-million plan to expand their use, according to an internal watchdog report released Tuesday [January 6, 2015].

The 8-year-old drone program has cost more than expected, according to a report by the Department of Homeland Security's inspector general, John Roth.

Rather than spend more on drones, the department should "put those funds to better use," Roth recommended. He described the Predator B drones flown along the border by U.S. Customs and Border Protection as "dubious achievers."

"Notwithstanding the significant investment, we see no evidence that the drones contribute to a more secure border, and there is no reason to invest additional taxpayer funds at this time," Roth said in a statement.

The audit concluded that Customs and Border Protection could better use the funds on manned aircraft and ground surveillance technology.

The drones were designed to fly over the border to spot smugglers and illegal border crossers. But auditors found that 78% of the time that agents had planned to use the craft, they were grounded because of bad weather, budget constraints or maintenance problems.

Drones Contribute Little to Arrests

Even when aloft, auditors found, the drones contributed little. Three drones flying around the Tucson area helped apprehend about 2,200 people illegally crossing the border in 2013, fewer than 2% of the 120,939 apprehended that year in the area.

Border Patrol supervisors had planned on using drones to inspect ground-sensor alerts. But a drone was used in that scenario only six times in 2013.

Time after time, we see the practical realities of these systems don't live up to the hype.

Auditors found that officials underestimated the cost of the drones by leaving out operating costs such as pilot salaries, equipment and overhead. Adding such items increased the flying cost nearly fivefold, to $12,255 per hour.

"It really doesn't feel like [Customs and Border Protection] has a good handle on how it is using its drones, how much it costs to operate the drones, where that money is coming from or whether it is meeting any of its performance metrics," said Jennifer Lynch, a lawyer for the Electronic Frontier Foundation, a San Francisco-based privacy and digital rights group.

The report's conclusions will make it harder for officials to justify further investment in the border surveillance drones, especially at a time when Homeland Security's budget is at the center of the battle over President [Barack] Obama's program to give work permits to millions of immigrants in the country illegally. Each Predator B system costs about $20 million.

No Silver Bullet

"People think these kinds of surveillance technologies will be a silver bullet," said Jay Stanley, a privacy expert at the American Civil Liberties Union. "Time after time, we see the practical realities of these systems don't live up to the hype."

Customs and Border Protection, which is part of Homeland Security, operates the fleet of nine long-range Predator B drones from bases in Arizona, Texas and North Dakota.

The agency purchased 11 drones, but one crashed in Arizona in 2006 and another fell into the Pacific Ocean off San Diego after a mechanical failure last year.

Agency officials said in response to the audit that they had no plans to expand the fleet aside from replacing the Predator that crashed last year. The agency is authorized to spend an additional $433 million to buy up to 14 more drones.

The drones—unarmed versions of the MQ-9 Reaper drone flown by the Air Force to hunt targets in Pakistan, Somalia and elsewhere—fly the vast majority of their missions in narrowly defined sections of the Southwest border, the audit found.

They spent most of their time along 100 miles of border in Arizona near Tucson and 70 miles of border in Texas.

Better Measures of Effectiveness Are Needed

Rep. Henry Cuellar (D-Texas) has promoted the use of drones along the border but believes the agency should improve how it measures their effectiveness.

Homeland Security "can't prove the program is effective because they don't have the right measures," Cuellar said in an interview. "The technology is good, but how you implement and use it—that is another question."

The audit also said that drones had been flown to help the FBI [Federal Bureau of Investigation], the Texas Department of Public Safety and the Minnesota Department of Natural Resources.

Such missions have long frustrated Border Patrol agents, who complain that drones and other aircraft aren't available when they need them, said Shawn Moran, vice president of the Border Patrol agents' union.

"We saw the drones were being lent out to many entities for nonborder-related operations and we said, 'These drones, if they belong to [Customs and Border Protection], should be used to support [its] operations primarily,'" Moran said.

Demand for Domestic Drones Fuels the Military-Industrial Complex

Tom Barry

Tom Barry is cofounder of the Center for International Policy, a nonprofit public policy research and advocacy think tank in Washington, DC. Barry directs the Center's TransBorder Project whose goal is to foster policy alternatives and improve understanding of transborder issues such as immigration, homeland security, border security, and the national security complex.

The continuing rise of Predator drones at home has been fueled by the bizarre merger of military influence in domestic affairs and the key role of border hawks in the politics of immigration reform. DHS's [Department of Homeland Security] early decision to tap generals involved in the military's own controversial overseas drone program to shape and direct the domestic drone program points to the increasing merger of the post-9/11 homeland security/border security complex with the military-industrial complex.

Drone proliferation at home will likely increase from a multibillion-dollar spending surge to boost "border security" as a result of congressional proposals to reform immigration policy.

At home and abroad, drone proliferation has benefited from a broad bipartisan consensus about the purported success of the US military's foreign deployment of Predator drones in counterterrorism operations by the Pentagon and intelligence apparatus. Drone proliferation at home is closely linked to military and CIA enthusiasm for what are formally called unmanned aerial vehicles (UAVs), or simply unmanned systems.

Government reports [have] pointed to the complete absence of any cost-benefit evaluations and efficiency assessments of the DHS drone program.

DHS decided—with virtually no reviews or evaluations—to purchase unarmed versions of the Predator drones used abroad for "signature strikes" (targeted drone killing). The department, whose mission includes "border security," has also relied on military bases along the land border and coastal waters to host its own drone fleet.

Reports Contradict Effectiveness

Since DHS began acquiring Predators, along with Predator variants called Guardians, from General Atomics nine years ago, this domestic drone program has proved an abysmal failure—whether measured by its effectiveness in immigration enforcement, drug control, or counterterrorism. A series of reports by the General Accountability Office, Congressional Review Service, and the DHS Inspector General's Office have documented the paltry achievements, the alarming strategic confusion, and near-systemic logistical and technical shortcomings of the DHS drone program.

These government reports pointed to the complete absence of any cost-benefit evaluations and efficiency assessments of the DHS drone program.

Yet these official reviews failed to shed any light on the department's controversial decision to deploy only the hugely expensive military-grade Predator drones and to enter into sole-source contracts with General Atomics to provide, maintain, and even operate the federal government's domestic drone fleet.

Nor did they probe the decision by DHS to hire military men to run the domestic drone program, despite their total lack of experience in law enforcement, border control, drug control, and immigration enforcement. Instead, from the start, DHS brought in generals with a history of procurement and management of the military's killer drones to hunt down immigrants and illegal drugs with Predator drones.

The continuing rise of Predator drones at home has been fueled by the bizarre merger of military influence in domestic affairs and by the key role of border hawks in the politics of immigration reform. The decision early on by DHS to tap generals involved in the military's own controversial overseas drone program to shape and direct the domestic drone program points to the increasing merger of the post-9/11 homeland security/border security complex with the military-industrial complex.

Drones Feature in Immigration Reform

Congressional proponents of immigration reform have included repeated references to their commitment to provide dramatically increased aerial surveillance of the southwestern border by Department of Homeland Security drones.

Prominent immigration reform advocates such as Sen. Charles Schumer (D-NY) and Cong. Henry Cuellar (D-Texas) insist that "continuous" and "24 hours, seven days a week" drone surveillance is a fundamental condition of successful immigration reform. Yet these and other border drone advocates don't point to the achievements of the current DHS program. Rather, like Cuellar, they point to the purported success of the US military's antiterrorist drone program.

"We gotta have efficiencies, effectiveness, accountability on how they're used," he said. "But again, keep in mind, look at the history how they've been used extremely well in the military," said Cuellar, who cochairs the Congressional Caucus on Unmanned Systems, commonly known as the "Drone Caucus."

The [Office of Air and Marine] strategic plan calls for a fleet of two dozen drones by 2015—a goal that seemed unlikely to be reached given budget-cutting and the abysmal performance record of the OAM drones.

The DHS drone program is run by the Office of Air and Marine (OAM), a division of the Customs and Border Protection (CBP), which also includes the Office of the US Border Patrol.

Prior to 9/11 and DHS's creation, the Border Patrol and the US Customs Service (the legacy agency that became ICE), the various Border Patrol and US Customs sector offices mainly tapped their planes and boats to do what these agencies have traditionally done, namely apprehended unauthorized immigrants and seize illegal drugs. Under OAM, the actual operations remain largely the same, although now framed in a new security, counterterrorism context. According to CBP, the mission of OAM is "to detect, interdict, and prevent acts of terrorism and the unlawful movement of people, illegal drugs and other contraband towards or across the borders of the United States."

OAM boasts that it "is the most experienced operator of Unmanned Aircraft Systems in the Homeland Security mission set on the world stage."

OAM currently has a fleet of 10 Predator and Guardian drones manufactured by General Atomics. The OAM strategic plan calls for a fleet of two dozen drones by 2015—a goal that seemed unlikely to be reached given budget-cutting and the abysmal performance record of the OAM drones.

Questions Worth Asking

The first and signature initiative of the newly created OAM was to enter into a collaborative venture with General Atomics for unmanned Predator drones for border security operations—the first of which was deployed from Ft. Huachuca Army Base in Sierra Vista, Arizona shortly after the founding of OAM. In April 2006, this first CBP Predator crashed and was totaled in the Arizona desert due to a control error by the remote piloting team contracted from General Atomics.

Since 2005, when CBP deployed its first major drone, the UAV program of DHS has been the subject of mounting concern and criticisms from the government's own oversight and research agencies, including the Congressional Research Service, the Governmental Accountability Office, and the DHS's own Office of Inspector General.

In addition to the types of questions about worth and efficiency noted above, CBP/OAM has failed to adequately answer the following questions:

1. Why it so quickly decided that a drone fleet was necessary for border security?

2. Why it decided that the Predator UAV was the best fit?

3. Why it has continued the exclusive relationship with General Atomics despite the dubious accomplishment of these expensive military-developed drones?

Predator Drones Get Special Treatment

In November 2012, CBP did sign a sole-source contract with General Atomics Aeronautical Systems to provide maintenance and operating crews for its current contingent of UAVs and to purchase as many as 14 additional drones. But there was little hope that the money could be found until drones became a core component to the "border surge" advocated by Sen. Schumer earlier this year.

Whether at home or in South Asia, Predators get special treatment by the federal government, benefiting from sole-source, no-bid contracts. In October, DHS signed a new sole-source contract with General Atomics Aeronautical Systems. The $443.1 million five-year contract includes $237.7 million for the purchase of up to 14 additional Predators and Predator variants, and $205.4 million for operational costs and maintenance by General Atomics teams.

CBP insists that there is only one "responsible source" for its drone needs and that no other suppliers or servicers can satisfy agency requirements for these $18 million drones.

In a November 1 statement titled "Justification for Other than Full and Open Competition," DHS contends that General Atomics Aeronautical Systems Inc.'s (GA-ASI) knowledge of the production, operation, and maintenance of the MQ-9 [Predator] is so unique that a transition of OAM UAS equipment to a UAS other than the MQ-9 or support services to a company other than GA-ASI "would notably impact the CBP UAS program," including "appreciably impacting national security through decreased interdictions of contraband (e.g., illegal narcotics, undocumented immigrants)."

Current
CONTROVERSIES

C H A P T E R 4

Should Commercial Drone Use Be Allowed?

Chapter Preface

For decades, Americans have enjoyed the hobby of flying model airplanes and copters with little worry about regulations or licensing requirements. As long as remote-controlled aircraft weigh less than fifty-five pounds, fly below four hundred feet, avoid airports, stay within sight, and are not used for commercial purposes of any kind, the Federal Aviation Administration (FAA) does not regulate their use.

Those are the strictures that would-be commercial drone operators found themselves chaffing against as small, affordable consumer drones became widely available and demand spiked for their use in photography, agriculture, and other commercial interests.

But even as hobby drones soared in popularity over the past few years, their commercial use remained strictly illegal and many drone users were breaking the rules without even realizing it. The FAA has long defined "commercial use" so broadly that simply uploading amateur drone video to YouTube—which an untold number of drone hobbyists have done—constitutes a violation that can draw fines of $10,000, and indeed has.

Meanwhile, a growing chorus of lobbyists from such diverse industries as construction, mining, film production, agriculture, energy, utilities, news media, real estate, and online retail began imploring the FAA to lift its ban on the commercial use of drones. In response, Congress gave the FAA a mandate to develop regulations for drone use and to open the nation's airspace to commercial drone traffic by September 30, 2015.

As it worked since 2012 to create the new rules, the FAA issued several hundred commercial drone operation permits on a case-by-case basis, primarily to law enforcement, universities, and agriculture groups, and it established a handful of sites around the country for commercial drone testing.

The agency has been roundly criticized for its slow pace in developing the guidelines and for missing several key progress benchmarks during the process, but a draft version of the long-awaited document was released for public comment in February 2015. As of this writing, it was unclear how heavily it might be revised or whether it would be enacted on schedule; some analysts think the rules are unlikely to be finalized before early 2017.

"Drones are an important technology for business, law enforcement, agriculture and more, but the lack of clear rules about small drones, the difference between commercial and a hobby drone, and how and where they can be used, is creating a serious threat to . . . safety," US senator Charles Schumer (D-NY) said in a press release after urging the FAA to expedite its rulemaking in the fall of 2014.[1]

FAA administrator Michael Huerta has defended his agency's progress, telling *Politico* that safety is exactly why the FAA has taken its time to get the drone issue right.

"There are proponents of unmanned aircraft, and they see huge potential of this technology—and for them, we can't move fast enough," Huerta said. "What they would like to see is free and open use of unmanned aircraft as soon as we can get there. On the other side," he added, "we have pilots—commercial pilots and general aviation pilots—who are very concerned that these are difficult to see, and they don't have a really good understanding of how they interact with other aircraft."[2]

---

1. Quoted in William Cole, "Drones Left Up in the Air," *Honolulu Star-Advertiser*, December 8, 2014.

2. Quoted in Jennifer Shutt, "FAA Administrator on the Future of Drones," *Politico*, November 30, 2014. http://www.politico.com/story/2014/11/drones-future-faa-michael -huerta-113214.html#ixzz3cu3H3ylQ.

If the FAA's rules are enacted as written in the February 2015 draft, drone users would have to take an airspace rules exam every two years and get an operator certificate, among other use criteria. (Those who fly model airplanes that meet existing guidelines would continue to be governed by them.)

The newly proposed rules would also effectively end the ban on commercial drones and allow them to fly at low altitudes within view of a ground-based pilot. Because that will essentially limit commercial drones to short-distance tasks, online retailers like Amazon who envisioned a shiny fleet of drones delivering packages to consumers' doorsteps remain out of luck, at least for now. Nevertheless, the proposed rules officially inaugurate the commercial drone era and represent a giant boon for the emerging drone economy.

The authors in this chapter explore the potential benefits and safety concerns of commercial drones and consider the question of whether commercial drone use should be allowed.

Commercial Drones Have Endless Potential

Rachel Janik and Mitchell Armentrout

Rachel Janik and Mitchell Armentrout wrote this viewpoint for the Medill News Service, a program of the Medill School of Journalism at Northwestern University in Evanston, Illinois.

The next time you feel the urge for fresh Mexican food, just look up. A taco-toting drone may be circling in the sky above you.

Researchers at the Darwin Aerospace laboratory in San Francisco have designed the Burrito Bomber, the world's first airborne Mexican food delivery system that would allow customers to have food parachuted right to their doorstep.

As fun as they may be to think about, such ideas aren't likely to be realized anytime soon. The Federal Aviation Administration [FAA] likely won't decide until 2015 the regulations to integrate burrito-bearing drones into urban airspace.

But the potential of a booming domestic drone industry for commercial purposes has entrepreneurs seeing dollar signs. A far stretch from the military strikes that most people typically associate with drones, developers have begun hatching a litany of ideas for unmanned air systems in the commercial sphere, controlled by civilians in American skies.

From conservation efforts and crop monitoring to Hollywood filming and even food delivery, experts anticipate the value of the commercial drone industry, already worth almost $14 billion per year, to skyrocket to more than $82 billion by

2025, according to Mario Mairena, government relations manager for the Association for Unmanned Vehicle Systems International [AUVSI].

"And that's a conservative estimate," Mairena said. "We're excited about where the industry is at right now."

Maybe the most exciting thing is that we don't yet know all the ways this technology is going to mature.

Though opponents decry the Big Brother-like intrusion of thousands of remote cameras roaming the sky, Mairena said the industry could create as many as 70,000 jobs in the first three years after the Federal Aviation Administration releases guidelines to integrate unmanned systems into national airspace, scheduled for 2015. A recent AUVSI industry report claims that for every year commercial drone integration into the national airspace is delayed, more than $10 billion in economic potential is lost.

Chris Anderson, co-founder of drone manufacturer 3D Robotics, said he expects the commercial drone market to boom once they get clearance to enter the skies.

"Maybe the most exciting thing is that we don't yet know all the ways this technology is going to mature," he said.

Reshaping the Way We Think

One of the most promising areas for growth in unmanned systems could be in agriculture, according to Anderson.

"It's really reshaping the way we think about farming, among other things," Anderson said. Using camera-equipped drones to monitor crops could save millions per year, he said, with $300 UAVs to check for disease and irrigation levels replacing $1,000 per hour manned aircraft flyovers.

"It makes American farmers that much more competitive," he said. Hollywood is also in on the push for commercial drone licensing. Howard Gantman, spokesman for the Motion

Picture Association of America, said the film industry has been lobbying for years for the right to use unmanned aircraft for aerial filming.

"It's safer than putting a camera operator up in a tall tree, it's cheaper than renting a helicopter for a day," Gantman said.

Opening scenes from the most recent James Bond film "Skyfall" were shot from drones, as were some scenes from "The Smurfs 2." Because those were filmed in Europe, producers were able to opt for a roughly $200 drone rather than hire a helicopter filming crew for more than $2,000 per hour.

"Flight crews can eat up huge portions of movie budgets," Gantman said.

One of the more well-known uses of drones is by police departments. Steve Gitlin, spokesman for drone manufacturer AeroVironment, said law enforcement appreciate the more budget-friendly surveillance capability as an alternative to helicopters. They also have been used for search and rescue missions and deployed to locate survivors in natural disasters.

For poor countries, the ability to aerially monitor national parks and protected lands is now possible with the advent of these more affordable, model-airplane sized UAVs.

"These systems can take care of the jobs that put people in harm's way," Gitlin said.

New Weapon Against Poachers

A promising new frontier for drone surveillance could save countless endangered species, as non-profits like World Wildlife Fund [WWF] embrace UAVs to monitor wildlife populations and track poachers.

Early in 2012, WWF began research into how small UAVs like the GPS-enabled Raptor drone could help nations like Nepal stop the illegal wildlife trade. The low-cost technology has been critical in developing countries with gravely at-risk animals like the Asian elephant, white rhino and tiger. For poor countries, the ability to aerially monitor national parks and protected lands is now possible with the advent of these more affordable, model-airplane sized UAVs.

WWF's efforts have attracted attention, and the non-profit is now expanding its UAV wildlife protection programs with the help of a $5 million Global Impact Award grant from Google.

Carter Roberts, CEO [chief executive officer] of WWF, said he hoped the grant would allow animal rights groups to create "an umbrella of technology" around endangered species threatened by wildlife trafficking.

"We face an unprecedented poaching crisis. Killings are way up. We need solutions that are as sophisticated as the threats we face. This pushes the envelope in the fight against wildlife crime."

Journalistic Tools: "This Is It"

Matt Waite, professor of journalism at the University of Nebraska-Lincoln, said when he saw a drone for the first time at a digital mapping conference in 2001, he was instantly inspired.

"I thought about all the natural disasters I had covered as a reporter and I thought, 'This is it,'" he said.

Despite his enthusiasm for the new technology, using them for commercial newsgathering remains illegal in the U.S. Still, Waite was interested in pursuing UAV's potential in the industry, and set up a Drone Journalism Lab at the University of Nebraska to allow students to experiment with drones.

But the anxiety over potential privacy abuses surfaced when a false rumor surfaced that celebrity gossip site TMZ was applying for a drone of its own, presumably to get stealthy paparazzi shots of unsuspecting stars.

Waite said he believes this fear of misuse reflects more of the public's distrust of the media as a whole, not the practical application of the technology.

"Using drones in journalism does not have to include stalking Lindsay Lohan," he said. "Responsible journalists should be aware of the rules."

Waite contends that the hot topic of drones will be old news once the regulations surrounding their use are finally hashed out in both the legislature and the courts system. He predicts UAVs will be used for some of the most boring—but vital—parts of journalism, like traffic reports.

Privacy Questions Remain

For civil liberties groups, unchecked use of UAVs poses serious privacy concerns. But many private sector uses have mostly positive potential, said Electronic Privacy Information Center's Amie Stepanovich. Newsgathering in public spaces and such uses as food delivery all represent a social good as long as video footage is recorded legally and all "incidental collection" of video—footage picked up by a drone conducting a job separate from its recordings capability—is disposed of promptly, she said.

"There are definitely a lot of innovative ways to use these machines, but how do you limit what information is collected?" said Jay Stanley, an ACLU senior policy analyst. "It changes the way people feel within their environment."

Such questions have been left to the FAA, an organization that has never dealt with privacy issues until now. The drone industry awaits comprehensive guidelines, expected to be released in 2015. "We all just want rules for the road," said the University of Nebraska's Waite. "Once we have those, we can operate."

Commercial Drone Use Will Benefit the US Economy

Darryl Jenkins and Bijan Vasigh

Aviation and airline analyst Darryl Jenkins has consulted for numerous government agencies and was a member of the Executive Committee of the White House Conference on Aviation Safety and Security. Bijan Vasigh is professor of economics and finance at Embry-Riddle Aeronautical University in Daytona Beach, Florida, and a managing director at Aviation Consulting Group LLC. They wrote this viewpoint for the Association for Unmanned Vehicle Systems International (AUVSI), an organization whose mission is to advance the unmanned systems and robotics community through education, advocacy, and leadership.

The purpose of this research is to document the economic benefits to the United States (U.S.) once Unmanned Aircraft Systems (UAS) are integrated into in the National Airspace System (NAS).

In 2012, the federal government tasked the Federal Aviation Administration (FAA) to determine how to integrate UAS into the NAS. In this research, we estimate the economic impact of this integration. In the event that these regulations are delayed or not enacted, this study also estimates the jobs and financial opportunity lost to the economy because of this inaction.

While there are multiple uses for UAS in the NAS, this research concludes that precision agriculture and public safety are the most promising commercial and civil markets. These two markets are thought to comprise approximately 90% of the known potential markets for UAS.

We conclude the following:

1. The economic impact of the integration of UAS into the NAS will total more than $13.6 billion in the first three years of integration and will grow sustainably for the foreseeable future, cumulating to more than $82.1 billion between 2015 and 2025;

2. Integration into the NAS will create more than 34,000 manufacturing jobs and more than 70,000 new jobs in the first three years;

3. By 2025, total job creation is estimated at 103,776;

4. The manufacturing jobs created will be high paying ($40,000) and require Technical baccalaureate degrees;

5. Tax revenue to the states will total more than $635 billion in the first 11 years following integration (2015–2025); and

6. Every year that integration is delayed, the United States loses more than $10 billion in potential economic impact. This translates to a loss of $27.6 million per day that UAS are not integrated into the NAS.

[Unmanned Aircraft Systems] are already being used in a variety of applications, and many more areas will benefit by their use.

Utility of UAS

The main inhibitor of U.S. commercial and civil development of the UAS is the lack of a regulatory structure. Because of current airspace restrictions, non-defense use of UAS has been extremely limited. However, the combination of greater flexibility, lower capital and lower operating costs could allow UAS to be a transformative technology in fields as diverse as urban infrastructure management, farming, and oil and gas exploration to name a few.

Present-day UAS have longer operational duration and require less maintenance than earlier models. In addition, they can be operated remotely using more fuel efficient technologies. These aircraft can be deployed in a number of different terrains and may be less dependent on prepared runways. Some argue the use of UAS in the future will be a more responsible approach to certain airspace operations from an environmental, ecological and human risk perspective.

UAS are already being used in a variety of applications, and many more areas will benefit by their use, such as:

- Wildfire mapping;

- Agricultural monitoring;

- Disaster management;

- Thermal infrared power line surveys;

- Law enforcement;

- Telecommunication;

- Weather monitoring;

- Aerial imaging/mapping;

- Television news coverage, sporting events, moviemaking;

- Environmental monitoring;

- Oil and gas exploration; and

- Freight transport.

Applicable Markets

There are a number of different markets in which UAS can be used. This research is concentrated on the two markets, commercial and civil, with the largest potential. A third category (Other) summarizes all other markets:

1. Precision agriculture;

2. Public safety; and

3. Other.

Public safety officials include police officers and professional firefighters in the U.S., as well as a variety of professional and volunteer emergency medical service providers who protect the public from events that pose significant danger, including natural disasters, man-made disasters and crimes.

With sensible regulations in place, we foresee few limitations to rapid growth in [those] industries [interested in UAS].

Precision agriculture refers to two segments of the farm market: remote sensing and precision application. A variety of remote sensors are being used to scan plants for health problems, record growth rates and hydration, and locate disease outbreaks. Such sensors can be attached to ground vehicles, aerial vehicles and even aerospace satellites. Precision application, a practice especially useful for crop farmers and horticulturists, utilizes effective and efficient spray techniques to more selectively cover plants and fields. This allows farmers to provide only the needed pesticide or nutrient to each plant, reducing the total amount sprayed, and thus saving money and reducing environmental impacts.

As listed above, a large number of other markets will also use UAS once the airspace is integrated. We believe the impact of these other markets will be at least the size of the impact from public safety use.

With sensible regulations in place, we foresee few limitations to rapid growth in these industries. These products use off-the-shelf technology and thus impose few problems to rapidly ramping up production. The inputs (i.e., parts) to the UAS can be purchased from more than 100 different suppliers; therefore, prices will be stable and competitive. The inputs to the UAS can all be purchased within the U.S., although these products can be imported from any number of foreign countries without the need of an import license. UAS have a durable life span of approximately 11 years and are relatively easy to maintain. The manufacture of these products requires technical skills equivalent to a baccalaureate degree. Therefore, there will always be a plentiful market of job applicants willing to enter this market. In summary, there are no production problems on the horizon that will impact the manufacturing and output of this product. Most of the barriers of potential usage are governmental and regulatory. For this study, we assume necessary airspace integration in 2015, on par with current legislation.

States with an already thriving aerospace industry are projected to reap the most economic gains [from UAS manufacturing and use.]

Covering and justifying the cost of UAS is straightforward. In the precision agriculture market, the average price of the UAS is a fraction of the cost of a manned aircraft, such as a helicopter or crop duster, without any of the safety hazards. For public safety, the price of the product is approximately the price of a police squad car equipped with standard gear. It is also operated at a fraction of the cost of a manned aircraft, such as a helicopter, reducing the strain on agency budgets as well as the risk of bodily harm to the users in many difficult and dangerous situations. Therefore, the cost-benefit ratios of using UAS can be easily understood.

Economic Benefit

The economic benefits to the country are enormous and were estimated as follows. First, we forecast the number of sales in the three market categories. Next, we forecast the supplies needed to manufacture these products. Using estimated costs for labor, we forecast the number of direct jobs created. Using these factors, we forecast the tax revenue to the states.

In addition to direct jobs created by the manufacturing process, there is an additional economic benefit. The new jobs created and the income generated will be spread to local communities. As new jobs are created, additional money is spent at the local level, creating additional demand for local services which, in turn, creates even more jobs (i.e., grocery clerks, barbers, school teachers, home builders, etc.). These indirect and induced jobs are forecast and included in the total jobs created.

The economic benefits to individual states will not be evenly distributed. The following 10 states are predicted to see the most gains in terms of job creation and additional revenue as production of UAS increase, totaling more than $82 billion in economic impact from 2015–2025.

In rank order they are:

1. California

2. Washington

3. Texas

4. Florida

5. Arizona

6. Connecticut

7. Kansas

8. Virginia

9. New York

10. Pennsylvania

It is important to note that the projections contained in this report are based on the current airspace activity and infrastructure in a given state. As a result, states with an already thriving aerospace industry are projected to reap the most economic gains. However, a variety of factors—state laws, tax incentives, regulations, the establishment of test sites and the adoption of UAS technology by end users—will ultimately determine where jobs flow.

Job Creation

By 2025, we estimate more than 100,000 new jobs will be created nationally. For the purposes of this report, we base the 2025 state economic projections on the current aerospace employment in the states. We also presume that none of the states have enacted restrictive legislation or regulations that would limit the expansion of the technology. These landscapes will likely shift, however, as states work to attract UAS jobs in the years following integration. Future state laws and regulations could also cause some states to lose jobs while others stand to gain jobs. In conclusion, while we project more than 100,000 new jobs by 2025, states that create favorable regulatory and business environments for the industry and the technology will likely siphon jobs away from states that do not.

The trend in total spending, total economic impact and total employment impact was investigated for 2015 through 2025. The total spending in UAS development and total economic and employment impacts are expected to increase significantly in the next five years. This study demonstrates the significant contribution of UAS development and integration in the nation's airspace to the economic growth and job creation in the aerospace industry and to the social and economic progress of the citizens in the U.S.

Commercial Drone Rules Should Be Less Restrictive

Troy A. Rule

Troy A. Rule is a law professor at Arizona State University's Sandra Day O'Connor College of Law.

For more than half a century, the Federal Aviation Administration [FAA] has piloted the development of sensible aviation regulation in the United States. Unfortunately, when Congress enacted legislation in 2012 directing the FAA to craft rules for small civilian drones, the agency entered uncharted territory.

Civilian drones are fundamentally different from manned aircraft. Many small drones can be purchased online for just a few hundred dollars and are designed to hover relatively close to the ground, well below where conventional planes and helicopters fly.

The FAA is working on federal civilian drone regulations, but in the meantime, the agency has outlawed any commercial uses of drones without express FAA authorization. This ban applies to hundreds of types of flying devices that are not even capable of reaching the minimal safe altitude of manned airplanes. Several times this year, FAA officials have issued cease-and-desist notices against ordinary citizens for flying small commercial drones just a few dozen feet above land.

The FAA's controversial crackdown on commercial drones drew attention last March [2014] when an administrative law judge for the National Transportation Safety Board ruled that the FAA lacked authority to fine a man $10,000 for using his drone to capture aerial footage of the University of Virginia for a promotional video. The judge hearing the case candidly pointed out that, under the FAA's expansive view of its own regulatory power, even the flight of a paper airplane or a toy balsa wood glider would fall within FAA jurisdiction. Shockingly, an NTSB opinion issued this week reversed that decision and implied that the FAA did possess regulatory authority over the flights of unmanned objects, regardless of their size, all the way down [to] the ground.

The FAA should be focused on those aspects of drone regulation that are most appropriately implemented at the federal government level.

A Troubling Decision

This new ruling is particularly troubling because the FAA still hasn't found a federal regulatory scheme capable of effectively integrating drones into the nation's airspace. A June audit report revealed that the agency was "significantly behind schedule" in meeting congressionally imposed deadlines for its development of civilian drone regulations. Frustrated at the FAA's snail-like pace, companies such as Amazon and Google have begun exporting their drone research activities to other countries.

Small drones are not built for lengthy interstate flights at altitudes where conventional airplanes fly, so why should a federal agency be the chief regulator of these devices? Rather than seeking to expand its regulatory jurisdiction all the way down to the ground, the FAA should advocate for itself a more limited role in a collaborative federal, state and local regulatory scheme tailored to the unique attributes of drone technologies.

A "Geo-Fence" for Safety

The FAA should be focused on those aspects of drone regulation that are most appropriately implemented at the federal government level. For instance, the agency could accelerate the development of national drone safety and performance standards analogous to the National Highway Traffic Safety Administration's manufacturing standards for motor vehicles. Among other things, these FAA standards could require that all commercial drones incorporate specific global positioning system features to ensure compatibility with a nationally standardized geo-fence network designed to keep drones out of the way of conventional aircraft. At least one leading drone manufacturer is already using "geo-fence" software to prevent operators from flying their drones into the airspace surrounding hundreds of airports around the world.

Most other facets of civilian drone regulation are better suited for lower levels of government. Several state legislatures have already enacted drone-related statutes, but states should be doing much more. In addition to creating registration and licensing programs for commercial drones and their operators, legislatures could enact laws that clarify the scope of landowners' rights to exclude drones from the airspace directly above their land. If tailored properly, these aerial trespass statutes could help to address a wide array of conflicts involving drones, including those involving law enforcement uses of drone devices.

Drone Zone Laws

Local governments are well-positioned to serve valuable functions in drone regulation as well. In particular, drone zoning laws adopted at the local level could permit wider use of drones in certain commercial or agricultural zones while imposing greater restrictions on drones above residential areas. Municipalities could even adopt temporary-use permit provisions to accommodate occasional drone use by real estate agents and wedding photographers without compromising landowner privacy. Regrettably, until the FAA signals that it does not intend to regulate these sorts of activities at the federal level, most local officials are unlikely to craft innovative drone policies within their communities.

The commercial drone industry is poised to take off in the United States, but it will largely remain grounded until the FAA embraces a narrower regulatory role and gets out of the way.

Banning Commercial Drones Is Not the Answer

Vivek Wadhwa

Vivek Wadhwa is a fellow at the Rock Center for Corporate Governance at Stanford University and director of research at the Center for Entrepreneurship and Research Commercialization at Duke University.

The Federal Aviation Administration recently released a report detailing more than 190 safety incidents involving drones and commercial aircraft. In response, Senator Dianne Feinstein (D-Calif.) has vowed to push legislation that would crack down on the commercial use of drones, also called Unmanned Aircraft Systems (UAS). India's Directorate General for Civil Aviation has already banned all use of drones in the country—even for civilian purposes.

There are valid concerns that the proliferation of drones will endanger commercial flights and cause serious accidents. The U.S. military is rightfully worried that drones will be weaponized as killing machines and become autonomous flying IEDs (improvised explosive devices) that target a specific individual by means of facial recognition.

Banning commercial drone use will not solve these problems; it will just give us a false sense of comfort and kick the can further down the road.

About two years ago, I wrote a *Washington Post* column in which I argued that we need to prepare ourselves for the "drone age." It isn't just the United States that is developing drone capabilities; governments and DIYers all over the world are doing the same, particularly the Chinese. This isn't all bad; there are many good uses for drone technologies.

To start with, there isn't yet a clear consensus on what a drone is. Is it something that flies and is remote controlled? If that is the case, should the FAA also ban remote-controlled airplanes and helicopters that hobbyists have flown happily and relatively safely for many years? The drone encounter that Senator Feinstein cited in a Senate Commerce Committee hearing as a reason to regulate commercial drone flights was reportedly just a pink toy helicopter.

Let's first acknowledge that drones will be common in our skies and that they will play an integral role in our economy and society.

Would Drone Bans Be Enforceable?

Then there is the practicability of enforcement. If the government should institute restrictions and penalties, who will enforce them? Will the police buy high-performance drones to shoot down illicit drones? Can we scramble the Air Force to blow a flock of $300 quadcopters out of the sky? Should we equip legions of young children with air rifles? Proposing laws without realistic hope of enforcement does nothing to solve the problems at hand.

Let's first acknowledge that drones will be common in our skies and that they will play an integral role in our economy and society. We know that drones are saving money and improving safety on many types of remote inspection such as that of distant pipelines and tall broadcast towers. Documentary filmmakers use drones to get aerial shots that are not affordable with a regular plane or helicopter. As well, start-ups like Matternet are pioneering the use of drones to deliver critical medical supplies to remote parts of the developing world. Drones could be used as long-haul cargo-delivery vehicles, allowing for more efficient point-to-point delivery of goods and materials. Then of course, companies such as Google and Amazon are developing drone delivery services that provide within-the-hour delivery of ordered goods—without putting any more traffic onto the streets or carbon into the skies.

So if we don't ban the drones, what can we do to prepare for them and weave their capabilities into a broader picture of economic development?

Collision-Avoidance Technology Is a Challenge

First, there needs to be a core technology framework for collision avoidance. This is no small problem. Even the best computer-vision algorithms struggle to navigate complex cityscapes. The vehicles in NASA's DARPA challenge weighed thousands of pounds and carried serious computational and sensor firepower. Yet they could barely navigate barren wastelands without flipping themselves over or running into a wall. So how will a drone the size of a shoebox carry enough intelligence to avoid hitting a building, a person, a car, a power line or, worst case, a commercial aircraft? It's a wonderful engineering challenge and worth the focus of some of our best minds.

Assuming we have collision-avoidance systems in place, how can we build a system of distributed air-traffic control for drones? It would obviously need to be computer-driven and automatic, and to include safety measures and emergency kill switches or other mechanisms to bring down a drone that is malfunctioning or poses a danger. We would need to plan for specific air corridors in city areas that are dedicated to drones and confine the drones to those places. Again, this is a huge engineering challenge, but not one that is insurmountable.

More Problems to Solve

We also need to build private and commercial air-defense systems, just as the military is developing, to shield our schools, homes, and businesses from drone surveillance or attack. I wonder whether force fields such as we saw on *Star Trek* may become a practical reality.

Beyond the technical issues, we need to debate what is socially acceptable and to create legal frameworks. Should the cameras of delivery drones be recording and saving all video footage as they enter into the airspace of a customer's home? For that matter, should drones be allowed to fly over private property at all—or should they be limited to public roads between droneports? Should we have the right to shoot down unauthorized drones on our property? If the Second Amendment grants the right of gun ownership to individuals for self-defense, then does it allow them to fly their own defensive drones?

These are issues we need to tackle—and soon. The drones are coming, whether we are ready or not.

Commercial Drones Could Threaten National Security

Michael McCaul

Texas Republican Michael McCaul is chairman of the US House of Representatives Subcommittee on Oversight, Investigations, and Management.

Unmanned aerial systems [UAS], commonly known as "drones," have been a game changer for our men and women serving in Iraq and Afghanistan. These systems have provided our troops with much needed "eyes in the sky" and have taken the fight to the enemy, eliminating some of the most dangerous Al-Qaeda terrorists. Drones have also increased our capabilities to secure our borders and aid first responders.

US Customs and Border Protection [CBP] began first looking at using drones back in 2004. Now, CBP owns ten UAS aircraft. These systems have been used to surveil drug smuggling tunnels; video dams, bridges, levees, and riverbeds at risk of flooding; and assist with the deployment of National Guard resources responding to local flooding. CBP has flown missions in support of the Border Patrol, Texas Rangers, US Forest Service, FBI [Federal Bureau of Investigation], and others. These systems have become a force multiplier for military operations and border security.

However, we are now on the edge of a new horizon: using unmanned aerial systems within the homeland. Currently, there are about 200 active Certificates of Authorization issued by the Federal Aviation Administration [FAA] to over 100 dif-

Michael McCaul, "Using Unmanned Aerial Systems Within the Homeland: Security Game Changer?," Statement to the House Subcommittee on Oversight, Investigations, and Management, July 19, 2012.

ferent entities, such as law enforcement departments and academic institutions, to fly drones domestically. . . .

The FAA plans to select six test sites around the country for the use of non-government drones this year and plans to allow the deployment of non-government drones nationwide by 2015.

> *The US government [is] concerned that these aerial vehicles could be modified and used to attack key assets and critical infrastructure in the United States.*

Government Agencies Are Lagging

While the FAA is responsible for ensuring these systems fly safely in US airspace, with only two and a half short years until drones begin to dominate the skies in the US homeland, no federal agency is taking the lead to deal with the full implications of using unmanned aerial systems and developing the relevant policies and guidelines for their use. This is despite the fact that four years ago the Government Accountability Office [GAO] recommended the Secretary of Homeland Security direct the TSA Administrator to examine the security implications of future, non-military UAS operations in the national airspace system and take any actions deemed appropriate.

GAO's recommendation was well founded because in 2004 TSA issued an advisory that described possible terrorist interest in using UASs as weapons. The advisory noted the potential for UASs to carry explosives or disperse chemical or biological weapons. It discussed how the Revolutionary Armed Forces of Columbia, or FARC, and Hezbollah were interested in acquiring UASs. While the advisory acknowledged there was no credible evidence to suggest that terrorist organizations planned to use these systems in the United States, it did state that the US government was concerned that these aerial vehicles could be modified and used to attack key assets and critical infrastructure in the United States.

Drones Pose Potential Threats

These concerns were validated just last week [July 2012] when a Massachusetts man agreed to plead guilty to attempting to damage and destroy federal buildings. The individual was arrested in September 2011 after an undercover FBI investigation revealed his plot to use multiple remote controlled aircraft laden with explosives to collapse the dome of the US Capitol and attack the Pentagon.

As if this plot wasn't frightening enough, cutting edge research out of the University of Texas at Austin has revealed yet more security vulnerabilities. Specifically, researchers from the Cockrell School of Engineering led by Dr. Todd Humphreys proved that civilian unmanned aerial systems can be hacked into and hijacked with a relatively small investment of money and time. These findings are alarming and have revealed a gaping hole in the security of using unmanned aerial systems domestically. Now is the time to ensure these vulnerabilities are mitigated to protect our aviation system as the use of unmanned aerial systems continues to grow.

The Department of Homeland Security [DHS] mission is to protect the homeland. Unfortunately, DHS seems either disinterested or unprepared to step up to the plate to address the proliferation of Unmanned Aerial Systems in US air space, the potential threats they pose to our national security, and the concerns of our citizens of how drones flying over our cities will be used including protecting civil liberties of individuals under the Constitution. For example, in discussions with my Subcommittee staff prior to this hearing, Department officials repeatedly stated the Department does not see this function (domestic use of drones) as part of their mission and has no role in domestic unmanned aerial systems. I strongly disagree.

A Call to Action

DHS's lack of attention about this issue is incomprehensible. It should not take a 9/11 style attack by a terrorist organization such as Hezbollah or a lone wolf inspired event to cause DHS to develop guidance addressing the security implications of domestic drones. It should not take a hearing to force DHS to develop policy when it comes to the security of our homeland. What it should take is responsible leadership willing to recognize a potential threat and take the initiative. DHS lacks that initiative. I am concerned DHS is reverting back to a pre-9/11 mindset, which the 9/11 Commission described as a lack of imagination in identifying threats and protecting the homeland.

We are disappointed DHS declined to testify today. This is simply another example of how DHS leadership is failing to get ahead of the curve on an issue which directly impacts the security of the United States. I hope that our witnesses' testimony will be a call to action for the Department. During today's testimony, we look forward to learning more about the security issues related to the domestic use of drones and what DHS needs to do to prepare for their widespread use.

Weaponized Hobby Drones Are Inevitable

Patrick Hruby

Award-winning journalist Patrick Hruby is an adjunct professor at Georgetown University and a fellow at the University of Texas.

Less than a month ago [December 2012], rumors that celebrity news and gossip website TMZ was interested in obtaining a paparazzi drone prompted privacy concerns and public debate about the appropriate personal and commercial uses of unmanned aerial vehicles.

Now, a new online video poses a more troubling question: What if civilian drones are equipped to shoot more than just pictures?

Titled "Citizen Drone Warfare" and posted to YouTube last week by an anonymous man calling himself "Milo Danger," the video shows a hobbyist drone equipped with a custom-mounted paintball pistol flying over a grassy field and peppering human-shaped shooting-range targets with pellets.

Following an attack pass by the drone, one of the targets sports three large red blotches on its head and neck area.

"I wanted to show an inevitability of what I think will happen with these drones," said "Milo," who lives on the West Coast and spoke to *The Washington Times* on condition of anonymity. "I'm not advocating bad activities. But I wanted to raise some of the ethical issues we need to think about with this new technology.

"We didn't post the footage of this, but some of the guys who worked with me on the project weren't afraid of being shot by paintballs. They wanted to see if they could escape the drone. The answer was, no, they could not."

Though Federal Aviation Administration [FAA] regulations do not explicitly mention the use of firearms on drones, they do prohibit any type of recreational flying or dropping objects from aircraft that endanger life or property.

The Drone Community Reacts

DIYDrones.com, a drone hobbyist website and online community that counts defense and aerospace engineers among its 32,000 members and averages more than 1.5 million page views a month, discourages using or modifying drones for any uses that are "potentially illegal or intended to do harm."

Defense experts have warned for years that small, commercially available drones could be used as weapons.

"We've banned the weaponized use of drones," said Chris Anderson, the site's founder. "So in our community, the reaction to this video is dismay. We're particularly interested in civilian uses of drones, things like search-and-rescue and filming sports teams. Obviously, putting a paintball gun on a drone doesn't help."

American Civil Liberties Union [ACLU] policy analyst Jay Stanley wrote on the organization's website that the video was "pretty scary" and America "cannot allow our skies to fill with flying robots armed with all manner of dangerous weapons."

Mr. Stanley also noted that defense experts have warned for years that small, commercially available drones could be used as weapons. In 2004, a New Zealand engineer managed to build a miniature cruise missile for less than $5,000, a project that subsequently was shut down by the nation's government because of security concerns.

Last month, a 27-year-old Massachusetts man was sentenced to 17 years in prison for plotting to attack the Pentagon and the Capitol with a remote-controlled model aircraft rigged with explosives.

"We've called for a ban on armed drones, and I think there's a broad consensus that we should not allow armed drones to be used domestically," said Mr. Stanley, the author of a report on drones and privacy. "The International Association of Chiefs of Police has recommended against it. I think this video likely will further cement that consensus."

"Terrifyingly Easy"

In the video, Milo wears sunglasses, a black baseball cap, a large American-flag bandanna that covers his face and a T-shirt reading "Dangerous Information"—the latter the name of a fledgling Web video series that explores topics such as picking locks and growing marijuana.

Holding a small, six-rotor hobbyist drone in his hand, Milo states that the realistic-looking handgun attached to the machine's undercarriage fires "non-lethal" 11 mm paintballs.

By the time the drone lands, [it] has hit all five targets repeatedly.

"Let me be clear, under no circumstances should you ever put a live firearm on a drone, a remote-controlled toy or any other vehicle," he says. "It's incredibly dangerous.

"Can a mail-order drone from a kit even handle the stress of rounds cycling through a gun? Is it accurate? Let's find out."

Flying about 15 feet above the ground and controlled by Milo with the help of an onboard video camera that transmits real-time images to a set of piloting goggles, the drone maneuvers around five human-shaped targets, the buzz of its electric engines mixing with the popping sound of the paintball gun discharging.

By the time the drone lands, Milo has hit all five targets repeatedly.

"If the question is, 'How easy is it to fly this drone?' the answer is, 'terrifyingly easy,'" he said. "The first time we flew it, we were able to put all of the paintball ammunition into a target 50 yards away from the operator—and 15 yards from the [drone]—in an area the size of a dinner plate."

Do-It-Yourself Drone Training

According to Milo, building the drone was nearly as straightforward. He purchased the drone and the paintball gun online, downloaded open-source piloting software and found instructions on how to get the drone up and running by running simple Internet searches for the terms "drones" and "DIY."

The entire project, he said, took no more than a dozen hours and cost less than $2,000.

"I'm not particularly handy," he said. "But I was able pick up this pretty high-end hobby as a completely inexperienced person and master it with a small budget in a couple of weeks. It was up and flying within a couple of sessions of working on it, and that's including trial and error and making mistakes."

The hardest part, Milo said, was centering the weight of the paintball pistol, which weighs approximately 2 pounds—roughly the same weight as many actual handguns.

"There would be some practical physical considerations to mounting a real gun," Milo said. "Many pistols have significantly greater recoil. However, some guns have very little. And the onboard computer for the drone tries to keep itself level even if you try to knock it out of the air.

"I don't think it would have problems staying in the air with many smaller firearms, but I don't encourage anyone doing that."

Unlike the autonomous human-hunting drones of dystopian science fiction—think "The Terminator" film series—Milo's drone flew by remote control [RC], the same way miniature dune buggies and toy airplanes are piloted by RC enthusiasts.

"With very little extra work, however, we could program it on a computer to fly on a path, fire on a fixed target and then fly home with little human intervention," he said. "This drone is capable of that."

The Future Is Soon?

Earlier this year, a different YouTube video appeared to show a homemade quad-rotor drone with a custom-mounted machine gun laying explosive waste to a group of mannequins.

The fun and valid uses of this technology are going to happen. But other possibilities are there.

Viewed more than 15 million times, the video turned out to be a hoax, part of a viral marketing campaign for the future-warfare video game "Call of Duty: Black Ops II."

"Drones are a hot topic," Milo said. "You can't look at the Internet without coming across a drone-related story. Most of them are about military drones or government and police agencies considering drones and their uses. But very infrequently do you see stories that cover the DIY maker approach.

"The fun and valid uses of this technology are going to happen. But other possibilities are there. Surveillance drones over American skies. Armed drones. Not just your local police but also your neighbors. I wanted to create a video that put the questions out there."

For the most part, drones currently are confined to the military—which reportedly has more than 7,500 vehicles in service—and hobbyists such as Milo, who are flying roughly double that number. Moreover, current FAA rules largely prohibit commercial drone use, while hobbyists are subject to strict guidelines: no flying above 400 feet, near populated areas or outside the operator's line of sight.

A federal law passed in February [2012], however, compels the FAA to allow drone use by police and emergency services later this year and allow "safe" commercial use by September 2015.

Video Sparks Consumer Interest

Drone advocates such as Mr. Anderson argue that the technology is akin to the personal computer, flexible enough to perform important and useful tasks ranging from crop-dusting to inspecting pipelines to extreme sports photography.

Milo said excited paintball players began contacting him within hours of his video being posted online.

"A ton of people are very excited, to the point of 'Shut up and take my money' and 'This is now on my Christmas list,'" he said. "People are interested in playing with this kind of toy."

Acknowledging the inevitability of increased drone use by the government and private citizens alike, Mr. Stanley said society needs to proceed with caution.

The Washington Times recently reported that because of privacy issues, the FAA appears likely to miss its self-imposed Dec. 31 deadline to choose six sites in states throughout the nation where drones will be put through a battery of safety and other tests before full commercialization is allowed.

"There is nothing like seeing actual video of something that might be an abstract concept to bring home the reality of the fast-paced technological era we are living in," Mr. Stanley said. "And this video is a reminder of how we really need to step up and deal with these issues, and not just sit back and let things happen on their own. Whether that's preventing guns from being placed on drones, or putting in rules to protect our privacy, we should decide if these are changes we want or don't want and protect ourselves as necessary."

Commercial Drones Must Be Thoroughly Regulated

Arthur Holland Michel

Arthur Holland Michel is codirector of the Center for the Study of the Drone at Bard College in New York, an interdisciplinary research, education, and art community working to understand unmanned and autonomous vehicles.

In 2012, when small drones, the kind that weigh just a few pounds and carry a small object (like a camera, or a burrito) became affordable, the idea of a drone-filled airspace began shifting from sci-fi fantasy to reality. But the passage toward integration was set to be turbulent.

Drones were more commonly thought of as the weaponized, ghostlike military spy aircraft that lurked over Pakistan, Yemen and Somalia, killing enemy militants and, occasionally, civilians and children. While these drones have little in common with small domestic drones, the public was spooked. Groups like the American Civil Liberties Union [ACLU] raised alarms. Fearing for privacy and safety, lawmakers from Washington state to Virginia rushed to propose legislation to limit or ban drones, even very small ones. The Federal Aviation Administration [FAA] stressed, sternly, that commercial drone use would be absolutely prohibited until 2015, when it would enact comprehensive—and strict—safety regulations. The agency reminded the public that private drone users were subject to restrictions, too.

Two years later, the drones are soaring, while the efforts to limit their use have stalled and the public debate has gone into a tailspin.

In June [2014], a company called Squadrone System started a Kickstarter campaign to fund a small multi-rotor drone called the HEXO+, which the company described as "an intelligent drone that follows and films you autonomously," perfect for making exciting action sports videos. Within a few hours, the campaign had raised more than three times its $50,000 target. When the campaign ended, the company had raised $1.3 million.

In state legislatures, drone regulation is one of the few issues that has enjoyed bipartisan support.

Drone Fever vs. Drone Fear

That same week, a company called APlus Mobile made its own Kickstarter campaign. Instead of a drone, the company proposed a Personal Drone Detection System—essentially, an anti-drone radar. "Our intent is to keep your privacy safe from your neighbors and people you may not know who are flying small drones near your home or office," it said. The campaign only managed to raise $1,435 of its $8,500 goal. It's clear: The drone is winning.

In state legislatures, drone regulation is one of the few issues that has enjoyed bipartisan support. In 2013, according to the ACLU, 43 states debated 96 drone bills; however, all but eight of these bills died in session. This year, just four out of 36 states that considered drone legislation have enacted any laws. This is not enough to keep pace with drone proliferation.

And lawmakers in Washington aren't jumping to regulate the drone. In fact, some have caught drone fever. Last month [July 2014], Democratic Rep. Sean Patrick Maloney of New York hired a photographer who used a drone to capture (admittedly rather stunning) aerial views of the congressman's wedding. Sen. Rand Paul, R-Ky., who filibustered Congress for

13 hours in protest of government drone use, owns a toy drone. When he flew it on Fox News, the look on his face was childlike.

Recommendations, Not Regulations

Even the FAA has been toothless. Desperate to prevent the midair meeting of a drone and a manned aircraft, the agency has released a number of policy statements intended to limit unsafe drone use. These statements include the ban on commercial use. But policy statements are not legally binding. They are recommendations, placeholders for the real, legally enforceable regulations that will come sometime after 2015. While private individuals and companies often respect federal agency policy statements, in the case of the FAA, droners, eager to get airborne, have openly flaunted them.

The FAA has attempted to enforce these policy statements through cease-and-desist letters and, in one case, a $10,000 fine. But these actions have been repeatedly struck down in court. The FAA's attempts at enforcement have therefore only served to highlight that it has its hands tied. Meanwhile, the rules that actually are legal (like keeping away from airports) are easy to break and difficult to enforce.

The domestic integration of drones must not be rushed. . . . The FAA needs time to develop an integration plan, a gargantuan task that will (and should) take several years.

At an industry level, the FAA and the droners have fallen into the all-too-familiar battle that pits regulation against the profit-efficiency motive. The drone industry, represented formally by the Association for Unmanned Vehicle Systems International, is frustrated that the FAA's foot-dragging is keeping the U.S. from launching into what will be a multibillion dollar industry. When I visited the association's annual trade show in May, people talked about the FAA as if it was a regulatory boogeyman.

The coexistence of federal regulations and a profit-hungry industry is never a happy one. "Each day that integration is delayed will lead to $27 million in lost economic impact," wrote Michael Toscano, the association's president, in a letter to the FAA in January. Mathematical fuzziness aside, the argument misses a point: Well-thought-out safety regulations, especially in the air, where stakes are high, have no price. Two years ago, this battle would have been unthinkable.

Addressing Complex Challenges Will Take Time

When used intelligently, or by professionals, drones are safe and useful. Recently, an amateur drone pilot found his lost grandfather in just 20 minutes; the authorities had been searching for three days. But if used stupidly, drones are dangerous. Just a few days after the missing grandfather was retrieved, Cal Fire almost had to suspend operations over the Plymouth wildfires because an amateur videographer was flying a drone in the area. Just because pretty much anybody can fly a drone doesn't mean that everybody should. The dangers of improper drone use are real.

The domestic integration of drones must not be rushed. It is naturally a challenging process, because drones present a set of complex challenges. The FAA needs time to develop an integration plan, a gargantuan task that will (and should) take several years. Safety ought to have priority over profits.

Calls for caution are not alarmism; they are legitimate. A vigorous and balanced debate in state assemblies, on Capitol Hill and in public forums is prerequisite to the development of sensible policies and norms. We are not seeing that debate. It has been squelched by the technological promise of kits like the HEXO+.

Alluring as it is, let's not get carried away with the drone. As the technology develops more quickly and the price drops further, the safety and privacy concerns will become more pressing. We need to be careful and patient. The drone will have its day. Let's make sure we are prepared for it when it does.

Organizations to Contact

The editors have compiled the following list of organizations concerned with the issues debated in this book. The descriptions are derived from materials provided by the organizations. All have publications or information available for interested readers. The list was compiled on the date of publication of the present volume; the information provided here may change. Be aware that many organizations take several weeks or longer to respond to inquiries, so allow as much time as possible.

American Civil Liberties Union (ACLU)
125 Broad St., 18th Floor, New York, NY 10004
(212) 549-2500
e-mail: info@aclu.org
website: www.aclu.org

Through activism in courts, legislatures, and communities nationwide, the American Civil Liberties Union (ACLU) works to defend the individual rights and liberties that the Constitution and laws of the United States guarantee to everyone. The ACLU website has an extensive collection of reports, briefings, and news updates related to the use of drones, with an emphasis on concerns about human rights, privacy, mass surveillance, police militarization, and civil liberties. Publications available from the ACLU include "Unchecked Government Drones? Not Over My Backyard," "The Unreal Secrecy About Drone Killings," and "ACLU Testifies on the Need for Regulation of Surveillance by Domestic Drones."

American Security Project (ASP)
1100 New York Ave. NW, Suite 710W, Washington, DC 20005
(202) 347-4267
website: http://americansecurityproject.org

The American Security Project (ASP) believes that America's current national security strategy is flawed and that it increases worldwide anti-Americanism and threatens the nation's ability to compete in the global marketplace. The organization hopes to increase public awareness of the true nature of the struggle between the United States and violent extremists so that the country might develop more effective policies and strategies to meet the threat. On its website, ASP publishes issue summaries, recent issues of *American Security Quarterly*, and reports, including *Understanding the Strategies and Tactical Considerations of Drone Strikes*. Under the link Issues/Asymmetric Operations/Strategic Effect of Drones, ASP publishes an annotated bibliography on drones.

Amnesty International USA
5 Penn Plaza, New York, NY   10001
(212) 807-8400 • fax: (212) 627-1451
e-mail: aimember@aiusa.org
website: www.amnestyusa.org

Amnesty International USA works to ensure that governments do not deny individuals their basic human rights as outlined in the United Nations Universal Declaration of Human Rights. The organization seeks greater transparency in the use of drones and opposes targeted killing without due process. Its website contains recent news, reports, and a searchable database of archived publications, including many on the impact of drones and drone policies.

Association for Unmanned Vehicle Systems International (AUVSI)
2700 S. Quincy St., Suite 400, Arlington, VA   22206
(703) 845-9671 • fax: (703) 845-9679
e-mail: info@auvsi.org
website: www.auvsi.org

The Association for Unmanned Vehicle Systems International (AUVSI) is a membership organization that supports the use of unmanned aerial systems such as drones and related technology. Members represent government organizations, industry, and academia and support the defense, civil, and commercial sectors. AUVSI publishes the monthly magazine *Unmanned*

Systems, which highlights current global developments and unveils new technologies in air, ground, maritime, and space systems, and *Mission Critical*, a quarterly electronic publication. The organization's website features extensive information about drones and other unmanned systems, regulatory efforts, and related issues.

Brookings Institution

1775 Massachusetts Ave. NW, Washington, DC 20036
(202) 797-6000 • fax: (202) 797-6004
e-mail: communications@brookings.edu
website: www.brookings.edu

Founded in 1927, the Brookings Institution conducts research and analyzes global events and their impact on the United States and US foreign policy. It publishes the quarterly *Brookings Review* and numerous books and research papers. Its website publishes editorials, papers, testimony, reports, and articles written by Brookings scholars, including "The Global Swarm: An International Drone Market," "The Predator Comes Home: A Primer on Domestic Drones, Their Huge Business Opportunities, and Their Deep Political, Moral, and Legal Challenges," and "When Can the US Target Alleged American Terrorists Overseas?"

Cato Institute

1000 Massachusetts Ave. NW, Washington, DC 2001-5403
(202) 842-0200 • fax: (202) 842-3490
website: www.cato.org

The Cato Institute is a libertarian public policy research foundation dedicated to peace and limited government intervention in domestic and foreign affairs. Cato publishes numerous reports and periodicals, including *Policy Analysis* and *Cato Policy Report*, both of which discuss US drone policy as both a domestic and foreign policy tool. Its website contains a searchable database of Institute articles, news, multimedia, and commentary, including the video "Game of Drones: Liberty and Security in the Age of Flying Robots" and the article "Look up in the Sky and See a Drone."

Center for Strategic and International Studies (CSIS)
CSIS Center for Strategic and International Studies
Washington, DC 20036
(202) 887-0200 • fax: (202) 775-3199
website: www.csis.org

The Center for Strategic and International Studies (CSIS) conducts research and develops policy recommendations on a variety of issues, including defense and security strategies, economic development, energy and climate change, global health, technology, and trade. The Center publishes *The Washington Quarterly*, recent articles from which are available at its website. CSIS publishes books, reports, newsletters, and commentaries targeted at decision makers in government, business, and academia. Website visitors can access articles on drones through the website's search engine, including "US Civil Drone Policy" and "The Alternatives to Drone Strikes Are Worse."

Council on Foreign Relations (CFR)
58 East 68th St., New York, NY 10021
(212) 434-9400 • fax: (212) 434-9800
e-mail: communications@cfr.org
website: www.cfr.org

The Council on Foreign Relations (CFR) specializes in foreign affairs and studies the international aspects of American political and economic policies and problems. Its journal *Foreign Affairs*, published five times a year, includes analyses of current conflicts around the world. Its website publishes editorials, interviews, articles, and reports, including the article "Why Did the CIA Stop Torturing and Start Killing?" and the report "Reforming US Drone Strike Policies."

Drone Project/Medill National Security Journalism Initiative
Medill School of Journalism
Media Integrated Marketing Communications
Evanston, IL 60208-2101
(847) 467-1882

e-mail: contact@nationalsecurityzone.org
website: http://droneproject.nationalsecurityzone.org

The Drone Project is part of the Medill National Security Journalism Initiative, a program at Northwestern University that provides working journalists and those in training with the knowledge and skills to report accurately, completely, and with context on issues related to defense, security, and civil liberties. The Drone Project website features dozens of informative articles about drones and drone policy written by student reporters, many of which have been published by McClatchy newspapers. The Drone Project website also features an interactive map that details the current status of drone legislation in each state.

Drone Safety Council (DSC)

e-mail: info@dronesafetycouncil.org
website: http://dronesafetycouncil.com

Formed in 2013, the Drone Safety Council (DSC) is an industry-standards body working to develop safety standards for commercial and civilian drones and unmanned robotic vehicles. The nonprofit organization is dedicated to addressing the growing concerns for the safety of commercial and civilian drone operators as well as the general public. The group's goal is to inform, investigate, and implement drone safety standards that will be adopted by drone manufacturers and by global governments for the safety of all concerned. The DSC website includes a wide variety of information about drone safety and current and pending regulations, in addition to updates on the group's efforts.

Human Rights Watch

350 Fifth Ave., 34th Floor, New York, NY   10118-3299
(212) 290-4700 • fax: (212) 736-1300
e-mail: hrwnyc@hrw.org
website: www.hrw.org

Founded in 1978, Human Rights Watch is a nongovernmental organization that conducts systematic investigations of human rights abuses in countries around the world. It publishes many books and reports on specific countries and issues as well as annual reports, recent selections of which are available at its website. Publications on drones include "What Rules Should Govern US Drone Attacks?," "A Dangerous Model: The US Should Reveal Its Legal Rationale for Drone Attacks," and "Anatomy of an Air Attack Gone Wrong."

The Rutherford Institute
PO Box 7482, Charlottesville, VA 22966-7482
(434) 978-3888
e-mail: staff@rutherford.org
website: www.rutherford.org

The Rutherford Institute is a conservative civil liberties think tank with a dual mission. It provides legal services in the defense of religious and civil liberties and seeks to educate the public on important issues affecting constitutional freedoms. The Institute supports strong civil liberties protections from constitutional invasions by domestic drones. Its website publishes news and commentary on the domestic use of drones, including "Key Cases: Drones" and "Roaches, Mosquitoes, and Birds: The Coming Micro-Drone Revolution," and commentary by its founder, constitutional attorney John W. Whitehead.

Bibliography

Books

Medea Benjamin — *Drone Warfare.* New York: OR Books, 2012.

Marjorie Cohn, ed. — *Drones and Targeted Killing: Legal, Moral, and Geopolitical Issues.* Charles City, VA: Olive Branch, 2014.

David Cortright, Rachel Fairhurst, and Kristen Wall, eds. — *Drones and the Future of Armed Conflict: Ethical, Legal, and Strategic Implications.* Chicago: University of Chicago Press, 2015.

Steven Hogan — *The Drone Revolution: How Robotic Aviation Will Change the World.* Seattle: CreateSpace, 2015.

Craig Issod — *Getting Started with Hobby Quadcopters and Drones: Learn About, Buy and Fly These Amazing Aerial Vehicles.* Seattle: CreateSpace, 2013.

Mark LaFay — *Drones for Dummies.* New York: Wiley & Sons, 2015.

Jerry LeMieux — *Drone Entrepreneurship: 30 Businesses You Can Start.* Phoenix, AZ: Unmanned Vehicle University Press, 2013.

Jonathan Rupprecht — *Drones: Their Many Civilian Uses and the US Laws Surrounding Them.* Seattle: CreateSpace, 2015.

P.W. Singer   *Wired for War: The Robotics Revolution and Conflict in the 21st Century.* New York: Penguin, 2009.

Richard Whittle   *Predator: The Secret Origins of the Drone Revolution.* New York: Henry Holt and Co., 2014.

Periodicals and Internet Sources

Hassan Abbas   "Are Drone Strikes Killing Terrorists or Creating Them?," *Atlantic*, March 31, 2013.

Hassan Abbas   "How Drones Create More Terrorists," *Atlantic*, August 23, 2013.

Amnesty International "Will I Be Next? US Drone Strikes in Pakistan," amnestyusa.org, 2013. www.amnestyusa.org.

Associated Press "Drone 'Containing Radiation' Lands on Roof of Japanese PM's Office in Tokyo," *Guardian* (UK), April 22, 2015.

Associated Press "Poll: Americans Skeptical of Commercial Drones," *Toledo Blade*, December 19, 2014.

Kelsey Atherton "FAA May Never Figure out Drone Rules," *Popular Science*, June 30, 2014.

Kelsey Atherton "This Is the FAA's Plan for Drone-Friendly Skies," *Popular Science*, November 8, 2013.

Ashley Balcerzak and Taylor Hiegel "Police Forces Struggle to Incorporate Drones," Medill School of Journalism Drone Project, March 18, 2013. http://droneproject .nationalsecurityzone.org.

Jeremy Barr "Journalists Await New Drone Regulations. And Wait, and Wait . . . ," poynter.org, January 30, 2014. www.poynter.org.

Tom Barry "Fallacies of High-Tech Fixes for Border Security—International Policy Report," Center for International Policy, April 2010. www.ciponline.org.

Tom Barry "How the Drone Warfare Industry Took Over Our Congress," AlterNet, November 30, 2011. www.alternet.org.

Peter Bergen and Jennifer Rowland "A Dangerous New World of Drones," CNN, October 8, 2012. www.cnn.com.

Rae Ellen Bichell "No Seat Belts Required: Drone Hobbyists Talk Safety," National Public Radio, October 26, 2013. www.npr.org.

Matt Bigler "Controversial Police Drone Inches Closer to Flight in San Jose," cbslocal.com, April 9, 2015. http://sanfrancisco.cbslocal.com.

Thomas Black   "Armed Drones Seen as
                    Dogfight-Ready in (Not-Too-Distant)
                    Future," Bloomberg Business, May 8,
                    2015. www.bloomberg.com.

Joshua Bleiberg   "Drones and Aerial Surveillance: The
                    Opportunities and the Risks,"
                    Brookings Institution, November 18,
                    2014. www.brookings.edu.

Joshua Bleiberg   "Should Rock Bands Use Drones?,"
                    Brookings Institution, November 5,
                    2014. www.brookings.edu.

Bloomberg   "Alibaba Drones Fly Over Beijing
Business   While Amazon Pleads for US Tests,"
                    February 2, 2015.
                    www.bloomberg.com.

Allie Bohm   "Drone Legislation: What's Being
                    Proposed in the States?," ACLU,
                    March 6, 2013. www.aclu.org.

Cory Booker   "Can US Drone Policy Finally Soar?,"
                    CNN, February 19, 2015.
                    www.cnn.com.

William Booth   "More Predators Fly US Border,"
                    Washington Post, December 1, 2011.

Rod Boshart   "Carter: US Drone Attacks Violate
                    Human Rights," Quad-City Times,
                    September 14, 2012.

Christopher   "The Future of Unmanned Aviation
Calabrese   in the U.S. Economy: Safety and
                   Privacy," Statement Before the Senate
                   Committee on Commerce, Science,
                   and Transportation, January 15,
                   2014. www.aclu.org.

CBS Local   "Drone Scare for LAX-Bound Flight
                   Reignites Safety Debate," February 9,
                   2015. http://losangeles.cbslocal.com.

Paul Cochrane   "Peaceful Drones," *MIT Technology
                   Review*, March 26, 2015.

David Cortright   "How Drones Are Changing Warfare:
                   License to Kill," *Cato Unbound*,
                   January 9, 2012.
                   www.cato-unbound.org.

David Cortright   "The Scary Prospect of Global Drone
                   Warfare," CNN, October 19, 2011.
                   www.cnn.com.

Catherine Crump   "Why Americans Are Saying No to
and Jay Stanley   Domestic Drones," *Slate*, February 11,
                   2013. www.slate.com.

Jeremy Diamond   "US Drone Strike Accidentally Killed
                   Two Hostages," CNN, April 23, 2015.
                   www.cnn.com.

Laura Donnelly   "Drones Could Be Used to Seek out
                   Arteries to Prevent Heart Attacks,"
                   Telegraph (UK), February 8, 2015.

Kimberlu Dozier   "Human Rights Groups Criticize US
                   Drone Program," *Huffington Post*,
                   October 22, 2013.
                   www.huffingtonpost.com.

Dronelife News — "How Sexy Headlines May Be Shaping the Drone Debate," July 30, 2014. http://dronelife.com.

Bill Gertz — "China Preparing for Drone Warfare: PLA Plans to Build 42,000 UAVs, Pentagon Says," *Washington Free Beacon*, May 8, 2015.

Ben Gielow — "AUVSI Tells Congress—Pace of UAS Integration Unacceptable," Association for Unmanned Vehicle Systems International, March 11, 2014. www.auvsi.org.

Andrew Griffin — "TGI Friday Drone Crashes into Woman's Face and Cuts It Open in Restaurant," *Independent* (UK), December 9, 2014.

Neema Singh Guliani — "Unchecked Government Drones? Not Over My Backyard," *The Hill*, March 24, 2015. http://thehill.com.

Gregory Hall — "Drones' Promise Weighed Against Privacy, Safety," *Courier Journal*, December 14, 2014.

Elizabeth Harrington — "Audit: DHS Drone Program Ineffective at Border Security," *Washington Free Beacon*, January 6, 2015.

Julian Hattem — "Drones Crash onto White House Agenda," *The Hill*, January 29, 2015. http://thehill.com.

W.J. Hennigan   "City in Virginia Passes Anti-Drone Resolution," *Los Angeles Times*, February 6, 2013.

Andres Jauregui   "'Drone Boning' Is Why You Can't Have Sex in Public," *Huffington Post*, December 22, 2014. www.huffingtonpost.com.

Leo King   "Mind-Controlled Drone Scientists Work on Groundbreaking Flight," *Forbes*, February 25, 2015.

David LaGesse   "If Drones Make You Nervous, Think of Them as Flying Donkeys," National Public Radio, March 31, 2015. www.npr.org.

Josh Lederman   "Secret Service to Conduct Drone Exercises Over Washington," Associated Press, February 24, 2015. http://hosted.ap.org.

Tammy Leitner and Lisa Capitanini   "How a Drone Could Spoof Wi-Fi, Steal Your Data," NBC Chicago, May 5, 2015. www.nbcchicago.com.

Barry Levine   "Drones Overhead in LA's Valley Are Tracking Mobile Devices' Locations," *Venture Beat*, February 23, 2015. http://venturebeat.com.

Daniel Lippman   "Drones Fly into the Political Ad Wars," *Politico*, February 7, 2015. www.politico.com.

Ryan Lovelace   "Drones in Our Future: On Our Border with Mexico, Both Drug Smugglers and the CBP Use Them," *National Review*, February 4, 2015.

Joan Lowy   "Battlefield Stigma Complicates Peaceful Drone Use at Home," Gazettenet.com, March 30, 2013. www.gazettenet.com.

Joan Lowy   "Proposed Rules for Drones Envision Routine Commercial Use," Associated Press, February 15, 2015. http://apnews.myway.com.

Michael B. Marois   "Creeps Embrace a New Tool: Peeping Drones," Bloomberg Business, May 5, 2015. www.bloomberg.com.

William Marra and Sonia McNeil   "Understanding 'The Loop': Humans and the Next Drone Generations," *Issues in Governance Studies*, August 2012. www.brookings.edu.

Gary Martin and Viveca Novak   "Drone Makers Push Congress to Open Skies to Surveillance," *Houston Chronicle*, November 24, 2012.

Mark Mazzetti and Matt Apuzzo   "Deep Support in Washington for CIA's Drone Missions," *New York Times*, April 25, 2015.

Kalaya'an Mendoza   "This Is How You Fight Drones," *Human Rights Now*, November 14, 2013. http://blog.amnestyusa.org.

Asher Moses | "Flying Drones a Safety Threat at Airports," *Sydney Morning Herald*, September 11, 2012.

Greg Nichols | "Swarm Robots Poised to Fly Amid Acquisitions and Military Investment," *Robotics/ZD Net*, April 14, 2015. www.zdnet.com.

Mickey Osterreicher and Alicia Calzada | "Have Drone, Will Gather News," *News Photographer*, January/February 2015.

Ed Pilkington | "Amazon Tests Delivery Drones at Secret Canada Site After US Frustration in British Columbia," *Guardian* (UK), March 30, 2015.

Avery Plaw | "Drone Strikes Save Lives, American and Other," *New York Times*, November 14, 2012.

Mark Prado | "Golden Gate Bridge Officials Want to Keep Drones Away from Span," *Marin Independent Journal*, April 24, 2015.

PRNewswire-USNewswire | "Drones Reduce Number of American Troops, Former Clinton White House Spokesman Robert Weiner and Defense Analyst Tom Sherman Say Liberals and Conservatives Should Both Advocate Them," October 10, 2014. www.prnewswire.com.

ProCon.org | "Drones—Pros and Cons," August 11, 2014. http://drones.procon.org.

Brad Reed   "The World's Tiniest Drone Shows
                 Privacy May Be Dead for Good,"
                 BGR, March 5, 2015. http://bgr.com.

Reuters   "Mini Army Drones Developed,"
                 March 10, 2015. www.reuters.com.

Barrie Rokeach   "As a Pilot, I'm Not Keen on Sharing
                 the Skies with Drones," *San Francisco
                 Chronicle*, May 13, 2015.

Alice Ross   "Is Congressional Oversight Tough
                 Enough on Drones?," Bureau of
                 Investigative Journalism, August 1,
                 2013. www.thebureauinvestigates
                 .com.

Luke Runyon   "As Rules Get Sorted Out, Drones
                 May Transform Agriculture Industry,"
                 National Public Radio, February 16,
                 2015. www.npr.org.

William Saletan "In Defense of Drones: They're the
                 Worst Form of War, Except for All
                 the Others," *Slate*, February 19, 2013.
                 www.slate.com.

Henry Samuel   "Drone Spotted Near Charlie Hebdo
                 as Ten More Fly Over Paris,"
                 Telegraph (UK), March 4, 2015.

Monica Sarkar   "Security from the Sky: Indian City
                 to Use Pepper-Spray Drones for
                 Crowd Control," CNN, April 9, 2015.
                 www.cnn.com.

Michael Schmidt "Drones Smuggle Contraband Over
                 Prison Walls," *New York Times*, April
                 22, 2015.

Connor Adams Sheets "Commercial Drones' Rise Seen as Growing Danger to Traditional Aircraft," *International Business Times*, April 25, 2014.

Aaron Smith "US Views of Technology and the Future—Science in the Next Fifty Years," Pew Research Center, April 17, 2014. www.pewinternet.org.

Andrew Stobo Sniderman and Mark Hanis "Drones for Human Rights," *New York Times*, January 30, 2012.

Jay Stanley and Catherine Crump "Protecting Privacy from Aerial Surveillance: Recommendations for Government Use of Drone Aircraft," ACLU, 2011. www.aclu.org.

Amie Stepanovich "The Future of Drones in America: Law Enforcement and Privacy Considerations—Hearing Before the Committee of the Judiciary United States Senate," US Government Printing Office, March 20, 2013. www.gpo.gov.

Laura Sydell "As Drones Fly in Cities and Yards, So Do the Complaints," National Public Radio, May 12, 2014. www.npr.org.

Daniel Terdiman "Flying Lampshades: Cirque du Soleil Plays with Drones," CNET, September 23, 2014. www.cnet.com.

Patrick Tucker   "The Nine Strangest Flying Robots
from the World's Biggest Drone
Show," *Defense One*, May 8, 2015.
www.defenseone.com.

Muhsin Usman   "How America Is Fueling
Radicalization of Muslims and How
to Reverse It," *Huffington Post*, July 6,
2012. www.huffingtonpost.com.

Steve Watson   "Security, Privacy Experts Testify to
Congress on Spy Drones," *Prison
Planet*, July 19, 2012.
www.prisonplanet.com.

John Watts   "Drone, Baby, Drone . . . If You Want
More Terrorists," Campaign for
Liberty, February 27, 2013.
www.campaignforliberty.org.

John Whitehead   "The Micro-Drone Revolution:
Roachbots, Ravens, Mosquitos, and
More," CNS News, April 15, 2013.
http://cnsnews.com.

Craig Whitlock   "FAA Proposes Rules for Drone Use;
Obama Issues Curbs on
Surveillance," *Washington Post*,
February 15, 2015.

Craig Whitlock   "How Crashing Drones Are Exposing
Secrets About US War Operations,"
Washington Post, March 25, 2015.

Ben Wolfgang   "Drone Privacy Scare," *Washington
Times*, February 15, 2012.

Index

A

Acheson, Ben, 30–33
AeroVironment (AV), 119, 146
Ahern, Gregory, 102–103
Air Line Pilots Association, 40
Airline safety and drones, 39–42
Air traffic control (ATC) procedures, 46
Al-Aulaqi, Anwar and Abdulrahman, 86
Al-Firdos bunker airstrike, 63
Ali, Entisar, 89
Al-Muslimi, Farea, 66
Al-Qaeda, 31, 59–60, 75, 84, 89, 164
Al-Qaeda in the Arabian Peninsula (AQAP), 66
Al-Qaeda in the Islamic Maghreb (AQIM), 66
Alston, Philip, 89
American Civil Liberties Union (ACLU)
   commercial drones, 169, 175
   law enforcement drones, 103, 104, 117, 131
   military drones, 28, 79, 81, 86, 93–94
American troop safety and drones, 56–58
Anderson, Chris, 145
Anti-drone activism, 124
Anti-US sentiment, 74
APlus Mobile, 176
Armentrout, Mitchell, 144–148
Assassination drones, 119–120
Asset management with drones, 110–111

B

Association for Unmanned Vehicle Systems International (AUVSI), 19, 145
Atlanta Journal Constitution newspaper, 84
The Atlantic magazine, 62

Badway, Aaron, 59–61
Balko, Radley, 120
Baltimore Sun newspaper, 126
Barry, Tom, 134–139
Beck, Charlie, 127
Behram, Noor, 79
Benjamin, Medea, 88–90
Bennett, Brian, 130–133
Bilodeau, Cloe, 59–61
Bin Laden, Osama, 60
Blair, Dennis, 89
Booby-trapped drones, 52
Borhian, Bruce, 128
Bowcott, Owen, 79
Bowden, Mark, 62
Brannen, Sam, 51, 54
Brown, Michael, 128
Bureau of Investigative Journalism (TBIJ), 65–66, 79–80
Burris, Keith C., 56–58
Bush, George W., 56, 82

C

California Air National Guard, 23
California Department of Forestry and Fire Protection (Cal Fire), 24
California v. Ciraolo (1986), 37

The Means to Grow Up

In *The Means to Grow Up*, author Robert Halpern describes the pedagogical importance of "apprenticeship"—a growing movement based in schools, youth-serving organizations, and arts, civic, and other cultural institutions. This movement aims to re-engage youth through in-depth learning and unique experiences under the guidance of skilled professionals. Employing a "pedagogy of apprenticeship," these experiences combine specific, visceral, and sometimes messy work with opportunity for self-expression, increasing responsibility, and exposure to the adult world.

Grounded in ethnographic studies, *The Means to Grow Up* illustrates how students work in unique ways around these meaningful activities and projects across a range of disciplines. Participation in these efforts strengthens skills, dispositions, and self-knowledge that is critical to future schooling and work, renews young people's sense of vitality, and fosters a grounded sense of accomplishment. In unearthing the complexities of apprenticeship learning, Halpern challenges the education system that is increasingly geared towards the acquisition of de-contextualized skills. *The Means to Grow Up* reveals instead how learning alongside experienced adults can be a profoundly challenging and complex endeavor for adolescents and offers readers an exciting vision of what education can and should be about.

Robert Halpern is Professor at the Erikson Institute for Graduate Study in Child Development.

Critical Youth Studies

Series Editor: Greg Dimitriadis

The Means to Grow Up

Reinventing Apprenticeship
as a Developmental Support
in Adolescence

Robert Halpern

Routledge
Taylor & Francis Group

NEW YORK AND LONDON

First published 2009
by Routledge
270 Madison Ave, New York, NY 10016

Simultaneously published in the UK
by Routledge
2 Park Square, Milton Park, Abingdon, Oxon OX14 4RN

Routledge is an imprint of the Taylor & Francis Group, an informa business

Typeset in Minion by EvS Communication Networx, Inc.
Printed and bound in the United States of America on acid-free paper by Edwards Brothers, Inc.

Library of Congress Cataloging in Publication Data
Halpern, Robert, 1951–
The means to grow up : reinventing apprenticeship as a developmental support in adolescence / Robert Halpern. — 1st ed.
p. cm. — (Critical youth studies)
Includes bibliographical references and index.
1. Apprenticeship programs—United States. 2. Adolescence—United States. I. Title.
HD4885.U5H35 2009
658.3'1240835—dc22
2008025200

ISBN 10: 0-415-96032-0 (hbk)
ISBN 10: 0-415-96033-9 (pbk)
ISBN 10: 0-203-88597-X (ebk)

ISBN 13: 978-0-415-96032-8 (hbk)
ISBN 13: 978-0-415-96033-5 (pbk)
ISBN 13: 978-0-203-88597-0 (ebk)

This book is dedicated to my own two apprentices.
You long ago surpassed your teacher.

Contents

Series Editor Introduction

Richard Sennett's recent book, *The Craftsman* (2008), alerts us to the powerful, persistent, and long-standing human need to do work that matters—work that is skilled, work that is deeply particular, work that is often for its own sake. Such work demands continuous trial and error—often over many years and many decades. Such work holds out the promise of pride in craft. And its practitioners can be found in a range of domains—from the skilled carpenter to the master musician to the expert engineer. As Sennett argues, this basic human need reaches back centuries.

Our contemporary economy, however, is making such craft-work increasingly anachronous. The fetish for "flexibility" makes the worker him- or herself continually useless. Skills are quickly acquired, temporarily applied, then discarded. The human cost is profound—the forging of deep self through deep craft.

Education has come to play a new and pernicious role here. Workers are now "life-long learners" and must be continually "retrained" to keep gainful employment. For many, education has been both the cause of and the cure to our contemporary economic dilemmas. The lack of "basic skills" that can be applied in multiple circumstances is the problem—and policies like No Child Left Behind and "skill and drill" pedagogies are the supposed cure. In fact, former Federal Reserve chairman Alan Greenspan (2007) concluded his sprawling, recent autobiography, *The Age of Turbulence*, with a plea for the importance of math education. Better math education, according to Greenspan, will help rectify the massive global, economic inequalities produced over the last several decades. It seems an anti-climactic note on which to end his tome—exposing, perhaps, the intellectual poverty of the project.

All of this makes Robert Halpern's new book, *The Means to Grow Up: Reinventing Apprenticeship as a Developmental Support in Adolescence*, so terribly important. In this beautifully written, carefully crafted, and thoughtfully argued book, Halpern shows us the pedagogical importance of "apprenticeship." That is, he argues for the importance of relationships forged in the "doing" of craft between novice and expert. Such pedagogical relationships span a range of domains. Halpern highlights the ways such apprenticeships work in arts (e.g., in video-making), in the sciences (e.g., in chemical engineering), as well as so-called "handwork" fields (e.g., in boat building). In each case, we see students working in particular and unique ways with adults around meaningful activities and projects.

Pedagogy, here, cannot be disentangled from its contexts of production. It cannot be reduced to a set of rules with a priori promises and pre-defined conclusions. Rather, the curriculum itself emerges from its very activities; in particular, purposeful, task-directed, work that ends in a tangible product—a painting, chemical solution, or boat. Assessment here is organic and emergent, as the teacher offers particular, nuanced, and context-bound responses to this ongoing work. *The Means To Grow Up* is filled with such examples, offering a different vision of what education can and should be about.

The implications of this move are profound. In particular, they offer a challenge to the long-standing notion that ones education should smoothly and ideally follow a K-16 track. In unearthing the complexities of apprenticeship learning, Halpern challenges the degradation of so-called "vocational" education, showing that—and more importantly, showing *how*—learning a craft with an experienced adult can be a profoundly challenging and complex endeavor. In this respect, he shares much with Mike Rose and his recent *The Mind at Work*—a book that looked to highlight the cognitive complexities embedded in a range of professions, from those of plumbers, to waiters, to hairdressers, and beyond. Like Rose, Halpern looks to redeem such work from those who would marginalize it. Moreover, Halpern shows us in stunning and expansive detail the ways such learning happens across multiple sites and settings—the complex trials and errors, successes and failures, triumphs, and frustrations which happen in these particular kinds of relationships.

In so doing, Halpern reinforces a critical vision of youth development—one at terrible risk today. As noted above, the notion of doing work well, often for its own sake, has been very much a part of our common human inheritance. Drawing on the writing of Erik Erikson, Halpern embeds such work in notions of youth development. In particular, he highlights the pedagogical importance of working though a project over time, refining ones craft over multiple such endeavors, apprenticing to someone more skilled. Such notions of youth development are at radical risk today—challenged by the imperatives of an education system increasingly geared towards the acquisition of de-contextualized "skills." In *The Means to Grow Up*, Halpern asks what such notions of education mean for young people today—young people both entering a competitive workforce as well as forging validated notions of self over time. Indeed, Halpern reinforces the mutually constituting nature of these issues. I, for one, can't imagine a more pressing question for our times.

Greg Dimitriadis
University at Buffalo, SUNY

References

Greenspan, A. (2007). *The age of turbulence: Adventures in a new world.* New York: Penguin Press.
Rose, M. (2004). *The mind at work: Valuing the intelligence of the American worker.* New York: Viking.
Sennett, R. (2008). *The craftsman.* New Haven, CT: Yale University Press.

Preface

What does it mean when large numbers of urban adolescents report that school is boring, their lives are boring, there is not enough to do, no choices that make sense? A young woman could be speaking for hundreds of thousands of peers when she tells Chavez and Soep (2005, p. 411): "At school, my body was in the classroom but my mind and heart were nowhere to be found. Every day I would come home from school and head straight for the television with a box of cereal. . . . At the age of sixteen I was just waiting around until I became rich and famous or fell off the face of the earth."

It is not as straightforward as it might seem to interpret these youthful feelings. Some youth may feel their lives to be restricted—by family, school, peers, or neighborhood. Some may be uncertain of what they could and should be doing, or where they might find good experiences. Some youth may feel that they are indeed simply waiting—for something to happen, for life to begin, or for the world to come to them. For some, expressions of boredom may mask doubts about whether they are equipped to tackle current tasks and begin moving toward adulthood. For some youth, such expressions may be protective, where past efforts to commit or take a risk have yielded little positive response.

Implicit in all these interpretations is the sense that young people cannot create vital experience and a sense of meaning on their own, nor find the means to move ahead; that they need adult support and involvement to do so. Yet I would argue that it is not adult support per se. I have been doing research on urban youth programs—settings with caring and attentive adults—for many years and have often heard (and observed) much the same expression of boredom from participating youth (Halpern, 1992; Halpern, Barker, & Mollard, 2002). I have come to believe that, though most youth programs are psychologically safe and mildly engaging settings for participants, in important ways they are not providing the experiences youth need to acquire or maintain a sense of vitality, real accomplishment, and movement.

There is, though, a distinctive sub-set of youth programs, and a small but growing group of high school programs, that are providing such experiences. These distinctive programs provide and/or link youth to settings in which they learn and practice the skills of a specific discipline, through increasingly responsible participation in the tasks characteristic of that discipline, under the guidance of a skilled professional (Rogoff, 1990). Some, though by no means all, describe what they provide as apprenticeship, and I have come to believe that the term, even separated from its historic connotations, is an apt one for capturing what is essential about them.

My specific interest in apprenticeship began in the spring of 2003, when I began a 30-month qualitative study of an exemplary initiative in Chicago, called After School Matters (ASM). ASM sponsors after-school apprenticeships for groups of inner-city high school students in such areas as literary, visual and performing arts, design (graphic, textile, etc.), journalism, video and computer technology, and culinary arts. Instructors are mostly young professionals whose identities are strongly rooted in their discipline. Participants spend the first months learning the basics of a discipline, through guided work on discrete products or performances characteristic of that discipline. Eventually they are required to integrate and demonstrate what they have learned in a culminating product or performance.

Though ASM apprenticeships are of relatively short duration (youth partici-pate three afternoons a week over the course of a school year or two), they appear to have a variety of interesting effects on the skills, dispositions, and sense of self of participating youth. Participants, for instance, begin to think more flexibly and approach tasks more carefully. They learn that problems or difficulties in a project are not a sign to quit but something to work through. They come to take more responsibility for themselves—their words, bodies, ideas, and reactions. Their public behavior becomes more mature, more appropriately assertive. They become more patient with themselves and others. They come gradually to give more of themselves to the projects they were working on. They begin to think more about what they need to do—in the present and the future, in this setting and sometimes in others.

These effects are clearly tied to the attributes of the After School Matters settings. The work is specific, visceral, disciplined, and sometimes messy. Youth learn what they need to know and to do as they go along, trying and correcting, observing and imitating others, seeking out resources. Instructors fill in, cor-rect and re-direct when it is important to do so. They treat participating youth maturely but matter-of-factly. They expect youth to be serious, to take the work seriously, and to share responsibility for successes and failures. Exposure to instructors gives participating youth a sense of different ways of being an adult, what it means to be passionate about a discipline and what it takes to become good at something.

Instructors and participants face difficulties in this work. Most youth bring years of passive learning to a context that demands the opposite, and often a diminished sense of themselves as capable learners. More vulnerable youth experience difficulties or setbacks as an attack on their selves, rather than a part of the work. Some cannot or will not permit themselves the luxury of becoming interested and excited about the work, of expressing their ideas and experiences through it. But though instructors are frustrated at times, and youth struggle in these settings, it is evident that these apprenticeships are working in important developmental terrain. Youth know that they are trafficking in adult feelings and responsibilities. The ASM apprenticeships do not unbind participating youths from often difficult lives. But they do get incorporated into those lives, becoming a new resource to draw on.

Given my experience with ASM, I began looking around for other examples of apprenticeship-like youth programming, not sure what I was likely to find, at the same time trying to place this type of experience in a larger context. I found the concept of apprenticeship woven into the literature in a number of fields— the learning sciences, cognitive science, cultural psychology, and anthropology, as well as vocational education. There seemed widespread agreement that apprenticeship is deeply rooted in human cultures and that it is a powerful learning and socialization model; as Collins, Brown, and Newman (1989, p. 491) put it, "the way we learn most naturally."

Out in the real world of social institutions, I noted a paradoxical, in some respects confusing, situation. Thoughtful observers argue that youth have become too isolated from the adult world, both from maturity-fostering experience and from realistic models of "grown ups whom [they] can imagine becoming and would like to become" (Meier, 2006, p. 74). The large majority of urban youth are not headed to college, especially not immediately. (Indeed in some major cities half of youth are not even graduating from high school.) The high school curriculum experienced by many youth is shallow and aimless. Yet there is an enduring cultural belief that preparing for college is the central, if not the sole, task of the high school years and that the problem with high schools is that they are not effective enough in helping with this task. The percentage of parents focused exclusively on four-year colleges for their children has actually increased over the past two decades.

Parents may not know better or may be reluctant to circumscribe their children's futures. But school staff should know. Rosenbaum (2002, p. 4) cites a survey finding that 57% of seniors in the bottom half of their class "reported that counselors urged them to attend college," even though their odds of acquiring a four year degree were slim. (At best about half of those who enroll in four year colleges graduate within six years—some believe the percentage to be much lower, closer to a third; Gray, 1997). As Rosenbaum puts it, many youth who think they are college bound are actually work bound, but since no one advises them as such they do not prepare for this reality.

Youth themselves plan, often vaguely and ambivalently, for college, not seeing any alternatives and having little specific idea of what they might actually strive to become. Most youth accurately believe themselves to be in a kind of holding pattern, except one with no airport at which to land. They know little, for instance, about the wide range of skilled and semi-skilled technical work—most of which requires a two year technical degree—that constitutes the largest part of the work force, nor about how one might convert creative interests and talents into a sustainable career. Employers meanwhile complain that, whatever their educational experiences, young people arrive at the work place unprepared for the cognitive, psychological, social and/or technical demands of work.

I will not be arguing in this book that American society should abandon the idea that any and all youth should strive for higher education. Even if imperfectly, that idea reinforces the ideal of equal educational opportunity. I will be arguing, nonetheless, that youth apprenticeship experiences set the foundation for and in some instances actually create more nuanced and grounded post-secondary pathways for many youth, across social class. What might at first glance seem a strategy for reproducing inequality—an academic pathway and extended adolescence for the most advantaged youth, a more vocational pathway and a push into the adult world for the less advantaged—is one means for addressing it.

It is argued, with some reason, that our educational institutions lack "reliable mechanisms that can make the future of children transparent enough for us to predict their ultimate post-school destinations" (Lewis, 2007, p. 342). High school guidance counselors with hundreds of young people in their caseloads know few of them well enough to advise on such life-defining decisions. Yet apprenticeship experiences are full of knowledge about participating youth, and the exact kind that is helpful in thinking about next steps.

But my arguments here are not just about preparation, nor even pathways. I am arguing for reintroducing a particular kind of developmental experience, one that might not seem intuitive to the times—and especially to an anyone-can-do-anything culture—but may be especially valuable just for that reason. Apprenticeship provides experience that young people can acquire in no other way. The experience is interesting because the disciplines scattered throughout the adult world and the work they embody are often interesting. There is a texture to this part of the culture, a kind of uneven terrain, that demands a lot more of the self than is demanded or allowed in almost any other setting of young people's lives.

Acknowledgments

I would like to thank the many individuals from apprenticeship programs and initiatives around the United States who shared their experience and insight with me. They made this book possible and are identified by name in the Appendix. I would also like to thank a number of foundations who provided partial support for my research and writing: The W. T. Grant Foundation, the Ewing Marion Kauffman Foundation, The Garfield Foundation, the Evelyn and Walter Haas, Jr. Fund, and the Wallace Foundation. My thanks to Adam Green and Rocking the Boat for permission to use the cover photo.

Introduction

For the young person with an interest in wood working, the shop must feel like a powerful invitation to competence, a pathway to achievement.
Rose (2004, p. 80)

Actually, I think kids come here and sometimes don't know who they are, but they discover it through the program. That's what happened to me.
William, a participant in The Food Project
(cited in Gale, 2006, p. 123)

In a small town in Oregon, Anna G., age 17, spends 10 hours a day over the course of a summer working with an archeologist at the U.S. Interior Department, Bureau of Land Management, conducting cultural resource surveys designed to identify and map sites needing protection from development. She analyzes topographic maps, completes archeological site inventories, prepares site sketches, photographs sites and artifacts, using GPS instruments and software for site mapping. In a small city in Wisconsin Andre M., age 17, leaves school at 1:30 p.m. each day and goes to work at a printing/graphics shop. There he works in digital and offset printing, helps with pre-press, press and binding operations, learns about paper and inks, and begins to master industry software. Andre takes complementary course work at the local technical community college, for which he receives both high school and college credit. At the end of two years, Andre will receive a Certificate of Occupational Proficiency from the state.

Anna and Andre are part of an interesting, but largely unexamined and unanalyzed phenomenon: the renewal and re-conceptualization of youth apprenticeship. In studios, workshops, theaters, laboratories, hospitals and clinics, government offices, farms, kitchens, bakeries, and boat yards, high school-age youth are apprenticing themselves to photographers, choreographers, graphic designers, small business owners, set designers, software engineers, civil engineers, chefs, master bakers, nurse practitioners, ecologists, veterinarians, chemists, master boat builders, horticulturists, teachers, and others. They are spending hundreds of hours in the adult world, learning and taking responsibility for adult tasks.

This book examines the renewal of youth apprenticeship in the United States. Drawing on my own and others' research I explore the reasons that apprenticeship seems to leave an "indelible impression" on so many who experience it (Sigaut, 1993, p. 105). I argue that apprenticeship creates a fruitful learning context, addresses adolescent developmental needs, and begins to fill a cultural void for this age period. The learning framework embodied in apprenticeship is both old, deeply rooted in cultures throughout history, and brand new, woven through the most current findings in cognitive science. That framework addresses through example some of the central problems with the central institution in young people's lives, that is, with school: its lack of meaning if not purpose, a dysfunctional motivational structure, fragmentation of knowledge and experience, and the separation of knowing from doing.

From a developmental perspective, apprenticeship experiences provide opportunity for the real accomplishment that Erikson (1968) noted as so important during adolescence. They create that transitional space where young people can be both playing and working, pretending to be and practicing at being what they might become and yet genuinely participating in a particular adult community (Winnicott, 1971; Csikszentmihalyi & Schneider, 2000). In a paradoxical way, the very structure of apprenticeship provides a foundation for self-discovery and its very specificity creates the conditions for broad growth in adolescents. Submitting (or at least assenting) to a tradition, its norms, rules, practices, and understandings, may not be easy for adolescents but, strangely enough, it suits them.

Why Call It Apprenticeship?

As I conducted background research for this book, I talked with individuals who wondered why I was using the term "apprenticeship." Although the experiences I will be describing are apprenticeship-like in spirit and dynamics, they are not formal Department of Labor-registered apprenticeships, nor could they be. Such apprenticeships require four thousand or more hours of work, take from three to six years to complete and serve adults almost exclusively. The experiences discussed here are an adaptation of what has become an adult institution to the middle years of adolescence, an unquestionably awkward adaptation as well as a compelling one.

I decided to use the term apprenticeship in part because I found it more accurate and more resonant than possible alternatives such as internship, experiential learning, and work-based learning. Experiential learning is too broad a term and tends not to reflect the centrality of entering into a specific discipline, craft or trade; in other words the focus on working and learning to get good at something specific. Internship and work-based learning are closer to what I will be discussing, but the former especially tends to offer more limited experiences, tends not to deliberately envision a gradually deepening immersion in a field, or to foster an identity tied to that field (even if a temporary one); nor does internship typically give youth any significant degree of responsibility. Work-based learning is the closest, but for me is a slightly confusing term because it has not always been clear what young people should be learning in a workplace (e.g., academic subjects or something else).

In an affirmative sense, I chose the term apprenticeship because it captures qualities in the experiences that explain why it works so well. These experiences provide youth a sense of joining and contributing to a tradition, as embodied in a specific discipline or civic sphere. Apprentices are, typically, working and learning in the setting in which a craft, trade or discipline is practiced. The knowledge and skills young people need to acquire are being used throughout the setting. Both adult and youth are active. They share responsibility for the work to be done and the products to be created, although each has a different role. The adult mentor is responsible for sharing his or her disciplinary knowledge and skills with youth. Youth are responsible for working hard to begin to become proficient at something specific, and for contributing to the community which they have joined. Young people's work, though developmental, is judged by the established standards of a discipline.

In a less direct, but no less important sense, participating youth are "apprenticing" themselves to the norms, rules, demands, and opportunities of the adult world. One program director describes the youth she works with as "apprentices to the [discipline] of rigorous thinking, problem-solving and collaborating" (Salvante-McCann, personal communication, February 5, 2007).[1] Young people are learning what it takes—and how hard it is—to get good at something. They are beginning to learn how adults construct careers. They are assuming specific identities, even if temporarily. They are having adult-like conversations, feelings, and relationships. Their responsibilities, and the experiences as a whole, are real enough. I am, finally, making a particular argument: that the less explicitly (or narrowly) vocational framework described in these pages reflects what apprenticeship needs to be or can be in the current context of American adolescence. Both providing apprenticeship-like experiences and framing such experiences as apprenticeship are valuable to urban youth. These experiences provide crucial ingredients for just what is missing for many youth at this time in history.

Organization and Overview of the Book

I begin my exploration of youth apprenticeship with two somewhat theoretical chapters. Chapter 1 reviews the literature on learning (and instruction) and illustrates how findings on the qualities of good learning environments are reflected in the attributes of apprenticeship. Chapter 2 discusses the developmental tasks and support needs of adolescents, focusing especially on those growing up under difficult circumstances, and illustrates the ways in which apprenticeship responds to those tasks and support needs. In both chapters I draw on my own and others' programmatic research to illustrate how the attributes of apprenticeship fit elements of theory. These two chapters nonetheless hold aside time and place to a large extent.

Chapters 3 and 4 describe current institutional contexts for and examples of youth apprenticeship—how and where it is actually working in practice. Chapter 3 examines the role of apprenticeship in current efforts to re-think and re-design high school. I describe the historical decline in apprenticeship and gradual growth in high school as a universal experience; discuss why and how high school has proved a poor fit for some youth; and discuss and illustrate through case examples the incorporation of apprenticeship experiences into the programs of an as yet still small number of high schools, in an effort to make learning experiences more relevant and engaging.

One of the most striking features of the renewed youth apprenticeship is its broad base and impetus in a range of arts, cultural, issue-oriented and other civic institutions, as well as in small businesses and public sector institutions and agencies. Chapter 4 describes and illustrates through case studies the breadth of sponsorship, purposes, and types of experience associated with this other strand of youth apprenticeship in the United States, and discusses some elements that appear to unite this diverse movement. In the last section of the book, chapters 5 through 7, I step back and reflect on youth apprenticeship: what the experience is like for youth, challenges and pleasures, how and where youth grow, questions and limitations.

Although the book is linear in design, with each section building on the prior one, in a figurative sense everything radiates out from the case studies. And though they are illustrative of general points made throughout the book, each is also its own story. Four case studies are tied in some way to high school education and/or high school reform: Berkeley Biotechnology Education, Inc. (BBEI), the Wisconsin Youth Apprenticeship Program (YAP), Roundabout Theater's education programs, and the Big Picture Schools. The remaining seven reflect the breadth of disciplinary work and fields. Three are in the arts: Artists for Humanity, Marwen Arts/Art at Work, and the Education Video Center. One is in the sciences: Apprenticeships in Science and Engineering (BBEI should be considered a science apprenticeship in important respects as well). Three more are in a heterogeneous category that I call handwork (although it oversimplifies what each is about): Rocking the Boat, The Food Project, and Careers Through Culinary Arts. In framing the case studies, I also draw on a number of other initiatives, including St. Louis Art Works and Riverz Edge Arts (Woonsocket, Rhode Island); the nationwide Research and Engineering Apprenticeship Program, the nationwide Science and Engineering Apprenticeship Program, and Project SEED (sponsored by the American Chemical Society and available nationwide); and a second boat-building program, Urban Boat Builders (Minneapolis-St. Paul).

With one exception, the case studies were developed through interviews, some 56 in all, with initiative directors, staff, and a handful with youth, supplemented by reports, descriptions, analyses, manuals, journals, dissertations, and other materials. A chronology of those interviewed is provided in Appendix A. The exception is BBEI, for which I depended heavily on the doctoral dissertation of the former initiative director, Amy Ryken. The other principle source of data for the book was a three-year study of Chicago's After School Matters (ASM), a citywide youth apprenticeship initiative, based at the time in some 35 high schools (Halpern, 2005, 2006a, 2006b). In this work two research assistants and I followed 24 separate apprenticeships, serving 480 youth in all, over the course of a school year each. That study included 300 hours of observation, 38 interviews with adult mentors, and 48 interviews with apprentices. All unattributed citations and descriptions in the book derive from the reports and field notes of that study.

A Diverse Enterprise with Some Common Dynamics

In some respects apprenticeship is as diverse as the disciplines it embodies. These include the visual and performing arts (and media arts), basic and applied sciences, including engineering, ecology and public health, graphic design, architecture, culinary arts, farming, carpentry, and selected industrial trades. Apprenticeships can be found in such deeply rooted traditions as cabinet making and boat building, and such new ones as biotechnology, social documentary, habitat restoration, and computer-based media production. Some are more conceptual, others more physical, some more technical or instrumental, others more aesthetic and expressive.

Sponsors of the new youth apprenticeships are also diverse. They include youth serving agencies, arts, cultural and civic organizations, high schools, universities, and businesses. Sponsors may provide an apprenticeship experience themselves, that is they may be or create a work place of sorts, or they may place youth with other public or private organizations. A few sponsors embrace apprenticeship as a "foundational philosophy," as Margaret Salvante-McCann of the Roundabout Theater Company puts it (p.c., February 5, 2007). Others view and use the term in a more practical frame. Individual mentors may be paid to do this work or volunteer. Youth likewise are often paid for their work, occasionally not. An individual youth may work with one adult or be part of the staff of a department. A youth may be in a studio surrounded by other apprentices working on similar projects. Some apprenticeships are built around teams, crews or ensembles. In some settings apprentices learn primarily from adult teachers; in others they may learn a good deal from more experienced peers.

Apprenticeships serve a wide range of youth with respect to background, educational status, and life experience. Most try to serve the diverse population of low- to moderate-income urban youth, and the majority of young people reached and served appear to belong to the large, neglected middle part of this population. Though many are weakly attached to school, they are nonetheless hanging on, not yet disconnected. Some youth have dabbled in street culture, but few are actively involved with gangs. Most either have vague or unrealistic plans for the future, often aiming too high given their educational accomplishments, and occasionally aiming too low.

Sponsors' primary interests and goals vary. In the majority of apprenticeships described in these pages, the historic framework—the learner's labor in exchange for an opportunity to learn a trade—is not central, though it is often one element. Many sponsors do wish, nonetheless, to give participants a novice's experience in a specific field; the first steps toward becoming a skilled scientist, ceramicist, actor, or community developer. Some wish to help young people find their passion or find themselves in the world, through the vehicle of a particular discipline. Some use the discipline of a specific field or practice, for example, farming or theater or boat building, as a vehicle for strengthening particular aspects of young people's selves: their selves as learners, their sense of efficacy or of voice, capacity for hard work, their sense of empathy or commitment to social justice, or their basic sense of trust. Relatedly, some are motivated by an interest in giving young people the tools to explore what they believe in, or to counter their pessimism about making a difference.

A handful of sponsors view apprenticeship as a vehicle for reforming the curriculum and pedagogy of high school in the United States. Sponsors have used apprenticeship as both a model for what more engaging, appropriate learning experiences should look like and as an actual element in re-designed high school experience. Apprenticeship has been an important component of the so called new vocationalism, a re-thinking of vocational-technical education to include a broader range of youth, experiences that cross-cut high school, college and work, and a broader, more flexible definition of vocation itself.

Attributes In Common

Though taking place in varied settings and involving different disciplines, youth apprenticeships provide similar learning and working experiences in important respects. Projects have real meaning and use—making a documentary about housing conditions, designing a logo for a business, surveying a fish habitat, growing organic produce to benefit low-income families. Greg Gale, associate director of The Food Project, notes that "If we do not farm well and productively, people go hungry, land lies wasted, and families do not have access to the life-giving produce we grow" (Gale, 2006, p. 11). Learning and work are structured to lead young people through complete production cycles. Constraints are characteristic of those found in professional work in the fields involved. Practices are sometimes "very precise, demanding and non-negotiable" (Hay & Barab, 2001, p. 295). Yet learning and producing processes have elements of uncertainty. Answers and solutions are not known ahead of time; unexpected difficulties are commonplace.

Apprentices learn through observation, imitation, trial and error, and reiteration; in other words through force of experience. The founder of Rocking the Boat, which includes boat building as one core activity (the others are maritime and conservation skills), notes that the instructors put tools in apprentices' hands right away, set them to work, and begin teaching and demonstrating as the apprentices work. Reflecting on his own experience as a novice boat builder, he says that "It's really abstract, and I wasn't able to understand it until I started doing it" (Green, p.c., June 22, 2006). Though professionalism and care are expected, perfection is not. Learning and work are defined by approximation; one gets to skill, to the final product or performance, in stages.

Teaching in apprenticeship is distinct in both aim and approach. The adult mentor does not drive the learning experience; is not at the center of it. (As Larson

& Hansen, 2005, put it, the mentor shares expertise but leaves agency with youth.) Yet s/he is critical to the experience and is involved in it in almost every way. Mentors sequence and control task demands, so apprentices can work on gradually more challenging products or exercises. They direct apprentices' attention, demonstrate and sometimes collaborate. A filmmaking instructor stops by a cluster of apprentices who are editing a video, sees that they are not aware of a particular capability of the editing software, brings it up on the screen and demonstrates its use. A mural instructor notes that "I would sit with them [the apprentices] and paint around the area [on the panel] where they were painting."

Mentors act as the embodiment of a discipline, and also as "exemplars," modeling skilled practice and the general behavior of one with that particular identity (i.e., scientist, dancer, filmmaker, chef, cabinet maker).[2] Apprentices may get to watch their mentors at work, addressing a problem, running a meeting, or simply interacting with others. The apprentice is motivated toward mastery in part by a desire to be like, even to "become", his or her teacher (Litowitz, 1993). The director of education for the Roundabout Theater notes that it is from their teaching artist mentors that young actors, directors, and set designers "take in the responsibility of being an artist at work" (Salvante-McCann, p.c., February 5, 2007).

The Experience of Apprenticeship and Its Effects: A Growing Experience

Apprenticeships are genuinely unprecedented developmental contexts for youth—about learning but not at all like school; serious and demanding, but accepting of struggles and mistakes; with both the substantive work and young people's own developing selves at the center of things. It takes time for youth to figure out what these experiences are about, how they work, what learning resources they provide and what the expectations will be. It takes time to accept being taken seriously but matter-of-factly. Apprentices experience a range of emotions and psychological states that are uncommon in other settings of their lives.

The no-excuse, matter-of-fact demandingness of apprenticeship can be jarring, especially for youth who have become accustomed to a passive role in school, minimal expectations from adults, and mixed or negative messages about their capabilities. It takes time for some youth to learn to trust the apprenticeship framework, including the very different relationship with adults. It is a challenge for some to be active, to work hard, to learn to work with care, to work deeply and to persist, whether to accept the idea that the quality of produce grown is critical, or to not stop working on a design with the first idea that comes to mind.

Some youth struggle with the realization that there is little room in apprenticeship for either bravado or self-abnegation; these are brushed aside by the demands and standards of the work. Some start out with what Larson (2004, p. 12) describes as "a naive sense of self-sufficiency," coupled with doubt about whether they can learn anything useful from others. Some lack patience, willingness, or psychological strength to start at the beginning in a field—to sweep up sawdust, bus tables, set up equipment in a lab—whether reacting to their parents' difficult lives or having internalized the American belief that everything should be easy. Some, though not many, are unwilling to subscribe to a tradition that they do not fully understand.

With time young people's sense of difficulty, disorganization, or just tentativeness is increasingly balanced by more complex feelings. What begin as external demands become internalized and no longer feel like impositions. Young people adjust to what they once thought they could not. Day in, day out, they get better at the work and begin to believe they can do it. They come to trust process more and learn to enjoy the routines of the setting. They become more comfortable with the distinctive feelings they experience in apprenticeship. As one ASM apprentice notes, "it sounds stupid, but being in the middle of a project, not knowing if, let alone how, it will turn out can be a good feeling." Youth report feeling that they are using their whole self, head, hand and heart.

While the demands of apprenticeship push grandiosity, posing, and fronting aside—there is little room for them—young people note being glad to be able to be themselves, to not have to pose or front or try to fit in. An apprentice in Chicago's Marwen Arts notes that "nobody is telling you to be any way. You do what you need to do" (Yenawine, 2004, p. 6). Not least, youth come to appreciate the new type of adult and new type of adult relationship they discover in apprenticeship. They like being around adults who enjoy their work, are passionate about a particular field and draw their identity from it.

What Apprentices Learn, How, and Why They Grow

As suggested above, youth bring varying personal resources to and are unquestionably affected differently by these experiences. It is neither easy to account for growth or for lack of it. Some youth seem more frozen and closed developmentally, some more fluid and open. Some find themselves suited to a particular discipline, others not so much. Some youth are more active in seeking meaning in the apprenticeship situation, others much less so. Timing is important. Each year in high school brings its own preoccupations; these shape how youth use after-school and summer activities, including how deeply they are prepared to commit to a project. Learning and growth are, also, incremental. Some disciplines have steep initial learning curves; others offer easy entry, with later levels of mastery requiring subtle skills that take years to master. Some abilities, especially those involving aesthetic judgment, grow slowly, and require familiarity with the larger body of work in a particular discipline.

Given such caveats, apprenticeship experiences appear to operate across a broad swath of developmental terrain. At a basic level, most youth find their way into the discipline at hand procedures, techniques, tools of the trade, vocabulary, basic concepts, behavioral norms, physical skills, view, and understanding of a field of practice itself. In many fields apprentices learn to make concrete representations of tentative thoughts and plans using customary techniques—sketch-books, lab journals, pencil drawings on a piece of wood, small-scale models, dark-room prints, or story-boards. With experience, apprentices become more efficient; the same task in the kitchen or laboratory or dark room takes half the time it did two months ago.

Apprentices exert gradually greater control over their own efforts, a kind of discipline-specific self-regulation; they are better able to steer those efforts. Apprentices working with a professional muralist on one project learn to work large, to keep the elements connected (Larson & Walker, 2006). A filmmaking apprentice uses a film-editing program in an innovative way. With time, the apprentice begins to learn how to look at things in a particular field to understand them, to recognize patterns, to know what is important, to sense when a work at hand feels right (Polanyi, 1966). For instance, the wood working apprentice develops what Rose (2004, p. 92) calls "cabinet sense."

To differing degrees, young people acquire skills in approaching and engaging tasks as such. They learn, for instance, to prepare before plunging in. They learn to get started or move ahead without waiting for instructions or guidance. Apprentices learn to attend to detail, to edit, and to revise. They learn to seek out needed information and to draw on others' experience. Apprentices grow more adept at working with a measure of uncertainty. They do not freeze when faced with problems and obstacles, and become able to view it as just part of the work.

Apprentices gain knowledge and skill in design and production processes. They learn to compress ideas to fit constraints—of time, materials, human resources, their own experience, or the marketplace. Youth working on commissioned art learn both "to figure out what the customer wants and how long it will take to produce it" (Motta, p.c., June 19, 2006). Apprentices learn to cope with contingencies, from wood splitting to a cast member's illness to bad weather at a critical point in the growing season. They learn about the creative process, for instance, that running into a dead end is part of the process. An ASM choreography apprentice notes learning that she will come up with the next sequence: "one idea leads to another."

Apprenticeship provides many kinds of meta-lessons, which flow directly from experience. In learning from their mistakes and successfully working through difficult problems, apprentices are also learning that they can do so. Boat-building apprentices learn to work with as well as work through mistakes—compensate for them, change and re-balance the design. In other words, they learn that mistakes go along with the imperfections of craftsmanship. In learning how to work as part of a team, apprentices learn what it means to be responsible to a team or ensemble, and what it means to make a contribution to a larger effort. A sound design apprentice working in theater notes that "I liked working behind the scenes where you can watch the show and know that you've contributed something. You know that without the sound you've designed, it wouldn't' be perfect, it wouldn't seem right" (Roundabout Theater Education Report, 2006, p. 12).

Some effects of apprenticeship experience can be described as self effects:

how young people view and understand themselves, including what they think they are capable of, what they enjoy and are good at; and how they approach the opportunities and difficulties in different settings, including willingness to take risks, work hard and be active. Apprenticeship may help ground adolescents' natural grandiosity, contribute to more accurate self-appraisal. For some youth, an apprenticeship experience seems to have a self organizing effect, pulling them together, waking them up, mobilizing their energies, in some instances providing a sense of direction. As an ASM photography apprentice notes, "it [being in the apprenticeship] kind of opens up your mind, and [makes you] think about what you are doing and where you want to go."

Apprenticeship and Policy Concerns

The richness, complexity, and incremental quality of apprenticeship experiences are difficult to convert to terms that fit policy discourse. Some of the effects discussed in the book nonetheless have obvious relevance to school achievement or work readiness. Of the sense of discipline acquired in his apprenticeship experience, one youth notes, for instance, "you can apply that to school and really bury down and get homework done when you need to get it done or study when you have to get that done" (Lehmann, 2005, p. 118). More globally, apprenticeship experiences lead some youth to re-evaluate how they are approaching high school. They may come to think more closely about what it might take to pursue particular disciplines or careers, and how much time and effort it takes to get good at a chosen endeavor. Richard Grausman, founder of the Careers through Culinary Arts program, notes that the more a young person learns in the kitchen the more he or she can understand a chef's expertise, what has gone into it (Grausman, p.c., December 21, 2006). In some instances, apprenticeship experiences open up paths to college. Youth make new adult relationships, enter into new networks, and are connected to new institutions, all of which may be located outside of their existing social world. The acquisition of this new capital comes at a crucial time, as apprentices are beginning the transition from high school to either further schooling or work or both.

Mechanisms Through which Apprenticeship Works

The mechanisms through which young people grow in apprenticeship are both straightforward and circular—in the best sense of the word. The growth one observes in youth derives from the demands of the work itself. Skill- and knowledge- building are almost incidental, bound up with the work. Growth in task related skills derives logically from the fact that tasks in apprenticeship are complex, contingent, and open-ended. Skills develop in apprenticeship because they have to—one is faced with a new or persistent problem, constraints of time, resources or materials (Rose, 2004).

The intricacy or complexity of tasks in apprenticeship, and the genuine need for resulting products, demand care and thus teach the apprentice to work more carefully.

The iterative, cyclical, and extensive nature of apprenticeship are reinforcing in many senses. Young people have the opportunity to—and they have to—work through a problem or practice a skill until they get it right. Working through complete production cycles gives the experience coherence and deepens its meaning. The pressure of real world deadlines focuses the attention and effort of both apprentice and mentor.

Young people's growth is reflected (and reflected back) in the growth of products and performances. It is motivating to be able to see the relationship between one's efforts and the results of those efforts. A boat-building instructor notes that the work is so compelling in part because "it is the combining of many different tasks to have this attractive, functional thing at the end" (Wenger, p.c., June 27, 2007). The sense of realness and genuineness of social contributions made also reinforce the experience: Rocking the Boat apprentices working (with other organizations) to restore New York's Bronx River saw the return of a beaver to the river for the first time in 200 years.

Growth through apprenticeship is spurred in part by the props of a particular discipline—its language, tools, customs, and characteristic setting. These structure growth, enable it, and provide meaning, connecting the apprentice to a tradition. The apprentice is surrounded by others doing the same or similar work. In a science lab or art studio or design firm, the apprentice can see and therefore learn from what others are trying to accomplish. Young people learn that the routines in which they are participating are the same as those of the most skilled adults in that discipline, and in some cases date back scores or even hundreds of years. The props of a discipline communicate the seriousness of what the apprentice is doing and affirm his or her right to be doing it. Working inside of a discipline both grounds and structures young people's aspirations. A painting apprentice may learn not just how to paint but who painters are, where and how they work, how art is bought and sold, how people train to become artists.

The adult mentor plays a number of important roles in contributing to apprenticeship effects. The mentor holds the discipline for the apprentice, controlling the challenges and keeping the work on the constructive side of difficulty. Apprentices acquire new cognitive, affective, and social dispositions in part through observing and imitating adult mentors. Identification with the mentor provides both a spur for mastery and a model for identity work. Who they are, what they've done, the path they've taken, and even how they behave is instructive, interesting, and often novel to apprentices. Coy (1989, p. 111) describes this as "the essence of what it is like 'to eat someone else's rice."

The Limits and Limitations of Apprenticeship

Apprenticeship has some inherent limitations and some that are a function of the broader sociocultural context in which it operates. The former are directly related to, and seemingly a consequence of, its strengths. These include its emphasis on learning through experience and de-emphasis on formal, didactic teaching, it's specificity, depth and its embeddedness. Learning through experience is neither easy nor obvious, especially early on. Novices may have difficulty observing their own behavior in a way useful to helping them re-organize it. They may not know what is important about what they are observing as they watch others at work. They often do not know how to use knowledge or techniques just taught or learned to solve problems. They may not know how to use practice to improve. A young person may not be in a setting long enough to move from the periphery to the middle of things, to move through the bottlenecks to mastery (Perkins & Salomon, 1989), or generally to move into a position to get a lot out of the work.

Pedagogy in apprenticeship is difficult to define and pinpoint, let alone codify. Mentors may not know how to access or articulate what lies behind their own expertise nor the tacit knowledge accumulated over time in their field. They may not realize how much they know. Teaching, like learning, is embedded in production processes and tied to immediate tasks and problems. It is difficult for mentors to find a balanced role, and often not clear what should be formally taught as opposed to learned through experience.

The specificity of apprenticeship is one of its most confounding qualities. Working deeply in a discipline is, inevitably, limiting as well as powerful. Situated knowledge and skill are, seemingly, most powerful in specific situations. Thought patterns, reasoning strategies, and heuristics learned in apprenticeship appear to be discipline-specific (in part because one is drawing on experience in that particular discipline to work one's way through problems). These qualities raise the question of how useful discipline-specific knowledge and thought patterns are in a world in which the role of disciplines as organizers of knowledge and experience are (perhaps) becoming less central.

Although it should already be clear that apprenticeship has much general value as a learning and developmental experience, is it worth the effort? The evidence accumulated in this book suggests that very specific learning and work experiences leave a deep imprint on still malleable selves. Young people carry the dispositions acquired in apprenticeship—to be active, resourceful, attentive to the context, sense of responsibility, capacity to think and work problems through, knowledge of one's strengths and limitations, and so forth—to other settings in their lives. Larson and Hansen (2005, p. 20) describe these as "gateway capabilities"; that is, as laying a foundation for those that will be needed later. The constraints to transfer seem rooted less in the specificity of what is acquired than in lack of recognition and support for growth from adults in other settings.

A Challenging Context

The societal context in which youth apprenticeship operates raises a very different set of questions. For instance, work has been noted to have become more fluid—a series of personal encounters, more abstract—involving manipulation of symbols and information, more focused on process and less reliant on specific (or fixed) content. Breadth of skills seems as or more important than depth. Substantive, discipline-specific knowledge and skills are not becoming entirely irrelevant. They are important to a number of growing occupations, including biotechnology/bioscience, nursing and new clinical and lab based technical occupations in the health care field (e.g., physical, occupational, respiratory, and other therapists, EKG and surgical technicians, etc.).

Paralleling the changing narrative of work is a narrative describing a less well-defined and less straightforward transition from high school to work or post-secondary education for the majority of American youth. Both the transition itself and the labor market as a whole lack transparency, and it is difficult for youth to make sense of the context in which they have to make decisions (Lehmann, 2005). I will argue, nonetheless, that apprenticeship experiences offer potential to help with this difficult process in a number of ways. In some instances they can nurture the beginnings of a career. For the many youth not ready to begin a career process, apprenticeship still provides experiences that help clarify educational and work-related decision-making processes, and introduce young people to the variety of adult work and disciplinary knowledge. And becoming a photographer or engineer or journalist even for a year or two enriches an adolescent's self and provides a bridge or interim identity for her as she strives to figure out who she is, who and what she wants to be.

The seeming fluidity and rapidly changing technologies of work suggest a shift in thinking about the traditional conceptions of apprenticeship and, less clearly, in the specific experiences provided. In some newer fields young workers are creating new traditions and practices, for example, they widely and freely share ideas, information, and technologies directly with each other. They are raising questions about the relevance of established bodies of knowledge and custom. Mastery is increasingly coming to be viewed as tentative and relational, an interaction of the individual's abilities, a particular task and a particular setting. If it is not fixed, it has to be regenerated.

I will examine as well questions about how apprenticeship fits with newer conceptions of adolescent development. Theorists are placing greater emphasis on individual initiative as an engine of development; arguing, for instance, that young people have to be "producers of their own development" (Larson, 2004, p. 2). It is notable that mentors in at least some of today's youth apprenticeships reflect the newer thinking about locus of initiative, ownership, and related dimensions. They balance sharing of their own knowledge and experience with recognition that youth want and need to discover principles and precepts for themselves. They balance the need to build on tradition with respect for young people's need for voice. The skilled and authoritative boatbuilding instructor for Rocking the Boat notes nonetheless that "I try to do as little to do as little as I can [in the shop] to have what I want happen, because what I want to happen is what the youth want to happen" (Kautz, p.c., March 9, 2007).

Systems Questions

As implied above, the re-emergence of youth apprenticeship has been an ad hoc, decentralized, idiosyncratic phenomenon. There is, obviously, no youth apprenticeship system, no directed public funding, certainly no public policies supporting it. For the most part, sponsors of apprenticeship do not see themselves as part of a new social movement, let alone an effort to renew a centuries old institution. They have come to the apprenticeship framework because it fits and makes sense.

One might argue that the vocational/technical education departments of schools and school systems are the most obvious bases for apprenticeship, and in fact vocational/technical education is experiencing something of a revival. Youth are more likely to seek out apprenticeship experiences if such experiences yield meaningful credit and fit into visible educational pathways. Yet as an institution, high schools have barely begun to attend to the need to bring stakeholders together to consider new pathways for youth. If, and as provision of apprenticeship spreads, it is likely to remain variable, growing out of local conditions, opportunities, resources, and institutional relationships.

Systemic issues, then, are present everywhere in the background of this loosely constructed field. Institutions with complementary strengths, interests and roles need to be able to find each other. Forums are needed for those in the education, youth development, school-to-work and work worlds to get together, compare notes and consider what they want to do together (if anything). As I discovered in working on the book, those working in individual initiatives could learn a good deal from each other, but there are no mechanisms for bringing stakeholders together to share experience. Many cities are full of untapped resources which could be mobilized in the cause of youth apprenticeship. Potential funders with a new interest in youth apprenticeship would not know where to direct that interest in most cities.

It should be noted that few mayors, governors, business leaders, or philanthropists are crying out for "more youth apprenticeship" for the nation's high school age youth. In Wisconsin, for instance, a superlative statewide youth apprenticeship program has had to fight for years to stay alive. Still, there is an urgent sense at every level of society that the United States must address the puzzle of adolescence, of young people going through the motions, barely hanging on in school without exactly knowing why, fantasizing about becoming rock stars or professional athletes, looking at the adult world with puzzlement and sometimes cynicism and, most critically, having little specific idea of what they might actually strive to become.

I

Theoretical Bases

1
Apprenticeship as a Teaching and Learning Framework

...how many times I observed novices talking to themselves as they took on a new task, or shaking head or hand as if to erase an attempt and try again.

Rose (2004, p. 198), describing cabinet-making apprentices

Apprenticeship is the way we learn most naturally.

Collins, Brown, & Newman (1989, p. 491)

Apprenticeship has lurked in the shadow of thinking about good learning environments for almost a century now. It serves as an implicit model for such foundational thinkers as Dewey, Montessori, Vygotsky, and Bruner and, more recently, as an explicit model for Gardner. It has proven to be a fruitful framework for recent generations of learning theorists. Sociologists and anthropologists have studied apprenticeship as a learning and an economic model (see, e.g., Geer, 1972; Goody, 1982; Lave, 1982; Coy, 1989).[1] A handful of philosophers, most notably Polanyi (1958, 1966), have employed it in reflecting on knowledge and skill.

Recently writers have begun to link apprenticeship to learning in two notable ways. Looking inward they have tied it to findings from neuroscience about how the mind and/or brain works. Human brains appear biologically, even evolutionarily, prepared for apprenticeship. This is illustrated in the role of mirror neurons and the importance of "mirroring"—observing and mentally imitating—in the learning process (Blakeslee, 2006). The predisposition begins early in life. Sheets-Johnstone (2000, p. 344) argues that "certain infant capacities ... joint attention, imitation and turn-taking ... are at the foundation of apprenticeship." At the other end of the continuum, writers have argued that learning is essentially a social (or shared) and situated process (deriving from the features of particular settings) and have used apprenticeship as a paradigm for that process (Lave & Wenger, 1991).

While apprenticeship seems to offer an attractive framework for thinking about learning (and teaching), it is not intended as such. Lave (1982, p. 182) captures this incongruity in his discussion of Liberian tailor apprentices, noting that "while it is clear that almost everyone who undertakes apprenticeship succeeds in learning tailoring ... it is extremely rare to observe situations in which either teaching or learning is the principle business of an interchange between master and apprentice." Teaching and learning in apprenticeship are embedded in practice and production. To an extent they are by-products of practice. They tend also not to rely so completely on language and, as implied above, sometimes not at all.

Good Learning Environments and the Foundational Theorists

The foundational theorists articulated themes that continue to be explored, in some cases a century later. They both drew on and adapted each others' ideas. In most important ways they agreed about learning. They believed, for instance, in learning through doing, through work on consequential, socioculturally meaningful activities, and in the need for learning through both head and hands. They saw a balanced role for learners and teachers in the initiation of and responsibility for learning, and viewed learning as rooted essentially in a particular community. They emphasized the centrality of motivation, locating it in the task itself, the desire to please significant adults and the values of a particular culture. To differing degrees they worried about schooling. Dewey and Montessori, for instance, recognized that schooling would be the dominant framework for learning in the twentieth century but were critical of its motivational structure, pedagogy and curriculum, and its isolation from the larger life of the society.

Dewey (1902, 1916, 1938) believed that young people were motivated to learn when they had some choice about what to study and some responsibility for how; when they worked on tasks that made sense to them, especially tasks that "really needed to be done"; and when they worked in the context of a community of shared endeavor. Although young people are active agents of their own learning, they are not the sole constructors of it. The curriculum should be organized around longstanding tasks, problems and questions, important social themes, culturally recognized disciplines and activities (what Dewey sometimes called learning through occupations). Moreover because Dewey saw the larger social environment changing rapidly, he believed that young people had to be prepared for an unpredictable future with new problems and new knowledge needs. In that light they had to be prepared to be lifelong learners, experimenters and problem-solvers.

If Dewey's theme was disciplined experience, Montessori's was purposefulness (Montessori, 1913, 1948). She argued that children learn best on serious, relatively concrete tasks over which they have some control; that the process of working on a task is itself motivating; and that tasks should echo the real world outside the classroom. She believed that learning should engage different senses and require a measure of exactness or precision. Mastery is, most of all, a matter of practice and repetition. The teacher's role is to set up the environment so that children can work independently, to observe and guide, intervening mainly when it is clear that a child cannot fruitfully solve a problem on his or her own (Lillard, 1972). In her writings on adolescence Montessori emphasized, in addition opportunity for creative expression (self-realization), experience with producing things, opportunity to choose one's work, and the design of experiences that addressed adolescents' need to build, feel part of and find a constructive role in a community (Montessori, 1978). Like Dewey, she believed that young people had to be prepared for a future likely to be very different than past and present.

Vygotsky in turn emphasized that thinking, and by implication learning, are fundamentally socially mediated. The immediate social environment and the culture as whole provide ingredients and mechanisms for both (Vygotsky, 1978; Bockarie, 2002). Yet what begins as a social process nonetheless becomes internalized at some point (or as Rogoff, 1994, would have it, appropriated). A young person's "potential" achievements, evoked through observation, imitation and in social interaction, are practiced until internalized as his or her own. The adult in some respects treats the young person as if she were more competent than she actually is. Vygotsky argued also for the specificity of learning, that it is "more than the acquisition of the ability to think; it is the acquisition of many specialized abilities for thinking about a variety of things (Vygotsky, 1978, p. 83). Adults have a particularly important role in helping immature learners connect every day knowledge to the specialized knowledge and skill found in specific technical arenas of a culture.

Drawing on Vygotsky, Bruner has argued for the importance of field or discipline as an organizer and structure for learning. Each discipline has its key questions, ideas, and procedures, a kind of tool-kit that, once grasped, make it easier to learn. Learning can be seen as movement gradually deeper into a discipline, at some point becoming a matter of identity (Bruner, 1973, 1996). Extending Vygotsky's work on cultural scaffolding, Bruner introduced the concept of teaching as scaffolding.[2] He points out the value of trial and error in giving the learner a better sense of possible outcomes but notes that novice learners also need assistance. The teacher, or "tutor," provides such assistance by coaching and modeling, and by "controlling [sic] those elements of the tasks that are initially beyond the learner's capacity, thus permitting him to concentrate on and complete only those elements that are within the range of competence" (Wood, Bruner, & Ross, 1976, p. 90). The teacher helps the learner recognize when his or her approach to a learning problem is likely to lead in the wrong direction. Bruner has recently emphasized also the value of tangible products, works ("oeuvres") and works in progress, in providing evidence of learning processes and generally making learning efforts more palpable (Bruner, 2003, p. 171).

In some of his writings Bruner, like his predecessors, explores the motivational basis of learning. He argues that young people are motivated to learn when they have opportunity for "deep immersion [sic] in a consequential activity—not a metaphor, not a simulation, not a vicarious experience" (1966, p. 69). They are motivated to learn when a particular idea, procedure or piece of information is worth knowing for some reason and when it is immediately usable.[3] They are motivated to learn also by a desire to emulate valued others and to participate in their culture—to be a part of a web of social reciprocity (Bruner, 1960, 1966).

Powerful Learning Environments

The work of the foundational theorists is echoed throughout the literature on learning and instruction. Although one would not know it from the persistence of the "curriculum wars" (see, e.g., Ravitch, 2000), there is substantial agreement among learning researchers about the attributes of good learning environments—those that are motivating and absorbing; in which youth actively seek understanding and mastery; in which they feel productive and develop a genuine, grounded sense of efficacy; and in which they develop a sense of affiliation with the setting, its goals and activities.

A good learning environment is, not surprisingly, one in which subject matter and tasks are interesting. That is most likely when learning content and tasks are anchored; that is, when they reflect problems encountered in actual work in a discipline or out in the world, and when the reason for work on tasks is immediate and more concrete than abstract. Tasks are more interesting when they are relatively novel, moderately complex and demanding and when, to the extent practicable, there is no pre-determined solution, rather a measure of uncertainty and risk (Pye, 1968; Sternberg & Lubart, 1995).[4]

Learning is more interesting when knowledge and skill are used in an integrated way, rather than in isolated fragments. Tasks invoke different faculties, head and hand, different modes of representation and different parts of the self (Eisner, 2002; Abbott & Ryan, 2001; Bereiter & Scardamalia, 1993; Gardner, 1991). Learning is more engaging when young people can connect it to their own lives and when, through it, they can connect themselves—their beliefs, questions, thoughts—to the larger world. It is more engaging, in other words, when tasks have value, whether personal, aesthetic, practical, civic or other.

A good learning environment is discipline-driven. There may be one or more than one discipline at hand. But each provides what Resnick (1989) calls an organizing structure for learning. This includes the distinctive repertoire of concepts, language, core understandings, questions, problems and ways of thinking of a discipline, as well as its distinctive procedures, tasks, tools, materials and products. It may include the dimensions or phases of work within the discipline, for example research, design, rehearsal, composition, layout, blueprint, template, rough draft, and so forth. It may include a curriculum of sorts, a learning sequence, with more complex tasks incorporating and building on what was learned in simpler ones. And it includes means for the learner to adopt the identity of one who works in that discipline, even if temporarily.

As important as a conceptual framework, and complementing it in important ways, is a social framework: the community created to support learning. In good learning environments the community is defined by a sense of safety, of shared responsibility and of interdependence. Learners feel safe to take risks, raise questions, venture opinions, disagree, and express enthusiasm. There is a sense of jointness (Tharp, 1993). Participants agree on the work of the setting—what they are trying to do. They learn and produce, think, solve problems, and generally work together. More experienced learners share knowledge and experience with newer ones. The latter nonetheless have a role in contributing to the work and the life of that community, of practicing—and contributing to—the work being done. The products of new learners' work are shared acknowledged, valued and celebrated (Lave & Wenger, 1991; Bereiter & Scardamalia, 1993; Rogoff, 1994; Cambourne, 2002; Palincsar & Herrenkohl, 2002; Head, 2003).

In the context of these conceptual and social structures, good learning environments afford plentiful time and opportunity for learners to work their way into the discipline at hand (Bereiter & Scardamalia, 1993; Bereiter, 2002). Learners can devote sustained attention to their work. They have plentiful opportunity for the trial and error, practice and experimentation that solidify emergent abilities (Pye, 1968). New learners have opportunity to observe more experienced learners and experts at work. They may work on simpler tasks but they can observe complex ones, so as to begin to develop "a conceptual model, or cognitive map" (Berryman, 1995, p. 196).

Gradually growing skill and experience set the stage for gradually deepening involvement with a discipline and growing responsibility for one's continued learning and learning products; what Rogoff (1994, p. 209) describes as the "transformation of participation itself." As learners gain skill, they need and want more opportunity to regulate their own effort, to control the direction and outcome of that effort. They may, nonetheless, have to be encouraged to use what they are learning in their own way, to generate their own hunches, approaches and solutions, to use their own knowledge, prior experience and personal strengths to address learning tasks or problems.

Assessment is interwoven with learning, practice and experimentation. Performance is assessed routinely. Mistakes are viewed as part of the learning process, rather than as evidence of failure. Feedback is immediate and misconceptions are corrected quickly. In formal assessments learners are asked to put their understanding to work, "explaining, solving a problem, building an argument, constructing a product" (Perkins, 1998, p. 41). Assessment emphasizes the processes leading to a solution and the lessons derived from it, as much as whether it is precisely right or wrong. Learners, then, have opportunity—and receive support—to reflect on themselves as learners and on the learning process.

The Role of the Teacher

The teacher obviously has substantial responsibility for creating and maintaining the conditions of learning described above. S/he embodies the discipline at hand and holds its full complexity for the learner. In a complementary vein, s/he establishes the tenor for the learning community being built. The teacher helps the new learner learn how to address tasks and problems in discipline-specific ways. Teachers "lend" learners their expertise, insight, and motivation. They do not hide their thoughts about the problem at hand but join in with novice learners. They model, through use, the language of a particular discipline; they demonstrate, make visible, the mental, physical, and affective processes involved in addressing the tasks of that discipline.[5] They demonstrate their own interest in and commitment to the material to be learned.

In his or her scaffolding role the teacher may help the learner get started with a task or project, by focusing the learner's attention, helping with a first step, or talking about process. S/he identifies promising elements to build on and controls those elements of a task that are beyond a learner's capability (Bockarie, 2002; Wood et al., 1976). Good teachers encourage learners to think more deeply, and to be active in their work, for example, to predict what might happen next, to identify rules, to link the immediate material to prior or associated material, to reflect on what and how they are learning. To be useful, scaffolding requires the teacher to know the learner well. S/he should have a sense of how a learner is best motivated, where and when that learner is most easily frustrated, what the obstacles are to moving ahead. S/he should be able "to generate hypotheses about the learner's hypotheses" and "a theory of [that particular] learner" (Wood et al., 1976, p. 97).

Parallels with Apprenticeship

There are correspondences with apprenticeship in almost every dimension of good learning environments described here. Learning in apprenticeship is rooted in a discipline. It has many sources: the teacher, other apprentices, specialized language and tools, the setting itself, and the demands of specific tasks and projects. Learning is experiential in the deepest sense. A young person is doing what he or she is supposed to be learning. Apprentices working on a mosaic mural learn how to choose and arrange tiles (and about the qualities of different types of tile) as they try to use them to realize a design. A community organizing mentor tells Larson and Hansen (2005, p. 16), "a lot of things with organizing you can't teach, you have to experience it …" A sustainable agriculture apprentice is simultaneously learning about plant growth and using that information to plant, care for and harvest vegetables.

Because of the obvious connection between knowledge and its use, the reason one is learning something in apprenticeship is self evident (Gardner, 1991). Youth sometimes have opportunity to connect the learning and work of their apprenticeship to their own lives or those of family and community. One young African American woman, for instance, joined a research project on cardiovascular disease in minority populations (AAS, 1997). Another young woman had an opportunity to clean up and restore a river that is an important part of her community but which had been viewed—and used—for decades primarily as a place to dump garbage.

Task Structure

Tasks in apprenticeship are involved and involving, with multiple steps. Before even starting work on a display case, wood-working apprentices have to identify key sections, determine dimensions and make multi-dimensional drawings of each, and make lists of needed materials and tools. One apprentice enumerates 125 steps—distinct procedures—in constructing the cabinet (Rose, 2004). In producing a "design package" for the electric service of a silver analysis laboratory, a young man has to "gather [sic] information about power requirements" for various kinds of equipment; apply that information to the design and choice of circuits, wire, circuit breakers, switches, etc.; create and present drawings and schematics for electricians to use (Hamilton & Hamilton, 1997, p. 687).

Apprentices face open-ended problems and shifting variables. The founder of a boat building apprenticeship notes that "even though we've built 17 boats here, the next boat we build we'll be scratching our heads and trying to figure out what to do at every turn" (Green, 2006, p.c.). Although apprentices learn and work by a set of rules, tasks often require one to feel one's way. Riordan (2006, p. 101) describes a visit to a pottery apprentice who is working on a large mosaic mural of his own design, involving a sea creature smashing through a wall: "Holding a slab of arching gray-green tentacle in his hands, he explained: 'I'm making waves of clay. If it were solid it would potentially explode because of the air bubbles. So that's why my tiles aren't solid.' I inquired, 'How did you know how to do that?' to which he replied, 'Well I'm learning as I go along.'"

Tasks are marked by real-world constraints. The demands of planting and harvesting a vegetable crop are complicated by lack of rain or too much of it. The apprentice farmer learns to track what sells at a farmers market, in order to plan for future seasons' planting. An apprentice working on a mural at a subway station, "carefully painting each brick in the background," is taking too much time and realizes that "he had to find a quicker approach" (Larson & Walker, 2006, p. 258). A young woman apprenticing to a first grade teacher struggles with the fact that young children arrive at school tired or hungry.

Tasks in apprenticeship have a sense of intentionality. An After School Matters photography instructor notes wanting his apprentices to come to understand that "even a photographer who just seems to be shooting has an inner project in mind." A boat building apprentice has to learn to read and interpret a blueprint because he or she has to act on it to take the next step in the process. Tasks lead to tangible products or performances which are often genuinely needed by someone—a business, a community, a particular population of people. Apprentices may be writing a movie script, preparing a marketing plan, building a boat, growing vegetables and then selling them in a farmer's market, analyzing a social or health problem to help shape a public agency's response, documenting an environmental problem, designing and making a piece of sculpture, answering a scientific question.

Tasks often require use of the whole self, different senses, physical and emotional as well as cognitive skills. An observer asks a cabinet-making apprentice how he decides the number of times to put a board through an automatic planing tool, and the apprentice "explains that you can hear when the board is even" (Rose, 2004, p. 75). In another context, wood-working apprentices judge how close to being finished a piece of furniture is by running their hands along it, sliding draws in and out, in effect making a "tactile" judgment (Bailey, Hughes, & Moore, 2004, p. 157).

Production as Curriculum

The curriculum in apprenticeship is embodied largely in the work, in the skills, practices, and products of that work. As Lave (1982, p. 182) puts it, "production processes have logic and order to them and these shape educational processes." Apprentices learn in two dimensions: by working gradually toward more complex tasks and full-scale production; and by working through complete production cycles, from conception to final product. These dimensions interact to create a gradually deepening learning and production experience. Rose (2004, p. 91) illustrates this in describing a cabinet-making apprenticeship. He writes that, with experience, "the emerging structure of the object" one is constructing "will itself aid recall and proper sequencing of behaviors."

In the early phases of an apprenticeship, youth may work on single elements of a multifaceted task or process, and on exercises, models, and lower cost projects. A program director describes it as "expanding the vocabulary of what they can use, what they can pull from" (Novello, p.c., July 6, 2007). In filmmaking an apprentice begins to learn about setting scenes by helping to film footage of possible locations, perhaps helping set up lighting, and eventually becomes responsible for filming a scene—lighting it, choosing shots and angles, placing the actors in it. St. Louis Artworks apprentices working on a sculpture commission "will work the first few weeks on 3-D designs doing models," ideas from which will be incorporated into the design of the formal model for presentation to the client (Block, p.c., August 1, 2006). A young woman apprenticed to a jewelry designer says that "she helped me get started on my own work; she would give me her left-over materials to learn with, that's how I made my first pieces" (Camacho, p.c., August 1, 2007).

Preliminary projects are used in part to gauge readiness for more complex ones. Apprentices with Urban Boatbuilders (St. Paul, Minnesota), for instance, are required to make a simple object (such as a wooden mallet, bevel gauge, or canoe paddle) that is judged to meet defined functional and aesthetic standards, before moving into full-scale production. The boat building instructor says that "I'll give them a block of wood and they have to do a series of things to that piece, for example cutting a bevel with three different tools to specific requirements, or cutting a piece so that it's square and they can keep their line" (Wenger, p.c., June ,27, 2007). Discussing how she and her staff gradually build and assess young people's skills, the director of an applied arts studio notes that "they're never put on a job till we know they're ready … it would be completely irresponsible and it would set the kid up to fail, which is exactly what we're not about" (Novello, p.c., July 6, 2007).

The production cycle creates a frame for an expanding set of tasks and skills. Generically, that includes a conceptualization phase, design phase, production phase, feedback and revision, and final product or performance. As the apprentice moves through this cycle, demands shift, work tempos change, and choices may narrow. What begins as a rough version of the final product or performance is gradually refined. Describing participants' experiences in the late phases of documentary production, Wahl (2006, p. 6) writes that "Rough cut screenings are an outpouring of the reactions of others. The challenge for the producers is to find ways to pull themselves back to their own sense of mission and purpose, to ask what they really think needs to be changed and what should be retained. And so the public moment of sharing the work provokes another round of private thinking and reflection as the product move to the next stage of refinement."

Learning Through Experience

Learning occurs through trial and error, practice and repetition, and increasingly close approximation. A lamp-making apprentice struggles for almost three weeks with the soldering iron, getting it, almost getting it, not getting it, almost getting it again. The founder of a boat building apprenticeship program notes that "the best form of introduction is to dive right in … It's really hard to learn anything without understanding why it's important to learn it (Green, p.c., June 22, 2006). Because the apprentice is usually working on a defined, clearly visible product, s/he can see and try to correct errors immediately, as s/he is working. The process is sometimes described as rough working or roughing in. Lave (1982, p. 184) has described it as a process of "successive approximation."

Early on especially, the apprentice learns through observering, listening to, and imitating others such as more experienced apprentices as well as teachers. In one instance, a more experienced lamp-making apprentice is helping a peer score and cut glass. The youth is afraid that she will shatter the scored glass when she bends it with the pliers, but a demonstration by the experienced apprentice gives her the confidence to proceed. (She looks as much relieved as proud after she succeeds in cutting a small piece.) In a graphic design studio, a small group is clustered around a computer where a peer is working on a design, talking as she works about what is working and not working with the piece (Novello, p.c., July 16, 2007).

Observation of "expertise-in-use" helps the apprentice understand more fully both the meaning of quality and the skills involved in a discipline (Collins et al., 1989, p. 456). For example, commenting on her experience observing the director-instructor's work, an apprentice filmmaker notes that "At first when I watched R directing a shot, I said, 'Why is he doing that? That doesn't make sense.' But when I see how the shot comes out, I say 'Oh, now I know why he did that.'" This apprentice is learning how much experience and judgment goes into a shot, helped by the instructor, who talks with her while he is setting up each shot. A new science apprentice says of her opportunity to sit in on some team and lab meetings: "Even though I don't participate, I'm sitting there and I'm kind of taking in what they're saying, and later on I sit down and I'm breaking down the arguments …" (Richmond & Kurth, 1999, p. 691).

Assessment as Organic to the Work

Assessment in apprenticeship focuses on practice and the products of that practice, what one writer calls the "scraps of the working process"—plans, corrections, working notes, ledgers, drafts, dead ends, unfinished works, "alternative takes" (Menger, 2006, p. 63). Assessment is often instructional rather than summative; that is, it takes the form of feedback pointing out elements that might need more work or correcting errors. Some feedback is ongoing, provided as the apprentice is practicing and/or working on tasks and products, and some episodic, when a draft or final product is ready. Feedback is geared to the apprentice's skill level. In a flamenco apprenticeship, for example, the instructor gives skilled dancers occasional, very specific technical feedback, a middle group ongoing feedback on technique, and struggling dancers both substantive and affective support.

Work on gradually more complex tasks and projects serves as visible evidence—and confirmation—of the apprentice's growth. Interim products and performances, complete as drafts or still in production, serve as touchpoints for apprentice and teacher. They are sometimes workshopped—made public through a discussion or demonstration or reading or viewing. A science apprentice, for instance, may present his or her ongoing work to the larger work group of students and faculty in a particular lab. Workshopping, a kind of protected judging, gives instructors a sense of apprentices' skills, their "best roles and means," as one puts it. It provides apprentices opportunity for learning both self-evaluation and evaluation of others' work. Culminating products or assignments from the teacher may ask the apprentice to draw on the range of knowledge and skills he or she has acquired. The young man cited earlier learning about the electrician's trade is "give … to produce a functional design package for its electrical services" (Hamilton & Hamilton, 1997, p. 686).

Mistakes and failure are seen as part of, and indeed critical to, the learning process in apprenticeship. A boat building instructor affirms that "Much of what they're doing is building on what they already know. If there are mistakes we'll address them as we go" (Wenger, p.c., June 27, 2007). George Shirley, a professional tenor and visiting artist with the St. Louis Opera Theater's high school apprenticeship program, tells an apprentice who is embarrassed by a mistake he has just made: "Do you know what a servomechanism is? A rocket is a servomechanism. Once it's launched, it constantly makes corrections to its course. And that's how human beings learn. Don't be afraid of failure; we learn by making mistakes. It's the only way we can get it right" (Miller, 2003, p. 3). At the same time, apprentices are encouraged to work with care, and "to keep working on things until they are right," as an ASM mural instructor describes it.

The Setting as a Key Learning Resource

The setting—whether workshop, studio, classroom, laboratory, a construction site, the wall of a building, a river, or prairie—provides important ingredients for the learning experience in apprenticeship. The setting is, typically, that (or like that) where a particular discipline, craft, or art form is actually practiced. Describing the graphic design studio at Artists for Humanity in Boston, an instructor notes that "its like a design firm, except for the amount of demonstration" (Vicin, p.c., January 8, 2007). The setting is defined in part by the specialized language of the field. As photography apprentices and instructors talk about mood, light, lenses, aperture settings, camera movements, composition, exposure, and film speed, they define that studio as a distinct setting.

Just as learning and producing are interwoven, the learning environment is embedded within—for all practical purposes is—the production environment. As James (2006, p. 7) notes, "it is often the cues and clues found in the work place, and not necessarily the work itself, that foster the understanding and completion of tasks."

The setting includes the materials that define the work—soil, plants, insects, shade and light in an urban farm. A former visual art apprentice understands the importance of learning about and experimenting with different materials, "learning what their limits are, how to push them further; there was always a demonstration and then letting us experiment" (Camacho, p.c., January 8, 2007). The setting includes the physical tools of a discipline, which shape the work in a host of specific ways. Tools are the vehicle through which purposes and skills are expressed, and also create immediate constraints. The setting may include the varied roles that define the work. For example, in a theater company there are not just actors and directors but writers, choreographers, set, costume, light and sound designers. The particular setting may include people with varying levels of status, knowledge, and experience, as in many science labs or in restaurant kitchens.

The climate in apprenticeship settings varies but is typically serious, somewhat intense but not tense. Apprentices often have both an inward focus—it is not uncommon to overhear them talking to themselves as they work—and an outward one, as they monitor their own work in relation to others. An apprentice's typical state is best characterized as intent. Rose (2004, pp. 110, 86) describes the workshop where apprentices are learning the electrical trade: "It's a relatively quiet place. The students talk some while they are working, check in on each other, consult, hang out—but not a lot… You could describe these students as patient but, though not inaccurate, patience doesn't quite capture the feel of the room." There is, typically, some shop talk, a rich mixture of "information, procedures, tricks of the trade," intermingled with banter and jokes. Informal talk serves as an "open channel" for information.[6]

Depending on the discipline, the apprentice may be surrounded by others, some more, some less advanced, all working on the same task or on different parts of a process or product. The apprentice sees the tasks to be mastered in all their "tangled" complexity, and at different stages of completion (Becker, 1972, p. 98). The apprentice can observe others' strategies and mistakes, and observe how the teacher looks at and evaluates others' work. A cabinet-making apprentice tells an observer: "You see work going on all around you. You see people making small, small mistakes and you learn from that" (Rose, 2004, p. 76). Apprentices are both "learning up" and "teaching down." An apprentice notes of the graduate students working around her in a science lab, "They're asking me questions, making me look at things from a different angle" (Richmond & Kurth, 1999, p. 689).

In this sense, apprenticeship is characterized by a distinct type of community. It is goal-directed, internally oriented, carries a clear set of norms, bears "a conception of excellence that is internal to a practice and expresses its ideals" (Strike, 2004, p. 227). Standards of quality work "are embedded in the work environment in which the novice participates," and are embodied in the performance and products of more experienced apprentices and teachers (Berryman, 1993, p. 390). A cabinet maker who takes high school-age apprentices into his workshop notes that he has developed his own "proficiency levels," involving tool use, perspective and mechanical drawings, hand skills, knowledge of wood, and of the business itself (Moore, 1986, p. 172).

The community keeps its members on track. A photography instructor describes it this way: "the kids kind of force each other to make art; those who are just shooting, with little thought, see what their peers are doing, and they begin to want to [work more deeply]." A sculpture apprentice notes of the studio experience, "It's hard to get away with anything when you have three of your best friends asking why you did that" (Sloan & Sosniak, 1985, p. 128).

Although roles and responsibilities are based on experience, participants work together to define and shape the work. They share responsibility for teaching and learning, for thinking through and problem solving, as well as for products. On one occasion, two mural apprentices stand in front of a panel discussing why it seems off balance. An experienced cabinet-making apprentice shows a younger one how to stand and how to push when using the backsaw in the miter box (Rose, 2004). As Resnick (1989, p. 13) puts it, apprenticeship-based communities allow for "skill to build up bit by bit, yet permit participation for the relatively unskilled, often as a result of the social sharing of tasks". Ultimately, the community in which apprenticeship unfolds serves to foster a particular identity in the apprentice. As Heathcote and Bolton (1996, pp. 2–3) write: "archeologists learn alongside their colleagues how to write group reports, how to take care as they sift or dig, and how to speculate with others about the age of historical objects... They also learn to become the sort of people that archeologists are."

The Adult Role

The adult mentor's deep knowledge of the field at hand, sense of intentionality and direction provide strong organizers for apprenticeship. A dance instructor notes that she has learned to think quickly while keeping the base of what she is trying to accomplish. Another dance instructor notes the importance of holding in mind the concepts one wants apprentices to work on or explore on a particular day, using the concept of "symmetry" as an example. Where formal teaching occurs it is a matter of necessity—the apprentice needs to know something in order to move ahead or to complete tasks central to the work at hand.

Adult feedback is usually informational, descriptive. A printmaking instructor tells an observer, "To say about a work or about a student 'oh, that's great' or 'oh, you're great' doesn't really mean anything to you or to the student" (Thomas, 2007, p. 781). When necessary, the adult mentor holds the difficulty of a discipline for the apprentice, so he or she does not feel overwhelmed. For example, an After School Matters flamenco instructor notes that "Our students don't realize how difficult it is, what they're doing; we don't really tell them." The instructor reassures the newer dancers by telling them to imagine doing it right, "pretend, until it becomes a part of you."

Teaching Commensurate with Experience

Teaching in apprenticeship, typically, involves generous instruction, correction, and assistance at the outset, declining as apprentices gain proficiency. This pattern reflects the best use of the teacher's time and effort, and the recognition that more experienced apprentices will be better at self monitoring, sensing errors and correcting themselves. For novices the teacher concentrates on modeling basic mental and physical dimensions of the work itself. In a filmmaking apprenticeship, a script breakdown session requires apprentices to ask themselves a number of questions about sequence, location, the logic of the narrative, and so forth, which the instructor asks early on, until the apprentices begin to learn to do it themselves.

The teacher is more active early on in structuring learning tasks. S/he may set up situations in which apprentices work on selected, simple products or exercises, and yet can still "see or directly experience or get the feel of things ... for themselves" (Ingold, 2005, p. 2). Teachers may give novices a feel for where they are heading—and how much work there is ahead—by letting them try a more complex procedure at the outset. Thomas (2007) describes how in the very first session printmaking apprentices have a chance to "pull" the printing press, the last and difficult step in the "detailed and demanding" printmaking process.[7]

For more experienced apprentices, the teacher's focus shifts to encouraging self-initiative, introducing qualitative dimensions of a field, fostering professionalism and identity. Teachers may focus more on encouraging apprentices to sustain their efforts, to think and work their way through problems, keeping the end in view. They may ask apprentices to explain plans, decisions and approaches to problems. An ASM teaching artist tells an apprentice: "You can't say [to me] its not working, you have to say how or why it's not working." Looking at a piece of unfinished work, she asks another apprentice "What is wrong with the use of space here?" Teachers help identify and nurture promising ideas, elements, lines of work, pushing apprentices to go further with them (Bereiter & Scardamalia, 1993, p. 149). They remind apprentices to draw on experience: An ASM instructor asks, "You guys, remember when we had this problem editing the last film?"

Teachers begin to discuss the subtleties of work in a field. An art instructor waits some weeks before talking with apprentices about how, in his own recent work, he was trying to explore the sublime. A photography instructor waits some weeks before discussing with apprentices the meaning of "light records what's really happening." The teacher encourages the apprentice to begin to think and act like an architect or chef or sculptor or boat builder. Thus the instructor in an ASM photography apprenticeship encourages one young woman who has immersed herself in the discipline to begin carrying her camera everywhere she goes. She tells an observer that now she looks at everything she sees as a potential composition.

Teaching by Walking Around

The bulk of instruction in apprenticeship is incidental, "teaching by walking around" as one ASM instructor puts it. For example, within a few minutes the instructor in a lamp-making apprenticeship demonstrates the proper use of the soldering iron to an apprentice who is about to begin soldering for the first time (including how to apply the iron—flat—and how to spread the liquid solder), shows another apprentice how to score glass, and another how to fit glass pieces together and re-cut where necessary. A boat building instructor notes that "I wouldn't say that what I do here is teaching, but learning certainly occurs. I will show them skills and give them pointers as they are developing those skills, if you call that teaching" (Wenger, p.c., June 27, 2007).

Some instruction takes the form of feedback as the apprentice works on a task. Howard (1982) describes it as "precise suggestion." After observing a group of apprentices struggle for twenty minutes with an editing problem, an ASM film-making teacher suggests, "why not try putting this close-up here?" Drawing on his store of tacit knowledge, a cabinet-making instructor tells one youth, who is clamping a drawer, "Not too tight. There's such a thing as a mechanic's feel where it's just right" (Moore, 1986, p. 166). Teachers confirm the results of an apprentice's action. They sometimes talk through the process at hand, ask questions that direct attention to a problem, or offer reminders that model a particular way of thinking. As an apprentice finishes work on a segment of a drawer, the cabinet-making teacher reminds him to measure and say the measurements aloud: "Mike call out '33 3/8, 33 3/4'" (Moore, 1986, p. 166).

Both teaching and feedback may take the form of demonstration. A film-making instructor may stop by a cluster of students who are editing a video, see that they are not aware of a particular capability of the editing software, bring it up on the screen, and demonstrate its use. A boat building instructor notes that "I do have certain days when I'll stop, do a demonstration on a joint or on mixing epoxy, tool sharpening—anything that requires a certain set of skills that are hard to learn experientially" (Wenger, p.c., June 27, 2007). On one occasion in a sculpture apprenticeship, the instructor is trying to demonstrate how to work on the mouth. She begins by drawing on newsprint on an easel, trying to describe the process, illustrating the planes. After a few minutes, she realizes that she needs to demonstrate: "So I don't know how to say it anymore. I lift it up [demonstrating on a bust]. So I cut it and pull up [Several kids: "Oh!"] ... What we're doing is we're catching a shadow" (McPhail, Pierson, Goodman, & Bunge Noffke 2004, p. 474).

Teachers direct apprentices' attention to particular dimensions of a task, process, or product. As one apprentice brings a print out of the darkroom for the instructor to comment on, the instructor asks her if she was moving when she took the photo, what the exposure was, and other questions that might explain problems with the print. A dance instructor tells an apprentice, "Elena, instead of concentrating so hard on your feet, I want to you to concentrate on your bounce; your feet are moving but the bounce isn't quite there." On occasion teachers use direct physical guidance, for example, placing a hand over the hand of the apprentice who is working with a tool, or, in dance, turning an apprentice's body in a particular direction or re-shaping an arm or leg. In some fields, such as visual arts, design, architecture, and cabinet making, they may teach and correct through sketching and drawing (teaching apprentices to use drawing to flesh out ideas).

A More Experienced Collaborator

The adult sometimes acts as an "experienced collaborator" (Larson & Hansen, 2005, p. 16). An ASM mural instructor notes that "I would sit with them [the apprentices] and paint around the area [on the panel] where they were painting." A graphic design mentor notes joining in to help finish jobs, in part to teach that "the beauty of a really good design is the last 10 percent, the finish—you know, you don't leave a word all alone on a line" (Novello, p.c., July 6, 2007). Motives for joining in the work are often practical. A boat building instructor notes that "I get involved [sometimes] because I want to make sure the skill-building and tasks are done efficiently" (Wenger, p.c., June 27, 2007).

Teachers use their own work as examples. A video/computer instructor, for example, may show a commercial he has developed and go through it frame by frame, describing and critiquing what he was aiming for. An art instructor may show slides of a project in which she had drawn variations of the same figure every day for several months, provoking a host of questions from apprentices, which may include, "Didn't you get bored?" Teachers sometimes share rough work, to give apprentices a feel for creative and production processes. Derek McLane, a well-known set designer who works with youth, notes that "The kids are fascinated by the amount of rough work I show them, the quick sketches I do when I am reading a play or talking to a director. There are a lot of dead ends in the design process and its important to get the ideas out. That's another lesson I think the kids benefit from" (Roundabout Education Report, 2006, p. 11).

Teachers share their aesthetic with youth, which may serve as youths' own initial aesthetic. For example, a cabinet-making instructor tells a cluster of apprentices that "Some cabinet-makers like a lot of face frame. I don't like as much" (Rose, 2004, pp. 85–86). An art instructor talks with apprentices about her commitment to public art and mural-making as a means of giving voice to the history and experience of communities that may lack voice. Some teachers try to expose youth to how they think about projects by talking about what they are doing as they work, or by "debriefing" with a young person who has just sat in on a planning or design activity.

Teachers will discuss what it is like to work as a professional in the discipline at hand. A photography instructor, for example, may gather apprentices to discuss the historic role of photography in print journalism, how assignments are made, and decisions the photographer has to make, such as how to decide on the degree of cooperation with the subject.

Teachers may also connect apprentices to the tradition in which they are working, for example, a group of lamp-making apprentices working in the arts and crafts style learn about and visit houses designed by Frank Lloyd Wright; a group of filmmaking apprentices watch and discuss films made by pioneering African American directors; a flamenco instructor offers a brief lecture about the distinct history and settlement of different parts of Spain, how these led to different dance forms and traditions, and where dance fits in community life.

2
Apprenticeship and the Tasks of Adolescence

In youth, then, the life history intersects with history.
Erikson and Erikson (1987, p. 657)

The studio's about growth. They're not working unless their stuff is changing and they're learning to make better things. You know, that's their job—to grow as artists.
A potter, on his apprentices Riordan (2006, p. 239)

American culture posits adolescence as a difficult developmental period. It is more accurate to say that American culture has difficulty with adolescents. Instead of treating youth matter of factly, we alternatively romanticize, infantilize, and scapegoat them. We trivialize the things that they take seriously and all but ignore their idealism. We isolate youth from the fullness and complexity of the adult world and then complain that they are unprepared for it. We have reduced the scope of activity in which young people might feel useful, and then proceeded to mourn the loss of the useful child.

Those who study adolescence and those who work with youth view it in a complex light. More than early and middle childhood perhaps, adolescence is a transitional time. One is beginning to look to the future (partly because one can do so cognitively) but is unsure what form one's life will take. It is a paradoxical time, of waiting and preparation, experimenting and making commitments, of recognizing social reality and questioning it. Adolescents can see the faults in the adult world more clearly than the demands of it. New kinds of developmental tensions emerge, new kinds of vulnerability to experience, tied to identity work. One wants to become oneself, "a person in one's own right" (Kleiber, 1999, p. 47), but one grows up with one's peers in a particular time and place. Individual attributes and developmental processes interact with the resources available in one's community and society, with economic trends and public policies. Opportunities, threats, and pressures vary enormously depending on where one is situated in one's society. Before they have even left childhood young people begin to recognize or at least to sense a narrative trajectory to their lives, one that feels partly open and partly set.

How, then, does apprenticeship interact with both the developmental tasks of adolescence and the contexts in which youth have to try to address those tasks? In this chapter I focus on the first part of this question, leaving for chapter 7 discussion of the second part. I argue that the attributes of apprenticeship fit well with the tasks and tensions of this age period, that apprenticeship is developmentally accurate in important ways. Tasks feel real and make sense. The youthful novice in a specific discipline is also a novice in many other respects. Apprenticeship provides a structure and some substance for the explorations of youth. Development of specific skills and work on broader identity are bound together; skills become incorporated into and change the self. It provides a means for youth to both test and accept reality, and sometimes transform it. Though very specific in many respects, apprenticeship is responsive to the multifacetedness of development. It attends to self-knowledge as well as knowledge of the world, autonomy as well as relatedness. It addresses just those domains in which youth are often unsure of themselves. And for more vulnerable youth it does so in a way that encourages a re-working of self without the need for self-repudiation.

Developmental Tasks

Larson (2002, p. 3) writes that "the inescapable developmental task of adolescents is to prepare themselves for adulthood." This broad task has many dimensions. Young people are loosening ties to family and seeking new sources of identification, choosing what to invest in, and learning how to do so effectively. They are learning to balance preoccupation with self and commitment to others, finding a balance between connectedness and autonomy, and learning to test perceptions against reality. They are gaining the experience needed to turn new capacities into actual skill and judgment, and developing habits and dispositions likely to be useful in adulthood. They are beginning to think about the adult world, to learn how it works, to make sense of it and to discern what their role in it might be. And through all these tasks, they are beginning to forge a distinct, coherent, grounded sense of self.

Most thinking about these tasks builds on—even when departing from—the work of Erik Erikson (1963, 1968, 1987). Erikson argued that the central task of adolescence is forging a sense of identity: who one thinks one is, what is important to do, what one is interested in and might be good at, what one is for and against, whom and what one might become. He described youth as a period of "rehearsal [for] the main performance, namely the individual's lasting identity in the adult world." Continued growth through these years requires the opportunity to apply the basic cultural tools acquired in middle childhood toward "real accomplishment, that is, achievement that has meaning" in the culture (1987, pp. 647, 622). Growth is driven in part by "positive identification with those who know things and know how to do things" (Erikson, 1968, p. 125).

Within the framework established by Erikson (and since elaborated by numerous others), the adolescent is exploring interests and discovering talents, experimenting with and trying on roles, allegiances, relationships, beliefs, activities and disciplines, in other words different "possible selves." At the same time, the young person is beginning to make choices and commitments, beginning to discover his or her own voice. He or she is beginning to reflect on and evaluate the larger culture, embodied in school, the media and other contexts. For instance, young people come to ask whether what is valued and how people are treated in school makes sense.

There are in these processes elements of resistance and rejection as well as affirmation. Youth are not just continuing to separate but to "transcend" the foundation of family in a search for new sources of identification (Kroger, 1996). They are asserting control over their lives. As Litowitz (1993, p. 194) puts it, "The desire to move beyond participation to responsibility is in itself an act of resistance, a resistance to being dependent and controlled by another." Yet, though making commitments is partly about taking ownership and responsibility, it is partly also about letting go and surrendering to particular endeavors (Kleiber, 1999).

Ultimately, the young person has to integrate old and new into a distinctive, coherent sense of self, one that ideally is optimistic yet realistic, and embodies a sense of continuity (Blos, 1979; Marcia, 1980; Csikszentmihalyi & Larson, 1984; Kroger, 1996). This distinctive sense of self—described as the true or enduring self—encompasses not just the meanings made of formative experience but an underlying psychological orientation to the world and a solidifying "inner compass ... for navigating the present and charting the future" (Hemmings, 2006, p. 133).

Actualizing New Capacities

Complementing the identity work of adolescence is a set of tasks best described as "actualizing" the new capacities that emerge during this age period. These include the ability to think (and therefore act) more complexly, flexibly and reflectively, to hypothesize, contextualize, and anticipate consequences. They include the related capacity to carry out more complex tasks: to plan, apportion time, sustain attention and effort, gather and organize information, monitor one's work, recognize problems, seek help when appropriate, revise as needed. Adolescence brings new capacities for self-management and self-regulation, for directing one's behavior, managing impulses, recognizing and expressing emotions. It brings new social capacities, for collaborating, considering (and taking) others' perspectives, listening to others and building on their ideas, and considering the effects of one's behavior on others (Costa & Kallick, 2000; Kroger, 1996; Larson, 2004; Schunk & Zimmerman, 1996).

Experience in different settings—one might say experience itself—provides the ingredients for identity work, for locating new sources of identification, for testing and anchoring ideas, fantasies and fears about who one might become. Just as important, it provides the means for converting new capacities into actual skills, habits, and judgment. Yet the specific qualities of experience direct how new capacities are actualized, transformed to skills, habits, and dispositions. Different settings evoke distinct capacities. To convert capacities to skills requires sustained use. And experience sometimes requires a translator to give it meaning.

Resources Needed to Support Work on Developmental Tasks

To work effectively on the tasks of adolescence requires both personal and social resources. Youth are far more than passive recipients of culture; they are active in shaping both their own lives and the world around them. Yet to be what Larson (2004) describes as producers of their own development, young people need to bring a range of personal attributes—a sense of curiosity, motivation, and agency, an openness to new experience, the sense of an open future, and a basic feeling of competence, of "alrightness," to cope with inevitable obstacles, false starts, and disappointment.

Even with such personal resources, young people need socially created opportunities—to discover talents, experiment and make commitments, contribute and to take responsibility, and generally to exercise growing capacities. They need access to a diverse portfolio of adults to support, guide, instruct, model and serve as new sources of identification. On their own, youth cannot acquire culturally important knowledge and traditions, cannot always know what is important within or about a particular experience, or indeed that an experience itself holds value. On their own, youth cannot escape self-preoccupation. They may not have the language or means, or feel permission, to analyze and give voice to their experiences.

Young people cannot consider possible realistic but interesting futures without exposure to concrete embodiments of those futures (Csikszentmihalyi & Schneider, 2000). In some measure they need breadth of exposure, the experience of "the diversity of human work and human knowledge that only a variety of experts can provide" (Kahn, 2006, p. 20). To develop new sources of identification, they need extended contact with individual adults skilled in and passionate about some area of life. More abstractly, the young person needs "societal structures standing ready to receive him, offering him that authentic credibility with which he can identify" (Blos, 1971, p. 975).

Because adolescents demand some ownership of their experiences, some psychological as well as social space, they are sensitive about adult involvement as well as sensitive to it. They want to imitate what adults do, but in their own way. They want to be treated maturely and taken seriously but also to be treated matter-of-factly and realistically. Youth want respect for their own intentions, but they want to know when those intentions are off track (Larson, 2004). They want to be granted some authority but they want it where it makes sense, they want to gain it gradually, and want it in a shared form (Hefner, 1988). Young people want adults to acknowledge and respect their idealism but also to help them put that idealism to practical use and debate it when necessary.

As with adult-youth relationships themselves, experiences designed by adults require a delicate balance. Youth want to be able to be themselves—and stay true to themselves—while learning to be something new. They want to trust what they are experiencing (Gregory, 1995). That includes feeling that one's efforts are real, in some sense; believing that those efforts are being evaluated honestly, on a defensible rather than arbitrary basis; and being able to express one's true self—questions, doubts, and vulnerabilities as well as pride in accomplishment. They want attention to their "selves" without an explicit, self-conscious focus on those selves. As one young man puts it, "I don't want t come into a place and find out someone is trying to raise my self-esteem" (Sisario, 2007, p. B8).

Distinctive Challenges Faced By Urban, Working-Class Youth .

A sizable minority of youth growing up today—and, certainly, a majority of working-class youth—lack access to the social resources and supports needed to address adolescent developmental tasks. A smaller but still notable number are personally vulnerable as well. Growing up in or near poverty, in a devalued and neglected neighborhood and perhaps a devalued group, seems especially to complicate the tasks of this age period. It increases the likelihood of a difficult early or middle childhood. It changes the normative calculus—including the potential costs—of both experimentation and commitment. It increases the costs of curiosity and ambition. It alters the normative balance between day-to-day preoccupations and long-term goals. In other words, it gives particular meanings to academic success, trying hard, and standing out in ways that compromise adolescent choices.

By the time they have reached high school, some young people's personal lives have been marked by the kinds of relational experiences, day-to-day pressures, unexpected life events and crises that pull children off track—preoccupied or erratic parenting, inordinate responsibility for care of self and siblings, loss of family members through separation or death, family or community violence, pressure from gangs, contact with police, juvenile justice, child welfare authorities. Such experiences can lead to questioning of self and mistrust of others (Lee, 1994; Nightingale, 1993), and can sap the psychic and physical energy needed to address the tasks of middle childhood and adolescence.

Loss of Support from Social Institutions

Even for the majority of working-class youth who have not experienced personally difficult early and middle childhoods, social institutions become less actively supportive, and social resources less available in general, as they move into adolescence. Young people's lives become too full of consequential accidents— the high school they happen to get into or do not get into, the corner they are on at the wrong moment, the opportunity that passes by because they did not see what it means.

As I discuss at length in chapter 3, schools are particularly problematic as developmental settings for many young people, and become steadily less welcoming as children advance in grade. Gregory (1994) found that youth who get off track in middle school attribute it to peer pressure, the freedom to misbehave, and the impersonal quality of the school culture—no one seems to care if they are there or not, doing well or not. These themes continue and often intensify in high school.

The majority of working-class high school students describe school as impersonal, teachers as needlessly controlling, arbitrary and disinterested, and learning experiences as "pointless, meaningless and menial" (Harter, 1996; McDonald & Marsh, 2004, p. 147). Youth feel both unknown and uncared for, and have little opportunity to experience "personal ownership of their participation" (Almeida & Steinberg, 2001; Larson, 2004, p. 3). Bullying and belittlement (by peers and teachers) further contribute to disengagement. In a qualitative study exploring the state of mind and preoccupations of mostly working-class teens in two high schools, Girod, Pardales, Cavanaugh, and Wadsworth (2005) found young people's defining emotional state to be fear—about their own futures, the state of the world, and their every day physical safety.

Many youths' experiences with school literacy, at the heart of schooling, are marked more by humiliation, shame and struggle than by pleasure (Fenwick, 2006). The damaging effects extend beyond reading and writing per se, to young people's view of themselves as capable learners. A sizable minority—close to 40%—of the youth I interviewed in my study of After-School Matters (ASM), report that they no longer believe in their own academic abilities. Some youth, struggling academically, come to see no point to academic work. Others believe academics to be important but, as Harter (1996) puts it, do not see how to recover their academic selves.

Youth and teachers seem to be out of step. In a poignant study in a largely Latino high school in Texas, Valenzuela (1999) describes a mismatch between young people's view and understanding of their school situation and that of even seemingly caring teachers. Teachers interpret young people's dress and deportment as "proving" that they do not care about school. For their part "youth who maintain that they don't care about school often mean something else," whether that they are fearful of the pain of doing poorly, wary of social embarrassment, or simply do not trust the setting enough to invest in it (Valenzuela, 1999, p. 70). Youth also cannot see why they should bother. Valenzuela offers the example of one responsive and caring journalism teacher, trying to introduce the possibilities of writing to his class. Yet the students protest that "nobody wants to learn what he's teaching ... he wants us to be writers and we don't wanna be ... he has a nice personality but what he teaches is not right" (p. 232).[1]

Restriction of Experience

Beyond school, working-class youth lack access to experiences that might counter fears, ground free-floating fantasies, and offer a nuanced picture of the possibilities, diversity, and complexity of the adult world. In urban areas at least, the problem is not an absolute lack of social resources for youth; most cities are full of them. Rather it is lack of connection between youth and those resources. In discussing their daily lives outside of school, youth describe a mixture of boredom and restlessness that they do not know how to do anything about. Of one young woman they interviewed, Chaskin and Baker (2005, p. 36) note that "Elisha expresses frustration with how she spends her time. She says she'd rather go to a 'teen program or something to help elevate my time, instead of sitting in the house bored, not doing nothing' … Her mother encourages her to find places to go, and makes specific suggestions, but Elisha believes that 'nothing is happening' … What she does know about seems too far away."

The immediate context of young people's lives limits the range of adults and the range of ways-of-being-adult that young people come into contact with, and thus their exposure to "the demands of personhood in a wide range of domains making up the adult community" (Shaw, 1996, p. 63). In a day-to-day sense many youth lack contact with adults who can say not just "Have you thought of trying this?", but "Come with me down this path a little way"; too few to say "You know, you can be serious about this." They lack opportunity also for rich, explanatory conversations with adults about work at hand, what Rose (2004, p. 86) calls "shop talk" and Heath (2000, p. 14) "talk with work."

Loss of Voice, Loss of Self

The absence of affordances—opportunities to work on, nurture, recognize a true, grounded self—seems to exacerbate the effects of peer pressure. Both in school and out of it adolescence brings a loss of voice—the ability and willingness to say and be what one truly thinks and believes, for many youth contributing to "false self behavior" and in turn loss of a sense of vitality (Harter, 1996, p. 37). Girls may hide their abilities and submerge their interest in academic material. As one young woman tells Valenzuela (1999, p. 71), "You kinda have to seem like you don't care because if you say something and it comes out sounding stupid, then everybody will say you're dumb." Boys, on the other hand, too often adopt the "inauthentic voice of bravado, posturing, foolish risk-taking and gratuitous violence" (Kimmel, 2006, p. 69).[2]

Too many girls and boys determine that the hypothetical benefits of making commitments and perhaps standing out—working hard in school, being intellectually curious, participating in organized out-of-school activities, demonstrating interest in some pursuit, seeking to go to college—are not worth the perceived social costs and occasional physical risks. Some youth unquestionably are held back by family, friends, or their own fears of "journeying beyond the familiar" (Musick, 1999, p. 4). Cairns, Leung, and Cairns (1995) describe a process that they call social synchronizing, in which youth coordinate or adjust their behavior and self-expectations to the peers immediately around them. In reflecting on the group loyalty that keeps low-income youth from striking out on their own,

MacLeod (1987) notes that they "disqualify" themselves, even before others have the opportunity to disqualify them.[3]

In spite of—and as a result of—discouraging and constraining experiences, many working-class youth articulate "wildly unrealistic expectations about their future" (Olson, 1997, p. 18). When asked what they think they'll be doing in 10 or 15 years, they mention either occupations that are very difficult to enter without enormous, sustained effort (e.g., medicine) or, more commonly, those involving a combination of rare gifts and/or luck (i.e., entertainment, professional sports).[4] Of one youth they interviewed Chaskin and Baker (2005, p. 34) note, "Hector doesn't have goals specified beyond graduating high school ... He can imagine being an artist, boxer or doctor [but it's] hard for him to imagine himself finishing a school after high school, since 'I might get kicked out because I'm usually get lazy and don't want to do nothing.'"

Perhaps most harmful for poor, urban youth are the social messages they receive—from the adults around them no less than from the media, more distant authorities, and the culture as a whole—that their presence in society is mostly destructive and that they will probably fail no matter what they try. Negative social labeling is so damaging in part because it exacerbates self-doubt, in part because it fosters a tendency to embrace rejection, in effect to identify with the negative label being applied (Erikson, 1987).

How and Why Apprenticeship Makes Developmental Sense

It is interesting, but hardly surprising, that the attributes of apprenticeship fit well with the tasks, preoccupations, and capacities of adolescence. Apprenticeship provides all kinds of ingredients for identity work: opportunity for both experimentation and commitment, for trying on roles and approaches to engaging the world, for learning about one's talents, interests, and limits. Reflecting the transitional quality of adolescence itself, activities are transitional in structure, both present- and future-oriented, embodying elements of both play and work (Winnicot, 1971). The demands of apprenticeship soften young people's egocentrism, without attacking their selves. Relationships with adults are grown up in some respects, appropriate to young people's lack of experience in others.

Apprenticeship provides a structure for adolescents' need to express, question, imagine, take risks, deconstruct, test limits, and make their own meaning. But it does so within a reasoned set of boundaries—the framework of a defined tradition and aesthetic and the example of an authoritative adult, committed to that tradition and to sharing his or her knowledge of it. Youth have to begin to fit their goals, needs and sometimes style into the constraints of a work setting. A coordinator in Wisconsin's Youth Apprenticeship Program notes of employers and mentors that "they have to know they can count on a young person to be there when scheduled to ... some kids think it's o.k. not to come if they call ahead, but that is not what is being [asked for]" (Nystrom, p.c., January 17, 2008).

For more vulnerable youth, apprenticeship addresses the normative tasks of adolescence without neglecting the harm that result from growing up under conditions of resource scarcity and social depredation. As will be seen in later chapters, apprenticeship re-builds capacity for trust and for openness to learning, strengthens young people's sense that they have something to say, are worthy of being listened to, and the sense that their aspirations and struggles matter to the larger world around them. But it does so indirectly, in the context of work and of relationships that are about something else.

Ingredients for Exploring Identity

The richness and solidity of a specific discipline provides in turn a solid base for exploring identity, whether an interim identity or one that becomes more enduring. A discipline provides a location in the broader culture, provides props such as tools, language, customs, traditions, work clothes, products and performances, and offers a ready-made community to belong to. Even if for a matter of months, the young person experiences what it is like to be an architect or chef—mentally, physically, and emotionally. Apprenticeship provides a way of engaging tasks, of using time and energy, in effect one way of being an adult. It has the texture a young person needs to learn about strengths and limits, what he or she likes or does not like.

Youth learn much more deeply about occupations they thought they knew and they learn about occupations and roles that they were unaware even existed. They sometimes learn that one can do something that others say is unrealistic: "Everyone always tells you 'There's no money in the arts ... It's so difficult, you're going to be a starving artist, there are no opportunities, blah, blah, blah ...' It's nice to know that that's not true, there is stuff you can do, that you are making a difference and really anything is possible" (*Teen Voices,* 2005, p. 2). Young people learn in detail the preparatory work that one needs to do to join a discipline, and can compare that to what they have been doing and plan to do in their educational lives. The apprentice also has opportunity to evaluate whether a particular discipline is for him or her. An apprentice in one of the scientific departments of a natural history museum observes that "I've seen my mentor working, and he seems to work really hard at what he does, but I think I need something a little more hands on" (Remer, 2006, p. 2).

The demands, discourse, and other elements of apprenticeship in a discipline contribute to self-knowledge. As apprentices learn to think more about what they are working on, they also think more about themselves, possibly because they are in a heightened state of awareness; their mind is active. An ASM photography apprentice notes that "it [being in the apprenticeship] kind of opens up your mind, and [makes you] think about what you are doing and where you want to go." Describing the graphic design studio in which she works as well as the broader organization, an apprentice with Artists for Humanity, a Boston-based organization, notes that "I know this might sound kind of cheesy. When you come here you're getting away from the world. You're coming here to find yourself. The people here actually challenge you and your thought process" (*Teen Voices,* 2005, p. 2).

Authentic Experience

Apprenticeship responds to adolescents' interest in authentic experience. Discussing the contribution of "on water" apprentices to cleanup and renewal of the Bronx River in New York, a Rocking the Boat instructor notes that "If we don't go out [on the river] and collect data then someone at Lehman College will not be able to do his scientific work" (Heyman, p.c. , March 19, 2007). A young woman working with an endocrinologist on a study of Cushing's syndrome collects sinus samples from patients and analyzes them under a microscope for telltale clues to a disease that causes serious health complications (Bauer, 2000).

At times youth have opportunity and responsibility to wrestle with the social and moral issues that are at the heart of a particular type of endeavor or even of Americans' common life. An apprentice in a lab that uses animals for research asks, "Should we really have the right to experiment and freeze animal tissue? I'm not sure, but when I was labeling the vials and kidney parts … I began to think that this animal was once alive …" (Reimer, 2006, p. 7). Reflecting on young people's work on a radio documentary about Abu Ghraib prison in Iraq, which included interviews with U.S. Marines, the story's producers write that "a whole lot of process hides behind youth media products—moments of fraught deliberation about how to tell a meaningful story that has the potential to upset assumptions and raise generative questions" (Soep, Meyano, & Kurwa, 2007, p. 10).

Roles too are authentic. Filmmaking apprentices are part of a production crew and are working with a production schedule. The common routines, for instance setting up or breaking down equipment, contribute to the sense of engagement in something real. The founders of Marwen Arts, Chicago, which provides arts apprenticeships, deliberately decided to locate its studios close to galleries and museums in order to link apprentices "to the community that inspires and contextualizes their activities. Despite the distance the students often travel from their neighborhoods and schools, the trip itself comes to symbolize the transformation encouraged by Marwen—from ordinary teens in often challenging surroundings to young artists and designers shaping their own futures" (Yenawine, 2004, pp. 5, 6).

Actualizing Capacities

Apprenticeship provides ingredients for youth to work on—to actualize—new capacities. Complex, multi-step tasks help apprentices learn, for instance, to attend as much to the front and back ends of the creation and production process, that is to preparation and revision, as to the heart of the process. (Adult mentors note apprentices' initial tendency to jump in without planning or "take one crack at a piece of work and then call it quits," as one describes it.) Preparing can involve the simple act of setting up equipment and materials. It can mean doing research (e.g., on the history of a community) or creating a storyboard or collecting computer-based images or rehearsing lines and getting into character. Engaging tasks deeply requires the young person to apportion his or her energy.

Youth have high standards and can be hard on themselves. At the same time, they can be impatient, and experience difficulty working on tasks that require reiteration. Apprenticeship taps into both of these tendencies simultaneously, smoothing them out. There is often no way around the process of approximation, getting there in stages. The detailed nature of the work, the specificity of action sometimes required, tools and materials themselves, require deliberateness and care, modulating impulsiveness. Weeding a vegetable field requires patience, pacing, and close attention to differences in a tangled mass of greens in front of one. Editing videotape requires painstaking transcription, as well as careful incorporation of segments of tape into material already inputted. In some disciplines, youth are required to follow exact procedures, whose logic may not be immediately clear. In science apprenticeships, they may have to repeat procedures that did not work well and wait patiently for results.

What Pye (1968) calls "the manner of doing things" in apprenticeship has a kind of integrity that young people appreciate. Boat building apprentices may feel "lectured to" but also feel valued when a boatbuilding instructor tells them "if you know it's supposed to be symmetrical, figure out what it takes to make it symmetrical ... If it's supposed to be varnished, not only should the varnish job look good, it should be done so it's going to last" (Wenger, p.c., June 27, 2007). That may mean preparing the surface with extra care, taking more time than one is inclined to. Pride in doing the work right is more powerful than any initial resentment at having to do so.

Softening Egocentrism

Apprenticeship decenters young people in a healthy way. It is not about them, not about their preoccupations. The focus is on the work at hand (rather than the adolescent per se). Performance is evaluated within the framework of standards that are part of an explicit, valued tradition. In apprenticeships where learning and production are collective activities, youth have to work on the idea that, as an ASM flamenco instructor notes, "you come together for one thing, and you have to do something well together ... it's not about you, but its all about you." Youth often quickly learn that, as the teaching artist in a graphic design studio puts it "if one of us screws up it is going to affect everyone" (Vicin, p.c., January 8, 2007). In a restaurant kitchen, youth have to learn to contribute to—and to take pride in—an end product that they may not even see leave the kitchen.

Collaborative work strengthens the capacity to take others' perspectives. An ASM mural instructor describes how work on the mural requires apprentices to step back on a regular basis to consider their work in relation to the whole. In work on a large collective canvas, a reinterpretation of Gauguin's "Where Do

We Come From? What Are? We Are We Going?", seven painting apprentices from Artists for Humanity have to learn to accommodate each others' styles, in effect to make room for each other (Stickgold, 2004).

Safe Contexts to Experiment, Commit, Succeed and Fail

Apprenticeship settings are, typically, psychologically safe contexts. The sense of purpose and shared endeavor contribute to this. The threshold for being accepted and for accepting others is lower than in school or the neighborhood, in part because the work creates common ground. While there is inevitably some teasing, it is rarely hurtful. An ASM apprentice notes, "I don't have to walk around with my head up [watching out for myself] or trying to get attention. You get attention for what you do." As another puts it, "It's good to be here, you don't have to worry about a teacher getting on you, or somebody messing with you in the hallway about dress code, you just come in here and relax, 'OK, I'm at work now." An apprentice in Marwen Arts notes that "nobody is telling you to be any way. You do what you need to do" (cited in Yenawine, 2004, p. 6).

The setting, though demanding, can feel protective in comparison to others in young people's lives. The graphic design apprentice cited earlier notes of her studio that "Anywhere else you go, they're going to be like 'What was she thinking when she got up this morning and put that on? What was she thinking when she painted that? Why did she do that?' Here they don't question it, they embrace it ..." (*Teen Voices*, 2005, p. 2). A Marwen apprentice, reflecting on her studio experiences there notes that "not a single teacher ever said 'no, you can't do that'" (Camacho, p.c., January 5, 2007).

Pressures in apprenticeship, though real, are shared and measured. Producing a live radio show every Friday evening, for example, leaves little room for moodiness after an argument with a girlfriend or boyfriend. Yet such personal issues will be attended to in other ways during the week. In art the common studio experience of critiquing and being critiqued by peers creates both pressure and safety in experimenting. One youth notes that "It's hard to get away with anything when you have three of your best friends asking you why you did that" (Sloan & Sosniak, 1985, p. 128). Youth have to learn to work on their own tasks, surrounded by others working on theirs. When a youth cannot get the teacher's attention, he or she will look around for help from peers. The instrumental basis for a new peer relationship often extends out to become more personal, but almost always stays respectful. One often observes joking, but never belittling.

Apprenticeship challenges—but also modulates—adolescents' sensitivity to be being evaluated, especially in public. When they feel they are in a safe setting, young people appear to value critical feedback from adults and peers as much or more as positive feedback. A young woman in a product design apprenticeship notes that "A couple of days ago, Alec [the designer with whom she is apprenticing] was here and I was freaking out because I wasn't on time for my deadline and he was like 'What do you think? We're going to stop everything for you?'

And I loved that because I know what he was saying was, 'You're great and you can do it'" (Daniel, 2007, p. 122).

For those youth who have come to believe that they are likely to fail at what they try—or that they themselves are failures—apprenticeship turns the concept on its head. The unsuccessful or partly successful effort goes with the territory, and can be evidence of growth—one is stretching, risking. An adult theater director tells the youth he is working with: "No one gives a damn if you fail. Don't be afraid to fail. If you fail, well, fail gloriously. Really fail. Put everything into it and make it a glorious failure" (Heath, 2000, p. 5).

By definition, being an apprentice means being on a long learning curve. The iterative nature of learning and production leads to frequent, low-stakes feedback. Over time, a young person may be providing help and feedback as often as he or she is receiving it. This complementarity changes the valence of the latter. The discomfort of exhibiting or talking publicly about one's work is coupled with visceral recognition that feedback strengthens a piece of work. After a "rough cut" screening of a documentary about the International Criminal Court, produced by youth through New York City's Educational Video Center, an audience member points out that "You talk about the idea starting in the nineteenth century, but then you fast forward to Nuremberg—it was confusing" (Wahl, 2006, p. 6). The production team may find the feedback provided through the screening to be a painful experience, but they also learn how important it is to the quality of the final product.

A Different Adult-Youth Relationship

Adult-youth relationships in apprenticeship are characterized by a sense of shared endeavor, or the sharing of an important activity, by a commitment to shared responsibility, and by processes of identification. Although these relationships are potent, in a developmental sense, they are also matter-of-fact. Youth may not be, and in many settings generally are not, treated as someone special. These relationships are also developmentally appropriate, in the sense of being calibrated by young people's growing skill and experience. Youth are afforded ownership and responsibility for the work at hand—as Rogoff (1994) puts it, both adult and youth are active—but within a reasoned framework. Adults know youth are learners but treat them *as if* they were engineers or theater artists or cabinet makers, knowing that some or many will not continue in that discipline beyond their apprenticeship

Adults as Exemplars

The adult in apprenticeship is authoritative, the embodiment of a discipline, and also an exemplar, modeling the practice, general behavior and affective commitment of one with that particular identity (i.e., scientist, dancer, filmmaker). A teaching artist on a mural-making project, observing that apprentices are taking a long time to settle down to work one day, picks up her brush and starts working on a section of the mural. The youth not surprisingly follow suit. A teaching artist with Artists for Humanity notes that she sometimes works on her own paintings alongside apprentices: "That way we are sharing passion for making art. It is during these moments, I think, that I make the most connection with the kids … [they see] that I'm doing what I love the best, and they're next to me and we can have these natural conversations" (Truong, p.c., December 8, 2006).

In the course of work or in response to specific questions, mentors talk about what it is like to work in a field, in effect to make a home in it. A young woman apprenticing in a fifth-grade classroom asks the teacher how she knew she wanted to do this work, and how she manages to feel good about it. The teacher responds that "[her commitment is reconfirmed] every day that I can reach a kid, when I can do that it is worth it" (Esme, p.c., November 26, 2007). One day an ASM photography mentor arrives at the apprenticeship from a shoot. This leads to a discussion of how one becomes a professional photographer, and the choices made along the way. At one point a teaching artist with New York City's Roundabout Theater must take a 10-week leave because she has been cast in a Yale Repertory Theater production. She brings her "renewed artistry" with her upon returning to her teaching work (Roundabout Education Report, 2005–2006, p. 10).

The adult has a kind of dual identity for youth. Another teaching artist with Roundabout puts it this way: "I know I am a teacher to the youth [in student production workshop] but I still want to be an artist there, I still want to have the flexibility that artists have, the joy in my work, the fun …" (Keith, p.c., April 19, 2007). The very fact that the mentor is a working professional, one who started out where youth are, and is living the difficulties and rewards of the work, helps break through whatever skepticism youth might have of adults. A painting teaching artist notes that youth "get excited when I am in a show—it is very sweet—they also see that I have my own life as an artist; that completely changes what they hear when I talk about art" (Truong, p.c., December 8, 2006).

Youth Ownership, But Reasoned

Adults recognize and draw on what apprentices bring in ways sensitive to their relative inexperience. An ASM photography mentor notes of her co-mentor that "he has control of things but he is always willing to go in different directions when the apprentices want to." In a dance apprenticeship, the mentors incorporate choreographic materials drawn from ethnic and national dances brought in by the students themselves. An art mentor steps back during a peer critique session, letting the group arrive at a helpful, specific critique, knowing that at some point an apprentices will get to the heart of what still needs to be worked on. The founder of a boat building apprenticeship notes that from the first day the staff "make it very clear that the shop is theirs to use" (Green, p.c., June 13, 2006).

Yet the ownership afforded youth is reasoned. A potter notes of one young man that he could have "come up with a million ways to construct Quinn's wall project [but] my goal was to get him to discover these things on his own and to stop him from making silly and stupid mistakes" (Riordan, 2006, pp. 239–240). A Roundabout Theater teaching artist notes that adults have to strike a balance between affording youth a sense of ownership of the work and helping nurture a sense of integrity derived from joining a tradition and internalizing its standards (Keith, p.c., April 19, 2007). Moreover, young people's own internal standards can be harsher than any external ones, so "you have to teach them at the same time to be forgiving of themselves" (Fleming, p.c., February 16, 2007).

From One Adult to Another

Apprentices are treated as adults and expected to behave as such; in effect to understand and enact professionalism. As a dance instructor told her apprentices: "you have to be on time, you have to get ready to dance, you have to do things you do not like, there are a couple of exercises that are boring, but you have to do it as part of the job." One of the teaching artists for Artists for Humanity notes that "it's a fine balance. I am a supervisor, I do need to assert authority in certain instances, when their attendance is inconsistent, when they're shirking the work, because we do pay them. But it's our responsibility to help them know what it is to be a professional ... I want to be supportive of their creativity and to help them grow in terms of mature art work" (Truong, p.c., December 8, 2006).

Adult-youth dialogue is mature, about the work at hand, or about the discipline itself. In a print-making workshop, instructors talk with youth about the idea that there are no right or wrong answers in making art; it is about self-expression, sometimes about pushing boundaries, but disciplined (Thomas, 2007). An ASM apprentice notes of a photography mentor that he keeps it matter-of-fact: "He lets you know if you're not going to work, you're not going to get better at this." An ASM art mentor lets her apprentices know that "Not every idea is necessarily a great idea. That's really [about helping them develop] the aesthetic sense ..." She pushes apprentices to articulate their intent in work on a particular piece, and (to the extent possible) to explain their choices.

When feedback includes some judgment, it is provided in ways that do not stop young people in their tracks. In commenting on the role of adult mentors during the project design phase an astronomy apprentice notes that "we have our own ideas, they tell us yes or no, but if they say no, they say 'well, why don't you try this, or this isn't going to work because ...'" (McCarthy, 2002, p. 34). Mentors do not make a big deal about mistakes. As he is preparing to print, a print-making apprentice begins to cover the rag paper with blankets but forgets to first lay news print to absorb excess paint: "Robert [the instructor] without alarm or irritation, reminded him about the steps in the print-making process and the reasons for the steps. 'Remember that stuff [the paint that has been applied to the Plexiglas] goes through newsprint like crazy' ..." (Thomas, 2007, p. 787).

A Relationship Defined by Jointness

The fact that the relationship is task-focused, not youth-focused, fosters "joint-ness," allowing mentor and apprentice to leave differences in authority and power at the margins of their relationship. In discussing the joint staff-youth problem solving in a boat building apprenticeship, Green (p.c., June 22, 2006) notes, "We [the staff] really don't know the answers to a lot of the things we come up against and we have to figure them out." Moreover, "It is important for the kids to know that the adults don't have all the answers." Describing the adult-youth relation-ship at Youth Radio, Chavez and Soep (2005, p. 420) note that while youth and adults "may not see eye to eye in what they want for a story", their focus is still on the story, "what the want their work together to accomplish." The task focus also decenters the relationship, changing the valence of feedback from adults to youth. The task or project is in process, it is unfinished. Correcting and improv-ing it as the work proceeds is integral to the process.

Mentors' demands for respect and attention are focused on the work, the field or discipline itself, the community of adults and apprentices; in other words it is not personal. Authority derives from and inheres in the traditions, procedures, tools, and methods of a discipline, in other words its cumulative experience, not in the mentor per se. An ASM flamenco instructor notes that "I'm very clear that I'm both their instructor and their choreographer, and I reserve the right to change things according to what I see best." Yet, the instructor continues, "I also let them know that some people's abilities are stronger and I will never put you in a place that you are weakened because of where I put you."

The mentor expects commitment, even if for just the duration of the ap-prenticeship experience. On one occasion, after repeatedly going through a series of steps in class, a flamenco teaching artist tells the group that "you guys are going to go to sleep with this in your head." Yet this teaching artist backs off when necessary. On another occasion, she tells the group "Ladies, you're coming along nicely, but this turn is psyching you out. I can see it." The commitment expected of youth includes openness to the experience as a whole. The founder of a martial arts center tells an observer that if "the teacher's job is to provide challenges that you [the apprentice] would not provide yourself ... the student's job is to be open—open-hearted, open-minded—to receive that challenge, and to talk openly so that we can develop the trust that allows that vulnerability to be o.k." (Musick, 1999, p. 39).

As noted in chapter 1, mentors will, when necessary, "hold" the challenges and demands of the work for apprentices. That often means helping to get and keep apprentices focused. In a flamenco apprenticeship, the teaching artist talks with apprentices about using a few minutes at the beginning of the afternoon to "collect yourself, and that is not running around or talking to friends, its just collecting yourself to get ready to work." On a number of occasions in my ASM research, I observed mentors reminding apprentices about what they were working on that day. A filmmaking mentor notes that he periodically talks with apprentices about "the work in front of them," meaning what they still need to do on a particular project. Mentors also remind youthful apprentices to draw on experience: "You guys, remember when we had this problem editing the last film?" Instructors are lending apprentices their experience and even their approach to work.

Attending to Young People's Selves

The task orientation of apprenticeships sometimes leaves less time for generic relationship-building, discussion, and exploration of personal issues than might be found in less structured youth programs. At the same time, generous blocks of time allow for solid relationships to develop, for trust to build, and for the work and the social elements to go together without stress. Once apprentices begin to feel safe, their worries, struggles, and life questions do filter into apprenticeships, and there are many informal moments for incidental discussion that can range from the most personal issues to the most abstract, from family relationships to aspirations to political ideology. An ASM photography mentor notes that "one day—I cannot remember what started it—something came up about my parents, about my dad, and [suddenly] she said, 'Oh, I wish I knew my dad, I never met my dad.' We started talking about it. She felt I was someone she could trust and if I thought it [her experience] was interesting, maybe it was interesting." Reflecting on the personal support and help she provides youth in her studio, a graphic design mentor asks, "How can you not? We've become a kind of weird family" (Vicin, p.c., January 8, 2007).

In some settings conversation is ubiquitous and leads in almost any direction. An ASM mural instructor comments that "there are discussions that we have while we are working together that are very casual but at the same time intense in terms of the things we talk about. They could be political discussions, they could be discussions about art, and about human nature ... I think it has something to do with the work that you are doing and you kind of concentrate on something and you kind of just forget who you are talking to ... I really cherish those conversations."

Attending to Vulnerability, But Indirectly

For those youth who carry a range of vulnerabilities into adolescence, adult-youth relationships in apprenticeship provide a corrective experience without adding to the labeling and categorizing that often contribute to the burden of vulnerability. Adults are not unaware of who youth are, the vulnerabilities and stresses in some youths' lives, the fact that some have received little adult attention and little recognition as individuals. Simply coming to know apprentices as individuals, and developing relationships with them leads to some sense of responsibility. In discussing one youth, an instructor tells this author, "He has called himself stupid in the past and I said 'Don't ever say that in front of me again."" Instructors are willing and able to help with personal struggles and support needs. But they do so incidentally and, one might say, indirectly.

While instructors are on youths' side, and may view their role in part as helping strengthen youths' belief in themselves, they do not see it as their mission to save, validate, lecture to, socialize, re-parent, or reform youth, and are not inclined to let the difficulties in youths' lives excuse them from the responsibilities of the work at hand. Reflecting on her apprentices' hunger to be both taken seriously and held accountable, the director of Riverz Edge Arts (Woonsocket, Rhode Island) notes that "these kids' lives are full of material for excuses, but you can't coddle that; then they'll always be making excuses" (Novello, p.c., July 6, 2007). An ASM instructor notes of the youth he works with, "they need something like, 'okay, here are your limits, but I am cool with the way you are.'"

Discourse associated with the work at hand sometimes indirectly addresses youths' sense of their lives. For example, a sculpture instructor tries to respond to young people's frustration with their busts by referring to the "voices in our head" that sometimes say "oh God, this is so ugly, I did such a bad job" and to encourage the apprentices by saying that "you can change the voices" and that they should say to themselves "this is sculpture, we're just making things and I'm trying ... when you're kinder to yourself, you'll be kinder to your art" (McPhail, Pierson, Goodman, & Bunge Noffke, 2004, p. 475).

II
Cases

3

Apprenticeship in the Framework of High School Reform

From the standpoint of the child, the great waste in the school comes from his inability to utilize the experiences he gets outside the school in any complete and free way within the school itself; while on the other hand he is unable to apply in daily life what he is learning at school. That is the isolation of the school—its isolation from life.

John Dewey (1902/1990, p. 75)

I have always thought it's hysterical that inside the school building we work really hard to make lessons that look and feel real, when all the while the real world is going on outside—and it's filled with history, social issues, work issues, scientific exploration, math, writing, technology and everything else.

Dennis Littky (2004, p. 113), co-founder, The MET.

Apprenticeship and schooling are in many respects two inherently opposed approaches to teaching, learning, and socialization. For instance, in school young people tend to be passive learners, with little control over what, how or where they will learn. Tasks are abstract, fragmented and short-term and work is individual. In apprenticeship young people are active learners with a measure of control over and a sense of ownership of their work. Tasks are embedded, relatively more concrete, often extended and involve joint effort. In school, young people are isolated from more experienced learners; in apprenticeship they are connected to them. In school, teachers monopolize teaching; in apprenticeship it is distributed. In school, teachers tend to hide what they know and can do; in apprenticeship they demonstrate it. In school young people work on many things, but superficially; in apprenticeship on a few things, but in depth.

This set of contrasts might seem to favor apprenticeship. Yet historically schooling arose for apparently good reasons, just as youth apprenticeship declined for many of the same reasons (Timmons, 1988). It is ironic, then, that apprenticeship (or apprenticeship-like learning) is now being proposed as an element in broader efforts to re-think and re-vitalize high school for millions of youth for whom schooling has become a discouraging experience. In this chapter, I describe the historical decline in apprenticeship and gradual growth in high school as a universal experience; discuss why and how high school has proved a poor fit for some youth; and illustrate through four case studies the perhaps surprising role of apprenticeship in efforts to re-think high school to make it more relevant and engaging.

The Decline of Youth Apprenticeship

As with schooling, there is historical irony in arguing for the re-introduction of apprenticeship into adolescence itself. For centuries it was a defining feature of the second decade of life. In pre-industrial Europe a youth would apprentice to a master of some craft or trade for a period of seven years, emerge as a journeyman, and be inducted into the guild that controlled practice in that craft or trade. Passage from apprentice to journeyman typically required production of a "masterpiece," a culminating product that required the range of skills of that trade or discipline.[1] In addition to specific skills, apprenticeship contracts often stipulated that the apprentice was to be taught some business skills (e.g., how to negotiate prices) as well as basic literacy and numeracy. Some masters took it upon themselves to foster moral principles and precepts to live by and a sense of place in the world.

Apprenticeship was not available to all youth, especially girls, and was not always a positive experience. Masters were sometimes slow to share their knowledge, and some were cruel. Indigent youth, placed through parish authorities, were frequently exploited in "blind alley" occupations (Sybolt, 1917). A sizable minority of apprentices never finished their terms (Hannawalt, 1993). Still, for many youth apprenticeship provided a "safe passage from childhood to adulthood in psychological, social and economic ways" (Rorabaugh, 1986, p. vii).

The European apprenticeship model was transplanted to the American colonies, but would not acquire the important role that it had held for European youth. Monopolistic craft guilds never took hold in the American context. A host of factors chipped away at apprenticeship as an institution: ideas such as democracy and equality; the expansion of schooling; social and economic instability, contributing to a fluctuating demand for labor; immigration, population mobility and, not least, changing technologies and patterns of production. Apprenticeship even became entangled in efforts to end slavery (and indenture more generally). In the pre-Civil War period a few of the states committed to ending slavery passed statutes requiring former slaves to go through a period of "apprenticeship" to their former masters. (After the war southern states also tried, but were not permitted, to use apprenticeship statutes to maintain control over former slaves; Douglas, 1921).

Over time, master craftsmen lost control of both entry into specific trades and the knowledge that was so valuable to them. Definitions of master, journeyman, and apprentice became more fluid (Laurie, 1997). New forms of apprenticeship did appear, for example, in engineering, iron ship building and boilermaking (Aldrich, 1999). But production was gradually becoming specialized and mechanized and craftsmanship, in all its meanings, coming to be seen as less important than efficiency.[2] The growing use of machines also had the perverse effect of devaluing physical, and especially hand, work (Rorabaugh, 1986). In the printing trade, for instance, steam-powered presses began to replace hand presses. As work shifted to factories, it was further fragmented into specialized tasks. The skills of many factory jobs could be learned "in the space of a few days or at most a few weeks" (Douglas, 1921, p. 109).

The emerging industrial economy had a complex effect on the lives of youth. Their contribution to the family economy remained important, but that sometimes meant seeking work far from home. Factories hired and cast out young workers with impunity, and few factory owners felt any responsibility to prepare them for the future. By the turn of the century, schools were beginning to claim that social role, and compulsory schooling laws were pulling more children and youth out of the labor market. Although schooling represented a new pathway into the workforce, and into such new occupations as clerking, accounting and teaching (Rorabaugh, 1986), most urban working-class youth left school before eighth grade and embarked on a series of short-term, dead-end jobs that rarely led to more skilled work. Douglas (1921, p. 107) noted that "[Ralph Waldo] Emerson himself would not have put much faith in the quality of self-reliance caused by carrying parcels, tending a cotton loom, stitching button holes, canning oysters, rolling cigarettes and opening doors." The majority of urban youth experienced a long period of churning and flux between leaving school and settling down (Modell, Furstenberg, & Hershberg, 1981).

The Century of the High School

By the first decades of the 20th century, formal apprenticeship had virtually disappeared as a feature of youth in the United States. Trade unions, and to a lesser extent employers, took control of apprenticeship, and the age of entry rose to 18 or 19, removing it from middle adolescence.[3] High school would gradually take its place as the defining institution of this age period, working reasonably well for some youth, not well for many others. Among other things, schooling shifted the locus of learning and socialization away from settings in which young people were "guided by adults to whom they were closely attached and from activities of significance in every day life" (Hymel, Comfort, Schonert-Reichl, & McDonald, 1996, p. 317). As Dewey put it (1902, p. 12) schools were "the one place in the world where it is most difficult to get experience."

Between 1890 and 1920 there were a variety of efforts to develop models of secondary schooling that prepared youth for work. These included manual training high schools and trade schools. The latter in particular were viewed as a substitute for apprenticeship in such trades as bricklaying, plastering, plumbing, carpentry, stone cutting, and machining. Most were private institutions with modest public support and they never took hold, in part because responsibility for them was never made clear, in part because they were deemed not real enough: "The [trade] school is essentially static, there is an air of business unreality about the work carried on… Try as teachers and students may, the feeling that they are playing at work rather than working is almost inescapable" (Douglas, 1921, p. 195).

Beyond their immediate limitations, such efforts failed to influence the development of high school as an institution. Unlike most European countries, which evolved differentiated secondary education systems with explicit structures for sorting youth along the way, the United States opted for a common high school experience, shaped by the ideals of equal educational opportunity and individual choice (LeTendre, Hofer, & Shimizu, 2003). Educators who tried to introduce more differentiated approaches found their work (sometimes unfairly) linked to the ideas of social Darwinists such as David Snedden and Charles Prosser, who believed it a waste of time and resources to expose the majority of youth to an academic education (Hyslop-Margison, 2001). In 1913 E. R. Cooley, the Illinois state school superintendent, introduced legislation to create a differentiated high school structure in Illinois, with a strong technical-vocational component modeled after that he had observed in a trip to Europe. He was rebuffed by teachers, educational reformers and organized labor, on the grounds that such a differentiated system was anti-democratic and would perpetuate class distinctions (Gittens, 1985). Dewey (1916, p. 318) argued that a differentiated high school system was not only likely to perpetuate social inequality and conflict but to promote "the feudal dogma of social predestination."

The comprehensive high school that emerged instead was designed "to accommodate a broad range of students" (LeTendre et al., 2003, p. 52). A core academic curriculum was loosely intended to prepare youth for college or work. Academic and vocational strands of schooling were separated both conceptually and structurally and would remain so throughout the century. Vocational education emerged as a second-tier, remedial track for students deemed less intellectually able, confirming the fears of those who had argued against a differentiated secondary education system.

By the mid-1920s the majority of youth were attending high school, a dramatic increase over a period of just two decades. By the late 1930s, with high schools becoming a last resort for unemployed youth, high school enrollment was nearly universal. Yet even as high school was becoming the norm, educators were already struggling with questions of relevance. The curriculum, adapted from the European "classical humanist" model, took on a life of its own (Kliebard, 1985). Vocational education remained a conundrum and vocational educators struggled for both an identity and a place in the school system. The idea that preparation for the world of work should be part of the high school experience for all or most youth would neither be embraced nor completely repudiated (Hyslop-Margison, 2001).

The ideal of high school as a vehicle for working-class youth to achieve their aspirations proved a myth for the majority of such youth. While the American school system permitted aspirations, it was mostly designed to sort children and youth (Timmons, 1988). The sorting that was done explicitly in Europe was simply done implicitly in the United States. Because it contradicted the ideals of the education system (and, moreover lacked transparency and logic), it led to confusion about purpose among those in the heterogeneous middle and to discouragement and a sense of stigma among those on lower tracks. The general academic track became little more than a holding place for millions of youth, leading neither to college nor vocation. For those moved to a lower track (a placement that was made as early as first grade for some children), it was difficult to get back to a higher one. Moreover, sorting took place at many levels of the school system. High schools in poor neighborhoods typically had fewer resources, fewer qualified teachers and a more restricted curriculum. The result was that, as a group, working class children had systematically less "opportunity to learn" (LeTendre et al., 2003, p. 79).

By the 1950s the consequences of what critics would later describe as mis-education were becoming entwined with a larger pattern of social, economic and cultural exclusion among youth growing up in an increasingly neglected and isolated central city. Such youth's lives were—as they continue to be—marked by a restriction of experience and limited exposure to the adult world outside their communities. As Cloward and Ohlin (1960) framed it, inner-city youth were growing up outside the opportunity structure of American society. Moreover, as Kenneth Clark (1964) argued, social forces ultimately had psychological consequences. Persistently damaging experiences in school and outside of it constituted a continuous assault on the selves of many urban, especially minority, youth.

The Re-Emergence of Apprenticeship

Apprenticeship would, surprisingly, re-appear in the late 1980s, precisely in response to efforts to re-think social arrangements for the large numbers of youths struggling, with little or no support from societal institutions, to find a pathway through adolescence to whatever came next. If such youths' high school experiences led nowhere in particular, their early labor market experience was marked by a series of unconnected low-level jobs punctuated by long periods of unemployment (Gregson, 1995). The William T. Grant Foundation sponsored a commission to identify new approaches to meeting the needs of some ten million youth that it called "the forgotten half," and youth apprenticeship was included among the resulting proposals (William T. Grant Foundation, 1988).

In 1990 Stephen Hamilton published *Apprenticeship for Adulthood*, a seminal book that broke through the frozen academic-vocational debate and set the tone for a decade of experimentation. Hamilton argued that the key to better meeting the needs of many—if not most—youth lay not in high school classrooms but in work-like learning and socialization experiences outside school walls, whether in workplaces or other settings. Hamilton argued for a balanced approach to such experiences, not too vocational nor too narrowly focused on the highest risk youth; and for youth to be in "constructively ambiguous roles as, simultaneously, workers with real responsibilities and learners" (p. 16). He noted also that creating meaningful apprenticeship experiences—and explicit pathways—could not be done piecemeal. It required creation of a formal system with high schools, businesses, community colleges and government working closely together.

Hamilton's work, along with that of a small group of like-minded researchers, some of whom looked to Europe and especially to Germany for inspiration, stimulated a debate about the potential value of a vocationally oriented youth apprenticeship system in the United States (see, e.g., Rosenbaum, 1992; Bailey, 1993; Hamilton, 1990; Kantor, 1994; Gregson, 1995). Debate concerned how trade-specific and generally how work-like youth apprenticeship should be; whether it could escape the stigma historically attached to vocational education; and whether it was realistic to expect businesses and trade unions to join school systems as genuine partners in youth development, given the short-term, profit-maximizing mentality of the former and the narrow, often parochial orientation of the latter.

Observers worried simultaneously that youth apprenticeship opportunities would exclude minority youth (just as registered apprenticeships excluded minorities) and that apprenticeship would become a new means for sidetracking them. Kantor (1994, p. 456), for instance, argued that "the introduction of work-oriented programs [including apprenticeship had] functioned over the years to fragment the curriculum and deepen the division between college-bound and non-college bound students." While youth advocates worried that businesses might exploit youth rather than teach them, businesses worried that they might invest in young people who would work for a year or two and leave, while unions worried that youth apprenticeship would create a new workforce of lower wage skilled workers.

Beyond these issues, the possibility of developing a vocationally oriented youth apprenticeship system was fundamentally constrained by the structure of the American school system. In countries such as Germany and Japan differentiated education, with some youth in technical tracks, was embedded in the culture (LeTendre et al., 2003). It was accepted by parents and educators as an appropriate way to meet young people's needs. Stakeholders believed, moreover, that specialization led to mastery. (Debate focused more on how early to require youth and their parents to choose a course of study, and how easily to permit switching.)[4] American parents—with the complicity of educators who could not or would not be honest with them—were far more reluctant to believe that a young person might be better suited for a technical education, beginning in high school. For this and other reasons (not least the persistent perception of it as a dumping ground) the number of youth concentrating in vocational/technical education, the likeliest base for apprenticeship, was steadily declining.

Conceptual and practical obstacles to youth apprenticeship were partially countered by political and business leaders' worry about the declining economic competitiveness of the United States in relation to those countries with strong vocational/technical education systems, and in which youth were explicitly prepared for the workplace (in other words those countries that some academic perceived to be unrealistic models for the United States). In his first State of the Union Address, President Clinton proposed spending a billion dollars over four years to dramatically expand youth apprenticeship. Governors discussed the idea at their national meetings, as did the Council of Chief State School Officers (a group of whom traveled to Germany, Denmark, and Sweden to learn about those countries' youth education and training systems).

During the 1990s youth apprenticeship was incorporated into numerous efforts to re-conceptualize vocational education and strengthen school to work pathways. Efforts had been underway since the late 1980s to create a "new vocationalism": to develop models that better integrated academic and vocational curricula, making the former more relevant and the latter both deeper and broader; to create work-based learning experiences, or at least to upgrade the technological resources of vocational education classrooms for a new economy; and to create new pathways from high school to high skill jobs and to technical community college. In this context youth apprenticeship was viewed as a kind of bridge, between types of learning experiences, school and workplace, and the high school and post-high school years. A small group of vocational education critical theorists promoted youth apprenticeship as "potentially transformative," uncovering problematic dimensions of school and work settings and, potentially, reinvigorating both (Gregson, 1995, p. 9).

Two pieces of federal legislation—the re-authorized Perkins Vocational Education Act of 1990 and the historic (but ultimately short-lived) School To Work Opportunity Act of 1994—served as a spur for a series of local experiments in workplace-based learning, some of which included youth apprenticeship.[5] In 1992 the U.S. Department of Labor initiated the School-to-Work/Youth Apprenticeship Demonstration, with 15 grantees around the country (Corson & Silverberg, 1994). During this same period Arkansas, Georgia, Maine, Oregon, and Wisconsin initiated their own youth apprenticeship programs. These typically involved partnerships among high schools, community colleges, and businesses, in fields thought to be most relevant to the state economy. In and around the city of Binghamton, New York, Stephen and Mary Hamilton (1993) were also working through a variety of design and implementation issues in a local demonstration that received attention in both the press and academic literature.

Findings from these first efforts to renew apprenticeship were mixed, would prove somewhat confounding, but suggested that it was worth working through the challenges (Johnson, 1997; Steinberg, 1998; Bailey, Hughes, & Moore, 2004). Workplaces were not inherently strong learning settings. Work experiences could be developmentally powerful but such experiences were not always deep enough. Workplace mentors had to be deliberately prepared—and sometimes reminded—to attend to youth learning needs. Knowledge and skill elements and progression needed to be made explicit. When youth lacked basic math, science, or other knowledge needed for an apprenticeship, it was not clear who should be responsible for helping them acquire it. In many instances mechanisms for communication between school staff and workplace mentors were ill defined.

Apprenticeship experience did lead some youth into the occupation at hand, typically through continued preparation in a technical college. But in urban contexts especially, apprenticeships proved to have more broadly developmental than specifically vocational value. Even when youth did not end up entering the vocational arena in which they had apprenticed, they acquired new cognitive and social skills, and new dispositions seen to be helpful to future schooling or work. The experience led at least some youth to re-commit to school. At the same time, youth in urban contexts also reported preferring even middling workplace experiences to those at school, noting that in the workplace people treated them with respect, assumed that they wanted to learn, assumed that they would regulate their own behavior and that they would seek help when they needed it. Youth valued the opportunity to get to know and work alongside adults, and the "real-ness" of the workplace setting (Olson, 1997; Steinberg & Almeida, 1998). Some youth made connections that compensated for their lack of access to informal job networks (Kantor, 1994).

Collectively, the findings from renewed apprenticeship experiments—especially Wisconsin's program—raised questions about the prevailing assumption among high school educators that if a young person did not identify a clear vocational interest it was better to keep him or her on a general, vaguely academic track (Phelps et al., 1999; Bailey et al., 2004). The findings also contradicted the fundamental assumption that high school should continue to be about preparing all youth for a four-year college. Findings from Wisconsin's program, for instance, indicated that integrating technical and academic learning did not deflect youth from higher education and had positive effects on persistence once youth embarked on a post-secondary program (Phelps et al., 1999).

Apprenticeship in the Current Context of High School Reform

By the turn of the 21st century, some educators had come to see the vocational education and school-to-work problems as part of a broader problem with high school as an institution. This concern has led to a decade of high school "redesign" efforts, focused in varying measures on content, pedagogy and organization and now, finally, just beginning to question basic assumptions, especially the idea that the goal of high school should be to prepare all or most youth for a four year college. While efforts to renew vocational education and strengthen school to work connections have continued, they have in some instances been subsumed into this broader reform movement. The consequences for youth apprenticeship have been varied. In some settings it (along with other elements of real world learning) has been grafted onto high school programs that have otherwise changed little. In other settings it has been part of a more fundamental re-design; and in a handful of cases it has served as a conceptual and practical lynchpin.

The Criticism of High School

As in every decade since the 1950s, urban and a growing number of suburban high schools have been criticized in recent years for being impersonal, fragmented, and alienating settings, marked by mediocrity and bled of meaning for many participating youth. A recent report by the National Academy of Sciences notes that urban high schools lose about half their students before graduation, and that the majority of youth who do not drop out are "chronically disengaged ... inattentive, exert little effort, do not complete tasks" (Stipek et al., 2004, pp. 18, 19, 101). Working-class youth describe a flattened curriculum that makes few demands on their minds and seems unrelated to their lives. Complex disciplinary knowledge and practice are over-simplified, reduced to textbook formats. Assignments are watered down. One close observer of high schools says that "When you look at the assignments these kids get, it is just appalling. A course may be labeled college preparatory English. But if the kids get more than three paragraph-long assignments it is unusual" (Haycock, cited in Arenson, 2007, p. A21). Short blocks of time for each class make it hard for teachers to formulate deep, sustained learning projects, and make it difficult for teachers to attend individually to their students—to listen to questions, concerns, or ideas (Steinberg, Sawanson, Knobloch, & Bobowick, 2001).

Youth report that they cannot make sense of school as a developmental setting (McDonald & Marsh, 2004). The majority of youth report that they are simply "going through the motions" (Olson, 1997, p. 14). Youth do not know why they are asked to work on certain tasks or learn what they are asked to learn, nor how tasks and subject matter relate to their lives or likely futures. They do know that they are being asked to attend to institutional agendas, not their own. They may or may not try to figure out and enact the language, responses, behaviors teachers are asking for. As they find it difficult to guess what teachers want, young people guard what they say or write. They rarely get to work on and therefore "find out what they [themselves] think" (Greene, 1995, p. 54). Passive, teacher dependent learning undermines "development of confidence in one's own sense making and problem-solving abilities" (Berryman, 1995, p. 193).

The assessment structure of high school—with learning, effort and growth processes reduced to single letters or numbers, and acquiring meaning primarily in social comparison—does not work for the majority of urban youth. Young people are set against each other in a competition which requires significant numbers of youth to feel like failures. Both the temporal structure of school and the over-arching approach to assessment make it more difficult for teachers and youth to develop strong relationships, and may be one reason that the majority of high school students "do not believe that their teachers either know or care about them" (Almeida & Steinberg, 2001, p. x). Perversely, the more students struggle academically and/or disengage, the less attention and support they get from school staff (Thomas, 2007).

School learning has been described as inert and "encapsulated" (Engestrom, 1991). Schools lack the connection to the larger world needed to allow young people to use or "activate" the knowledge they are acquiring; and in a complementary vein schools make little effort to identify let alone link youth to knowledge resources outside the standardized curriculum. Given the enormous vocational consequences of choices made in high school, as an institution it is strangely removed from and largely unconnected to the world of work (Grubb, 1995).[6] A young person interested in becoming an artist or an engineer will rarely have experiences in school that give him or her a concrete sense of the tasks and daily work of those careers.

The majority of teachers and guidance counselors continue to talk about vocational-technical education in a deprecating way, despite the facts that over half of students are on a general (i.e., non-college) track and only about 20% of those entering ninth grade will earn a four-year college degree. Guidance counselors rarely have enough knowledge of individual youth to help them plan next steps and anyway often lack up-to-date information on the local job market (Olson, 1997). In a broader vein, neither counselors nor teachers nor schools as a whole seem to know how to support the personal exploration, shifting about, commitment and re-commitment that underlie identity work (Kroger, 1996).

Re-Thinking High School

These criticisms have led to a strong sense among some stakeholders that it is time to re-think the nature and organization, if not the purpose, of high school. In this context, apprenticeship is playing two modest roles, one figurative and the other literal. In the former capacity, apprenticeship has been used as both a foil for schooling and a model for re-imagining learning in high school. Lave (1996, p. 150) writes, for instance, that "the informal practices through which learning occurs in apprenticeship are so powerful and robust that this raises questions about the efficacy of standard formal educational practices in schools." Hatano and Oura (2003, p. 26) observe that "unlike in school settings, novices [in apprenticeship-like settings] are not expected to solve problems all by themselves." Gardner (1991, p. 125) argues that "the best chance for an education leading to understanding lies in the melding of certain features of apprenticeships with certain aspects of schools...."

Writers have translated the attributes of apprenticeship into equivalent school-based terms. They have argued for learning to be deeper rather than broader. They have sought to infuse curricula with more meaning for students, by organizing it around longer-term projects that require planning, team-work and application of knowledge to "real world" tasks and problems, ones that are genuinely unfinished, and for which there are many possible solutions. They have argued that learning should be based in "complex, realistic and relevant environments" (deKock, Sleegers, & Voeten, 2004, p. 146), and therefore have urged high school educators to look outside the school building for curriculum and learning experiences. As Castellano, Stringfield, and Stone (2003, p. 245) put it, "Communities abound with work and learning opportunities, and these have power to transform the entire curriculum." Reformers have argued for continuous, low-stakes assessment, linked directly to learning projects and activities; and for achievement itself to be re-conceptualized as more fluid, partial and iterative. As Meier (2006, p. 74) notes, young people "must see that adults care about getting things right for reasons beyond scores."

Reformers have argued also for learning in high school to be less teacher driven and more genuinely participatory; and for new teacher roles, to include facilitating, demonstrating, modeling, and encouraging reflection. They have urged educators to ask themselves what professionals engaged in particular disciplines do in their daily work—what procedures and tools they use, what kinds of observations and inferences they make, etc.—and use that as a basis for the design of learning. One educator argues for the importance of simple exposure to adults skilled in different fields: "it does not matter what the adults are expert in ... if it's carpentry or sewing or cooking ... or physics or chemistry ... adolescents need to experience the diversity of human work and human knowledge that only a variety of experts can provide" (Garzzini, cited in Kahn, 2006, p. 20). It has even been suggested that high schools should function more like traditional apprenticeship guilds, "an association dedicated to excellence in some particular human endeavor, some particular practice, such as music, sport or mathematics" (Strike, 2004, p. 225).

Incorporating Apprenticeship: Different Purposes and Approaches

In actual practice, apprenticeship continues to occupy only a very modest place in high school education in the United States. With one prominent exception, Wisconsin's Youth Apprenticeship Program, no city, county, or state school systems have incorporated it into their overall high school structure. Rather, it is an idiosyncratic presence in a handful of schools of many types—multi-industry vocational campuses, single focus vocational high schools, regional career/technical education centers, large comprehensive high schools with embedded career or occupational academies or similar specialized programs, and the new "small" high schools, one-third to one-half of which have occupational or disciplinary themes.[7]

Some high schools incorporate apprenticeship in a clearly vocational framework. Youth make a commitment, even if tentative, to an occupational area—biotechnology, information technology, printing or graphic arts, automotive, health care, or some other. They might spend from 10 to 15 hours a week in a workplace, for one or two years, taking complementary technical coursework at the high school or a local community college. Apprentices in some fields are supported to continue in their chosen field after graduation whether in college or work, with high school pathways connected to subsequent ones.

Other high schools incorporate apprenticeship not as preparation for a specific profession or skilled trade but as a platform for very different kinds of learning experiences than are available in school.[8] Apprenticeship may be designed to ground, round out and extend students' other learning experiences; to stimulate and ground thinking about college; and/or to foster real-world skills. Sponsoring high schools nonetheless emphasize the value of exposure to particular occupations and types of workplaces, giving youth a concrete sense of the variety of work, what different jobs entail and how careers evolve, and a measure of self-knowledge in relation to personal strengths, limitations, preferences, and dislikes.

In whichever context—more vocational in purpose or less so—apprenticeship might be integrated with the larger high school experience a lot, a little or not at all. In a handful of schools "work and classroom are each a half of whole" (Crary, p.c., December 7, 2007). In the Big Picture schools, described shortly, young people's apprenticeship experiences organize much of the learning in the school. More commonly, apprenticeships will influence curriculum and pedagogy (of technical classes especially) to some degree, but that still depends on whether apprenticeships are concentrated in one field or spread out across many. The external partners of themed high schools may have their own after-school and/ or summer apprenticeship programs, which serve to extend their school-based work for those youth who can participate.

Apprenticeship in a Vocational Context

Vocational education (now often called career and technical education) has, finally, begun to gain a measure of respect, or least to be dismissed less quickly as a model and idea. Provided through a wide range of school structures, it has been revived by its embrace of new career fields such as biotechnology/bioscience, computer- and design-related disciplines, and by the revised conceptual foundation in the so-called new vocationalism. This foundation envisions a broad range of youth participating in programs that cross-cut high school, college, and career, in which learning is personalized yet embedded in a community of practice including peers, teachers and work site supervisors, and in which there is plentiful hands on experience in different settings (Ryken, 2002, p. 23). It assumes also a narrowed distance between academic and technical education, with the two feeding and reinforcing each other. For instance, math, science, and English requirements for youth on technical tracks have already increased, with applied courses in these areas adding conceptual material (Stone & Aliaga, 2005).

Apprenticeship is a good fit with this broader conceptualization of vocational education, especially as an extension of the century-old model of school-based shops, studios, labs, and kitchens. In theory, programs without apprenticeships can create work-like learning conditions. In some fields youth can work on the types of tasks and with the types of equipment they would encounter in the workplace. In many others, though, it is not possible. A young man apprenticing with materials engineers for a local transit authority, learning to monitor and diagnose stress on tracks and equipment, simply could not find this experience in school. With exceptions (see, e.g., Gentry, Rizza, Peters, & Hu, 2005), school-based instructors are likely to be professional teachers, not working professionals. Resource constraints have prevented school-based programs from keeping up with changes in practice and technology in various industries. Not least it is very difficult to re-create the pressures, problems, unpredictability, and general dynamics of work settings inside a school. Being in the workplace day in and day out builds a store of practical knowledge that cannot be acquired any other way (Kraus, p.c., January 28, 2008).

Vocational/technical education programs are, in fact, increasingly including a year or more of apprenticeship in their curricula. Estimates vary, in part due to differences in definition, but it appears that anywhere from 15% to 25% of youth concentrating in vocational/technical education have a semester or more of serious, apprenticeship-like experience in work settings (Stone & Aliaga, 2005). Some apprenticeships focus on longstanding and emerging industrial trades, including automotive maintenance and repair, sheet metal work, welding, machining, HVAC (heating, ventilation and cooling), electro-mechanics, industrial drafting, printing and less commonly carpentry; some on relatively newer fields such as criminal justice/forensic sciences, telecommunications, financial services and especially the rapidly growing fields of information technology, biotechnology/bioscience, graphic design, and health care/health sciences.

Apprenticeship experiences vary in breadth and therefore in relative emphasis on exposure to a field as a whole. In drafting and design, for instance, apprentices might focus on mechanical, engineering or architectural specializations or learn something about all three. In programs focused on the health professions, students might apprentice in specific roles such as nursing, diagnostic imaging, pharmacy, physical or occupational therapy. Or they may rotate through stations in a hospital or outpatient setting. Youth enrolled in FACES for the Future, a partnership between Oakland's Children's Hospital (California) and six area high schools, participate in a three-year sequence that includes applied science classes, a series of eight- week "clinical rotations" in different hospital departments, and an extended clerkship (an in depth, paid experience in one specialty). Participants receive high school credits for the clinical work in the hospital or its outpatient clinics.

CASES

A Local Partnership: Berkeley Biotechnology Education Inc.

One example of a vocational initiative in a newer field, incorporating apprenticeship in a key role, is Berkeley Biotechnology Education Inc (BBEI), a partnership between two Berkeley (California) area high schools, a group of local corporations (primarily drug and biotechnology companies), academic and government labs, and a local community college.[9] The BBEI program includes four specialized, lab-based high school courses during the junior and senior years, a summer-long apprenticeship between those two years, and a year of focused community college coursework accompanied by a second apprenticeship experience. Apprenticeships are shaped in part by personalized learning plans and explicit performance objectives. They are also guided to differing degrees by industry skill standards. Apprentices meet weekly in groups to reflect and process the experience. The full three-year program leads to an accelerated AS (associate of science) degree in bioscience or biotechnology.

Within BBEI apprenticeship is viewed as a key component of an integrated whole, in which "knowledge and experience in one component take on value and new meaning when connected with activities in other components" (Ryken, 2001, p. 46).[10] The basic lab skills acquired in high school biotechnology courses make the apprenticeship experience more fruitful. It in turn gives more meaning to theoretical science classes in microbiology in high school, both of which provide a strong foundation for the year-long community college and apprenticeship experience. When knowledgeable adults engage youth in more than one context it allows for skills to grow from different sources. Young people have multiple opportunities—and different kinds of opportunities—to acquire a particular skill or master a particular concept.

Youth learn for the first time in the high school laboratory all the procedures and tools they will use again on a regular basis in apprenticeship: scientific notation, pipetting, streaking, sterile/aseptic techniques, plating, how to use a spectrophometer, a hemocytomter, how to do cell count, and so forth. Acquiring lab skills not surprisingly makes young people want to use them. The interplay in this model between ideas and procedures, content, and tools seems to deepen each. As one mentor describes it, "The tools [sometimes] give you a way back to the content."

Within the relatively defined field of bioscience, apprenticeships vary in tenor and pace. Youth have worked on such activities as fermentation production, toxicology testing for new pharmaceuticals, and plant genetic engineering. They have worked in quality control departments and purification departments. One young woman worked in a lab developing bioengineered blood clotting factors for people with hemophilia. Some work is more dramatic, other work more mundane but still critical to a particular problem or process. Time pressures are greater in production facilities than in research laboratories, and mentors sometimes harder to pin down. Across the board, young people spend time learning to document their procedures and findings accurately and in detail—this is pounded in until it becomes second nature. One youth points out that "GLPs [good laboratory practices] are long and boring, but they are essential in making sure the rack studies go smoothly" (Ryken, 2001, p. 71).

Given the design of BBEI, as a deliberately complementary and in some places interlocking set of experiences, it is difficult to separate out the effects of apprenticeship as such. Young people bring different personal goals and tasks to the program, use it and benefit from it in different ways. For some it reinforces and enables plans, for others it alters them. Some youth discover that they want to go directly into the labor force, others that they need much more education to achieve their goals.

In the context of this larger developmental process, apprenticeship teaches both skills and lessons. It creates "occasions where students confront ideas, forms, procedures, relationships and feelings, and make sense of their presence in the workplace …" (Ryken 2001, p. 78). Young people learn when, how, and of whom to ask questions, and, more generally, that these are settings designed for asking questions. They learn to appreciate knowledge as fluid not fixed. Young people report being struck by one-on-one attention from their mentors, the very fact that a mentor is focused on them. They seemingly enjoy the mixture of positive feedback and critique that goes with the work. Youth are proud also of being relied on, of handling important experiments, meeting difficult deadlines. One young man describes a "crunch" in which he and a supervisor had to work urgently to prepare plants for a client's research: "It was just me and my supervisor that pulled it off—768 plants got sent to the field for studies. Each plant went through our hands as we genetically transformed them" (Ryken, 2001, p. 135).

BBEI illustrates the ways in which young people's workplace experiences can filter into their school lives and influence educational practices. As one teacher puts it, "the culture of apprenticeship pervades the whole program" (Ryken, 2001, p. 109). The new habit of asking questions often extends into the classroom. One young man who apprenticed in a hospital research lab notes that his apprenticeship carried over to school because [sic] "you feel like you know what you are doing … people might come to you and ask you for help and you are able to take a stand and say this might be an easier way to do that" (Ryken, 2001, p. 128). At least a few of the high school science teachers involved in the program have changed their own classroom practices to more closely reflect those found in professional lab and production settings. A teacher illustrates this in commenting that "They are working together all the time [in class]. We tell them it is o.k.…. They get to know each others' strengths and weak points" (Ryken, 2001, p. 108). For their part, mentors note the enlivening effect of having high school youth in the lab.

Challenges in the BBEI experience cluster in a few predictable areas. One is in making sure the elements work together. A high school biotechnology teacher notes, for instance, that it is difficult to connect the apprenticeships to the classroom because tasks in the former are so specific and young people are doing a wide variety of things. A second is variability in young people's use of the experience as a learning resource. Some youth build on the routines of the work to explore more deeply; others stay at the level of routine and procedure, in part because they feel comfortable at this level. A third challenge, then, centers on some mentors' lack of time to explain both procedures themselves and the reasons for procedures. In one company, for instance, a mentor reportedly did not "have the time to talk about how things are engineered or … what happens if there is a pH failure, what's behind it …" (Ryken , 2001, p. 67). When they have the time, mentors appear to enjoy sharing their knowledge with youth: "In the micro[biology] class they were talking about micro I.D.s. It was difficult for them to grasp... I took out an API strip and had them observe how to do it" (Ryken, 2001, p. 68).

A Distinctive Statewide System: Wisconsin Youth Apprenticeship Program

Although there was much talk in the 1990s of recreating a European-style youth apprenticeship system in the United States, one state, Wisconsin actually tried to do so. The Wisconsin Youth Apprenticeship Program (YAP), initiated in 1991 and still running, comes closest of any program in the United States to embodying the elements and procedures in (as well as the issues and problems presented by) a full-scale system. YAP operates under the auspices of the Department of Workforce Development and works through local partnerships among high schools, technical community colleges and employers. Partnerships in turn operate under a set of state requirements that include a match of 50% of their state grant. Much of that match comes from participating companies, who make a significant financial commitment that includes the apprentice's wages and the supervisory/teaching time of one or more mentors.

YAP currently serves about 2000 high school juniors and seniors from 306 of Wisconsin's 430 school districts, clustered into 34 local partnerships. The program has been through periods of rapid growth (amidst national acclaim) and threats to its existence, due to loss of legislative support. It appears to have weathered those threats and is recovering the funding base lost in recent years.[11] Support for YAP from immediate stakeholders—parents, employers, high school administrators and youth themselves—has been consistent through all the reversals of the larger policy and funding environment.

The YAP model includes a paid workplace apprenticeship in one of a number of technical or service fields, and a series of four classes in that field (one per semester) taken at the high school or at a technical community college. Students choose either a one-year/450 hour or two-year/900 hour apprenticeship, typically 10 to 15 hours per week during the school year and, for some, full time during school breaks and summers. Youth both fulfill requirements for high school graduation and are skill-certified by a state agency and/or industry council. Articulation agreements link the high school experience to the relevant technical community college program. Fields include health care (including, but not limited to, nursing, diagnostic imaging technicians, pharmacy technicians, and rehabilitative therapy aides), financial services, information technology, biotechnology, printing, design and drafting (engineering, architectural, graphics), automotive, manufacturing (machining, production, logistics), welding, agriculture, and tourism.[12]

Early on there was some ambivalence about whom YAP was intended to serve. Staff and other stakeholders agreed that it was well suited for youth who needed other ways to learn, but debated whether that meant primarily non-college bound, technical college bound or any and all youth. The consensus arrived at was that it should remain open in whom it targeted and that it should be designed to keep young people's post-high school options open. Although participants in YAP take some technical coursework they are not placed on technical tracks as such. Some are on an academic track, some a technical one, and some on a dual academic-technical track.

Youth receive high school credits for both the work-based and classroom-based portions of the program and, through an articulation agreement, up to 12 credits of that high school course work can be applied toward an associate degree at a technical community college. (The technical college system has also approved changes to allow high school teachers to teach introductory level technical courses for college credit.) Youth who complete an apprenticeship and demonstrate a defined set of skills in their chosen field receive a Certificate of Occupational Proficiency from the state.

Staffing for YAP includes an overall coordinator for the regional/local partnership, a part-time coordinator at each high school (typically, a counselor or technical education teacher), and a designated community college contact. Partnership coordinators might be based in the community college, a Chamber of Commerce, or in the offices of one of Wisconsin's regional education consortia. Their main responsibilities include recruiting employers, maintaining articulation agreements, helping with placements, and making sure courses are available for apprentices. The school-based coordinator does student recruitment, scheduling, oversees quarterly performance reviews (described below), makes sure credits are recorded and meets with parents, among other program tasks. Apprentices have an on site mentor with primary responsibility for shaping the work and learning experience; in most placements other employees become informal mentors as well.

Although apprenticeship begins junior year, planning for it obviously has to start earlier. Youth and parents have to learn about why, how, and for whom the program might make sense, what apprenticeship entails and enough about different fields open to the youth to choose one. YAP staff can demonstrate with years of data that program participation does not narrow young people's future choices and actually helps provide a sense of direction; parents nonetheless often have numerous questions and, unless an older child has been in the program, some doubts. Sometimes complicated scheduling is needed to balance YAP with other requirements. The state program director notes that school coordinators virtually have to create "individualized curriculum maps" for youth (Crary, p.c., December 7, 2007). Work schedules have to account for academic requirements and course choices have to account for work schedules.

One of the hallmarks of YAP is detailed industry skills standards (in the form of checklists with three levels of competency) developed by representatives from each industry. The standards convey what industry leaders across the state see as important basic skills needed in their respective fields. They serve as an implicit curriculum outline, guiding teaching and learning in the workplace and the classroom.[13] The skills standards work as a kind of harness on the natural variability among work sites and situations in any field. They remind work place mentors and others to assure movement in apprentices' tasks and responsibilities over time. They give youth a much more specific sense of what particular kinds of jobs entail. Not least they provide the basis for certifying apprentices' competency, in a format recognized and accepted by businesses across the state.

Reading through each set of standards reinforces the idea that an occupation is more than work, that it represents a distinctive human endeavor, with its own rich language and practices. Printers speak of competence in image transfer and assembly, flexography, rotogravure, and key line paste-ups. Apprentices have to demonstrate the ability to strip/register a four-color process, to cut half-tone blocks out, to demonstrate sheet-wise, work and tumble, work and turn. Drafting and design apprentices must demonstrate mastery of CAD (Computer Assisted Design), they must apply the principles of orthographic projection in creating a drawing, create assembly drawings, interpret geometric and tolerance symbols, make section view and isometric working drawings.

Although apprentices' work schedules vary widely, there is a tendency to begin work either very early in or toward the end of the school day. Youth also sometimes work weekends if that fits the work setting. Employers may or may not be flexible about the time of day youth will be there, but they almost universally require a predictable and fixed schedule. Juniors, typically, have more trouble getting in required hours than seniors, one reason for the emergence of one-year apprenticeships in some fields.

At the front end of their experience, apprentices may have to spend six to eight weeks learning "how things are done in a business—processes and procedures" (Braun, p.c., January 25, 2008). The speed with which apprentices move into the heart of the work varies by field and setting. Apprentices usually have some core roles and ongoing responsibilities. For instance, one youth apprenticing in information technology was part of a team that was reconfiguring and "changing over" a hospital's computer network. At the same time, sponsors are encouraged to rotate youth through different areas or stations, to expose them to the full production or service process and to assure that they have opportunity to develop the range of competencies on skills checklists. A printing apprentice, for example, will be rotated through pre-press, press, binding and finishing, and production support. A hospital-based apprentice might work in a few different types of clinics, in different roles, as well as the hospital pharmacy.

Apprenticeship-related courses are taken at participants' own high school, a neighboring high school or a local technical community college. Local partners occasionally contract for instructors, when none are available. Some fields have defined course sequences, for example health care specialties that require basic courses on medical terminology, physiology, and body structure. Courses are occasionally delivered through ITV (instructional television) in deference to the low numbers in a particular field at a high school. In a relatively early study, focused on printing apprenticeships, students reported that their printing courses were more challenging than their academic ones and sometimes more interesting, for example a course on "graphic arts chemistry" (Orr, 1995).

Apprentices have a quarterly performance review, with mentors joined by local program coordinators and parents. For parents, seeing and hearing what their children are doing in apprenticeship transforms their sense of what this experience is about and, on occasion, their sense of what their children are capable of. Schedules for recording competencies acquired on the skills checklists vary, as do the specific means for ascertaining competence, a longstanding issue in the program. A printing mentor notes that "I give the student a job to run. I go through and check the color intensity, position, straightness and squareness. I look at the accuracy and precision of the job" (Orr, 1995, p. 76). Because of the sizable number of discrete skills listed in some fields (automotive lists over 300), mentors usually certify—observe or test—clusters of skills on a series of occasions.

Benefits

In part due to the breadth of fields, apprenticeship in the YAP context has worked well for a range of youth, from those clearly interested in a specific field to those who primarily needed and wanted other ways to learn (Knox, 1998). In one study, 80% of apprentices reported that their interest in that field had deepened and that they would continue studying and working in it. But even those who learned that they did not like a field often felt that what they learned was important to their future. Youth note, for instance, learning to work more quickly and "to work with what you have" (Orr, 1995, p. 64). They note greater awareness of their own strengths and limitations, for example, lack of study skills. They also note acquiring a better sense of direction or at least greater confidence in being able to find a career. The state program director notes that through participation in YAP "kids figure out what learning is all about, 'why I'm learning this', because they apply it directly … they're choosing to take an extra math class so they can feel more competent with people they respect in the field." She continues, "these kids are so thrilled [by what they are learning at work], they come back and they help other students" (Crary, p.c., December 7, 2007).

A series of studies over more than a decade has found that participation in YAP does not deflect youth from higher education pathways—three quarters of graduates go to a technical or four year college—and has positive effects on persistence in both technical and four year colleges (Orr, 1995; Knox, 1998; Phelps et al., 1999). Participating youth are somewhat more likely than peers to choose a two-year college to start with and to combine school and work. A longstanding coordinator who has followed hundreds of youth observes that they are more focused than peers once they get to college, and "even when they are not sure what they want to do they seem to know how to think about it" (Kraus, p.c., January 28, 2008).

One distinctive benefit of YAP is the enduring relationships youth develop with the employers with whom they apprentice. Some two-thirds of participants continue working part-time or return for summer employment to those businesses. Youth have been provided funding for college, computers to use, and other supports. Coordinators recite numerous cases of youth coming back to work at a company after college. One youth, for example, is now a loan officer at the bank at which he apprenticed years ago. For their part, employers note a variety of benefits of participating in YAP. Those that have taken apprentices for some time come to believe that "they are training their future workforce (Crary, p.c., December 7, 2007). Employers note the energy and creativity young people bring to the work setting and that having a youth apprentice around increases morale. Employers have re-thought their internal training programs to include more cross training. They have noted also that mentors' own work performance sometimes improves as a result of serving in that role and that, like their apprentices, some mentors just "blossomed" (Orr, 1995). As one employer puts it, "what started out as a civic duty turned out to be quite beneficial for us" (Phelps & Jin, 1997, p. 19).

...And Challenges

In addition to the challenges associated with survival in a sometimes difficult state fiscal climate, YAP has also experienced a range of practical challenges and learned lessons about its strategic choices. It has been difficult in recent years to recruit apprentices for fields viewed historically as blue collar or as tied to manufacturing. For example, although printing has changed enormously, with computer-guided processes playing an important role, it is still viewed as a blue collar trade. The stigma attached to industrially oriented fields is based partly on the belief that they are shrinking and partly on the belief that they do not offer opportunity for advancement. The former belief is only partly accurate, the latter is mistaken; work in older fields offers as much and sometimes more opportunity for advancement than do newer ones.

Although more youth are opting for one-year apprenticeships, most program leaders and some employers continue to believe that two years are necessary. It can take a few months for youth to learn the processes associated with work places, and even longer to learn how to learn in them. Even with mastery of discrete skills, it takes time and experience to be exposed to—and therefore add to one's working memory—the range of problems that can come up. As a coordinator puts it, "isolated skills are only a part of growing competence" (Nystrom, p.c., January 17, 2008).

Overall responsibility for an apprentice's learning is not always clearly defined. One early study found that it is left too much up to apprentices themselves to integrate disparate experiences, especially school- and work-based experiences (Orr, 1995). In some instances school coordinators and mentors are not relieved of enough other responsibility to afford the time needed for their roles. Youth report occasionally having to remind mentors that they are there to train and learn (Scribner & Wakelyn, 1997). On the other hand, the best work sites train youth to be active, "to approach a tech and say 'hey, I have some free time, is there something I can help with?'" These work sites socialize youth "to take charge of their own learning" (Kraus, p.c., January 28, 2008).

It has been challenging to maintain a collective sense of ownership of a program with many voluntary partners—high school faculty, community college faculty, numerous individual employers, and mentors. The legislative appropriation for the program covers only a portion of the total cost of running it— less than half. While the partners value the program, it is not at the core of their missions. Each partner has to make a commitment to YAP out of its own operating budget, which means in part that each has to weigh the value of the program against other priorities. Especially for high schools, which should be the base for the program, it has been impossible to maintain technical expertise in so many fields on a core faculty, or to provide courses in a field in which only a few students are working. Yet high schools also do not want to "lose" their students to the technical college because there are staffing and funding implications. In a tight funding environment (with declining enrollment in some districts) "teachers and departments are fighting for students" (Braun, p.c., January 25, 2008).

While needing to continuously work to maintain political support, monetary, and psychological commitment of partners across the state, program leaders have learned that local partnerships require care and maintenance as well. Though a statewide program with a common structure, YAP has what one partnership coordinator calls "a local texture" shaped by the local and regional economy, institutional relationships and parents. Local labor markets are not static and the YAP program has had to learn to respond to shifts in demand, with employers coming and going. A number of informants observe that apprenticeship is more closely tied to the economy, more sensitive to it, than is schooling, for better or worse.

In summary, YAP is both valued by those who have been involved, and remains marginal in important respects. It survives, and thrives in places, due to the commitment of partners who have diverse missions and priorities. Because there are not enough YAP participants (in a particular high school or across the state) to force a re-thinking of high school structure "young people practically do this on top of full schedules, not as an alternative" (Crary, p.c., December 7, 2007).

Less Vocationally Oriented Models

Two additional strands of school-sponsored youth apprenticeship grow out of high school reform as a whole. The first is apprenticeship tied to the defining theme in one of hundreds of new themed high schools around the country. Common themes include visual, performing or media arts, one or more basic or applied sciences, a design-related field, business, law, technology per se, community development, social justice, health careers, culinary arts, environment, marine and maritime studies, and international studies. The specificity of apprenticeship experiences are influenced by the type of theme, whether an occupational field or discipline, or a more general principle or domain of social concern. For instance, in the marine/maritime academy located in Sandy Hook, New Jersey, youth have a substantive senior year work experience with such nearby institutions as the National Oceanic and Atmospheric Administration and the Coast Guard. Themed high schools are also somewhat more likely to include apprenticeship when they have an external partner. The partner might not only play a role in shaping a school's mission and curriculum, but provide apprenticeships in its area of expertise. This is the case, for instance, with Roundabout Theater in its work in New York City.

The final strand of school-based apprenticeship is tied to that segment of the small high school movement that has tried to thoroughly reconfigure high school. In this group of schools, some of which also embody themes, apprenticeship is one among a number of equally significant reforms. In addition to small size (500 or fewer students) these include greater flexibility in time use; clustering of students in family-like groups (advisories); more collaborative and interdisciplinary project work; individualization of learning plans; and some form of authentic assessment.

Apprenticeship experiences in this distinct group of high schools, as in themed high schools, tend to serve some vocational purposes and some broader philosophical ones. Even when emphasized vocational purposes are subsumed in a broader rationale focused on the multidimensional value of real world learning, of getting young people out into the adult work and social world. Larry Rosenstock, principal in the 1990s of the Rindge School of the Technical Arts in Cambridge, Massachusetts, put it this way: "Work has authenticity and relevance, which leads, from my experience, to engagement. So we need to preserve that part of vocational education but greatly diminish narrow training for specific jobs. There's very little role for that, in my opinion, at the secondary level" (cited in Olson, 1997, p. 34).

The new small high schools that incorporate apprenticeship—whether themed or non-themed—typically do so during the junior or senior year. In non-themed high schools the field or discipline chosen is individualized, based on a young person's interests. In most programs students have an on-site, volunteer mentor who is a professional in the discipline involved. Most programs require that students work on extended projects that are part of the core work of the host organization (i.e., they do not do clerical work). Students are often required to keep a journal or other record of their experiences, and there may be additional written assignments addressing specific questions. Some schools have distinct learning goals for apprenticeships, others do not. Some require students to develop learning plans for their apprenticeship (with the help of their advisory teacher), others do not. In either case, there is typically some kind of "showcase" or "exhibition" of the student's experience and products at defined intervals, and there might be a formal assessment framework, for either or both self-assessment and/or peer and teacher assessment.

Roundabout Theater: Apprenticeship in The Context of Themed High Schools

The range of ways in which external partners can give substance to themes is illustrated by the work of Roundabout Theater, one of New York City's premier non-profit theater companies. Roundabout's education department has founded one high school and worked with a number of others, most recently Bronx Theater High School and the Brooklyn School for Music and Theater. In Roundabout's high school work apprenticeship serves a number of functions—vocational and non-vocational, real and metaphorical. The former director of Roundabout's education department describes apprenticeship as a "foundational philosophy" for all its work, and in this she does not exaggerate (Salvante-McCann, p.c., February 5, 2007).

In the first instance, apprenticeship serves as the frame for professional development work with teachers. Classroom teachers are apprenticed to resident teaching artists from Roundabout, with the goals of both learning to use theatrical principles, elements, and practices in the classroom and of building a school-based theater company. (Roundabout staff describes it as turning classrooms into theaters and theaters into classrooms.) As teachers gain theater knowledge and experience, they join with Roundabout teaching artists in mentoring youth. Experienced youth, in turn, have opportunities to mentor younger ones. In mounting productions, youth also work alongside Roundabout technical staff, who join resident teaching artists throughout the pre-production period. The ultimate goal at this level is a self-sustaining, largely youth run production company within a school.

Roundabout extends its school-based work by offering its own apprenticeship programs, VOICES and Student Production Workshop (SPW), based at its own theater facilities. Youth (from the two partner high schools as well as from others throughout the city) who discover a passion and talent for theater may be invited to audition for either program. In distinct ways each prepares youth for careers in the theater arts. Each program operates under the direction of a lead teaching artist. VOICES is more closely modeled on the traditional conservatory. Youth with prior theater experience audition, learn and practice theater craft using the workshop model. SPW, the newer of the two programs, is more youth-driven and serves a broader population of youth, many deemed at educational risk. In both programs, young people create and mount their own productions, and have access to the wide range of theater expertise under Roundabout's wing.

Theater as Metaphor for Teaching and Learning

Resident teaching artists' classroom work is guided by a model called the Theatrical Teaching Framework. This framework has two dimensions. The first, more conceptual, emphasizes the power of theater in opening up new worlds to youth. Theater has a long history and provides a unique set of tools for crystallizing cultural issues, raising up archetypal human struggles, and exploring the human condition. The second, practical dimension focuses on helping teachers explore the parallels between teaching and theater and learn to incorporate elements of theater into their own classroom practices. Dramatic elements such as theme, plot, spectacle, and character are seen to have correspondences in classroom teaching and learning situations. Like good theater, good teaching is argued to include inciting incidents, dramatizing lessons, identifying point of view, creating an effective narrative, a lesson with a resolution (moment of truth), and use of spectacle to make learning more interesting. Teachers learn to use rehearsal as a new element in their preparations. They learn about the value of revision. A set designer says that "teachers are impressed by the number of revisions that a designer executes. We just keep doing it over and over until its right" (McClane, 2006, p. 11).

Roundabout staff use Dorothy Heathcote's theatrical teaching model, known colloquially as "the mantle of the expert," as an additional underpinning for the school-based work (Heathcote & Bolton, 1996). Although this model also treats classrooms metaphorically as small theaters, it focuses more on the learner and his or her role. Heathcote's premise is that young people learn best by assuming the identity and stance of experts—"acting" as experts—in a discipline. Learning is partly, if not largely, about becoming the kind of person that an historian or scientist or writer is. As Salvante-McCann (p.c., May 21, 2007) puts it, "if kids are going to learn history they have to be historians, act as if they were historians; it is a kind of performance ..."

Roundabout teaching artists are theater professionals (typically, actors, directors, or playwrights) who themselves learn this new role through a kind of apprenticeship itself, to Renee Flemings, the director of instruction and curriculum development and to a small cadre of "master" teaching artists. Flemings (p.c., February 16, 2007) notes that one of her central goals is to help new teaching artists learn to let teachers or youth—whomever they are working with at a particular moment—take the lead in making choices, in effect to teach from behind. There is a deliberate kind of parallel process envisioned. Salvante-McCann notes that "the way in which the artists engage kids is absolutely determined by the way in which we engage the artists" (p.c., May 21, 2007). As Flemings puts it, "everyone is a work in progress."

Teaching artists introduce the Theatrical Teaching Framework and Heathcote's mantle-of-the-expert through summer institutes and in extended residencies during the school year, which include workshops for teachers and classroom-level coaching and support. They set up mock classrooms for teachers to rehearse new practices and provide each other feedback. For instance, a teaching artist may have a group of teachers stage a scene from a play and then link that back to classroom processes. Teaching artists reportedly approach support for individual teachers as they would a theatrical project itself. They study the teacher, the students, and the situation and decide what the story is and how they will work with a particular class. They work also to find the most helpful balance between a focus on theater craft and a focus on the teacher's own agenda and preoccupations.

Theater sometimes plays a more direct role in classroom work, with teaching artist and classroom teacher jointly exploring a whole play or segment with students, through mini-productions in a particular class. For instance, students may read through and discuss a script or do some acting exercises as preparation for an assignment. In a fuller manifestation, a group of teachers and youth mimic the full pre-production phase of a play, with specific disciplines assuming particular roles. In a science class, for instance, youth might become lighting designers; in math, set designers; in history, costume designers; and in English, playwrights and actors.

Teaching artists note a number of challenges in serving as master to the teacher's apprentice. The new frameworks introduced for teaching and learning in some instances help teachers begin to see their work in a new light. They serve to re-energize teaching, learning, and classroom life. At the same time, not all teachers are willing or able to forge a dramatic new teaching self. Teachers in general are unaccustomed to working together in teams and groups, a dynamic at the core of theater. Younger teachers reportedly are more likely to be open to Roundabout's ideas. Experienced teachers sometimes feel that teaching artists lack credibility to help strengthen teaching and learning. Salvante-McCann reflects that the work together can "only happen in a relationship," and even then "either the teacher is ready , willing and able to apprentice him or herself to that artist or they're not and the things that get in the way are all the baggage of the teaching profession … they don't have the time, they don't get it, they don't see the reason, they have to get ready for the regents exam" (p.c., February 5, 2007, May 21, 2007).

Roundabout teaching artists' other key role involves support for theater productions, and for use of productions to build self-sustaining theater companies. Teaching artists try to expose as much of the school community as they can to the production process and make it an integral part of school life. Of a typical core group of about 10 teachers with whom Roundabout might work most closely in the classroom, perhaps half will become involved in theater production at a school. The teaching artist will often work with one or more key school staff in a joint directorial role. Roundabout teaching artists in technical areas such as sound, lighting, and set design will join productions at key points to work with youth responsible for that area of production. A sound designer, for instance, describes his work with a two person team: "I helped them understand how to work with and talk to a director. I trained them on the [control] equipment, to run the sound board … I taught them a little bit about signal flow, choosing music, its thematic role, how music sets a mood, sound effects. One time I brought in a blueprint of a theater in which I had to choose the location of the speakers, and talked with them about the problem I faced …" (Rummel, p.c., March 2, 2007).

Youth Apprenticeship in the Theater

As with its school-based programs, Roundabout's own youth programs are guided by a conceptual framework, except in this case the framework is apprenticeship itself. Salvante-McCann (p.c., undated), the former education director, writes that "The entire history of theater production in the West, until recently, was founded on the apprentice-master relationship. Theater artists didn't *study* in a school; they under*studied* a mature, experienced actor or designer. Actors climbed the theater company ladder, from juvenile parts to mature leading roles. The process mirrors the four step process so famously outlined by Vygotsky (a theater director before he became a psychologist), which to simplify boils down to 'Teacher does; student watches. Teacher does, student helps. Student does, teacher helps. Student does, teacher watches.'" Echoing Heathcote, Salvante-McCann notes that "we treat [youth] as theater artists, we use all the language of the theater; they *are* theater artists for their time with us ... We tell our teaching artists that you haven't taught the lesson until the young people teach you" (p.c., February 5, 2007).

VOICES Renee Flemings, still active as an actor and playwright, is both principal teaching artist and theatrical director for VOICES. "Tech" apprentices—in sound, lighting, set design, stage management—also have technical professionals as teachers. The program is designed for youth with some experience in theater, who give evidence of being serious about strengthening their craft (Flemings, in Roundabout Education Report, 2006, p. 5). VOICES is at once like a conservatory and like a small theater company, with the same goals, roles, activities, and work cycles. Youth have to audition to join, a process which includes a letter of intent and recommendations.

The program works through both an open-ended teaching-learning progression and defined production cycles, of which there may be more than one during a year. In the early part of the year, Flemings leads workshops on specific theater skills, with a focus on both acting and writing. On any afternoon youth may work with a segment of text, their own or from an established play, and talk through what it means, how it might be played, the effect of choices on what is conveyed. Actors learn and practice specific acting approaches, some based on well-known acting teachers such as Meisner, Strasberg, and Augusto Boal. Through many of the exercises and activities during this time, youth are building an ensemble.

Flemings (p.c., February 16. 2007) describes a learning process structured to begin with "a discussion of what a thing is—a concept, a particular activity, etc., then a modeling of it in practice, then a use of it in some real activity, such as the scene of a play, then a discussion and reflection again," connecting it to the whatever the company members are working on. She focuses in part on encouraging apprentices to articulate why they have made certain choices and decisions. She focuses also on the different kinds of trust needed as director or actor, or in specific technical roles. One needs to be able to trust oneself, one's experience and instincts, yet also trust others in their roles. Her teaching and learning philosophy is strongly constructivist: "I don't know about you, but I hate when people tell me what I'm supposed to know ... Let me figure it out. Even if you model it for me, let me figure it out and give it a name, then it's something that I own."

Flemings sets time aside to talk about theater, from its traditions to the practical aspects of making a living, the audition process, where to get information on auditions, what equity work is, where acting opportunities reside. Flemings talks with youth about her own current projects and invites them to come see her working. She wants them to see in a concrete way that "it is possible to make this a career, a life, that it can be real." VOICES apprentices sit in periodically on Roundabout productions in different phases of pre-production as well as when they are in production. They observe first-hand the technical and artistic problems that come up and the choices made by the director, technical staff and actors, an irreplaceable learning experience and a crystallizing experience for some. On one occasion, for instance, youth are able to observe Derek McLane, a renowned set designer, go through a "tech" for a production of *The Three Penny Opera*. Through this experience youth see that theater is what Salvante-McCann (p.c., February 5, 2007) calls "a live environment" with the elements being moved around, dropped, and added.

VOICES apprentices draw on both their own work and on existing plays in selecting productions, under the directorial guidance of Flemings. For one production, for instance, they put together specific scenes from a number of classic plays, with the intent of "showing [sic] their common humanity with characters from many different periods and cultures" (Flemings, in Roundabout Education Report, 2006, p. 5). As the ensemble moves into production, youth in different roles (including directorial apprentice) work both with Flemings herself and with various Roundabout staff and teaching artists as needed. For example, the stage manager has access to a professional stage manager to learn how to manage different parts of the job, from creating a timeline to plotting out rehearsal schedules with the director to running production meetings. Tech professionals sit in as needed on production meetings.

Flemings notes that "I hand the responsibilities over slowly." She will model the director's role—telling the apprentice what she is looking for—as the apprentice director learns what it means to be responsible for the vision of the production. Yet it is, also, just when youth are working on a production that the preparatory work sinks in, and youth begin to take hold of what they are doing. Of one particular production, Flemings notes that "by the time we got close to tech time the youth would know 'its time to get real', they would be ready in that circle for warm-up, they would have script in hand, they would ask 'Can I go over my blocking?' That's the transition. I would see them go from 'Oh, this is fun' to a regard for what they have to do."

Flemings notes that it is part of the teaching artist's job to model the behavior and emotional state needed for the work, particularly a certain openness to experience. She notes also that a critical part of her job at times is to create a little bridge between what an apprentice has to do, to meet the demands of the work and go further with it, and what they think they can do. She offers the example of two young women who were unable to let go physically and make the transformation necessary to really inhabit particular characters in *Uncle Vanya*. Flemings chose to have the girls improvise being animals, to "unfreeze" them—one to become a rat, the other a rhino. She worked with them and pushed them until they caught the physical manifestations of each animal: "Ileana just let your shoulder drop and see how you feel." Then, the young women were able to transfer this physical learning to the characters. Calling what she did a kind of trick, Flemings notes nonetheless that "it was a really powerful experience for them. They had learned how to change your self into someone else."

Student Production Workshop Student Production Workshop is a new program at Roundabout. Its work is structured by the goal of mounting a full-scale theatrical production each year. If in VOICES youth are apprenticed primarily to the lead teaching artist and secondarily to theater as a whole, in SPW the relative emphasis is reversed. Youth take on all the roles that would be found in a professional theater company. They write the script for the play to be produced (and any music and songs to be included), direct, cast, act, stage manage, design the set, design and run lighting and sound, run their own rehearsals, and so forth. A second goal of SPW is to create a self-sustaining, youth led company, with theater knowledge and experience in effect held by the company, and with more experienced youth mentoring new company members. Alvin Keith, an experienced theater, film, and television actor who is the teaching artist for SPW, describes it as spreading out the master-apprentice model (p.c., April 19, 2007).

Theater training in SPW takes place in the context of work on a production. Keith notes that during the first year of the program he took on a more authoritative directorial role, because there was so much about theater that workshop members did not know. During the second year he stepped back somewhat, giving the student director the freedom to decide when and how to call on him. He notes that "we turn it [responsibility for different parts of the work] over as much as we can ... we try to make the line between being more active and less active as organic as possible." As workshop members have come to feel more secure in their knowledge and assumed fuller control of the production, they have been able to see Keith more as part of the production team. Teaching takes place in the course of co-participation. Keith notes that "our relationship is something that seems to be constantly evolving."

Keith believes that he serves the role of both teacher and model—of the professional as artist—for youth. He shares his personal philosophy about theater directly and through example. At the heart of this is the idea that theater is "about discipline and about art." As Salvante-McCann (p.c., February 5, 2007) notes, it is "from the teaching artist that the young person takes the responsibilities of being an artist at work." The creative element, the unique self brought to writing or interpretation, requires the discipline if it is to be expressed. Keith notes, too, that there has to be joy in the work: "I want them to feel that here in this space we are safe and we can have fun." Another theme that Keith emphasizes is theater as community, not just working together, important in itself, but being responsible for both oneself and for others, and buying in to a common goal.

As in VOICES, youth in SPW build skills through the workshop structure. Keith has company members write and act single scenes. Or they may take a scene from an existing play and discuss it from different angles. There are, also, physical exercises—as in VOICES, Keith notes that it is difficult for some youth to open up, put their bodies in the service of acting, "even something as simple as doing a warm-up, practicing breathing." Youth, again, have opportunities to observe Roundabout productions in various stages of preparation, and access to technical professionals.

In Keith's vision for student production workshop, the onus shifts from him to youth, element by element, from warm ups to theater exercises to script editing to production tasks and problems. Echoing other Roundabout staff, he notes that his role is to "present opportunities to youth … letting them make their choices, but for the things that it makes sense for them to have choices about." Lighting design apprentices are not asked to put up lights and run the light board until they have had had a set of experiences that ready them technically for these tasks. Once production work starts, youth have full responsibility except for scheduling the involvement of technical professionals, which is done by one of Roundabout's education staff. There is a youth director and a core of youth who have learned how to run their own production meetings. In wrestling with the complexity of a theater production, youth learn how complex such productions are. Technical and artistic problems come up all the time, something which helps the youth learn that "problems are not personal, they're part of putting on a production" (Keith, p.c., April 19, 2007).

Summary

Suffused through Roundabout's work—both school- and workshop-based—is the tension between a deep belief in, love for, and desire to promote theater itself and the belief that theater provides a powerful means to promoting other ends. Roundabout's education staff keep an eye out for youth who appear to be viable candidates for a life in the theater and try to create pathways to deeper theater involvement and next steps within the organization's programs They may at times deliberately place a youth in different roles, to assure that he or she experiences the day in, day out work of professionals in that role. Youth not uncommonly start off in one role and are shifted to another. It may take a nudge from a teaching artist who can see what a youth is not yet ready or able to see in themselves: talent in one direction or another. Teaching artists have to learn to gauge where each youth is in the developmental process. Flemings notes that she sometimes asks herself, "Am I being too easy or too hard on them?"

Yet while Roundabout's master teachers are committed to nurturing the next generation of theater artists, they are realistic—and realistic with youth—about how difficult it is to make a career in theater. Referring to Roundabout's school-based work, the director of Roundabout's education department, notes that "we're not just interested in teaching theater for theater's sake. We know that theater helps kids reach their potential all around and we know how to do theater better than we know how to do anything else" (Millar, p.c., October 15, 2007). For at least some youth themselves, the apparatus and content of theater—the chance to dramatize, to act or re-enact what one is learning—serve to ground learning, to make it less seemingly abstract.

Woven through all of Roundabout's work is the conviction that theater—with it stories, processes, varied roles, individual and collective demands—provides a powerful framework for learning, self-development and identity, that it is, in fact, a kind of disciplined version of life itself. It allows for both the playing out of core human dilemmas and the reframing of them. An example of this can be found in the treatment that student production workshop youth chose for a play about New Orleans, to be performed as a benefit for victims of Hurricane Katrina. The young woman who co-wrote and directed the production for Roundabout's black box theater notes that "We wanted to do a play about the culture and life-style of New Orleans, and include things like music, food and voodoo. In the play a New Yorker goes down and takes a tour of the place ... It was a benefit for Katrina victims, but I did not want to do a play about Katrina. I wanted the audience to see New Orleans for what it is—a beautiful place" (Navarro, cited in the Roundabout Education Report, 2007, p. 15).

In VOICES, SPW and the school-based work, teaching artists strive to give youth a sense of ownership of the work with which they are involved and a sense of integrity about it, derived from the feeling of knowing, participating in and internalizing the traditions of the theater. Salvante-McCann (p.c., May 21, 2007) notes that "adolescents, more than any other age group, need to make their own theater." In joining a tradition, youth extend it with their own creative interpretations. In describing his involvement with one particular production through student production workshop, a young man notes that "I wrote some songs for it that gave the characters a chance to talk to the audience about what they were thinking—like Brecht does with Epic theater" (Roundabout Education Report, 2006, p. 13). This young man feels and, in fact is, connected to one the 20th century's great playwrights.

Apprenticeship as an Organizing Experience

A handful of high school models around the country have made apprenticeship-like experience the centerpiece of their educational programs, with youth learning and working off campus throughout all or most of the high school experience. As with Roundabout, the sponsors of these models believe that being, even if for only a period of time, an actor or printer or field biologist has value at many levels. Such experience helps youth discover what they love to do and begin to understand what it will take to do it well. It provides an outlet for young people's desire to contribute and enriches the culture. Yet sponsors also, or even primarily, believe that the prevailing model of teaching and learning in high school is fundamentally flawed, in part because of its lack of connection to the real world, in part because it ignores or denies young people's own interests, developmental preoccupations and idealism, in short their selves.

Over the past half century there have been a number of models of more experience-based high school education. For many decades the paradigmatic example was New York City's City as School (CAS), an almost 40-year-old program now being replicated in other cities. CAS, which (along with a handful of other schools or models no longer in existence) actually grew out of the educational ferment of the 1960s, serves about 900 youth on campuses in four boroughs. Students, typically, spend three or four days a week off campus in apprenticeship-like learning and producing roles. They also attend classes on campus created by CAS teaching staff, or college courses. Students are helped to choose off campus experiences and college courses, and more generally helped to design their high school programs, by teachers designated as Resource Coordinators.

Over the past decade CAS has been supplanted as an exemplar by a model called the Big Picture schools. The Big Picture model was elaborated at The MET, an alternative high school in Providence, Rhode Island, led by Dennis Littky and Elliot Washor. Within the Big Picture model apprenticeship is an important element in a singular effort to re-invent high school—to re-think everything from the common curriculum, how time is organized, how and where learning takes place, and the kinds of learning that are seen as important, to how achievement is conceptualized and measured, the roles of teachers and the role of the world outside the school.

Big Picture Schools: Apprenticeship at the Core

The founders of Big Picture believe that academic and applied learning should be treated as complementary parts of a whole: each is more powerful when connected to the other. Yet the role of each in Big Picture is distinct. Academic learning is enlisted to address real world problems and tasks. Applied learning is enlisted because it is a good vehicle for teaching young people how to use knowledge, learn to think, and become resourceful learners. By implication, applied learning—what is usually called technical or vocational learning—should be part of the curriculum for all youth, not treated as a second tier option (Majkowski & Washor, 2007).

Philosophically, the Big Picture model holds that all young people—even those who have had negative experiences with schooling—want to learn and can be trusted to shape their own learning experiences. Young people will work hardest to learn when they value the object of their learning; when learning is hands on, when it combines hand, heart, and mind; and when they have a real need—a reason—to do so. As Littky (2004, p. 8) puts it, "They say knowledge is power. We say the use of knowledge is power." By implication, educators must look outside the walls of the school for learning resources, involving a range of adults and institutions in the educational process; "teachers cannot and should not bear this responsibility alone" (Littky, 2004, p. 123). As a Big Picture mentor argues, putting youth "out in the world [impels them] to deal with the way they think about themselves and their future and their work and the people around them and their own skills" (cited in Riordan, 2006, p. 255).

The general elements of the Big Picture model include: small schools, personalized learning plans, small advisory groups that stay together for four years with the same faculty advisor, multifaceted and authentic assessment, and an emphasis on building and nurturing community, starting inside the school and extending outward.[14] Central to the model is Learning Through Internship (LTI; Littky and Washor considered using the term "apprenticeship" but worried that its connotations were too narrowly vocational.) All students spend two days a week throughout their high school career learning from and working with mentors in a range of small and mid-sized businesses, academic settings (e.g., science or computer science labs), government agencies, workshops, studios, hospitals, human service and community development organizations, advocacy organizations, arts organizations, and other non-profits.

Youth have learned about and done public health research, preventive health outreach and health education (on smoking, AIDS, STDs, fetal alcohol syndrome, nutrition). They have learned about and practiced public policy analysis and public interest law. They have learned about and practiced veterinary medicine, physical therapy, marine biology, medical research, auto repair, culinary arts, photography, metal work, arts administration, early childhood education, graphic arts, computer science, social documentary, television production, and a range of business roles. Interns have worked as artists' assistants. One intern worked in the Providence mayor's office learning how the mental health system is organized and analyzing unmet mental health needs. Another was part of a team that was re-designing Radio Shack's retail stores.

A student will, typically, have three or four internship experiences over the course of four years and, although each is seen as valuable in its own right, it is the total internship experience that is understood to be the key to young people's growth. The process begins in ninth grade with activities designed to help young people identify potential interests—a deceptively difficult but also deceptively interesting task for many youth. Young people will do preliminary research into careers and disciplines associated with those interests, contact and visit potential placement sites, shadow and interview potential mentors about the daily work, the development of their careers, and why they chose a particular field. (Each school has a database of scores of established internships.) Students' sense of possible internships is broadened through learning about other students' internship experiences—in advisory, through exhibitions, and through informal conversation.

Once a student chooses an internship, it serves as an organizer for his or her learning activity for that segment of the school year. (The length of internships varies widely, from as little as a quarter to a year or more.) The faculty advisor works with the student and his or her on site mentor to develop a plan that incorporates Big Picture's broad learning goals in five domains: communication, social reasoning, quantitative reasoning, empirical reasoning and personal qualities,[15] and each student's individualized learning plan. Advisors are responsible for helping students identify academic content relevant to an internship and for assuring that students have access to needed academic resources. Mentors are oriented by school staff and have a manual to help guide their work with youth. Advisors visit internship sites regularly, working with the mentor and student around issues that arise on either side of that relationship.

The first few weeks of an internship (called "anthropology") are spent studying and learning about the work of the mentor and the organization. After that youth generally begin working on defined projects, developed with the support of the mentor. These projects anchor the experience. They are intended to be "rigorous," involving the core work of the discipline at hand, and "authentic," either genuinely needed by the host organization, addressing a real community or societal need, or embodying a creative process that leads to a full-scale product. Projects must include associated learning activity in relevant disciplines and research of some sort. (An internship project may itself be a research study. For example, a youth working with the Narragansett Bay Commission studied how pollution, population growth, and water treatment interacted to affect water quality.)

Majkowski and Warsor (2007, p. 3) capture the interplay of elements in one internship, mentored by a professional photographer, centered on creating a photo portfolio of an old mill in Providence: "Over a period of 10 months, from August through April, Cory photographed the mill, perfecting his photography and, with his [mentor] studied the physics of light and lighting and the lenses and chips that process it. He studied the chemistry of producing the photographs from old-fashioned cameras and film processing, and the nature of composition in art. He consulted with other photographers, read and researched, and spent long hours at various times of the day taking scores of photographs and analyzing their technical and aesthetic quality."

The mentor's role in Big Picture internships is in most respects similar to that in other types of apprenticeships—to teach the intern the basics of the discipline involved, the procedures, concepts and language, the tradition and organizational context, and to help as needed with technical problems. A young man interning in a pottery studio is designing and constructing a mosaic tile wall, depicting a sea scene with an aquatic creature bursting through the wall. In the process he and his mentors (a husband and wife team) together confront a series of technical problems—for example, figuring out how to make waves of clay and to glue mosaic tiles to dry wall—that they work through together. Through the work itself, they try to help him learn about art making—how to approach projects, to visualize the final product, to decide when something is done (Riordan, 2006).

Mentor, advisor, and student share responsibility for identifying relevant "generic" academic content and connections to Big Picture's common learning goals. This task is both crucial to the Big Picture model and inherently difficult. The same qualities that make learning through internship so powerful—its specificity and embeddedness—complicate efforts to link it to broad learning goals. Each type of internship draws on a distinct body of knowledge applied in distinctive ways, and builds a fairly specific set of skills. The intern in the pottery studio, described above, is acquiring the range of visual motor skills and sensibilities needed for "hand-building"; he is learning the properties of clay, to mix glazes, to fire ceramic ware. These are very different skills and sensibilities than those developed by a student in a kindergarten classroom, learning about teaching and curriculum, about observing children and scaffolding their learning, about schools as institutions and about particular dimensions of child development. Broad constructs have distinctive meanings in different contexts. A printing apprentice operating a complex machine called a digital die cutter says that he "needs patience, concentration, focus" (Lupe, p.c., November 26, 2007). A young woman learning about childcare provision also describes the need to be patient, but in relation to the shifting moods and temperamental differences of the infants and toddlers she cares for (Riordan, 2006).

Every three months during the school year, students organize the work they have been doing (at their internship and on campus) and present it at an exhibition, attended by their advisor, peers in their advisory, their mentor, parents, and others from the campus community. Exhibitions help young people see where they are—in that particular discipline or field, in relation to their own personal goals, and in their growth in relation to Big Picture learning goals. Students explain the reasoning that went into projects, discuss problems faced and how they addressed them, present findings and interim products, reflect on what they have learned (about themselves as well as the work), and generally "defend" the work. Fellow students, staff and parents ask questions, suggest further work that is needed, help reflect on and validate progress, and help formulate follow-up plans. Questions and comments may ask students to explain how they arrived at a plan or reached a conclusion, where their evidence is, why they stopped where they did, or what enabled them to break through a problem.[16]

Although exhibitions help pull each experience together for students, LTI coordinators and advisors have to work together with students to make the movement from internship to internship constructive. Students can get stuck at any point. Some freshman have difficulty identifying interests, may be unwilling or unable to commit to a type of internship or to call an identified placement or, on occasion, to leave the building to make that first trip to a placement. A few youth panic when they get to a placement and see busy adults, talking, dressing, and perhaps looking different from them. One young man describes how he felt the first week: "Everyone but me is white. What will they think? How will I work here?" (Lupe, p.c., November 26, 2007). Youth can fail to know how to build on an initial experience to forge the next.

Internship patterns vary. The majority of youth take a year or more to arrive at an internship that might be identified as pivotal. The first one or two will be more experimental, the latter one or two marked by deeper involvement and often deeper learning. One young woman interested in the work of diagnostic imaging technicians had two faltering internships at two different hospitals before she found a setting in which the staff took her up, involving her in patient care, teaching her about the role of different types of imaging in diagnosis and treatment, training her in procedures and reading film. In this setting she was able to make a substantive commitment, doing helpful research on shielding. The young printing apprentice mentioned above found a home—and staff would say found himself—with his second internship, at the printing and graphic design firm. Over time he has been given steadily more responsibility for the range of work in the shop. The Chicago Big Picture principal observes that "the whole company has become his mentor" (Nambo, p.c., November 26, 2007).

A series of internships may not seem obviously connected, or appear to form a logical progression; they may involve one or more false starts. But there is often a developmental coherence to even an unruly sequence. Each internship yields lessons, including a measure of self-knowledge, that help a student plan and pick the next one, and use it more fully. The first one or two or three internships prepare a student for a fourth, which crystallizes what course a young person wants to follow, or turns out to be a pivotal experience in some other way. For one young woman in Chicago, herself undocumented, an internship at a community agency that advocated for the rights of day laborers and undocumented workers led to recognition that she was most interested in why Latinos struggled with education. She subsequently interned with a local college program designed to help Latino youth continue into post-secondary education, producing a documentary focused on young adults who had managed to go on, to be used by the program in its outreach efforts. Another young woman in Chicago, who thought she was interested in nursing, had one internship at a women's health clinic and a second at a WIC clinic before a summer teaching experience led her to see a potential vocation in teaching. One day in particular, when a substitute was present, she took on a central teaching role and was able to reach and help children—just a few years younger than she—struggling with reading and other work. In her senior year, she interned in a fifth-grade classroom, watching and working with a particularly dedicated teacher. As a Chicago Big Picture principal notes, "there's something happening when you go from one to another—you discover where you belong" (Nambo, p.c., November 26, 2007).

Although internship in the Big Picture context is more a means to an end than an end in itself, and moreover is one among a number of interrelated learning elements, adults and youth point to distinctive effects deriving from it. At a basic level, young people learn to try something new, for some a difficult, even terrifying idea. They become more active and resourceful learners. As one youth notes, "before I had a feeling of not knowing things. I had to ask people what's going on. Now I find it out for myself" (Learning Journeys, 2000). Out of sheer necessity young people learn to manage their time and effort, becoming self-organizers. Littky observes that by the time youth are seniors in high school "they know how to get places on time, they know how to get things done, they know how to talk to adults, they know how to talk on the phone, they know how to write, they're kind, considerate ..." (Learning Journeys 2000). A youth in Providence notes that "I know how to drop things and pick them up" (S, p.c., April 6, 2006). Riordan (2006) observes that young people gradually figure out when (and how much) to count on themselves and when others in working on tasks.

Being responsible to and for others reportedly brings young people out of themselves. A New York City principal observes that internship experiences strengthen young people's ability "to put themselves in others' places, recognize and make sense of others' perspectives" (Decker, p.c., January 24, 2007). Reflecting on a fifth-grade teaching experience, a young woman notes realizing that "I can be a link between their [the children's] world and a bigger one" (Esme, p.c., November 26, 2007. In an exhibition presentation that I observed, a young woman in Providence draws on her own memories of kindergarten to imagine how the children she works with must be feeling: "I remember that feeling, of being lost."

The effects of internship experience resonate both inward and outward. Over the course of four years, students might develop relationships with numerous adults other than their teachers; not just mentors but co-workers on site at apprenticeships, adults in other settings who provide critical information or with whom they have to work on their projects. This social capital often proves helpful in the transition from high school to college or work. At the same time, young people's work contributes to the larger social world of which they are becoming a part. At his own initiative, a young man interning in operations at a local airport analyzed the historic pattern (location, direction, etc.) of bird kills, a major safety hazard. His findings led to changes in air traffic control: "they actually changed the use of the runaways as a result of the work of a 15-year- old kid" (Adler, p.c., June 7, 2006). A youth interning in the Bronx (New York) Public Defender's office did the research and then developed a "quick call" list that lawyers could use on the spot at arraignment hearings to propose alternatives to jail. An architect rehabilitating a high school drew on one intern's knowledge of high schools as physical, learning, and social environments.

Growth across developmental domains is uneven, yet seems to even out over time. A young man working in an artificial intelligence lab at Brown University learns to work independently, but remains hesitant to ask questions and inarticulate in explaining his work. These achievements come later in his high school experience, and some growth only becomes evident in young people's post-high school lives. Youth realize that they have learned to do research, to find resources, or to assess their own work in progress. A Chicago Big Picture principal describes the effect of the learning and work experiences youth have over three or four years as "breaking barriers," from the physical ones trapping them in their neighborhood, to the psychological ones that limited their sense of who they could become (Nambo, p.c., November 26, 2007). Ultimately, for some, apprenticeship experiences yield a changed sense of self and an awareness of not being the person they thought they were.

Big Picture staff and youth themselves grapple continuously with a number of issues. One is defining the appropriate balance between adult (mentor or advisor) and apprentice responsibility in assuring a fruitful learning and work experience. Big Picture staff learn over time both to genuinely trust the process and that trusting young people's ability to shape their learning experiences does not imply abdication of adult responsibility. A Providence principal describes it as "a constant shifting back and forth" (Hempel, p.c., June 8, 2006). While some youth struggle to adjust to being relied on, others become all too adept at assuming responsibility without adult involvement. As Riordan (2006, p. 149) asks of one young woman, was she responsible "to the detriment of her learning process?" Riordan argues that a particularly important—and difficult—adult task is to "create the necessary risk or tension required for learning" (p. 289).

Adults and youth sometimes struggle to create organic links between internship experiences and Big Picture's broad learning goals; and more generally between internship experiences and a variety of academic content. An advisor notes that it can be difficult for youth "to mine the experience for academic content—our culture simply doesn't connect the academics of school with the world outside of it" (Sylvia, p.c., February 28, 2007). Using a variety of learning experiences to deepen academic knowledge is especially difficult for youth who arrive at a Big Picture school with weak literacy and math skills. As one advisor put it, these youth face invisible but real hurdles every day.

Mentors are at times unsure of their responsibility for identifying relevant academic content and connections to Big Picture's broad learning goals. These latter responsibilities can be a source of anxiety and occasionally a source of frustration (Riordan, 2006). Because adult responsibility is diffuse, youth are off campus and learning contexts vary widely, it can be difficult to calibrate progress; difficult even to determine if a young person is taking adequate advantage of learning opportunities and resources.

Advisors struggle with the question of what to do when an internship setting itself does not provide the ingredients for a good learning experience. Mentors vary in available time and commitment. While one couple, potters, tell an observer that "we'll teach them everything we know. And anything we don't know we'll figure out together," another reflects that she mentored a young woman "halfway" (Riordan, 2006, p. 235). Even forewarned, new mentors sometimes fail to anticipate the extent of their responsibility to youth. A setting might be an inherently poor match for a young person, or a poor match at that point in their development. One teacher speaks of the difficulty of "finding that fine balance between a site and a kid" (Sylvia, p.c., February 28, 2007). Youth nonetheless note learning from unsuccessful internships, about themselves and about the demands of particular jobs. One, for instance, learned that if she wanted to be a pastry chef she had to get up at four in the morning. Among other kinds of growth, young people get better over time at judging potential internship settings.

Undefined Potential and Many Issues

The initiatives described here are tiny islands on a broad sea. As a Big Picture teacher in New York City notes, "we're 300 kids in a million kid system" (Luria, p.c., February 28, 2007). Yet, collectively, these initiatives provide important substance for re-imagining learning in high school. They make an implicit argument about the kinds of learning tasks—and rewards— that motivate youth. None of the initiatives find youth disengaged or inattentive, exerting little effort or just going through the motions; in fact the opposite. Youth are not always sure where an apprenticeship will lead, but they usually feel that the experience is a vital one and is helpful to them in building a base for the future.

Apprenticeship reminds those interested in high school reform that it is not just about changing what happens inside classrooms during the school day but also about connecting high schools and students to other resources and pulling other stakeholders into the educational experience. Where apprenticeship has been incorporated the high school has come to serve as a mediator, linking young people to outside learning and work settings (Rahm, 2002). Responsibility for teaching and learning has been more widely "dispersed ... throughout a community" (Knox, 1998, p. 45). New relationships among institution and sectors have been created, as well as new social connections for youth.

In some settings apprenticeship has influenced what happens inside the school itself. It has broken through the vocational-academic divide in curriculum and led to changes in pedagogy. In both the BBEI and Wisconsin YAP initiatives youth have brought work-site issues back to the classroom. The YAP program director reports that "we've got kids who encourage their high school instructors to go to the work-site to observe" (Crary, p.c., December 7, 2007). In BBEI, teachers on the academic side of the curriculum began to think about vocation in a different way. As a Big Picture teacher argues, "the prevailing view is you just go to school to go to school and then you learn everything you need for the job on the job. This doesn't make sense ... the kind of thinking used at work has to be a part of school" (Luria, p.c., February 28, 2007).

Challenges in Incorporating Apprenticeship

If the examples provided in this chapter illustrate how fruitful it can be to incorporate apprenticeship into high school education, they also make clear that there are challenges to doing so in more than a modest way. These challenges are practical, bureaucratic and philosophical. Some are distinct to apprenticeship, others characteristic of any effort to reform or re-think schooling. As implied above, some pertain to the still unfinished agenda of creating more coherent pathways from high school to post-secondary education, training or work.

In immediate terms, assuring that young people have good learning experiences in businesses, non profit organizations, government agencies and higher education institutions requires specially devoted staff, ground work, attention to detail in planning, close monitoring, and often working through or around bureaucratic hurdles. In larger, school-wide programs it has proven challenging to place and then to support the hundred or more students who may be out in apprenticeship at any one time, as well as their mentors. Maintaining existing apprenticeship sites and cultivating new ones requires a great deal of work.

High school apprenticeship programs sometimes use volunteer mentors. They may be willing but busy. When they offer to volunteer, they may not realize how different a "master-apprentice" role is to a typical, content free mentoring relationship. Those who are not in education themselves (i.e., college professors or teachers) are likely to have little experience in creating rigorous learning experiences, especially for high school-age youth. Such factors contribute to wide variability in the quality of young people's learning and work experiences (Riordan, 2006).

Evidence from Wisconsin's YAP and from Big Picture schools suggests that apprenticeship remains a hard sell for parents. Despite evidence to the contrary, parents continue to fear that apprenticeship will divert their children from college preparation experiences. Knox (1998, p. 129) observes that parents of YAP participants tend to look "for subjects not competencies when evaluating their children's education." They worry, legitimately in some instances, about fitting apprenticeship into schedules with numerous requirements. The principal of a Chicago Big Picture school that serves a mostly Latino population notes that parents are sometimes uncomfortable with the apparent lack of easily visible and translatable learning experience, and a tendency (based on personal experiences) to set learning and work in opposition to each other. Participating in exhibitions and seeing how seriously the approach is taken helps.

The dispersal of responsibility associated with high school apprenticeship programs creates the challenge of assuring that young people are on track, having good learning experiences and having some opportunity to connect apprenticeship and school experiences. High school staff struggle with the question of much responsibility to give students for shaping both their apprenticeship experience and the linkage of that experience to school work. Staff have debated how much mentors should know and have to worry about a high school's broad learning goals and agenda; conversely how active high school teaching staff should be in shaping the on site experience; and how best to link apprenticeship experiences to classroom experiences. As the BBEI case study illustrates, creating linkages between classroom and work sites has been easier in contexts with a single occupational or disciplinary focus. Where youth participate in all kinds of apprenticeships high school staff have struggled to incorporate those experiences into classroom life. This difficulty is alleviated somewhat in high schools with individualized learning plans.

School-based educators sometimes report difficulty getting a detailed enough picture of young people's apprenticeship experiences to be able to link them to classroom work. A complementary problem for teachers, advisors and, to an extent mentors, has been to determine the right level at which to focus field-based disciplinary learning. Stakeholders in the sciences, for instance, seem to believe that it should be at a more applied level than that found in school, but not at such an every-day level that it does not include learning concepts, principles, etc.

Findings from both Wisconsin YAP and Big Picture, as well as from other school-based initiatives, indicate that it is too often left up to youth to put the pieces together—of their schedule, of the elements of their learning program, even of adult responsibility for supporting their learning. Youth in Alberta, Canada's RAP (Registered Apprenticeship Program) reported being unsure of expectations, not clear about how to make decisions regarding apprenticeship choices and coursework, and unaware of the implications of making certain decisions. They lacked help, in other words, about the context in which they were making decisions (Lehmann, 2005).

For these reasons perhaps, youth tend to describe the school-based and workplace-based elements of their education as distinct learning experiences (Bailey et al., 2004). Thus a young woman in the Alberta program mentioned above notes that "Going to work and going to school are two different things" (Lehmann, 2005, p. 120). Even in programs like Wisconsin's YAP, designed to be integrated, youth reported that though they learned a lot at work they saw little connection to what they learned at school, nor were they sure what the connection was supposed to be (Scribner & Wakelyn, 1997). Young people sometimes find that they are expected to think—and to learn—differently at school and at their apprenticeship (Moore, 2005). They learn that, for almost any activity, there is a school way and then there is a real world way. Put in generous terms, they prefer to value each setting for what it is and what it provides.

The variability and specificity of learning in apprenticeship create all kinds of translational challenges for schools which use it in a broad way. Almost all Big Picture schools, for instance, are subject to the regulations of the school systems of which they are a part. Regulations often require translating qualitatively rich, complex learning experiences into standardized units (e.g., subject-specific credits recognized by the state education agency) that do not fit those experiences. Likewise, Big Picture schools often have to adapt to accountability frameworks, such as demonstrating "average yearly progress" on aggregate test scores, that don't match their individualized learning processes and outcomes. A Big Picture principal in New York City notes, for instance, most youth "get on track eventually, and whatever time they've lost gets [transformed], accelerates into something powerful ... Yet because of the New York City structure, which requires the orderly accumulation of credits, we have to make sure they don't get too lost along they way." He adds that, in spite of support for innovative high school models in the city, the freedom to innovate comes with a high cost: "everybody is going to be living or dying by their numbers" (Decker, p.c., January 24, 2007).

From the perspective of some partner organizations working with themed high schools, it has been difficult to adapt to flux and turnover at the school level, and the broader instability of the school system itself. Roundabout staff, for instance, had to fight for the attention and active support of even those principals who invited Roundabout in as a partner. Salvante-McCann (p.c., February 5, 2007, May 21, 2007) notes that "principal buy in is absolutely crucial; if you don't have it you're dead in the water." At the same time, the principal of one school "felt he had other things he needed to get to before turning to us," and Roundabout has been through three principals at another school: "Each time there's a transition our work has to be re-negotiated, and during the first transition year we have to pull back."

Both non-school partner organizations and principals in schools that incorporate apprenticeship report feeling constantly buffeted by change in policies and priorities, restructuring, new initiatives begun without consultation with those affected. Big Picture was barely getting underway in two sites in Chicago when the district decided the model did not make sense as part of a high school redesign initiative. Partners like Roundabout report that being a part of the work of the schools is a process of continuous adaptation. For instance, during one recent school year professional development days were all but eliminated, making it impossible to run workshops for teachers. During recent periods in which small themed schools came under increased pressure to improve test scores, Roundabout teaching artists were swept aside: "Where teachers and administrators had been open to theater integration before, there was a high sense of risk around our programming and a stronger desire on the part of the school to retreat into the safety zone of skill and drill" (from an undated Roundabout proposal for financial support for school partnership work). Recently, the New York City schools decided to shift art-related funding from outside partners to school-based art teachers.

Finally, efforts to make apprenticeship-like experience a more regular and integral part of high school experience have to await a more forceful re-examination of core premises: first and foremost, that the goal of high school education should be to prepare all young people immediately and directly for college; second, and related, that all or most high school learning should take place inside the walls of high school buildings. For all the hand wringing about drop out rates and disengagement in high school, no political or social space has yet been created for debating these assumptions.

The example of apprenticeship can contribute to needed debate about what is important for young people to know and be able to do. Its implicit argument for—and actual illustration of—multiple pathways to adult competence, and its valuing of different kinds of experience, raise new questions about the meaning of equal educational opportunity. Calling some youth "college bound" and others "non-college-bound" masks the need for serious commitment to youth across a continuum of learning goals and experiences; in other words the need to create middle pathways that reflect the large number of technical disciplines and jobs that are neither high skilled nor unskilled (Lewis, 2007). These pathways, some through technical community college, may just be emerging. But they need social validation, and that will only occur with a significant cultural shift that is not yet occurring. The principal of a Big Picture high school in New York City puts it this way: "I'm not a believer that every kid should go to college, at least no right away, but that's not something I can say very often or out loud" (Decker, p.c., January 24, 2007).

4

The Broader Base
of Apprenticeship Experiences

Hard, meaningful work is a painful and precious gift to deliver to young people.

Greg Gale, The Food Project (2006, p. 6)

One striking feature of youth apprenticeship in the United States is its broad base and impetus in a range of both youth-focused and arts, design, scientific, and cultural institutions not directly connected to public schooling. Sponsors do valued creative, cultural, technical, or civic work in domains that easily interest and engage youth. They often have a strong mission, skilled and passionate adult staff and real work for participants to do. In this chapter I describe and illustrate through case studies the breadth of sponsorship, purposes, and types of experiences associated with this other major strand of renewed youth apprenticeship, and discuss some elements that appear to unite this diverse movement. Case studies describe apprenticeships in the arts and youth media, basic and applied sciences and a heterogeneous category that I am calling hand-work, and that includes boat building, sustainable agriculture, and culinary arts. In fact, all the apprenticeships that I describe in this chapter involve hand-work to some degree, or at a minimum are hands on.

As will be seen, apprenticeship experiences are organized in different ways. Some sponsors design and run their own studio-, lab- or field-based experiences; others place youth in existing work settings, usually after providing a preparatory experience of some sort; and a handful do both. Some sponsors provide apprenticeships within the framework of a central youth development mission. Others are adult professional or trade organizations that have extended their own mission to include work with youth, turning intuitively to apprenticeship as the framework for youth involvement. Those that incorporate their work with youth into ongoing adult activities have discovered that it is not difficult to find a place for youth and that it enriches and extends their own work when they do so.

To varying degrees and in varying combinations, sponsors are motivated by a desire to provide youth a visceral experience of what it is like to work in a particular field (or on a particular type of public issue), and perhaps interest them in that field; to provide youth some experience of success in a specific discipline, experience in which they can "find their passion"; to provide youth an outlet for making a contribution to their community or society; and/or, at a practical level, to get some needed work done. Ideologies also vary widely. Sponsors might be committed to nurturing entrepreneurial skills among youth who would otherwise lack access to such skills, or alternatively nurturing young people's commitment to addressing social and economic injustice.

Some sponsors emphasize the benefits to local communities (or to the market place) of the work produced by apprentices. Public art, social documentary, radio production, growing and distributing food, environmental assessment and similar activities have obvious public benefit. Apprentices help restore prairie, wetlands, and rivers, protect bridges from corrosion, study climate change, and illuminate the causes off neighborhood violence and ways to address it. They help chip away at basic scientific and technical problems. They contribute to—and even help design—public health campaigns. Disciplines take on new meaning for youth when turned to social purposes. Apprentices from St. Louis Artworks (Missouri) were commissioned by a local community development organization to provide artwork for two new residences for the elderly. The youth interviewed residents about their lives, trying to get a sense of what was important to them, took photos and then painted portraits that incorporated something about each subjects' life. After being exhibited at the St. Louis Art Museum, the portraits were hung in the residence hall outside each resident's room. The portraits not only captured residents' individuality but also fostered a small measure of independence by helping some find their rooms without assistance.

Most apprenticeships described in these two chapters reflect the in-between qualities outlined in chapters one and two. They balance work-like responsibilities and tasks with learning and with opportunity for self-exploration. They are demanding but protective. They are about getting good at something specific, but with an eye toward supporting adolescent development in a broad way. In some contexts there is a formal progression, in stages, from pre-apprenticeship to more formal apprenticeship, with broadening and more work-like responsibilities. Youth who proceed beyond the trial period commonly receive a stipend or hourly wage. Being paid is important to participants (and sometimes to their families) and communicates to them that their contribution is valued. The director of an arts organization notes, for instance, that by paying youth to make art "we are telling them that their ideas have value, that art has value, and that being a creative person has value" (Henao, 2005, p. 6).

In some apprenticeships youth are both learning (and learning about) a specific professional role, learning about other roles in that setting, and learning about the organizational and economic contexts for that role. For example, a youth working with an etymologist in a natural history museum may have opportunity to learn about the work of the primatology, paleontology and mineralogy departments, as well as about museums and their mission. Because of where that youth is located he or she is getting what Remer (2006) calls an inside view of those disciplines. While apprenticing to a chef, a youth might also learn about the restaurant business. Working in a theater company, a young person might help with marketing and selection of projects as well as production itself (see, e.g., Heath, 2000).

Some sponsors view their work as a complement to young people's school experience, others as a counter-weight to that experience. Sponsors routinely emphasize that their settings are "not school" in important ways. For instance, adults and youth are working together and may be working on a project in which no one has the answer, and the outcome of the work is genuinely uncertain. Many sponsors are nonetheless committed to helping youth think about and/or plan for college, and may play an active role in the college search and application process. Some sponsoring organizations, especially in the arts and sciences but in technical fields such as culinary arts as well, have relationships with networks of colleges and link apprentices as appropriate directly to them.

Apprenticeship in the Arts, Media Arts, and Design

The creative disciplines provide a major arena for youth apprenticeship. These include literary, visual, and performing arts (and associated crafts), media arts and design.[1] Each discipline itself encompasses varied professional roles and types of work and work settings. An apprentice in photography may be learning and working in fine arts photography, social and documentary photography, architectural photography, conservation photography (in a museum), or some other specialized area. Organizations such as Chicago's Dreaming Tree Productions and New York City's Ghetto Film School train youth in dramatic filmmaking, while those such as New York City's Education Video Center train them in social documentary. An apprenticeship might be based in a youth-centered or professional studio, media labs or workshops, non-commercial or commercial firms, or out in the streets of a community.

Depending on the discipline and context, youth may pursue their own creative vision (individually or in groups) or work primarily on commissioned projects or jobs. Work in design fields is typically more circumscribed than that in fine arts, and somewhat more likely to involve institutional or commercial clients. Work in graphic design studios, for instance, usually entails a defined job for a specific client—a foundation's annual report, printed logos, stationary, the design of a new web site. In Sweat Equity Enterprises (New York City), a program that provides apprenticeships in consumer product design, youth have designed "shoes for Skeechers, watches for Timex, package designs for Dr. Miracles Hair Care Products, skateboards for Zoo York…" (Daniel, 2007, p. 68). Work in media arts is especially varied in purpose, with equally strong traditions in creative or imaginative work and in documentary or journalism.

Arts apprenticeships, typically, begin with a period of studio-based (or as appropriate field-based) technical preparation, often unpaid. This introductory period might include assessment of apprentices' entering skills, basic technical instruction, and provision of background: the history of a field, its changing technologies and approaches, and aesthetics. Some programs or settings have two or three levels of induction, with a paid apprenticeship at the most advanced level. In Boston's Artists for Humanity all participants, including those who will apprentice in graphic design and photography, start with a 72-hour experience in the painting studio. In San Francisco's Youth Radio, youth begin with 12 weeks of introductory learning and work in different elements of radio production, including use of the web and music production. They may continue with a second 12-week course and then join production teams in the newsroom, doing research on a topic, lining up interviews, writing scripts, learning sound engineering, and eventually pitching and producing their own stories (Chavez & Soep, 2005).

Because the period of formal preparation in many arts apprenticeship settings is abbreviated, a central principle in this broad arena is empowering youth to make their own creative choices within a reasoned framework. This framework is provided, in most instances, by the teaching artist and includes the traditions of a discipline, its collective beliefs about what constitutes good technique and good work. It is tempered, especially (but not solely) in media arts, by the increasing integration of established disciplines and emergent ones, that is, of longstanding conventions and standards with new technologies and formats. In many instances youth are leading adults into these new forms of artistic, design and cultural practice.

Beyond (or perhaps as a part of) teaching and serving as the holders of tradition and standards, adults face the difficult task of using their knowledge carefully—of the world, of the social issue a group of youth is working on, of how work is likely to be received by an audience, and so forth—carefully. For instance, youth apprenticing in media arts not infrequently choose topics that have personal resonance to them or to youth in general; and also topics that involve issues of social equity or social justice. In such instances adults have the complex task of simultaneously respecting young people's choices and interpretations and nudging them toward more complex understandings. This task often includes bringing young people out of or away from themselves, putting the story or the commission at the center. A central principle of the Education Video Center is getting the story right. Adult producers at one youth radio initiative note that "we are not in the business of soliciting stories we agree with. The ones that challenge our own personal politics are among the most important we can produce" (Soep, Mayeno, & Kurwa, 2007, p. 10).[2]

Arts apprenticeships strive to convey a balanced sense of art as personal expression, vocation and identity and art as a means to earn a living. Susan Rodgerson, the founder of Boston's Artists for Humanity, notes that "Just because you're doing art doesn't mean it's not a job. Creativity is serious business" (Jain, 2003, p. 66). Earning a living through making art is a regular topic of conversation between teachers and apprentices. Arts-based apprenticeships may include formal discussions of the kinds of work one might pursue in the arts and what it means to be both an artist and entrepreneur to some degree. They may include discussion of "how to interact with clients in a way that is sensitive to their needs and yet they respect what you bring to the table" (Yu, p.c., June 8, 2007). Mentors themselves serve as models of the ways in which artists combine personal work and commercial or non-profit work to create sustainable careers, a practice which is increasingly common in the arts and has been described as crossover.

The entrepreneurial model in arts apprenticeships in some instances extends beyond individual youth to the organization as a whole. A sponsoring organization might try to fund a portion of its budget through commissions, ploughing a certain percentage back into the organization and sharing the rest with youth. The corporations, businesses or foundations that commission work typically see this as an opportunity to support productive activities outside of the traditional youth programming framework. In one commissioned project, apprentices from St. Louis Artworks, mentored by artists from the St. Louis Craft Alliance, created a "collage mural" in which hand-drawn and digital images were transferred to digital film and then overlaid on ceramic tile using a heat-based sublimation process. The tiles were put on concrete boards and hung in local corporate offices, with the clients (CitiCorps, Missouri Foundation for Health) choosing the theme.[3]

While sponsors of arts apprenticeships work to help youth see how they might make a career in particular art forms, they also often aim to help youth look at the larger culture more critically. The media and design arts bring youth into direct contact with the manipulation of ideas and information by large corporations; with stereotypes about particular people and groups; and sometimes with the limitations of their own educational experiences. Adults involved often strive to encourage youth to engage popular culture more actively and especially more critically. This latter goal is not easily achieved; young people are more likely to internalize and mimic popular culture than to critique and reject it (Mayer, 2007).

On the other side of this equation, arts apprenticeship raises the issue of relationship between artist and audience, how important it is for work to be understood by others. Youth struggle with this issue at a number of levels. They question, for example, why they have to keep working on a project until it is clearly comprehensible to others. They question why they have to adapt what they are doing to others' sensibilities or backgrounds. They question why they should compromise their principles to satisfy an audience. In a complementary vein, youth sometimes wonder what they have to say or contribute, and what their own sources of creativity can or should be.

Collectively, apprenticeships in this diverse arena convey to youth their potential to simultaneously enrich the larger culture, alter it and contest it. While young people's work can be very personal, at times too much so, it is often acute, given young people's sensitivity to authenticity and inauthenticity. On some topics or issues, especially those close to their daily lived experience, young people express a distinct point of view, one that adults would not likely uncover. On other, especially larger, topics youth do not necessarily differ from adults. Rather "the conclusions they come to and the recommendations they make are very mature; they are not 'youth' conclusions or recommendations" (Fauntleroy, p.c., January

4, 2007). Yet adults who work with youth in this field—as in related ones—note that the work turns young people's "immaturity" from a liability to an asset.

CASES

Artists for Humanity

Artists for Humanity (AFH) is a youth arts organization founded in 1991 by Susan Rodgerson. It provides paid apprenticeships in painting, sculpture, photography, graphic design, and silk-screening, serving about 100 youth in a large new facility containing exhibit space as well as studios, built specifically for the organization. Youth work in the studios three afternoons a week during the school year and five afternoons a week during the summer. Teaching artists are active professionals in their respective fields. The organization has a dual mission, encouraging young people's artistic development and introducing them to the commercial and entrepreneurial side of making art. (AFH strives to fund about half the total budget through commissions.) Behind these direct goals is that of nurturing young people's trust in both themselves and the world around them. Rodgerson notes that "What kids need to see is that when you have faith, the world opens up to you. It's really a metaphor for trusting life" (Woodman, 2003, p. 12).

Participants initially spend 72 hours, or two to three months, as unpaid students in the painting studio. The assumption is that what is learned in painting transfers to other arts. This is a trial period for both the youth and the organization. The painting studio is a large, open space with six teaching artists working with groups of about 10 to 12 participants each. A handful of youth in each mentoring group are still in the trial stage of the work, most others are working on their own projects. The director of the painting studio notes that one advantage of this arrangement of space is that apprentices "get to see six very different artists, six different models of being an artist" (Gibbs, p.c., December 7 2006). A few of the teaching artists use the AFH studios for their own work. One notes that "I work on my paintings right here; it shows that I'm focusing on my work. It's better to paint together than for me to just tell them things" (*What Kids Can Do*, 2006).

Many youth arrive at AFH with some drawing experience, but almost none with painting experience. Youth are "thrown into the work right away" as the associate director puts it (Motta, p.c., June 19, 2006). The first painting assignment, in acrylic, is a self-portrait. Teaching artists use the assignment to assess basic drawing, composition and perceptual skills, and to begin a gain a sense of who a young person is. Starting youth off working right away is used also to communicate commitment to their own expressive vision, a theme throughout AFH's work. A painting teaching artist notes that most new participants need substantial basic instruction in almost every area: composition, creating expressive lines, values and tones, light and shadow, color choice, and juxtaposition. She notes, for instance, that she restricts youth to the primary colors to start off, so that they can learn gradually to manage and mix color (Truong, p.c., December 8, 2006). The remaining painting projects during the trial phase are determined by youth themselves. That ongoing work is used as the primary vehicle for feedback from teaching artists and more experienced peers. This teaching artist notes that "youth really work off of each other, get inspiration, make social ties and through that are challenged by each other." There are regular formal peer critique sessions set up in the studio. As she puts it, youth experience many "layers of mentoring."

Youth who successfully negotiate the first phase of the work move into formal paid apprenticeships in one of the studios. Youth have some choice, but are constrained by the availability of openings in a studio, and nudged in particular directions by teaching artists, whose experience helps them determine where a young person will fit. Those who go into the photography and sculpture studios often have prior interest and experience. That is not usually the case with graphic design. Youth in that studio may spend some weeks both learning to use computer-based image editing tools (e.g., Adobe's Photoshop and Illustrator) and such basic concepts as placement, proportion, layout, fonts, the relationship of form and function. They practice and begin applying skills associated with different stages of a project.

Studios have distinct climates and pressures, and differing balances between personal and commercial work. Painting and sculpture fall more toward the personal end of the continuum, photography is balanced, and graphic design is mostly commercial. Design projects are typical of the field—an annual report from the Boston Globe Foundation, the photography and design work for the *Boston Globe's* teen newspaper (*Teens in Print*), letterhead for a corporation. Youth from any studio can be recruited for specific commissions. The painting teaching artist notes that while the majority of painting apprentices are "individual minded" and prefer to pursue their own work, they also feel "honored" when approached to work on a commission (Truong, p.c., December 8, 2006).

Across studios, AFH teaching artists note embedding instruction and assessment into the flow of the work. The painting teaching artist notes that "it's good to set up a structure with basic expectations and rules, a level of respect for community norms, but to be open to the learning that is naturally occurring throughout the process." She notes that "I jump in at the teachable moments or when I see a young person is struggling in some way, for example to create a particular mood." She may comment on the style or technique that seems to be emerging in an apprentice's work and where that work seems to be going: "I check in with them to go through these different thoughts, to help them reflect on where their work is going" (Truong, p.c., December 8, 2006). The graphics teaching artist notes that, given the time pressures of multiple commissions, "there is often no time to stand up and start talking about the use of color … it's much more part of the work: 'what do you think of this?', 'why don't we look at this?'… [At times] it may be the whole group teaching and learning at once."

During busier phases of work on commissions teaching is nonetheless "catch as catch can" (Vicin, p.c., January 8, 2007).

Teaching artists emphasize the importance of art resources—books, slides, trips to museums and galleries—as teaching aides and tools to stimulate and broaden apprentices' imaginations. The painting teaching artist notes having to create ballast to counter "this prevailing comic style, a very graphic style, in the studio right now." The graphics teaching artist notes reminding apprentices that visual stimulation, references and ideas are all around—in magazines, the media, the work of different artists, work in museums: "It's all about the store of memories one can draw on ... images from different parts of the culture."

Apprentices learn how to negotiate and manage work on commissions alongside adult staff, both the teaching artists and a small marketing staff. A commission begins with adult staff and apprentices meeting with clients to define and shape a project. Participants learn through these meetings how important this formative process is to a project. Their job here is to listen carefully to clients, ask questions that will help clients articulate what they are looking for, and often to translate a verbal idea into a visual one. Graphics studio clients, for instance, may want an image or logo to express who they are or to capture an organization's mission. Youth will start off working on simpler commissions, perhaps creating trial designs. Youth join in negotiating and then work under real deadlines and have to communicate with clients as the work goes along. The graphic design teaching artist notes that the studio "runs pretty much like a design firm, except for the amount of demonstration" (Vicin, p.c., January 8, 2007). Youth understand that adults will join in the project work at selected points and will give it a final check.

Although AFH is not a youth-led organization, youth are taken seriously and their artistic vision and intentions are respected, in commissioned work as well as personal projects. Teaching artists let apprentices know directly and indirectly that, as the graphics teaching artist puts it, "this is their studio, their workplace." Youth are encouraged to see themselves as "co-owners of the enterprise" (*What Kids Can Do*, 2006, p. 1). Hourly wages are supplemented by a percentage of revenue from commissions: 50% of commissions generated by adult staff; 80% for commissions they generate themselves. The associate director notes that they try to create a sense of collective responsibility and "everyone working together toward common goals" (Motta, p.c., June 19, 2006).

Exhibiting is an important part of the larger experience at AFH as it provides exposure, a chance to sell work, and an opportunity to learn to talk about one's work in a public venue. Apprentices exhibit in AFH's own space or in space that AFH has chosen in various parts of Boston. (As with commissioned work, marketing staff and teaching artists themselves seek out exhibit space.) Apprentices' work might be placed in a corporate setting, hotel lobby, restaurant, store, or other public space. For instance, a team of photography and graphic design apprentices created a series of silk-screen panels on urban animals—chipmunks, squirrels, and skunks—and exhibited them at a local restaurant.

This project, although not intended as commercial, turned out to have some commercial success. One teaching artist recently proposed creating a mural for the community room at a women's shelter, and is taking responsibility for seeking funding for the project. For the window of a well-known department store honoring Black History Month, AFH apprentices created welded steel human figures draped with clothes depicting historical black fashions (*What Kids Can Do*, 2006).

From a staff perspective, participating in AFH has a significant effect on young people's sense of themselves. A teaching artist notes that "it's new for youth to challenge themselves in this way and to see for themselves what they are capable of ... also to see that their creativity is appreciated ... there are people who love their openness and honesty." Youth who have a chance to exhibit gain confidence as people they don't know praise work and sometimes buy it. The associate director notes that youth really begin to believe that "the whole world is open to them" (Motta, p.c., June 19, 2006). He adds that "they learn how to work hard to get better at one thing, so they have an idea that whatever they decide to do, they know what it takes to become proficient." The teaching artist who oversees the painting studio observes that youth also gain perspective on their own talent: "they see how hard other kids are working who are also very good artists" (Gibbs, p.c., December 7, 2006). He sees youth as becoming more serious and more able to "put in the work, regardless of when"; and more willing to put themselves in an uncomfortable situation in making art.

Because of the important role of commissions, the tension between art as personal expression and art as commodity, that is between fine art and commercial art, is a chronic theme within AFH. Corporate clients, for instance, tend to be conservative in their artistic tastes, an issue with which some painting apprentices struggle. The painting teaching artist "lets [youth] know that work on a commissioned project can be a tremendous learning experience, even though they will not always be pursuing their own vision" (Truong, p.c., December 8, 2006). Behind the specific struggle with compromising one's vision in commissioned work, youth struggle with the broader question of how important it is to be responsive to audience, in general. Teaching artists play an exemplary role in helping youth with this dilemma, sharing both the struggles and fruits of their own work and talking about they way they have resolved the questions of whom and what they are working for.

Marwen Arts/Art at Work

Marwen Arts is a youth arts organization in Chicago that provides studio-based instruction to a wide age range of children and youth from throughout the city. Marwen sponsors a paid summer apprenticeship program called Art at Work, for 15 high school juniors and seniors who have a strong foundation of studio work and are interested in exploring art as a field of study and work. The program has three components, deliberately conceived to be complementary. The first is a collective, commissioned art or design project, under the supervision and tutelage of a Marwen teaching artist. The second is a mentored placement in a professional setting that incorporates arts and design-related disciplines. The third is college and career workshops, during which time is also set aside for youth to process and reflect on experiences in the two production settings.

The goals of Art at Work include furthering young people's skills and identity as developing artists, helping them see and feel what it might mean and might take to pursue a career in the arts, and helping in a variety of specific ways with college planning. The director of the program notes that it is designed both to illuminate and create the next steps for youth who seem to have an interest in an arts career and, for some youth, to correct the "romantic image of the starving artist" (Anselmo, p.c., December 19, 2006). In a general way, the program is designed to push youth who already have a set of core art-making skills out of the Marwen nest a bit and connect them to new mentors throughout Chicago's art and design communities. Marwen's overall program director notes that "we send them out into the world to act as public agents, knowing there is support back here ... they're always linked back to the umbilicus of the program" (Lundius, p.c., April, 19, 2007).

Art at Work is also guided by Marwen's overall philosophy for developing young artists. As the senior program director puts it, "We have the responsibility to give youth genuine autonomy in the choices they make, within a carefully considered framework ... More and more we see our job as being very clear about the appropriate number of choices for them to have to consider within any given learning opportunity, even moment to moment" (Lundius, p.c., April 19, 2007). While apprentices need space for their own personal expression, they also need active adult mentors to modulate the creative experience.

Collective Projects The collective art projects worked on by apprentices over the years include: murals at two subway stations, one painted, the other based on photographic images transposed onto large boards; the design and embellishment (with sculptures that they created) of a garden next to the Marwen facility; and the design of murals for Marwen itself, one using ceramic mosaic tiles, the other a photography-based collage. These projects have engaged youth in the distinct challenges in creating both public and site specific work. Art at Work apprentices have to learn to link their own ideas to those of fellow apprentices and translate them into to the varied rationales for doing public art, from engaging people's imaginations, to strengthening a sense of community, humanizing or beautifying a site, or symbolizing its history. They have to take into account the physical and functional nature of a site, local zoning ordinances, community preferences and sensitivities, and how potential purposes and qualifiers relate to a client's goals. Each project also embodies a specific technical domain. On a mosaic mural, for instance, youth learn about the aesthetic and physical qualities of different types of tile, dimensions of color (hue, tone, intensity, temperature), the relationship of background and foreground, and how to use tile to realize an artistic goal. They learn to select, cut and "sand" tile, lay it out on graph paper, and for a smaller group, how to grout.

The teaching artist for the mosaic mural project is a young Mexican American woman with a growing local reputation as a public artist who is herself a former Art at Work apprentice. For participating youth, she is the embodiment of how one can find pathways into the adult world of art making and, if one wishes, use art to engage the world in different ways. She prepares youth for the work by introducing them to both the tradition of public art and to the phases in a project. She shows slides depicting projects that she has worked on in different stages of completion, so youth can visualize the project more concretely. This also helps participants understand what kinds of ideas and energies are central at each phase as well as "how exactly things are made" (Gaspar, p.c., July 2, 2007). As the group begins the design phase, she stimulates youth with slides of a variety of murals and public art, and visits to other mural sites.

The teaching artist notes that she works in public art because she is interested in the collaborative process, and she extends that to teaching. She teaches and shares her experience in part through dialogue, while working alongside youth on specific tasks. She notes that in the process of working on a mural there is always a lot of problem solving involved, "so I turn it around. I ask them for help—'What do you think about this? How do you think we should take care of this? ... How much glass here? How much ceramic? Which of these five different blues?' It allows them to take ownership; it allows me to step back and them to step up" (Gaspar, p.c., July 2, 2007). Yet she also modulates apprentices' responsibility. While she makes sure that "youth do everything that I do on a project," she takes a more central role as project work becomes more technical, working with apprentices in smaller teams and managing the process very closely, using handfuls of youth in carefully defined roles. A small group of the most skilled youth, for instance, will help her with installation (where it is necessary to work quickly since the grout will dry).

The teaching artist works with participants on their individual artistic goals. In this she draws on her own formative experience: "I try to get them to think about what language they want to express themselves with ... I remember as a young artist I was stuck in painting for a long time and I finally broke away. [So] I try to encourage them to try different mediums" (Gaspar, p.c., July 2, 2007). In sharing with youth her personal values as a professional, including her commitment to the civic and community dimensions of art and the benefits of working collaboratively, she provides another level of ideas for them to consider as they move into the next phase of their development.

Individual Placements Apprentices work in a range of commercial and non-profit organizations and with individual artists and designers. Youth have, for instance, worked in architectural firms doing research on "green" design and construction, learning to construct scale models of buildings or other structures, and as part of a team working with clients to select interiors for a project. One young man built on pre-existing photography skills to learn about and practice architectural photography. He became familiar with use of wide angle lenses, such issues as perspective control, achieving depth of field (e.g., using a small aperture and longer exposure time), different types of shots (recording versus interpreting), and different purposes at different stages of a project, illuminating a site for designers, photographing models, and so forth. Another youth, working for an architectural firm that had a commission to re-design local public housing, studied the history of housing in the affected neighborhoods, did research on and made models of possible facades. A mentor in that firm reflects that "the work [in architecture and design] is sometimes conceptual, sometimes applied and sometimes social" (Yu, p.c., June 8, 2007).

Youth have worked in museums learning the skills of curating—recording, cataloguing, and preserving collections, doing background research for, helping design and mount exhibits, designing and participating in public education. A preservation project in a photography museum required one youth to learn about the causes of photo deterioration, how to physically handle and store old photographs and prints, as well as how to digitize them. This project required archival research into the history of photography and individual photographers' biographies, and afforded opportunity to read photographers' own statements about their work. Youth have worked as assistants to individual artists in their studios, on commissioned public art projects (typically murals) and in art galleries. A young woman worked in costume and set design for a dance company. Another young woman, apprenticing at an industrial design firm, designed a model for a cell phone that ended up being used by the firm. Apprentices have brought their artistic and design skills to bear on projects in non-arts settings such as zoos and children's museums.

Marwen has built a roster of organizations and mentors that take Art at Work apprentices year in and year out, and the program director matches youth to sites based on her knowledge of both, as well as youths' own stated goals for an apprenticeship. Marwen staff pay close attention to this network, in large part because it multiplies the resource base Marwen can bring to bear on its work with youth, and in a complementary vein links Marwen to the larger art and design community in Chicago. The program director works with mentors in sponsoring organizations to assure that apprentices' projects involve substantive work, meet an organizational need (are not make-work) and are tailored to individual youth.

In the weekly workshops that constitute the third component of Art at Work, participants have an opportunity to reflect on the issues coming up in their sites. These have ranged from the common (and central) issue of fitting one's own artistic vision into a project's or organization's needs without feeling that one is selling oneself short, to figuring out how to share one's ideas in a context with busy teams of adults, to questions about the value of the academic approach a curator takes. Challenges have included translating studio experience and skills to more practical and applied art or design, and figuring out how one's seemingly distinct skills are relevant to the mundane tasks common to most workplaces.

The combination of a collective experience in which one can join others in a common project, an individual experience in which one owns the work done and products created, albeit in a context of another organization's ongoing work, and a reflective experience, allowing apprentices to process and problem solve in a safe setting, works well for youth. In the collaborative work of public art, youth learn about "chipping in—what does the project need to move ahead?" Youth learn how to conceptualize and work on big projects, "to experience collective achievement, they learn that collaboration works out well, comes together and can yield a beautiful product" (Gaspar, p.c., July 2, 2007). Reflecting on the false starts and dead ends in one common design project, a young woman notes learning that in the creative process "you have to do some work that will not pay off because you never know what will turn out to be the idea that takes" (Camacho, p.c., January 8, 2007).

The diverse group of individual placements nurture a range of skills and sensibilities, reach and affect youth in diverse ways. Some, for instance, learn to find a creative space within the constraints of a project or job. One youth apprenticing in architecture learned about how architects balance function, site context, and aesthetics in helping an architect shape a design for a new store. Youth in a number of settings experience first hand—physically, intellectually, and emotionally—the rhythm and pressures of project work. The young woman who worked with the costume and set designers of a dance company notes that she learned through experience the enormous preparation and background work that goes into the production as it is seen on stage. The young photographer whose work included cataloguing historical photographs and documentary material for the Museum of Contemporary Photography was deeply moved by his direct contact—physical in some instances—with the history of the field.

The timing of the Art at Work apprenticeship, for the most part during the summer before senior year, works well for college planning. It leads some youth to an earlier start and many youth to a more focused planning process. It clarifies interests; a former participant notes having "that shock of realization: 'whoa, I think I want to do this as a living'" (Camacho, p.c., January 8, 2007). Like Artists for Humanity, Art at Work provides a pathway for youth to take on increasingly responsible roles inside the organization itself. Some graduates have returned to Marwen during college and after to serve as mentors and teaching artists. Not least, Art at Work provides young people with connections to Chicago's art and design communities, in some instances fostering relationships that continue for years. The public art teaching artist notes that she has recommended several youth to colleagues working on public art projects around Chicago. One young man who had been placed as an assistant with a prominent local artist, Tony Fitzpatrick, was hired back for four summers. This young man pursued his fine arts studies at Cooper Union in New York City and, when he graduated, had an exhibition at Marwen: "Tony was the first person to walk up and buy a painting and one by one the paintings sold ..." (Lundius, p.c., April 19, 2007).

Education Video Center

The Education Video Center (EVC), founded in 1984 by Steve Goodman, provides pre-apprenticeships and apprenticeships in video-based social documentary. Its two main programs are Documentary Workshop ("Doc Workshop"), a two-stage, semester- or year-long pre-apprenticeship experience; and YO-TV, an advanced program for a small group of apprentices who are paid to produce both short and full-length documentaries, working 15 hours a week over the course of one year. YO-TV apprentices may be recent high school graduates and usually have some sense that they want to pursue media-related work professionally. EVC is based in its own video lab in an alternative high school in New York City.

Goodman and his staff have a multifaceted vision for the program. This includes helping youth master the documentary form; strengthening young people's sense that social inequities are not fixed but can be addressed, through media as well as through other means, and the sense that they personally can contribute to social change; and, relatedly, strengthening young people's belief that they have a right to ask questions of others and question the world around them. Making documentaries unfreezes young people's sense of that world, in part because it "defamiliarizes the familiar" (Goodman, 2001, p. 4). Chen, Goodman, and Riel (2003, p. 6) note that youth "may walk past an abandoned lot every day and not really think very much about it, but when they look at it through the camera, it can become the subject of their inquiry." EVC's goal in this sense is get youth in the habit of looking beyond what is immediately visible, to think about its origin but also "to imagine that which is not present" (Goodman, 2005, p. 216).[4]

The components of the EVC vision and mission vision derive in part from the adult staff's values and experiences, in part from what they have learned over the years about the youth that participate in EVC. The Doc Workshop instructor notes that "most of our kids are disenchanted with the education system. They know something's wrong, they're angry at times about it, but by the time they get to us they're juniors and seniors ... they don't see themselves going to college yet they also don't see what their options really are" (Neptune, p.c., April 27, 2007). Many youth are "far more fluent in spoken language than in written, have little experience using libraries, and are suspicious of information generated by sources outside their neighborhood" (Goodman, 2003, pp. 38, 48). Most youth also reportedly enter EVC with a pessimistic view of the possibilities of social change, and of their own potential to alter the "social conditions that shape their lives." In both an objective and a subjective sense they are poorly informed about important issues that affect their own and their families' lives. In a practical sense, youth often lack the most basic skills of inquiry, including doing research, weighing evidence, and linking what they observe to any framework, question, social issue or body of knowledge.

Doc Workshop meets four afternoons a week for three hours at a time. It involves sustained "video-based inquiry into a social issue" in the community (Goodman, 2003, p. 37) Participants learn and practice the range of skills involved in producing a documentary, from narrowing in on a topic to doing background research, gathering video and audio, writing, editing, rough cut screening, and final editing. They also learn to conduct interviews, to handle equipment, and to develop an argument using both the narrative and the audio-visual elements of the documentary. They learn "to pose their own questions and search for answers to them" (Goodman, 2003, p. 37), to become "critical" viewers and reviewers, evaluating information for accuracy and truthfulness.

Doc Workshop leads participants to full production in steps. Classroom-based instruction, experimentation, practice, and role-playing are mixed with some live interviewing on the streets, followed by a production exercise and then by the full production itself. Adult staff get cameras into the hands of youth fairly quickly so that they can play with what they will soon be working on and begin to understand the work ahead of them.[5]

Instructors lead "active viewing" exercises in which youth analyze photographs, completed documentaries, and movies, sometimes without accompanying sound. The instructor may ask youth how the subjects in a photo are represented, what message the photographer is trying to convey and with what technique (Goodman, 2005). She might ask youth what makes the interview they have just watched successful, or what a documentary-maker was trying to do with a particular juxtaposition. Photos are used in part to illustrate how images deliver information and shape a story, and to make the point that a documentary camera operator employs "a similar aesthetic sensibility as a still photographer" (Goodman, 2005, p. 212). These exercises foster the habit of looking closely at images (and media in general), questioning their intent and technique.

In practical exercises during the early weeks, youth learn interviewing techniques, they learn to use story boards and begin to learn about developing a treatment—a written description of a project that includes its themes, chapters or segments, how that story will be told and why it is important to make (Baudenbacher & Goodman, 2006). Youth are also beginning to learn about formal aspects of composition, from types of camera shots to use of angles, light and shadow, and placement in the screen. An instructor helps a group understand the role of different kinds of camera shots by comparing them to words—each conveys a different meaning.[6]

While they are learning basic practical skills and a acquiring a conceptual foundation, they begin meeting to identify a focus for their documentary. At this point participants are divided into crews (of about five or six) that will stay together through the whole documentary making process. Ideas will be jointly tested and worked through together. Crews decide whom to interview and how an interview will be shot. Much of the editing is done in smaller teams of two or three. Initially, the crew generates and then begins to evaluate a list of possible topics, exploring and questioning each. Youth are asked to defend their choice: to address why a topic would make a good documentary, what questions it would answer, why someone might want to view a documentary on that topic.

Adults play an active role in helping youth choose and refine the subject of their documentaries. The Doc Workshop instructor shares her experience about "what a good subject is" and will try to help them "see down the road to what will give them a sense of satisfaction in the end" (Neptune, p.c., April 27, 2007). More often than not topics emerge from young people's own life experiences. Doc Workshop documentaries have focused on such topics as housing conditions, school conditions, out of wedlock childbearing, guns, policing, stress, death, and bereavement. One typical documentary, on anger, emerged from a discussion of fighting. Most of the youth had fought and they wondered: How did I learn to fight? Why did I learn to fight? Another focused on domestic violence in teen relationships. This documentary ranged across the psychological, sociological and legal dimensions of this problem, and from the immediate—what to do when one is in an abusive relationship—to the philosophical—what is the social and legal history of domestic violence in the United States?

Instructors use the early weeks of work on a documentary to continue formal teaching, with the emerging project as material. The instructors discuss specific conventions of the documentary form, and work with youth to create the narrative that will sustain an argument and line of inquiry. They push youth "to think through and not accept" conventional wisdom, stereotyped thinking, or the apparent reality presented in the mainstream media. Adult staff also "hold" the project until youth are ready to take over, reminding them of steps in tasks, schedules and deadlines (Goodman, 2003, pp. 56, 58; Goodman, p.c., January 3, 2007).

Learning tends to be clustered around key elements of and phases in the production process. Toward the front-end, instructors emphasize the centrality of interviewing: "We're only allowed to ask questions—that's our tool—so we have to use it ..." (Youth Powered Video, 2006). Participants learn to prepare for interviews, equipping themselves with specific questions and some background knowledge. They work on learning to ask open-ended questions, to speak clearly, to pay close attention, and to build on responses, asking for specific examples when appropriate. They work on not interrupting while maintaining the flow of give and take; on making good use of unpredictability; and engaging the interviewee but keeping oneself out of the interview.

Editing calls on two different sets of skills—technical and narrative. Youth learn to use software (e.g., iMovie and Final Cut) with a host of capabilities. They log—transcribe—footage ("cover shot of Marta picking up her baby with narration over it ... establishes Marta with her baby Fernando"), work with time codes and frames, learn how to import footage, learn to move sequences around on the timeline, and to add layers of audio below the line. Using these tools, youth learn how to forge a narrative structure, provide background, create dramatic tension, and a point of view. Individual scenes, edited by one or two youth, are put up on a wall, arranged, viewed, and re-arranged. They are taught to think and argue through the purpose of particular scenes, defending the incorporation or exclusion of characters or specific quotes. One youth tells another: "You forgot to put in a good point. You asked him does he still ride the train [after a fare increase] and he said 'Yeah, I have to'" (Youth Powered Video, 2006).

Rough cut (in sequence but far from seamless) screenings play a critical role in the production and learning processes. Here the production team receives the bulk of feedback from a select audience asked to provide both support and critique. Youth are required to wrestle with understandings different from their own, to weigh feedback, and at times to acknowledge that what they had thought was nearly done is not yet so. They begin to understand that the audience is a kind of participant in the documentary production process.

The Doc Workshop instructor notes that there is often a "nearly complete transformation of the piece between the rough cut and final screening; that is when they put in a lot of hours and they're there nearly all the time" (Neptune, p.c., April 27, 2007). The instructor notes that "I get a lot of 'oh well, I'm done', when they've really strung together a lot of quotes. Now they realize that there are these next levels—the narrative, the logical flow of the documentary. . and the nuances … There's a slump because they've realized they have so much more work to do." Yet, the audience feedback is also motivating; it begins to make clear that the work is consequential.

Throughout the stages of the work, adult roles shift back and forth between teacher and co-worker. Teaching "is always related to something that youth are working on" (Goodman, p.c., January 3, 2007). Adults may work alongside youth, for instance, while they are shooting footage or editing. Adult staff emphasize that decision-making power is shared, while adults give youth as much responsibility as they are prepared for. Accountability is personal: "They [youth] may go out in the field with professional mentors, but the mistakes they make—and what they learn from them—are entirely their own" (Goodman, 2001, p. 4).

YO-TV

YO-TV documentaries follow a similar progression overall, but at a deeper level given their larger topics, longer time frame, and more experienced teams of participants. Topics and themes are, typically, less personal, in part because these documentaries are commissioned (or at least have organizational clients; clients have included museums, human rights groups, public broadcasters). Documentaries have focused, for instance, on human rights and the International Criminal Court (I.C.C.), Hurricane Katrina and its aftermath, immigration and the experience of undocumented workers. With fewer time constraints, research and interviewing are more extensive. For the documentary on the International Criminal Court, youth attended I.C.C. planning meetings at the United Nations, consulted with Teacher College faculty and students developing and human rights curriculum, and met with staff from different human rights groups. A YO-TV crew made a documentary on Hurricane Katrina, flying to New Orleans to film footage, interview displaced residents and officials. In preparing for their trip, the crew did background research on city planning, the local and regional economy.

In discussing her role, a YO-TV instructor notes that even with experienced youth she has to make sure youth have access to certain ideas, "what they would not necessarily get from doing research on line ... broadening their sense of the kinds of resources out there in the world" (Fauntleroy, p.c., January 4. 2007). The instructor notes the need to focus on gaps in broad technical skills. She helps participants learn to set up shot lists, practice with verité interview technique, learn to adjust questions on the fly, or practice experimenting with camera angles. The instructor notes that teaching continues all the way through the production process, but after the first stages happens largely in the course of production: "those teaching moments that happen spontaneously" (Fountleroy, p.c. Jabuary 4, 2007).

Reflection and critique are integral parts of the work in both Doc Workshop and YO-TV. Built into the program are regular occasions for youth to step back and assess specific work they have done. Growth is documented through portfolios and formal assessment rubrics. Portfolios include interview outlines, edited samples of videotape, drafts of written narration, critical reviews, logs, journals and other artifacts of the work. For example, included in the portfolio of a young man who had worked on a documentary on housing conditions were phone logs illustrating his persistence in attempting to reach respondents, letters of inquiry that he had written to housing officials, interview questions, and interview samples (Goodman & Tally, undated, p. 3).

Portfolio roundtables provide an opportunity for youth to consolidate and reflect on their growth and struggles, decisions made along the way, what they learned about themselves and the issues they studied; and for staff, parents, visiting artists and others to join in that reflection. On one occasion, a young woman looks back self-critically on her interview with a particular homeless man: "Why did I ask that? It had nothing to do with what we were discussing." One can see in observing her that she realizes she had been uncomfortable and was not listening, and that she is also proud that she worked through this issue in subsequent interviews (Youth Powered Video, 2006).

Young people's work on documentaries is affirmed by public showings, and EVC staff work hard to find venues for finished work. The YO-TV documentary on the I.C.C. was shown at a Human Rights Watch international film festival. The YO-TV documentary on Katrina was screened at the Tribeca Film Festival. Goodman (p.c., January 3, 2007) notes that youth "don't get the whole picture until they've been through the whole process ... once they've done the work, shown it to an audience and see what the impact is, they begin to realize what they've been a part of ... that they've made something" that goes out into the world, and contributes. One youth notes that "it feels great knowing you left a mark on people's consciousness" (Baudenbacher & Goodman, 2006, p. 170).

Growth and Challenge In an immediate sense, young people's growth through participation in Doc Workshop and YO-TV reflects the tasks of the work. Young people usually do learn both how to ask questions and to persist—to follow-up when needed. They learn to prepare, especially to do the background research that leads to a much more informed interviewing process, and they come to "really feel the impact of that—when you come prepared" (Neptune, p.c., April 27, 2007). Youth learn to tell a story combining words, visual images and music. They begin to develop inquiry skills, although staff believe that these take longer to mature than the time permitted for these projects. Youth learn to revise, and revise again, at times a frustrating experience. One young man notes: "There were times I just wanted to walk away" (Goodman, 2001, p. 5). Conversely, youth learn about how to end a production. It is not easy to know when—or accept that— one has explored a topic as much as one can, given time and other constraints, gathered enough footage, spent enough time editing, come close enough to the product one imagines. And relatedly, they learn that at some point "products stand on their own, without explanation" (Wahl, 2006, p. 7).

Growth in the various skills associated with documentary work can be seen to be emblematic of broader growth. When a young person learns to ask questions, he or she is also learning to raise questions, to be more active in the world around him or her. One participating youth notes learning that "you don't have to be older to think about certain things, think about certain topics, about certain issues" (Goodman, 2005, p. 217). Interviewing others stimulates self-reflective processes, a kind of dialogue in which youth become more aware of what they themselves think about a particular question. Youth come to see problems as malleable not fixed, the social world as constructed, and also as a source of information.

Video documentary works well as a vehicle for young people's growth because it is simultaneously a structured experience, an iterative one and an open one. Starting with Steve Goodman, EVC staff also deeply trust youth. Adult staff believe they have knowledge and experience to share with youth. Yet while they are committed to "equipping the kids," as one puts it, they genuinely believe that youth bring distinctive strengths to documentary making and that adults do not have the answers. The Doc Workshop instructor notes that "each time we do a documentary the structure is different, the problems are different, we need a different plan. It can be difficult but it is crucial to get youth to really feel and understand that this is their documentary" (Neptune, p.c., April 27, 2007).

Work in crews teaches youth to count on each other and to be responsible to others. A YO-TV instructor notes that over time youth no longer need rules and policies; they "come to understand what is required of them" (Fauntleroy, p.c., January 4, 2007). Young people pull and push each other, build on each others' ideas, reflect on and argue about the work. The collective intelligence and perspective brought to each documentary affects its course and outcome. Youth learn also that a collective vision can have just as much integrity as an individual one. Collective work de-centers youth. In working on documentary topics that they personally did not favor and may not have been interested in youth learn to how to engage—to become interested in and motivated by—work that is not of their own choosing. One youth notes that "I didn't like the topic [homelessness] at the beginning but I learned a whole lot about it and I think it was a good experience" (Youth Powered Video, 2006).

Goodman and other staff note two key constraints on the work. The first is participating youths' often weak educational backgrounds. Goodman (p.c., January 3, 2007) offers the example of "a skill like reading a *New York Times* article, digesting its content and integrating that into a forthcoming interview" as the type of growth that comes only slowly to youth. Documentary production requires a good deal of writing and some reading, and as a formal literacy experience this kind of documentary production appears to have mixed effects. It renews young people's sense of ownership of literacy to a moderate extent. But it does not—because it cannot—address basic gaps in literacy skills, gaps that are the result of a lifetime of mis-education. Some youth shy away from writing tasks such as logging videotape throughout their time at EVC, leaving them to peers. Even as they struggle with writing, some or many youth do not to come to see more clearly their lack of basic skills.

The second constraint is a relatively limited time frame for work with some participating youth. About half or more of Doc Workshop participants stay with EVC for only a semester. A documentary can be completed in that time, and it is helpful for this group of youth to experience the whole documentary cycle. But most youth are not only novices at this work, they barely begin to "wake up" over a semester. The iterative and reflective elements of EVC's work do not have time to really take hold. Shifting a young person's center of gravity is a gradual process.

Apprenticeships in the Sciences

Apprenticeships in the sciences encompass a wide range of basic and applied experiences and a fairly consistent apprenticeship structure across disciplines. Most apprenticeships take place during the summer, are full-time for eight to ten weeks and come with a stipend. Some provide the option of participation for a second summer. Apprenticeships are based in university, commercial, government, or non-profit settings, in labs, production facilities, and clinics or out in the field. Mentors likewise are in varied roles as scientists. A particular initiative may have some government funding, for example from the National Science Foundation or the military, and will often rely on contributions from the mentor and his or her institution (including the stipend). Corporations not surprisingly are active in supporting science apprenticeships, foundations somewhat surprisingly less so.

Science apprenticeships generally have a balanced emphasis on providing a specific, in depth learning experience and on striving to interest youth in scientific careers. The majority of sponsors explicitly or implicitly target economically disadvantaged youth and/or youth of color. For instance, the American Chemical Society's *Project SEED*, in operation for almost four decades, requires applicants' family income to be at or below 200% of the official poverty level. The Research and Engineering Apprenticeship Program (REAP), administered by the Academy of Applied Sciences, and the Science and Engineering Apprenticeship Program (SEAP), administered by the American Society for Engineering Education, both funded by the U.S. military, also target what they describe as socially and economically disadvantaged youth. The Environmental Protection Agency and the U.S. Department of Agriculture have apprenticeship programs based in their research facilities and also strive to recruit under-represented youth to those initiatives.

In about 40 universities around the country, specific units, research groups, or labs sponsor science apprenticeship programs (about half of which make efforts to recruit youth from groups under-represented in the sciences). These programs often focus on specific themes, for example nanoscience at the Nanoscale Science and Engineering Graduate Group at the University of California, Berkeley, and acoustics and electromagnetics at the Applied Research Lab at the University of Texas at Austin. By way of contrast, the Apprenticeships in Science and Engineering, part of Portland State University's Saturday Academy, places youth in all kinds of settings, across many fields.

Explicit attention to disadvantaged youth in many initiatives is premised on the assumption that many such youth cannot "see themselves as scientists or mathematicians or engineers" (AAS, 2001, p. 5). It is through the visceral experience of being in a professional science setting, working alongside practicing scientists, being scientists for that two months, that young people begin to imagine it as possible. One REAP mentor notes that the experience seems to help "jump start" young people's futures (AAS, 2001, p. 26). A science teacher notes of three Project SEED apprentices from his school that it was only when they actually "moved around in this other world for eight weeks" that they became able to envision themselves working in it, and "if you can't envision it you may never get there" (quoted in Di Fulco, 1998, p. 1). For some Project SEED apprentices this was "the first time they had seen women in science" (Project SEED, 1996, p. 2).

Goals The central substantive goals of science apprenticeships are helping youth learn what "doing science" is really like, outside the school classroom, and introducing youth to both the distinctive culture of science, and range of ways of being a scientist. Sponsors argue that young people tend to misapprehend science in characteristic ways, whether believing, for example, that it is nothing but the drudgery of measuring the same thing in precisely the same way over and over, or that it about making striking discoveries of brand new phenomena. Sponsors thus emphasize "the way scientific ideas are generated and validated ... the scope and nature of research ... the norms which guide [scientists'] actions " (Richmond & Kurth, 1999, p. 678). They emphasize things that scientists do that young people in school usually can not, for example, generating one's own questions, "looking for flaws in experiments [or] finding ways to verify the validity of new methods" (McCarthy, 2002, p. 18). Comparing his laboratory experience to that at school, one apprentice notes how different it is to do live experiments, with unpredictable outcomes (AAS, 1997, p. 10).

Though students often have experience with one or more lab-based courses at school, the demands of work environments—lab or field—are of a completely different nature. These settings require greater specificity, care and depth, in preparing materials and media, in carrying out procedures, making observations, collecting specimens, culturing, testing (e.g., different conditions), measuring, plotting, graphing, calculating, recording (of procedures and observations). Youth are treated as staff. They are entrusted with sensitive and sophisticated equipment. One young man notes that "not many kids can say that they played with a shock tube [used to study gas combustion processes] at the age of 18 and played with a $5000 oscilloscope ..." (Huang, 2008) Mentors assign articles or proposals to read. Youth join the weekly lab or work group conference and sit in on brown bag presentations by graduate students or faculty.

Science is, obviously, a diverse enterprise; each scientific field is a distinct discipline in its own right, with its own concepts, language, problems and methods. Applied sciences such as engineering, computer science, medicine and ecology typically involve different settings, kinds of problems and end-points than more basic ones. Youth typically work on ongoing studies or projects; less commonly propose and carry out their own work. Apprentices' projects are as diverse as the fields in which they work. Youth have studied the effects of methamphetamine on locomotor activity, variant strains of streptococcus pneumonia, how particular chemical compounds bend light, the patterns of glacial winds, galactic structures, basic processes in magnetism, and specific public health problems. A young man at the EPA's research lab in Raleigh, North Carolina, worked on a study quantifying the frequency of children's hand-to-mouth contacts to determine their exposure to pollutants. Youth have tested new instruments, engineered new polymers, helped develop new drugs, clarify basic biological processes, developed tests of water quality at coal-fired power plants, contributed data to the study of climate change, monitored and/or restored habitats. In the Nature Conservancy's summer apprenticeship program, for instance, teams of youth are assigned to nature preserves around the northeast, where they live and work alongside stewardship staff and scientists (from such fields as marine restoration, lepidoptery, and ornithology). Apprentices might work on shellfish restoration in bays and estuaries; tracking and counting bird populations, banding birds, and collecting data on their surroundings; grassland and prairie renewal.

Apprentices in most initiatives bring their work to a conclusion by organizing it as a poster and presenting it at a symposium or conference. This event may be internal to the particular initiative or part of the larger work in a field. For example, each fall Project SEED apprentices present their posters at local, regional, and national American Chemical Society meetings. Apprentices have on occasion been co-authors or received acknowledgements in published scientific papers.

What Youth Learn Sponsors of science apprenticeships are careful to recognize these as circumscribed experiences. REAP program principles state that apprentices "must contribute to the work at hand, understand their contribution and, in general, understand what was accomplished" (AAS, 2000, p. 42). In a similar vein, Project SEED principles state that apprentices "don't have to understand the whole picture at first, as long as they understand what they did and why, in the course of the summer" (Project SEED, 2007, p. 15). A great deal of learning is procedural, corresponding to the bulk of day-in, day-out work, and due as well to apprentices' varied experience with the disciplines in which they work. Youth nonetheless experience being "contributing members of a scientific community" (Richmond & Kurth, 1999, p. 678). The program director at the University of Texas' Applied Research Lab notes that he wants apprentices "to touch everything in the [scientific] process." And he has found that apprentices "really disappear into the organization" (cited in Green, 2006).

Youth become aware that in any field there are a number of choices about how to approach key questions, what to work on and specialize in, where to work. Youth discover that they love or alternatively that they lack the temperament to work on abstract or on basic questions. One apprentice notes learning that "I like the experience of discovering new things, such as finding a large prime number" (AAS, 2001, p. 22). Youth sometimes have no idea that a particular area of science, for example paleo-oceanograpghy, even exists, let alone why it is important to society. More applied experiences give youth a sense of how science is used to meet social needs, solve public or commercial problems.

Science apprenticeships often help youth acquire a more differentiated sense of what doing something useful means in science. In some apprenticeships, youth have an opportunity to work on a project that has immediate public utility. One young woman, for example, conducted research to test the effectiveness of chloride sensors embedded in bridges. Such sensors would help provide warning of looming structural weaknesses in steel structures supporting a bridge. In other situations, youth are making a discrete contribution to a large-scale enterprise or long-term project, such as building DNA libraries in genomics. Here usefulness remains internal to the work, with its social utility a long way off, and difficult even to predict.

A common theme in youth and mentor feedback is how helpful these experiences are in clarifying the process of preparing for college, especially in learning about the range of possibilities, from two year technical programs, in pharmacy, nursing, biotechnology or other fields, to four year regimens in a particular basic or applied science.[7] Apprentices have opportunities to work with and get to know both graduate and undergraduate students. This contact gives youth a very specific sense of the early phase of scientific careers. Older students are usually honest about the pros and cons of careers in science and helpful about college options. A REAP apprentice notes that his experience served as a kind of preview of what a career in scientific research would be like.

Even full time, the two-month time frame places constraints on the work designed for and with apprentices. Mentors worry, for instance, about youth not getting the big picture in a particular field. In their feedback to AAS, a number of REAP mentors comment on the difficulty of working through all phases of a scientific project, however bounded, over the course of two months, and argue for something more closely resembling a year-round apprenticeship, with the summer as a start up or pre-apprenticeship. Project SEED mentors have argued as well for a more extensive experience or at least some kind of systematic follow In that light youth who participate again for a second year report jumping in quickly, being given more responsibility for the work of the setting at hand, and feeling more clearly that they belong. They also report the experience to deepen their commitment to science (Project SEED, 1997, pp. 1–2).

CASES

Apprenticeships in Science and Engineering

Apprenticeships in Science and Engineering (ASE) is part of Portland State University's Saturday Academy and has been in operation since 1990. It serves about 150 Oregon high school-age youth each summer, in full-time, eight week, paid apprenticeships. Apprenticeships are based in public agencies, non-profits, universities, and corporations, in such fields as archaeology, biology (zoology, botany, molecular/cell biology), biomedicine/nursing, chemistry, computer science, earth science, ecology, engineering (civil, chemical, electrical, etc.), math, oceanography, and physics. Apprentices work under the tutelage of a mentor, either on specially designed projects or, more typically, as part of a team working on an existing project.

During the school year, the ASE program director works to recruit sponsoring organizations and mentors. The majority of both return from year to year. The sponsoring organization is responsible for paying the apprentice's stipend, and for preparing a description of the project on which the apprentice will be working, including some specific tasks, and the kinds of knowledge and skill that the apprentice will be working on. Academic scientists typically draw funding from ongoing grants, and occasionally include a line item for an ASE apprentice. For instance, a biology professor at Reed College included a line item for an ASE apprentice in a National Science Foundation proposal, subsequently funded.

Youth have to apply to ASE, a competitive process that includes an essay on why they would like to apprentice in a particular area (based on brief descriptions of that coming summer's apprenticeships). ASE strives to recruit a diverse pool of youth, and a national college preparation program called Upward Bound helps by referring some youth as applicants. Once accepted, youth select three preferences, under the guidance of the ASE program director. Mentors review applications, interview the youth interested in working with them and select an apprentice. Apprentices participate in an initial ASE orientation that helps prepare them for what to expect at their sites, how to interact with mentors and others and generally how to get the most out of the experience. They also sign an agreement outlining expectations of them, which include timeliness, commitment to necessary background reading and maintenance of a daily log of their work and experiences.

Mentors, who volunteer their time (as well as their organization's resources), receive a handbook and can participate in an optional orientation. ASE pays high school teachers to serve as monitors. They will visit each apprenticeship site twice during the summer and e-mail or call in more regularly. ASE sponsors a mid-summer conference in which apprentices participate in workshops led by scientists from a range of fields. At the end of the summer, apprentices participate in a symposium, presenting their work, together with any findings, in the form of poster sessions. Below are brief descriptions of the work outlined for selected ASE apprenticeships (Apprenticeships in Science and Engineering, Program Office).

Oregon Department of Fish and Wildlife:

"The Apprentice will receive 'hands on' training in fish habitat and population survey techniques, fisheries management programs, and computer skills related to natural resource management. Tasks will include quantifying fish habitat, capturing fish with nets and with electrofishing equipment, taking fish measurements, counting and identifying fish on videotapes, entering and analyzing data, and working with fish enhancement projects in lakes, streams and riparian areas."

Portland State University (Research on Viruses of Extremophiles)

"This position involves the purification, characterization and identification of DNA sequences of viruses taken from hydrothermal environments. This is important to determine the genetic diversity of viruses in a relatively simple ecosystem ... the apprentice may collect samples from hot springs in Lassen Volcanic National Park. S/he will purify DNA from these samples both by extraction and directly using the polymerase chain reaction ... The apprentice will then purify this DNA and determine its sequence. This sequence will be analyzed and compared to other samples using a personal computer."

Rockwell Collins Flight Dynamics, Mechanical Design Department

"[The apprentice] will learn the basics of 3-D modeling of parts, from which s/he will produce drawings using the company's computer aided design (CAD) software. The apprentice will get a hands on experience in a dynamic mechanical design department developing hardware for use in modern transport aircraft."

Portland, Oregon Health and Science University

"The clinical group [The Cardiac Fluid Dynamics and Imaging Lab in Pediatric Cardiology] sees patients with all forms of congenital heart disease

...The apprentice will build and develop a flow model (using rubber valves, pumps, tubing, etc.) Designed to mimic cardiac disease and scan it with clinical ultrasound scanners capable of Doppler flow mapping. This will lead to improved cardiac diagnosis. Tasks include literature reviews, scanning, modeling, evaluating statistics and digital image manipulation."

Multnomah County Oregon, Facilities and Property Management Division

"The apprentice will gain exposure to and understanding of the fundamental construction process that is important to all design professionals ... S/he will gain: gain an understanding of different construction delivery methods, both CM/GC and traditional low bid methodologies ... the application of construction documents into work plans ... knowledge of various codes that dictate design and construction processes; an understanding of construction procedures and how to find the appropriate information needed to interpret specifications and drawings; and an understanding of the role of the architect/engineer, contractor and owner ... The apprentice will participate in inspection and testing activities needed to confirm quality of work..."

A Few Examples Although the above makes clear there is no typical ASE apprenticeship, a few examples provide the texture of young people's experiences. One is with a plant ecologist at Oregon State University. A recent summer's project focused on restoring native wetland prairie in the Willamette Valley. Partial funding for this project comes from the Army Corps of Engineers, which has an interest in expanding habitat for endangered species. A sub-project involves comparing use of fire and hand removal to clear the prairie of non-native species and woody materials. One particular apprentice's work included collection of field data, called cover measurements, and development of procedures for identifying plants at different early stages of growth. At the time of the apprenticeship the research team was monitoring 60 small plots, each of which needed periodic measurements along certain lines.

The apprentice had to learn to identify specific species for counting (he was responsible for learning the characteristics of about 20 species) and to measure the percentage of a plot covered by a particular species, using a template developed by the project team. In describing this work, the mentor notes that it was exacting, requiring close observation, pattern recognition, and generally great attention to detail. It could also be strenuous, in the sense that data collection in the field had to proceed regardless of weather conditions. Another task assigned to this apprentice was to grow plants from the seedling stage, removing and then "pressing" them at one-day intervals, to provide a visual representation of a plant's size at each age. (His mentor told me that the research team uses this "tool" to the present day, even though it is more common in the field to use photos.)

As is common in ASE apprenticeships, the mentor assigned readings to fill in the larger background necessary for work on this project. These included material on the history of prairies, and how they were maintained in nature historically. The mentor notes that she involved the apprentice also in her contacts with the public agencies that would use the data being collected for their own policy purposes. She told me that one thing you cannot really understand in a field like ecology until you get into the workforce is how people working in different roles, institutions, and agencies interact.

A second example is an apprenticeship with an oceanography professor, Deborah Clark, also at Oregon State. She is engaged in a paleoceanography project, collecting and analyzing sediments off the coast of Chile in an effort to reconstruct ocean history and relate that to climate. A chemical oceanographer by training, she works with a colleague who is a geological oceanographer. The apprentice's project this past summer involved analyzing the chemical composition of sediments (looking especially for organic carbon, organic nitrogen and biogenic silica). She had to learn two different procedures, one of which involved burning up a sample and measuring gaseous residues (carbon dioxide and nitrogen gas) and the other using chemical re-agents to leech off the silica. The former, an established procedure, primarily involved great care and attention to detail in preparing samples, and careful measurement of results. The latter was a new procedure for the lab (adapted from work elsewhere that had been described in a scientific paper), was difficult to learn and more unpredictable. The mentor notes that for every sample the apprentice had to do a kind of mini-experiment, for example, by leeching the sample for varying lengths of time. For both sets of procedures, the apprentice was responsible for keeping a detailed record of both procedures and results in a notebook. The mentor noted the importance of all the data being accounted for and traceable back to the bench work.

As with the previous example the mentor assigned some reading in paleoceanography. In addition, the apprentice helped out with, and was in a variety of ways exposed to, other work taking place in the lab. For instance, she helped prepare solutions for a graduate student studying copper concentrations in seawater. He was heading out to the field and was under a tight deadline. The mentor invited the apprentice to seminars and thesis hearings. As she noted to me, she wanted the apprentice to get a sense of the breadth of the oceanography field, and be able to put the work of that lab in a larger context. She also wanted the apprentice to be able to participate in the different kinds of activities entailed in doing science.

A third, longstanding, apprenticeship (10 ASE apprentices over the years) is with a forestry professor at Oregon State University, Steve Strauss, who does research in the field of forest biotechnology. Apprenticeship projects with his research group, which includes post docs, graduate students and technicians, have focused on specific problems deriving from the ongoing work of the group in genetic engineering of poplar trees and other plants (an acknowledged controversial subject). The professor says he chooses the project "from some question in our work" because "it doesn't make sense for them to create something out of thin air; they don't know enough about the field." Apprentices have contributed to work on identifying, studying the role of and inducing the switches that turn genes on and off. They have focused on the question of how long it might take for the tree's "immune system" to recognize a newly inserted gene as alien and, in effect, shut it down. One apprentice studied the process of RNA interference, an important new area of genetic work.

Apprentices' daily work has varied and includes a variety of laboratory tasks such as pouring gels, culturing tissues, and some field tasks that might include collecting samples or even planting trees. Apprentices have to master, at a basic level, the chemical procedures in genetic engineering, such as how enzymes and buffers are used and how DNA sequencing is done. In an interview the professor notes that he tells prospective apprentices that they will be "50% drone, 50% scientist." They have to "organize themselves," execute the experiment chosen, retrieve data, and if necessary (and it is often necessary) figure out what they did wrong. He emphasizes to apprentices that they will eventually—late in the summer—have to present and defend their work to the team, a protected version of what any scientist would do. Apprentices are supervised on a day-in, day-out basis by any or many of the members of the professor's research team.

As formal mentor, the professor sets aside times during the summer to talk with the apprentice about both the biotechnology field and about science. He emphasizes that science is both the "hundreds of details, from how you pipette properly to how you make up the chemistry of a control for a particular experiment" and the broad questions scientists wrestle with, about rationale for particular lines of work, choices made, and "where your work fits in the universe." He talks with apprentices about presenting scientific work, a separate and important part of the larger process. He notes a tendency for apprentices to present their work as a series of actions—"first I did this and then I did this"—and that he teaches them that one has to present work in the order of its logic, beginning with the why of it.

This professor reports that he treats apprentices in a no nonsense fashion. They are expected to work not on the clock but like he or any scientist does: "If you screw up the experiment, well then you've got to do it again ... there's a lot of personal responsibility as a scientist; you're in this because, for now at least, this is your identity, you want to know the answer ... [yet] it's hard for a kid to say to himself, well, I won't be able to make soccer tonight because I've got to finish this experiment." The professor makes sure apprentices feel like full members of his laboratory team, for instance inviting them to participate in weekly lab-wide meetings. He emphasizes to apprentices the value of their work to what the lab is doing. Because of the sensitivity of his work, he focuses on ethics and values as well as on the formal science of work on the genetic modification of organisms, and the differences between human genetics, agricultural genetics, and forestry.

As these three examples illustrate, ASE apprentices have regular contact with top-flight scientists, at times working along side them in the lab or in the field. Through their work they begin to understand the range of specializations and roles within what might already seem a specialized area of science. Apprentices working with the forestry biotechnology group described above might meet a forest hydrologist, a professor of "harvest operations" and a specialist in environmental and resource economics. In a comment echoed by her peers, the oceanography mentor notes that while science classes in school provide a global view of scientific fields they do little or nothing to help youth learn about the breadth of and differentiation within scientific professions.

The forestry biotechnology mentor told me that "young people's thinking about what they're doing changes radically in just those two months, from these crazy, simple notions [of science] that they get in high school to some level of real appreciation for the complexity, pressures, issues." Apprentices learn that what seems boring and routine is connected to what is most interesting; the two sides of the work are interdependent. They learn also that there are reasons for established procedures. As one ASE mentor notes, some apprentices are skeptical "that everything needs to be done a certain way or even needs to be done; maybe it's a little adolescent rebellion, maybe kids are a little more critical these days." He emphasizes to apprentices that "when you do things in the lab or in the field what you do is dictated by the biology of how long it is going to take" (Strauss, p.c., May 24, 2007).

Hand-Work: This Crucial Human Activity That Has Been Lost

In the course of my research, I discovered a handful of apprenticeship initiatives that emphasized the value of difficult physical work in general and of hand-work in particular. These programs operate in different spheres—boat building, cabinet-making, sustainable agriculture, culinary arts. Their core ideas are not just about working hard or working with one's hands as such. Hand-work is valued because it is most explicitly hands on and because it allows for visceral expression of what Rose (2004) calls "mind at work." In the case studies that follow, hands on work provides the foundation, allowing other kinds of work to happen. These in turn deepen the meaning of the hands on work itself.

Staff in the initiatives described here note they usually have to overcome misapprehensions that apprentices bring from growing up in this culture. In particular, hard physical work is viewed as menial and stigmatizing. Apprentices with The Food Project (TFP), described shortly, not only had to overcome this prejudice in their own minds, but sometimes in the minds of peers. As one of TFP's adult leaders notes of a particular cohort, "At first it was difficult for the young people, it was so new, and none of their peers thought it was a reasonable thing to do. I think they felt pretty ostracized in the community; they'd come home dirty and tired" (Chang, 2005, p. 5).

Sponsors emphasize the value of sheer physical labor to varying degrees. In reflecting on what they learned in a study of Youth Build, a construction apprenticeship, Hahn and Leavitt (2004, p. 58) note that one of the most striking findings was "the power of physical, visible work ... there is something vital about the sheer physicality of the work performed by these young people." Physical tasks and challenges teach lessons that cannot be learned in other ways. Young people are proud of overcoming physical obstacles. Apprentices learn about their own bodies, become more aware of them, more centered on them in constructive ways. The physical invokes visual-tactile senses, perceptual skills, close observation and a host of attributes not found in other types of apprenticeships.

Working with one's hands often means working with and through tools, an important element in these apprenticeships. Mentors teach youth that tools are critical to effective work in most fields, that they have their own histories, fit specific tasks, solve specific problems and, themselves, have required considerable skill to develop. Tools have pride of place, and competence in a field is partly about competence in tool use. Skill in the kitchen, for instance, is expressed first of all through the speed and dexterity of young people's knife work.

Boat Building and On Water Apprenticeships

Urban Boatbuilders (UBB) in St. Paul, Minnesota, and Rocking the Boat (RTB) in the Bronx, New York, teach urban youth the boat building craft. Rocking the Boat, in addition, has a complementary on water/conservation program. The adult staff of both programs describe boat building as a compelling activity, and the boat itself as a charismatic object, as one RTB instructor puts it (Kautz, p.c., March 9, 2007). The UBB boat building instructor reflects that "it just so happens that boats demand a lot of our kids; they [the boats themselves] also do much of the inspiring. I don't have to be a cheerleader, it's this thing that you're producing that helps drive you to persevere and to strive for craftsmanship" (Wenger, p.c., June 27, 2007). Taking a boat that one has built out on the water (remembering at the same time what it looked like at different stages), feeling its solidity and seaworthiness, is a powerful confirmatory experience, hard to come by for many urban youth.

Urban Boatbuilders serves a somewhat older and notably vulnerable population of youth—a number have been incarcerated in the local juvenile correction system, where some had their first experience with UBB's work. Rocking the Boat serves a cross-section of mostly low- and some moderate-income youth from the Bronx. The two are structured differently, UBB with a three-stage apprenticeship structure (junior, senior, and shop apprentices), and RTB with two levels, and with experienced apprentices doing more teaching than producing. While both programs emphasize learning through trial and error, immersion into full-scale boat building occurs more quickly in RTB. In UBB novices participate in a three month basic curriculum and complete a preliminary project that must meet a functional and aesthetic standard before moving into boat production, in part because most of UBB's boats are produced for clients: "They have to demonstrate to themselves and to us that they have capabilities they'll need once they start working on the boat" (Wenger, p.c., June 27, 2007).

Both programs share a number of principles: a premium on craftsmanship;

respect for the processes of the work; youth ownership (of the work and of the shop itself) within a framework of adult cognizance; taking and treating youth seriously. The UBB boat building instructor notes that one young man who had grown up in Somalia was surprised when they put a plane in his hand the first day. In the culture he came from, a young person spends months or years observing master boat builders before being given responsibility; "but he said that he felt we believed in him, we trusted him, and over time he came to believe in himself" (Wenger, p.c., June 27, 2007). Staff of both programs value hand-work and believe that it is a crucial human activity that has been lost. As an RTB boat building instructor observes, "what makes us human is our ability to make things, fundamentally, with our hands."

Rocking the Boat

I have chosen Rocking the Boat for a case study largely because I came to know it better. In many places staff or youth could easily be speaking for their counterparts in UBB. Founded by Adam Green, RTB runs two programs that create a complementary whole. The first is a traditional wooden boat building program, the second an on water program (using the boats built in the workshop) that includes basic seamanship and environmental work on the Bronx River. During the school year, youth participate in one or the other program for a minimum of one semester, three hours a day for three days a week, although many continue for a year or more, in what is described as pre-apprenticeship. A smaller number (10 or so at a time) continue on to become formal apprentices. This latter group serve as mentors and teachers to newer participants and continue to develop their own boat building skills.

The boats that youth build are based on traditional 14 to 21 foot long wooden craft used on New York area waterways during the 18th and 19th centuries. The program during the school year uses an array of modern tools, including power tools. The summer program, based at an historic site on the Hudson River, uses traditional tools of those earlier eras. The boat building shop is staffed by an instructor and four or five apprentices, who typically have two or three years of experience. They work alongside groups of 12 to 16 youth. Both Green and the boat building instructor believe that youth have to feel and take ownership of the shop. As Green notes, "we make it very clear that the shop is theirs to use" (p.c., June 22, 2006). The boat building instructor notes also that adults try to foster a "self-governing shop" (Kautz, p.c., March 9, 2007). Each semester the group develops its own shop rules, addressing issues of attendance, behavior, shop safety, clean up, and so forth.

A particular group of youth may be starting work on a new boat or may work on one that has been under construction for some weeks. Boat plans use a long established vernacular, primarily a series of lines and a matrix of numbers that are translated into three different visual perspectives. The boat building process itself reflects a sequence and procedure that has changed little over time. The boat is drawn out full-scale in three different perspectives on sheets of plywood that are painted white, in a traditional process called lofting. These patterns in turn are transferred on to the oak that will be used to build the spine of the boat. The boat is built upside down on a mold derived from the two-dimensional plywood.

During the first few weeks, youth will work with and learn to handle the range of tools and equipment, from block planes and sanding tools to various kinds of saws and chisels. New apprentices are given the full run of tools and tasks right away. Green notes that "In general we don't do too much talking [about boat building]. I try to keep that to a bare minimum and have the kids just get right into it and explore it … It's really abstract and I wasn't able to understand it until I started doing it." Youth will receive some instruction on use of larger, more complicated tools and equipment, but demonstrations occur at moments in time when tools or procedures are about to be needed. For example, youth will receive instruction in how to steam a plank and bend it to the boat's skeleton at the point at which that skill becomes needed. There are also some discrete modules that staff introduce periodically. Oar making is one, understanding wood another—hard and soft woods, different kinds of grain patterns, colors, textures, and what information each provides; different ways of cutting up a tree, where wood is stronger.[8]

Youth, typically, work in clusters of two or three, and there may be three or four tasks going on in the shop at once. All the apprentices in the shop may meet at the beginning of the day or the week to coordinate, since elements of the boatbuilding process depend on each other. Apprentices work alongside the newer youth, providing physical assistance and guidance, and demonstrating technique. The boat building instructor looks to see where he is needed, for example, when a youth is "fighting" a tool or seems apprehensive (or overly cavalier) about using it. He notes that work with tools is clearly about skill but is partly about finding a mix of certainty and caution, "kids exercising their ability to recognize danger and confronting some of their fear—power tools make a lot of noise and seem dangerous" (Kautz, p.c., March 9, 2007).

Some feedback and suggestion is directed toward trying to get youth to think ahead to next steps. The boat building instructor notes that when youth first arrive they "don't really think more in advance than the next hour or day … so we're using that work on the boat to get that forethought going." He notes that some of his comments are intended simply to encourage and reassure youth. A surprising number "seem never to have had any positive feedback." He observes also that youth seem to get more out solving problems themselves. He cites an occasion on which a youth was struggling with the hand-plane but kept working it and eventually "figured it out" (Kautz, p.c., 3/9/07).

RTB staff view the boat building process as being in part about learning to approach tasks in a way that is characteristic of work in a boat building shop. For instance, youth need to learn to make and work through mistakes: "When we are building a boat we have this amazing luxury to make mistakes—it's just wood; if it's off on one side we can make it off on the other side" (Green, p.c., June 22,

2006). Making mistakes is critical to learning to work through the problems that inevitably come up. The boat building instructor notes that "for every instance in which you can figure out the grain, there's another where it's all over the place and you can't get [the wood] to not tear out with a hand blade ... and so, until you gain an understanding that 'wow, this isn't my fault,' there is frustration."

Growth and Challenges RTB staff describe growth in participating youth that seems a mixture of the personal and technical. In a specific sense, youth learn how to use a variety of tools, they learn to choose the right tool for a particular task, how a boat is put together, how and why it floats, and what makes a good boat. They learn some technical drawing, painting and some trigonometry. They learn to communicate using numerical information. They figure some things out for themselves, for example, how to work the grain of a piece of wood. They learn to explain the boat building process; it is not a mystery to them anymore. Youth grow modestly in a variety of ways reflective of the nature of the workshop—in the capacity to stay centered, to focus on what is front of them; in the capacity to think ahead, to think about where they are heading, and what steps are next. One apprentice notes that "I won't play as much as I used to [when I'm working on a task], I have to make sure that what I'm doing is right on the money" (Remer, 2007, p. 30).

Green believes that one of the most important ideas that youth incorporate through boat building is "a sense that a problem isn't something you need to accept or deny or get angry about ... it's being able to look at the situation, analyze it, make sense of it and figure out how to fix it." Youth are learning also to adjust and accommodate, through working with the imperfections in the wood, in their own and in others' craft. Less directly, but just as critically, some youth learn a lot about themselves, and in particular that they *can* learn new skills. As the boat building instructor puts it, youth come to see that "what they learn to do here is really not that different than what they'll be able to do elsewhere in the world, with their minds or with their hands" (Kautz, p.c., March 9, 2007).

Difficulties youth face seem to complement the ways in which they grow. Some are uncomfortable with feeling inexperienced. Some are impatient with themselves or others, or with the processes of the work. Some have difficulty maintaining concentration. The boat building instructor describes it as an inability to focus for a long enough period to figure something out. Or as Adam Green puts it, "they'll be planing and staring out the window." Too many youth enter the shop with a reflexive tendency to immediately give up when faced with a problem. The wood may not cooperate with a tool, there will be knots or it is difficult to figure out which way the grain is going. As Green puts it, "It's just immediately 'How do you do this?' before they have even looked around. You want to say to them, 'Just stop and look at it and you'll see the answer...'"

Both staff and youth themselves suggest why boat building seems such a powerful experience. To start, it is physical. The boat building instructor observes that youth seem to get special satisfaction from the non-power tools and processes, such as hand-planing and sanding. It is, also, visible. An alumnus notes that "every day we would finish working on the boat, I would look at the boat and say to myself 'I helped get us this far'" (Remer, 2007, p. 30). Green notes that boat building is both well-defined and open ended. RTB's social worker describes the work as "a compilation of rituals." Yet though the steps and techniques have been established for decades and centuries, each boat presents new problems. The plans and the tools might be the same but the wood will be different and the young people interpreting the plans and using the tools will be different, "and we can't always remember how we did it the last time and that's fine" (Green, p.c., June 22, 2006). It is not one of those situations in which the teacher knows the answer but is hiding it from learners. As Green puts it, the adult staff "really *don't* know the answers to a lot of the things we come up against and that fact seems important to youth ... there's just this very realistic, genuine quality to the process."

RTB's On Water Programs In RTB's on water program youth use the boats built in the workshop in the service of a variety of environmental conservation and restoration projects. They learn enough basic seamanship to get them safely around the waters of the Bronx River. The instructor is the former captain of *The Clearwater* and herself started out as an apprentice on that boat. Youth learn basic boat handling, safety, and care, for example, checking equipment before heading out on the water and procedures for responding to an overboard situation; basic navigation, including using landmarks, reading and using tide tables and nautical charts, calculating current, reading nautical charts, reading a compass, and learning the math needed to take bearings. Youth learn to plan their trips, for example, factoring in the timing of currents and determining how long it will take to reach a site; and once on water to pay attention to their surroundings, to know where they are; the instructor observes that "it is especially important on the water to think before you act, to be mindful, to recognize that you are in an unfamiliar environment ... you have to learn everything you can about it." She teaches in part by positing situations youth could face as they are on the water in different parts of the river. When they are on the water she will ask apprentices to stop every once in a while, look up and ask what can happen and what they would do (Heyman, p.c., March 9, 2007).

The seamanship instructor reflects that "the outdoor environment is, strangely, very alien to these kids." She notes that "you see a few kids who are afraid of the water and by the end of the semester they're not even thinking about it." Youth learn "to do what they need to without being intimidated—you row to where you need to." This sounds basic enough, but to physically master and come to understand a new environment adds another dimension to young people's lives. (More than a few youth cannot swim when they join the program and that becomes part of the challenge and accomplishment for them.) Seamanship and environmental work are woven together. The conservation instructor, a former park ranger, notes that as youth learn to navigate and explore the river they learn about its features and significance as an environment; its economic, cultural and ecological role; how it has been used and mistreated historically. They become stewards of that environment, and learn in that way what the concept means (Archino, p.c. February 23, 2007).

A number of organizations, studies, and projects depend on RTB's on water work. RTB apprentices act as field staff for the Bronx River Alliance, for university-based ecologists and biologists and for city parks department staff charged with care and maintenance of waterways. Work includes surveying fish populations, monitoring water quality, monitoring for invasive fish or plant species, environmental "remediation" and habitat restoration. Youth learn how to analyze water samples for oxygen content, salinity, and other attributes; to keep records of their field work; and restoration and remediation techniques. They plant marsh grasses, create and maintain oyster beds, and have helped pull every imaginable type of object out of the water, from cars to washing machines. RTB teams follow prescribed protocols and develop their own ideas for contributing to project goals. In one project, for instance, they interviewed people who fish the river to see what was being caught.

Youth sometimes struggle psychologically with remediation work, because it involves cleaning up problems created by others' behavior and indifference, and the actions of corporate agents over which they feel little control (i.e., governments and businesses letting sewage and industrial waste overflow into the river). The environmental instructor notes that "since we're working in the river, almost everything we're doing is after the fact, remediating spills, re-planting plants that have been deliberately removed" (Archino, p.c., February 23, 2007). Yet RTB's youth have also been part of and been able to see for themselves the significant improvement of the river habitat, including the return of fish and animals not seen for decades or centuries. In one instance, an experienced apprentice was heavily involved in a project to re-introduce river herring (ailwives) to the river, lost for 400 years because of damming at multiple points. In another poignant example, a beaver had been spotted on the river for the first time in some 200 years, the result of collaborative work by a number of organizations, including RTB.

As with boat building, the on water apprenticeship experience appears to have both specific and broad effects. About one in five youth go into environmental studies or work in some form. For these as well as for other youth, the experience expands what they think they can do and therefore might do: "If you want to be a marine biologist there's nothing about growing up in the South Bronx that eliminates that possibility" (Archino, p.c., February 23, 2007). Youth become more open to possibilities. A recent program alumnus puts it as follows: "When I was younger I just felt that life was handed to you one way and that way was how it would stay forever, but joining the program opened my eyes to new experiences, new environments, new people, different cultures; it just changed my perspective on life" (Remer, 2007, p. 15).

RTB's social worker notes that it is important not to minimize how important the whole RTB program—boat building and on water—is as welcoming, safe, and accepting (Kiss, p.c., December 4, 2006). RTB staff treat the program as a separate and distinctive space in young people's lives, though program staff will help with school problems as needed and will help arrange school credit for participation when that fits a high school's curriculum. One important reason for youth governance in the boat building shop is in fact to set it apart: "In many ways we want to stay away from anything that reminds them too closely of school … If they get reminded of school they just shut off" (Green, p.c., June 22, 2006). For many youth RTB's indoor and outdoor spaces are some of the few places in their lives without worry, threat, or verbal abuse, spaces where they do not have to worry about defending themselves. As one youth tell the social worker, "this is the time when I don't have to think about that stuff."

The Food Project

The Food Project (TFP) provides apprenticeship-like experiences in a handful of fields connected to growing, preparing and distributing food. A diverse group of youth work on a 31 acre farm in Lincoln, Massachusetts, an "urban learning farm," and three smaller plots in the Dorchester neighborhood of Boston, in an urban kitchen in which food is prepared for distribution to homeless shelters and soup kitchens, as well as for catered events, available in a small number of stores, and at two TFP-sponsored farmer's markets (in Dudley Square and downtown Boston). Youth work as farmers, volunteer leaders, food preparers, nutrition educators, de facto agricultural extension agents, ecologists, small business people, community organizers, service providers, and advocates. A majority of the 250,000 pounds of organic produce grown and harvested each year is donated to homeless shelters, food pantries, and soup kitchens. Another significant portion is set aside for the community supported agriculture (CSA) program, in which Boston area residents purchase shares of the farm's total production, entitling them to a certain amount of produce on a regular basis.

Greg Gale, the program director, writes that TFP gives youth "the opportunity to contribute purposefully to society by growing food for the hungry and caring for the land. Through this work they are challenged to step outside the story of who they are or have been and try on a new way of thinking, acting or being" (2006, p. 9). The TFP experience is designed to be both specific and systemic, to immerse youth in each dimension of agriculture and at the same time to help them think broadly, to understand more deeply how our approach to agriculture leads in the end to misdistribution and hunger for some, and how that approach itself is symptomatic of larger social and economic issues.

Sixty youth enter TFP's summer youth program (earning $150 a week), organized into 10 person crews with crew leaders (usually college students) and assistant crew leaders (drawn from earlier summers). About half these youth will continue working with TFP during the ensuing school year and of this group half again will become formal apprentices, some of whom, again, will eventually be hired as TFP staff. Participating youth come from a variety of communities and backgrounds, a pattern which represents a deliberate decision by program leaders and an important dimension of program experience.

First year participants are in the fields every day except Wednesday, when they are at homeless shelters and soup kitchens. They learn to sow seeds, transplant and propagate, hoe, weed and harvest, both by hand and using hand tools; to test and improve soil; irrigate, trellis and prune. They build wash stations and learn to pack produce. They learn the nutritional value and uses of a variety of vegetables, herbs and fruits, about crop rotation, soil fertility and health, for example, improving the chemical balance or building organic matter through cover cropping. Youth that work with TFP during the year will participate in the full cycle of preparing seed plants in the winter and spring (in the greenhouse and rooftop garden at the farm).

On a typical day in the field, the farm manager will let each crew know how much acreage it needs to cover, over what time frame. Schedules are regular, part of the larger structure of TFP as a whole. Harvesting occurs, for example, on Tuesdays and Thursdays for four hours. After lunch on those days, the master farmer will provide feedback to crews and give a "harvest rating." Often in the early weeks crews get a low score, perhaps a 4 out of 10, and "they're absolutely shocked because we don't have grade inflation" (Gale, p.c., August 7, 2006). At the end of the summer "there will almost always be a week when the farmer gives a 9 or 9.5 and the whole place erupts in applause and the farmer will explain why—no bruised produce came in this week and everything is on time."

The field work is physically difficult and at times unrelenting. Youth get dirty and sweaty; it can be hot or raining. Gale notes that "almost everybody will tell us that they almost quit the first week." Youth quickly learn that growing and harvesting food require a set of attribute that include not only toleration of discomfort but pacing—the ability to sustain a level of effort over many hours; attention to detail at many points—one wants to pick the weeds and leave the herbs or young vegetables; and at times the ability to gather one's resources for an intense effort. Vegetables grow slowly, at a pace that itself teaches about patience and the different kinds of care needed at different points. Yet, at times, a great deal of produce may be ready and need harvesting, seemingly all at once—a team may be responsible for harvesting a thousand pounds of summer squash in one day. The adjustment youth have to make is also individual—some youth work too slowly, with too much attention to detail; "they only go a foot at a time because they notice everything." Others charge ahead. Some struggle with weeding, some with determining when a vegetable is ready to harvest.

Adult staff, older apprentices, and crew leaders teach in large part by example, working alongside the crew, demonstrating particular techniques or a sustainable pace of work. Crew leaders will encourage, exhort, and challenge, for instance, when the crew needs to finish a row. Crew leaders are themselves mentored by adult staff. They learn to lead, to step back a little from the work, to be very specific about expectations, to use playful approaches to challenge youth, to give youth strategies for persevering and to read when it is time to throttle back (Gale, 2005).

On selected afternoons youth participate in a social curriculum that examines hunger and homelessness, teaches about community-building, social justice, and service to others and includes structured time for self exploration. In a weekly straight talk session, crew members take turns sitting in the middle of a circle as their peers and the crew leader offer feedback, and they have a chance to respond.[9] Some straight talk discussion focuses on how the crew as a whole is functioning and how it might operate more effectively.

This dimension of TFP's work is designed to nurture in youth a kind of social concern that ties thoughts and feelings to action; to "break down the 'business as usual' social patterns youth carry with them into new situations" and encourage youth to reflect on what they are doing (Gale, 2006, p. 12); and to introduce a particular conception of accountability, part individual, part collective. As Gale puts it, "youth are encouraged to ask themselves not just how am I operating but how is our crew operating." Conversation is designed as well to break down the protective shell that many youth bring to the program, one that seems necessary in other contexts but is an impediment on the farm and in the other settings in which TFP operates. As a staff member puts it, for some youth the psychological distance between their neighborhoods and the farm is even greater than the physical distance.

Throughout the program TFP staff emphasize the dignity of physical labor and the fact that the work youth do is genuinely needed. Gale (2000, p. xx) notes motivating newer youth by letting them know that "believe it or not you're needed—you may not *feel* needed in terms of how you've been treated [in other settings], but *we* need you and people need you beyond here ... we will train you to be able to do whatever it takes to step into that ... being of use means a lot." The extension of the work into food preparation, delivery and service to those who are homeless and/or hungry is both concretely important and symbolic. A day after being in the field, youth may be at a shelter preparing meals using the vegetables they harvested the previous day. Growing food to meet real and basic needs, combined with awareness that these needs should not exist in a wealthy society, are equally important.

Formal Apprenticeships The first summer's work leads for some youth to further involvement with TFP, during the school year and in subsequent summers. During the year youth work at the farmers market, in the Green House at the farm, in shelters or leading volunteers at the farm site. With experience, youth can be selected into apprenticeships in one of four areas: rural agriculture, urban agriculture, farmers' market, food preparation, and urban education and outreach. All apprentices play some role teaching and leading youth on the first year crews, and the majority do some community education and outreach. Youth are in some sense apprenticing to TFP itself, both its interconnected components and its distinct way of building a productive and useful community and addressing social concerns.

Apprentices at the main farm in Lincoln work with the farm manager, crew leaders, and other adult staff to lead and carry out farm operations, work with volunteers and summer youth program participants. Youth apprenticing in urban agriculture are responsible for production at the three urban sites and work at the new urban learning farm, used to provide education and guidance to community residents growing vegetables on their own plots. Urban farming requires extensive soil analysis, the preparation of raised plant beds if the soil is contaminated, and distinct planting strategies. Apprentices help prepare planting schedules, lead younger youth in agricultural work, weigh and record produce. Because the urban farms are located in residential neighborhoods, apprentices explain the work to neighborhood residents and address concerns or questions. They work with community residents and organizations to address security issues and examine how the presence of the farm plot can contribute to broader community development.

Apprentices in TFP's kitchen work under the tutelage of culinary staff to prepare food for delivery to a handful of homeless shelters and soup kitchens, as well as for catered events; and also work on a new commercial product line started with salsa and pies, using vegetables from the farm. They learn basic culinary skills, food safety, and some marketing. Farmers' market apprentices work with the market manager to run TFP's two markets, in Dorchester and downtown Boston, both of which sell produce grown by TFP itself. They are responsible for working with farm staff as well as other vendors at the market, arranging produce, pricing it, recording and analyzing sales. Apprentices need to know about the produce being sold—its taste and nutritional value, preparation, possible uses. Their mentor describes this as a very "public" apprenticeship, "high paced, intense, a lot of things happening at once, people to interact with, exchanges going on" (Burns, p.c., February 9, 2007).

Urban education and outreach apprentices' responsibilities include technical assistance to neighborhood residents with their own community gardens; presentations on food and nutrition issues in varied community settings; work with other organizations on environmental problems such as lead contamination and on food policy issues such as support for locally grown food; and advocacy on food issues with local and state government. Youth plan and lead public education/awareness events, for example community lunches; help local gardeners with questions about soil improvement or remediation, use of pesticides, or sustainable agriculture methods; work with other organizations to measure and map levels and locations of lead in a neighborhood.

Apprenticeships are distinguished by the amount of responsibility youth have, the variety of tasks for which they are responsible, and the teaching and leadership role they assume. Apprentices are exemplars for newer youth. They join their adult mentors in reflecting on program design, thinking about and sharing ideas for improving farm, market and kitchen operations. The urban grower notes that "we ask youth to step up, but gradually ... Within TFP there's this ladder, and youth know that as you move through our programs expectations are going to increase." Performance-related issues that might have been left unnoted earlier are brought up immediately (Andrews, p.c., February 7, 2007).

TFP's framework for supporting youth development is at once conservative and subversive. It uses a basic human activity—hard, physical, agricultural work—as a foundation for deliberately shaking loose young people's sense of themselves and for exploring difficult social issues. The natural and social worlds also serve as contrasting bases for youth to learn about mastery and achievement. One does not master the natural world, but works "in partnership with it." Still, "human beings can have mastery over some things, like decontaminating urban garden plots from lead and other toxins" (Rossi, 2003, p. 2). Getting the work done is important—it will meet real social needs—and "standards are in place because we want them to get the work done" (Gale, 2005, p. 6). But although adult staff are demanding of youth and exacting in their expectations, they complement this pressure by assuring that TFP is a safe place for youth. Young people are never blind-sided; demands have reasons.

TFP is guild-like in its internally-oriented standards and emphasis on community. Gale notes that "it's very empowering to be part of a community pulling hard in the same direction" (p.c., August 6, 2007). As in a guild, there is a hierarchy with the larger body of work visible to all. Doing one kind of work leads to the next. Youth participating in one element of the organization's work can see how it relates to other elements. Yet TFP also differs from traditional guilds in that participants at all levels have a voice, and all practices are open to criticism. An urban agriculture apprentice tells an observer that "At The Food Project you are invited, nobody is discriminated against, and they make you feel good ..." One youth notes that "this is a world that allows you to speak and not be criticized for your thoughts" (cited in Gale, 2006, p. 22).

TFP appears to work at different levels for youth. When one young woman is asked what she gained from her work on a summer crew she responds "Patience ...take your anger out on the weeds" (*What Kids Can Do*, 2007, p. 1). Youth learn to deal with if not love the hard work, and seeing the effect of that work gives it meaning. A young woman tells Andrews (2001, p. 8) that "[you are] going to the shelters and you're seeing all these people who would not normally have this healthy organic food ... and you serve it to them...." Participation in all the stages of production and then in the preparation and distribution of food also strengthens young people's capacity to see connections. Youth come to see that how the soil is treated affects the quality of produce, and that how agriculture is organized in the United States affects people's access to high quality food. One youth notes that "The Food Project does so much more than just farming, so there's just that expansive aspect about it. There's so much, you gotta take a lot of it away" (Andrews, 2001, p. 16). As Gale puts it, "our work integrates in a society that disintegrates" (2006, p. 9).

Youth evince a deepening commitment to TFP and its goals become theirs as well. The urban grower notes that "I'm constantly amazed at what they're willing to do to be part of this experience. I'm thinking of one young woman who has to leave her house in Dorchester at 5 every morning to make sure she gets to the farm on time. To see a 15 year old doing that every day is pretty remarkable" (Andrews, p.c., February 7, 2007). A young woman participating in "carrot day," one of TFP's public education efforts promoting locally grown food, notes that "I am, at times, prompted to do strange things in the name of the Food Project. For instance, last August I found myself dressed up in a homemade eggplant costume, passing out carrots to complete strangers, urging them to eat locally" (Perkins-High, 2007).

There is a sense of growing up in a community, with all the mutual supports and responsibilities that entails. Gale describes a young man who helped out a peer missing a lot of work, calling to make sure he was out of bed in the morning and then calling again to make sure he was at work. Investment in the TFP community as a whole also deepens. An apprentice notes that "This is my third summer with them and I feel very connected to the community, like I belong here. They've invested in me and I've invested in them too … I think you start off thinking that it's a good job, makes money and is fun and different than other jobs kids get, but then it becomes much more than that. The work draws you in, it starts to mean a lot to you" (Borisova, 2005, pp. 1, 14).

Careers Through Culinary Arts

The Careers Through Culinary Arts Program (CCAP) was founded in 1990 by Richard Grausman, a well-known chef and food educator. CCAP runs high school-based programs during the school year in a number of cities, sponsors competitions for scholarships, and runs a summer-long, paid apprenticeship program for youth in New York City. Youth selected for the summer program have to have demonstrated some commitment to culinary work—and some passion for food—through prior experience in school, other CCAP programs, or elsewhere. Youth receive one or two weeks of orientation and are then placed in restaurants or institutional food service operations (e.g., corporate dining rooms, museums). They work 30 hours a week, on average, mostly in the kitchen but occasionally also in the dining room. A number of participating restaurants are among the best known in New York City.

Since its inception, CCAP has had a particular commitment to bringing young people of color into culinary work. Grausman believes that both parents and educators dissuade youth who otherwise might be—and in many cases actually are—drawn to culinary arts. The context for such reservations is a general loss in American culture in the belief in starting at the beginning and working one's way up in a field. Young people themselves "want to be chefs right away, they don't want to peel carrots." Some working-class parents use entry level work as a kind of bogeyman to keep their children in school: "if you stay in school and graduate you won't have to do the things your parents and grandparents did." This further stigmatizes the idea of starting at the beginning and working one's way up (Grausman, p.c., December 21, 2006). Grausman's experience with scores of youth over more than a decade belies these beliefs. He has found that early commitment to a culinary career, which includes both education and good work experience, significantly increases the odds that a young person will advance in the field. One CCAP mentor, who has observed the careers of a number of young professionals in her role overseeing food services at the Museum of Modern Art, agrees. She notes that on the road to becoming a chef "it is critical to spend time working in others' kitchens" (Grace, p.c., January 16, 2007).

Restaurant kitchens are, nonetheless, notoriously challenging learning and work environments. There is a lot going on simultaneously and everything moves at high speed—tasks, instructions, language, and movements. A complex set of roles and discrete activities have to fit together in time and sequence. Tasks are both mundane and precise; attention to detail is critical. Chefs have distinctive culinary philosophies and food preparation approaches—down to the way they dice vegetables. Keeping with tradition, it is apprentices' responsibility to learn as much as they can about the way their mentor does things: "the right way to do anything in the kitchen is the way the chef does it" (Grausman, p.c., December 21, 2006). Chefs vary also in their interest in teaching and passing on their knowledge. It depends in part on their own apprenticeship experiences, in part on their temperament. The mentor from the Museum of Modern Art notes that "in big production, high volume kitchens like ours some chefs want to teach, others have less interest, and some simply lack time" (Grace, p.c., January 16, 2007). Another mentor reflects "you catch a cook on a bad day and you might not learn anything" (Borenkoff, p.c., January 30, 2007). In kitchens, then, the apprentice has to learn to hold his or her own, for instance, being assertive in claiming a piece of equipment, and sometimes to fight for learning opportunities.

CCAP staff have developed an orientation program that does as much foreshadowing as possible before placing youth in a commercial kitchen. At a practical level, youth learn some of the basic skills that put a young person in a better position to progress in the kitchen, especially knife skills, food handling, and safety. Beyond such skills, staff emphasize the idea that "acting right" in a work environment opens the door to growth in responsibilities and opportunity to learn. In that light they discuss with youth the many specific behaviors that sideline young entry level workers—showing up late or not at all, non verbal behavior communicating resentment at being asked to do unpleasant tasks, sitting down in the middle of a shift, or sneaking out for a smoke. CCAP staff emphasize the importance of letting the chef know that one has come to the kitchen to work and learn, for instance through expressions of interest in and curiosity about food and food preparation. And they emphasize the general importance of communication: "always ask, never assume." Grausman (p.c., December 21, 2006) observes that "I've had some fabulous technicians that couldn't express themselves; when they needed help they didn't know how to ask for it, they couldn't communicate ... so they would leave when things got hard." CCAP staff continue meeting regularly with youth over the course of the summer, having learned from experience that "you can't just open a door and push someone through it" (Grausman, p.c., December 21, 2006). These meetings provide opportunity to share and process work experiences, talk about new foods discovered and about some of the challenges experienced, such as working at the speed demanded in a professional kitchen.

Once placed with a restaurant or institutional food service operation, youth might spend the bulk of their time at one or two food preparation stations, or be rotated through many stations, a week or two at a time They will start the summer working at the preliminary stages of food preparation and move only gradually to involvement with the end product, the plated dish. Youth learn to make stock from scratch, the basics of roasting and baking. They might learn to serve food, to prepare menus and order food from suppliers, keeping in mind what ingredients are available at what prices and estimating amounts of ingredients needed. They will learn about food storage and re-use. Youth learn to judge the quality of ingredients. They are introduced to new foods and ingredients and learn how these are used in a range of recipes. They learn the role of different utensils, how to use specialized equipment, and perhaps most important how the kitchen works—the role of each station, how staff interact, how the hierarchy works. Over the course of the summer, some youth—probably a minority of the full cohort of 40 or so—will experience the opportunity to "add their own judgment into the mix" (Mitchell, p.c., December 8, 2006).

Mentors focus to differing degrees on teaching about work behavior in general and what it means to be—to think and act like—a professional. One mentor notes that "if necessary we will teach youth about punctuality, work behavior, but if we feel they are not here to do anything we won't keep them; this is the real world." He and his staff nonetheless take responsibility for teaching the working through, planning, and anticipating that they consider basic but that they are aware is "not so basic" for youth: "when you're done with whatever tasks you have then you should be jumping in to help somebody out ... at the end of the day you have to break down your station, do all the cleaning—like any chef or cook will do ... know what you're doing the next day, study the menu you're going to be working with, know what items you'll need, check to make sure they're available here" (Borenkoff, p.c., January 30, 2007).

Mentors and youth themselves describe growth in craft, including knife skills, speed, accuracy, food handling, and general dexterity. One youth notes that he has learned "to be fast but not so fast that you mess up." A second notes that "Chef compliments everything that I do when I plate a tomato salad; 'it's beautiful,' as he would say in Polish" (CCAP Exit Survey, 2007). Youth acquire a deeper, more differentiated knowledge of foods and ingredients, for example the distinctions among the herbs that are used in recipes. Some youth note developing a closer, richer relationship to food. Youth learn to work in a complex, fast-moving environment: "If you survive in the kitchen you'll come out being

a multi-tasker, capable of precision, of orchestrating the pieces [of a meal] ..."
(Grausman, p.c., December 21, 2006). Youth begin to understand the unusual
balance between hierarchy and teamwork in kitchens, and the critical role of
communication in negotiating this structure.

Some youth come to see the kitchen as an inherently unfriendly environment—communication to be too gruff, people too busy to pay attention, chefs
too busy to provide feedback. Some are not able to get beyond the repetitive
nature of the work, especially in high volume kitchens. Progress toward greater
responsibility is sometimes slow: "you're not going to be asked to handle expensive ingredients until you've proven yourself" (Mitchell, p.c., December
8, 2006). Many other youth get a charge from the energy of a kitchen. Youth
with a natural or deep seated interest in food—how it tastes, how it looks, what
can be done with it—seem especially to get a lot out of the work. Grausman
(p.c., December 21, 2006) believes that this passion helps youth stay motivated
through the mundane, repetitious dimensions of the work. They are in a setting
that holds the things they are most excited about, as well as the manual labor
that has less meaning.

Grausman (p.c., December 21, 2006) observes that "work itself matures a
young person quite rapidly. He or she all of a sudden understands that life isn't
just days going by; there is suddenly something to focus on and to achieve...."
Youth seem somewhat surprised at their own perseverance, surprised that they
are both held accountable and can actually rise to the challenge. One notes, "I
can't believe I got up and was there on time every day"; another that "although
I woke up at 4:45 a.m., it felt good to walk the dark streets and know I am going
to work" (Mitchell, p.c., December 8, 2006; CCAP Exit Survey, August, 2007).
Youth learn also to navigate the difficult choices that come with responsibility;
one youth learns, for instance, how to work through the irreconcilable demands
of a supervisor who accepts no excuses for being late and a mom who needs him
to stay home for a few hours to care for a sibling. A handful of youth comment
on learning to get a lot out of the setting, for instance, always having a notebook
handy to record important information (CCAP Exit Survey, August, 2007).

Youth note valuing the experience of meeting people from a range of backgrounds and experiences. Most CCAP apprentices have never been inside of
let alone dined in a restaurant like the one they have been placed in. For some
it is "a culture shock of sorts," as the program coordinator notes (Mitchell, p.c.,
October 23, 2006). Girls and youth of color sometimes found themselves to be
"the only one in the kitchen."

Yet the people participants meet and work with sometimes become the core
of a new social network. More generally, CCAP's own network of restaurants
and institutional food service settings is helpful to youth who will continue
apprenticing, or go to culinary school and then return to the kitchen. CCAP
staff help youth figure out paths into a very competitive industry, help with the
recommendations and scholarships that will be critical to some youth and, most

critically, stay in touch, for those moments when doubts or problems place a youth at risk of giving up.

Conclusions

The case studies in this chapter capture, first of all, the richness, variety, and depth potentially available to youth in American culture, the work that it takes to place, and the value of placing youth in the middle of that richness. There is so much to learn in any specific arena of human endeavor. Each provides a singular window into the adult world, while offering lessons about that world as a whole. Apprenticeships in the arts give youth a disciplined voice; those in the sciences, a sense of contributing to a gradually expanding knowledge edifice. Some fields emphasize physical processes and artifacts, others more abstract sociological and legal ones. Youth are required to wrestle with questions at the heart of a discipline, for example, the relationship of artist to audience, the kinds of science that contribute most to societies' well-being, and the relationship between economic systems and quality of life for the majority of citizens.

Just as an object under water provides the skeleton for the growth of a reef, apprenticing in a discipline seems to provide that skeleton for young people. Each discipline provides unique structures for growth, in addition to the common ones found across fields. In RTB and TFP, for instance, there is a beginning-to-end quality to the work—from harvesting the wood to using it in boat building; from planting the seed to preparing and distributing the harvested food. As Adam Green puts it, it is critical to know where things come from; that they just don't magically appear in finished form. The purpose of work in the sciences is different than that in the arts, confirmatory or disconfirmatory rather than expressive, as are the nature and role of iteration, the sources of pressure in the work and constraints on innovation.

Apprenticeships re-create to an extent the steps from the bottom of a field to the middle of it. As Lave and Wenger (1991) put it, youth move from the periphery to the middle. Yet these are also telescoped experiences, with practice and real use overlapping. In some fields, especially the sciences, the experience of being in a professional setting, working alongside practicing professionals, enables young people begin to imagine it as possible for them. The work young people do is genuinely needed; by implication they themselves are genuinely needed. When an Art at Work mentor working with a team of youth on a public art project asks a young woman "How do you think we should handle this?" she is not engaging in an exercise. Youth are really, as noted earlier, co-owners of the enterprise.

The case studies confirm and give meaning to the truism that young people have much to contribute to our common life. This idea has seemed, at times, a kind of rhetorical device for including youth in society, one neither examined very closely nor thought through carefully. But the rich, specific, and varied contributions made by young people's work in the varied fields described here, the ways in which youth work, and their willingness when necessary to stick with the work under sometimes difficult circumstances, make it clear that this truism is a profound one. An especially notable theme is mentors' surprise at how much an apprentice has brought, contributed to and even altered the work of an enterprise; and the not infrequent comment that the mentoring experience has led them to look at their own work "with new eyes," as one scientist puts it (Academy of Applied Science, 2000, p. 21).

Not least, the case studies make clear the institutional resources available to be mobilized for youth. Because it is diverse and decentralized, the collection of sponsors described here is hardly visible as an important developmental resource. Yet when viewed as a collective it offers significant potential as a base for experience. And unlike many school-sponsored apprenticeships, this other group is not constrained by competing agendas, bureaucratic requirements, or role limitations. It is, as a whole, a lively group of institutions. The Food Project's Greg Gale (2005, p. 5) notes that "Almost every day feels like we have new and different challenges to face." As the TFP farmers market supervisor notes, "over time the organization has discovered the pieces it needed" (Burns, p.c., February 9, 2007). What is interesting is that these are much less standardized settings than school, but work as well or better.

III

Reflecting on Apprenticeship

5

The Experience of Apprenticeship
From Both Sides

Some youth just take a little longer to realize what's going on …
   An Artists for Humanity teaching artist

It now seems more like a practice to me.
   An After School Matters photography apprentice

In this chapter I examine the difficulties and rewards of the apprenticeship experience from the perspective of both apprentices and instructors.[1] From the former, one discerns a mixture of frustration early on with the difficulty or demandingness of the work, incipient pride at coping and persisting, and growing enjoyment of the routine of the work itself. It takes time for youth to learn to use these settings for what they can provide. In general, apprentices report on their experience in a way that conveys a sense of being more viscerally alive in these than in other settings of their lives. The challenges—faced by apprentices and instructors alike—derive from the internalized models of learning and striving that youth bring with them to apprenticeships, from young people's shifting psychological states, and from the limited time frames in relation to both the specific demands of becoming skillful and larger processes of growth.

Apprenticeships are genuinely unprecedented developmental contexts for youth—about learning but not at all like school; serious and demanding, but accepting of struggles and mistakes; with both the substantive work and young people's own developing selves at the center of things. Youth may be aware at the outset that, as learning and working experiences, these are more interesting than what is typically available to them. But they rarely understand what they are getting themselves into and are often surprised by both the demands and the opportunity itself. It takes time for youth to figure out what these experiences are about, how they work, what learning resources they provide and what the expectations will be. Steinberg (2000, p. 9), for instance, describes young people "who, for the first time, found themselves getting help to do something well, rather than being judged to do it badly." It takes time to accept being taken seriously but matter-of-factly. Apprentices experience a range of emotions and psychological states that are uncommon in other settings of their lives.

For some youth, apprenticeship may be a requirement of their chosen curricular track or, as in the case of Big Picture Schools, of the school itself. For many others, these are voluntary experiences. In either case youth approach them with different interests in mind—exploring a discipline, simple curiosity, the promise of a stipend, something to add to a college application, or just something engaging to do after school or in the summer. As one After School Matters participant notes, "it's a lot better than going home to sleep or hanging out some more with my friends." Choosing to join an apprenticeship program can, nonetheless, mean going against the grain of friends and family, for whom a particular activity might sound strange. Youth not infrequently hear "Why do you want to do that?" and may be teased if an activity does not fit gender stereotypes.

Instructors, too, experience a variety of distinctive challenges, some related to who youth are and what they bring to the apprenticeship, some to the flexible nature of their role, some to the constraints created by relatively limited time to nurture professional skills and habits, in the face of practical deadlines. There is no defined master-apprentice model for work with youth under the conditions outlined in chapters three and four. At times these are novel experiences for instructors as well as for their apprentices. Mentors may have little prior experience in youth work. A science mentor with Oregon's Apprenticeship in Science and Engineering notes that "you get the impression that high school students are going to be difficult to work with ... I was surprised at how easy it was to talk to A and how mature she was. She would tell me when she didn't understand something; it was very simple...."

Personal Challenges and Growing Pleasure

Young people approach apprenticeship in varied ways, related to the novelty of the discipline, their own temperamental style, and their experience with learning and new settings. Rocking the Boat's Adam Green notes that "you see kids who are particularly excited and open and dive right in," and others who are passive and hang back in the early weeks (p.c., June 22, 2006). For some youth, the experience catches right away. Others take much longer to ignite. Marwen's public art teaching artist notes of one young woman that "when I first met her I thought, 'Why does she want to do this?' She ended up being one of my rock stars ... she went on to help one of my colleagues and me with a project at O'Hare airport, and now she really wants to do mosaics on her own" (Gaspar, p.c., July 2. 2007).

Difficulties of the Novice Phase

Apprentices often describe the first weeks as tough or frustrating. Culinary apprentices note the difficulty of staying on their feet for hours, cutting themselves with their knives as they try to keep up, remembering who is who in the kitchen. Science apprentices struggle with the seeming inflexibility of procedures, the need to attend to detail and the time it takes for experiments to unfold. Some fields are more difficult to grasp and learn one's way around in. One young man, working for a geneticist, writes in his journal "Different bacteria strains, varying growth media, millions of lab tools—sometimes I'm just overwhelmed" (Richmond & Kurth, 1999, p. 681). An apprentice working in a civil rights organization describes not understanding at times what the adults are talking about at meetings: "So, it's difficult. That's the most challenging thing—basically not understanding about civil rights issues … I try to take notes … And I'm like, 'What do I write? Is this important?'" (Riordan, 2006, p. 95). Reflecting on a community organizing experience for youth, Larson and Hansen (2005, p. 345) note that "Impacting human worlds is difficult and we think it likely that many youth do not become adept at it."

Youth sometimes have difficulty adjusting to the rules and norms of workplaces and of work itself, whether dress codes and hierarchy, the directness of feedback, the busyness of mentors and colleagues, or basic responsibility and accountability frameworks. For some youth, the challenge is as basic as "just showing up, calling if you're going to be late or absent" (Wenger, p.c., June 27, 2007). An After School Matters (ASM) art instructor talks about needing to be explicit about "why it is important to come on time, at 3, not 3:05 or 3:30, because they just don't seem to understand, they say 'oh, I had to go to the store to get a candy bar.' I think the least of my worries is the artwork." An Artist for Humanity teaching artist notes that "Some youth just take a little longer to realize what's going on; sometimes they realize it after they leave" (Vicin, p.c., January 8, 2007). Renee Flemings of Roundabout Theater echoes that thought: "It takes a while for some kids to get what this is about. They're kids, they think they can come to rehearsal late" (p.c., February 16, 2007); Flemings notes that most youth do eventually get it, "if they have to be late for some reason they'll let me know, instead of 'I'll show up when I show up.'"

Not Like School

The director of St. Louis Artworks notes that the most difficult aspect of the experience for apprentices in her program is "to understand the difference between being at school and being at work … You can't hold back, you can't put your head down and nap" (Block, p.c., August 1, 2006). Youth report surprise that, unlike school, in these settings one cannot fake it, cheat or "skate through." A Big Picture apprentice notes that: "You can cheat your way through other high schools and you can cheat your way through elementary and middle school, but here you cannot cheat at all. It's impossible. When you have to stand in front of everyone and do your exhibition, you've got to have something" (Steinberg, 2000 p. 10). When the director of Riverzedge Arts tells participants at the "72-hour" review that she knows they have been fooling around "they're stunned that I know. That's when it hits them: 'this I really serious'" (Novello, p.c., July 6, 2007).

The contrast with school extends to difficulty adjusting to a learning context in which one is expected to be active. Instructors attribute this difficulty to young people's lifelong experience as passive learners, accustomed to being told not just what to do but what to think. A documentary instructor who, during the early weeks, has youth discuss and evaluate the qualities of photos and completed documentaries, notes that with each group "there's a day when they turn on me: 'You didn't teach us anything so how do you expect us to do this?'" The instructor reflects that "It's like a mutiny, but an important one," for it is at this moment that the group begins to realize how different this setting is than others they are accustomed to (Neptune, p.c., April 27, 2007).

Youth sometimes struggle to hear and use feedback, whether because of how it feels, or simply because it suggests that they have a lot more work to do. Thus a young man struggles to assimilate the comments of a print-making instructor who tells him, "Add more to it, make it more personal, what does this have to do with you?" (Thomas, 2007, p. 782). Or youth become frustrated when, as is not uncommon in workplaces, they are asked to prepare a product which is then revised by someone else: "Like the last time I was there I had to cut up a layout of a mat. It was basically a big puzzle ... and I'm tracing everything out, and I taped everything together, and then once I gave it to one of the designers he changed the whole thing" (Larson & Walker, 2006, p. 253).

The dysfunctional lessons brought from other experiences operate across all the dimensions of work and learning. Youth with little or no recognition, and perhaps little more than criticism, for efforts in the past get discouraged easily, by the need to keep working on a task or product, or by the time it takes to become proficient at particular skills. The director of Riverzedge Arts notes having to reassure youth that they will begin to feel differently: "Rome wasn't built in a day—you've only been here six months" (Novello, p.c., July 6, 2007). An ASM instructor observes that apprentices tend to give up easily in part because they experience no genuine accountability in school or elsewhere; they are just pushed around, threatened or ignored. Another notes that the apprentices spend the whole day "being controlled in so many ways ... they go through the halls all the time people yelling at them." She is surprised because "it is much more effective to appeal to their maturity ... and trust them with some responsibility." Youth sometimes need to be told explicitly that collaborating is not cheating, that failing at a task does not make one a failure.

Youth with difficult personal histories or a sense of social marginalization may have little tolerance for the feelings that accompany being a novice. Cohen (1999, p. 145) suggests that the experience of struggle with a new task "plays back [earlier] experiences of exclusion and marginality." More immediately a Rocking the Boat on water instructor notes that "it's hard enough for teenagers to do some of the thankless work here, but it is much harder when you grow up in a place where a lot of people feel that somebody owes them something" (Heyman, p.c., March 9, 2007). In general, investing in an activity, risking one's self, would seem to require a basic sense of competence, of "alrightness," to begin with.

The Challenge of Opening Up

Mentors from a number of initiatives note that it is difficult for youth to open up to the varied experiences in apprenticeship, to drop the protective shell they carry around and that seems necessary in other contexts. An Artist for Humanity teaching artist notes that "a lot of them have this tough facade and don't like to talk about their feelings or what they're about ... the first identity project, the autobiographical project, is difficult for many kids ... I feel like there's this mask they put on for the world" (Truong, p.c., December 8, 2006). As Greg Gale of The Food Project puts it, "an opposite kind of self is required" in these settings than in others (p.c., August 7, 2006).

The difficulty of opening up, taking risks, letting go can be seen in almost any field. A boat-building instructor observes that "It's hard to do things that are or seem intimidating, [for instance] to cut an expensive piece of wood. They don't want to make a mistake" (Wenger, p.c., June 27, 2007). It is especially evident in apprenticeships requiring self-expression, those in which youth have to write, draw, act, move, think up, and imagine freely. Youth struggle with the vulnerability—the fear of ridicule—that accompanies exposing their thoughts and ideas to others. Young people who have been warned their whole life to edit themselves may be suddenly told to do the opposite. A Roundabout teaching artist observes that some apprentices "are so aware of themselves, and everything around them, that they're almost paralyzed" (Keith, p.c., April19, 2007). He adds that it is hard for some to let go: "they want to be vulnerable but they just can't be—that's why the safe space."

Youth struggle in a number of ways with the creative process. It is never easy to start a new project, or to sit in front of a blank page, to wait for what comes next. Youth lack the experience to trust that ideas will come. An ASM painting apprentice notes the difficulty—and scariness—of "thinking about, deciding what to do next when we start a new project." As discussed in chapter 4, apprentices sometimes have difficulty breaking through the imagery and stereotypes of the popular media in which they are immersed every day. They tend to act like "little media drones," as one ASM teaching artist says. Drawings and images often simply reflect back the media and advertising images young people see. Or young people bring a graphic style that can limit the growth of their painting or drawing.

A related challenge, notable in apprenticeships involving self-expression, involves learning how to draw on personal experience—more generally on what is inside one—to fuel but not define a product or performance. To an extent, apprentices' difficulty in transforming material is due to the very relentlessness of popular media, and perhaps to the degradation of language in the music that some apprentices listen to. To an extent it is psychological—apprentices sometimes use these experiences to explore deeply personal dimensions of their life experience. In one youth radio story, for instance, a young woman explores "whether her Peruvian father truly understood the effects on her life of his decision not to speak Spanish in the home" (Chavez & Soep, 2005, p. 413). There is also a developmental dimension. Young people tend to be internally focused and somewhat egocentric in filtering or making sense of the world around them. In discussing script writing, a filmmaking apprentice notes that "It's a completely different thought process than just writing down your own thoughts, when you're trying to get in the head of the character and think like they think" (Dowdy, Birney, & Reedus, 2004, p. 20).

A Growing Experience

With time young people's sense of difficulty, disorganization, or just tentativeness is increasingly balanced by more complex feelings. What begin as external demands become internalized and no longer feel like impositions. Young people adjust to what they once thought they could not. Day in, day out, they get better at the work and begin to believe they can do it. They learn to manage their frustration and "use their emotions [sic] as information" (Larson & Walker, 2006, p. 259). They get used to the language, and to exercises and structures that at first cause discomfort. In discussing peer critiques, an ASM teaching artist notes that "we would try to get them to use the vocabulary, you know, values and tones, line quality, the weight of the picture, elements, things like that. So they would get used to using that kind of language, and then the meaning would start coming out...."

Young people come to enjoy the distinctive feelings they experience in apprenticeship. A photography apprentice describes pleasure in the total experience of shooting photos: "When I am outside, roaming around, just being able to take the picture, that's the fun part, just having the experience of holding the camera the correct way, adjusting the focus...." For a young woman in a biology lab, the lab begins to feel more like home.

Apprentices across the disciplines talk about the importance of routine as a pathway into the work—the physical acts of setting up, handling and taking apart equipment, and the basic care of materials and equipment, preparing, laying out, cleaning and maintaining. Apprentices become acclimated to the setting in part through daily routines and rituals. These contribute to a sense of predictability and reliability, and contribute to apprentices' understanding of practice and discipline. When a youth walks into a kitchen, she begins to know who will be stationed at different spots, what others will be working on and how to slot herself into the complex set of tasks underway. In a flamenco apprenticeship, the warm up not only prepares the muscles, but pulls the dancers in. If they were distracted before, the warm up gets them engaged. Over the course of 10 to 15 minutes, 20 individuals become one ensemble.

Apprentices begin to develop a necessary minimal level of skill or conditioning. The budding photographer begins to feel like a photographer at heart, the young scientist like a scientist. There are more extended productive periods. In a complementary vein, apprentices come to see that these are safe settings to demonstrate competence, express vulnerability, worries, anger, to not have to pose; apprentices know that, as one put it, "no one is going to rip on them." In discussing the climate of the photography studio an ASM apprentice notes that "We would get around week five, everyone would start working independently, it would get like pretty quiet in the room and people were still talking and doing other things, but that is when it started feeling like a cohesive group to me. That is when people are comfortable and they are not worried about what other people are doing."

Apprentices begin to learn to trust process more. They report coming to appreciate that the demands of the work are tempered by its emphasis on approximation; the fact that a product or performance will eventually take shape, that one gets there gradually, in stages. In science apprenticeships, youth come to understand the reasons for what initially seem to be needlessly painstaking procedures. Young people talk about how different an experience feels when they have some extended time to work on it, a sense that it is really done, not just stopped by the time available. An ASM filmmaking apprentice describes how it is difficult to get into editing, especially on a day when he is "riled up" from school, but then he settles down "and suddenly I look up and it is six o'clock."

Youth describe a growing desire to get something out of the experience. A filmmaking apprentice from another initiative reports that "When we first got into it we thought, 'yeah, this is going to be so cool.' And then the hours that you put in and how it takes away from other things... And you really want to get something out of it" (Dowdy, Birney, & Reedus, 2004, p. 20). Youth begin to see that the work they have put in is paying off. An ASM flamenco apprentice puts it well, noting that "it is very hard but you get more out of it than you think, you get more out of it than you asked for." For those who do apprenticeships after school, it becomes something to look forward to. As an ASM photography apprentice puts it, "you know, it's a long, hard day [at school] and you're so bored, then you come to photography and you laugh, you have conversation, you do this work...."

Meeting responsibilities becomes a source of pride as well as a burden. An astronomy apprentice: "I was the guy that had to do the paddle and constantly tweak it to try to keep it on the slit for like ... a dozen 10 minute exposures. So I would sit there for, you know, like 10 minutes with my eye glued to this eyepiece desperately trying to keep it on the slit when you can't see the slit and can hardly see the object ... so it was really tough. And I think probably that's what I'll remember most, just sitting there for 10 minute exposures with my neck cramping up ... but in the end it was definitely worth it because we got the data we needed" (McCarthy, 2002, p. 37).

Apprentices are able after a while to reflect on their own growth. An ASM mural apprentice mentions learning how to transfer an outline to a bigger platform and learning how to mix paints to create the color he wants. He describes learning to see differences in colors that he would not have been attentive to before. A theater apprentice mentions learning how to use the whole stage, and learning to separate himself from his own emotions and adopt the emotional state of the character he is portraying. A filmmaking apprentice learns to not get too attached to a particular shot or scene, but to view it in relation to its contribution to the story and narrative. Youth in a number of initiatives speak of the pleasure of discovering that they liked something that they may have known little about. A sound design apprentice with Roundabout Theater notes that "To tell the truth, it really surprised me that I liked theater so much. I liked working behind the scenes where you can watch the show and know you contributed something. You know that without the sound you've designed it wouldn't be perfect" (Roundabout Education Report, 2006, p. 12).

Youth come to recognize the learning in apprenticeship as both different and sometimes more powerful. Contrasting her experience in a New York City design apprenticeship with that at school a young woman tells an interviewer that "I feel like they [school staff] don't include us ... They made it up, they already made it, it's already tested ..." (Daniel, 2007, p. 137). Apprentices note that the volitional nature of learning in apprenticeship contributes to growth. An ASM apprentice reflects that "I grew up more, the interest in the program made me different as opposed to school where you have to do it; in the program it is a choice."

Learning also feels more purposeful to youth. For example, though both school and many apprenticeships require writing, and involve learning to write more effectively, apprentices describe the writing process in apprenticeships as more interesting. It is not just the varied forms—a script, a particular type of poem, a journalistic piece summarizing an interview, a statement of philosophy or intent in relation to some artwork—but the greater control over content and the clear use of the writing. An observer notes of the writing done for a youth radio program that "This isn't just writing so you can get the five paragraph essay down. You're going to be producing something that's going to be consumed by the public—at the very minimum on the [program] web site and possibly on National Public Radio" (Mahiri, 2007).

Not least, youth come to appreciate the new type of adult and new type of adult relationship they discover in apprenticeship. They like being around adults who enjoy their work, are passionate about a particular field, and draw their identity from it. An ASM apprentice notes that she likes the instructors' honesty: "they [the instructors] hold nothing back, they don't sugar-coat." Another notes liking that instructors do not condescend, and generally refrain from blatant use of power: "they don't come at you with this attitude like I'm an adult, listen to me." Apprentices like that instructors have serious conversations with them. An ASM photography apprentice describes one of her instructors as follows: "Mr. D. has a very intelligent conversation with you ... other teachers look down at you, like 'you're just a kid, you won't understand.'" A number of apprentices note liking that the instructors really listen to them: "they hear what you say." They are surprised that an instructor really takes their ideas seriously, turns them over, critiques them as well as praising them. A handful of apprentices comment on instructors' commitment to each apprentice's needs: "if they [the instructors] are talking to someone, they'll tell you to hold on for a minute, and then they'll come over."

Instructors' Work: Challenges and Rewards

Apprenticeships are also challenging and growing experiences for mentors. Challenges are practical, developmental, psychological, and cultural. They include calibrating expectations, deciding what is most important to teach and work on, given time constraints, and figuring out the right balance of responsibility for learning and producing. Challenges can include combating the models of teaching and learning young people acquire in school, coping with lack of basic skills, and sometimes coping with young people's physical and psychological state after a day at school. Mentors may need to reach youth who have experienced significant loss or other trauma and they often struggle to understand, if not accept, young people's priorities and values.

Mentors in a number of initiatives note the importance of finding the right balance or mix, of methods, content, expectations, and instructor activism. They have to work to figure out at what level to teach and what to choose to convey. The dilemma derives from their having a good deal of knowledge and experience and a relatively limited amount of time. It derives from the inherent difficulty of making explicit one's implicit knowledge. A painting mentor describes the challenge as "taking an almost infinitely complex craft and aesthetic and reducing it down—and then what do you reduce it down to?" (Fesmire, p.c., July 31, 2007). It also takes instructors, especially new ones, some weeks to figure out what apprentices know and can do. A few note having to be less theoretical and conceptual over time.

Mentors struggle—in the positive sense—with how much to let apprentices "wander in the wilderness" before stepping in, and how much to contribute themselves to make a product better. Mentors have to decide when to be more active, with such comments as "you could try..." or "why don't you try..."—a kind of gentle push to next level—and when to hold back. The majority are aware of a need to encourage apprentices to take responsibility for the process and product of each apprenticeship. Yet, as one notes, "sometimes you give them too much creative freedom at the beginning, you wasted a lot of time, and they began to get overwhelmed." An ASM art instructor notes that "Not every idea is necessarily a great idea. That's really [about helping them develop] the aesthetic sense ... which is one of the issues I've had with a lot of apprenticeships."

Mentors note challenges in working with youth on those skills and dispositions that call on new developmental capacities such as planning and persisting. An ASM filmmaking instructor notes that a big challenge is "to get them to do the pre-production, to think ahead about what is coming down the line; pre-production is all planning." Lack of experience means that an apprentice might go with his or her first idea simply because he or she does not yet know that other ideas will follow. An ASM art instructor observes that, especially given the structure of learning in high school, helping youth "understand the process of trial and error and failure as a way of exploring is very difficult." A colleague overseeing a multi-panel mural notes: "They paint for 30 minutes and say 'o.k.

I'm done, and I'll say ... the shapes of this needs work, you need to change this color or this shade, and there is a lot of teeth-sucking and sighing, but most of the time they are up for it."

Because youth are in a fluid period developmentally, consistency can be an issue. Young people's responses—and sense of responsibility—to a setting may vary from day to day. An Artist for Humanity teaching artist notes that youth "sometimes need reminding of what they are doing here (Vicin, p.c., January 8, 2007). This developmental pattern is exacerbated in school year programs in which young people can arrive at apprenticeship tired and/or psychologically worked up. Youth can invest in the work after school and manage to get engaged, but episodically; productive activity breaks down easily. An ASM instructor observes that "at the end of a difficult school day, they'll go through the motions and they'll want to be there, but having the physical energy to pull off some of the stuff, and inspiring them has been difficult." On some days apprenticeships function in the territory between distraction and engagement. Adam Green of Rocking the Boat describes the challenge as keeping apprentices centered on what they are doing: "They'll be planing and staring out the window" (p.c., June 22, 2006). The director of a product design apprenticeship program observes that "young people's motivation and focused attention ... seemed to go in and out" (Daniel, 2007, p. 71).

The mixed backgrounds, capacities, and motives of apprentices mean that mentors often have to adjust initial expectations of who apprentices will be and what is possible to accomplish. An ASM dance instructor notes that "I thought they would be like me in high school, we did not like being there but we listened to everybody...." Instructors may have to adjust to the residue of a poor general education or lack of basic skills. A boat building instructor notes that "it's amazing how many seniors in high school cannot read a ruler" (Wenger, p.c., June 27, 2007). In describing her personal struggle to figure out at what level to teach, an ASM art instructor notes that "when we were their ages, we were rendering things naturalistically and we knew about artists. Part of it is having to almost not use our own experience as a basis...."

Mentors note struggling to find a balance in working with psychological impediments to learning and growth, for example, in helping apprentices "drop the facade" which, as noted earlier, is protective elsewhere but gets in the way in these apprenticeships. An ASM dance instructor notes: "You see kids in high school and you see their downfall and how they could avoid so many pitfalls if they just paid attention to themselves and did not care about fashion and all this gang stuff going on." Between a peer culture that can hold youth back and, in some instances, lives marked by loss and disruption, "you learn that you have to go against a whole world of things, as one ASM instructor puts it. A handful of youth remain unable to engage no matter how much an instructor reaches out. An ASM flamenco instructor tells a young woman: "You are the quietest person I have ever met in my life, and I cannot even see you sometimes in class.

You have to get my attention, because I know you are not getting the steps. You have to grab me and get my attention."

Mentors Are Growing Too

While mentors are learning about and adjusting to the youth they work with, they are simultaneously figuring out their role for themselves. Mentors do not have any extended socialization into a particular professional identity, as, for example, do teachers. They have different levels of prior experience with youth, varied understandings of their role and varied "working" models of being a teacher. This contributes to wide variability in how mentors define their role. Some are more process-oriented, others more product-oriented. Most are authoritative rather than authoritarian. Some consciously see themselves as a model; others deliberately do not want that responsibility. There is variability in how close instructors wish to become to apprentices, and in how much they want to learn about apprentices' total lives. One ASM poetry instructor, for instance, reports that she receives calls from her apprentices almost every night for support or advice on a range of issues. Most other mentors would not feel this to be part of their work.

For the great majority of mentors, work with youth is one part, often a modest part, of a larger professional life. Mentors describe it as rewarding but draining. They note that it takes time to figure out how mentoring youth should relate to their other work. A documentary filmmaker who is also an Education Video Center instructor notes that "the dialogue between my teaching self and my creating self is important" (Neptune, p.c., June 27, 2007). A teaching artist with Artists for Humanity notes that she is "still working on" finding a balance between her own work and her role as teacher. She notes that "the work [with youth] is so fulfilling that it is easy to be thinking about it all the time ... it can be very draining emotionally and physically ... On the other hand I'm learning a lot, I am more aware of what I know because I have to talk about it in a way that makes sense to other people" (Truong, p.c., December 8, 2006).

Mentors across disciplines note that having an apprentice helps them step back from their work, whether to think more consciously about specific tasks, what they know, a project, or the nature of the work. Especially in the arts and design fields, mentors believe that their work with youth is stimulating, young people's experimentation and energy contagious. The AFH teaching artist cited above reflects that "in some ways [the apprentices'] work really does influence mine, there's a natural give and take." A RiverzEdge teaching artist notes that "since coming here the range of what I can appreciate has broadened exponentially—being in art school for six years you become accustomed to a narrow sensibility of what good art is" (Fesmire, p.c., July 31, 2007). Derek McLane, a set designer who works with youth through Roundabout Theater, notes: "You recognize your own worth as an artist when you see you've excited a student intellectually and they suddenly realize that theater might offer them another path to learning" (Roundabout Education Report, 2006, p. 11).

A Master at Work

In the course of my own research with After School Matters and in the case studies for the book, I met many masters at work. These were mentors who, through trial and error, through memories and emulation of good teachers from their own formative experiences, or through instinct, had found a mix of strategies that reached youth, pushed them, and brought them inside a field. Here I have chosen to describe one who I found to be truly a master-full. She is a flamenco teacher and artist named Cecilia Barrioso (C), and, at the time of my research, she was teaching in a basement dance studio at Farragut High School on the southwest side of Chicago. The apprenticeship, part of After School Matters, took place three afternoons a week after school. The studio, which seemed converted from a large basement storage room, smelled like pesticide. Old pipes (some that seem to be leaking) ran across the ceiling. C and her apprentice dancers made the best of it, not complaining, C noting that she likes being tucked away in her own corner of the giant school.

Farragut is a tough, sometimes chaotic high school serving a mixed but strongly divided Latino and African American population. All but a few apprentices in the company are Latino (three are African American). A handful have worked with C the previous year and are committed to flamenco, another handful participated in a summer flamenco class taught by C; the rest have little or no dance experience. The latter group's interest and motivation vary. The apprentices come in all shapes, sizes, and ages and are a diverse group, in terms of self-presentation. Some are so shy that they can barely pick their head up and speak in public, others are extroverted and dramatic; a few seem old for their ages.

C is in her 30s, with a long history of professional dance and teaching. C is a natural teacher and motivator and clearly holds the affection of the apprentices. She is deeply committed to bringing the apprentices into the flamenco tradition and pushing them to accomplish what they themselves often do not believe they can. She tells me that "I find a challenge when people tell me I can't do it … and literally one day a girl said in class 'I can't do it'. So, I calmly went step by step, and I slowly sped it up, and she got it. And I turned to the class and said, 'Can you believe she said to us I can't do it? Sometimes you need a little help and that's why I'm here." Yet she also tries to balance the traditional discipline of the dance studio with recognition that these youth need someplace safe, and partly relaxing; something they can enjoy as their own.

Goals The apprenticeship introduces youth to Spain's diverse cultural heritage, expressed through dance—the *Jota*, from the north of Spain, which uses castanets, reflects that region's mixed Celtic and Greek influences and which can be lively and exuberant or the calm and sedate, energetic or intricate; and Flamenco, from the south of Spain, with its Gypsy and Moorish influences, a typically strong and austere form, that emphasizes heel work, hand-clapping, body posture, arm positions, hand movements, but includes a variation called *Guajiras* (of Cuban origin), done with fans and hats, embodying a gentler and more lyrical style. The apprenticeship is geared toward and ends in two public performances, one in winter, a second in spring.

C has a number of specific goals for the apprentices' experience: "In addition to giving them what I call a crash-course in the art, I'm also trying to get expression, I'm trying to get [them to have] a feel for the pieces, to teach the musicality." She wants apprentices to move beyond being themselves, and inhabit a dance persona. Yet knowing that it takes years to become technically skilled, and knowing that many apprentices will be with her for only a year or two, C primarily wants the apprentices to develop affection for the dance, have the pleasure of performing, and have flamenco become a small part of themselves. She wants to connect them to a tradition that will enrich their lives, and give them a source of dignity.

C notes that she wants apprentices to learn to work hard and to learn to see the connection between working hard and obtaining a concrete result. She believes the work they do, day-in and day-out, will give them a sense of physical integrity and some new physical skills, for example, training their minds to communicate with their bodies. One additional goal of this apprenticeship is to teach apprentices group responsibility, and to try to foster group identity. C notes that "Basically you're with a bunch of strangers that you really don't know well, and you come together for one thing, and you have to do something well together … it's not all about you, but it's about all of you."

Getting Organized One of C's more immediate tasks each year is to begin shaping this diverse group of individuals into an ensemble or company, as she notes "to create group unity as quickly as possible." In the early weeks, she makes sure the dancers learn and use each other's names. It takes a few weeks for apprentices to warm up to each other, and some are in fact hesitant to take the initiative to get to know others. Within a few weeks, the apprenticeship has lost three apprentices to work—they tell C that they need to earn more money. Soon two more apprentices are lost to transportation difficulties, having no way to get home after class. While attrition abates, absence from class remains a problem. After a few apprentices simply disappear for a week or two without explaining absences, C feels the need to have a talk about attendance. She reminds the group that every class builds on previous ones and adds elements toward performance and that apprentices are counting on each other. Not showing up is not simply a personal decision. C feels compelled to tell the group that unexcused absences could mean not participating in the performance.

The Studio Experience: Teaching and Learning The climate in the dance studio is absolutely serious and purposeful, but also relaxed, with humor mixed in from both instructor and apprentices (the latter an indication of feeling safe). Class starts each day as all dance classes seem to, with dancers drifting in, changing, maybe doing a little stretching (less than adult dancers). The timing and rhythm of the warm-up exercises are set by the castanets used by each dancer, and the random clicking of castanets, becoming gradually more persistent, is part of the informal lead in, as the dancers get ready. The warm-up serves a number of purposes: It gets the apprentices engaged and brings them to the same place. It converts 20 individuals into one ensemble. It is the same every day; the sameness contributes to apprentices' understanding of practice and discipline, and it contributes to a sense of predictability and reliability in this apprenticeship.

The learning experience is built on repetition, accretion, and sequence. Each new set of steps, of movements, builds on previous ones. Whatever is learned each day will be repeated as part of class every day hence, until it becomes automatic. The class is working toward the performance, and C has the whole set of dances in mind, adding small pieces each day and each week. The class works on a small piece of choreography until they get it right. Larger chunks of choreography are introduced each week as the class moves toward performance. C "holds" the larger picture—and the size of the challenge—for the apprentices, so they do not feel overwhelmed: "Our students don't realize how difficult it is, what they're doing; we don't really tell them." She tries to reassure the newer dancers by telling them to imagine doing it right, pretend, until "it becomes part of you."

There is a progression in C's emphases. The first weeks focus mostly on mastery of basic steps and forms, introduction to the different dance traditions and music, conditioning, and kinesthetic awareness. Gradually C adds attention to use of space, sense of direction, speed of steps and movement, partnering, breathing, foot, arm, leg and body positions, and technique. One afternoon, for instance, the focus is on moving to and through diagonals, and on teaching the dancers to use the direction of their head or body to create impressions of movement through space, for example, a diagonal impression. On another day, the dancers practice working in different combinations, to get them used to (as well as to test out) the varied combinations they will be put in for performance. In later weeks C adds attention to stage presence and stage-craft, for example, facial expressions (encouraging some girls to relax, others to smile, others to express emotion), entrances and exits, and holding a line (one of the dances uses four lines of dancers in sequence).

Woven through each week's classes are mini-lectures about the history and social role of different types of dances—*Sevillana, Guajira, Jota, Bolero*—and discourse on the nature and spirit of flamenco. Each type of dance demands different physical skills, spirit and sentiment. The *Sevillana*, for instance, is integral to fiestas and ferias (week-long fairs) and is usually a dance for couples. The spirit of the *Guajira* is more feminine and showy, and the shawl is used flirtatiously. Talking about flamenco one day, C tells the apprentices that its essence is "absolute control." C also uses costumes—shawls, bowler hats, skirts—to help the dancers come to inhabit the spirit of each tradition. (C is reported to scour second-hand shops for dresses and costumes, and her mother helps her fit and adjust them to each dancer.) One afternoon a few weeks before the performance, she gives the dancers an informal lesson in how to wrap the shawls correctly—she tells them that it is like a dress you are wearing, not like you are hanging laundry.

C explains the sense and meaning of the steps, what each dance is about (what animates it, gives it life), and sometimes the story of the particular music that they are dancing out. She does this to help the dancers develop a character, to understand the emotional import of particular steps and movements, and because in these dances each movement has a symbolic meaning. For one dance, the story of a young man during the Spanish Civil War who has been arrested by soldiers for his political beliefs and is being taken away, probably to be killed, she tells some of the dancers, "you're part of the military," and others "you're part of the resistance." She asks the apprentices to use whatever they need to to feel the anger in their hand and arm gestures, meant to represent the firing of rifles. She tells a group of dancers "think of the image of someone carrying power," for a particular set of movements. Part of what C is trying to convey is that even when a movement—a step, a walk, a use of the arms, a bend, seems familiar, it is not; it is not ordinary, it is to be carried out differently than in every day life.

Specific Teaching Techniques C's teaching strategy is multifaceted and flexible. She describes, demonstrates, guides, implores, jokes, and scolds. She teaches with her voice (she is a master of inflection), her body, arms, legs, words, sounds, and gestures. She uses verbal and visual analogies, visual descriptions of movement, physical and verbal humor. She shapes or adjusts the dancers' arms, legs, feet, heads, backs, and stomachs. She notes that "People hear in different ways and you have to figure out five different ways to say one thing;" and that "there have been times when I have had them literally talk it out, because I cannot get them to understand [what I am asking with a particular instruction or demonstration]."

Verbal instructions and guidance come in all forms: words, numbers, sounds meant to represent rhythms and emphases, counts, clapping—bam *bam*, bam bam ba di da *dam* ... bam-ba-da-dida-*da* .. ba-*da*-di-di-di-*da* ...bah, dah, dah, boom ... beem, beem, beem, 1,2,1 ... 6, 7, **8-9-10** ... 6-7, 8-9-**10**,11-**12** ... **12**-1-2, 3,4,5,6,7,8,9,10 ... **12**, 1, 2, 3,4,5, **6-7-8-9-10**. To emphasize a movement where the dancers have to turn their heads on a particular count: 1-2, *head,* 3-4. C uses verbal cues to prepare the dancers for a sequence: "And ..." "And *one* ..." "Ready? Let me see it ..." "Focus ..." "O.K., together, *and* ..." also "Think!" ... "Again!" ... "Who's number one? Come on and rock and roll. Let's *go.*" She uses verbal directions to control tempo or rhythm: "Walk, walk, walk, walk, walk"; on a particular turn with the shawl held out: "slow ... slow ... milk it for all its worth." She uses verbal and physical repetition to train the dancers' bodies, their muscles and nerves, to do the work automatically—"again," she says and "again."

C tries to get dancers' minds to communicate with their bodies. She makes this explicit by isolating body parts in her instructions, and by repeatedly telling the dancers to talk to their bodies as a whole and to specific body parts: "use the foot, the foot knows where it's going" … "straight-bend-straight-cross, tell it to yourself and then tell it to your foot" … "one leg listens to you, the other leg doesn't quite listen to you yet; yell at it 'Straight! Straight!'" … "you have to talk to your feet, I'm leaving your upper body alone so you can talk to your feet." Sometimes C tries to free a dancer from concentrating too hard on a body part, so that he or she can focus more on the movement guiding it.

As illustrated, C uses analogies of all sorts to describe what she wants from a particular sequence of movements or section of a dance. In trying to get the dancers to understand moving at angles through space, she talks about dance as geometry. To describe what she wants from one hand movement, she tells the class, "when you drop your arms, ladies, it doesn't come from dropping your hand, it comes from changing your angle." For a sequence that involves pairs of dancers doing contrasting thrusts up and down with their hands as they face each other, she tells them to act like a couple angry at each other. For two forceful steps that occur between the main beats of a song she asks the class to imagine firecrackers going off, in unexpected, rapid succession. In one sequence she tries to get the dancers to understand the spirit of one dance segment by telling them to convey quiet self assurance—"I know…," which suddenly ends with a dramatic break—"and another thing…."

C also uses her own talent for physical comedy to teach what not to do. For example, for one sashaying movement requiring the dancers to keep their heads at a steady height she demonstrates what she does not want by acting like a rider on horseback. One day she runs across the studio to a far corner and waves dramatically to the dancers with both arms in an effort to show them where they should be facing. And she uses verbal humor as a critique or reminder—"Wednesday is really important, we'll be blocking out the dance; if you miss class I'll put you in the back, and for those of you who like the back, I'll put you in the front." Referring to the lack of needed bounce in the steps in a particular dance, she tells the class "I see nobody jumps on their beds anymore." On one occasion, to get the dancers to work as a group, she asks if they've watched Captain Nemo, then says, "so you know how fish swim, as a school, together." Continuing, she asks if they've watched the wild animal specials on National Geographic, then says, "you know what happens to animals that stray from the group." The dancers laugh, but get the point.

In other words, C uses anything she can think of to get to the dancers, whether to get them to understand what she is after, or to create an image in their heads, or to get them to learn to be someone other than themselves for particular roles or to illustrate the arch or dynamic of a particular movement. And she adjusts her teaching strategy depending on what is coming back from the group. On a day when the class seems not be to concentrating, she uses her voice differently, does more demonstrating, provides more feedback, and generally pulls them together through sheer expenditure of energy and force of will.

Individualizing C has an eye both for the group and for each dancer, with the bulk of feedback going to the latter. She simultaneously instructs the class, teaching and detailing steps, and provides an almost constant stream of very specific feedback to individual dancers about the position of an arm or foot or leg, the shape of a movement—"A, point your foot," "S, look up," "N, your timing," "T, shoulders," "E, instead of concentrating so hard on your feet, I want you to concentrate on your bounce; your feet are moving but the bounce isn't quite there." She will sometimes move a dancer to a different spot in the group, to get her more involved, to encourage her to lead, or to place her next to a more skilled or motivated dancer. Occasionally, she will isolate individual dancers for a moment or two, for example, to listen to the sound of their feet striking the floor in a dance requiring very particular toe-heel-flat combinations. The immediacy, consistency, and constancy of corrections contribute strongly to the improvement of dancers' technique. After a dancer has successfully made an adjustment, she confirms that it is correct—"There, that's much better."

C teaches different sub-groups of apprentices differently, the skilled dancers getting very specific technical feedback, and also feedback related to their expected leadership role in the ensemble; the middle group getting probably the most constant feedback, on every aspect of their technique—limb positions, foot and arm work, etc. To allow for movement within the ranks of the class, she has created four lines of dancers for one of the dances to be performed, with each having slightly more difficult steps. This allows her to move dancers up and down, depending on how they are faring in class.

C expects commitment; on one occasion, after repeatedly going through a sequence of steps that the class is just not getting, she tells the dancers that "You guys are going to go to sleep with this in your head...." Yet she pays attention to limits, backing off when necessary. On another day, as the dancers repeat a particular piece that they are not quite getting, three, than four, than five times, she tells them, "Ladies, you're coming along nicely, but this turn is psyching you out—I can see it."

C summarizes her teaching approach as follows: "I tend to go with the flow with what I see is their capabilities. I try to challenge them and I give them time to absorb, and if I can't figure out the right words, the right actions, the right way to teach [a step], then I modify it or take it out. In addition to giving them what I call a crash-course in the art, I'm also trying to get expression, I'm trying to get a feel for the piece, to teach the musicality... And try to do it respectfully to the art. I adjust it according to their abilities. And I'm very clear that I'm both their instructor and their choreographer, and I reserve the right to change things according to what I see the best, and I also let them know, that some people's abilities are stronger and that I will never put you in a place that you are weakened because of where I put you. I want them to feel confidence within the piece, I really dislike recital pieces where everyone is facing front and doesn't move anywhere, very boring. And there's the challenge of learning how to move through shapes, keeping in line, learning how to watch."

Challenge and Growth In reflecting on the challenges she faces in this work, C notes the difficulty of creating one unified company, the periodic lack of leadership from within the group, and the lack of energy and seeming passivity of the apprentices at times, in the face of the hard work needed to get ready for performance. C notes that it can be difficult to get individuals to relate to and become comfortable with each other, even in partnering. C relies on experienced dancers to step up—to choose to dance in the front row, to work with new dancers, to volunteer to demonstrate a step, to encourage and exhort—but at times no one seems willing. In a more general way C notes, with her characteristic humor, that in some years it simply takes too much work to get youth to take responsibility for themselves or the larger experience: "I still think of them as kids, because here we are getting ready for the performance, and I set all their costumes out and they sat in the center of the stage and said, 'I don't know where my clothes are!' And I'm thinking 'ahhh,' I'm like their mom."

A basic challenge has been inspiring the collective energy needed day-in and day-out: "They'll go through the motions and they'll want to be there, but having the physical energy to pull off some of the stuff, and inspiring them has been difficult." Individual apprentices' energy and engagement rise and fall, and while some are ready to work hard on a particular day, others are not. C notes that she is constantly trying to decide whether to wait for someone, to scale back, or to keep moving, and that there is a sacrifice both ways. Ultimately, C recognizes, these are teens, growing up under often difficult conditions, struggling with issues that she tries to account for (and help with when she can), while not letting them undermine the collective work. Occasionally, she finds herself dealing with more than she expected: One apprentice, unmarried, tells C that she was "tremendously happy" when she thought she was pregnant, and became very depressed when she learned she was not.

On the other side of these challenges is the growth that C sees in the apprentices, that is apparent to an observer, and that the apprentices themselves describe in interviews. Mastering flamenco is not easy. One apprentice notes that "the first semester was tough, I never got it rhythmically"; another that "I don't get the feeling of dancing to the music." And this is clearly the hardest that many of the apprentices have ever worked physically. An apprentices tells me that "I'm tired after I get home, my feet hurt"; another reports that "when I get home I eat dinner, watch a little T.V., then start to work [on homework] but suddenly my head's down."

When the apprentices first start they are uncomfortable—with their bodies and with the idea of appearing clumsy or making a mistake in public. Over time, this discomfort diminishes, and the apprentices reflect a steadily emerging sense of physical confidence, and pride in their bodies. They move more freely, with a greater sense of rhythm, with more expression, and with greater strength. C notes that "every year you can see most of them evolve and change, from the beginning, where they are unsure and unsettled [to] the end when they are doing things that they didn't pick up easily in the beginning of the class... They just gain confidence. Hopefully they can take that outside the [studio]." An apprentice notes that: "When I first started it was so difficult, I felt like I was doing everything wrong, but I kept working every day and I got it a little by little."

And apprentices note gaining a sense of accomplishment simply through hard work itself. One notes that it took time to learn to appreciate the work, and that "it grew [on me]." Another notes that "I like it when C. says 'again ... again', when she has us do over the whole thing, I like her attitude ... when I struggle she'll keep teaching me the same step until I get it. Some days I'm tired, I don't want to listen, she gets me to pay attention." Over the last few weeks before a performance, an observer watches the class in rehearsal, going over a section of dance again and again, some looking ready to drop, but managing to keep pulling themselves together.

When asked about what they liked most about this apprenticeship experience, apprentices mentioned different aspects: "the warm ups" ... "the heel work, dancing with the shawls" ... "meeting new people and learning about music" ... "that you can send a message through body movement." But the story often came back to the lead instructor: One apprentice spoke for a number of the others when she said, simply, "being with C, the way she teaches steps, her attitude, because it gives us energy."

The performance at the closing ceremony—surprisingly accomplished, moving, genuinely artistic—serves very much as a culmination; until then the apprentices have been working on all the pieces of the whole, all the different kinds of preparation—dance itself, learning to work the stage, costumes—but have not put it all together. There is no substitute for the tension created by the lights, the music over the auditorium speaker system, the audience, the timed entrances and exits, the rush of costume changes. That is when the apprentices really begin to feel like dancers. C puts it best: "And for that one moment, they're special—you'll find them right after the show, prancing around in their costumes. That [experience] to them means more than anything."

6

Benefits of Participation
in Apprenticeship

It takes a lot of thoughtful effort to learn to do something without thinking ...

Howard (1991, p. 82)

Wherever I go I look at things and think "that would be an interesting
picture."

An ASM photography apprentice

In this chapter I explore the effects of participation in youth apprenticeship and
the mechanisms leading to those effects. My goal here is to map the terrain on
which apprenticeship operates, not to make claims in traditional scientific terms.
For one thing, I have learned over decades of work that discrete experiences are
integrated into complex, evolving selves in ways that are poorly understood,
difficult to parcel out and hard to measure. It is difficult to anticipate what the
scores of discrete things apprentices learn might turn into; for instance when a
flamenco apprentice says that "I've learned that I can send a message through
movement of the body."

As a practical matter, none of the experiences drawn on in this book have been
subject to formal outcome evaluation. The bulk of research on apprenticeship
(including my own) is qualitative, with rich descriptions of teaching, learning
and producing processes, and reflections by youth, mentors, program directors
and researchers themselves. What evidence of effects is found in this research
is suggestive. In its favor, it is consistent across settings and studies. It also has a
good deal of face validity—it makes sense in relation to the learning and producing experiences on which it is based. In some instances, as in my own research,
observers describe growth over time in specific ways that would seem unlikely
in the absence of these specific experiences. In addition to evidence embodied
in ongoing processes and concrete products, some is found in performance on
tasks selected by mentors to assess knowledge and skill, what Gardner (1991)
describes as "landmarks of growth."

Evidence of growth can be found in how apprentices approach tasks, how
they talk about the work and themselves, and in how mentors describe apprentices. For instance, the language young people use to describe their work is at

once concrete and expressive, rich with detail. This language provides a window into the experience. Evidence is implicit in the demands of the work itself. An achievement—or a personal sense of achievement—is often the culmination of a learning and producing experience. Working on a task or project evokes a particular set of skills and capacities, contributes to their further development, and is simultaneously a demonstration of them. For instance, when an apprentice participates in or leads a group of other apprentices, he or she is simultaneously learning and demonstrating the attendant group skills. The fact that apprentices have a chance to play with a particular profession in their minds, and in practice, is both a defining part of the experience and an effect of it.

Apprenticeship experiences nonetheless reach and affect youth to widely varying degrees. Disciplines have different learning curves and, as pointed out in chapter five, youth have varying capacities to use these settings as developmental resources. Time in apprenticeship and timing in young people's lives influence effects. For each participating youth, growth across domains is uneven (although, as I noted in the Big Picture case study, often evens out over time). Growth is tentative in some instances. Altering young people's habits, predispositions, reactions, dominant feelings and modes of thought require persistent immersion in the apprenticeship environment and reinforcement from outside of it. For the most vulnerable youth, each week's and each month's gains have to be re-confirmed.

Although the focus here is on individual effects, the work of apprentices yields a variety of social benefits. That work ameliorates environmental problems, meets community needs, addresses social justice problems, contributes to scientific and other forms of knowledge, supports others' well-being and development through teaching and care giving, and enriches American culture with artistic products. Apprenticeship also activates—mobilizes—a variety of latent cultural resources for supporting adolescent development. As apprentices do their work in the community, they connect to and pull in all kinds of resources. Workplaces benefit also. As the Wisconsin Youth Apprenticeship Program illustrates, adults report that having an apprentice in their workplace is energizing and enriching. Work with apprentices sometimes changes mentors' understanding and view of and commitment to youth.

Categorizing Benefits

The findings presented in this chapter suggest that apprenticeship experiences operate across a broad swath of developmental terrain, from very specific and contextually rooted skills to the most basic ways of talking, acting and thinking. In my own work with After School Matters, I identified three broad kinds of growth deriving from participation in apprenticeship: in discipline-specific knowledge, skills, and sensibilities; in approaching and carrying out tasks, including group or collaborative work on tasks; and in what I called "self effects"—ways of talking, acting, thinking, identity and sense of self, including self-as-learner and self-as-maker. I employ these categories again here, but have further broken out each, to include clusters of effects that bear their own conceptual labels, for example, growth in interpersonal skills and sensibilities and meta-lessons under growth in task-related skills.

In creating and employing categories to discuss effects of youth apprenticeship, I faced a problem that, when looked at slightly differently, is not a problem but an important finding itself. Many examples of effects cut across specific categories; moreover, effects in each category interact to shape and reinforce each other. Kleiber (1999, p. 106) notes, for instance, that "pushing through constraints to take action ... contributes both to a sense of competence and to an incorporation of that action pattern into one's identity." Similarly, learning to work with care within a discipline plants the seed for a more general disposition to do so, and affects one's sense of oneself. The ability to keep re-investing oneself in the work one is doing reflects both skill in addressing difficult tasks and growth in the self. Bereiter and Scardamalia (1993) point out that some self-regulatory knowledge and skill is a domain-specific version of general skills: one is learning how to work best in that particular domain. The capacity to invest in tasks and desire to make meaning from them are likewise both general and domain-specific achievements. As Steve Goodman of the Education Video Center points out, when a young person learns to ask questions s/he is also learning to raise them.

Policy Relevant Categories

Much recent debate about investment in supports for youth has focused on the need to improve high school graduation rates, get more youth into college and/ or foster skills that will be needed in the so called new economy. Youth apprenticeship initiatives serve these aims directly to varying degrees, but indirectly in many ways. Much if not all of the growth I describe here is policy relevant, even when I do not be label it as such. This includes such basic skills as punctuality and time management, mid-level skills such as producing good quality work within time constraints, and such higher order skills as thinking flexibly, applying past experience, and gathering data relevant to the problem at hand. It also includes psychological dispositions and social skills. And it includes growth in young people's store of social capital. At the same time, it is less clear that apprenticeship experiences can strengthen basic literacy and numeracy skills, although they can and do strengthen young people's sense of ownership of these domains.[1]

Disciplinary Knowledge, Skills, and Sensibilities

Engagement in a discipline nurtures the growth of specific procedural knowledge and skills; encourages use of the associated technical, procedural, and aesthetic vocabulary; and, over time, nurtures the growth of "qualitative" judgment or sensibilities specific to that discipline. One gradually learns how to think, choose, strategize, act, and generally work around in a discipline. One comes to understand what it means to work as a professional in that discipline, within a task or project, day to day and over time. Yet acquiring a high level of proficiency in most disciplines takes years of work, sometimes thousands of hours of tutelage, practice, and performance (see, e.g., Bloom, 1985; Ericsson, 1996).

In apprenticeships that last somewhere between 300 and 900 hours, young people might acquire basic techniques, technical and aesthetic vocabulary and key concepts. They may begin to control their new skills; to use, if not master, the tools of a discipline; to be able to solve some design or production problems; to talk and act (and occasionally to see or think) like a graphic designer or photographer or field biologist. A boat building instructor notes that the work becomes that much easier, more effective when he can say to an apprentice, "Hey can you go shave that keel?" (Kautz, p.c., March 19, 2007). That request implies some knowledge and experience, as well as common understanding of what the task is about.

But apprentices are just beginning to be able to see what is more important and what less, or what the keys to a field might be. A graphic design mentor describes apprentices' growth in skill as "patchy," deeper in a few areas, much shallower in others (Hodge, p.c., July 31, 2007). Aesthetic judgment especially grows slowly, and requires familiarity with the larger body of work in a particular discipline. In printing, for instance, choice of fonts and placement of words on a page takes time to master. An ASM photography instructor notes that "the concept of contrast you cannot really teach, you can only look at something over and over again ... seeing prints over and over, you get familiar with the way things react to the chemistry, to the light ... some people can make a print in 10 minutes and it is absolutely perfect, but you cannot do that when you have only been printing for a year."

Basic Skills

Early accomplishment often means learning to use the tools of a trade. A science apprentice notes that "M ... taught me how to filter solution and to use the shaker ... I learned how to use a rubber stopper with parafilm ... how to label and store the vials" (Richmond & Kurth, 1999, p. 682). In some fields tools have become more complex, taking longer for apprentices to gain access to and master—think of the Big Picture apprentice in Chicago given responsibility for a digital die cutter and the young man who learns to use an oscilloscope. The resulting sense of accomplishment is perhaps that much stronger.

In many fields apprentices learn to make concrete representations of tentative thoughts and plans using customary techniques—sketch-books, lab journals, pencil drawings on a piece of wood, small-scale models, darkroom prints, or story boards. These serve many purposes. In the RiverzEdge graphic design studio, the mentor emphasizes the value of hand drawn sketches at the front end of a project as a means for the young designer to slow down and explore an idea before jumping in to execute it on the computer (Hodge, p.c., July 31, 2007).

Sketches and similar visuals are a low-cost vehicle for exploring and testing an idea, trying out an alternative, in other words for making a strategic choice.

As they learn to use the tools of their trade, apprentices are also beginning to learn the tricks of that trade: how best to cut a piece of glass without breaking it, how to overlay colors on each other on a print, how to keep an interview going with connected questions, what to quickly look for in evaluating a photographic print. Perkins (1981) describes these as heuristics. For instance, an astronomy apprentice learns to use "a trick of computer image processing" to improve the quality of photos he needs to test his hypothesis (McCarthy, 2002, p. 70). Bailey, Hughes, and Moore (1995, p. 155) illustrate with a cabinet-making apprentice who has to saw pieces of lumber for a chest of drawers. Instead of "measuring each piece [sic] individually, he measured one carefully and then used it as a template for the others."

Growing Control Over the Work

With experience, apprentices become more efficient; the same task in the kitchen or laboratory or dark room takes half the time it did two months ago. The cabinet-making apprentice learns to estimate length with a glance, and likewise to judge symmetry, squareness, and proportion. He or she is beginning to develop "cabinet sense" (Rose, 2004). Apprentices become more strategic in their use of time and energy. They will not spend as much time as a novice on a minor task, or repeat the same strategy without trying to figure out what went wrong initially. A young pianist notes learning how to use practice more fully, "what I had to do, what I had to prepare" (Sosniak, 1985, p. 47). A young community problem solver learns how to identify and reach whomever it is that can assure action on a problem (Adler, p.c., June 7, 2006).

Apprentices exert gradually greater control over their own efforts, a kind of discipline-specific self-regulation; they are better able to steer those efforts. Apprentices working with a professional muralist on one project learn to work large, to keep the elements connected (Larson & Walker, 2006). The director of St. Louis ArtWorks notes that apprentices begin to think in a less linear way about design problems and creative options, to both think "outside the box" and to "bring outside the box ideas into a process with a structure" (Block, 2006, p.c., August 1, 2006). Apprentices become more resourceful in those efforts. Youth working in design and the arts are able to recognize and draw from a wide array of visual resources and images, to transform those into elements of a design, to transform ideas into physical forms.

Deepening Understanding

Apprenticeship experience leads to gradual change in the young person's perception of and thinking about the object of his or her work—whether a poem or film, a field of vegetables, a design, a performance, or a discipline as a whole. A

young painter with Artists for Humanity notes that "Ever since I started painting I look at the world as more detailed, more beautiful. I see a can on the street
or something and that looks like art to me, but again that's how it changed me"
(*Teen Voices*, 2005, p. 2). Science apprentices begin to understand—not just
use—technical language and to grasp more deeply the problems they are working on (Richmond & Kurth, 1999). An agricultural intern thinks about soil in
a completely different way. The apprentice is learning how to look at things to
understand them (Polanyi, 1966). Participants in a sculpture apprenticeship learn
how to look closely at facial features, for example, seeing geometric shapes in
them. The dancer begins to understand the structure of a piece of choreography.
ASM community development apprentices are observed over time to view their
neighborhood in a more complex way, no longer relying on stereotypes, but
talking about its many qualities.

In some contexts growth in technical skills and understanding contribute to
a shift in qualitative (i.e., aesthetic) judgment. Apprentices learn, for instance, to
bring out the qualities of the material with which they are working (Pye, 1968).
An ASM dance apprentice learns to recognize which piece of music gives greater
resonance to a piece of choreography. In photography such skills as achieving
depth of field, establishing proper contrast by juggling negative size, developer
time, and choice of filter have both technical and aesthetic dimensions. In filmmaking, the same goes for such skills as foreshadowing, creating a mood through
use of specific visual images (motifs), learning to manipulate scene sequence,
and learning about the relationship between visual and auditory dimensions of
a scene. Apprentices gain a firmer sense of what makes a photo or a movie work,
and likewise whether a particular photo or movie "works." As described above,
apprentices gradually begin to understand that the challenge is to translate life
to print or film or physical structure, itself a qualitative problem of figuring out
what the essence of something is, or what defines it.

Joining a Discipline

Apprentices demonstrate mastery in part by joining the debate about ideas and
practice in the field in which they are working. In formulating their own stories
and approach to radio (and to other media), young people also critique prevailing norms about what good radio is. In an ASM photography apprenticeship, a
young man creates a composition with a picture of Jesus Christ atop a kitchen
sink that one of the instructors uses to initiate a discussion of the impact of
controversial art on viewers. The instructor seems to be arguing for restraint and
a sense of responsibility. To their credit, a number of apprentices speak up in
disagreement, and use examples of photographs by professional photographers
to make the point that a lot of art can be seen to offend somebody, and that it is
difficult to draw the line.

Growth within a discipline is shaped to an extent by its distinct learning curve.
Some disciplines, like dance or laboratory work in sciences, have a steep initial

learning curve; others, like painting or photography, a deceptively easy entry but many layers of knowledge and skill to work through. (In agricultural work, dance, and a few other more physical disciplines a period of physical conditioning accompanies or precedes technical work.) Instructors describe or imply a point at which some apprentices "step inside" a discipline or art form, inhabit it rather than going through the motions of working at it. A flamenco teacher describes the process as capturing the spirit of flamenco. Youth begin to think like a professional in that field: An ASM filmmaking apprentice notes that she has learned to ask herself the questions that her mentor asks her, about the logic of the narrative, the hooks on which the movie will turn, and so forth.

Growth in Approaching and Carrying Out Tasks

The nature of tasks in apprenticeship creates distinct potential for growth in task-related skills. This growth is observable in both cognitive and affective dimensions of work on tasks, for different stages in work on a task or project, and in managing contextual influences on task completion. Apprentices learn to do the kind of work and engage in the kind of thinking needed at each stage in the task cycle, and to manage their feelings through the process. They learn how to work alone and with others.

Getting Going and Moving Ahead

At the front end, apprentices get better at preparing for work on a new or ongoing task. An ASM flamenco instructor notes observing change in how her apprentices "get ready to do things": gather themselves to prepare for class or rehearsal or to learn a new step. A science apprentice notes that, in preparing a protocol for an experiment, "even the most simplistic things you have to really outline, go into detail with" (Richmond & Kurth, 1999, p. 683). Mentors in a number of initiatives note that it is a critical sign of growth when apprentices get to work without waiting for instructions or a push from the mentor. This seems part of becoming more purposeful about the work. Renee Flemings of Roundabout Theater describes a transformation in how youth approach the work, from "oh, this is fun" to "o.k., what do I have to do [to make this production work]?" (p.c., February 16, 2007).

Mentors note that youth gradually get better at continuing to move ahead when faced with problems and obstacles. This ability has a cognitive dimension— staying open, spreading out possibilities, making links, drawing on bits and pieces of knowledge (Boshuizen, 2003)—and a psychological one. Adam Green of Rocking the Boat notes that an important sign of growth in participating youth is when they are not stopped short by a problem but are able to view it as just part of the work. Apprentices grow more comfortable working with constraints—having to meet deadlines, to share equipment, to use materials at hand, to sacrifice an idea to keep a project moving. As noted in chapter three, a Wisconsin Youth Apprenticeship Program (YAP) participant learns "to work with what you have" (Orr, 1995, p. 64). Youth become better able to cope with the unforeseen and uncontrollable—lack of rain for one's crops, a cloudy sky or too much moonlight on the night one has time reserved on a telescope. Apprentices learn to sort out what they can and cannot control, to adjust goals, scale back ambitions, and compensate.

Working Under Pressure

Apprentices learn to work under different kinds of pressure—many tasks needing to be done, time pressures, competing priorities. An apprentice with The Food Project notes that "you can't just focus on one thing because if you do, everything else goes to waste" (Andrews, 2001, p. 16). A biotechnology apprentice reports that "while my samples were cooking (figuratively speaking) I would be making up the work groups on the computer for my samples that day or I might record the weights of sample dishes that I will be using in the future" (Ryken, 2001, p. 69). Young people are often particularly surprised by the time pressures of the work setting, and note time management as one of the more important skills acquired. And as this last example illustrates, in learning time management apprentices are also learning to manage their own productivity. As a young chef apprentice notes, he has learned "to be fast, but not so fast that you mess up" (CCAP, 2007).

With experience, youth get better at managing the rhythm of ongoing projects and of work itself, including their investment in that work. Youth in The Food Project's first year crews learn to work at a sustainable pace that will take them through a day in the fields. Youth acquire the simple but helpful capacity "to pick up a thread," not start from scratch each day or each week. Apprentices learn to keep working on their own work in progress, equal measures persistence and endurance; to keep investing themselves physically and mentally in the work. A young sculptor notes that "the thing about being an artist is that you just have to keep doing it" (Sloan & Sosniak, 1985, p. 136). They learn that some seemingly wasted effort is necessary. As the Marwen Arts apprentice cited in chapter four learned, "you have to do some work that will not pay off because you never know what will turn out to be the idea that takes" (Camacho, p.c., January 8, 2007). Apprentices learn to judge the right amount of persistence. An ASM mural apprentice notes learning "not to give up on stuff too early, to give it a chance," meaning to keep working on a section of the mural until the effort is not returning as much.

Working With Uncertainty

Apprentices grow more adept at working with a measure of uncertainty, for instance, working on tasks whose end point may not be clear, while trying to manage the risks inherent in the work. They learn to balance planfulness with openness to "the unanticipated opportunities that inevitably emerge in the context of action" (Eisner, 1999, p. 114). At the same time, they acquire the patience to stay with a task until it is complete, which can mean revising a documentary, repeating an experiment, staying in the kitchen until the equipment is cleaned, stored and ready for the next day or in the field until the weeds are removed. That sometimes means staying with tasks that are unpleasant or frustrating, in part by giving them meaning. One youth tells Larson and Walker (2006, p. 17): "You just have to analyze why you're frustrated and then go out and find a solution." It sometimes means deciding when a task is done, knowing that at some point one has to let go, for reasons of time, resources, diminishing returns, and let a product or performance stand on its own.

Young people in apprenticeship learn to become "masters of their own attention" (Bruner, 1966, p. 116). A handful of ASM apprentices note learning to pay attention to what they are doing, to not get distracted. A number note learning to put worries aside and/or to work when they are not in the mood: "If I've had a bad day in school I'm like 'I don't want to be here right now'. But as the day goes on you just let it go ... I've learned to just be here, not to worry about what happens when I get home, what will happen with my friends...." A photography apprentice notes that when she feels lazy, for example, not doing an assignment, she is more likely to tell herself that she must get in the habit of working hard, and adds "so I have been pushing myself more."

Working With Care

Youth in the apprenticeships described in these pages acquire the habit of working with care. This habit is expressed in different ways—attending to detail in learning to portray a character, being exact in counting the seedlings in a monitoring plot in the woods, slowing down while painting a boat hull. As noted in chapter four, apprentices in the sciences may not understand early on the importance of following a procedure exactly as laid out or measuring a quantity exactly as prescribed. Working with care translates into commitment to getting whatever one is working on right. Rose (2004) calls this principled action. He cites as an example a young electrician apprentice who makes sure the electrical wiring inside the wall is laid and secured correctly, even though it will be invisible. Working with care includes staying with the work until it is good enough. An ASM mural instructor, in reflecting on how his apprentices have grown, notes that "They don't lie to themselves too much and say 'oh, I am done' ... they know when something looks good or looks bad, and they are honest with themselves about their own work."

Apprenticeship experience fosters an instrumental resourcefulness that is both inner- and outer-directed. Resourcefulness is reflected in an interest in examining one's own ideas (Eisner, 2002) as well as those of others. It includes the willingness to experiment A photography apprentice notes that "If I see it [the print] is too light, I've learned to experiment, without bothering Mr. D.

every two seconds." It includes a disposition to "find out things for myself" as the Big Picture apprentice put it. A science apprentice notes learning "how to teach myself ... [my mentor's] emphasis on logic and method will enable me to solve almost any problem" (AAS, 1999, p. 2). Apprentices get better at tapping into other people's expertise and drawing them in to help with a project, and more generally at doing whatever it takes to secure whatever they need to do a particular job. It includes using feedback. An ASM mural apprentice notes that "if they [the instructors] are hard, I am like, man, now I know I have to really concentrate and really add value to the picture."

As should be clear, growth of discipline-specific skills and growth of skill in thinking about, thinking through, approaching and carrying out tasks become easily intertwined as one tries to describe them. The graphic design apprentice who learns to spend time sketching by hand at the beginning of a project—instead of just jumping in without thinking—learns both how to start a design project and the general importance of "slowing down" one's work process. As an apprentice becomes more efficient, accurate and strategic in a field he or she is better able to regulate the risks on specific tasks. Being able—learning—to step back and judge one's own work-in-progress is partly dependent on familiarity with what "good" work is in a specific domain. When mural apprentices learn how to make art within the constraints of a pre-specified design they are learning something both specific to muraling and more general (Larson & Walker, 2006). Learning to prepare for a day's work—warming up correctly for a dance class, preparing one's paints and brushes for work on a mural—is both a discipline-specific skill and a more general one.

Interpersonal Skills and Sensibilities

Some apprenticeship experiences strengthen capacities to work collaboratively with others, and to work as part of a defined community (Hefner, 1988; Larson, 2004; Larson, Hansen, & Walker, 2005; Chavez & Soep, 2005). Apprentices learn to contribute and commit to shared goals. An ASM theater apprentice notes that "some people you just cannot work with, but my tolerance has gotten a little better. I say, 'I'm looking to the prize at the end of the road; I want to get there; so I'll work with this person.'" Youth learn how to provide feedback constructively. On one occasion an ASM apprentice, unbidden, walks over to another, points to a drawing she was working on, and says it reminded him of a particular piece of work by a well-known artist, suggests a refinement, and then says "it's really good." On another occasion I observed an art apprentice gently ask another if he felt that the work was finished, then point out how much he liked the way the piece divided up space before commenting on parts that seemed unfinished.

Apprenticeships involving collective work contribute to "a deeper grasp of the complementarily between self and others" (Larson, 2004, p. 9). A Rocking the Boat alumna notes that her collaboration with other youth in the program created "a sense of self-reliance and [at the same time] dependency on others.

You really have a sense of yourself and your effect on others" (Remer, 2007, p. 19). Apprenticeships can strengthen capacity for give and take, for instance arguing one's point of view while also listening to others and building on their ideas. A Roundabout teaching artist notes that "youth learn to respect a director who is their own age" (Keith, p.c., June 19, 2007). Youth acquire the capacity to consider the effects of their behavior on others, and to put themselves in another's shoes. One ASM filmmaking apprentice notes learning to thank others: "little things, like sending thank you notes to actors who auditioned but didn't get cast." Not least, youth learn the basic importance of communicating needs (not expecting others to read one's mind). As one youth puts it, "I learned that you need to talk to others, you need to explain to them what you want" (Larson, 2004, p. 10).

Meta-Lessons

As apprentices learn to work more proficiently in a particular field and more effectively on tasks in general, they are simultaneously learning lessons about work in that field and about work more generally. Learning how to do something and learning about doing it are not easily separable. The apprentice who learns to work with constraints is learning about doing so. The apprentice who learns that some wasted effort is necessary in testing a scientific idea or making a painting is acquiring the capacity to waste some effort and realizing its value and necessity. The difference is in the reflective and self-reflective quality of this cluster of effects. The director of a design apprenticeship notes, for instance, that with experience young people learn to talk about their work, describing the ideas behind it, processes, problems they faced and so forth (Daniel, 2007).

Time spent working in a field affords young people a more accurate and differentiated view of that field. A young graphic designer begins to understand how client driven design work often is. A young woman apprenticing in a soil biophysics lab notes learning that the job of a scientist "is as much to explain an idea to his or her colleagues as it is to keep it to himself" (Richmond & Kurth,1999, p. 683). Apprentices learn that work in any discipline comes as a package: "many things you love also have parts you hate" (Levine, 2002, p. 32). Beginning to learn in a field feeds recognition of how much there is to learn and the motivation to do so. Discussing young people's experience in the kitchen, Grausman (p.c., 12/21/06) observes that "the more they begin to learn the more they can appreciate expertise and what goes into it ... sometimes it's when they try to replicate [what a chef has done] and they can't, they begin to appreciate the chef's expertise."

Young people learn about the meaning and arc of careers. One young woman apprenticing with ASE, for example, comes to understand the long horizon of a science career, why someone might work for years on a problem. Apprentices in commercial kitchens and university laboratories see staff at many different levels, gaining a specific sense of what it looks and feels like to start at the beginning in a field and progress to higher levels within it. As young people come to see how deep any field is, they may realize that they are working on or near "the surface of things," as one ASM apprentice put it. They come to understand more deeply and specifically what it means to be and what it takes (including how long it takes) to get good at something

Apprentices in a number of initiatives note surprise at how much work goes into products and performances—a box of vegetables, a community meeting, or a 15-minute dance. A theater apprentice learns not only how to rehearse but that rehearsal is important: "I never saw anything in a real theater before. I just thought you came out from backstage and did it" (Roundabout Education Report, 2006, p. 14). They come to understand more viscerally the relationship between the quality of work and the quality of products. Gale (2005), for instance, notes how youth in The Food Project come to see the relationship between the quality of their work in the fields and the quality of the produce harvested, and further why it is important to grow quality produce.

Young people learn that one cannot just do things. They require thinking through. Photography apprentices learn that, as an ASM photography mentor puts it, "until you start thinking ... you are not making interesting images." Of one participant in a documentary video project, Goodman (2003 p. 91) notes: "When he came into video arts he thought it was gong to be easy ... He finally realized that it was important to do his work. He had to sit down and think about the kind of questions he had to ask. He asked deeper questions. This was work. He learned that he, Julius, could work."

Lessons can be, and often are, empowering as well as humbling. Apprentices working on social documentaries, in youth radio, in sustainable agriculture, in community development, civil rights, and related fields come to see that there are means—organizations, laws, political processes—for affecting social reality and addressing injustice. They learn "that they have the power to change things and there's this system to do it, as opposed to saying 'I'm a victim and this sucks'" (Adler, p.c., June 7, 2006). Apprentices note coming to realize that the products of their work can reach out to and affect other people. An ASM documentary apprentice: "I realized that I can reach out to people with my writing, and [that] my words can actually change people or have an effect on them." An apprentice in flamenco notes, "I've learned that you can send a message through movement of the body." Yet apprentices also learn about constraints and limits. An astronomy apprentice, learning about such limitations as available time (on needed equip-ment), mechanical breakdown and human error, notes that "it lets you realize what the people in NASA have to go through to, you know, make a project work" (McCarthy, 2002, p. 36).

Apprentices in a number of fields note learning that working on a project, whether a laboratory experiment, a field study or a community problem, is messy and results not always definitive. This was, nonetheless, an especially notable theme among science apprentices. One observes that "rather than the world of miraculous discoveries and innovative, quick problem-solving I expected, I encountered long, meticulous data collection in which clear patterns didn't necessarily emerge" (Moilanen, 1996, p. 11). Another reports that "I always assumed that once you start on something, it's always a disaster or a total success. There were no gray areas in between. For me, I think I'm pretty much in that gray area, which I never suspected would happen" (Richmond & Kurth, 1999, p. 685). Yet these youth, like those in other fields, also learn that when hypotheses are not supported or results are murky they are contributing to knowledge in a field; they are connected to long-term threads of work. Dr. Kenneth Alexander, a physician mentor for the REAP program, notes of an apprentice who worked in his lab (studying the human papillomavirus) that "she learned about the feeling of pride and success when an experiment works, but also a bit about how experimental failure is a call to persistence and patience" (Academy of Applied Sciences, 2000, p. 7).

Apprentices develop a more differentiated understanding of work on complex tasks. For instance, apprentices working on a video documentary learn that work at different stages of a project calls on different capacities, creativity early on, focused work in the middle and then assessment and revision later. Apprentices may learn that "a problem isn't something you either need to accept or deny or get angry about," but rather work through (Green 2006, p.c., June 22, 2006). They may learn that some of what they need to know they will get through experience. A young man learning auto repair notes that although he had read about how to do a brake job "step by step" in a manual, the manual did not "show you what to do if the bolt's rung off or ...rusted up ... it makes the repair a whole lot more difficult. And you [have to] learn through somebody else's experience" (Evanciew & Rojewski, 1999, pp. 43–44).

Not least, young people in the initiatives described here learned a great deal about reciprocity; about how an individual can affect a whole group; that they can learn from others, and that exchanging knowledge and experience is possible: If they help others, those others will help them. Yet apprentices also come to recognize that others do not automatically understand their goals and intentions. As the young director in an ASM filmmaking apprenticeship notes, he learned that he can't just tell the actors what to do, he has to explain what he wants, show them.

Self Effects

This is a broad but critical domain. It includes changes in the way young people present themselves to others; changes in how they view and understand themselves, including what they think they are capable of, what they enjoy and are good at; and changes in how young people approach the opportunities and difficulties in different settings, including willingness to take risks, work hard and be active. For some youth, an apprenticeship experience seems to have a self-organizing effect, pulling them together, waking them up, and mobilizing their energies, in some instances providing a sense of direction. In observing youth before and after the experience, one not infrequently sees a tighter, better defined, though not closed off, self. For some youth apprenticeship has a self-recognizing effect: young people find or locate themselves in the array of choices about identity.

In some instances apprenticeship helps young people learn to name, to give language to their experiences, a basis for beginning to figure out the meaning of those experiences (Worthman, 2002). For instance, they can begin to articulate why a particular experience has been important or problematic. Less directly, self effects include adolescents' subjective experience of the immediate and broader social world, what they think of it and where they think they fit into it (Shaw, 1996). The painting studio director at Artists for Humanity captures the range and subtlety of self effects when he notes that "they're just not exactly the same kids" who walked in the door a year or two or three ago (Gibbs, p.c., December 7, 2006).

Acting In and On the World

A number of program directors note changes in what might be called presentation of self, in both work and other situations. The director of St. Louis Art Works describes growth in apprentices' ability to "introduce themselves to any guest or client, look them in the eye, shake their hand, introduce themselves, explain what they're making and why" (Block, p.c., August 1, 2006). An apprentice who has to interview people for a documentary feels both more comfortable and more entitled to do so. In effect, he comes to believe that he has the "right to be curious, to ask questions, to discuss, to imagine how things could be different" (Claxton, 2007, p. 120). An ASM flamenco mentor notes that "[between] the time these kids started and now they have changed—the way they sing, the way they sit, they way they get ready to do things." One dancer's way of walking and holding herself was inhibiting her progress in dance, and the mentor could not see the physical reason, but it seemed linked to how she was feeling. Somehow over the weeks dance had the effect of unblocking this, and there was a total change in the way she carried and presented herself.

In After School Matters, I observed apprentices begin to use language and share their thoughts more carefully and responsibly—be specific in asking for assistance, hold off on a wisecrack, be less belittling or sarcastic, focus comments on the work itself. I observed apprentices begin to pay closer attention to and take more responsibility for themselves in a variety of ways—their words, bodies, ideas, reactions. Their public behavior became more serious, more appropriately assertive, and more attuned to the situation they were in. ASM apprentices also commonly describe themselves as becoming less shy: "I would have been the shy person, sitting back and not saying anything. Now sometimes I'll raise my hand and volunteer to read my work" … "I guess I used to be real shy, I never used to talk. Now I'm talking to more people, even those I don't know" … "I give my opinion more to people because I would be real quiet."

Giving More of Oneself and Getting More Out of Experience

As described earlier, apprentices come to approach both tasks and others differently over time. They become more patient with themselves and others. They gradually give more of themselves to the projects they are working on, especially in apprenticeships involving self-expression. An apprentice describes a willingness to embrace the serious side: "I like to see people doing stuff they are good at." A filmmaking apprentice notes that "when we first got into it we thought, 'yeah, this is going to be so cool'. And then the hours that you put in and how it takes away from other things ... And then you [realize that you] really want to get something out of it" (Dowdy, Birney, & Reedus, 2004, p. 20). Young people want to use the new skills they are acquiring, exemplified by the young photographer who carries her camera with her everywhere.

Youth learn that it is "o.k. to do new things," as one ASM instructor puts it, that trying to act in the world, to take a few risks, is not going to lead to negative feedback, ridicule or trouble. An ASM choreography apprentice describes a new willingness to try activities: "try it, try it, if you don't like it, fine, but go with it." Over time youth begin to bring real emotion and feelings (in other words, more of their real selves) to creative and expressive work. Alvin Keith of Roundabout Theater notes that "across the country kids are scared of failure, scared of being mocked and laughed at, but these kids have taken on that challenge" (p.c., April 19, 2007).

A Grounded Sense of Competence

Being good at something, having a specific set of deepening skills, gives youth a much more grounded sense of competence. It is not always a general sense—one instructor calls it "a specific kind of invincibility" (Wenger, p.c., June 27, 2007)—but it provides a foundation for more general growth. This instructor notes that "the more they get under their belt the more they think they can do." This kind of self-confidence sometimes comes most slowly to a young person him or herself. An ASM apprentice tells me that "everybody looks at me like I am a team leader because J gives me responsibilities, but I don't know what they see, I guess my energy." It is through the demands of apprenticeship that young people learn that they are able to work harder than they thought, that they actually can lead a team, that they can draw on their personal experience to explore universal issues. A culinary apprentice notes that "when I look back it seemed so hard [at first] but now I can see I did it" (Mitchell, p.c., December 8, 2006). The director of an arts-focused program that does a lot of commissioned work notes that "when these kids succeed at a project, especially a difficult one, they walk the earth taller, I don't know any other way to put it" (Novello, p.c., July 6, 2007).

Modulating Egocentrism, Fostering Sociocentrism

On the other side of this equation, apprenticeship helps ground adolescents' natural grandiosity, and contributes to more accurate self-appraisal. An ASM theater apprentice notes that "when you see other kids with some talent you think about your own talent differently." An ASM apprentice notes learning that "the whole world is not focused just on me." The demands of giving feedback and supporting peers in a painting studio lead apprentices to be more sensitive to other people's individuality. As one painting apprentice notes, these demands have made her "a more open person" (*Teen Voices*, 2005, p. 2). The demands of fields like print and broadcast journalism lead apprentices to learn to put aside their "selves" and listen to what another has to say about an issue. Youth working in agricultural or boat building or documentary crews, in dance or theater companies, learn to place their "self" in the service of a collective goal. That includes acceding to a shared vision, accepting an assigned role, trusting a collective process, learning to compromise and link one's vision to those of others. As Greg Gale of The Food Project put it, youth learn to ask themselves not just how they are doing but how the crew is doing.

A Vehicle for Forging Identity

Identity work in apprenticeship can be subtle or dramatic, specific or comprehensive. The principal of a Big Picture school in Chicago notes that for some youth such work is as basic as it gets: "I am not who I thought I was" (Nambo, p.c., November 26, 2007). It is often more discrete. A young woman whose family immigrated to the United States from Bosnia when she was 11 years old describes feeling lost and like "the foreigner" until she discovered photography, began getting good at it, and receiving recognition for her work. It gave her a base for beginning to redefine herself. Salvante-McCann of Roundabout (p.c., February 5, 2007) describes a young woman who had been floating along, "You know—the typical struggle freshman and sophomores have in committing themselves to their own future. She stood in the back of the theater [one day] and she looked around and she said 'I can do this,' and so you just had a sense that she was picturing herself as an adult in the profession."

Identity processes embody a mixture of self-recognition and of beginning to sense what is distinct about oneself. A theater apprentice notes that "Before I came to Roundabout I was a bit lost—I didn't understand myself" (Roundabout Education Report, 2007, p. 15). A design apprentice reflects that "I no longer feel that something is missing. I'm not searching so hard anymore" (Daniel, 2007, p. 77). A science apprentice reports that "the biggest influence" her experience had was on her "views and insights regarding myself … It gave me an inner intensity that has kept me with a burning desire to succeed and accomplish" (Project SEED, 1996, p. 2). Describing young pianists, for instance, Sosniak (1985) notes that as they move through adolescence, they begin to learn that their music making is personal; they have to find their own identity as pianists, in sound, in choice of music; and so forth.

Finding and working in a discipline that one loves can act as anchor as one negotiates challenges during this time of life. This was the case with an Art at Work apprentice, for whom photography played this role. The son of Mexican immigrants who traveled back and forth between Mexico and the United States, he struggled to stay engaged in school but grew to be passionate about photography. With the encouragement of his photography teachers and his own success, he gradually began to think more expansively about his life. He applied and was accepted into the School of the Art Institute and, though not feeling at home there, was staying with it at the time of this writing.

Self-definition and social recognition complement and reinforce each other. An ASM filmmaking apprentice reports that "now in school people see me as a video person, whereas before I was just this creepy little girl ... now people, when they need something done with video, they'll come to me." Cassandra, a young woman from Artists for Humanity notes of her apprenticeship experience that "it definitely helped me with my individuality. Cassandra is somebody; Cassandra is an artist; Cassandra is a person that people can look up to" (*Teen Voices*, 2005, p. 2). Young musicians, artists, and others begin to want to be recognized as such; to make that identity public. That happens in public exhibits and performances, sometimes also through visible symbols of a particular identity. Participants in Youth Build, a construction-based apprenticeship for older youth, were proud to be seen around the neighborhood in their dirty work clothes and tool belts (Hahn & Leavitt, 2004).

Even for those who do not find a personal home in a discipline, apprenticeship provides a sense of direction. An ASM photography apprentice notes that "it [being in the apprenticeship] kind of opens up your mind, and [makes you] think about what you are doing and where you want to go." A young woman who had apprenticed in radio production notes that "the biggest impact Youth Radio had on me was that it gave me a sense of direction. I learned what opportunities were out there for me ..." (Gonzalez, cited in Jenkins, 2007). Apprenticeship can be a self-organizing experience, something noted by a number of Big Picture advisors with whom I spoke. As the mother of a REAP science apprentice tells his mentor, his apprenticeship experience "helped pull his thoughts and goals together" (AAS, 2000, p. 18).

Identity work in apprenticeship is sometimes about recognizing that one can join the adult world, be accepted by adults, and still be oneself. Greg Gale of The Food Project notes that when adults step back with youth and reflect on their growth, youth are inclined to say "'You're not looking at the person who I truly am.' And we say 'I think we're looking at who you really are; I think you just haven't been able to share it elsewhere'" (Gale, 2000). At the same time, it can be about learning to express resistance to the culture that is imposed on one, and about acquiring the courage to try to change it, whether through words, images and stories or through physical acts, as with the TFP apprentice, dressed in an eggplant costume, passing out information on the value of purchasing locally grown food.

Learning, Schooling, and Vocation

In some contexts, apprenticeship strengthens young people's sense of themselves as learners, for instance their willingness to explore—and interest in exploring—new ideas or fields; their belief that in novel learning or work situations they can figure out what they need to know and locate needed resources; their interest in sharing and talking about what they have learned; and their basic sense that they are learners, that being a learner is an important part of being oneself. This comes through particularly clearly where apprenticeship is part of a broader effort to re-think learning, as in Big Picture schools (Levine, 2002; Littky, 2004; McPhail, Pierson, Goodman, J., & Bunge Noffke, 2004).

It leads some youth to re-evaluate how they are approaching high school. They may come to realize generally how much they still have to learn (Grausman, p.c., December 21, 2006). The may come to think more closely about what it might take to pursue particular disciplines or careers, and how much time and effort it takes to get good at a chosen endeavor. As one former program director notes, "By participating in these experiences students come to understand that they actually have educational and career decisions to make" (Ryken, 2001, p. 79).

At a practical level, apprenticeship broadens youths' awareness of the breadth of careers people pursue. This was an especially prominent theme in science apprenticeships. Youth participating in the Research and Engineering Apprenticeship Program noted not only being unaware that certain specializations existed but that the particular ways of working on scientific problems existed (AAS, 2000). A photography apprentice with Artists for Humanity describes how her experiences there countered the skepticism she had experienced previously about pursuing a career in the arts: "Everyone always tells you 'There's no money in the arts ... It's so difficult, you're going to be a starving artist, there are no opportunities, blah, blah, blah...' It's nice to know that that's not true, there is stuff you can do, that you are making a difference and really anything is possible" (Teen Voices, 2005, p. 2).

The proportion of youth who pursue studies in the field in which they apprentice varies by field. It appears to be higher in the sciences, moderately high in visual arts, more sporadic in other fields. Anecdotally, it is not uncommon for staff to point out youth who go on to study and work in the field at hand. For instance, Gale (p.c., January 25, 2007) discusses one young woman who worked for a few years with The Food Project and went on to study community nutrition at Cornell's School of Agriculture and Life Sciences. The conservation mentor for Rocking the Boat notes surprise and pleasure at how many of the youth he has worked with go on to study in an environment-related field.

Although apprenticeship experiences cannot—nor do they have the mandate to—strengthen basic literacy or numeracy skills, in using literacy and math as tools apprentices sometimes come to value them—and language itself—differently. A radio production apprentice notes that "This isn't just writing so that you can get the five paragraph essay down. You're going to be producing something that's going to be consumed by the public—at the very minimum on the Web site and possibly on national Public Radio" (cited in Mahiri, 2007). Youth may recover a fragile sense of reading and/or writing as pleasurable activities. In his study of a theater apprenticeship, Worthman (2002) notes that young people's understanding of the possibilities of writing changed more than did their historic struggles with it. I found the same in ASM journalism and social documentary apprenticeships, both of which required a good deal of writing. Apprentices may, in effect, come to see the uses of literacy, numeracy, and academic knowledge.

A handful of those interviewed for this book emphasized the fact that apprenticeship experiences add to young people's store of social capital, opening up educational as well as work possibilities. Youth make new adult relationships, enter into new networks, are connected to new institutions, all of which may be located outside of their existing social world. The acquisition of this new capital comes at a crucial time, as apprentices are beginning the transition from high school to either further schooling or work or both. As mentors and others get to know a particular young person they become invested in helping him or her plan for post-secondary education or work. Mentors may be active, for instance, in helping apprentices see how they can pursue a discipline in college and in linking them to resources to make that process work. An apprentice with Boston's Artists for Humanity notes that "My mentor wrote me an amazing letter that I think got me into college [the School of the Art Institute in Chicago], so its influenced my life" (*Teen Voices*, 2005, p. 2).

Mechanisms at Work: A Virtuous Circle

In important respects the mechanisms leading to the kinds of growth described here are self-evident, even circular: The growth one observes in youth derives from the demands of the work itself. Skill- and knowledge-building are almost incidental, bound up with the work. The founder of Rocking the Boat notes that "the process itself—building the boat—does a lot of the skill-building work for you. Rather than saying, 'I want to build skills one through ten,' we'll just build the boat and one through ten will develop" (Green, p.c., June 22, 2006). Of a pottery apprentice an observer notes: "the challenges he named are also the skills he needs to acquire to propel him forward" (Riordan, 2006, p. 104).

The intricacy or complexity of tasks in apprenticeship, and the genuine need for resulting products, demand care and thus teach the apprentice to work more carefully. Apprentices in a summer astronomy apprenticeship are observed to learn both care and patience through the meticulous acts of gathering and recording data (McCarthy, 2002). Rose (2004, pp. 7172) is struck by one young man's deliberateness and care in penciling in the location of structural supports for a wooden cabinet: "Every time he slides the framing square from one increment of the line to another he checks it at several points, his face turned slightly, eye close to the wood. Then he runs his pencil slowly along the rule, pulls his head back and checks again ... The exact placement of the supports matters, and it is one the last tasks in the long life of this valued project."

A Set of Mutually Reinforcing Attributes

The iterative, cyclical, and extensive nature of apprenticeship are reinforcing in many senses. The fact of having extended periods of time to work in one field, on one or a few projects, allows for the practice, the working and re-working that contribute to a gradually deepening learning experience. There are numerous opportunities to return to the same material. Young people have the opportunity to—and they have to—work through a problem or practice a skill until they get it right. Reflecting on his students' biotechnology apprenticeships a high school teacher notes that they "do things over and over again. It forces them to reach a standard, more so than I can do in the classroom" (Ryken, 2001, p. 120).

Growing skill allows the apprentice to get more out of his or her work and to want to get more out it. As a young person gets better at preparing a culture in a lab, filming a scene, taking or processing a photograph, s/he exerts more control over the attendant work. And may become more passionate about it as well. As Chen, Goodman, and Riel (2003, p. 8) argue, passion is as much or more an "outcome of being effective at something" as a "precursor to it." Working through the problems associated with complex tasks, especially tasks that one has a hand in designing, contribute an authentic sense of efficacy, which itself feeds further commitment. Ownership of one's mistakes contributes to ownership of what one learns from them.

Cognitive and affective processes interact to reinforce each other in apprenticeship. The complex feelings (and sense of being more fully alive) evoked by deep engagement with tasks are self-reinforcing. Learning to be patient and to be careful, whether editing video, working with clients to determine what they want from an art commission, or conducting an experiment in a lab, have affective correlates that reinforce those tendencies. As apprentices learn to work through feeling frustrated and stuck, they come to feel less frustrated and stuck.

The fact that the work results in concrete products or performances provides important reinforcement as well. It is motivating to be able to see the relationship between one's efforts and the results of those efforts. The product embodies one's effort and growth. An ASM photography mentor notes that "Some of these kids I don't think have ever made anything ... physical, something that they can actually hold in their hand and realize they've completed all the steps in the process to get to that point...." A boat building instructor notes that the work is so compelling in part because "it is the combining of many different tasks to have this attractive, functional thing at the end" (Wenger, p.c., June 27, 2007). Public performance, presentation, use or sale of products communicates that one's work is of interest to others and has social value (Honig & McDonald, 2005).

The mutually reinforcing qualities of apprenticeship extend to the demands it makes on the self. Learning and growth stick in part because apprenticeship tends to involve the whole self in tasks and projects, to call on many capacities and senses. Activity cycles between thinking and acting. Thinking is often embedded in physical activity, giving it a more solid aspect, while physical activity itself leads to new patterns of thought. In some unspecified way, learning is integrated more viscerally into the self.

Growth Through Demands and Responsibility

As Richard Grausman of CCAP notes in chapter 4 the demands and responsibilities of apprenticeship "mature a young person quite rapidly." Life is suddenly no longer "just a series of days going by." The feeling of being relied on is a powerful one. A Wisconsin YAP regional coordinator whose son apprenticed in information technology notes that "he just blossomed—they treated him no differently than all the other staff ... One weekend he was called in to help with a critical Y2K [year two thousand] problem, and you could feel his pride" (Kraus, p.c., January 28, 2008).

Norms and expectations are at a high level. A design mentor notes that "being exposed to real working professionals and real industry ... having this burden to design up to that [level] ... and asking you at a young age to trade up ... sobers a kid up in a way that's very powerful" (Daniel, 2007, p. 106). The pressure of real world deadlines focuses apprentices' and mentors' attention and effort. The mentor assumes—rightly or wrongly—that the apprentice is serious about the work at hand. A potter who served as mentor to an apprentice from a Big Picture school notes that "The studio's about growth. They're not working unless their stuff is changing and they're learning to make better things. You know, that's their job—to grow as artists" (Riordan, 2006, p. 239).

Because apprentices have a sense of responsibility for projects, they are more likely to imbue those projects with meaning. When a project has meaning it more deeply engages the person working on it; there is a deeper emotional as well as intellectual commitment (Abbott & Ryan, 2001). Responsibility for the setting itself can breed investment in it. When young people are given both physical freedom in and responsibility for a space they treat it, its tools, materials, and other participants respectfully (Thomas, 2007).

Growth Through the "Props" of a Discipline

Growth through apprenticeship is spurred by the props of a particular discipline—its language, tools, customs, and characteristic setting. These structure growth, enable it, and provide meaning, connecting the apprentice to a tradition.

An ASM community development mentor notes that as her apprentices acquire more language and concepts to make sense of their community (and society) their work deepens and they begin to feel connected to the field itself. Sense of belonging (in a specific setting or in a field itself) and growing competence go hand in hand, reinforce each other. A science apprentice says, "I'm more comfortable in the lab, and I can go in by myself without anyone being there and know what I'm supposed to be doing ... It's just more welcoming now, I guess" (Richmond & Kurth, 1999, p. 688).

Apprentices are sometimes participating in longstanding practices and rituals, by doing so re-affirming them, carrying them on and joining the community that practices them. In his study of a carpentry workshop in a Los Angeles high school Rose (2004, p. 69) writes that "Some of the work the students do maintains the shop itself. They clean machinery, cut and store wood stock, and make simple tools like sanding blocks—the same activity you would have found in a 19th century workshop." As Polanyi (1958) argues, some of the growth through apprenticeship derives from the very act of submitting to the rules and demands—in other words to the reality—of the discipline at hand.

The props of a discipline—the language, tools, setting—communicate the seriousness of what the apprentice is doing and affirm his or her right to be doing it. A young man says of an expensive, sophisticated piece of astronomy equipment, "I can't believe I'm using this; I can't believe I'm getting to do this" (McCarthy, 2002, p. 33). When a group of print-making apprentices visit the studio of a professional graphic designer, they are impressed by how much it resembles their own studio; the experience helps them feel that they too are serious people doing serious work. The props of a discipline can physically and cognitively organize a young person. A Big Picture principal describes a previously disorganized and distractible young man, apprenticing at a yacht building shop: "He's got his work bench there, it's one of the most beautiful things you've ever seen; he's got his tools organized, and the way he did his work—he was documenting and photographing his project..." (Adler, p.c., June 7, 2006).

The Setting Protects and Teaches

As noted throughout, learning in apprenticeship is often social; the apprentice surrounded by others doing the same or similar work. In a science lab or art studio or design firm the apprentice can see and therefore learn from what others are trying to accomplish. The presence of others leads to "uninvited" help. A science apprentice notes of other students and staff in the lab, "They're asking me questions, making me look at things from a different angle" (Richmond & Kurth, 1999, p. 689). The apprentice can participate in critiques involving others, allowing for learning that is close but not too close. When tasks are shared youth learn not just about themselves but about themselves "in relation to others" (Musick, 1999, p. 35). An ensemble theater production requires each participant to consider his or her own actions in relation to those of others, and in particular the impact of his or her actions on others (Worthman, 2002).

The setting—as with the experience as a whole—is full of tacit messages. One, for example, is that "this way of engaging tasks, of using time and energy, is one way of being an adult." Another is that becoming good at something is a slow, sometimes tedious process, but one that is manifest, and trustworthy in a concrete way. Still another is that the adolescent is being taken seriously not because of some special category he or she belongs to but because he or she is present, working and learning.

Dissonance and Accommodation

A number of observers have argued that growth in youth apprenticeships occurs in part through an encounter with new, unfamiliar demands, an experience of "dissonance," and gradual adaptation (see, e.g., Larson &Walker, 2006; Riordan, 2006). Rose (2004, p. 88) observes that "As students take on projects like the display case or the kitchen cabinet, they often find themselves at the current limits of their ability, and it is at those limits that further aspects of carpentry develop." The process of adapting—of learning—is deeper in adolescence than earlier in life due to new cognitive capacities. A young person struggles to master new demands. With some measure of mastery he or she can step back to see what has been accomplished, perhaps deriving lessons from the experience.

The opportunities and demands of apprenticeship settings encourage self-evaluation and re-evaluation. Youth are constantly testing their perceptions against reality (Hefner, 1988). An ASM theater apprentice says that "when you see other kids with some talent you think about your own talent differently." In a complementary vein, young people look inward a bit more, learning to use their own growth as a criterion and motivator, rather than the too often superficial affirmation or approbation of peers.

A New Self-Narrative

The focus in apprenticeship on the work at hand (rather than the adolescent per se) communicates a number of things, most importantly that the adolescent is a person who can and should be doing this work. Apprentices are "recognized," at the right level, in the right way. In the matter-of-fact but serious discussion that occurs around the work in process—the praise, critique, questions, suggestions—apprentices have the experience of being taken seriously, but treated matter-of-factly. This in turn encourages apprentices to take themselves more seriously but matter-of-factly. Apprentices value the fact mentors trust them to do whatever they need to do to carry out the work. The photography apprentice values the fact that s/he has been entrusted with expensive professional equipment; the dance apprentice becomes a choreographer by being entrusted to choreograph work for the final performance.

For weeks or months the apprentice may act right but not feel right. In science apprenticeships young people are observed to use the language and discourse of a discipline well before they truly understand it; they are practicing being "real" scientists (Richmond & Kurth, 1999) As the ASM flamenco apprentice quoted in chapter five notes "You fake it until you make it." Apprentices have to grow into their new identity. But at some point it sticks, in part because the apprentice has decided that he or she wants to become the kind of person a scientist or photographer or documentary maker is. Moreover, young people's selves are not just enriched but altered by the history of the discipline and the setting they have joined; that history becomes part of their own. An apprentice photographer becomes kin to the long line of great photographers that preceded her.

Even when the apprentice decides that a discipline is not for him or her, the experience seems to increase the menu of possible future selves the youth can imagine becoming. Speaking about one of his students, apprenticing in the Materials Management Department of a local hospital, a Big Picture advisor notes that this young man's work setting "offers a lens through which to see his own future in a way that a math class or a history [class] can't" (Riordan, 2006, p. 215). For more vulnerable youth, apprenticeship experiences provide a measure of discontinuity from earlier experience without directly threatening the underpinnings of existing self-identity. They address the problem that Erikson (1987, p. 637) describes as "a decided disbelief in the possibility that time may bring change, and yet also a vivid fear that it might."

Young people's direct experiences have metaphorical equivalents that can seem just as powerful at times. The finished boat is "a visual representation of potential ... a reminder [to youth] of what they can do with their lives" (Wenger, p.c., June 27, 2007). The slow, almost invisible but steady growth of a vegetable crop parallels that of its young caretakers, communicating as well that growth takes its time. As young people learn to use specific tools in a discipline, they metaphorically acquire a broader set. One Youth Build participant notes that "okay, like they gave me the tools ... It's not just the construction tools, but they're giving you other tools, how to deal with issues, with feelings, with anger, with patience, cause when I came here I didn't have none of that but they stripped me down and it's great" (Ferguson, 1996, p. 100).

The Mentor's Role

As described earlier, the mentor plays a number of important roles in contributing to apprenticeship effects. The mentor holds the discipline for the apprentice, controlling the challenges and keeping the work on the constructive side of difficulty. A pottery mentor says of his apprentice that "my goal was to get him to discover ... things on his own and to stop him from making silly and stupid mistakes" (Riordan, 206, pp. 239–240). In his study of a filmmaking apprenticeship, Larson (2004, p. 16) observed that "Although adults exercised quite a bit of control, they did so in ways that helped keep youth in a channel of engagement."

In a youth radio apprenticeship, adults create a constructive tension between youth as learners and youth as adult-like producers, needing to make high quality broadcasts (Chavez & Soep, 2006).

Apprentices acquire new cognitive, affective and social dispositions in part through observing and imitating instructors. They learn to give feedback by imitating the feedback style and language of the instructor—how it is couched, when to be practical, when to ask a question. An Educational Video Center apprentice has internalized the philosophy of the organization about the value of documentary work, noting when asked that "it is to take the things we see in our daily lives but do not notice and by putting them on film showing a different perspective" (Youth Powered Video, 2006). Youth begin to internalize the mentor's enthusiasm for the discipline at hand, his or her matter-of-fact approach to problems. This process is partly unconscious. Yet it seems also that "habits of mind are contagious" (Claxton, 2007, p. 118).

On occasion mentors can embody a lifetime of experience for youth in a specific lesson. When a professional jazz saxophonist joins the musicians of a teen theater company, he talks with them about the importance of the spaces between notes, which he describes as stillness. One youth asks him about the stillness in his own music and he replies that "I'm leaving space for others, but more than that, I'm waiting for my moment to come in, even when I don't know when that happens" (Worthman, 2002, p. 36). Mentors can sometimes deliver messages that might not be heard if coming from a parent or teacher. In a conversation with a youth about how he arrived at his position, a chef notes (without apparent irony) "nobody hands anything to you on a plate; whatever it is you want to do it takes a lot of effort on your part" (Learning Journeys, 2000).

Identification with the mentor provides both a spur for mastery and a model for identity work. Who they are, what they've done, the path they've taken and even how they behave is instructive, interesting and often novel to apprentices. An artist who had apprenticed in Marwen's Art at Work notes that it was in being mentored by "and just being around" people who had made art their life that she "could see it's possible" (Gaspar, p.c., July 2, 2007). The youth she works with know her journey and know also that at one point in her life she was where they are now. Another former Marwen apprentice notes that "we learned from the professionality of our teachers ... there's a certain level they just operate at; also they are models, you are learning how to get to that point ... the adults lead you into new areas simply by what they are interested in and introduce you to; now I'm getting into street art" (Camacho, p.c., January 8, 2007).

Apprentices in a number of programs comment on instructors' passion for their discipline. Young people like being around adults who "value you getting better at what *they* do," as one youth puts it (Gentry, Rizza, Peters, & Hu, 2005, p. 63). A science apprentice asks, "why is my mentor, who is the most brilliant person I have ever encountered, I mean why is he here? The reason he is here is because this is what he loves to do" (Richmond & Kurth, 1999, p. 692). An ASM apprentice notes of her instructor that "he's just this powerful journalist and I like the way he writes." For some apprentices the process of identification is a spur to growth. The apprentice is motivated toward mastery by a desire to be like, even to "become" his or her teacher (Litowitz, 1993). A Rocking the Boat alumna notes that "watching [Adam Green, the director] pursue his own vision has inspired her to go after what she wants in life" (Remer, 2007, p. 19).

As the mentor gains legitimacy for the youth, so does his or her perspective, on work, problem-solving, and eventually broader issues. For example, when revising and correcting is an integral part of the mentor's approach to tasks, that may gradually be "adopted" and internalized by youth, becoming an aspect of their own approaches. When a mentor says, "If you think you're done after high school, think again," a young person may hear those words differently, perhaps really hear them for the first time. Rose (2004) notes how young electrical apprentices adopt their instructors' pride in the proper laying of electrical wiring inside a wall, knowing that the work will never be seen but internalizing the electrician's sense that what is important is that he or she knows. As one ASM mentor told me, the most gratifying thing was "when a kid says, 'I was thinking about what you said...'."

As an embodiment of the adult world, and often a very different one than a youth might have experienced up to that point, the mentor helps shift his or her subjective experience of that world. Working closely with the mentor makes the adult work world feel more human, less distant and monolithic (Daniel, 2007). The mentor, like the apprenticeship experience as whole, may help resolve contradictions between what youth are told and what they have observed and experienced about the value of effort and commitment, the costs and benefits of tasking risks. Roundabout Theater teaching artists' evident respect for youth, and commitment to a relational model in work with them, may be just as powerful as the structure of the discipline in shaping young people's developing selves. Yet even the fact that youth may not be treated as someone special, though sometimes difficult for them, is helpful. As a CCAP staff member notes of her culinary apprentices, "by the end a lot of them take great pride in 'I'm just like everyone else [in the kitchen], I'm a worker'" (Mitchell, p.c., December 8, 2006).

7

The Limits and Limitations of Youth Apprenticeship

We do not make things anymore and most sensible people will go to university and emerge as knowledge workers. Those who do not will be confined to the twilight world of the call center and fast food restaurant.
A British government minister (cited in Unwin, 2004, p. 150)

In this chapter I reflect on questions raised by my own and others' explorations of youth apprenticeship. In an immediate sense, these are questions about the limitations of apprenticeship as a learning model, including some that relate to its specificity. In social and perhaps policy terms, there are questions about the definition, meaning and role of youth apprenticeship in relation to the changing nature of work and the demands youth face as they move toward adulthood. As Gardner (1991) suggests, apprenticeship seems old fashioned. Breadth of education is viewed as more valuable than depth in today's world. Although it might seem that the demands youth face as they move toward adulthood are evolving in ways that make apprenticeship less attractive, I argue that apprenticeship (paradoxically) fosters the kinds of dispositions currently viewed as essential for youth. For some it actually creates the beginning of a pathway into adulthood. The problem with apprenticeship is whether it can find a place in a culture that seems antithetical to it in many respects.

Reflecting on the limitations of youth apprenticeship requires some overgeneralization. As should be clear, there is significant variability among apprenticeship settings, a feature that itself is both a strength and a limitation. Apprenticeships vary not only in disciplinary base but in sense of purpose and authenticity, type of setting, time frame, intensity, rhythms of work, and many other dimensions. Time pressures are routinely greater in commercial production settings than in studios or laboratories, and mentors often more distracted by deadlines and multiple tasks.

Apprenticeships that take place in youth-centered settings differ in characteristic ways than those that take place in adult work settings. In the former, for instance, it typically takes longer for adult mentors to establish—and ongoing work for them to sustain—a sense of purposefulness, seriousness and productivity (Daniel, 2007). When teens are surrounded by other teens, they tend to act like teens. In adult work settings, youth are "outnumbered" and have less room and less time to adjust and few or no other peers to fool around with. Mentoring looks and feels different in different disciplines. On average, for instance, artists as mentors are different in temperament and approach than scientists. Their model of growth and learning is seemingly less linear. One tells an observer that "I'm not as impressed with the ability to go from A to B without causing a ruckus as someone else would be" (Riordan, 2006, p. 236).

Limitations Inherent to Apprenticeship

Many of the limitations inherent to apprenticeship represent the flip-side of its strengths. This is illustrated particularly clearly in the learning process, including the distinctive role of teachers and teaching. It is illustrated as well in the specificity of apprenticeship—its strong roots in a specific discipline, its emphasis on depth rather than breadth, and its practical quality. It might seem a truism, but any specific type of developmental experience has strengths and limitations. Youth need a portfolio of good experiences of different types. The specificity of apprenticeship, in particular, constitutes a limitation primarily when it is compelled to carry more than its share of good developmental experience.

The Learning Model

As argued in chapter 1 and illustrated in subsequent chapters, apprenticeship is in many respects a powerful learning model. There is a match "between the nature of competence and the process by which it is acquired, shared and extended" (Wenger, 1998, p. 102). Learning in apprenticeship is experiential; young people learn by doing. It involves immersion, fostering specific skills by immersing youth in contexts that demand them (Bereiter & Scardamalia, 2003). As Adam Green of Rocking the Boat puts it, RTB throws new apprentices fully into the work right away, believing that this is the best way to learn. (Youth in commercial production settings may also be thrown into the work because of time pressures and deadlines.) The learning model in apprenticeship is iterative, marked by increments of trial and error, false starts, the gradual accretion of knowledge and skill, by routine and by practice and more practice. Not least, the process of learning and the resources for learning are distributed throughout the learning and production setting.

These characteristic features are to an extent different ways of describing the same process. And their limitations are also connected. Learning in apprenticeship can at times seem inefficient, sometimes too routinized, needlessly painful and drawn out. Even with mastery of discrete skills, it takes time and experience to be exposed to—and therefore add to one's working memory—the range of problems that can come up in a discipline. And as a Wisconsin Youth Apprenticeship Program (YAP) coordinator puts it, "isolated skills are only a part of growing competence" (Nystrom, p.c., January 17, 2008).

Novices in a discipline do not automatically learn from experience. As discussed in chapter 5, they have to learn how to do so, a process which itself takes time. For instance, novices have difficulty observing their own behavior in a way useful to helping them re-organize it. They may not know what is important about what they are observing as they watch others at work. They often do not know how to use knowledge or techniques just taught or learned to solve problems. They may not know how to use practice to improve. Although it is inherently difficult to know when a product or task is finished in apprenticeship, it is especially difficult for novices to know; likewise discerning the important dimensions of tacit knowledge, that which is not easily named or shared.

To the degree that motivation and mastery reinforce each other, the novice may have a more difficult time motivating him or herself. The depth of a field can be daunting to some youth. And some apprentices never get the opportunity to enter deeply into a field. A young person may not be in a setting long enough to move from the periphery to the middle of things, to move through the "bottlenecks" to mastery (Perkins & Salomon, 1989) or generally to move into a position to get a lot out of the work. Mentors have occasionally restricted full participation because they viewed the work of the discipline as a whole, or a particular project, as too complex and specialized or too sensitive. Project deadlines—particularly multiple short deadlines—sometimes constrain participation. A mentor in a civil rights organization, commenting on why she did not bring an apprentice to a meeting with a local police department, notes that her week has simply been too hectic (Riordan, 2006, p. 143). Apprentices sometimes have to negotiate increased responsibility (Ryken, 2006).

In some circumstances simple immersion in the work of a discipline may not provide enough background or information for youth to acquire important conceptual foundations. As Gardner (1991, p. 125) argues, when apprenticeship does not provide the background knowledge and framework that surrounds a particular set of tasks it "may result in people who are practically competent but not adequately reflective about what they do." This problem can be seen in apprenticeships in the natural sciences where growth sometimes stays at the level of procedure, not changing apprentices' conceptual understanding of higher order principles, or their ability to use science creatively (Crawford, Bell, Blair, and Lederman, 1999; Hay & Barab, 2001). Some of the participants in the Berkeley Biotechnology Education, Inc. (BBEI) program, notably those in production rather than research settings, noted wishing for more explanation for some of the procedures they were carrying out (Ryken, 2001). As discussed in chapters 4 and 5, getting to the essence—grasping the main goals and concepts—of such abstract fields as community development or social action is also especially difficult.

Even with experience and growing skill, the kind of practice required to get good at something is not necessarily enjoyable. Practice is more complex than is often anticipated. It is in some respects mindless, yet requires concentration to be profitable; "it is sheer repetition, but always different from one [instance] to the next" (Howard, 1982, p. 158). In general the affective and skills pay off of the apprenticeship experience is cumulative and often not felt for months. It can also be subtle, not easily "seen" and appreciated by those not directly involved. As Sloan and Sosniak (1985, p. 136) point out, "If you don't have the self-motivation and the self-discipline to continue doing it, no one cares."

There is a developmental dimension to the learning challenges described here. The attributes of apprenticeship that make it appealing to youth at times interact uneasily with others that do not fit the developmental characteristics of youth itself. If the novice stage of learning and work in a discipline is inherently difficult, it is especially so for youth, who may lack both patience and the experience to know that striving for mastery will become less frustrating with time. The discipline and single-mindedness required for practice and reiteration do not fit well with the fluidity of young people's attention. Identity is forged partly through experimentation. Adolescents try out different roles, sample different kinds of experiences, question themselves and others, take risks and test limits. Yet it is forged equally through commitment—of sustained energy and attention to some domain (or domains), whether academic, artistic, athletic, vocational, or other. Such commitment "delimits the potential for growth ... [a youth] cannot become a plumber or a nurse or a poet unless he pays considerable attention to the skills required for plumbing, nursing or writing poetry" (Csikszentmihalyi & Larson, 1984, p. 13).

Teaching

Pedagogy in apprenticeship is difficult to define and pinpoint, let alone codify. Mentors may not know how to access or articulate what lies behind their own expertise nor the tacit knowledge accumulated over time in their field.[1] They may not realize how much they know. Teaching, like learning, is embedded in production processes and tied to immediate tasks and problems. It is difficult for mentors to find a balanced role, and often not clear what should be formally taught as opposed to learned through experience. As noted in chapter 5, mentors, at times, have to adjust the pace of work, increase the scaffolding and explicitness of feedback provided to novices. In a design apprenticeship focused on consumer products, mentors eventually created design notebooks to serve as a bridge between where most youth were and professional standards. The notebooks included checklists (e.g., what needed to be in final technical drawings), simple heuristics and formulas (e.g., with respect to proportions), anatomical outlines for shoes and clothes, and so forth (Daniel, 2007).

The fact that mentors are first and foremost professionals in a field is a great strength of apprenticeship but it means that mentors have a divided identity, with sometimes strong or sometimes weak self-identities as teachers (and therefore strong or weak sense of responsibility to teach). Richard Grausman of CCAP contends that "if you put somebody in the hands of a good chef or sous chef, that person will have had experience teaching, but a mentor who is new in the kitchen may not be ready to teach or may be insecure about sharing his or her knowledge" (Grausman, p.c., December 21, 2006). As with seeking responsibility, an apprentice may have to let adult mentors know clearly that "I want to learn this," as one youth puts it (Taylor & Watt-Malcolm, 2007, p. 38).

Mentors vary in how they view and use their authority, with some more reluctant than others to be authoritative. In some apprenticeships the adult still resembles the traditional "master" who is deliberately and systematically sharing knowledge and experience. In others the adult is a volunteer "mentor" with a much less defined role vis-à-vis an apprentice. In the latter case, commitment to apprentices is more matter of personal choice and availability of time than of defined responsibility invested in professional role (Riordan, 2006).

The Specificity of Apprenticeship

The specificity of apprenticeship is one of its most confounding qualities. Working deeply in a discipline is, inevitably, limiting as well as powerful. Disciplines historically have been central to how cultures organize learning, knowledge and adult endeavor. They embody a particular "vision of human achievement" (Kahn, 2006, p. 21). By implication, thought patterns, reasoning strategies and heuristics learned in apprenticeship appear to be discipline-specific (in part because one is drawing on experience in that particular discipline to work one's way through problems). Knowledge and skill acquired in apprenticeship are, seemingly, most useful in specific situations. Even literacy and math skills used are often particular—the applied math of the carpenter or boat-builder, the very specific form that writing takes when one is recording lab procedures, logging videotape or narrating a documentary.

These qualities raise two questions. First, how useful is discipline-specific knowledge in a world in which the role of disciplines as organizers of knowledge and experience is perhaps becoming less central? (Put another way, disciplines appear to be relatively fixed, while instrumentally useful knowledge and skill appear to be changing rapidly.) I address this question later in the chapter. Second, to what extent does apprenticeship have general value as a learning and developmental experience? In the language of learning theory, to what extent do the discipline-specific knowledge and skill acquired in apprenticeship transfer?

In one sense transfer is inherently problematic. Most knowledge and skill, wherever and however organized, is "context bound and full of circumstantial links to the setting and occasion" (Saloman & Perkins, 1989, p. 120). What people know and can do is rooted not just in their minds but in the features—the demands, opportunities, and relational characteristics—of the contexts they inhabit (Gonczi, 2001). Apprenticeship, though, seems especially context-bound and is often deliberately rooted and specific, not incidentally so. The knowledge shared by adults is what is needed in that setting, even at a particular moment or for a specific procedure. Bailey, Hughes, and Moore (2004, p. 118) use the example of a surgical technician apprentice being taught to set up "a very specialized anesthesiology machine" to ask whether the effort it took was worthwhile. Their answer is mixed: they note that, though this particular knowledge is very specific, the young woman is learning a great deal more through her participation in the distinctive community of the operating room, for instance, how surgeons, anesthesiologists, and nurses collaborate around a common goal; and perhaps more specifically about why attention to detail and care in carrying out tasks are important.

The findings in chapter 6 suggest also that apprenticeships operate on more than one level for youth. At the practical level, they are very specific and concrete, although they do demand that youth take what they have learned on one problem in a particular setting and apply it to the next problem in that setting. But they also operate at a meta-level, fostering such general qualities as persistence, resourcefulness, and what Dennis Littky of Big Picture calls mindfulness. Transfer of even these qualities is not straightforward. As pointed out in chapter 3, youth tend to treat each setting in their lives as distinct; they do not try to make connections or ask what new ideas or approaches they can bring from one setting to another.[2] But as youth who have participated in apprenticeships continue to mature, in other words over time, they seem better able to tap into those experiences, to draw on the broader skills and habits developed through them.

Youth Apprenticeship and the Changing Nature of Work

How do the discipline-specific experiences of apprenticeship map onto an evolving workplace, especially for the large group of youth who will be entering into what has been described as semi-skilled work? Changes in work have been characterized in different ways, in part because observers tend to focus on different trends. For instance, work has been noted to have become more fluid—a series of personal encounters; more abstract—involving manipulation of symbols and information; more focused on process and less reliant on specific (or fixed) content. Berryman (1993, p. 365) emphasizes rapidly changing production technologies, open-ended problem pathways, more non-routine situations, demand for customized solutions and products. Studies of work in specific manufacturing settings seem to confirm these generalizations. One study examining the demands on workers (mostly high school graduates) in medical equipment, steel-making, and valve manufacturing plants found common demands across all three, notably "diagnostic, trouble-shooting and team problem solving" skills, with breadth of skills as important as depth (Lewis, 2007, p. 339).

Substantive, discipline-specific knowledge and skills are not becoming entirely irrelevant. They are important to a number of growing occupations, including biotechnology/bioscience, nursing and new clinical and lab based technical occupations in the health care field (e.g., physical, occupational, respiratory and other therapists, EKG and surgical technicians, etc.). Yet even in many scientific, technical and design-oriented disciplines important knowledge and procedures are evolving rapidly (Boshuizen, 2003). A graphic design mentor describes his field as marked by both changing technology and a growing talent pool with wider access to key technology (Hodge, p.c., July 31, 2007). He cites as an example animation, a rapidly growing field which has become computer-based and no longer requires unique hand work skills. Some traditional trades are changing more rapidly than in the past. Electrical work, for instance, increasingly requires an understanding of electronics, handling of delicate materials (e.g., signal-carrying conductors) and work with technical professionals in other fields such as computer systems (Racca & Roth, 2001).

Some observers argue that the question of whether or not deep substantive knowledge and skill in a particular discipline is still relevant is not as critical as that of what to do about the de-skilling of work in general (see, e.g., Fleming, Harley, & Sewell, 2004; Fenwick, 2006). They argue that that although the new economy is said to be a knowledge economy, the bulk of new technical work, as well as the substantial segment of the economy involving service work, is routine and low-skilled. Work at lower skill levels tends to be characterized by "hyper levels of accountability and monitoring generated by obsession with 'total quality control'"; and in some settings by "contradictory procedures, conflicting directions [and] multiple interpretations" of what quality means (Fenwick, 2006, pp. 458–459). Studies in this vein point to surprising feelings of isolation in the workplace and disappointment about lack of opportunity for growth in the job (Eisenhart, 1992). The more pessimistic characterization of today's work place reflects a growing "skills polarization" in the workforce, between high skill elites and a minimally skilled mass of workers (Lewis, 2007).

Educational Implications

In spite of differences in the characterization of work itself, those who study or practice technical education tend to agree about the implications of changes in the nature of work for skill demands. By most accounts, institutions responsible for preparing youth should concentrate on fostering a new set of generic skills: flexibility, adaptability and the capacity to improvise; self-initiative and an entrepreneurial orientation; the ability to find and manage information and to analyze unfamiliar tasks, to work in teams, acquire new skills as needed, and to communicate effectively, especially with people whose vocabulary, frame of reference and work knowledge one does not share (Fuller, 1996; Murname & Levy, 1996; Silbereisen, 2003). Less immediately, youth should be (somehow) prepared to be the creators and managers of their own unique careers. A handful of observers emphasize the need for creativity, although definitions vary widely (including creative use of the self in various work places).

We should not be unreflective about this vision of needed skills and dispositions. In my own view, their generic quality is problematic. It seems to undermine the possibility of a strong identity, a sense of vocation, in both learning and work. Berryman 1993, p. 370) argues that "the idea of 'generic' workplace skills is something of a conceptual swamp." It is unclear not only whether it is possible to deliberately and directly foster such skills, and if so how, but whether they really exist at all in disembedded form. At a less philosophical level, "successfully to carry out certain jobs might appear to depend" exactly upon not using some of the skills listed above (Halliday, 2000, p. 163).

Even the idea that work is becoming more process-oriented, and therefore content free, is belied to an extent by U.S. Bureau of Labor analyses of where (beyond entry-level service occupations) job growth will be greatest. Some growth indeed will be in such jobs as systems analysts and information processing technicians. But other growing fields include nursing and "allied" health care roles, biotechnology/bioscience, and design-oriented fields, as well as selected construction trades. There is growing awareness that work at the margins of the economy in the creative and cultural fields also provides an option for at least some youth. The majority of artists and other creative workers already spend some time in commercial, non-profit and "community" work (Markusen, Gilmore, Johnson, Levi, & Martinez, 2006).[3]

A more explicitly political implication would be that the American education system must do a better job of addressing the skills polarization that has occurred, creating strong educational experiences in the large middle area between high skills and no skills, the area that is usually defined as technical. Although close to three-fourths of the decent-paying new jobs created over the next decade will not require a four year college degree, they will require a solid, substantive education and solid basic literacy skills. In other words, as work continues to bifurcate a deep, substantive education is possibly becoming more important, yet one that is not too narrowly technical. A graphic design mentor I interviewed observes that the best solutions to design problems are informed, even if indirectly, by an individual's broad knowledge of history, culture, other fields. He notes, moreover, that "if they [young people] don't have some broader education they're just going to be hired help in a way" (Hodge, p.c., July 31, 2007).

A Role for Youth Apprenticeship

If apprenticeship-like experience is not a perfect fit with new skills needed for work, it seems a better fit than school, at least than school as customarily organized. As the findings in chapter 6 make clear, apprenticeship provides a good means of fostering many of the generic, seemingly substance-free skills thought to be critical to the 21st century. To cite just one attribute, as apprentices learn to work on open-ended problems with more than one possible solution, within a context of time, resource or client-directed constraints, they are learning skills central to much of the new work they will supposedly be facing. Apprentices' distinct capacity to learn through observation and imitation, and their growth in the general qualities discussed earlier and in chapter 6, may be important attributes to bring to new workplace situations (in which one must play close attention to what is going on around one). Not least, acquiring the habit of what Pye (1968) describes as workmanship should be useful for many kinds of work.

Creating Micro-Pathways

Paralleling the changing narrative of work is a narrative describing a less well-defined and less straightforward transition from high school to work or post-secondary education for the majority of American youth. Both the transition itself and the labor market as a whole lack transparency. Youth cannot "see through the system to plot a course" toward an intermediate or longer term goal" (Hamilton & Hurrelmann, 1994, p. 331). It is difficult for youth to understand the context in which they have to make decisions (Lehmann, 2005). In the United States two-thirds of white youth and close to 90% of youth of color will not earn a four year college degree. For these youth, and even for some of those who finish college, the transition to an adulthood marked by full time work and an identifiable career is unpredictable. Employers experiment with youth, while youth experiment with employers, a trial and error process that is costly on both sides. The process of moving toward adulthood becomes more individualized and contingent. With fewer "structural bridges between school and work [most] youth must rely substantially on their own resources" (Mortimer, Vuolo, Stadd, Wakefield, & Xie, 2008, p. 46). Such resources are shaped by race, social class, community and related variables.

Apprenticeship experiences offer potential to help with this difficult process in a number of ways. In some instances they can nurture the beginnings of a career. Youth are more likely to consider a particular work experience the beginning of a career when it is a rich and interesting experience, often the case in apprenticeship (Mortimer et al., 2008). A young person's apprenticeship experience can provide a potential employer a sense of the relevant experience and skills s/he brings to a job, something rarely provided by school transcripts. For the many youth not ready to begin a career process, apprenticeship still provides experiences that help clarify educational and work-related decision-making processes, and introduces young people to the variety of adult work and disciplinary knowledge. Work in a particular discipline helps a young person begin to understand the structure of the adult work and institutional world. And, as described in chapter 6, it contributes to identity work. Becoming a photographer or engineer or journalist even for a year or two enriches an adolescent's self and provides a bridge or interim identity for her as she strives to figure out who she is, who and what she wants to be.

Apprenticeship Re-Conceptualized?

Assuming the value of apprenticeship-like experience for youth, a number of factors point to a need to view it in open, flexible ways. A few I have noted—the changing conditions of work, new types of work and more individualized and varied pathways from adolescence to adulthood. An additional factor is philosophical, deriving from the application of critical social theories and post-modern frames to work in general and apprenticeship itself. All together these factors are linked by the changing meanings of knowledge, of experience and mastery, even of work itself.

The seeming fluidity and rapidly changing technologies of work suggest a shift in thinking about the purposes of apprenticeship and, less clearly, in the specific experiences provided. Countries in Europe that include youth apprenticeship as part of a school to work system have begun to make this shift. They are viewing apprenticeship less as a rigid model of vocational training and more as "a launching pad for different career pathways ... an outfitter for individual expeditions into the more and more de-regulated occupational territories of the labor market" (Heinz & Taylor, 2005, p. 13). As I suggested above, in the current occupational context apprenticeship might serve more to clarify and direct young people's movement into the labor force or into particular post-secondary educational programs. Working in a discipline alongside skilled professionals makes the adult work world feel more human, less distant and monolithic (Daniel, 2007).

The emergence of new professions, many involving new digital technologies, and the growth of the creative/cultural sector add to an already strengthening sense that young people are leading their older peers into the future. Young workers are creating new traditions and practices, for example they widely and freely share ideas, information and technologies directly with each other. They are raising questions in some fields about the relevance of established bodies of knowledge and custom. Mastery is increasingly coming to be viewed as tentative and relational, an interaction of the individual's abilities, a particular task and a particular setting. If it is not fixed, it has to be regenerated. Continual shifts in technology, knowledge and skill demands make growing numbers of workers "perpetual apprentices," but often apprentices with no masters (Ainley & Rainbird, 1999, p. 4).

Changes in the conditions of work, the practical meaning of mastery, and the role of tradition and hierarchy are echoed in a new discourse on apprenticeship. Observers argue that the goal should not be to get the apprentice to move toward the master's conception of skill, aesthetics, and so forth, but for him or her to have greater access to performance itself (Lave & Wenger, 1991). In a more democratic apprenticeship "no role has all the responsibility for knowing or directing, and no role is by definition passive" (Rogoff, 1994, p. 213). The apprentice should be supported to take what s/he is learning and use it in his or her own way (Hung, 1999).

Concepts long associated with apprenticeship—mastery, conventions, completion—are being contested especially strongly in creative fields. Menger (2006, p. 60) observes that "Instead of habits, bits of learned techniques, fidelity to reality and inherited constraining conventions, the artistic realm becomes more and more that of individualistic originality ... a growing insistence on personal sincerity, on individual fidelity to one's inner world of feeling and experience ... in a word, with insistence on authenticity." Youthful artists are combining disciplines, creating new ones (e.g., performing visual arts), creating and drawing on symbols not meant to be widely understood, and resisting calling their works finished.

A more explicitly political perspective holds that culturally defined or discipline-specific practices are not fixed or inevitable, but constructions that serve specific social purposes. Such purposes include, for example, maintaining economic privilege, controlling entry into a profession and exploiting workers' lack of power to set living wages. Although this critique of the structure of work does not apply directly to the youth apprenticeship experiences described in this book, it does imply that youth apprenticeship has to be emancipatory in spirit (Habermas, 1972). At a minimum it has to place the specifics of work in a larger moral and political perspective, and in particular to afford the apprentice insight into the social and economic forces which shape his or her life.

The new discourse surrounding apprenticeship has parallels in an emergent discourse on adolescent development and learning. Theorists are placing greater emphasis on individual initiative as an engine of development; arguing, for instance, that young people have to be "producers of their own development" (Larson, 2004, p. 2). This is a delicate concept, for though it implies youth initiative and control, it also hints that youth are somehow more on their own. (In this it echoes the 21st century skills formulation of youth as needing to be "creators of their own careers.") Taking a page from Erikson, theorists are also arguing again that youth is the time of life when the roots of social reconstruction are planted. As Erikson (1962, p. 24) put it, "it is the young who carry in them the power to confirm those who confirm them, to renew and regenerate, to disavow what is rotten, to reform and rebel...."

It is notable that mentors in at least some of today's youth apprenticeships reflect the newer thinking about locus of initiative, ownership and related dimensions. They balance sharing of their own knowledge and experience with recognition that youth want and need to discover principles and precepts for themselves. They balance the need to re-affirm tradition with respect for young people's need for voice. The skilled and authoritative boat building instructor for Rocking the Boat notes nonetheless that "I try to do as little to do as little as I can [in the shop] to have what I want happen, because what I want to happen is what the youth want to happen" (Kautz, p.c., March 19, 2007). One of the mentors in a youth radio program argues for the value—and even necessity— of interdependence between adults and youth in youth media apprenticeships: "neither party could carry out the work alone even if they wanted to" (Soep, p.c., July 23, 2007). In a teen theater production company in Chicago, the script for each production is "gleaned, made up entirely of the teenagers' writing and incorporates [sic] the movement, dance and music of the rehearsals." The process draws on and transforms the lived experience of participating youth to create "new cultural items" (Worthman, 2002, p. 8).

The best mentors do not seem even to need a balance-of-power lens, or perhaps they constantly adjust the balance. As Alvin Keith, the Roundabout Theater teaching artist, put it "we try to make the line between being more active and being less active as organic as possible" (p.c., April 19, 2007). In that light, the proposed, or in some cases emergent, shift in the locus of authority in apprenticeship sits uneasily with the assumption that apprentices have to be willing to submit (or at least assent) to the norms and rules of a specific tradition. Or perhaps it simply illustrates that any social institution is in part a product of its time, just as is each youth.

Where Apprenticeship Fits

Apprenticeship provides for something missing in American adolescence. Put differently, it provides the spark for something already present but undefined in youth. It suggests the means for youth to have a solid, developmentally appropriate experience. It is one of the few ways still available to youth to experience what it is like to be an adult, psychologically, socially, viscerally. It confirms the value of creating micro-pathways to support next steps and helping more generally with identity work. Apprenticeship may seem a bit old fashioned, as Gardner (1991) has stated. But it is also points to the kinds of youthful achievement that could be given meaning in American culture.

If the re-emergence of youth apprenticeship answers some questions about American arrangements for adolescence, it raises others. For the most part, current apprenticeship experiences are discrete. With an exception or two, they are not tied to a formal, well-defined and culturally sanctioned educational/vocational pathway. Youth in some instances can and do get high school and/or community college credit for their apprenticeship experiences. A few initiatives, like BBEI, cross over from high school to post-secondary. But no U.S. initiatives, not even Wisconsin's, feed directly into formal, registered apprenticeship systems.[4] It is too often unclear what young people might do with their new skills, dispositions, and self-knowledge when a particular experience ends. It is often up to mentors and youth themselves to build on an apprenticeship experience.

Where, then, ought apprenticeship reside, in relation to other institutions and goals for youth? How "real" do the tasks of apprentices have to be—and in what senses real? In 1990 Stephen Hamilton argued that youth apprenticeship experiences could have only the most modest effects on young people's lives unless they were part of a larger system, a formal set of structures and pathways that linked the worlds of schooling, work and youth development. Even if Hamilton was correct, I do not envision a formal, centralized youth apprenticeship structure in the United States, or even 50 state systems. I believe that youth apprenticeship as described in this book will remain a decentralized phenomenon, with many sources of expression. As chapters 3 and 4 illustrate, some of that expression will be tied to schools—and especially to a revived vocational/technical education impulse—and some not. Yet even if and as provision of youth apprenticeship remains variable, growing out of local conditions, opportunities, resources, and institutional relationships, systemic issues will impress themselves on this loosely constructed field. In fact, they already have.

Potential stakeholders from the education, youth development, school-to-work and work worlds will have to be brought together to discuss interests, roles, definitions, and so forth. As I discovered in working on the book, those working in individual initiatives could learn a good deal from each other, but there are no mechanisms for bringing stakeholders together to share experience. Many cities are full of untapped resources which could be mobilized in the cause of youth apprenticeship. That in turn will require intermediaries similar to Chicago's After School Matters, which not only gives youth apprenticeship an identity in Chicago, but pulls together many funding sources, provides a general structure for apprenticeships in the form of a set of principles, recruits, contracts with, places and supports professionals from throughout the Chicago area.

Hamilton's argument does need attending to at the experiential level. If the institutions in young people's lives do not relate to each other—in fact, even seem to work at cross purposes—discrete experiences will have less impact than they otherwise might. For instance, where local school systems have youth apprenticeship programs the relationship between young people's school experiences and their apprenticeship experiences is too often discordant. Young people report both thinking and learning very differently in the two types of settings, and sometimes resist efforts to tie to the two together. The case studies in chapter 3 suggest that it is possible for classroom and work-site experiences to enrich each other. This will require much deeper relationships among institutional partners than has been achieved in initiatives up to the present, something that (as the Wisconsin YAP experience indicates) will in turn require far more goading than has occurred in current partnerships.

It is, then, not yet clear whether or where apprenticeship can be made integral to our culture's arrangements for youth, particularly those growing up under difficult conditions. It is possible that involving a greater number and variety of adults and adult institutions in supporting young people's growth will be self-reinforcing. Apprenticeship—and apprentices—tend to mobilize and activate latent resources from their surrounding communities, a wonderful kind of value added. Apprenticeship tends to feed on itself, with former apprentices helping support the learning and growth of new ones. The challenge for youth apprenticeship is whether it can find a place in a culture that seems antithetical to it in so many respects.

Conclusion

But in youth the tables of childhood dependence begin slowly to turn: no longer is it for the old to teach the young the meaning of life. It is the young who, by their responses and actions, tell the old whether life as represented to them has some vital promise, and it is the young who carry the power to confirm those who confirm them ...

Erik Erikson (1968, p. 258)

Whatever you grow up with you turn into.

An ASM filmmaking apprentice

For many youth today it is difficult to find experiences that make sense, that combine some challenge, novelty, and a measure of control and yet are rooted in the larger culture. As the young woman quoted by Chavez and Soep at the outset implies, too many teens are waiting around either to become famous or to fall off the face of the earth. For whatever reasons—deference, misapprehension, preoccupation, economic necessity, indifference—adults seem to have abdicated. A great quantity of youthful idealism, energy, imagination, questioning, pushing at boundaries has no place to go. Conversely, a host of potential cultural resources to support youth themselves remain latent, not knowing where to go or even that they might be resources.

The ideas and initiatives described in this book offer a way past this conundrum, through the renewal and reinterpretation of an old institution. In modest terms, apprenticeship provides occasion for adults to stay involved with youth in a way that makes sense, and conversely new links for youth to the adult world. In some respects the whole adult world becomes a resource: In the course of work on an Education Video Center documentary, a homeless man permits a young woman to interview him a second time; she had been too shy to ask questions the first time she tried.

Apprenticeship does its developmental work in domains in which youth are unsure of themselves. It provides grounding, structure, and some substance for the explorations of youth. The task focus decenters the young person, providing a vehicle for escaping self preoccupation. Even as apprenticeship nurtures self, it does so by taking the young person out of and beyond the self (Nakamura, 2001). These are settings in which youth can not only try out particular identities and perhaps find their distinct voice, but in which they can deliberately and viscerally learn lessons not available elsewhere. Apprenticeship allows for some fluctuation in commitment. And yet it helps young people see where, how and into what they might grow (Csikszentmihalyi & Larson, 1984).

For some youth apprenticeship may well be primarily a safe, moderately engaging space—a kind of engaged moratorium. For some, it serves to organize their daily life or to put other settings, such as school or neighborhood, in perspective. For some youth, apprenticeship is formative in the most basic sense of the word. An Artists for Humanity apprentice, accepted by the School of the Art Institute in Chicago, tells the teaching artist who mentored him, "I don't think you realize how much I'm going to miss this place. I don't think I'll ever be able to find this kind of set up again, where I'm actually paid and respected to create; where my voice is actually heard, where I don't have to prove to anyone that 'I'm worthy of entering your institution'" (Vicin, p.c., January 8, 2007).

Proposing a greater role for apprenticeship in adolescence raises many questions, but most are questions that need to be addressed anyway. Some pertain to the systemic context for youth apprenticeship—or better put the lack of a systemic context. In a country in which high school educators rarely speak to community college educators, let alone those in the business world, there is much "systems" work to do. Even within the high school itself, bringing vocational/technical education into the heart of the so-called academic curriculum has barely begun to happen.

Apprenticeship surely will have greater meaning in the long run if it has some kind of cultural sanction—if it both "counts" and is widely recognized as valuable. Apprenticeship is, nonetheless, only one element of a necessary cultural re-alignment in supporting adolescent development. Americans have to pay closer attention to young people in a host of ways. Of these, none is more important than recognizing and addressing disparities in social resources among youth. As Lewis (2007) points out with respect to formal education, it is not just having a good education system that makes a country competitive, it is how, and especially how widely, the goods provided through that system are distributed. In the United States those goods are distributed unequally, needlessly marginalizing large numbers of youth and weakening society as a whole.

Neither apprenticeship nor any other approach is going to fully compensate for the years of institutional and social neglect experienced by some American youth. If it is difficult to convince such youth that they are capable of taking their place in a "new and wider world," it is even more difficult to convince them that they are "entitled to a place in that world" (Musick, 1999, p. 22). Actually, such convincing cannot be done; it has to come from experience, day-over-day; from feedback that does not question the self (or try to affirm it) but that communicates the concreteness of development and focuses on the seriousness of the work at hand. Witnessing others who are knowledgeable, engaged, and passionate about what they do is always a revelation. Joining them, on the other hand, can seem risky, not least because, in their very commitment, these others appear as vulnerable as they do competent. Yet joining skilled adults in some body of work is also interesting, and it is just this quality that we sometimes underestimate in our arrangements for youth.

Appendix

A Chronology of Interviews for the Book

4/6/06   Kristen Hempel, Big Picture Schools, Providence, Rhode Island

4/7/06   Dennis Littky, Big Picture Schools, Providence, Rhode Island

5/8/06   Molly Schmitz, Director, Apprenticeships in Science and Engineering, Portland, Oregon

5/31/06   Adam Green, Founder and Director, Rocking the Boat, Bronx, New York

6/7/06   Charles Adler, Big Picture School Principal, Providence, Rhode Island

6/8/06   Chris Hempel, Big Picture School Principal, Providence, Rhode Island

6/13/06   Adam Green, Founder and Director, Rocking the Boat, Bronx, New York

6/19/06   Andrew Motta, Associate Director, Artists for Humanity, Boston

6/19/06   Abby Remer, Coordinator, Career Intervention Network, New York City

6/22/06   Adam Green, Founder and Director, Rocking the Boat, Bronx, New York

6/27/06   Allison Fetter, St. Louis Opera Theater, St. Louis, Missouri

8/1/06   Priscilla Block, Director, St. Louis ArtWorks, St. Louis, Missou

8/7/06   Greg Gale, Program Director, The Food Project, Lincoln, Massachusetts

10/23/06   Kathleen Mitchell, Careers Through Culinary Arts Program, New York

12/4/06   Barbara Kiss, Social Worker, Rocking the Boat, Bronx, New York

12/7/06   Rob Gibbs, Painting Studio Director, Artists for Humanity, Boston

12/8/06   Kathleen Mitchell, Careers Through Culinary Arts Program New York

12/8/06   Quyen Truong, Painting Teaching Artist, Artists for Humanity, Boston

12/19/06   Gina Anselmo, Director, Art at Work, Marwen Arts, Chicago

12/21/06   Richard Grausman, Founder and Director, Careers Through Culinary Arts Program, New York

1/5/07   Steve Goodman, Founder and Director, Educational Video Center, New York

1/8/07   Claudia Vicin, Graphics Teaching Artist, Artists for Humanity, Boston

1/9/07   Paulina Camacho, Alumnus, Art at Work, Marwen Arts, Chicago

1/16/07   Meg Grace, Executive Chef, Museum of Modern Art, CCAP Mentor, New York

1/25/07   Greg Gale, Program Director, The Food Project, Lincoln, Massachusetts

1/29/07   Sam Decker, Principal, The Bronx Guild Big Picture School, New York

1/30/07   Steve Borenkoff, CCAP Mentor, New York

2/5/07   Margie Salvante-McCann, Director, Education Program, Roundabout Theater, New York

2/7/07   Danielle Andrews, Urban Grower, The Food Project, Lincoln, Massachusetts

2/9/07   Bob Burns, Farmers Market Manager, The Food Project, Lincoln, Massachusetts

2/14/07   Monica Pless, Urban Agriculture Mentor, The Food Project, Lincoln, Massachusetts

2/16/07   Renee Flemings, Lead Teaching Artist, Education Program, Roundabout Theater, New York

2/23/07   Tony Archino, Environmental Instructor, Rocking the Boat, Bronx, New York

2/28/07   Deborah Clark, Apprenticeships in Science and Engineering, Mentor, Portland, Oregon

2/28/07   Al Luria, Staff, The Bronx Guild Big Picture School, New York

2/28/07   Dana Sylvia, Staff, The Bronx Guild Big Picture School, New York

3/9/07   Chris Kautz, Boat Building Instructor, Rocking the Boat, Bronx, New York

3/9/07   Samantha Heyman, On Water Instructor, Rocking the Boat, Bronx, New York

4/19/07   Alvin Keith, Teaching Artist, Education Program, Roundabout Theater, New York

4/27/07   Miriam Neptune, Documentary Workshop Instructor, Educational Video Center, New York

5/18/07   Alyssa Simon, Internship Coordinator, Pablo Neruda High School, New York

5/21/07   Margie Salvante-McCann, Director, Education Program, Roundabout Theater, New York

5/24/07   Steve Strauss, Apprenticeships in Science and Engineering, Mentor, Portland, Oregon

6/8/07   Simon Yu, Art at Work, Marwen Arts, Chicago, Mentor

6/13/07   Katherine Baker, Art at Work, Marwen Arts, Chicago, Mentor

6/27/07   Phil Wenger, Boat Building Instructor, Urban Boat Builders, St. Paul, Minnesota

7/2/07   Maria Gaspar, Public Art Teaching Artist, Art at Work, Marwen Arts, Chicago

7/16/07   Michelle Novello, Founder and Director, Riverz Edge Arts, Woonsocket, Rhode Island

7/31/07   Brad Fesmire, Teaching Artist, Riverz Edge Arts, Woonsocket, Rhode Island

8/6/07   Brian Hodge, Teaching Artist, Riverz Edge Arts, Woonsocket, Rhode Island

9/6/07   Lissa Soep, Adult Producer, Youth Radio, San Francisco

10/15/07 David Millar, Education Program Director, Roundabout Theater, New York

11/26/07 Alfredo Nambo, Back of the Yards Big Picture School, Chicago

11/26/07 Esme and Lupe, Students, Back of the Yards Big Picture School, Chicago

12/7/07   Cathy Crary, State Director, Wisconsin Youth Apprenticeship Program, Madison,

12/20/07 Nell Daniels, Director, Sweat Equity Workshop, New York City

1/17/08   Judy Nystrom, Regional Director, Wisconsin Youth Apprenticeship Program, Madison

1/25/08   Connie Braun, Regional Director, Wisconsin Youth Apprenticeship Program, Madison

1/25/08   Darla Burton, Regional Director, Wisconsin Youth Apprenticeship Program, Madison

1/28/08   Diane Kraus, Regional Director, Wisconsin Youth Apprenticeship Program, Madison

Notes

Introduction

1. From here on, personal communications will be designated p.c. in citations.
2. Throughout the book I will use the terms "teachers," "instructors," and "mentors" interchangeably, depending on the fit and the particular initiative being discussed or drawn on. The important point is that the adult's primary role is sharing his or her knowledge and experience in a specific substantive field, and serving as a particular kind of adult model. The adult-youth relationship may well broaden, and often does. But that is not the point of the relationship.

Chapter 1

1. Esther Goody's (1982) description the "seven ages" of the Daboya weaver, an almost lifelong apprenticeship beginning in earliest childhood, is one of the most detailed and interesting descriptions of deepening participation in an important socio-cultural practice that has been written. Boys' involvement in the trade shifts gradually from play to work and is always developmentally appropriate. Skill demands and broader maturity demands go hand and hand.
2. Vygotsky focused more directly on the role of culture in organizing learning (and in effect tutoring and scaffolding the young) than on the role of individual adults).
3. At one point in his writing, Bruner describes the situated learning and teaching characteristic of apprenticeship in his reflections on the "Kung in Africa. He notes that "one virtually never sees an instance of teaching taking place outside the situation where the behavior to be learned is relevant" (Bruner, 1973, pp. 11, 12).
4. Recent findings from neuroscience reinforce the idea that "the brain ... handles real, complex situations more easily than it does artificially contrived ones" (Ryan, 2000, p. 6).
5. Howard (1982, p. 60) notes that "often a single demonstration is worth a thousand metaphors or synonyms to communicate the meaning of a technical word or phrase."
6. Historical accounts of apprenticeship note a good deal of informal conversation in smaller trade shops, and some settings "buzzed with opinion on religious, social and political reform" (Laurie, 1997, p. 37).
7. This process includes drawing the image or design, "registering" it with tape to the bottom of a Plexiglas sheet, preparing a paint palette, painting the image on the Plexiglas, preparing rag paper, setting up for the roller press (covering the back of the painted image with newsprint and then a blanket), and "pulling" the roller press (Thomas, 2007).

Chapter 2

1. In the course of discussing an after-school drama and literature program for youth, Worthman (2002, p. 136) too notes that participants speak of having had opportunity to learn to write in school but "blowing it off" [sic] because "it didn't seem important at the time."
2. Girls seem better able—or perhaps feel freer—than boys to seek haven in academic work, in part because such work is viewed as feminine.
3. Although MacLeod's study of "leveled aspirations" focused on boys' experiences, there is evidence, as Valenzuela and others have found, that this dynamic holds as well for girls.
4. The grandiosity of youth has long been remarked upon. It is, nonetheless, seemingly fed rather than chipped away at by popular culture. An October 2005 survey of Washington, D.C. area teens by the Kaiser Family Foundation and the *Washington Post* found that 31% of teens thought it very or fairly likely that they would be famous someday (the same percentage as a nation-wide sample).

Chapter 3

1. In practice, apprenticeship was a more flexible institution than some historical accounts suggest. Likewise guilds played a more variable role than some accounts suggest. Epstein (1998), for instance, argues that broader social and economic conditions, shifting markets, changing production technologies and the whims of political authorities could strongly affect both institutions. In general, guilds exerted their greatest control from the 12th to the 17th century, with political authorities gaining steadily more influence after that, exerting their authority through an array of statutes (Aldrich, 1999).

2. Mumford (1952, p. 62), exaggerating somewhat, argued that the craftsman was distinguished by control over his work: 'He took his own time … reflecting and planning as he went along, lingering over the parts that interested him most …The craftsman, like the artist, lived in his work, for his work, by his work…'

3. Timmons (1988, p. 50) argues that early 20th-century trade unions faced a number of challenges with respect to apprenticeship. They rightly viewed control of apprenticeship as one source of leverage in their struggle with the owners and management of corporations. Yet "they also knew that apprenticeship needed re-thinking" and that schools had to play some role. Corporate leaders viewed "technical schools" as a possible way to dilute the role of trade unions, with their putatively foreign, i.e., socialist, connections, but could never fully secure the agreement of educators to push such schools. Instead, they created their own internal training programs.

4. Although placement in Germany is based on elementary grades and teacher recommendation, parents are also involved in the decision: "If a student wants to go to gymnasium and work hard under stressful conditions, he or she can do that. But, many parents or teachers would counter, what would be the point. If the *realschule* or *hauptschule* provide training that a student is interested in and the school atmosphere is relaxed, why bother with the *gymnasium*?" (Le Tendre et al., 2003, p. 63).

5. The former promoted new approaches that could serve as a platform for apprenticeship, for example, tech prep, sometimes described as "2 & 2," which entailed creation of a coherent technical education experience combining the last two years of high school and two years of community college. The School to Work Opportunity Act, which would survive barely six years, was intended to shift vocational education reform into a higher gear. It called for "performance-based" education and training (in the last two years of high school), leading to "portable credentials" and better preparing youth for their first jobs in the new high-skill careers (Phelps, Knox, & Griggs, 1999).

6. Bailey (1993) points out that there is no parallel for workplaces to the well developed networks that link high schools to college admissions offices; also that, while the high school transcript has a clear meaning to college admissions officers, it typically has very little meaning to employers. And as Fenwick (2006, p. 455) notes, high school educators should, but usually don't want to know what happens to youth "educated in particular ways when they enter the labor market."

7. This is a rough estimate; no one has actually tried to count the percentage of small high schools that are themed.

8. These high schools, typically, use the term "internship" rather than apprenticeship. But as will be seen in the case studies later in the chapter, I am interested in those high schools that create and support substantive experiences in specific disciplines.

9. Apprenticeship sponsors include the local Department of Public Health, a government genome institute, the Lawrence Berkeley Laboratories, Libby, Novartis, Bio-Rad Laboratories and, Bayer among others.

10. The description of this initiative relies heavily on Amy Ryken's dissertation *Content, Pedagogy, Results: A Thrice Told Tale of Integrating Work-based and School-based Learning*, School of Education, University of California, Berkeley, 2001. Dr. Ryken is also the former director of the initiative. I am grateful for her willingness to let me use this unique material.

11. Wisconsin was one of eight states to receive the first round of grants under the School to Work Opportunity Act of 1994. It was, in fact, used as a model in the federal legislation. YAP thrived along with the policy and political interest in school to work and reconceptualized vocational education. When federal funding ended in 2000, the state initially increased its commitment to $3 million, but in recent years a difficult budgetary environment in Wisconsin has led to an erosion in funding.

12. YAP began with apprenticeships in printing, and expanded gradually to more fields as it found

its footing. Printing was chosen as the initial industry for the program because it was a growing field and demanded skilled workers able to adapt to regular changes in technology.

13. In the first years of YAP, state staff worked with industry experts and high school staff to develop detailed curricula for the complementary course work. That has given way to course outlines, which allow easier adaptation to changing knowledge and technology.

14. There is a sizable literature on the Big Picture model, describing the workings of full model, its implementation, core challenges, students' experience, lessons learned, and so forth. In this case study, I focus largely on the internship experience, bringing in other elements as they are related. A number of Big Picture schools struggle with the questions of how, without formal coursework and with an emphasis on depth rather than breadth in learning, to assure that young people acquire a core of knowledge and skills needed to meet state standards, pass high stakes tests and graduate. Some, additionally, struggle to assure that youth acquire the conceptual underpinnings—not just procedural knowledge—in academic disciplines. There is, relatedly, debate within the Big Picture community about what it means for a young person to be ready to graduate. My emphasis here will be on just the apprenticeship experience and other elements as they relate to it.

15. These broad domains encompass a number of competences, e.g., taking in and expressing information, verbally and in writing; understanding diverse perspectives, citizenship, cooperation, and conflict resolution; testing ideas, collecting and interpreting data, various kinds of measurement, and so forth.

16. As with many other Big Picture components, exhibitions are potentially rich occasions for social learning. Other students who are present gain a much more concrete sense of work in a field that they may know little about. They learn to provide feedback and offer suggestions in helpful ways. The framework they use to provide feedback helps them think about their own work. For instance, in considering the extent to which a peer has demonstrated "ownership" of the internship experience a young person is stimulated to apply that criterion to their own experience.

Chapter 4

1. Including poetry, painting and drawing, public art, photography, silk-screening, printmaking, sculpture, ceramics, metal-work, theater, dance, dramatic and documentary filmmaking, radio production, print journalism, graphic art/design, digital arts, fashion design, industrial design (including design of consumer products), advertising, and architecture.

2. In San Francisco's Youth Radio youth work alongside adult producers and sound engineers, some of whom are program graduates. Chavez and Soep (2005) describe model as a "pedagogy of collegiality." Within this framework youth and adults learn from each other and are mutually dependent on each other. Each contributes something unique to the work—young people a fresh perspective and sensitivity to issues and emerging currents in culture, adults professionalism, life and technical experience, and a measure of wisdom.

3. Commissioned work is real yet protected to some degree. A few sponsoring organizations are thus trying to more directly test the feasibility of finding a niche in an already competitive market-place. The aforementioned St. Louis ArtWorks has started a business of its own, called ArtWorks Enterprise (the first component of which is Boomerang Press), which will serve as a base for revenue generating activity in support of the organization. Experienced apprentices work for Boomerang Press, creating and selling holiday cards and other types of themed note cards, calendars and similar products, and providing print services. The executive director notes that "it's hard to know where to try to compete; the marketplace … is very tough beyond commissioned work" (Block, personal communication, August 1, 2006).

4. Goodman is, additionally, committed to exploring through EVC what literacy means in an era in which more reading and writing take place through media other than books and, within a more flexible framework. A key question is whether and how engaging in literacy activity in visual and digital media might strengthen young people's sense of connection to literacy in its traditional sense.

5. A group of three youth—a scout, an interviewer, and a camera operator—might be sent out on the streets of Manhattan to conduct interviews on a specific topic. They will soon realize how difficult it is to approach and engage complete strangers. On one occasion a young man acting as scout looks to be held back by an invisible barrier; "I can't do it, it's too embarrassing," he tells his peers. He and the interviewer switch roles (Youth Powered Video, 2006).

6. Camera-work embodies a set of skills and judgments that include choosing where to position the camera and microphone, previewing the angles and perspective of a shot and what will reside inside the frame, choosing light settings, given light conditions, planning for camera movement, anticipating action. Each of these and other qualitative elements has to correspond to the setting—indoors or out—the goals of the interview and the mood of the broader documentary.

7. Science apprenticeship programs are in fact successful in bringing disadvantaged youth into the sciences. A late 1990s study of the American Chemical Society's Project SEED found that two thirds of participants majored in basic and applied sciences in college, in addition to chemistry such fields as medicine, nursing, biology, psychiatry, and pharmacology.

8. RTB cuts down and planes some of its own lumber, in part to give youth a sense of the complete cycle of the work, and a sense that materials, even finished products, come from somewhere; they do not just magically appear on store shelves.

9. Straight talk is guided by a set of principles that include balancing positive and negative, being kind, honest, detailed, and selective and, for those on the receiving end, "looking up," "opening up," and "storing up" (Gale, 2006, p. 46).

Chapter 5

1. I rely especially heavily here on an extended series of interviews done with After School Matters apprentices over the course of my research.

Chapter 6

1. One can, nonetheless, see how apprenticeships that use reading, writing, and mathematics as tools can strengthen critical aspects of literacy and numeracy. For instance, Stipek (2004, p. 77) discusses mathematics proficiency as a mixture of conceptual understanding, procedural fluency, strategic competence, adaptive reasoning, and "productive disposition." Apprenticeships that use math can presumably influence all but the first of these.

Chapter 7

1. Michael Polanyi (1966) reflected cogently on the difficulties of identifying and sharing tacit knowledge. In discussing his thesis in "The Tacit Dimension"—that we inevitably know more than we can tell—he points to a paradox: We integrate the particulars into a whole when are understanding something, but we comprehend an entity in part by "relying on our awareness of its particulars" (p. 13). More recently, Bereiter and Scardamalia (1993) noted that in many fields it would take a highly skilled observer to articulate rules that even approximate expert behavior.

2. A study of a youth apprenticeship program in Alberta, Canada found, nonetheless, that what transfer did occur was usually from work to school, rather than from school to work (Lehmann, 2005).

3. Missing in this sector of the economy are institutional structures to help this group of workers, when starting out, to construct careers that combine personal and commissioned work; and to help commercial and non-commercial firms understand the ways in which creative individuals can contribute to their work.

4. In Alberta Canada's apprenticeship program, called RAP (Registered Youth Apprenticeship), youth can potentially get credit for one year of formal apprenticeship training in a trade, but they must graduate from high school. For a description and discussion see Lehmann (2005).

References

AAS (Academy of Applied Sciences). (1997). *Research and Engineering Apprenticeship Program Annual Reports.* Concord, NH: Academy of Applied Science.

AAS (Academy of Applied Sciences). (1999). *Research and Engineering Apprenticeship Program Annual Reports.* Concord, NH: Academy of Applied Science.

AAS (Academy of Applied Sciences). (2000). *Research and Engineering Apprenticeship Program Annual Reports.* Concord, NH: Academy of Applied Science.

AAS (Academy of Applied Sciences). (2001). *Research and Engineering Apprenticeship Program Annual Reports.* Concord, NH: Academy of Applied Science.

Abbott, J., & Ryan, T. (1999). Constructing knowledge, reconstructing schooling. *Educational Leadership, 57*(3), 66–69.

Abbott, J., & Ryan, T. (2001) *The unfinished revolution: Learning, human behavior, community, and political paradox.* Alexandria, VA: Association for Supervision and Curriculum Development.

Ainley, P., & Rainbird, H. (Eds.). (1999). *Apprenticeship: Towards a new paradigm of learning.* London: Kogan Page.

Aldrich, R. (1999). The apprentice in history. In P. Ainley & H. Rainbird (Eds.), *Apprenticeship: Towards a new paradigm of learning.* London: Kogan Page.

Almeida, C., & Steinberg, A. (2001). Introduction. In C. Almeida & A. Steinber (Eds.), *Connected learning communities: A toolkit for reinventing high school.* Boston: Jobs for the Future.

Andrews, D. (2001). *Growing sites: The use of gardening and farming in youth development projects.* A major paper submitted to the Faculty of Environmental Studies in partial fulfillment of the requirements for the Magisteriate in Environmental Studies. York University, Ontario, Canada.

Arenson, K. (2000). The learning gap. *New York Times,* April 9, p. A21.

Bailey, T. (1993). Can youth apprenticeship thrive in the United States? *Educational Researcher, 22*(3) 4–10.

Bailey, T., Hughes, K., & Moore, D. T. (2004). *Working knowledge: Work based learning and education reform.* New York: Routledge.

Baudenbacher, G., & Goodman, S. (2006). *Youth powered video: A hands on curriculum for teaching documentary.* New York: Educational Video Center.

Bauer, E. (2000, June 29). Young scientists sample real-world research. *American News Service, Berkshire Publishing Group.*

Becker, H. (1972). A school is a lousy place to learning anything in. *American Behavioral Scientist, 16*(1), 85–105.

Bereiter, C. (2002). *Education and mind in the knowledge age.* Hillsdale, NJ: Erlbaum.

Bereiter, C. & Scardamalia, M. (1993). *Surpassing ourselves.* Chicago: Open Court.

Bereiter, C., & Scardamalia, M. (2003). Learning to work creatively with knowledge. In E. de Corte (Ed.), *Powerful learning environments: Unravelling basic components and dimensions.* Amsterdam: Pergamon.

Berryman, S. E. (1993). Learning for the workplace. *Review of Research in Education, 19*(1), 343–401.

213

Berryman, S. (1995). Apprenticeship as a paradigm of learning. In N. Grubb (Ed.), *Education through occupations in American high schools. Volume I: Approaches to integrating academic and vocational education.* New York: Teachers College Press.

Bloom, B. (Ed.). (1985). *Developing talent in young people.* New York: Ballentine.

Blos, P. (1971). The child analyst looks at the young adolescent. *Daedulus, 100,* 961–978.

Blos, P. (1979). *The adolescent passage: Developmental issues.* Madison, CT: International Universities Press.

Bockarie, A. (2002). The potential of Vygotsky's contribution to our understanding of cognitive apprenticeship as a process of development in adult vocational and technical education. *Journal of Career and Technical Education, 19*(1), 47–66.

Borisova, I. (2005). Understanding youth involvement and commitment to socially responsible work. Lincoln, MA: The Food Project. Retrieved August 2007, from http://www.case-web.org/assets/cases/abstract_10.pdf

Boshuizen, H. (2003, January 31). *Expertise development: How to bridge the gap between school and work.* Acceptance address of the professorship in Educational Technology at the Open Universiteit Nederland.

Bruner, J. (1960). *The process of education.* Cambridge, MA: Harvard University Press.

Bruner, J. (1966). *Toward a theory of instruction.* Cambridge, MA: Harvard University Press.

Bruner, J. (1973). *The relevance of education.* New York: W. W. Norton.

Bruner, J. (2003). The culture of education. In M. Gergen & K. Gergen (Eds.), *Social construction: A reader.* Thousand Oaks, CA: Sage.

Cairns, R. C., Leung, M., & Cairns, B. D. (1995). Social networks over time and space in adolescence. In L. J. Crockett & A. C. Crouter (Eds.), *Pathways through adolescence: Individual development in relation to social contexts.* Mahwah, NJ: Erlbaum.

Cambourne, B. (2002). Conditions for literacy learning. *The Reading Teacher, 55*(8), 758–762.

CCAP (Careers Through Culinary Arts Program). (2007). *Exit Survey, 8/07.*

Chaskin, R. J., & Baker, S. (2005). *Negotiating among opportunity and constraint: The participation of young people in out-of-school-time activities.* Unpublished manuscript Chicago: The Chapin Hall Center for Children at the University of Chicago.

Chavez, V., & Soep, E. (2005). Youth radio and the pedagogy of collegiality. *Harvard Educational Review, 75*(4), 409–434.

Chen, M., Goodman, S., & Riel, M. (2003). A discussion of how student media production can transform teaching and learning. *Cable in the Classroom,* June, 6–9.

Clark, K. (1964). *Dark ghetto.* New York: Harper and Row.

Claxton, G. (2007). Expanding young people's capacity to learn. *British Journal of Educational Studies, 55*(2), 115–134.

Cloward, R., & Ohlin, L. (1960). *Delinquency and opportunity.* Gkencie, IL: Free Press

Cohen, P. (1999). Apprenticeship a la mode? In P. Ainley & H. Rainbird (Eds.), *Apprenticeship: Towards a new Paradigm of learning.* London: Kogan Page.

Collins, A., Brown, J., & Newman, S. E. (1989). Cognitive apprenticeship: Teaching the crafts of reading, writing, and mathematics. In L. Resnick (Ed.), *Knowing, learning, and instruction: Essays in honor of Robert Glaser.* Hillsdale, NJ: Erlbaum.

Corson, W., & Silverberg, M. (1994). *The school-to-work transition and youth apprenticeship: Lessons from the U.S. experience.* New York: Manpower Demonstration Research Corporation.

Costa, A., & B. Kallick (2000). *Habits of mind.* Alexandria, VA: Association for Supervision and Curriculum Development.

Coy, M. (1989) *Apprenticeship: From theory to method and back again.* Albany: State University of New York Press.

Crawford, B., Bell, R. L., Blair, L., & Lederman, N. G. (1999, March). *The impact of science apprenticeships on student conceptions of the nature of science and scientific inquiry.* Paper presented at the Annual Meeting of the National Association for Research in Science Teaching, Boston.

Csikszentmihalyi, M., & Larson, R. (1984). *Being adolescent.* New York: Basic Books.

Csikszentmihalyi, M., & Schneider, B. (2000). *Becoming adult.* New York: Basic Books.

Daniel, N. (2007). *Sweat equity enterprises: The convergence of design education, youth development and situated learning.* Dissertation submitted to the Program in Teaching and Learning, School of Education, New York University.

deKock, A., Sleegers, P., & Voeten, M. (2004). New learning and the classification of learning environments in secondary education. *Review of Educational Research, 74*(2), 141–170.

Dewey, J. (1902/1990). *The school and society.* Chicago: University of Chicago Press.

Dewey, J. (1916). *Democracy and education.* Chicago: University of Chicago.

Dewey, J. (1938). *Experience and education.* New York: Collier Books.

Douglas, P. (1921). *American apprenticeship and industrial education.* New York: AMS Press.

Dowdy, J., Birney, S., & Reedus, N. (2004). College bound filmmakers: The journey to a screening. *High School Journal, 88*(1), 14–27.

Eisenhart, M. (1992). Review of the book *The first real job: A study of young workers. Anthropology and Education Quarterly, 23*(4), 336–340.

Eisner, E. (1999). The misunderstood role of the arts in human development. In B. Pressisen (Ed.), *Teaching for intelligence.* Arlington Heights, IL: Skylight.

Eisner, E. (2002). *The arts and the creation of mind.* New Haven, CT: Yale University Press.

Engelfried, C. (2006). Staffing the Montessori high school: What's so special about the specialist? *NAMTA Journal, 31*(1), 287–295.

Engestrom, Y. (1991). Non scolae vitae discimus: Toward overcoming the encapsulation of school learning. *Learning and Instruction, 1*(3), 243–259.

Ericsson, K. (1996). *The road to excellence.* Hillsdale, NJ: Erlbaum.

Erikson, E. (1962). Youth: Fidelity and diversity. *Daedalus, 91*, 5–27.

Erikson, E. (1963). *Childhood and society.* New York: W.W. Norton.

Erikson, E. (1968). *Identity: Youth and crisis.* New York: W.W. Norton.

Erikson, E. H., & Erikson, K. T. (1987). The confirmation of the delinquent. In S. Schlein (Ed.), *A way of looking at things: Selected papers from 1930 to 1980.* New York: W.W. Norton.

Erikson, E. H., & Erikson, K. T. (1987). Late adolescence. In S. Schlein (Ed.), *A way of looking at things: Selected papers from 1930 to 1980.* New York: W.W. Norton.

Erikson, E. H., & Erikson, K. T. (1987). A memorandum on identity and Negro youth. In S. Schlein (Ed.), *A way of looking at things: Selected papers from 1930 to 1980.* New York: W.W. Norton.

Evanciew, C. (1994). *Emerging themes in youth apprenticeship programs: A qualitative study.* Paper presented at the American Vocational Association Conference, Dallas, TX, December 9–13.

Evanciew, C., & Rojewski, J. (1999). Skill and knowledge acquisition in the work place: A case study of mentor-apprentice relationships in youth apprenticeship programs. *Journal of Industrial teacher Education, 36*, 24–53.

Fenwick, T. (2006). Work, learning, and education in the knowledge economy: A working-class perspective. (Review of the books *Hidden knowledge: Organized labour in the information age, reading work: Literacies in the new workplace, and voices from the margins: The stories of vocational high school students.*) Curriculum Inquiry, 36(4), 453–466.

Ferguson, R. (1996). *Youth build in developmental perspective.* Cambridge, MA: MIT, Department of Urban Studies.

Fleming, P., Harley, B., & Sewell, G. (2004). A little knowledge is a dangerous thing: getting below the surface of the growth of 'knowledge work' in Australia. *Work, Employment & Society, 18*(4), 725–747.

Flemings, R. (2006). Roundabout Theater Education Report, p. 5.

Fuller, A. (1996). Modern apprenticeship, process and learning: Some emerging issues. *Journal of Vocational Education and Training, 48*(3), 229–247.

Gale, G. (2005). Youth program design: Call notes. Best practices teleconference series. Academy for Educational Development. Retrieved May 17, 2007, from http://www.thefoodproject.org/uploaded files/teleconf/2_16_05notes.pdf

Gale, G. (2006). *Growing together.* Lincoln, MA: The Food Project.

Gardner, H. (1991). *The unschooled mind.* New York: Basic Books.

Geer, B. (Ed.). (1972). *Learning to work.* Beverly Hills, CA: Sage.

Gentry, M., Rizza, M., Peters, S., & Hu, S. (2005). Professionalism, sense of community and reason to learn: Lessons from an exemplary career and technical education center. *Career and Technical Education Research, 30*, 47–85.

Girod, M., Pardales, M., Cavanaugh, S., & Wadsworth, P. (2005). By teens, for teachers: A descriptive study of adolescence. *American Secondary Education, 33*(2), 4–19.

Gittens, J. (1985). *The children of the state: Child labor reform and education in Illinois, 1818–1980s.* Chicago: Chapin Hall Center for Children.

Gonczi, A. (2001). *Advances in educational thinking and their implications for professional education.* Working Paper 01-14. Australia: UTS Research Center for Vocational Education and Training.

Goodman, S. (2001). Behind the video camera: Student video makers learn new roles as agents of change. *What Kids Can Do* (news series), Volume 1, Number 5. San Rafeal, CA: Edutopia.

Goodman, S. (2003). *Teaching youth media.* New York: Teachers College Press.

Goodman, S. (2005). The practice and principles of teaching critical literacy at the Education Video Center. *National Society for the Study of Education Yearbook* (pp. 206–228). Chicago: National Society for the Study of Education.

Goodman, S., & Tally, B. (undated). The tape's great but what did they learn? *The Independent: Film and Video Monthly.*

Goody, E. (Ed.). (1982). *From craft to industry.* London: Cambridge University Press.

Green, T. (2006). High school grads experiment with science at the Applied Research Lab. Retrieved from University of Texas Applied research Laboratory, http:// www.utexas.edu/reseacrh/students/apprentice.html

Greene, M. (1995). *Releasing the imagination.* San Francisco: Jossey Bass.

Gregory, L. (1994). The "turnaround" process: Factors influencing the school success of urban youth. *Journal of Adolescent Research, 10*, 136–154.

Gregson, G. (1995). The school-to-work movement and youth apprenticeship in the U.S.: Educational reform and democratic renewal? *Journal of Industrial Teacher Education, 32*(3), 7–29.

Grubb, N. (1995). Resolving the paradox of the high school. In N. Grubb (Ed.), *Education through occupations in American high schools. Volume I: Approaches to integrating academic and vocational education.* New York: Teachers College Press.

Habermas, J. (1972). *Knowledge and human interests.* Boston: Beacon Press.

Hahn, A., & Leavitt, T. (2004). *Life after YouthBuild.* Waltham, MA: Brandeis University Heller School for Social Policy and Management, Center for Youth and Communities.

Halliday, J. (2000). Critical thinking and the academic vocational divide. *The Curriculum Journal, 11*(2), 159–175.

Halpern, R. (1992). The role of after-school programs in the lives of inner-city children. *Child Welfare, 61*(3), 215–230.

Halpern, R. (2005). *A qualitative study of After School Matters: Interim report.* Chicago: Erikson Institute.

Halpern, R. (2006). *A qualitative study of After School Matters: Final report.* Chicago: Erikson Institute.

Halpern, R. (2006). After School Matters in Chicago: Apprenticeship as a model for youth programming. *Youth and Society, 38*(2), 203–235.

Halpern, R., Barker, G., & W. Mollard. (2002). Youth programs as alternative spaces to be: A study of neighborhood youth programs in Chicago's West Town. *Youth and Society, 31*(4), 469–505.

Hamilton, M. A., & Hamilton, S. (1997). When is learning work-based? *Phi Delta Kappan, 78*(9), 676–681.

Hamilton, M. A., & Hamilton, S. (1997). When is work a learning experience? *Phi Delta Kappan, 78*(9), 682–689.

Hamilton, S. (1990). *Apprenticeship for adulthood: Preparing youth for the future.* New York: Free Press.

Hamilton, S., & Hurrelman, K. (1994). The school-to-career transition in Germany and the United States. *Teachers College Record*, 329–344.

Hannawalt, B. (1993) *Growing up in medieval England.* New York: Oxford.

Harter, S. (1996). Teacher and classmate influences on scholastic motivation, self-esteem, and the level of voice in adolescents. In J. Juvonen & K. Wentzel (Eds.), *Social motivation: Understanding school adjustment.* New York: Cambridge University Press.

Hatano, G., & Oura, Y. (2003). Commentary: Reconceptualizing school learning using insight from expertise research. *Educational Researcher, 32*(8), 26–29.

Hay, K., & Barab, S. (2001). Constructivism in practice: A comparison and contrast of apprenticeship and constructionist learning environments. *The Journal of Learning Sciences, 10*(3), 281–322.

Head, G. (2003). Effective collaboration: Deep collaboration as an essential element of the learning process. *Journal of Educational Enquiry, 4*, 47–62.

Heath, S. (2002). Three's not a crowd: Plans, roles, and focus in the arts. *Educational Researcher, 30*(7), 10–17.

Heath, S. (2000). Making learning work. *Afterschool Matters, 1*, 33–45.

Heathcote, D., & Bolton, G. (1996). *Drama for learning: Dorothy Heathcote's mantle of the expert approach.* Westport, CT: Greenwood Press.

Hefner, K. (1988). The evolution of youth empowerment at a youth newspaper. *Social Policy, 19*, 21–24.

Heinz, W. R., & Taylor, A. (2005). Learning and work transition policies in a comparative perspective: Canada and Germany. In N. Bascia et al. (Eds.), *International handbook of educational policy.* New York: Springer Verlag

Hemmings, A. (2006). Navigating cultural crosscurrents: (Post)anthropological passages through high school. *Anthropology & Education Quarterly, 37*(2),128–143.

Henao, L. (2005). An entrepreneur draws success out of teens. *The Boston Globe,* September 4.

Huang, T. (2008). Interview. University of Texas, Applied Research Lab. Retrieved January 15, 2008, from http://www.arlut.utexas.edu/education/video/Tiger_experience.mov

Hung, D. (1999). Activity, apprenticeship, and epistemological appropriation: Implications from the writings of Michael Polanyi. *Educational Psychologist, 34*(4), 193–205.

Hymel, S., Comfort, C., Schonert-Reichl, K., & McDougall, P. (1996). Academic failure and school dropout: The influence of peers. In K. Wentzel & J. Juvonen (Eds.), *Social motivation: Understanding children's school adjustment.* New York: Cambridge University Press.

Hyslop-Margison, E. (2001). An assessment of the historical arguments in vocational education reform. *Journal of Career and Technical Education, 17*.

Ingold, T. (2005). *Apprenticeships and social learning.* Paper presented at the Situated Learning within Post Secondary Education Workshop, Aberdeen, Scotland, 15 January.

Jenkins, H. (2007). Interview with Reina Gonzales, Youth Radio apprentice. The power of cllegial pedagogy: An interview with Youth Radio. August 21. Retrieved from http://www.henryjenkins.org/2007/08/the_power_of_collegial_pedagog.html

Johnson, E. (1997). *Benefits of school to work program participation: Perceptions of students and comparison of pre- and post grades and attendance.* Dissertation submitted to the Graduate Faculty of Virginia Polytechnic Institute, Blacksburg, VA.

Kahn, D. (2006). The key lessons of the third adolescent colloquium. *NAMTA Journal, 31,* 1–25.

Kantor, H. (1994). Managing the transition from school to work: The false promises of youth apprenticeship. *Teachers College Record, 95*(4), 442–461.

Kimmel, M. (2006). A war against boys? *Dissent, 53*(4), 65–70.

Kleiber, D. (1999). *Leisure experience and human development: A dialectical interpretation.* New York: Basic Books.

Kroger, J. (1996). *Identity in adolescence: The balance between self and other.* London: Routledge.

Larson, R. (2002). Globalization, societal change, and new technologies: What they mean for the future of adolescence. *Journal of Research on Adolescence, 12,* 1–30.

Larson, R. (2004). *Adolescents' experience in social institutions: Unlocking youth's (tremendous) potentials for growth.* Article prepared for the conference Positive Development: Linking Individuals, Communities, and Social Policies, Weimar, Germany, October.

Larson, R., & Hansen, D. (2005). The development of strategic thinking: Learning to impact human systems in a youth activism program. *Human Development, 48,* 327–349.

Larson, R., & C. Walker. (2006). Learning about the real world in an urban arts youth program. *Journal of Adolescent Research, 21*(3), 244–268.

Laurie, B. (1997). *Artists into workers.* Urbana: University of Illinois Press.

Lave, J. (1982). A comparative approach to educational forms and learning processes. *Anthropology and Education Quarterly, 13*(2), 181–187.

Lave, J. (1996). Teaching, as learning, in practice. *Mind, Culture, and Activity, 3*(3), 149–164.

Lave, J., & Wenger, E. (1991). *Situated learning: Legitimate peripheral participation.* Cambridge, MA: Cambridge University Press.

LeTendre, G., Hofer, B., & Shimizu, H. (2003). What is tracking? Cultural expectations in the U.S., Germany, and Japan. *American Educational Research Journal, 40,* 43–89.

Lehmann, W. (2005). "I'm still scrubbing the floors": Experiencing youth apprenticeships in Canada and Germany. *Work Empowerment Society, 19,* 107–129.

Levine, E. (2002). *One kid at a time: Big lessons from a small school.* New York: Teachers College Press.

Levine, M. (2002). College graduates aren't ready for the real world. *The Chronicle Review, 51*(24), 11.

Lewis, T. (2007). Social inequality in education: A constraint on an American high-skills future. *Curriculum Inquiry, 37*(4), 329–349.

Lillard, P. (1972). *Montessori: A modern approach.* New York: Schocken.

Litowitz, B. (1993). Deconstruction in the zone of proximal development. In E. A. Forman & C. A. Stone (Eds.), *Contexts for learning: Sociocultural dynamics in children's development.* New York: Oxford University Press.

Littky, D. (2004). *The big picture: Education is everyone's business.* Alexandria, VA: Association for Supervision and Curriculum Development.

MacLeod, J. (1987). *Ain't no making it: Leveled aspirations in a low-income neighborhood.* Boulder, CO: Westview Press.

Mahiri, J. (2007). *Yoth radio schooling education experts: Media pioneer Youth Radio generates a model for education engagement.* Battle Creek, MI: The Kellogg Foundation.

Majkowski, C., & Washor, E. (2007). *Perspectives on relevance and the quest for rigorous student learning: Balancing life to text and text to life.* Unpublished Manuscript.

Marcia, J. (1980). Identity in adolescence. In J. Adelson (Ed.), *Handbook of adolescent psychology.* New York: Wiley.

Markusen, A., Gilmore S., Johnson, A., Levi, T., & Martinez, A. (2006). *Crossover: How artists build careers across commercial, non profit and community work.* Minneapolis: Hubert Humphrey Institute for Public Affairs, University of Minnesota, October.

Mayer, V. (2007). The perils and promise of youth media production, *Journal of Communication, 57*(2), 404–407.

McCarthy, D. A. (2002). *An exploratory study of advanced astronomy camp.* Master's thesis at the Department and Curriculum, University of Wisconsin-Madison.

McDonald, R., & Marsh, J. (2004). Missing school: Educational engagement, youth transitions, and social exclusion. *Youth and Society, 36*(2), 143–162.

McPhail, J. C., Pierson, J. M., Goodman, J., & Bunge Noffke, J. (2004). Creating partnerships for complex learning: The dynamics of an interest-based apprenticeship in the art of sculpture. *Curriculum Inquiry, 34*(4), 463–493.

Meier, D. (2006). Undermining democracy. *Dissent, 53*(4), 71–75.

Menger, P. (2006). Profiles of the unfinished: Rodin's work and the varieties of incompleteness. In H. S. Becker, R. R. Faulkner, & B. Kirschenblatt-Gimblett (Eds.), *Art from start to finish.* Chicago: University of Chicago Press.

Miller, S. (2003). The teaching tenor. *St. Louis Post Dispatch,* March 2, p. 3.

Modell, J., Furstenberg, F., & Hershberg, T. (1981). Social change and transitions to adulthood in historical perspective. In T. Hershberg (Ed.), *Philadelphia: Work, space, and group experience in the 19th century.* New York: Oxford University Press.

Montessori, M. (1913). *The Montessori method.* New York: Frederick Stokes.

Montessori, M. (1948). *The discovery of the child.* New York: Oxford University Press.

Montessori, M. (1978). *From childhood to adolescence.* New York: Schocken.

Moore, D. T. (1986). Learning at work: Case studies in non-school education. *Anthropology and Education Quarterly, 17*(3), 166–184.

Mumford, L. (1952). *Art and technics.* New York: Columbia University Press.

Murname, R., & Levy, F. (1996). *Teaching the new basic skills.* New York: Free Press.

Musick, J. (1999). *New possibilities for youth development: Lessons from beyond the service world.* Chicago: Erikson Institute.

Nakamura, J. (2001). The nature of vital engagement in adulthood. *New Directions for Child and Adolescent Development, 93,* 5–18.

Olson, L. (1997). *The school to work revolution.* Upper Saddle River, NJ: Addison Wesley.

Orr, M. T. (1995). *Wisconsin youth apprenticeship program in printing: Evaluation 1993–1995.* Boston: Jobs for the Future.

Palincsar, A., & Herrenkohl, L. (2002). Designing collaborative learning contexts. *Theory Into Practice, 41,* 26–32.

Perkins, D. (1998). *The intelligent eye: Learning to think by looking at art.* Santa Monica, CA: Getty Center for Education in the Arts.

Perkins, D. N., & Salomon, G. (1989). Are cognitive skills context-bound? *Educational Researcher, 18,* 16–25.

Polanyi, M. (1958). *Personal knowledge.* Chicago: University of Chicago Press.

Polanyi, M. (1966). *The tacit dimension.* New York: Doubleday.

Project SEED. (1996, July). *Executive summary of Summer I Evaluation Study.* Washington, DC: American Chemical Society.

Pye, D. (1968). *The nature and art of workmanship.* Cambridge, MA: Cambridge University Press.

Rahm, J. (2002). Emergent learning opportunities in an inner-city youth gardening program. *Journal of Research in Science Teaching, 39*(2), 164–184.

Ravitch, D. (2000). *Left back: A century of failed school reforms.* New York: Simon & Schuster.

Remer, A. (2006). *Inside view: High school internship program at the American Museum of Natural History.* New York: Unpublished Manuscript.

Remer, A. (2007, December). *Rocking the Boat: Long term impact on participants' lives after completing the program.* Unpublished Report.

Resnick, L. (1989). *Knowing, learning, and instruction.* Hillsdale, NJ: Erlbaum.

Richmond, G., & Kurth, L. (1999). Moving from outside to inside: High school students' use of apprenticeships as vehicles for entering the culture and practice of science. *Journal of Research in Science Teaching, 36*(6), 677–697.

Riordan, M. (2006). *Discovering the core of experiential education: How Big Picture School students learn through internships.* Dissertation Submitted to the Department of Teaching and Learning, School of Education, New York University.

Rogoff, B. (1990). *Apprenticeship in thinking.* New York: Oxford University Press.

Rogoff, B. (1994). Developing understanding of the idea of communities of learners. *Mind, culture, and activity: An International Journal, 1*(4), 209–229.

Rorabaugh, W. J. (1986). *The craft apprentice.* New York: Oxford University Press.

Rose, M. (2004). *The mind at work.* New York: Viking.

Rosenbaum, J. (2002). *Beyond empty promises: Policies to improve transitions into college and jobs.* Unpublished Paper, Northwestern University.

Rossi, H. (2003). On fertile ground. *Sojourners Magazine,* November-December. Retrieded January 15, 2007, from http://www.sojo.net/index.cfm?action=magazine.article&mode=printer_friendly&issue=soj0311&article=031120

Roundabout Education Report. (2005–2006). p. 10. New York: Roundabout Theater Company.

Ryken, A. E. (2001). *Content, pedagogy, results: A thrice told tale of integrating work-based and school-based learning.* Unpublished doctoral dissertation, School of Education, University of California, Berkeley.

Ryken, A. E. (2006). "Goin' somewhere": How career technical education programs support and constrain urban youths' career decision-making. *Career and Technical Education Research, 31*(1), 49–71.

Solomon, G., & Perkins, D. (1989). Rocky roads to transfer: Rethinking mechanisms of a neglected phenomenon. *Educational Psychologist, 24*(2), 113–142.

Scardamalia, M., & Bereiter, C. (1993). *Surpassing ourselves: An inquiry into the nature and implications of expertise.* Chicago: Open Court.

Schunk, D., & Zimmerman, B. (1996). Modeling and self-efficacy influences on children's development of self-regulation. In J. Juvonen & K. Wentzel (Eds.), *Social motivation: Understanding school adjustment.* New York: Cambridge University Press.

Scribner, J. & Wakelyn, D. (1997).*Youth apprenticeship experiences in Wisconsin: A stakeholder-based evaluation.* Paper presented at the American Educational Research Association Meeting, Chicago, March.

Seidel, S., Aryeh, L., & Steinberg, A. (2002). *Project-based and experiential learning in after-school programming.* Cambridge, MA: Project Zero, Harvard Graduate School of Education.

Shaw, T. (1996). The ethnographer as youth's apprentice. *Journal of Child and Youth Care Work, 11*, 61–71.

Sheets-Johnstone, M. (2000). Kinetic tactile-kinesthetic bodies: Ontogenetical foundations of apprenticeship learning. *Human Studies, 23*, 343–370.

Sigaut, F. (1993). Learning, teaching, and apprenticeship. *New Literary History, 24*, 105–114.

Silbereisen, R. K. (2003). Contextual constraints on adolescents' leisure. *New Directions for Child and Adolescent Development, 99*, 95–101.

Sisario, B. (2007). In the Bronx, a film school with a ghetto name. *New York Times*, September 13, B8a.

Sloan, K., & Sosniak, L. (1985). The development of accomplished sculptors. In B. S. Bloom (Ed.), *Developing talent in young people.* New York: Ballantine.

Soep, E., Mayeno, B., & Kurwa, N. (2007). Social justice youth media. In W. Ayers, T. Quinn, & D. Stovall (Eds.), *Handbook of social justice in education.* Mahwah, NJ: Erlbaum.

Sosniak, L. A. (1985). Learning to be a concert pianist. In B. S. Bloom (Ed.), *Developing talent in young people.* New York: Ballantine.

Steinberg, A. (1997). Making schoolwork more like real work. *Harvard Education Letter, 13*(2) 6–9.

Steinberg, A. (2000). Forty-three valedictorians: Graduates of the MET talk about their learning. Boston: Jobs for the Future.

Steinberg, A., & Almeida, A. (1998). CLC toolkit. Newton, MA: The National Center for Mental Health Promotion and Youth Violence Prevention.

Sternberg, R., & Lubart, T. (1995). *Defying the crowd: Cultivating creativity in a culture of conformity.* New York: Free Press.

Stipek, D . (2004). *Engaging schools: Fostering high school students' motivation to learn.* Committee on Increasing High School Students' Engagement and Motivation to Learn. National Research Council. Washington, DC: The National Academies Press.

Stone, J., & Aliaga, O. (2005). Career and technical education and student-to-work at the end of the century: Participation and outcomes. *Career and Technical Education Research, 30*(2), 125–144.

Strike, K. (2004). Community, the missing element of school reform: Why schools should be more like congregations than banks. *American Journal of Education, 110*(3), 215.

Sybolt, R. (1917). *Apprenticeship and apprenticeship education in colonial New England and New York.* New York: Arno Press.

Taylor, A., & Watt-Malcolm, B. (2007). Expansive learning through high school apprenticeship: Opportunities and limits. *Journal of Education and Work, 20*, 27–44.

Teen Voices. (2005, April) An interview with Artists for Humanity. Volume 15. Retrieved February 2, 2007, from http://www.teenvoices.com/issue_current/tvartgallery1.html

Tharp, R. G. (1993). The institutional and social context of educational practice and reform. In E. A. Forman, N. Minick, & C. A. Stone (Eds.), *Contexts for learning: Sociocultural dynamics in children's development.* Cambridge, UK: Cambridge University Press.

Thomas, E. (2007). Student engagement and learning in a community-based arts classroom. *Teachers College Record, 109*(3), 770–796.

Timmons, G. (1988). *Education, industrialization and selection.* London: Routledge.

Unwin, L. (2004). Growing beans with Thoreau: Rescuing skills and vocational education from the UK's deficit approach. *Oxford Review of Education, 30*, 147–160.

Valenzuela, A. (1999). *Subtractive schooling.* Albany, NY: SUNY Press.

Vygotsky, L. (1978). *Mind in society.* Cambridge, MA: Cambridge University Press.

Wahl, E. (2006). Educational video center: A mission to a methodology. The National Alliance for Media Arts and Culture. Retrieved August 2, 2006, from http://www.namac.org/, and retreived January 4, 2007, from http://www.bigpicture.org/publications/2007archives/PerspectivesonRelevance_V4_07.doc.pdf

What Kids Can Do. (2006). Common ground: Young people harvest food and community. Retrieved January 26, 2007, from http://www.whatkidscando.org/shorttakes/foodproject.html

What Kids Can Do. (2007). Teens transform Boston as urban arts pioneers. Retrieved April 14, 2006, from http://www.whatkidscando.org/studentwork/artistsforhumanity.html

William T. Grant Foundation. (1988). *The forgotten half: Pathways to success for America's youth and young families—Final report.* Washington, DC: The William T. Grant Foundation Commission on Work, Family and Citizenship.

Winnicot, D. (1965). *The family and individual development.* London: Tavistock.

Winnicot, D. (1971). *Playing and reality.* London: Tavistock.

Wood, D., Bruner, J., & Ross, G. (1976). The role of tutoring in problem solving. *Journal of Child Psychology and Psychiatry, 17*(2), 89–100.

Woodman, T. (2003). Drawing on experience—Teen arts program's first participants return to mentor others. *Boston Herald,* December 15.

Worthman, C. (2002). *Just playing the part: Engaging adolescents in drama and literacy.* New York: Teachers College Press.

Yenawine, P. (2004). *Addressing the needs of youth in fuel: Giving youth the power to succeed* (pp. 2–20). Chicago: Marwen Arts.

Youth Powered Video. (2006). *A hands on curriculum for teaching documentary.* New York: Education Video Center.

Index

W9-CHQ-144

(*continued on back*)

Nonlinear Regression Analysis
and Its Applications

Nonlinear Regression Analysis and Its Applications

Douglas M. Bates

Department of Statistics
University of Wisconsin
Madison, Wisconsin

Donald G. Watts

Department of Mathematics
    and Statistics
Queen's University
Kingston, Ontario, Canada

WILEY

JOHN WILEY & SONS

New York   Chichester   Brisbane   Toronto   Singapore

Library of Congress Cataloging in Publication Data:

Bates, Douglas M.
    Nonlinear regression analysis and its applications / Douglas M.
Bates, Donald G. Watts.

      p. cm.—(Wiley series in probability and mathematical
statistics. Applied probability and statistics)
    Bibliography: p.
    Includes index.

    ISBN 0-471-81643-4
    1. Regression analysis. 2. Linear models (Statistics)
3. Parameter estimation. I. Watts, Donald G. II. Title.
III. Series.
QA278.2.B375 1988
519.5'36--dc19

88-6065
CIP

Printed in the United States of America

10 9 8 7 6 5 4 3 2

To

Mary Ellen	Valery
Barbara	Lloyd
Michael	Megan

PREFACE

"Reading maketh a full man, conference; a ready man, and writing; an exact man."

— *Francis Bacon*

In this book we have tried to give a balanced presentation of the theory and practice of nonlinear regression.

We expect readers to have a working knowledge of linear regression at about the level of Draper and Smith (1981) or Montgomery and Peck (1982). Nevertheless, to provide background material and to establish notation, we give a summary review of linear least squares in Chapter 1, together with a geometrical development which is helpful in understanding both linear and nonlinear least squares. On the practical side, we discuss linear least squares in the context of modern computing methods and present useful material for checking the assumptions which are involved in regression and for modifying and improving fitted models. In Chapter 2 we discuss how nonlinear models can arise, and show how linear regression methods can be used iteratively to estimate the parameters. We also show how linear methods can be used to make approximate inferences about parameters and nonlinear model functions: again, the geometry is emphasized. The practical aspects of nonlinear estimation are discussed fully in Chapter 3, including such topics as getting starting values, transforming parameters, derivative-free methods, dealing with correlated residuals and with accumulated data, and comparing models.

In Chapter 4 we cover special methods for dealing with multiresponse data, and in Chapter 5, special techniques for compartment models in which the response function is specified as the solution to a set of linear differential equations.

In Chapter 6 we discuss improved methods for presenting the inferential results of a nonlinear analysis, using likelihood profile traces and profile t plots. Finally, in Chapter 7 we present material concerned with measuring how badly nonlinear a particular model–data set situation is. This chapter is helpful in understanding and appreciating the geometry of nonlinear least squares — and indeed, of linear least squares.

Extensive displays of geometrical constructs have been used to facilitate understanding. We have also used continuing examples so that readers can follow the development of ideas in manageable steps within familiar contexts.

All of the data sets used in this book are *real*, that is, the data were obtained from genuine physical, chemical, and biological experiments. We are grateful to the many authors, researchers, and publishers who gave permission to quote their data. In particular we would like to thank Don deBethizy, Rick Elliott, Steve Havriliak, Nico Linssen, Dave Pierson, Rob Stiratelli, Marg Treloar, and Eric Ziegel. We also acknowledge helpful comments made by participants in courses at Dalhousie University, Queen's University, and the University of Wisconsin, where the book was tested in class.

We are grateful to David Hamilton for stimulating discussions and collaborations, to Gunseog Kang for exemplary service in proofreading, and to Steve Czarniak, Mary Lindstrom and Dennis Wolf who also helped in proofreading.

The book was composed electronically using the *troff* text formatting language on the Statistics research computer at the University of Wisconsin–Madison. The figures were produced using the **S** language for statistics and graphics and both text and graphics were typeset on a Linotronic L300 using the PostScript language. We are appreciative of the good work done by Bea Shube and her colleagues at Wiley and by Bill Kasdorf of Impressions.

Considerable research was involved in developing the material in this book, and we thank the Natural Sciences and Engineering Research Council of Canada and the United States National Science Foundation for support.

Finally, we thank our wives for their continued love and encouragement.

June, 1988   Douglas M. Bates
                                                      Donald G. Watts

CONTENTS

3. Practical Considerations in Nonlinear Regression   67

Nonlinear Regression Analysis and Its Applications

CHAPTER 1.

Review of Linear Regression

"Non sunt multiplicanda entia praeter necessitatem."
(Entities are not to be multiplied beyond necessity.)

— *William of Ockham*

We begin with a brief review of linear regression, because a thorough grounding in linear regression is fundamental to understanding nonlinear regression. For a more complete presentation of linear regression see, for example, Draper and Smith (1981), Montgomery and Peck (1982), or Seber (1977). Detailed discussion of regression diagnostics is given in Belsley, Kuh, and Welsch (1980) and Cook and Weisberg (1982), and the Bayesian approach is discussed in Box and Tiao (1973).

Two topics which we emphasize are modern numerical methods and the geometry of linear least squares. As will be seen, attention to efficient computing methods increases understanding of linear regression, while the geometric approach provides insight into the methods of linear least squares and the analysis of variance, and subsequently into nonlinear regression.

1.1 The Linear Regression Model

Linear regression provides estimates and other inferential results for the *parameters* $\boldsymbol{\beta} = (\beta_1, \beta_2, \ldots, \beta_P)^T$ in the model

$$Y_n = \beta_1 x_{n1} + \beta_2 x_{n2} + \cdots + \beta_P x_{nP} + Z_n$$

$$= (x_{n1}, \ldots, x_{nP})\boldsymbol{\beta} + Z_n \tag{1.1}$$

In this model, the random variable Y_n, which represents the *response* for *case n*, $n = 1, 2, \ldots, N$, has a *deterministic* part and a *stochastic* part. The deterministic part, $(x_{n1}, \ldots, x_{nP})\boldsymbol{\beta}$, depends upon the parameters $\boldsymbol{\beta}$ and upon the *predictor* or *regressor variables* x_{np}, $p = 1, 2, \ldots, P$. The stochastic part, represented by the random variable Z_n, is a *disturbance* which perturbs the response for that case. The superscript ^{T} denotes the transpose of a matrix.

The model for N cases can be written

$$Y = X\boldsymbol{\beta} + Z \tag{1.2}$$

where Y is the vector of random variables representing the data we may get, X is the $N \times P$ matrix of regressor variables,

$$
X =
\begin{bmatrix}
x_{11} & x_{12} & x_{13} & \cdots & x_{1P} \\
x_{21} & x_{22} & x_{23} & \cdots & x_{2P} \\
\cdot & \cdot & \cdot & & \cdot \\
\cdot & \cdot & \cdot & & \cdot \\
\cdot & \cdot & \cdot & & \cdot \\
x_{N1} & x_{N2} & x_{N3} & \cdots & x_{NP}
\end{bmatrix}
$$

and Z is the vector of random variables representing the disturbances. (We will use bold face italic letters for vectors of random variables.)

The deterministic part, $X\boldsymbol{\beta}$, a function of the parameters and the regressor variables, gives the mathematical model or the model function for the responses. Since a nonzero mean for Z_n can be incorporated into the model function, we assume that

$$E[Z] = 0 \tag{1.3}$$

or, equivalently,

$$E[Y] = X\boldsymbol{\beta}$$

We therefore call $X\boldsymbol{\beta}$ the *expectation function* for the regression model. The matrix X is called the *derivative matrix*, since the (n,p)th term is the derivative of the nth row of the expectation function with respect to the pth parameter.

Note that for linear models, *derivatives with respect to any of the parameters are independent of all the parameters.*

If we further assume that Z is normally distributed with

$$\mathrm{Var}[Z] = E[ZZ^T] = \sigma^2 I \tag{1.4}$$

where I is an $N \times N$ identity matrix, then the joint probability density function for Y, given $\boldsymbol{\beta}$ and the *variance* σ^2, is

$$
\begin{aligned}
p(y \mid \boldsymbol{\beta}, \sigma^2) &= (2\pi\sigma^2)^{-N/2} \exp\left[\frac{-(y - X\boldsymbol{\beta})^T (y - X\boldsymbol{\beta})}{2\sigma^2} \right] \\
&= (2\pi\sigma^2)^{-N/2} \exp\left[\frac{-\| y - X\boldsymbol{\beta} \|^2}{2\sigma^2} \right]
\end{aligned}
\tag{1.5}
$$

where the double vertical bars denote the length of a vector. When provided with a derivative matrix **X** and a vector of observed data **y**, we wish to make inferences about σ^2 and the P parameters $\boldsymbol{\beta}$.

Example: PCB 1

As a simple example of a linear regression model, we consider the concentration of polychlorinated biphenyls (PCBs) in Lake Cayuga trout as a function of age (Bache et al., 1972). The data set is described in Appendix 1, Section A1.1. A plot of the PCB concentration versus age, Figure 1.1, reveals a curved relationship between PCB concentration and age. Furthermore, there is increasing variance in the PCB concentration as the concentration increases. Since the assumption (1.4) requires that the variance of the disturbances be constant, we seek a transformation of the PCB concentration which will stabilize the variance (see Section 1.3.2). Plotting the PCB concentration on a logarithmic scale, as in Figure 1.2*a*, nicely stabilizes the variance and produces a more nearly linear relationship. Thus, a linear expectation function of the form

$$\ln(\text{PCB}) = \beta_1 + \beta_2 \text{ age}$$

could be considered appropriate, where ln denotes the natural logarithm (logarithm to the base *e*). Transforming the regressor variable (Box and Tidwell, 1962) can produce an even straighter plot, as shown in Figure 1.2*b*, where we use the cube root of age. Thus a simple expectation function to be fitted is

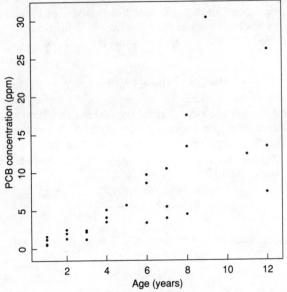

Figure 1.1   Plot of PCB concentration versus age for lake trout.

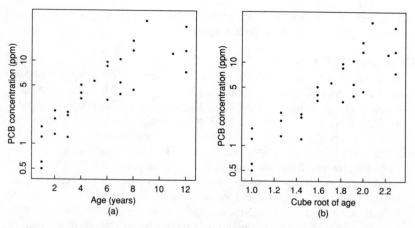

Figure 1.2   Plot of PCB concentration versus age for lake trout. The concentration, on a logarithmic scale, is plotted versus age in part *a* and versus $\sqrt[3]{\text{age}}$ in part *b*.

$$\ln(\text{PCB}) = \beta_1 + \beta_2 \sqrt[3]{\text{age}}$$

(Note that the methods of Chapter 2 can be used to fit models of the form

$$f(\mathbf{x}, \boldsymbol{\beta}, \boldsymbol{\alpha}) = \beta_0 + \beta_1 x_1^{\alpha_1} + \beta_2 x_2^{\alpha_2} + \cdots + \beta_P x_P^{\alpha_P}$$

by simultaneously estimating the conditionally linear parameters $\boldsymbol{\beta}$ and the transformation parameters $\boldsymbol{\alpha}$. The powers $\alpha_1, \ldots, \alpha_P$ are used to transform the factors so that a simple linear model in $x_1^{\alpha_1}, \ldots, x_P^{\alpha_P}$ is appropriate. In this book we use the power $\alpha = 0.33$ for the age variable even though, for the PCB data, the optimal value is 0.20.) ■

1.1.1   The Least Squares Estimates

The *likelihood function*, or more simply, the *likelihood*, $l(\boldsymbol{\beta}, \sigma \mid \mathbf{y})$, for $\boldsymbol{\beta}$ and σ is identical in form to the joint probability density (1.5) except that $l(\boldsymbol{\beta}, \sigma \mid \mathbf{y})$ is regarded as a function of the parameters conditional on the observed data, rather than as a function of the responses conditional on the values of the parameters. Suppressing the constant $(2\pi)^{-N/2}$, we write

$$l(\boldsymbol{\beta}, \sigma \mid \mathbf{y}) \propto \sigma^{-N} \exp\left[\frac{-\parallel \mathbf{y} - \mathbf{X}\boldsymbol{\beta} \parallel^2}{2\sigma^2} \right] \tag{1.6}$$

The likelihood is maximized with respect to $\boldsymbol{\beta}$ when the *residual sum of squares*

$$S(\boldsymbol{\beta}) = \parallel \mathbf{y} - \mathbf{X}\boldsymbol{\beta} \parallel^2$$

$$= \sum_{n=1}^{N} \left[y_n - \left(\sum_{p=1}^{P} x_{np}\beta_p \right) \right]^2 \tag{1.7}$$

is a minimum. Thus the *maximum likelihood estimate* $\hat{\beta}$ is the value of β which minimizes $S(\beta)$. This $\hat{\beta}$ is called the *least squares* estimate and can be written

$$\hat{\beta} = (X^T X)^{-1} X^T y \tag{1.8}$$

Least squares estimates can also be derived by using sampling theory, since the least squares estimator is the minimum variance unbiased estimator for β, or by using a Bayesian approach with a noninformative prior density on β and σ. In the Bayesian approach, $\hat{\beta}$ is the mode of the marginal posterior density function for β.

All three of these methods of inference, the likelihood approach, the sampling theory approach, and the Bayesian approach, produce the same point estimates for β. As we will see shortly, they also produce similar regions of "reasonable" parameter values. First, however, it is important to realize that the least squares estimates are only appropriate when the model (1.2) and the assumptions on the disturbance term, (1.3) and (1.4), are valid. Expressed in another way, in using the least squares estimates we assume:

(1) The expectation function is correct.
(2) The response is expectation function plus disturbance.
(3) The disturbance is independent of the expectation function.
(4) Each disturbance has a normal distribution.
(5) Each disturbance has zero mean.
(6) The disturbances have equal variances.
(7) The disturbances are independently distributed.

When these assumptions appear reasonable and have been checked using diagnostic plots such as those described in Section 1.3.2, we can go on to make further inferences about the regression model.

Looking in detail at each of the three methods of statistical inference, we can characterize some of the properties of the least squares estimates.

1.1.2 Sampling Theory Inference Results

The least squares estimator has a number of desirable properties as shown, for example, in Seber (1977):

(1) The least squares estimator $\hat{\beta}$ is normally distributed. This follows because the estimator is a linear function of Y, which in turn is a linear function of Z. Since Z is assumed to be normally distributed, $\hat{\beta}$ is normally distributed.

(2) $E[\hat{\beta}] = \beta$: the least squares estimator is unbiased.

(3) $\text{Var}[\hat{\beta}] = \sigma^2 (X^T X)^{-1}$: the covariance matrix of the least squares estimator depends on the variance of the disturbances and on the derivative matrix X.

(4) A $1-\alpha$ *joint confidence region* for $\boldsymbol{\beta}$ is the ellipsoid

$$(\boldsymbol{\beta} - \hat{\boldsymbol{\beta}})^T \mathbf{X}^T \mathbf{X}(\boldsymbol{\beta} - \hat{\boldsymbol{\beta}}) \le Ps^2 F(P, N-P; \alpha) \tag{1.9}$$

where

$$s^2 = \frac{S(\hat{\boldsymbol{\beta}})}{N-P}$$

is the *residual mean square* or *variance estimate* based on $N-P$ *degrees of freedom*, and $F(P, N-P; \alpha)$ is the upper α quantile for Fisher's F distribution with P and $N-P$ degrees of freedom.

(5) A $1-\alpha$ *marginal confidence interval* for the parameter β_p is

$$\hat{\beta}_p \pm \mathrm{se}(\hat{\beta}_p) \, t(N-P; \alpha/2) \tag{1.10}$$

where $t(N-P; \alpha/2)$ is the upper $\alpha/2$ quantile for Student's T distribution with $N-P$ degrees of freedom and the standard error of the parameter estimator is

$$\mathrm{se}(\hat{\beta}_p) = s \sqrt{\{(\mathbf{X}^T\mathbf{X})^{-1}\}_{pp}} \tag{1.11}$$

with $\{(\mathbf{X}^T\mathbf{X})^{-1}\}_{pp}$ equal to the pth diagonal term of the matrix $(\mathbf{X}^T\mathbf{X})^{-1}$.

(6) A $1-\alpha$ confidence interval for the expected response at $\mathbf{x}_0$ is

$$\mathbf{x}_0^T\hat{\boldsymbol{\beta}} \pm s\sqrt{\mathbf{x}_0^T(\mathbf{X}^T\mathbf{X})^{-1}\mathbf{x}_0} \; t(N-P; \alpha/2) \tag{1.12}$$

(7) A $1-\alpha$ confidence band for the response function at any $\mathbf{x}$ is given by

$$\mathbf{x}^T\hat{\boldsymbol{\beta}} \pm s\sqrt{\mathbf{x}^T(\mathbf{X}^T\mathbf{X})^{-1}\mathbf{x}} \; \sqrt{P\,F(P, N-P; \alpha)} \tag{1.13}$$

The expressions (1.12) and (1.13) differ because (1.12) concerns an interval at a single specific point, whereas (1.13) concerns the band produced by the intervals at all the values of $\mathbf{x}$ considered simultaneously.

1.1.3 Likelihood Inference Results

The likelihood $l(\boldsymbol{\beta}, \sigma \mid \mathbf{y})$, equation (1.6), depends on $\boldsymbol{\beta}$ only through $\| \mathbf{y} - \mathbf{X}\boldsymbol{\beta} \|$, so likelihood contours are of the form

$$\| \mathbf{y} - \mathbf{X}\boldsymbol{\beta} \|^2 = c \tag{1.14}$$

where c is a constant. A likelihood region bounded by the contour for which

$$c = S(\hat{\boldsymbol{\beta}}) \left[1 + \frac{P}{N-P} F(P, N-P; \alpha) \right]$$

is identical to a $1-\alpha$ joint confidence region from the sampling theory approach. The interpretation of a likelihood region is quite different from that of a confidence region, however.

1.1.4 Bayesian Inference Results

As shown in Box and Tiao (1973), the Bayesian marginal posterior density for $\boldsymbol{\beta}$, assuming a noninformative prior density for $\boldsymbol{\beta}$ and σ of the form

$$p(\boldsymbol{\beta}, \sigma) \propto \sigma^{-1} \tag{1.15}$$

is

$$p(\boldsymbol{\beta} \mid \mathbf{y}) \propto \left\{ 1 + \frac{(\boldsymbol{\beta} - \hat{\boldsymbol{\beta}})^{\mathrm{T}} \mathbf{X}^{\mathrm{T}} \mathbf{X} (\boldsymbol{\beta} - \hat{\boldsymbol{\beta}})}{\nu s^2} \right\}^{-(\nu + P)/2} \tag{1.16}$$

which is in the form of a P-variate Student's T density with *location parameter* $\hat{\boldsymbol{\beta}}$, *scaling matrix* $s^2(\mathbf{X}^{\mathrm{T}}\mathbf{X})^{-1}$, and $\nu = N - P$ degrees of freedom. Furthermore, the marginal posterior density for a single parameter β_p, say, is a univariate Student's T density with location parameter $\hat{\beta}_p$, scale parameter $s^2\{(\mathbf{X}^{\mathrm{T}}\mathbf{X})^{-1}\}_{pp}$, and degrees of freedom $N - P$. The marginal posterior density for the mean of $\mathbf{y}$ at $\mathbf{x}_0$ is a univariate Student's T density with location parameter $\mathbf{x}_0^{\mathrm{T}}\hat{\boldsymbol{\beta}}$, scale parameter $s^2\mathbf{x}_0^{\mathrm{T}}(\mathbf{X}^{\mathrm{T}}\mathbf{X})^{-1}\mathbf{x}_0$, and degrees of freedom $N - P$.

A *highest posterior density* (HPD) region of content $1 - \alpha$ is defined (Box and Tiao, 1973) as a region R in the parameter space such that $\Pr\{\boldsymbol{\beta} \in \mathrm{R}\} = 1 - \alpha$ and, for $\boldsymbol{\beta}_1 \in \mathrm{R}$ and $\boldsymbol{\beta}_2 \notin \mathrm{R}$, $p(\boldsymbol{\beta}_1 \mid \mathbf{y}) \geq p(\boldsymbol{\beta}_2 \mid \mathbf{y})$. For linear models with a noninformative prior, an HPD region is therefore given by the ellipsoid defined in (1.9). Similarly, the marginal HPD regions for β_p and $\mathbf{x}_0^{\mathrm{T}}\boldsymbol{\beta}$ are numerically identical to the sampling theory regions (1.10, 1.12, and 1.13).

1.1.5 Comments

Although the three approaches to statistical inference differ considerably, they lead to essentially identical inferences. In particular, since the joint confidence, likelihood, and Bayesian HPD regions are identical, we refer to them all as *inference regions*.

In addition, when referring to standard errors or correlations, we will use the Bayesian term "the standard error of β_p," when, for the sampling theory or likelihood methods, we should more properly say "the standard error of the estimate of β_p."

For linear least squares, any of the approaches can be used. For nonlinear least squares, however, the likelihood approach has the simplest and most direct geometrical interpretation, and so we emphasize it.

Example: PCB 2

The PCB data can be used to determine parameter estimates and joint and marginal inference regions. In this linear situation, the regions can be summarized using $\hat{\boldsymbol{\beta}}$, s^2, $\mathbf{X}^T\mathbf{X}$, and $v = N - P$. For the ln(PCB) data with $\sqrt[3]{\text{age}}$ as the regressor, we have $\hat{\boldsymbol{\beta}} = (-2.391, 2.300)^T$, $s^2 = 0.246$ on $v = 26$ degrees of freedom, and

$$\mathbf{X}^T\mathbf{X} = \begin{bmatrix} 28.000 & 46.941 \\ 46.941 & 83.367 \end{bmatrix}$$

$$(\mathbf{X}^T\mathbf{X})^{-1} = \begin{bmatrix} 0.6374 & -0.3589 \\ -0.3589 & 0.2141 \end{bmatrix}$$

The joint 95% inference region is then

$$28.00\,(\beta_1 + 2.391)^2 + 93.88\,(\beta_1 + 2.391)\,(\beta_2 - 2.300)$$
$$+ 83.37\,(\beta_2 - 2.300)^2 = 2\,(0.246)\,3.37 = 1.66$$

the marginal 95% inference interval for the parameter β_1 is

$$-2.391 \pm (0.496)\,\sqrt{0.6374}\,(2.056)$$

or

$$-3.21 \le \beta_1 \le -1.58$$

and the marginal 95% inference interval for the parameter β_2 is

$$2.300 \pm (0.496)\,\sqrt{0.2141}\,(2.056)$$

or

$$1.83 \le \beta_2 \le 2.77$$

The 95% inference band for the ln(PCB) value at any $\sqrt[3]{\text{age}} = x$, is

$$-2.391 + 2.300\,x \pm (0.496)\,\sqrt{0.637 - 0.718\,x + 0.214\,x^2}\,\sqrt{2\,(3.37)}$$

These regions are plotted in Figure 1.3.   ■

While it is possible to give formal expressions for the least squares estimators and the regression summary quantities in terms of the matrices $\mathbf{X}^T\mathbf{X}$ and $(\mathbf{X}^T\mathbf{X})^{-1}$, the use of these matrices for computing the estimates is not recommended. Superior computing methods are presented in Section 1.2.2.

Finally, the assumptions which lead to the use of the least squares estimates should always be examined when using a regression model. Further discussion on assumptions and their implications is given in Section 1.3.

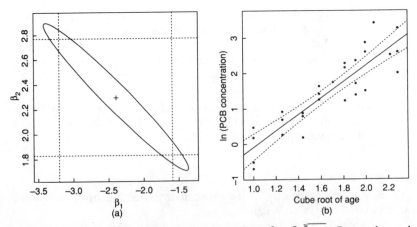

Figure 1.3 Inference regions for the model $\ln(\text{PCB}) = \beta_1 + \beta_2 \sqrt[3]{\text{age}}$. Part *a* shows the least squares estimates (+), the parameter joint 95% inference region (solid line), and the marginal 95% inference intervals (dotted lines). Part *b* shows the fitted response (solid line) and the 95% inference band (dotted lines).

1.2 The Geometry of Linear Least Squares

The model (1.2) and assumptions (1.3) and (1.4) lead to the use of the least squares estimate (1.8) which minimizes the residual sum of squares (1.7). As implied by (1.7), $S(\beta)$ can be regarded as the square of the distance from the data vector **y** to the expected response vector **Xβ**. This links the subject of linear regression to Euclidean geometry and linear algebra. The assumption of a normally distributed disturbance term satisfying (1.3) and (1.4) indicates that the appropriate scale for measuring the distance between **y** and **Xβ** is the usual Euclidean distance between vectors. In this way the Euclidean geometry of the *N*-dimensional response space becomes statistically meaningful. This connection between geometry and statistics is exemplified by the use of the term *spherical normal* for the normal distribution with the assumptions (1.3) and (1.4), because then contours of constant probability are spheres.

Note that when we speak of the linear form of the expectation function **Xβ**, we are regarding it as a function of the parameters **β**, and that when determining parameter estimates we are only concerned with how the expected response depends on the *parameters*, not with how it depends on the *variables*. In the PCB example we fit the response to $\sqrt[3]{\text{age}}$ using linear least squares because the parameters **β** enter the model linearly.

1.2.1 The Expectation Surface

The process of calculating $S(\beta)$ involves two steps:

(1) Using the P-dimensional parameter vector $\boldsymbol{\beta}$ and the $N \times P$ derivative matrix $\mathbf{X}$ to obtain the N-dimensional *expected response vector* $\boldsymbol{\eta}(\boldsymbol{\beta}) = \mathbf{X}\boldsymbol{\beta}$ and

(2) Calculating the squared distance from $\boldsymbol{\eta}(\boldsymbol{\beta})$ to the observed response $\mathbf{y}$, $\|\mathbf{y} - \boldsymbol{\eta}(\boldsymbol{\beta})\|^2$.

The possible expected response vectors $\boldsymbol{\eta}(\boldsymbol{\beta})$ form a P-dimensional *expectation surface* in the N-dimensional response space. This surface is a linear subspace of the response space, so we call it the *expectation plane* when dealing with a linear model.

Example: PCB 3

To illustrate the geometry of the expectation surface, consider just three cases from the ln(PCB) versus $\sqrt[3]{\text{age}}$ data,

$\sqrt[3]{\text{age}}$	ln(PCB)
1.26	0.92
1.82	2.15
2.22	2.52

The matrix $\mathbf{X}$ is then

$$\mathbf{X} = \begin{bmatrix} 1 & 1.26 \\ 1 & 1.82 \\ 1 & 2.22 \end{bmatrix}$$

which consists of two column vectors $\mathbf{x}_1 = (1, 1, 1)^T$ and $\mathbf{x}_2 = (1.26, 1.82, 2.22)^T$. These two vectors in the 3-dimensional response space are shown in Figure 1.4b, and correspond to the points $\boldsymbol{\beta} = (1, 0)^T$ and $\boldsymbol{\beta} = (0, 1)^T$ in the parameter plane, shown in Figure 1.4a. The expectation function $\boldsymbol{\eta}(\boldsymbol{\beta}) = \mathbf{X}\boldsymbol{\beta}$ defines a 2-dimensional expectation plane in the 3-dimensional response space. This is shown in Figure 1.4c, where the parameter lines corresponding to the lines $\beta_1 = -3, \ldots, 5$ and $\beta_2 = -2, \ldots, 2$, shown in Figure 1.4a, are given. A parameter line is associated with the parameter which is varying so the lines corresponding to $\beta_1 = -3, \ldots, 5$ (dot–dashed lines) are called β_2 lines.

Note that the parameter lines in the parameter plane are straight, parallel, and equispaced, and that their images on the expectation plane are also straight, parallel, and equispaced. Because the vector $\mathbf{x}_1$ is shorter than $\mathbf{x}_2$ ($\|\mathbf{x}_1\| = \sqrt{3}$ while $\|\mathbf{x}_2\| = \sqrt{9.83}$), the spacing between the lines of constant β_1 on the expectation plane is less than that between the lines of constant β_2. Also, the vectors $\mathbf{x}_1$ and $\mathbf{x}_2$ are not orthogonal. The angle ω between them can be calculated from

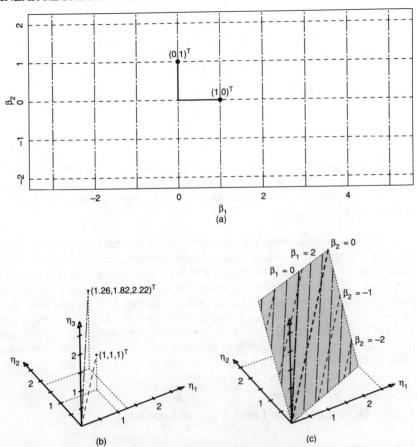

Figure 1.4 Expectation surface for the 3-case PCB example. Part *a* shows the parameter plane with β_1 parameter lines (dashed) and β_2 parameter lines (dot–dashed). Part *b* shows the vectors $\mathbf{x}_1$ (dashed line) and $\mathbf{x}_2$ (dot–dashed line) in the response space. The end points of the vectors correspond to $\boldsymbol{\beta} = (1, 0)^T$ and $\boldsymbol{\beta} = (0, 1)^T$ respectively. Part *c* shows a portion of the expectation plane (shaded) in the response space, with β_1 parameter lines (dashed) and β_2 parameter lines (dot–dashed).

$$\cos \omega = \frac{\mathbf{x}_1^T \mathbf{x}_2}{\| \mathbf{x}_1 \| \ \| \mathbf{x}_2 \|}$$

$$= \frac{5.30}{\sqrt{(3)(9.83)}}$$

$$= 0.98$$

to be about $11°$, so the parameter lines on the expectation plane are not at right angles as they are on the parameter plane.

As a consequence of the unequal length and nonorthogonality of the vectors, unit squares on the parameter plane map to parallelograms on the expectation plane. The area of the parallelogram is

$$\| \mathbf{x}_1 \| \; \| \mathbf{x}_2 \| \sin \omega = \| \mathbf{x}_1 \| \; \| \mathbf{x}_2 \| \sqrt{1 - \cos^2 \omega}$$

$$= \sqrt{(\mathbf{x}_1^T \mathbf{x}_1)(\mathbf{x}_2^T \mathbf{x}_2) - (\mathbf{x}_1^T \mathbf{x}_2)^2} \qquad (1.17)$$

$$= \sqrt{|\mathbf{X}^T \mathbf{X}|}$$

That is, the *Jacobian determinant* of the transformation from the parameter plane to the expectation plane is a constant equal to $|\mathbf{X}^T \mathbf{X}|^{1/2}$. Conversely, the ratio of areas in the parameter plane to those on the expectation plane is $|\mathbf{X}^T \mathbf{X}|^{-1/2}$. ∎

The simple linear mapping seen in the above example is true for all linear regression models. That is, for linear models, straight parallel equispaced lines in the parameter space map to straight parallel equispaced lines on the expectation plane in the response space. Consequently, rectangles in one plane map to parallelepipeds in the other plane, and circles or spheres in one plane map to ellipses or ellipsoids in the other plane. Furthermore, the Jacobian determinant, $|\mathbf{X}^T \mathbf{X}|^{1/2}$, is a constant for linear models, and so regions of fixed size in one plane map to regions of fixed size in the other, no matter where they are on the plane. These properties, which make linear least squares especially simple, are discussed further in Section 1.2.3.

1.2.2   Determining the Least Squares Estimates

The geometric representation of linear least squares allows us to formulate a very simple scheme for determining the parameters estimates $\hat{\boldsymbol{\beta}}$. Since the expectation surface is linear, all we must do to determine the point on the surface which is closest to the point $\mathbf{y}$, is to project $\mathbf{y}$ onto the expectation plane. This gives us $\hat{\boldsymbol{\eta}}$, and $\hat{\boldsymbol{\beta}}$ is then simply the value of $\boldsymbol{\beta}$ corresponding to $\hat{\boldsymbol{\eta}}$.

One approach to defining this projection is to observe that, after the projection, the residual vector $\mathbf{y} - \hat{\boldsymbol{\eta}}$ will be *orthogonal*, or *normal*, to the expectation plane. Equivalently, the residual vector must be orthogonal to all the columns of the $\mathbf{X}$ matrix, so

$$\mathbf{X}^T (\mathbf{y} - \mathbf{X}\hat{\boldsymbol{\beta}}) = 0$$

which is to say that the least squares estimate $\hat{\boldsymbol{\beta}}$ satisfies the *normal equations*

$$\mathbf{X}^T \mathbf{X} \hat{\boldsymbol{\beta}} = \mathbf{X}^T \mathbf{y} \qquad (1.18)$$

Because of (1.18) the least squares estimates are often written $\hat{\boldsymbol{\beta}} = (\mathbf{X}^T \mathbf{X})^{-1} \mathbf{X}^T \mathbf{y}$ as in (1.8). However, another way of expressing the estimate, and a more stable way of computing it, involves decomposing $\mathbf{X}$ into the product of an orthogonal matrix and an easily inverted matrix. Two such decompositions are the QR decomposition and the singular value decomposition (Dongarra et al., 1979, Chapters 9 and 11). We use the QR decomposition, where

$$X = QR$$

with the $N \times N$ matrix Q and the $N \times P$ matrix R constructed so that Q is orthogonal (that is, $Q^T Q = QQ^T = I$) and R is zero below the main diagonal. Writing

$$R = \begin{bmatrix} R_1 \\ 0 \end{bmatrix}$$

where R_1 is $P \times P$ and upper triangular, and

$$Q = [Q_1 \,|\, Q_2]$$

with Q_1 the first P columns and Q_2 the last $N - P$ columns of Q, we have

$$X = QR = Q_1 R_1 \qquad (1.19)$$

Performing a QR decomposition is straightforward, as is shown in Appendix 2.

Geometrically, the columns of Q define an *orthonormal*, or *orthogonal*, basis for the response space with the property that the first P columns span the expectation plane. Projection onto the expectation plane is then very easy if we work in the coordinate system given by Q. For example we transform the response vector to

$$w = Q^T y \qquad (1.20)$$

with components

$$w_1 = Q_1^T y \qquad (1.21)$$

and

$$w_2 = Q_2^T y \qquad (1.22)$$

The projection of w onto the expectation plane is then simply

$$\begin{bmatrix} w_1 \\ 0 \end{bmatrix}$$

in the Q coordinates and

$$\hat{\eta} = Q \begin{bmatrix} w_1 \\ 0 \end{bmatrix} = Q_1 w_1 \qquad (1.23)$$

in the original coordinates.

Example: PCB 4

As shown in Appendix 2, the QR decomposition (1.19) of the matrix

$$X = \begin{bmatrix} 1 & 1.26 \\ 1 & 1.82 \\ 1 & 2.22 \end{bmatrix}$$

for the 3-case PCB example is

$$\begin{bmatrix} 0.5774 & -0.7409 & 0.3432 \\ 0.5774 & 0.0732 & -0.8132 \\ 0.5774 & 0.6677 & 0.4700 \end{bmatrix} \begin{bmatrix} 1.7321 & 3.0600 \\ 0 & 0.6820 \\ 0 & 0 \end{bmatrix}$$

which gives [equation (1.20)]

$$w = \begin{bmatrix} 3.23 \\ 1.16 \\ -0.24 \end{bmatrix}$$

In Figure 1.5a we show the expectation plane and observation vector in the original coordinate system. We also show the vectors q_1, q_2, q_3, which are the columns of Q. It can be seen that q_1 and q_2 lie in the expectation plane and q_3 is orthogonal to it. In Figure 1.5b we show, in the transformed

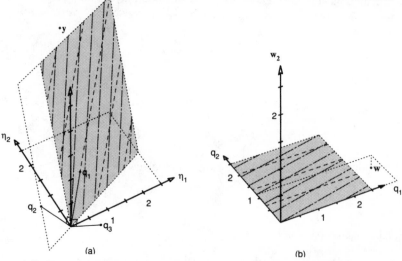

(a)   (b)

Figure 1.5 Expectation surface for the 3-case PCB example. Part a shows a portion of the expectation plane (shaded) in the response space with β_1 parameter lines (dashed) and β_2 parameter lines (dot–dashed) together with the response vector y. Also shown are the orthogonal unit vectors q_1 and q_2 in the expectation plane, and q_3 orthogonal to the plane. Part b shows the response vector w, and a portion of the expectation plane (shaded) in the rotated coordinates given by Q.

coordinates, the observation vector and the expectation plane, which is now horizontal. Note that projecting $\mathbf{w}$ onto the expectation plane is especially simple, since it merely requires replacing the last element in $\mathbf{w}$ by zero. ■

To determine the least squares estimate we must find the value $\hat{\beta}$ corresponding to $\hat{\eta}$. Since

$$\hat{\eta} = X\hat{\beta}$$

using (1.23) and (1.19)

$$R_1\hat{\beta} = \mathbf{w}_1 \tag{1.24}$$

and we solve for $\hat{\beta}$ by back-substitution (Stewart, 1973).

Example: PCB 5
For the complete $\ln(\text{PCB})$, $\sqrt[3]{\text{age}}$ data set,

$$R_1 = \begin{bmatrix} 5.29150 & 8.87105 \\ 0 & 2.16134 \end{bmatrix}$$

and $\mathbf{w}_1 = (7.7570, 4.9721)^T$, so $\hat{\beta} = (-2.391, 2.300)^T$. ■

1.2.3   Parameter Inference Regions

Just as the least squares estimates have informative geometric interpretations, so do the parameter inference regions (1.9), (1.10), (1.14) and those derived from (1.16). Such interpretations are helpful for understanding linear regression, and are essential for understanding nonlinear regression. (The geometric interpretation is less helpful in the Bayesian approach, so we discuss only the sampling theory and likelihood approaches.)

The main difference between the likelihood and sampling theory geometric interpretations is that the likelihood approach centers on the point $\mathbf{y}$ and the length of the residual vector at $\eta(\beta)$ compared to the shortest residual vector, while the sampling theory approach focuses on possible values of $\eta(\beta)$ and the angle that the resulting residual vectors could make with the expectation plane.

1.2.3.1   The Geometry of Sampling Theory Results
To develop the geometric basis of linear regression results from the sampling theory approach, we transform to the $\mathbf{Q}$ coordinate system. The model for the random variable $W = \mathbf{Q}^T Y$ is

$$W = R\beta + \mathbf{Q}^T Z$$

or

$$U = W - R\beta \tag{1.25}$$

where $U = Q^T Z$.

The spherical normal distribution of Z is not affected by the orthogonal transformation, so U also has a spherical normal distribution. This can be established on the basis of the geometry, since the spherical probability contours will not be changed by a rigid rotation or reflection, which is what an orthogonal transformation must be. Alternatively, this can be established analytically because $Q^T Q = I$, so the determinant of Q is ± 1 and $\| Qx \| = \| x \|$ for any N-vector x. Now the joint density for the random variables $Z = (Z_1, \ldots, Z_n)^T$ is

$$p_Z(z) = (2\pi\sigma^2)^{-N/2} \exp\left[\frac{-z^T z}{2\sigma^2} \right]$$

and, after transformation, the joint density for $U = Q^T Z$ is

$$p_U(u) = (2\pi\sigma^2)^{-N/2} |Q| \exp\left[\frac{-u^T Q^T Q u}{2\sigma^2} \right]$$

$$= (2\pi\sigma^2)^{-N/2} \exp\left[\frac{-u^T u}{2\sigma^2} \right]$$

From (1.25), the form of R leads us to partition U into two components:

$$U = \begin{bmatrix} U_1 \\ U_2 \end{bmatrix}$$

where U_1 consists of the first P elements of U, and U_2 the remaining $N-P$ elements. Each of these components has a spherical normal distribution of the appropriate dimension. Furthermore, independence of elements in the original disturbance vector Z leads to independence of the elements of U, so the components U_1 and U_2 are independent.

The dimensions ν_i of the components U_i, called the *degrees of freedom*, are $\nu_1 = P$ and $\nu_2 = N-P$. The sum of squares of the coordinates of a ν-dimensional spherical normal vector has a $\sigma^2\chi^2$ distribution on ν degrees of freedom, so

$$\| U_1 \|^2 \sim \sigma^2\chi_P^2$$

$$\| U_2 \|^2 \sim \sigma^2\chi_{N-P}^2$$

where the symbol $\sim$ is read "is distributed as." Using the independence of U_1 and U_2, we have

$$\frac{\| U_1 \|^2 / P}{\| U_2 \|^2 / (N-P)} \sim F(P, N-P; \alpha) \tag{1.26}$$

since the scaled ratio of two independent χ^2 random variables is distributed as Fisher's F distribution.

The distribution (1.26) gives a reference distribution for the ratio of the squared component lengths or, equivalently, for the angle that the disturbance vector makes with the horizontal plane. We may therefore use (1.25) and (1.26) to test the hypothesis that $\boldsymbol{\beta}$ equals some specific value, say $\boldsymbol{\beta}^0$, by calculating the residual vector $\mathbf{u}^0 = \mathbf{Q}^T\mathbf{y} - \mathbf{R}\boldsymbol{\beta}^0$ and comparing the lengths of the components $\mathbf{u}_1^0$ and $\mathbf{u}_2^0$ as in (1.26). The reasoning here is that a large $\| \mathbf{u}_1^0 \|$ compared to $\| \mathbf{u}_2^0 \|$ suggests that the vector $\mathbf{y}$ is not very likely to have been generated by the model (1.2) with $\boldsymbol{\beta} = \boldsymbol{\beta}^0$, since $\mathbf{u}^0$ has a suspiciously large component in the $\mathbf{Q}_1$ plane.

Note that

$$\frac{\| \mathbf{u}_2^0 \|^2}{N-P} = \frac{S(\hat{\boldsymbol{\beta}})}{N-P} = s^2$$

and

$$\| \mathbf{u}_1^0 \|^2 = \| \mathbf{R}_1\boldsymbol{\beta}^0 - \mathbf{w}_1 \|^2 \tag{1.27}$$

and so the ratio (1.26) becomes

$$\frac{\| \mathbf{R}_1\boldsymbol{\beta}^0 - \mathbf{w}_1 \|^2}{Ps^2} \tag{1.28}$$

Example: PCB 6

We illustrate the decomposition of the residual $\mathbf{u}$ for testing the null hypothesis

$$H_0 : \boldsymbol{\beta} = (-2.0, 2.0)^T$$

versus the alternative

$$H_A : \boldsymbol{\beta} \neq (-2.0, 2.0)^T$$

for the full PCB data set in Figure 1.6. Even though the rotated data vector $\mathbf{w}$ and the expectation surface for this example are in a 28-dimensional space, the relevant distances can be pictured in the 3-dimensional space spanned by the expectation surface (vectors $\mathbf{q}_1$ and $\mathbf{q}_2$) and the residual vector. The scaled lengths of the components $\mathbf{u}_1$ and $\mathbf{u}_2$ are compared to determine if the point $\boldsymbol{\beta}^0 = (-2.0, 2.0)^T$ is reasonable.

The numerator in (1.28) is

$$\left\| \begin{bmatrix} 5.29150 & 8.87105 \\ 0 & 2.16134 \end{bmatrix} \begin{bmatrix} -2.0 \\ 2.0 \end{bmatrix} - \begin{bmatrix} 7.7570 \\ 4.9721 \end{bmatrix} \right\|^2 = 0.882$$

The ratio is then $0.882/(2 \times 0.246) = 1.79$, which corresponds to a tail probability (or p value) of 0.19 for an F distribution with 2 and 26 degrees of freedom. Since the probability of obtaining a ratio at least as large as 1.79 is 19%, we do not reject the null hypothesis. ∎

A $1 - \alpha$ joint confidence region for the parameters $\boldsymbol{\beta}$ consists of all those values for which the above hypothesis test is not rejected at level α. Thus, a

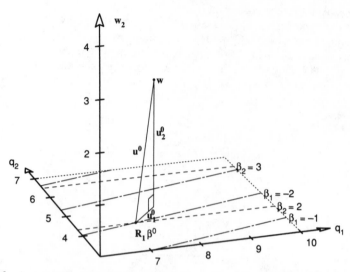

Figure 1.6   A geometric interpretation of the test $H_0 : \beta = (-2.0, 2.0)^T$ for the full PCB data set. We show the projections of the response vector w and a portion of the expectation plane projected into the 3-dimensional space given by the tangent vectors q_1 and q_2, and the orthogonal component of the response vector, w_2. For the test point β^0, the residual vector u^0 is decomposed into a tangential component u_1^0 and an orthogonal component u_2^0.

value β^0 is within a $1 - \alpha$ confidence region if

$$\frac{\| u_1^0 \|^2 / P}{\| u_2^0 \|^2 / (N - P)} \leq F(P, N - P; \alpha)$$

Since s^2 does not depend on β^0, the points inside the confidence region form a disk on the expectation plane defined by

$$\| u_1 \|^2 \leq Ps^2 F(P, N - P; \alpha)$$

Furthermore, from (1.24) and (1.27) we have

$$\| u_1 \|^2 = \| R_1(\beta - \hat\beta) \|^2$$

so a point on the boundary of the confidence region in the parameter space satisfies

$$R_1(\beta - \hat\beta) = \sqrt{Ps^2 F(P, N - P; \alpha)} \; d$$

where $\| d \| = 1$. That is, the confidence region is given by

$$\{ \beta = \hat\beta + \sqrt{Ps^2 F(P, N - P; \alpha)} \; R_1^{-1} d \mid \| d \| = 1 \} \tag{1.29}$$

Thus the region of "reasonable" parameter values is a disk centered at $R_1 \hat\beta$ on the expectation plane and is an ellipse centered at $\hat\beta$ in the parameter space.

Example: PCB 7

For the ln(PCB) versus $\sqrt[3]{age}$ data, $\hat{\boldsymbol{\beta}} = (-2.391, 2.300)^T$ and $s^2 = 0.246$ based on 26 degrees of freedom, so the 95% confidence disk on the transformed expectation surface is

$$\mathbf{R}_1\boldsymbol{\beta} = \begin{bmatrix} 7.7570 \\ 4.9721 \end{bmatrix} + 1.288 \begin{bmatrix} \cos\omega \\ \sin\omega \end{bmatrix}$$

where $0 \le \omega < 2\pi$. The disk is shown in the expectation plane in Figure 1.7a, and the corresponding ellipse

$$\boldsymbol{\beta} = \begin{bmatrix} -2.391 \\ 2.300 \end{bmatrix} + 1.288 \begin{bmatrix} 0.18898 & -0.77566 \\ 0 & 0.46268 \end{bmatrix} \begin{bmatrix} \cos\omega \\ \sin\omega \end{bmatrix}$$

is shown in the parameter plane in Figure 1.7b. ∎

1.2.3.2 Marginal Confidence Intervals

We can create a marginal confidence interval for a single parameter, say β_1, by "inverting" a hypothesis test of the form

$$H_0: \beta_1 = \beta_1^0$$

versus

$$H_A: \beta_1 \ne \beta_1^0$$

Any β_1^0 for which H_0 is not rejected at level α is included in the $1-\alpha$

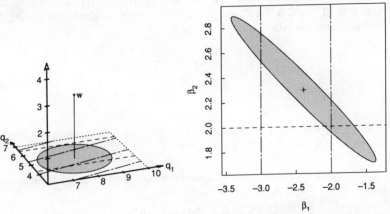

Figure 1.7 The 95% confidence disk and parameter confidence region for the PCB data. Part a shows the response vector **w** and a portion of the expectation plane projected into the 3-dimensional space given by the tangent vectors $\mathbf{q}_1$ and $\mathbf{q}_2$, and the orthogonal component of the response vector, $\mathbf{w}_2$. The 95% confidence disk (shaded) in the expectation plane (part a) maps to the elliptical confidence region (shaded) in the parameter plane (part b).

confidence interval. To perform the hypothesis test, we choose any parameter vector with $\beta_1 = \beta_1^0$, say $(\beta_1^0, \mathbf{0}^T)^T$, calculate the transformed residual vector $\mathbf{u}^0$, and divide it into three components: the first component $\mathbf{u}_1^0$ of dimension $P-1$ and parallel to the hyperplane defined by $\beta_1 = \beta_1^0$; the second component u_2^0 of dimension 1 and in the expectation plane but orthogonal to the β_1^0 hyperplane; and the third component $\mathbf{u}_3^0$ of length $(N-P)s^2$ and orthogonal to the expectation plane. The component u_2^0 is the same for any parameter $\boldsymbol{\beta}$ with $\beta_1 = \beta_1^0$, and, assuming that the true β_1 is β_1^0, the scaled ratio of the corresponding random variables U_2 and U_3 has the distribution

$$\frac{U_2^2/1}{\parallel U_3 \parallel^2/(N-P)} \sim F(1, N-P)$$

Thus we reject H_0 at level α if

$$(u_2^0)^2 > s^2 F(1, N-P; \alpha)$$

Example: PCB 8

To test the null hypothesis

$$H_0: \beta_1 = -2.0$$

versus the alternative

$$H_A: \beta_1 \neq -2.0$$

for the complete PCB data set, we decompose the transformed residual vector at $\boldsymbol{\beta}^0 = (-2.0, 2.2)^T$ into three components as shown in Figure 1.8 and calculate the ratio

$$\frac{(u_2^0)^2}{s^2} = \frac{0.240}{0.246}$$

$$= 0.97$$

This corresponds to a p value of 0.33, and so we do not reject the null hypothesis. ∎

We can create a $1-\alpha$ marginal confidence interval for β_1 as all values for which

$$(u_2^0)^2 \leq s^2 F(1, N-P; \alpha)$$

or, equivalently,

$$|u_2^0| \leq s\, t(N-P; \alpha/2) \tag{1.30}$$

Since $|u_2^0|$ is the distance from the point $\mathbf{R}_1\hat{\boldsymbol{\beta}}$ to the line corresponding to $\beta_1 = \beta_1^0$ on the transformed parameter plane, the confidence interval will include all values β_1^0 for which the corresponding parameter line intersects the disk

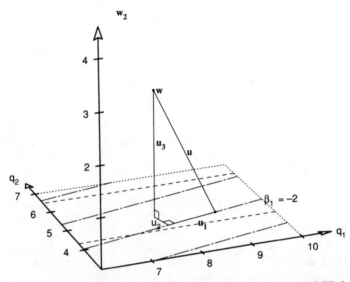

Figure 1.8 A geometric interpretation of the test $H_0 : \beta_1 = -2.0$ for the full PCB data set. We show the response vector **w**, and a portion of the expectation plane projected into the 3-dimensional space given by the tangent vectors $\mathbf{q}_1$ and $\mathbf{q}_2$, and the orthogonal component of the response vector, $\mathbf{w}_2$. For a representative point on the line $\beta_1 = -2$ the residual vector **u** is decomposed into a tangential component $\mathbf{u}_1^0$ along the line, a tangential component u_2^0 perpendicular to the line, and an orthogonal component $\mathbf{u}_3^0$.

$$\{\mathbf{R}_1\hat{\boldsymbol{\beta}} + s\, t(N-P;\alpha/2)\mathbf{d} \mid \|\mathbf{d}\| = 1\} \tag{1.31}$$

Instead of determining the value of $|u_2^0|$ for each β_1^0, we take the disk (1.31) and determine the minimum and maximum values of β_1 for points on the disk. Writing $\mathbf{r}^1$ for the first row of $\mathbf{R}_1^{-1}$, the values of β_1 corresponding to points on the expectation plane disk are

$$\mathbf{r}^1(\mathbf{R}_1\hat{\boldsymbol{\beta}} + s\, t(N-P;\alpha/2)\,\mathbf{d}) = \hat{\beta}_1 + s\, t(N-P;\alpha/2)\,\mathbf{r}^1\mathbf{d}$$

and the minimum and maximum occur for the unit vectors in the direction of $\mathbf{r}^1$; that is, $\mathbf{d} = \pm \mathbf{r}^{1T}/\|\mathbf{r}^1\|$. This gives the confidence interval

$$\hat{\beta}_1 \pm s\, \|\mathbf{r}^1\|\, t(N-P;\alpha/2)$$

In general, a marginal confidence interval for parameter β_p is

$$\hat{\beta}_p \pm s\, \|\mathbf{r}^p\|\, t(N-P;\alpha/2) \tag{1.32}$$

where $\mathbf{r}^p$ is the pth row of $\mathbf{R}_1^{-1}$. The quantity

$$\mathrm{se}(\hat{\beta}_p) = s\, \|\mathbf{r}^p\| \tag{1.33}$$

is called the *standard error* for the pth parameter. Since

$$(\mathbf{X}^T\mathbf{X})^{-1} = (\mathbf{R}_1^T\mathbf{R}_1)^{-1}$$
$$= \mathbf{R}_1^{-1}\mathbf{R}_1^{-T}$$

$\|\mathbf{r}^p\|^2 = \{(\mathbf{X}^T\mathbf{X})^{-1}\}_{pp}$, so the standard error can be written as in equation (1.11).

A convenient summary of the variability of the parameter estimates can be obtained by factoring $\mathbf{R}_1^{-1}$ as

$$\mathbf{R}_1^{-1} = \text{diag}(\|\mathbf{r}^1\|, \|\mathbf{r}^2\|, \ldots, \|\mathbf{r}^P\|)\mathbf{L} \qquad (1.34)$$

where $\mathbf{L}$ has unit length rows. The diagonal matrix provides the parameter standard errors, while the *correlation matrix*

$$\mathbf{C} = \mathbf{L}\mathbf{L}^T \qquad (1.35)$$

gives the correlations between the parameter estimates.

Example: PCB 9

For the ln(PCB) data, $\hat{\boldsymbol{\beta}} = (-2.391, 2.300)^T$, $s^2 = 0.246$ with 26 degrees of freedom, and

$$\mathbf{R}_1^{-1} = \begin{bmatrix} 5.29150 & 8.87105 \\ 0 & 2.16134 \end{bmatrix}^{-1}$$

$$= \begin{bmatrix} 0.18898 & -0.77566 \\ 0 & 0.46268 \end{bmatrix}$$

$$= \begin{bmatrix} 0.798 & 0 \\ 0 & 0.463 \end{bmatrix}\begin{bmatrix} 0.237 & -0.972 \\ 0 & 1 \end{bmatrix}$$

which gives standard errors of $0.798\sqrt{0.246} = 0.396$ for β_1 and $0.463\sqrt{0.246} = 0.230$ for β_2. Also

$$\mathbf{C} = \begin{bmatrix} 1 & -0.972 \\ -0.972 & 1 \end{bmatrix}$$

so the correlation between β_1 and β_2 is -0.97. The 95% confidence intervals for the parameters are given by $-2.391 \pm 2.056(0.396)$ and $2.300 \pm 2.056(0.230)$, which are plotted in Figure 1.3a. ∎

Marginal confidence intervals for the expected response at a design point $\mathbf{x}_0$ can be created by determining which hyperplanes formed by constant $\mathbf{x}_0^T\boldsymbol{\beta}$ intersect the disk (1.31). Using the same argument as was used to derive (1.32), we obtain a standard error for the expected response at $\mathbf{x}_0$ as $s\|\mathbf{x}_0^T\mathbf{R}_1^{-1}\|$, so the confidence interval is

$$\mathbf{x}_0^T\hat{\boldsymbol{\beta}} \pm s\|\mathbf{x}_0^T\mathbf{R}_1^{-1}\|\ t(N-P;\alpha/2) \qquad (1.36)$$

Similarly, a confidence band for the response function is

$$\mathbf{x}^T\hat{\boldsymbol{\beta}} \pm s \parallel \mathbf{x}^T\mathbf{R}_1^{-1} \parallel \sqrt{P\,F(P, N-P; \alpha)} \qquad (1.37)$$

Example: PCB 10

A plot of the fitted expectation function and the 95% confidence bands for the PCB example was given in Figure 1.3*b*. ∎

Ansley (1985) gives derivations of other sampling theory results in linear regression using the *QR* decomposition, which, as we have seen, is closely related to the geometric approach to regression.

1.2.3.3 The Geometry of Likelihood Results

The likelihood function indicates the plausibility of values of $\boldsymbol{\eta}$ relative to $\mathbf{y}$, and consequently has a simple geometrical interpretation. If we allow $\boldsymbol{\eta}$ to take on any value in the N-dimensional response space, the likelihood contours are spheres centered on $\mathbf{y}$. Values of $\boldsymbol{\eta}$ of the form $\boldsymbol{\eta} = \mathbf{X}\boldsymbol{\beta}$ generate a P-dimensional expectation plane, and so the intersection of the plane with the likelihood spheres produces disks.

Analytically, the likelihood function (1.6) depends on $\boldsymbol{\eta}$ through

$$
\begin{aligned}
\parallel \boldsymbol{\eta} - \mathbf{y} \parallel^2 &= \parallel \mathbf{Q}^T(\boldsymbol{\eta} - \mathbf{y}) \parallel^2 \\
&= \parallel \mathbf{Q}_1^T(\boldsymbol{\eta} - \mathbf{y}) \parallel^2 + \parallel \mathbf{Q}_2^T(\boldsymbol{\eta} - \mathbf{y}) \parallel^2 \qquad (1.38) \\
&= \parallel \mathbf{w}(\boldsymbol{\beta}) - \mathbf{w}_1 \parallel^2 + \parallel \mathbf{w}_2 \parallel^2
\end{aligned}
$$

where $\mathbf{w}(\boldsymbol{\beta}) = \mathbf{Q}_1^T\boldsymbol{\eta}$ and $\mathbf{Q}_2^T\boldsymbol{\eta} = \mathbf{0}$. A constant value of the total sum of squares specifies a disk of the form

$$\parallel \mathbf{w}(\boldsymbol{\beta}) - \mathbf{w}_1 \parallel^2 = c$$

on the expectation plane. Choosing

$$c = Ps^2 F(P, N-P; \alpha)$$

produces the disk corresponding to a $1 - \alpha$ confidence region. In terms of the total sum of squares, the contour is

$$S(\boldsymbol{\beta}) = S(\hat{\boldsymbol{\beta}}) \left\{ 1 + \frac{P}{N-P} F(P, N-P; \alpha) \right\} \qquad (1.39)$$

As shown previously, and illustrated in Figure 1.7, this disk transforms to an ellipsoid in the parameter space.

1.3 Assumptions and Model Assessment

The statistical assumptions which lead to the use of the least squares estimates encompass several different aspects of the regression model. As with any statistical analysis, if the assumptions on the model and data are not appropriate, the results of the analysis will not be valid.

Since we cannot guarantee *a priori* that the different assumptions are all valid, we must proceed in an iterative fashion as described, for example, in Box, Hunter, and Hunter (1978). We entertain a plausible statistical model for the data, analyze the data using that model, then go back and use *diagnostics* such as plots of the residuals to assess the assumptions. If the diagnostics indicate failure of assumptions in either the deterministic or stochastic components of the model, we must modify the model or the analysis and repeat the cycle.

It is important to recognize that the design of the experiment and the method of data collection can affect the chances of assumptions being valid in a particular experiment. In particular *randomization* can be of great help in ensuring the appropriateness of all the assumptions, and *replication* allows greater ability to check the appropriateness of specific assumptions.

1.3.1 Assumptions and Their Implications

The assumptions, as listed in Section 1.1.1, are:

(1) *The expectation function is correct.* Ensuring the validity of this assumption is, to some extent, the goal of all science. We wish to build a model with which we can predict natural phenomena. It is in building the mathematical model for the expectation function that we frequently find ourselves in an iterative loop. We proceed as though the expectation function were correct, but we should be prepared to modify it as the data and the analyses dictate. In almost all linear, and in many nonlinear, regression situations we do not know the "true" model, but we choose a plausible one by examining the situation, looking at data plots and cross-correlations, and so on. As the analysis proceeds we can modify the expectation function and the assumptions about the disturbance term to obtain a more sensible and useful answer. Models should be treated as just models, and it must be recognized that some will be more appropriate or adequate than others. Nevertheless, assumption (1) is a strong one, since it implies that the expectation function includes all the important predictor variables in precisely the correct form, and that it does *not* include any unimportant predictor variables. A useful technique to enable checking the adequacy of a model function is to include replications in the experiment. It is also important to actually manipulate the predictor variables and randomize the order in which the experiments are done, to ensure that *causation*, not *correlation*, is being determined (Box, 1960).

(2) *The response is expectation function plus disturbance.* This assumption is important theoretically, since it allows the probability density function for the random variable Y describing the responses to be simply calculated from the probability density function for the random variable Z describing the disturbances. Thus,

$$p_Y(\mathbf{y} \mid \boldsymbol{\beta}, \sigma^2) = p_Z(\mathbf{y} - \mathbf{X}\boldsymbol{\beta} \mid \sigma^2)$$

In practice, this assumption is closely tied to the assumption of constant variance of the disturbances. It may be the case that the disturbances can be considered as having constant variance, but as entering the model multiplicatively, since in many phenomena, as the level of the "signal" increases, the level of the "noise" increases. This lack of additivity of the disturbance will manifest itself as a nonconstant variance in the diagnostic plots. In both cases, the corrective action is the same—either use weighted least squares or take a transformation of the response as was done in Example PCB 1.

(3) *The disturbance is independent of the expectation function.* This assumption is closely related to assumption (2), since they both relate to appropriateness of the additive model. One of the implications of this assumption is that the control or predictor variables are measured perfectly. Also, as a converse to the implication in assumption (1) that all important variables are included in the model, this assumption implies that *any important variables which are not included are not systematically related* to the response. An important technique to improve the chances that this is true is to randomize the order in which the experiments are done, as suggested by Fisher (1935). In this way, if an important variable has been omitted, its effect may be manifested as a disturbance (and hence simply inflate the variability of the observations) rather than being confounded with one of the predictor effects (and hence bias the parameter estimates). And, of course, it is important to actually manipulate the predictor variables not merely record their values.

(4) *Each disturbance has a normal distribution.* The assumption of normality of the disturbances is important, since this dictates the form of the sampling distribution of the random variables describing the responses, and through this, the likelihood function for the parameters. This leads to the criterion of least squares, which is enormously powerful because of its mathematical tractability. For example, given a linear model, it is possible to write down the analytic solution for the parameter estimators and to show [Gauss's theorem (Seber, 1977)] that the least squares estimates are the best *both individually and in any linear combination*, in the sense that they have the smallest mean square error of any linear estimators. The normality assumption can be justified by appealing to the central limit theorem, which states that the resultant of many disturbances, no one of which is dominant, will tend to be normally distributed. Since most experiments involve many operations to set up and measure the results, it is reasonable to assume, at least tentatively, that the disturbances will be normally distributed. Again, the assumption of normality will be more likely to be appropriate if the order of the experiments is randomized. The assumption of normality may be checked by examining the residuals.

(5) *Each disturbance has zero mean.* This assumption is primarily a simplifying one, which reduces the number of unknown parameters to a manageable level. Any nonzero mean common to all observations can be accommodated by introducing a constant term in the expectation function, so this assumption

is unimportant in linear regression. It can be important in nonlinear regression, however, where many expectation functions occur which do not include a constant. The main implication of this assumption is that there is no systematic bias in the disturbances such as could be caused by an unsuspected influential variable. Hence, we see again the value of randomization.

(6) *The disturbances have equal variances.* This assumption is more important practically than theoretically, since a solution exists for the least squares estimation problem for the case of unequal variances [see, e.g., Draper and Smith (1981) concerning weighted least squares]. Practically, however, one must describe how the variances vary, which can only be done by making further assumptions, or by using information from replications and incorporating this into the analysis through generalized least squares, or by transforming the data. When the variance is constant, the likelihood function is especially simple, since the parameters can be estimated independently of the nuisance parameter σ^2. The main implication of this assumption is that all data values are *equally unreliable*, and so the simple least squares criterion can be used. The appropriateness of this assumption can sometimes be checked after a model has been fitted by plotting the residuals versus the fitted values, but it is much better to have replications. With replications, we can check the assumption before even fitting a model, and can in fact use the replication averages and variances to determine a suitable *variance-stabilizing* transformation; see Section 1.3.2. Transforming to constant variance often has the additional effect of making the disturbances behave more normally. This is because a constant variance is necessarily independent of the mean (and anything else, for that matter), and this independence property is fundamental to the normal density.

(7) *The disturbances are distributed independently.* The final assumption is that the disturbances in different experiments are independent of one another. This is an enormously simplifying assumption, because then the joint probability density function for the vector Y is just the product of the probability densities for the individual random variables Y_n, $n = 1, 2, \ldots, N$. The implication of this assumption is that the disturbances on separate runs are not systematically related, an assumption which can usually be made to be more appropriate by randomization. Nonindependent disturbances can be treated by generalized least squares, but, as in the case where there is nonconstant variance, modifications to the model must be made either through information gained from the data, or by additional assumptions as to the nature of the interdependence.

1.3.2   Model Assessment

In this subsection we present some simple methods for verifying the appropriateness of assumptions, especially through plots of residuals. Further discussion on regression diagnostics for linear models is given in Hocking (1983), and in the books by Belsley, Kuh, and Welsch (1980), Cook and Weisberg (1982), and Draper and Smith (1981). In Chapter 3 we discuss model assessment for nonlinear models.

1.3.2.1 Plotting Residuals

A simple, effective method for checking the adequacy of a model is to plot the studentized residuals, $\hat{z}_n / s\sqrt{1 - h_{nn}}$, versus the predictor variables and any other possibly important "lurking" variables (Box, 1960; Joiner, 1981). The term h_{nn} is the nth diagonal term of the "hat" matrix $\mathbf{H} = \mathbf{X}(\mathbf{X}^T\mathbf{X})^{-1}\mathbf{X}^T = \mathbf{Q}_1\mathbf{Q}_1^T$, and $\hat{z}_n$ is the residual for the nth case,

$$\hat{z}_n = y_n - \hat{y}_n$$

A relationship between the residuals and any variable then suggests that there is an effect due to that variable which has not been accounted for. Features to look for include systematic linear or curvilinear behavior of the residuals with respect to a variable. Important common "lurking" variables include time or the order number of the experiment; if a plot of residuals versus time shows suspicious behavior, such as runs of residuals of the same sign, then the assumption of independence of the disturbances may be inappropriate.

Plotting residuals versus the fitted values $\hat{y}_n$ is also useful, since such plots can reveal outliers or general inadequacy in the form of the expectation function. It is also a very effective plot for revealing whether the assumption of constant variance is appropriate. The most common form of nonconstant variance is an increase in the variability in the responses when the level of the response changes. This behavior was noticed in the original PCB data. If a regression model is fitted to such data, the plot of the studentized residuals versus the fitted values tends to have a wedge-shaped pattern.

When residual plots or the data themselves give an indication of nonconstant variance, the estimation procedure should be modified. Possible changes include transforming the data as was done with the PCB data or using weighted least squares.

A quantile–quantile plot (Chambers et al., 1983) of the studentized residuals versus a normal distribution gives a direct check on the assumption of normality. If the expectation function is correct and the assumption of normality is appropriate, such a normal probability plot of the residuals should be a fairly straight line. Departures from a straight line therefore suggest inappropriateness of the normality assumption, although, as demonstrated in Daniel and Wood (1980), considerable variability can be expected in normal plots. Normal probability plots are also good for revealing outliers.

Example: PCB 11

Plots of residuals are given in Figure 1.9 for the fit of $\ln(\text{PCB})$ to $\sqrt[3]{\text{age}}$. Since the fitted values are a linear function of the regressor variable $\sqrt[3]{\text{age}}$, the form of the plot of the studentized residuals versus $\hat{y}$ will be the same as that versus $\sqrt[3]{\text{age}}$, so we only display the former. The plot versus $\hat{y}$ and the quantile–quantile plot are well behaved. Neither plot reveals outliers. ∎

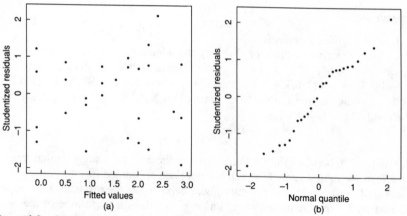

Figure 1.9   Studentized residuals for the PCB data plotted versus fitted values in part *a* and versus normal quantiles in part *b*.

1.3.2.2   Stabilizing Variance

An experiment which includes replications allows further tests to be made on the appropriateness of assumptions. For example, even before an expectation function has been proposed, it is possible to check the assumption of constant variance by using an analysis of variance to get averages and variances for each set of replications and plotting the variances and standard deviations versus the averages. If the plots show systematic relationships, then one can use a variance-stabilizing procedure to transform to constant variance.

One procedure is to try a range of power transformations in the form (Box and Cox, 1964)

$$
y^{(\lambda)} = \begin{cases} \dfrac{y^{\lambda}-1}{\lambda} & \lambda \neq 0 \\[2mm] \ln y & \lambda = 0 \end{cases}
$$

We calculate and plot variances versus averages for $y^{(\lambda)}$, $\lambda = 0, \pm 0.5, \pm 1, \ldots$ and select that value of λ for which the variance appears to be most stable. Alternatively, for a random variable Y, if there is a power relationship between the standard deviation σ and the mean μ such that $\sigma \propto \mu^{\alpha}$, it can be shown (Box, Hunter, and Hunter, 1978; Draper and Smith, 1981; Montgomery and Peck, 1982) that the variance of the transformed random variable $Y^{1-\alpha}$ will be approximately constant.

Variance-stabilizing transformations usually have the additional benefit of making the distribution of the disturbances appear more nearly normal, as discussed in Section 1.3.1. Alternatively, one can use the replication information to assist in choosing a form of weighting for weighted least squares.

Example: PCB 12

A plot of the standard deviations versus the averages for the original PCB data is given in Figure 1.10a. It can be seen that there is a good straight line relationship between s and $\bar{y}$, and so the variance-stabilizing technique leads to the logarithmic transformation. In Figure 1.10b we plot the standard deviations versus the averages for the ln(PCB) data. This plot shows no systematic relationship, and hence substantiates the effectiveness of the logarithmic transformation in stabilizing the variance. ∎

1.3.2.3   Lack of Fit

When the data set includes replications, it is also possible to perform tests for *lack of fit* of the expectation function. Such analyses are based on an analysis of variance in which the residual sum of squares $S(\hat{\beta})$ with $N - P$ degrees of freedom is decomposed into the *replication* sum of squares S_r (equal to the total sum of squares of deviations of the replication values about their averages) with, say, v_r degrees of freedom, and the *lack of fit* sum of squares $S_l = S(\hat{\beta}) - S_r$, with $v_l = N - P - v_r$ degrees of freedom. We then compare the ratio of the lack of fit mean square over the replication mean square with the appropriate value in the F table. That is, we compare

$$\frac{S_l/v_l}{S_r/v_r} \quad \text{with} \quad F(v_l, v_r; \alpha)$$

to determine whether there is significant lack of fit at level α. The geometric justification for this analysis is that the replication subspace is always orthogonal to the subspace containing the averages and the expectation function.

If no lack of fit is found, then the lack of fit analysis of variance has served its purpose, and the estimate of σ^2 should be based on the residual mean

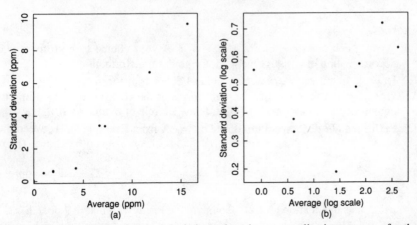

Figure 1.10 Replication standard deviations plotted versus replication averages for the PCB data in part a and for the ln(PCB) data in part b.

square. That is, the replication and lack of fit sums of squares and degrees of freedom should be recombined to give an estimate with the largest number of degrees of freedom, so as to provide the most reliable parameter and expected value confidence regions. If lack of fit is found, the analyst should attempt to discover why, and modify the expectation function accordingly. Further discussion on assessing the fit of a model and on modifying and comparing models is given in Sections 3.7 and 3.10.

Example: PCB 13

For the ln(PCB) versus $\sqrt[3]{\text{age}}$ data, the lack of fit analysis is presented in Table 1.1. Because the p value suggests no lack of fit, we combine the lack of fit and replication sums of squares and degrees of freedom and take as our estimate of σ^2, the residual mean square of 0.246 based on 26 degrees of freedom. If there had been lack of fit, we would have had to modify the model: in either situation, we do not simply use the replication mean square as an estimate of the variance. ■

Table 1.1　Lack of fit analysis of the model fitted to the PCB data

Source	Degrees of Freedom	Sum of Squares	Mean Square	F Ratio	p Value
Lack of fit	9	1.923	0.214	0.812	0.61
Replication	17	4.475	0.263		
Residuals	26	6.398	0.246		

Exercises

1.1 Write a computer routine in a language of your choice to perform a QR decomposition of a matrix using Householder transformations.

1.2 Draw a picture to show the Householder transformation of a vector $\mathbf{y} = (y_1, y_2)^{\mathrm{T}}$ to the x axis. Use both forms of the vector $\mathbf{u}$ corresponding to equations (A2.1) and (A2.2). Hint: Draw a circle of radius $\| \mathbf{y} \|$.

1.3 Perform a QR decomposition of the matrix $\mathbf{X}$ from Example PCB 3,

$$\mathbf{X} = \begin{bmatrix} 1 & 1.26 \\ 1 & 1.82 \\ 1 & 2.22 \end{bmatrix}$$

using $\mathbf{u}$ as in equation (A2.2). Compare the result with that in Appendix 2.

1.4 (a) Perform a QR decomposition of the matrix

$$\mathbf{D} = \begin{bmatrix} 0 & 1 \\ 0 & 1 \\ 0 & 1 \\ 1 & 1 \\ 0 & 1 \end{bmatrix}$$

and obtain the matrix $\mathbf{Q}_1$. This matrix is used in Example α-pinene 6, Section 4.3.4.

(b) Calculate $\mathbf{Q}_2^T \mathbf{y}$, where $\mathbf{y} = (50.4, 32.9, 6.0, 1.5, 9.3)^T$, without explicitly solving for $\mathbf{Q}_2$.

1.5 (a) Fit the model $\ln(\text{PCB}) = \beta_1 + \beta_2$ age to the PCB data and perform a lack of fit analysis of the model. What do you conclude about the adequacy of this model?

(b) Plot the residuals versus age, and assess the adequacy of the model. Now what do you conclude about the adequacy of the model?

(c) Fit the model $\ln(\text{PCB}) = \beta_1 + \beta_2$ age $+ \beta_3$ age^2 to the PCB data and perform a lack of fit analysis of the model. What do you conclude about the adequacy of this model?

(d) Perform an extra sum of squares analysis to determine whether the quadratic term is a useful addition.

(e) Explain the difference between your answers in (a), (b), and (d).

CHAPTER 2.

Nonlinear Regression: Iterative Estimation and Linear Approximations

"Although this may seem a paradox, all exact science is dominated by the idea of approximation."

– Bertrand Russell

Linear regression is a powerful method for analyzing data described by models which are linear in the parameters. Often, however, a researcher has a mathematical expression which relates the response to the predictor variables, and these models are usually nonlinear in the parameters. In such cases, linear regression techniques must be extended, which introduces considerable complexity.

2.1 The Nonlinear Regression Model

A nonlinear regression model can be written

$$Y_n = f(\mathbf{x}_n, \boldsymbol{\theta}) + Z_n \tag{2.1}$$

where f is the expectation function and $\mathbf{x}_n$ is a vector of associated regressor variables or independent variables for the nth case. This model is of exactly the same form as (1.1) except that the expected responses are nonlinear functions of the parameters. That is, for nonlinear models, *at least one of the derivatives of the expectation function with respect to the parameters depends on at least one of the parameters.*

To emphasize the distinction between linear and nonlinear models, we use $\boldsymbol{\theta}$ for the parameters in a nonlinear model. As before, we use P for the number

32

of parameters.

When analyzing a particular set of data we consider the vectors $x_n, n = 1, 2, \ldots, N$, as fixed and concentrate on the dependence of the expected responses on θ. We create the N-vector $\eta(\theta)$ with nth element

$$\eta_n(\theta) = f(x_n, \theta) \qquad n = 1, \ldots, N$$

and write the nonlinear regression model as

$$Y = \eta(\theta) + Z \qquad (2.2)$$

with Z assumed to have a spherical normal distribution. That is,

$$E[Z] = 0$$

$$\text{Var}(Z) = E[ZZ^T] = \sigma^2 I$$

as in the linear model.

Example: Rumford 1

Count Rumford of Bavaria was one of the early experimenters on the physics of heat. In 1798 he performed an experiment in which a cannon barrel was heated by grinding it with a blunt bore. When the cannon had reached a steady temperature of 130°F, it was allowed to cool and temperature readings were taken at various times. The ambient temperature during the experiment was 60°F, so [under Newton's law of cooling, which states that $df/dt = -\theta(f-T_0)$, where T_0 is the ambient temperature] the temperature at time t should be

$$f(t, \theta) = 60 + 70e^{-\theta t}$$

Since $\partial f/\partial \theta = -70te^{-\theta t}$ depends on the parameter θ, this model is nonlinear. Rumford's data are presented in Appendix 1, Section A1.2. ∎

Example: Puromycin 1

The Michaelis–Menten model for enzyme kinetics relates the initial "velocity" of an enzymatic reaction to the substrate concentration x through the equation

$$f(x, \theta) = \frac{\theta_1 x}{\theta_2 + x} \qquad (2.3)$$

In Appendix 1, Section A1.3 we present data from Treloar (1974) on the initial rate of a reaction for which the Michaelis–Menten model is believed to be appropriate. The data, for an enzyme treated with Puromycin, are plotted in Figure 2.1.

Differentiating f with respect to θ_1 and θ_2 gives

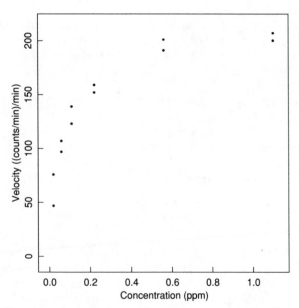

Figure 2.1 Plot of reaction velocity versus substrate concentration for the Puromycin data.

$$\frac{\partial f}{\partial \theta_1} = \frac{x}{\theta_2 + x}$$

$$\frac{\partial f}{\partial \theta_2} = \frac{-\theta_1 x}{(\theta_2 + x)^2}$$

(2.4)

and since both these derivatives involve at least one of the parameters, the model is recognized as nonlinear. ■

2.1.1 Transformably Linear Models

The Michaelis–Menten model (2.3) can be transformed to a linear model by expressing the reciprocal of the velocity as a function of the reciprocal substrate concentration,

$$\frac{1}{f} = \frac{1}{\theta_1} + \frac{\theta_2}{\theta_1}\frac{1}{x}$$

$$= \beta_1 + \beta_2 u$$

(2.5)

We call such models *transformably linear*. Some authors use the term "intrinsically linear," but we reserve the term "intrinsic" for a special geometric property of nonlinear models, as discussed in Chapter 7. As will be seen in Chapter 3, transformably linear models have some advantages in nonlinear regression because it is easy to get starting values for some of the parameters.

It is important to understand, however, that a transformation of the data involves a transformation of the disturbance term too, which affects the assumptions on it. Thus, if we assume the model function (2.2) with an additive, spherical normal disturbance term is an appropriate representation of the experimental situation, then these same assumptions will not be appropriate for the transformed data. Hence we should use nonlinear regression on the original data, or else weighted least squares on the transformed data. Sometimes, of course, transforming a data set to induce constant variance also produces a linear expectation function in which case linear regression can be used on the transformed data.

Example: Puromycin 2

Because there are replications in the Puromycin data set, it is easy to see from Figure 2.1 that the variance of the original data is constant, and hence that nonlinear regression should be used to estimate the parameters. However, the reciprocal data, plotted in Figure 2.2a, while showing a simple straight line relationship, also show decidely nonconstant variance.

If we use linear regression to fit the model (2.5) to these data, we obtain the estimates

$$\hat{\beta} = (0.005107, 0.0002472)^{\mathrm{T}}$$

corresponding to

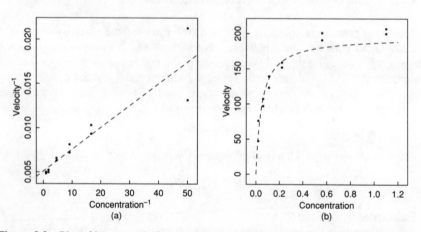

Figure 2.2   Plot of inverse velocity versus inverse substrate concentration for the Puromycin experiment with the linear regression line (dashed) in part a, and the corresponding fitted curve (dashed) in the original scale in part b.

$$\hat{\theta} = (195.8, 0.04841)^T$$

The fitted curve is overlaid with the data in the original scale in Figure 2.2b, where we see that the predicted asymptote is too small. Because the variance of the replicates has been distorted by the transformation, the cases with low concentration (high reciprocal concentration) dominate the determination of the parameters and the curve does not fit the data well at high concentrations. ∎

This example demonstrates two important features. First, it emphasizes the value of replications, because without replications it may not be possible to detect either the constant variance in the original data or the nonconstant variance in the transformed data; and second, it shows that while transforming can produce simple linear behavior, it also affects the disturbances.

2.1.2   Conditionally Linear Parameters

The Michaelis–Menten model is also an example of a model in which there is a conditionally linear parameter, θ_1. It is *conditionally linear* because the derivative of the expectation function with respect to θ_1 does not involve θ_1. We can therefore estimate θ_1, conditional on θ_2, by a linear regression of velocity on $x/(\theta_2 + x)$. Models with conditionally linear parameters enjoy some advantageous properties, which can be exploited in nonlinear regression.

2.1.3   The Geometry of the Expectation Surface

The assumption of a spherical normal distribution for the disturbance term Z leads us to consider the Euclidean geometry of the N-dimensional response space, because again we will be interested in the least squares estimates $\hat{\theta}$ of the parameters. The N-vectors $\eta(\theta)$ define a P-dimensional surface called the *expectation surface* in the response space, and the least squares estimates correspond to the point on the expectation surface,

$$\hat{\eta} = \eta(\hat{\theta})$$

which is closest to y. That is, $\hat{\theta}$ minimizes the residual sum of squares

$$S(\theta) = \| y - \eta(\theta) \|^2$$

Example: Rumford 2

To illustrate the geometry of nonlinear models, consider the two cases $t = 4$ and $t = 41$ for the Rumford data. Under the assumption that Newton's law of cooling holds for these data, the expected responses are

$$\eta(\theta) = \begin{bmatrix} 60 + 70e^{-4\theta} \\ 60 + 70e^{-41\theta} \end{bmatrix} \quad \theta \geq 0$$

Substituting values for θ in these equations and plotting the points in a 2-dimensional response space gives the 1-dimensional expectation surface (curve) shown in Figure 2.3.

Note that the expectation surface is *curved* and of *finite extent*, which is in contrast to the linear model in which the expectation surface is a plane of infinite extent. Note, too, that points with equal spacing on the parameter line (θ) map to points with unequal spacing on the expectation surface. ∎

Example: Puromycin 3
As another example, consider the three cases from Example Puromycin 1: $x = 1.10$, $x = 0.56$, and $x = 0.22$. Under the assumption that the expectation function (2.3) is the correct one, the expected responses for these substrate values are

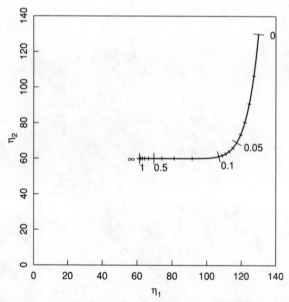

Figure 2.3 Plot of the expectation surface (solid line) in the response space for the 2-case Rumford data. The points corresponding to $\theta = 0, 0.01, 0.02, \ldots, 0.1, 0.2, \ldots, 1, \infty$ are marked.

$$\eta(\theta) = \begin{bmatrix} \dfrac{\theta_1(1.10)}{\theta_2 + 1.10} \\[2mm] \dfrac{\theta_1(0.56)}{\theta_2 + 0.56} \\[2mm] \dfrac{\theta_1(0.22)}{\theta_2 + 0.22} \end{bmatrix} \qquad \theta_1, \theta_2 \geq 0$$

and so we can plot the expectation surface by substituting values for θ in these equations. A portion of the 2-dimensional expectation surface for these x values is shown in Figure 2.4. Again, in contrast to the linear model, this expectation surface is not an infinite plane, and in general, straight lines in the parameter plane do not map to straight lines on the expectation surface. It is also seen that unit squares in the parameter plane map to irregularly shaped areas on the expectation surface and that the sizes of these areas vary. Thus, the Jacobian determinant is not constant, which can be seen analytically, of course, because the derivatives (2.4) depend on θ.

For this model, there are straight lines on the expectation surface in Figure 2.4 corresponding to the θ_1 parameter lines (lines with θ_2 held con-

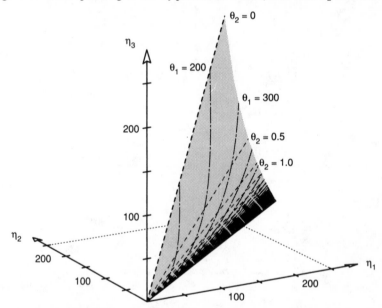

Figure 2.4 Expectation surface for the 3-case Puromycin example. We show a portion of the expectation surface (shaded) in the expectation space with θ_1 parameter lines (dashed) and θ_2 parameter lines (dot–dashed).

stant), reflecting the fact that θ_1 is conditionally linear. However, the θ_1 parameter lines are neither parallel nor equispaced. The θ_2 lines are not straight, parallel, or equispaced. ■

As can be seen from these examples, for nonlinear models with P parameters, it is generally true that:

(1) the expectation surface, $\eta(\theta)$, is a P-dimensional *curved surface* in the N-dimensional response space;
(2) parameter *lines* in the parameter space map to *curves* on the curved expectation surface;
(3) the *Jacobian determinant*, which measures how large unit areas in θ become in $\eta(\theta)$, is *not constant*.

We explore these interesting and important aspects of the expectation surface later, but first we discuss how to obtain the least squares estimates $\hat{\theta}$ for the parameters θ. Nonlinear least squares estimation from the point of view of sum of squares contours is given in Section 2.4.

2.2   Determining the Least Squares Estimates

The problem of finding the least squares estimates can be stated very simply geometrically—given a data vector $\mathbf{y}$, an expectation function $f(\mathbf{x}_n, \theta)$, and a set of design vectors $\mathbf{x}_n$, $n = 1, \ldots, N$

(1) find the point $\hat{\eta}$ on the expectation surface which is closest to $\mathbf{y}$, and then
(2) determine the parameter vector $\hat{\theta}$ which corresponds to the point $\hat{\eta}$.

For a linear model, step (1) is straightforward because the expectation surface is a plane of infinite extent, and we may write down an explicit expression for the point on that plane which is closest to $\mathbf{y}$,

$$\hat{\eta} = Q_1 Q_1^T \mathbf{y}$$

For a linear model, step (2) is also straightforward because the P-dimensional parameter plane maps linearly and invertibly to the expectation plane, so once we know where we are on one plane we can easily find the corresponding point on the other. Thus

$$\hat{\beta} = R_1^{-1} Q_1^T \hat{\eta}$$

In the nonlinear case, however, the two steps are very difficult: the first because the expectation surface is curved and often of finite extent (or, at least, has edges) so that it is difficult even to find $\hat{\eta}$, and the second because we can map points easily only in one direction—from the parameter plane to the expectation surface. That is, even if we know $\hat{\boldsymbol{\eta}}$, it is extremely difficult to determine the parameter plane coordinates $\hat{\boldsymbol{\theta}}$ corresponding to that point. To overcome these difficulties, we use iterative methods to determine the least squares estimates.

2.2.1   The Gauss–Newton Method

An approach suggested by Gauss is to use a linear approximation to the expectation function to iteratively improve an initial guess $\boldsymbol{\theta}^0$ for $\boldsymbol{\theta}$ and keep improving the estimates until there is no change. That is, we expand the expectation function $f(\mathbf{x}_n, \boldsymbol{\theta})$ in a first order Taylor series about $\boldsymbol{\theta}^0$ as

$$f(\mathbf{x}_n, \boldsymbol{\theta}) \approx f(\mathbf{x}_n, \boldsymbol{\theta}^0) + v_{n1}(\theta_1 - \theta_1^0) + v_{n2}(\theta_2 - \theta_2^0) + \cdots + v_{nP}(\theta_P - \theta_P^0)$$

where

$$v_{np} = \left. \frac{\partial f(\mathbf{x}_n, \boldsymbol{\theta})}{\partial \theta_p} \right|_{\theta^0} \qquad p = 1, 2, \ldots, P$$

Incorporating all N cases, we write

$$\boldsymbol{\eta}(\boldsymbol{\theta}) \approx \boldsymbol{\eta}(\boldsymbol{\theta}^0) + \mathbf{V}^0(\boldsymbol{\theta} - \boldsymbol{\theta}^0) \tag{2.6}$$

where $\mathbf{V}^0$ is the $N \times P$ derivative matrix with elements $\{v_{np}\}$. This is equivalent to approximating the residuals, $\mathbf{z}(\boldsymbol{\theta}) = \mathbf{y} - \boldsymbol{\eta}(\boldsymbol{\theta})$, by

$$\mathbf{z}(\boldsymbol{\theta}) \approx \mathbf{y} - [\boldsymbol{\eta}(\boldsymbol{\theta}^0) + \mathbf{V}^0 \boldsymbol{\delta}] = \mathbf{z}^0 - \mathbf{V}^0 \boldsymbol{\delta} \tag{2.7}$$

where $\mathbf{z}^0 = \mathbf{y} - \boldsymbol{\eta}(\boldsymbol{\theta}^0)$ and $\boldsymbol{\delta} = \boldsymbol{\theta} - \boldsymbol{\theta}^0$.

We then calculate the *Gauss increment* $\boldsymbol{\delta}^0$ to minimize the approximate residual sum of squares $\| \mathbf{z}^0 - \mathbf{V}^0 \boldsymbol{\delta} \|^2$, using

$$\mathbf{V}^0 = \mathbf{QR} = \mathbf{Q}_1 \mathbf{R}_1 \qquad [\text{cf. (1.19)}]$$

$$\mathbf{w}_1 = \mathbf{Q}_1^{\mathrm{T}} \mathbf{z}^0 \qquad [\text{cf. (1.21)}]$$

$$\hat{\boldsymbol{\eta}}^1 = \mathbf{Q}_1 \mathbf{w}_1 \qquad [\text{cf. (1.23)}]$$

and so

$$\mathbf{R}_1 \boldsymbol{\delta}^0 = \mathbf{w}_1 \qquad [\text{cf. (1.24)}]$$

The point

$$\hat{\boldsymbol{\eta}}^1 = \boldsymbol{\eta}(\boldsymbol{\theta}^1) = \boldsymbol{\eta}(\boldsymbol{\theta}^0 + \boldsymbol{\delta}^0)$$

should now be closer to $\mathbf{y}$ than $\boldsymbol{\eta}(\boldsymbol{\theta}^0)$, and so we move to this better parameter value $\boldsymbol{\theta}^1 = \boldsymbol{\theta}^0 + \boldsymbol{\delta}^0$ and perform another iteration by calculating new residuals $\mathbf{z}^1 = \mathbf{y} - \boldsymbol{\eta}(\boldsymbol{\theta}^1)$, a new derivative matrix $\mathbf{V}^1$, and a new increment. This process is repeated until convergence is obtained, that is, until the increment is so small that there is no useful change in the elements of the parameter vector.

Example: Puromycin 4

To illustrate these calculations, consider the data from Example Puromycin 1, with the starting estimates $\theta^0 = (205, 0.08)^T$. The data, along with the fitted values, residuals, and derivatives evaluated at θ^0, are shown in Table 2.1.

Collecting these derivatives into the derivative matrix V^0, we then perform a QR decomposition, from which we generate $w_1 = Q_1^T z^0$ and then solve for δ^0 using $R_1 \delta^0 = w_1$. In this case, $\delta^0 = (8.03, -0.017)^T$ and the sum of squares at $\theta^1 = \theta^0 + \delta^0$ is $S(\theta^1) = 1206$, which is much smaller than $S(\theta^0) = 3155$. We therefore move to $\theta^1 = (213.03, 0.063)^T$ and perform another iteration. ■

Example: BOD 1

As a second example, we consider data on biochemical oxygen demand (BOD) from Marske (1967), reproduced in Appendix 1, Section A1.4. The data are plotted in Figure 2.5. For these data, the model

$$f(x, \theta) = \theta_1 (1 - e^{-\theta_2 x}) \tag{2.8}$$

is considered appropriate.

Using the starting estimates $\theta^0 = (20, 0.24)^T$, for which $S(\theta^0) = 128.2$, produces an increment to $\theta^1 = (13.61, 0.52)^T$ with $S(\theta^1) = 145.2$. In this case, the sum of squares has increased and so we must modify the increment as discussed below. ■

Table 2.1 Residuals and derivatives for Puromycin data at $\theta = (205, 0.08)^T$.

n	x_n	y_n	η_n^0	z_n^0	v_{n1}^0	v_{n2}^0
1	0.02	76	41.00	35.00	0.2000	-410.00
2	0.02	47	41.00	6.00	0.2000	-410.00
3	0.06	97	87.86	9.14	0.4286	-627.55
4	0.06	107	87.86	19.14	0.4286	-627.55
5	0.11	123	118.68	4.32	0.5789	-624.65
6	0.11	139	118.68	20.32	0.5789	-624.65
7	0.22	159	150.33	8.67	0.7333	-501.11
8	0.22	152	150.33	1.67	0.7333	-501.11
9	0.56	191	179.38	11.62	0.8750	-280.27
10	0.56	201	179.38	21.62	0.8750	-280.27
11	1.10	207	191.10	15.90	0.9322	-161.95
12	1.10	200	191.10	8.90	0.9322	-161.95

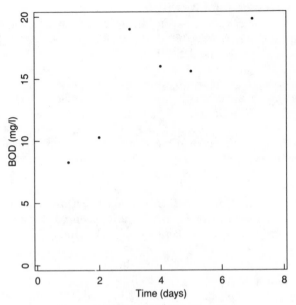

Figure 2.5   Plot of BOD versus time

2.2.1.1   Step Factor

As seen in the last example, the Gauss–Newton increment can produce an *increase* in the sum of squares when the requested increment extends beyond the region where the linear approximation is valid. Even in these circumstances, however, the linear approximation will be a close approximation to the actual surface for a sufficiently small region around $\eta(\theta^0)$. Thus a small step in the direction δ^0 should produce a decrease in the sum of squares. We therefore introduce a *step factor* λ, and calculate

$$\theta^1 = \theta^0 + \lambda\delta^0$$

where λ is chosen to ensure that

$$S(\theta^1) < S(\theta^0) \qquad (2.9)$$

A common method of selecting λ is to start with $\lambda = 1$ and halve it until (2.9) is satisfied. This modification to the Gauss–Newton algorithm was suggested in Box (1960) and Hartley (1961).

Example: BOD 2

For the data and starting estimates in Example BOD 1, the value $\lambda = 0.5$ gave a reduced sum of squares, 94.2, at $\theta = (16.80, 0.38)^T$.   ■

Pseudocode for the Gauss–Newton algorithm for nonlinear least squares is given in Appendix 3, Section A3.1, together with implementations in GAUSS™, S, and SAS/IML™.

2.2.2 The Geometry of Nonlinear Least Squares

Geometrically a Gauss–Newton iteration consists of:

(1) approximating $\eta(\theta)$ by a Taylor series expansion at $\eta^0 = \eta(\theta^0)$,
(2) generating the residual vector $z^0 = y - \eta^0$,
(3) projecting the residual z^0 onto the tangent plane to give $\hat{\eta}^1$,
(4) mapping $\hat{\eta}^1$ through the linear coordinate system to produce the increment δ^0, and finally
(5) moving to $\eta(\theta^0 + \lambda \delta^0)$.

The first step actually involves two distinct approximations:

(1) the *planar* assumption, in which we approximate the expectation surface $\eta(\theta)$ near $\eta(\theta^0)$ by its tangent plane at $\eta(\theta^0)$, and
(2) the *uniform coordinate* assumption, in which we impose a linear coordinate system $V(\theta - \theta^0)$ on the approximating tangent plane.

We give geometrical interpretations of these steps and assumptions in the following examples.

Example: Rumford 3

For the 2-case Rumford data set of Example Rumford 2, we plot y and a portion of the expectation surface in Figure 2.6. The expectation surface is a curved line, and the points corresponding to $\theta = 0.01, 0.02, \ldots, 0.2$ are unevenly spaced.

For the initial estimate $\theta^0 = 0.05$, a Gauss–Newton iteration involves the linear approximation

$$\eta(\theta) \approx \eta^0 + v\delta$$

where $\delta = (\theta - 0.05)$, η^0 is the expectation vector at $\theta = 0.05$,

$$\eta^0 = \begin{bmatrix} 60 + 70e^{-4\theta} \\ 60 + 70e^{-41\theta} \end{bmatrix} = \begin{bmatrix} 117.31 \\ 69.01 \end{bmatrix}$$

and v is the derivative vector at $\theta = 0.05$,

$$v = \begin{bmatrix} -70(4)e^{-4\theta} \\ -70(41)e^{-41\theta} \end{bmatrix} = \begin{bmatrix} -229.25 \\ -369.47 \end{bmatrix}$$

The Taylor series approximation, consisting of the tangent plane and the linear coordinate system, is shown as a solid line in Figure 2.6. This replaces the curved expectation surface with the nonlinear parameter coordinates by a linear surface with a uniform coordinate system on it.

Next we use linear least squares to obtain the point $\hat{\eta}^1$ on the tangent line which is closest to y. We then calculate the *apparent* parameter incre-

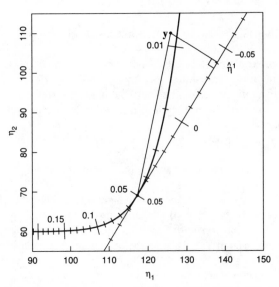

Figure 2.6 A geometric interpretation of calculation of the Gauss–Newton increment using the 2-case Rumford data. A portion of the expectation surface (heavy solid line) is shown in the response space together with the observed response **y**. Also shown is the projection $\hat{\boldsymbol{\eta}}^1$ of $\mathbf{y} - \boldsymbol{\eta}(0.05)$ onto the tangent plane at $\boldsymbol{\eta}(0.05)$ (solid line). The tick marks indicate true positions on the expectation surface and linear approximation positions on the tangent plane.

ment δ^0 corresponding to $\hat{\boldsymbol{\eta}}^1$ and from this obtain $\theta^1 = \theta^0 + \delta^0$. For this example,

$$\mathbf{z}^0 = \begin{bmatrix} 126 \\ 110 \end{bmatrix} - \begin{bmatrix} 117.31 \\ 69.01 \end{bmatrix} = \begin{bmatrix} 8.69 \\ 40.99 \end{bmatrix}$$

so $\hat{\boldsymbol{\eta}}^1 = (138.1, 102.5)^T$, $\delta^0 = -0.091$, and $\theta^1 = 0.05 - 0.091 = -0.041$.

It is clear that the linear approximation increment is too large, since $\theta^1 = -0.041$, whereas we can see from the points on the expectation surface that $\hat{\theta}$ is near 0.01. We must therefore use a step factor to reduce the increment before proceeding. ■

Example: Puromycin 5

For a two parameter example, we consider the data and the starting values from Example Puromycin 4. Since the response space is 12-dimensional, we cannot picture it directly, but we can represent the salient features in the 3-dimensional space spanned by the tangent plane and the residual vector. We do this in Figure 2.7, where we show a portion of the curved expectation surface, the residual vector, and the approximating tangent plane. It can be seen that the expectation surface is only slightly curved, and so is

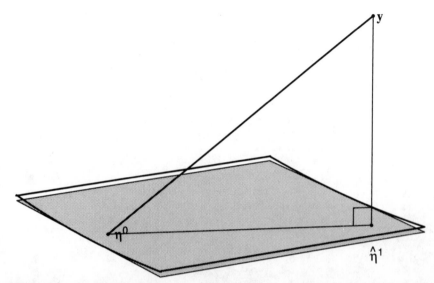

Figure 2.7 A geometric interpretation of calculation of the Gauss–Newton increment using the full Puromycin data set. We show the projection of a portion of the expectation surface into the subspace spanned by the tangent plane at $\boldsymbol{\eta}^0$ (shaded) and the residual vector $\mathbf{y} - \boldsymbol{\eta}^0$. The region on the expectation surface is bordered by the heavy solid lines. Also shown is the projection $\hat{\boldsymbol{\eta}}^1$ of the residual vector onto the tangent plane.

well approximated by the tangent plane.

In Figure 2.8a we show the parameter curves for $\theta_1 = 200, 210, 220, 230$ and $\theta_2 = 0.06, 0.07, \ldots, 0.1$ projected onto the tangent plane, and in Figure 2.8b the corresponding linear approximation lines on the tangent plane. It can be seen that the linear approximation lines match the true parameter curves very well. Also shown on the tangent planes are the points $\boldsymbol{\eta}^0$ and $\hat{\boldsymbol{\eta}}^1$, and in Figure 2.8a the projection of the curve $\boldsymbol{\eta}(\boldsymbol{\theta}^0 + \lambda \boldsymbol{\delta}^0)$ for $0 \leq \lambda \leq 1$. The points corresponding to $\lambda = 0.25, 0.5$, and 1 $(\boldsymbol{\eta}^1)$ are marked.

Because the planar and uniform coordinate assumptions are both valid, the points $\hat{\boldsymbol{\eta}}^1$ and $\boldsymbol{\eta}^1$ are close together and are much closer to $\mathbf{y}$ than $\boldsymbol{\eta}^0$. In this case, a full step $(\lambda = 1)$ can be taken resulting in a decrease in the sum of squares as shown in Example Puromycin 4. ∎

Example: BOD 3

As a second two-parameter example, we consider the data and starting values from Example BOD 1. In Figure 2.9 we show a portion of the curved expectation surface, the residual vector, and the approximating tangent plane in the space spanned by the tangent plane and the residual vector. It can be seen that the expectation surface is moderately curved, but is still apparently well approximated by the tangent plane. In this ex-

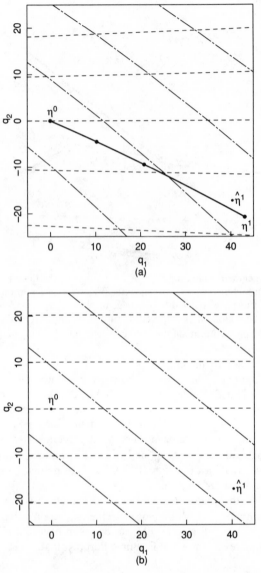

Figure 2.8 A geometric interpretation of calculation of the Gauss–Newton increment using the full Puromycin data set (continued). The points $\boldsymbol{\eta}^0$ and $\hat{\boldsymbol{\eta}}^1$ are shown in the tangent planes together with the parameter curves in part a and the linear approximation parameter lines in part b. In part a we also show the projection $\boldsymbol{\eta}^1$ of the point $\boldsymbol{\eta}(\boldsymbol{\theta}^0 + \boldsymbol{\delta}^0)$. The curve (heavy solid line) joining $\boldsymbol{\eta}^0$ to $\boldsymbol{\eta}^1$ is the projection of $\boldsymbol{\eta}(\boldsymbol{\theta}^0 + \lambda\boldsymbol{\delta}^0)$ for $0 \le \lambda \le 1$. The points corresponding to $\lambda = 0.25$ and 0.5 are marked.

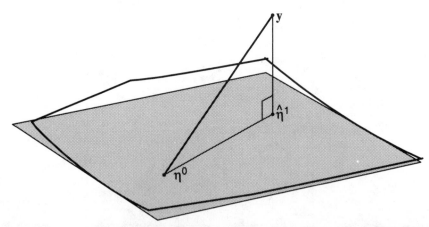

Figure 2.9 A geometric interpretation of calculation of the Gauss–Newton increment using the BOD data set. We show the projection of a portion of the expectation surface into the subspace spanned by the tangent plane at $\boldsymbol{\eta}^0$ (shaded) and the residual vector $\mathbf{y} - \boldsymbol{\eta}^0$. The region on the expectation surface is bordered by the heavy solid lines. Also shown is the projection $\hat{\boldsymbol{\eta}}^1$ of the residual vector onto the tangent plane.

ample, the edge of the finite expectation surface is shown as the angled solid line along the top edge of the surface.

In Figure 2.10*a* we show the parameter curves for $\theta_1 = 20, 30, \ldots$ and $\theta_2 = 0.2, 0.4, \ldots$ projected onto the tangent plane. In Figure 2.10*b* we show the corresponding linear approximation lines on the tangent plane. In this case, the linear approximation lines do not match the true parameter curves well at all. Also shown on the tangent planes are the points $\boldsymbol{\eta}^0$ and $\hat{\boldsymbol{\eta}}^1$, and in Figure 2.10*a* the projection of the curve $\boldsymbol{\eta}(\boldsymbol{\theta}^0 + \lambda \boldsymbol{\delta}^0)$ for $0 \le \lambda \le 1$. The points corresponding to $\lambda = 0.25, 0.5$, and 1 ($\boldsymbol{\eta}^1$) are marked.

Because the uniform coordinate assumption is not valid this far from $\boldsymbol{\theta}^0$, the points $\hat{\boldsymbol{\eta}}^1$ and $\boldsymbol{\eta}^1$ are widely separated, and in fact $\boldsymbol{\eta}^1$ is farther from $\hat{\boldsymbol{\eta}}^1$ than is $\boldsymbol{\eta}^0$. In this case, the reduced step, $\lambda = 0.5$, is successful, as was shown in Example BOD 2. ■

To summarize, geometrically we are using local information to generate a tangent plane with a linear coordinate system dictated by the derivative vectors, projecting the residual vector onto that tangent plane, and then mapping the tangent plane coordinates to the parameter plane using the linear mapping.

2.2.3 Convergence

We have indicated that the Gauss–Newton iterative method is continued until the values of $\boldsymbol{\theta}$ on successive iterations stabilize. This can be measured by the size of each parameter increment relative to the previous parameter value, which

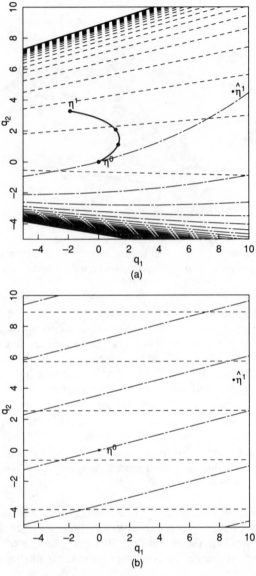

Figure 2.10 A geometric interpretation of calculation of the Gauss–Newton increment using the BOD data set (continued). The points $\boldsymbol{\eta}^0$ and $\hat{\boldsymbol{\eta}}^1$ are shown in the tangent planes together with the parameter curves in part a and the linear approximation parameter lines in part b. In part a we also show the projection $\boldsymbol{\eta}^1$ of the point $\boldsymbol{\eta}(\theta^0 + \boldsymbol{\delta}^0)$. The curve (heavy solid line) joining $\boldsymbol{\eta}^0$ to $\boldsymbol{\eta}^1$ is the projection of $\boldsymbol{\eta}(\theta^0 + \lambda\boldsymbol{\delta}^0)$ for $0 \leq \lambda \leq 1$. The points corresponding to $\lambda = 0.25$ and 0.5 are marked.

is the basis for one of the common criteria used to declare convergence (Bard, 1974; Draper and Smith, 1981; Jennrich and Sampson, 1968; Kennedy and Gentle, 1980; Ralston and Jennrich, 1978). Another criterion for convergence used, for example, in SAS (SAS Institute Inc., 1985), is that the relative change in the sum of squares on successive iterations be small. Himmelblau (1972) recommends that both these criteria be used, since compliance with one does not imply compliance with the other. However, compliance even with both relative change criteria does not guarantee convergence, as discussed in Bates and Watts (1981b). Kennedy and Gentle (1980) mention a relative step size criterion as well as relative change in the sum of squares and gradient size criteria. Chambers (1977) quotes several other criteria, including the size of the gradient, the size of the Gauss–Newton step, and the fact that the residual vector should be orthogonal to the derivative vectors; but no scale is suggested.

The main criticism of these criteria is that they indicate lack of progress rather than convergence. In most cases, of course, lack of progress occurs because a minimum is encountered: nevertheless, situations can occur where the parameter increment and sum of squares convergence criteria indicate lack of progress and yet a minimum has not been reached.

Examination of the geometry of nonlinear least squares provides a better procedure for determining convergence (Bates and Watts, 1981b). We know that a critical point is reached whenever the residual vector $\mathbf{y} - \boldsymbol{\eta}(\boldsymbol{\theta})$ is orthogonal to the expectation surface and therefore to the tangent plane to the expectation surface at $\boldsymbol{\eta}(\boldsymbol{\theta})$. We can thus adopt orthogonality of the residual vector to the tangent plane as a convergence criterion.

In practice, it would be unusual to obtain exact orthogonality in the presence of numerical roundoff, and we do not want to waste effort calculating small changes in the parameter vector while trying to achieve perfect orthogonality. We therefore need to establish a *tolerance level* which we can use to declare the residual vector to be "sufficiently orthogonal." One way to do this is to consider the statistical variability in the least squares estimates.

If we assume that the tangent plane forms a good approximation to the expectation surface near $\hat{\boldsymbol{\theta}}$, so a likelihood region for $\boldsymbol{\theta}$ roughly corresponds to a disk on the tangent plane with a radius proportional to $\sqrt{S(\hat{\boldsymbol{\theta}})}$, then we can measure the relative offset of the current parameter values from the exact least squares estimates by calculating the ratio of the length of the component of the residual vector in the tangent plane to $\sqrt{S(\hat{\boldsymbol{\theta}})}$. When this ratio is small, the numerical uncertainty of the least squares estimates is negligible compared to the statistical uncertainty of the parameters.

Unfortunately, this criterion involves the unknown least squares vector $\hat{\boldsymbol{\theta}}$. We therefore modify the criterion by substituting the current estimate, $\boldsymbol{\theta}^i$, for $\hat{\boldsymbol{\theta}}$, and measure the scaled length of the tangent plane component of the residual vector relative to the scaled length of the orthogonal component of the residual vector at $\boldsymbol{\theta}^i$. This leads to a *relative offset convergence criterion*

$$\frac{\| \mathbf{Q}_1^T (\mathbf{y} - \mathbf{\eta}(\mathbf{\theta}^i)) \| / \sqrt{P}}{\| \mathbf{Q}_2^T (\mathbf{y} - \mathbf{\eta}(\mathbf{\theta}^i)) \| / \sqrt{N-P}} \qquad (2.10)$$

where $\mathbf{Q}_1$ and $\mathbf{Q}_2$ are the first P and last $N-P$ columns respectively of the matrix $\mathbf{Q}$ from a QR decomposition of $\mathbf{V}$. The criterion is related to the cotangent of the angle that the residual vector makes with the tangent plane, so that a small relative offset corresponds to an angle near 90°.

To declare convergence, we require the relative offset to be less than 0.001, reasoning that any inferences will not be affected materially by the fact that the current parameter vector is less than 0.1% of the radius of the confidence region disk from the least squares point.

Example: Rumford 4

We illustrate the convergence criterion and its development with the 2-observation Rumford example. We wish to test whether the parameter value $\theta = 0.01$ could be considered a point of convergence. Figure 2.11 shows a portion of the expectation surface, the observation point $\mathbf{y}$, and the tangent plane at $\mathbf{\eta}(0.01)$. Also shown is the component of the residual vector in the tangent plane, $\mathbf{Q}_1^T \mathbf{z}$, and the component orthogonal to the tangent plane, $\mathbf{Q}_2^T \mathbf{z}$. The tangent plane component is large relative to the orthogo-

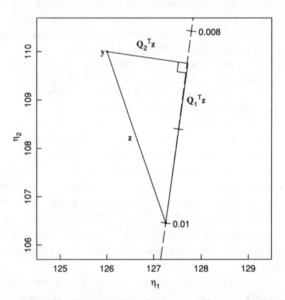

Figure 2.11 A geometric interpretation of relative offset using the 2-case Rumford data. A portion of the expectation surface (dashed line) is shown in the expectation space together with the residual vector $\mathbf{z}$ and its projections into the tangent plane ($\mathbf{Q}_1^T \mathbf{z}$) and orthogonal to the tangent plane ($\mathbf{Q}_2^T \mathbf{z}$).

nal component, having a relative offset of 1.92, and so we conclude that the residual vector at $\theta = 0.01$ is not sufficiently orthogonal for us to accept $\theta = 0.01$ as the converged value. ■

Convergence implies that the best estimates of the parameters have been obtained, under the assumption that the model is adequate. Before characterizing the precision of the estimates using inference intervals or regions, therefore, we should check the residuals for signs of model inadequacy. A complete discussion of the practical aspects of nonlinear regression is given in Chapter 3, but in the interests of completeness in analyzing the Puromycin and BOD data, we simply plot the residuals versus the fitted values and using probability plots before continuing.

Example: Puromycin 6
Convergence for the Puromycin data was declared at $\hat{\theta} = (212.7, 0.0641)^T$, with $s^2 = 119.5$ on 10 degrees of freedom. Studentized residuals from the least squares fit are plotted in Figure 2.12 versus fitted values in part a and as a normal probability plot in part b. Although there is one relatively large residual, the overall fit appears adequate, and so we proceed to develop parameter inference regions. ■

Example: BOD 4
Convergence for the BOD data was declared at $\hat{\theta} = (19.143, 0.5311)^T$, with $s^2 = 6.498$ on 4 degrees of freedom. Studentized residuals from the least squares fit are plotted in Figure 2.13 versus fitted values in part a and as a normal probability plot in part b. Since the residuals are well behaved, we proceed to develop parameter inference regions. ■

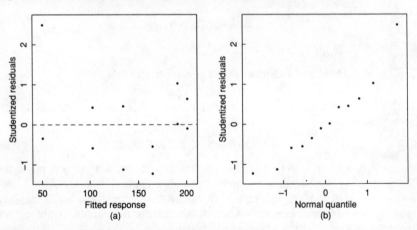

Figure 2.12 Studentized residuals for the Puromycin data plotted versus fitted values in part a and versus normal quantiles in part b.

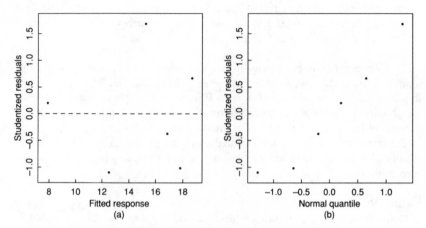

Figure 2.13 Studentized residuals for the BOD data plotted versus fitted values in part *a* and versus normal quantiles in part *b*.

2.3 Nonlinear Regression Inference Using the Linear Approximation

In the Gauss–Newton algorithm for calculating $\hat{\boldsymbol{\theta}}$, the derivative matrix $\mathbf{V}$ is evaluated at each iteration and used to calculate the increment and the convergence criterion. It is natural, then, to apply the linear approximation to *inference* for nonlinear models with the derivative matrix evaluated at the least squares parameter estimates. This yields approximate likelihood, confidence, or Bayesian HPD regions, based on

$$\boldsymbol{\eta}(\boldsymbol{\theta}) = \boldsymbol{\eta}(\hat{\boldsymbol{\theta}}) + \hat{\mathbf{V}}(\boldsymbol{\theta} - \hat{\boldsymbol{\theta}}) \qquad (2.11)$$

2.3.1 Approximate Inference Regions for Parameters

Recall that in the linear case, a $1 - \alpha$ parameter inference region can be expressed as [cf. (1.9)]

$$(\boldsymbol{\beta} - \hat{\boldsymbol{\beta}})^{T}\mathbf{X}^{T}\mathbf{X}(\boldsymbol{\beta} - \hat{\boldsymbol{\beta}}) \leq Ps^2 F(P, N-P; \alpha) \qquad (2.12)$$

Geometrically this region results because the expectation surface is a plane and the residual vector is orthogonal to that plane, so the region of plausible values on the expectation plane is a disk. Taking the disk through the linear mapping relating points on the expectation plane to points on the parameter plane, then maps the disk to an ellipsoid on the parameter plane.

Approximate inference regions for a nonlinear model are defined, by analogy with equation (2.12), as

$$(\boldsymbol{\theta} - \hat{\boldsymbol{\theta}})^T \hat{\mathbf{V}}^T \hat{\mathbf{V}} (\boldsymbol{\theta} - \hat{\boldsymbol{\theta}}) \leq P s^2 F(P, N-P; \alpha) \qquad (2.13)$$

or equivalently

$$(\boldsymbol{\theta} - \hat{\boldsymbol{\theta}})^T \hat{\mathbf{R}}_1^T \hat{\mathbf{R}}_1 (\boldsymbol{\theta} - \hat{\boldsymbol{\theta}}) \leq P s^2 F(P, N-P; \alpha) \qquad (2.14)$$

where the derivative matrix $\hat{\mathbf{V}} = \hat{\mathbf{Q}}_1 \hat{\mathbf{R}}_1$ is evaluated at $\hat{\boldsymbol{\theta}}$. The boundary of this inference region (2.14) is [cf. (1.28)]

$$\{\boldsymbol{\theta} = \hat{\boldsymbol{\theta}} + \sqrt{P s^2 F(P, N-P; \alpha)} \; \hat{\mathbf{R}}_1^{-1} \mathbf{d} \mid \; \|\mathbf{d}\| = 1\} \qquad (2.15)$$

Similarly, the approximate standard error for θ_p is s times the length of the pth row of $\hat{\mathbf{R}}_1^{-1}$ [cf. (1.33)]. Approximate correlations and standard errors for the parameters are easily calculated by factoring $\hat{\mathbf{R}}_1^{-1}$ into a diagonal matrix [cf. (1.34)] giving the lengths of the rows of $\hat{\mathbf{R}}^{-1}$ and a matrix with unit length rows as described in Section 1.2.3. The parameter approximate correlation matrix is calculated as in (1.35).

Example: Puromycin 7

Convergence for the Puromycin data was declared at $\hat{\boldsymbol{\theta}} = (212.7, 0.0641)^T$, with $s^2 = 119.5$ on 10 degrees of freedom and

$$\hat{\mathbf{R}}_1 = \begin{bmatrix} -2.4441 & 1568.7 \\ 0 & 1320.3 \end{bmatrix}$$

The 95 and 99% approximate joint inference regions were obtained by evaluating (2.15) with $\mathbf{d} = (\cos \omega, \sin \omega)^T$ and are plotted in Figure 2.14. To calculate approximate marginal inference intervals, we factor

$$\hat{\mathbf{R}}_1^{-1} = \begin{bmatrix} -0.4092 & 0.4861 \\ 0 & 0.0007574 \end{bmatrix}$$

$$= \begin{bmatrix} 0.6354 & 0 \\ 0 & 0.0007574 \end{bmatrix} \begin{bmatrix} -0.6439 & 0.7651 \\ 0 & 1.0000 \end{bmatrix}$$

so the approximate standard errors are 6.95 and 8.28×10^{-3} and the approximate correlation between θ_1 and θ_2 is 0.77. A 95% approximate marginal inference interval for θ_2, for example, is

$$0.0641 \pm \sqrt{119.5} \, (0.0007574) \; t(10; 0.025)$$

or 0.0641 ± 0.0185. The 95% marginal inference intervals for both parameters are shown as dashed lines in Figure 2.14. ∎

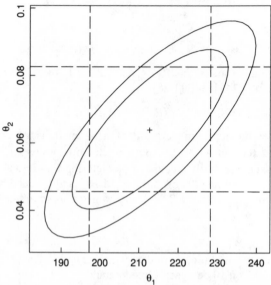

Figure 2.14 Parameter approximate inference regions for the Puromycin data. We show the least squares estimates (+), the parameter joint 95 and 99% inference regions (solid lines), and the marginal 95% inference intervals (dashed lines).

Example: BOD 5

Convergence for the BOD data was declared at $\hat{\boldsymbol{\theta}} = (19.143, 0.5311)^T$, with $s^2 = 6.498$ on 4 degrees of freedom and

$$\hat{\mathbf{R}}_1 = \begin{bmatrix} -1.9556 & -20.4986 \\ 0 & -12.5523 \end{bmatrix}$$

giving approximate standard errors of 2.50 and 0.203.

The 95 and 99% approximate joint inference regions are plotted in Figure 2.15 together with the 95% approximate marginal intervals. Note that the regions include negative values for θ_2, and such values are not physically meaningful. The approximate correlation between θ_1 and θ_2 is -0.85. ■

When there are more than two parameters, it is not possible to plot the joint approximate inference region, and so it is common to summarize the inferential situation by quoting the approximate marginal inference intervals and the parameter correlation matrix and by making pairwise plots of the inference region. More exact methods for summarizing the inferential situation are presented in Chapter 6.

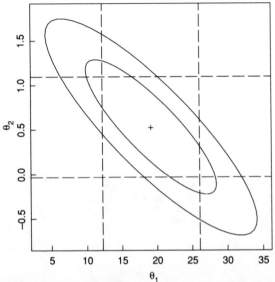

Figure 2.15 Parameter approximate inference regions for the BOD data. We show the least squares estimates (+), the parameter joint 95 and 99% inference regions (solid lines), and the marginal 95% inference intervals (dashed lines).

Example: Isomerization 1

Data on the reaction rate of the catalytic isomerization of n-pentane to isopentane versus the partial pressures of hydrogen, n-pentane, and isopentane as given in Carr (1960) are presented in Appendix 1, Section A1.5, and plotted in Figure 2.16. A proposed model function for these data is

$$f(\mathbf{x},\boldsymbol{\theta}) = \frac{\theta_1\theta_3(x_2 - x_3/1.632)}{1 + \theta_2 x_1 + \theta_3 x_2 + \theta_4 x_3}$$

Parameter estimates and summary statistics are given in Table 2.2, and residual plots versus the partial pressures and the fitted values in Figure 2.17. The plots show the residuals are generally well behaved. The summary statistics suggest potential difficulties, since some of the correlations are extremely high and some of the standard errors produce approximate 95% intervals which include negative values, but the parameters must be positive to be physically meaningful. The pairwise plots of the parameter approximate 95% inference region, given in Figure 2.18, clearly extend into negative parameter regions. ■

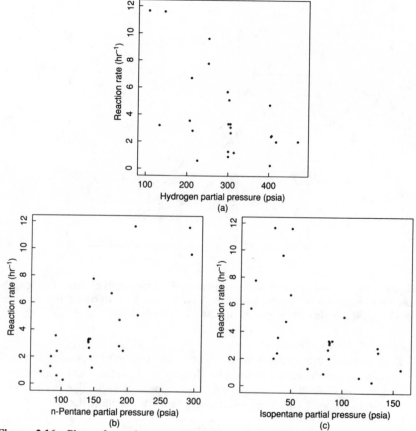

Figure 2.16 Plots of reaction rate of the isomerization of n-pentane to isopentane versus the partial pressures of hydrogen in part a, n-pentane in part b, and isopentane in part c.

Table 2.2 Parameter summary for the isomerization data.

Parameter	Estimate	Standard Error	Approximate Correlation Matrix			
θ_1	35.92	8.21	1.000			
θ_2	0.0708	0.1783	−0.805	1.000		
θ_3	0.0377	0.0998	−0.840	0.998	1.000	
θ_4	0.167	0.415	−0.790	0.998	0.995	1.000

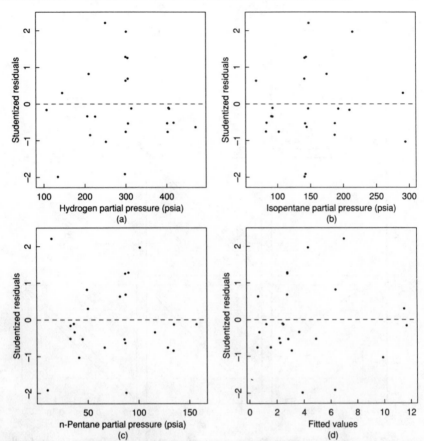

Figure 2.17 Studentized residuals for the isomerization data are plotted versus the partial pressures of hydrogen in part a, isopentane in part b, and n-pentane in part c, and versus the fitted values in part d.

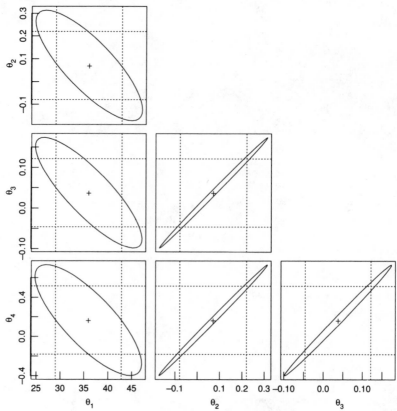

Figure 2.18 Pairwise plots of the parameter approximate 95% inference region for the isomerization data. For each pair of parameters we show the least squares estimates (+), the parameter approximate joint 95% inference region (solid line), and the approximate marginal 95% inference intervals (dotted lines).

2.3.2 Approximate Inference Bands for the Expected Response

Linear approximation inference intervals and bands for the expected response in nonlinear regression can be generated using the analogs of the equation for linear regression, (1.11) and (1.12). In those equations, we simply replace the estimated value $x_0^T \hat{\beta}$ by $f(x_0, \hat{\theta})$, the matrix X by $\hat{V}$, and the derivative vector x_0 by

$$v_0 = \left. \frac{\partial f(x_0, \theta)}{\partial \theta^T} \right|_{\hat{\theta}}$$

The $1 - \alpha$ approximate inference interval is then

$$f(\mathbf{x}_0,\hat{\boldsymbol{\theta}}) \pm s \parallel \mathbf{v}_0^T \hat{\mathbf{R}}_1^{-1} \parallel t(N-P;\alpha/2) \qquad \text{[cf. (1.36)]}$$

and the $1-\alpha$ approximate inference band is

$$f(\mathbf{x},\hat{\boldsymbol{\theta}}) \pm s \parallel \mathbf{v}^T \hat{\mathbf{R}}_1^{-1} \parallel \sqrt{P\,F(P,N-P;\alpha)} \qquad \text{[cf. (1.37)]}$$

Example: Puromycin 8

For the Puromycin data, the estimated response at $x = 0.4$ is 183.3 and the derivative vector is $\mathbf{v} = (0.8618, -394.9)^T$, so that, using $\hat{\mathbf{R}}_1^{-1}$ from Example Puromycin 6, $\mathbf{v}^T \hat{\mathbf{R}}_1^{-1} = (-0.3526, 0.1198)$. The inference band at $x = 0.4$ is then $(171.6, 195.0)$. A plot of the approximate 95% inference band is given in Figure 2.19. The band gradually widens from zero width at $x = 0$ to a constant width as $x \to \infty$. ∎

Example: BOD 6

The estimated response function for the BOD data and the approximate 95% inference band is plotted in Figure 2.20. The band widens from zero width at $x = 0$, narrows around $x = 4$ and then gradually approaches a constant width as $x \to \infty$. ∎

Inference bands for nonlinear models behave quite differently from those for linear models. In the above examples, because the functions are constrained

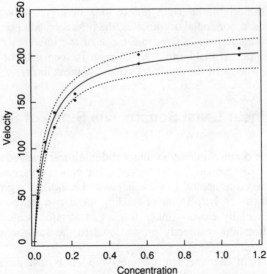

Figure 2.19 Approximate 95% inference band for the Puromycin data. The fitted expectation function is shown as a solid line, and the 95% inference band is shown as a pair of dotted lines.

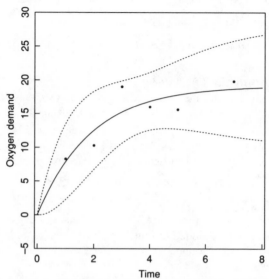

Figure 2.20   Approximate 95% inference band for the BOD data. The fitted expectation function is shown as a solid line, and the 95% inference band is shown as a pair of dotted lines.

to go through the origin, the bands reduce to 0 there. Also, because the model functions approach horizontal asymptotes, the inference bands approach asymptotes. These characteristics differ from those of the inference bands for linear models as exemplified in Figure 1.3. There it is seen that the bands are narrowest near the middle of the data, and expand without limit.

2.4   Nonlinear Least Squares via Sums of Squares

Sums of squares occur explicitly in linear and nonlinear least squares because of the assumptions of normality, independence, and constant variance of the disturbances. It is therefore natural to view linear and nonlinear regression via sums of squares, which can help in understanding these two topics. The likelihood approach is especially closely linked to sum of squares contours, because the loglikelihood function is directly proportional to the sum of squares function $S(\theta)$.

An important characteristic of linear models is that the sum of squares function $S(\beta)$ is quadratic. Because of this, contours of constant sums of squares are well-behaved regular curves or surfaces, such as ellipses and ellipsoids, and so the loglikelihood function can be completely summarized by:

the minimum value of the sum of squares function, $S(\hat{\beta})$, the location of the minimum of the sum of squares function, $\hat{\beta}$, and the second derivative (Hessian) of the sum of squares function,

$$\frac{\partial^2 S(\beta)}{\partial \beta \partial \beta^T} = X^T X$$

Furthermore, all these quantities can be determined analytically. For nonlinear models, however, the sum of squares function is not regular or well behaved, and so it is difficult to summarize the loglikelihood function.

2.4.1 The Linear Approximation

Linear approximations of the expectation function are used to determine increments while seeking the least squares estimates, and to determine approximate inference regions when convergence has been achieved. The linear approximation to $\eta(\theta)$ based at θ^0, (2.6), produces a linear approximation to the residual vector $z(\theta)$, (2.7), and hence a *quadratic* approximation $\tilde{S}(\theta)$ to the sum of squares function $S(\theta)$, since

$$S(\theta) = \| y - \eta(\theta) \|^2$$

$$= z(\theta)^T z(\theta) \approx \tilde{S}(\theta)$$

$$= [z^0 - V^0(\theta - \theta^0)]^T [z^0 - V^0(\theta - \theta^0)] \qquad (2.16)$$

$$= z^{0T} z^0 - 2z^{0T} V^0(\theta - \theta^0) + (\theta - \theta^0)^T V^{0T} V^0(\theta - \theta^0)$$

$$= S(\theta^0) - 2[y - \eta(\theta^0)]^T V^0(\theta - \theta^0) + (\theta - \theta^0)^T V^{0T} V^0(\theta - \theta^0)$$

The location of the minimum of $\tilde{S}(\theta)$ is

$$\theta^1 = \theta^0 + (V^{0T} V^0)^{-1} V^{0T} z^0$$

which gives the Gauss–Newton increment.

Note that the quadratic approximation (2.16) is not the second order Taylor series approximation to $S(\theta)$ based at θ^0. The Hessian in the Taylor series approximation includes a term involving the second order partial derivatives of the model function with respect to the parameters (see Section 3.5.1).

Contours of the approximate sum of squares function (2.16) are ellipsoids centered at θ^1 and of the form

$$(\theta - \theta^1)^T V^{0T} V^0 (\theta - \theta^1) = c$$

Of particular interest is the approximating contour

$$(\theta - \theta^1)^T V^{0T} V^0 (\theta - \theta^1) = z^{0T} V^0 (V^{0T} V^0)^{-1} V^{0T} z^0$$

which passes through θ^0. If this contour is close to the actual sum of squares contour which passes through θ^0, then we can expect that θ^1 will be close to the optimal value of θ.

Example: Rumford 5

In Figure 2.21 we plot the sum of squares function, $S(\theta)$, for the Rumford data as a solid line. Superimposed on the plot is the approximating quadratic, $\tilde{S}(\theta)$, obtained by taking a linear Taylor series approximation to the expectation function at $\theta^0 = 0.02$, shown as a dashed line.

A careful examination of $S(\theta)$ shows that it is not a parabola but is asymmetric, with a steeper rise to the left of the minimum than to the right. The closeness of $S(\theta)$ to a parabola indicates the small degree of nonlinearity of this model–data set combination. The minimum of the approximating parabola is at 0.008, and so the Gauss–Newton increment is $0.008 - 0.02 = -0.012$. ■

Example: Puromycin 9

In Figure 2.22 we plot sum of squares contours, $S(\theta)$, for the Puromycin data, shown as solid lines, and the location of the minimum, shown as +. Also shown, as a dashed line, is the ellipse derived from the linear approximation to the expectation function at $\theta^0 = (205, 0.08)^T$. The approximating paraboloid has the same value and curvature at θ^0 as the true sum of squares surface, and so the location of the minimum of the paraboloid, denoted by *, is used as the apparent minimum of the true sum of squares surface. The Gauss increment is therefore the vector joining the starting point θ^0 to the point indicated by *.

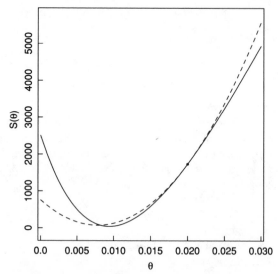

Figure 2.21 Sum of squares function for the Rumford data. The true sum of squares curve is shown as a solid line, and the parabola from the linear approximation at $\theta^0 = 0.02$ is shown as a dashed line.

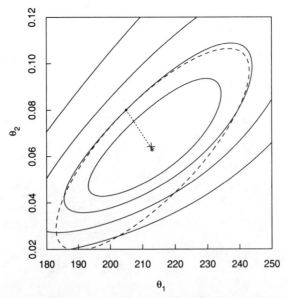

Figure 2.22 Sum of squares contours for the Puromycin data. True sum of squares contours are shown as solid lines, and the elliptical approximate contour from the linear approximation at $\boldsymbol{\theta}^0 = (205, 0.08)^T$ is shown as a dashed line. The location of the minimum sum of squares (+) and the center of the ellipse (*) are also shown. The dotted line is the Gauss–Newton increment.

Because the model–data set combination is not badly nonlinear, the sums of squares contours are quite elliptical, and the minimum of the approximating paraboloid is near the minimum of the true sum of squares surface. ∎

Example: BOD 7
In Figure 2.23 we plot sum of squares contours, $S(\boldsymbol{\theta})$, for the BOD data, shown as solid lines, and location of the minimum, shown as +. Also shown, as a dashed line, is a portion of the ellipse derived from the linear approximation to the expectation function at $\boldsymbol{\theta}^0 = (20, 0.24)^T$. The center of the ellipse is indicated by *.

In this example, the ellipse is a poor approximation to the true contour. The center of the ellipse is not close to the minimum of the true sum of squares surface and furthermore has a true sum of squares greater than that at $\boldsymbol{\theta}^0$. ∎

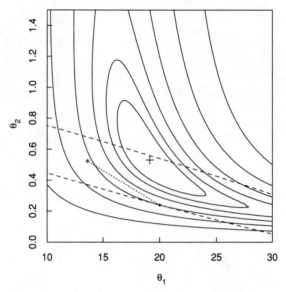

Figure 2.23   Sum of squares contours for the BOD data. True sum of squares contours are shown as solid lines, and a portion of the elliptical approximate contour from the linear approximation at $\boldsymbol{\theta}^0 = (20, 0.24)^T$ is shown as a dashed line. The location of the minimum sum of squares (+) and the center of the ellipse (*) are also shown. The dotted line is the Gauss–Newton increment.

2.4.2   Overshoot

The next iteration is carried out from the location of the apparent minimum of the sum of squares surface—provided, of course, that $S(\boldsymbol{\theta}^1)$ is less than $S(\boldsymbol{\theta}^0)$. In the Rumford example and in the Puromycin example, because the nonlinearity is moderate, the sum of squares at $\boldsymbol{\theta}^1$ is less than that at $\boldsymbol{\theta}^0$, and so we can proceed to iterate from $\boldsymbol{\theta}^1$. For the BOD example, however, the sum of squares at $\boldsymbol{\theta}^1$ is greater than that at $\boldsymbol{\theta}^0$, so we have overshot the minimum. By incorporating a step factor, so that only a fraction of the increment is used, we can find a point with a smaller sum of squares, as described in Section 2.2.1.

2.5   Use of the Linear Approximation

In this chapter we have used the linear approximation in two ways:

(1) to obtain a Gauss–Newton increment, and
(2) to obtain linear approximation inference regions.

For (1), the linear approximation is useful because the increment it generates can be checked by comparing $S(\theta^0 + \delta^0)$ to $S(\theta^0)$. If the sum of squares increases, we modify the increment with a step factor. Furthermore, the approximation is updated at each iteration.

For (2), the linear approximation provides inference regions which are easy to calculate and present for any number of parameters. However, the regions are based on only one approximation (at $\hat{\theta}$), and we cannot easily check their adequacy.

The extent to which the approximate regions adequately delineate the regions of reasonable parameter values is determined by the adequacy of the linear approximation to the expectation function. We have noted in Section 2.2.2 that the linear approximation involves two distinct components: the *planar assumption* whereby the expectation surface is approximated by the tangent plane, and the *uniform coordinate assumption* whereby the true parameter coordinate system is approximated by a uniform system. Both these aspects influence the adequacy of the approximation for inference; they are discussed more fully in Chapter 6, where we present profile likelihood methods for determining and displaying more accurate inference regions, and in Chapter 7, where we present methods for measuring nonlinearity.

We hasten to warn the reader that *linear approximation regions can be extremely misleading.*

Exercises

2.1 Write a computer routine in a language of your choice to perform nonlinear least squares using the Gauss–Newton approach. Take the function, its derivatives with respect to the parameters, and starting values as input to the routine. If necessary, use the pseudocode in Appendix 3, Section A3.1 for guidance.

2.2 Use a nonlinear least squares routine to fit a model of the form $\beta_1 + \beta_2(\text{age})^\alpha$ to the ln(PCB) data. Use starting values of $(-2.4, 2.3, 0.33)^T$ (the least squares estimates for β_1, β_2 for $\alpha = 0.33$ from Example PCB 2).

2.3 (a) Plot the expectation surface for the Rumford model, using the design $x = (7, 28)^T$. Mark the points on the expectation surface corresponding to the values $\theta = 0, 0.01, \ldots, 0.1, 0.2, \ldots, 1.0, \infty$. Compare this expectation surface with the one based on the design $x = (4, 41)^T$ plotted in Figure 2.3. Which design has smaller overall intrinsic nonlinearity? Which design has smaller overall parameter effects nonlinearity?

(b) Plot the expectation surface for the Rumford model, using the design $x = (12, 14)^T$. Mark the points on the expectation surface corresponding to the values $\theta = 0, 0.01, \ldots, 0.1, 0.2, \ldots, 1.0, \infty$. Compare this expectation surface with the one based on the design $x = (4, 41)^T$ plotted in Figure 2.3 and with that from part (a). Which design has smallest overall intrinsic nonlinearity? Which design has smallest overall parameter effects nonlinearity?

(c) What kind of design would have zero intrinsic nonlinearity everywhere? Why?

(d) Would the design in part (c) have zero parameter effects nonlinearity? Why?

2.4 (a) Plot the expectation surface for the linear model $\ln(\text{PCB}) = \beta \ln(\text{age})$ for the design age = 5, 10. Mark the points on the surface corresponding to $\beta = 0, 1, 2, 3$.

(b) Compare this expectation surface and its properties with those of the nonlinear Rumford model shown in Figure 2.3.

(c) Compare this expectation surface and its properties with those of the nonlinear Rumford model plotted in Problem 2.3.

2.5 (a) Generate the expectation vector, the residual vector, the sum of squares $S(\boldsymbol{\theta}^0)$, and the derivative matrix $\mathbf{V}^0$ for the data and model from Appendix 4, Section A4.1, at the starting values $\boldsymbol{\theta}^0 = (2.20, 0.26)^T$.

(b) Calculate the increment $\boldsymbol{\delta}^0$ and $S(\boldsymbol{\theta}^1)$, where $\boldsymbol{\theta}^1 = \boldsymbol{\theta}^0 + \lambda \boldsymbol{\delta}^0$, for $\lambda = 0.25, 0.50$, and 1.0. Is a step factor less than 1 necessary in this case?

2.6 (a) Use the fact that, for the model in Problem 2.5, θ_1 is conditionally linear, and generate and plot exact sum of squares contours for the data in Appendix 4, Section A4.1. (That is, for any specified value of θ_2, it is possible to use linear least squares to obtain the conditional estimate $\tilde{\theta}_1$ and to calculate the values of θ_1 which produce a specified sum of squares. By specifying the sum of squares to be that corresponding to a contour value, it is possible to generate the exact coordinates of points on the contour.) Let θ_2 go from 0.12 to 0.3 in steps of 0.01, and use contour values corresponding to 50, 75, and 95% confidence levels. Mark the location of the minimum on the plot.

(b) Compare these contours with those in Figure 2.23. Which data set suffers most from nonlinearity?

(c) Since the data are from the same type of experiment with the same model, how can this difference be explained?

2.7 Plot the point corresponding to $\boldsymbol{\theta}^0$ and the increment $\boldsymbol{\delta}^0$ from Problem 2.5 on the contour plot from Problem 2.6. Mark the points corresponding to the values $\lambda = 0.25, 0.5$, and 0.75 on the increment vector. Is a step factor less than 1 necessary in this case?

2.8 (a) Use the data, model, and starting values from Problem 2.5 in a nonlinear estimation routine to obtain the least squares parameter estimates.

(b) Calculate and plot the linear approximation joint and marginal inference regions on the plot from Problem 2.6.

(c) Are the linear approximation inference regions accurate in this case?

CHAPTER 3.

Practical Considerations in Nonlinear Regression

"Rationally, let it be said in a whisper, experience is certainly worth more than theory."

– Amerigo Vespucci

Nonlinear estimation, like all data analysis procedures, involves many practical considerations. In this chapter, we discuss some techniques which help ensure a successful nonlinear analysis. The topics include model specification, preliminary analysis, determination of starting values, transformations of parameters and variables, other iteration schemes, convergence, assessment of fit and modification of models, correlated residuals, accumulated data, comparison of models, parameters as functions of other variables, and presentation of results. A case study in which we illustrate many of the techniques presented in this chapter is given in Section 3.13. The important practical problem of designing experiments for nonlinear models is discussed in the final section.

3.1 Model Specification

An important step in any nonlinear analysis is specification of the model, which includes specifying both the expectation function and the characteristics of the disturbance.

3.1.1 The Expectation Function

Ideally, physical, biological, chemical, or other theoretical considerations will lead to a *mechanistic* model for the expectation function. The analyst's job is then to find the simplest form of the model and the parameter estimates which provide an adequate fit of the model to the data, subject to the assumptions about the disturbance. Note that it is not necessary for the expectation function to be stated as an explicit function of the parameters and the control variables. In Chapter 5 we discuss an important class of models, known as compartment models, in which the expected response is given by the solution to a set of linear differential equations. Special techniques, developed in that chapter, can be used to avoid solving explicitly for the expectation function in terms of the parameters and independent variables.

In other situations, the expectation function may be the solution to a non-linear differential equation or an integral equation which has no analytic solution. Then the value of the expectation function must be determined numerically for any given parameter values for a regular nonlinear least squares program to be used. In such situations, numerical parameter derivatives or a derivative-free optimization procedure will often have to be used to calculate the least squares estimates. However, as discussed in Caracotsios and Stewart (1985), when an expectation function is obtained from the solution to a set of ordinary differential equations, the parameter derivatives of the expectation function can be determined from the sensitivity functions for the system of differential equations. These functions are evaluated numerically at the same time as the solution of the differential equations is evaluated.

Example: α-Pinene 1

The decomposition of α-pinene was investigated by Fuguitt and Hawkins (1945, 1947), who reported the concentrations of five reactants as a function of time, at a series of reaction temperatures. In Appendix 1, Section A1.6, we present the data for the run at 189.5°C.

We discuss these data in Chapters 4 and 5 and fit a model which is specified by a set of linear differential equations. As discussed in Chapter 5, the parameters in such models can be estimated very easily, due to the ease with which they can be specified and the ease with which the responses and the derivatives with respect to the parameters can be evaluated. As will be also shown in Chapter 5, however, the linear differential equation model does not provide an adequate fit to the α-pinene data.

Stewart and Sorensen (1981) analyzed the complete data set reported by Fuguitt and Hawkins (1945, 1947), and proposed a model consisting of a set of five nonlinear differential equations

$$\frac{df_1}{dt} = -(\theta_1 + \theta_2)f_1 - 2\theta_3 f_1^2$$

$$\frac{df_2}{dt} = -\theta_4 f_2 + \theta_5 f_4$$

$$\frac{df_3}{dt} = \theta_1 f_1$$

$$\frac{df_4}{dt} = \theta_2 f_1 + \theta_4 f_2 - \theta_5 f_4 - 2\theta_6 f_4^2 + 2\theta_7 f_5$$

$$\frac{df_5}{dt} = \theta_8 f_1^2 + \theta_6 f_4^2 - \theta_7 f_5$$

where f_i, $i = 1, \ldots, 5$, represent the theoretical responses at time t.

There is no analytic solution to this set of differential equations, and so we must use numerical procedures. For given values of $\boldsymbol{\theta} = (\theta_1, \ldots, \theta_8)^T$, the differential equations would be integrated numerically using, say, a Runge–Kutta integration routine (Conte and de Boor, 1980). The numerical estimates of the responses, $\mathbf{f}(t)$, and the observed responses $\mathbf{y}(t)$, at the observation times, could then be used to calculate residuals from which an appropriate estimation criterion can be evaluated.

We discuss the choice of estimation criterion for multiresponse data in Chapter 4. Methods for obtaining derivatives of the response functions at the observation times by means of the "sensitivity functions"

$$\frac{\partial f_i(t)}{\partial \theta_p} \qquad i = 1, , \ldots, 5 \quad p = 1, \ldots, P$$

are given in Caracotsios and Stewart (1985). The derivative matrix $\mathbf{V}$ can then be calculated from the sensitivity functions. ∎

In other situations, a mechanistic model may not be advanced by the researcher, in which case the statistician will be called upon to suggest an equation. One approach is to ask the researcher to search through the literature to see if models have been proposed. If not, the statistician and the researcher can apply their modeling skills and develop a plausible mechanistic model. Failing this, the statistician must formulate a model which has the same sort of behavior as the data. If the data rise monotonically to an asymptote, perhaps a Michaelis–Menten, exponential rise, or logistic model might be appropriate. If the data peak and then decay towards zero, perhaps a double exponential, a Michaelis–Menten model with a quadratic term in the denominator, or a gamma function would be suitable.

Finally, if there are several sets of data, it may be possible to use the self-modeling approach of Lawton, Sylvestre, and Maggio (1972). This approach has been used in modeling spirometer curves which give the volume of air expelled from the lungs as a function of time for a number of subjects, and in modeling the creatine phosphokinase serum levels in patients suffering myocardial infarctions (Armstrong et al., 1979).

3.1.2 The Disturbance Term

All nonlinear estimation programs are based on specific assumptions about the disturbance term, usually that the disturbance is additive and normally distributed with zero mean, constant variance, and independence between cases (see

Section 1.3). Checking assumptions on the disturbance term is considerably easier and more sensitive if the data include replications at some or all of the design points. It is helpful if the experimental runs have been randomized, although many nonlinear experiments involve sequential measurements of the response, so that randomization may not be feasible.

At the initial stage, it is generally possible to check only one of the assumptions on the disturbance, namely constancy of variance. If there are replications, one can simply plot the data and look to see if the spread of the data tends to systematically increase or decrease with respect to any of the predictor variables. Alternatively, one can use an analysis of variance program to obtain averages and estimated variances and standard deviations for the replicated responses and then plot the variances or standard deviations versus the average, again looking for any systematic relationship, as discussed in Section 1.3. If none is apparent, then it may be tentatively assumed that the variance is constant and the analysis can proceed; if there is a relationship, then oftentimes a simple power transformation such as square root, logarithm, or inverse will stabilize the variance. Even without replications, some visual indication of constancy of variance can be gained from a data plot but this is not as definitive as when replications are available.

Note that transforming the data also involves transforming the expectation function. Thus, if there is a well-justified expectation function for the response but the data should be transformed to induce constant variance, then the same transformation should be applied to the expectation function to preserve the fundamental relationship. (See Section 3.9 for an example.) This is discussed more fully in Carroll and Ruppert (1984), where the Box–Cox transformations (Section 1.3.2) are applied to both the observed responses and the expected responses using the same transformation parameter λ. The optimal value of λ is determined by maximum likelihood. Alternatively, one can use weighted least squares (Draper and Smith, 1981) if a reasonable decision can be made about how the variance changes with respect to the response.

After a model has been fitted, it is possible to perform further checks on the disturbance assumptions by examining the residuals, as described in Sections 1.3, 3.7, and 3.8. It is also possible to check adequacy of the model and to compare rival models, as discussed in Section 3.10.

3.2 Preliminary Analysis

Having decided on a suitable expectation function (or set of plausible expectation functions) and a transformation of the data (and the expectation function, if necessary), we need to provide a computer program with the expectation function in some form and, unless numerical derivatives or derivative-free methods are used, its derivatives with respect to the parameters. Naturally, the expectation function and derivatives must be *correctly specified* and *correctly coded*, but (as most nonlinear analysts know from experience) a great many errors occur at this stage.

One way to ensure that the function is correctly specified and correctly coded is to use a separate program or even a calculator to evaluate the function at one or two distinct design points then compare these values with those from the nonlinear estimation routine. The same technique can be used for the derivatives, of course, but a better procedure is to compare the analytic derivatives from the routine with numerical derivatives obtained from finite differences of the expectation function (see Section 3.5.3). These comparisons are done on the basis of the relative differences between the derivatives calculated in the two ways. If v_{np} is the analytic derivative for case n and parameter p while $\tilde{v}_{np}$ is the finite difference approximation, then the relative difference is

$$\frac{|v_{np} - \tilde{v}_{np}|}{|v_{np}|} \quad \text{if } v_{np} \neq 0$$

$$|v_{np} - \tilde{v}_{np}| \quad \text{if } v_{np} = 0$$

Verifying that the relative differences are small not only provides a check on the derivatives, but, indirectly, a check on the expectation function, because a discrepancy between the numerical derivatives and the analytic derivatives can be due to either incorrect specification or coding of the analytic derivatives, or due to incorrect specification or coding of the expectation function, or both.

When coding the function, and especially when deriving and coding the derivatives, it is good practice to use temporary variables and the chain rule for derivatives, as demonstrated below. This helps avoid algebraic errors, which can occur when trying to reduce a function to its simplest form.

Example: Isomerization 2

For the isomerization data of Example Isomerization 1, the function

$$f(\mathbf{x}, \boldsymbol{\theta}) = \frac{\theta_1 \theta_3 (x_2 - x_3 / 1.632)}{1 + \theta_2 x_1 + \theta_3 x_2 + \theta_4 x_3}$$

is considered appropriate. To code the function and its derivatives, suppose the variables x_1, x_2, x_3 are coded as $X(1)$, $X(2)$, $X(3)$, and the parameters as $THETA(1)$, $THETA(2)$, $THETA(3)$, and $THETA(4)$. Then we can code the function simply and accurately by introducing the temporary variables

```
NUMX  = X(2)  - X(3)/1.632
DENOM = 1.0 + THETA(2)*X(1)  + THETA(3)*X(2)
      + THETA(4)*X(3)
RATIO = NUMX/DENOM
```

so the function becomes

```
F  = THETA(1)*THETA(3)*RATIO
```

Next, introducing the temporary variable

```
FD = - F/DENOM
```

the derivatives become (denoting $\partial f/\partial\theta_1$ by F1 and so on),

```
F1 = THETA(3)*RATIO
F2 = FD*X(1)
F3 = THETA(1)*RATIO + FD*X(2)
F4 = FD*X(3)                                    ■
```

It is also important to check that the data being analyzed are valid. That is, one must always ensure that the correct numerical values of the response and predictor variables have been entered into the machine. Probably the most effective way to check this is to plot the response versus each predictor variable, making sure that the response behaves the way it should with respect to each of the predictor variables.

3.3   Starting Values

One of the best things one can do to ensure a successful nonlinear analysis is to obtain good starting values for the parameters—values from which convergence is quickly obtained.

Several simple but useful principles for determining starting values can be used:

(1) interpret the behavior of the expectation function in terms of the parameters analytically or graphically;
(2) interpret the behavior of derivatives of the expectation function in terms of the parameters analytically or graphically;
(3) transform the expectation function analytically or graphically to obtain simpler, preferably linear, behavior;
(4) reduce dimensions by substituting values for some parameters or by evaluating the function at specific design values; and
(5) use conditional linearity.

We discuss each of these techniques in turn, and illustrate them with specific examples. For further discussion on obtaining starting values, see Ratkowsky (1983).

3.3.1   Interpreting the Expectation Function Behavior

One of the advantages of nonlinear regression is that the parameters in the expectation function are usually meaningful to the scientist or researcher. This meaning can be graphical, physical, biological, chemical, or in some other appropriate form, and can be very helpful in determining starting values. Initial estimates for some of the parameters may be available from related experiments. Also, plotting a nonlinear expectation function using various values for the parameters is an extremely beneficial exercise, because in this way one becomes familiar with the function and how the parameters affect its behavior.

Sometimes starting values can be obtained by considering the behavior near the origin or at other special design values. For example, letting $x = 0$ gives the initial value of $\theta_1 + \theta_2$ for the model $f(x, \theta) = \theta_1 + \theta_2 e^{-\theta_3 x}$, and letting $x \to \infty$ gives the asymptote θ_1 (assuming $\theta_3 > 0$).

Example: Puromycin 9

In the Michaelis–Menten expectation function, $f = \theta_1 x / (\theta_2 + x)$, the parameter θ_1 is the asymptotic velocity of the enzymatic reaction, and so can be estimated by the maximum observed data value, y_{max}, or by eye from a plot. Graphically, θ_1 represents the asymptotic value of f as $x \to \infty$. Similarly, θ_2 represents the half-concentration, i.e. the value of x such that when the concentration reaches that value the velocity is one-half its ultimate value. For the Puromycin data, $y_{max} = 207$ provides a good starting value for θ_1. From a plot of the data (Figure 2.1), or simply from a listing, it can be seen that the observed velocity reaches $y_{max}/2$ at a concentration of about 0.06 and so this value can be used as a starting value for θ_2. ∎

3.3.2 Interpreting Derivatives of the Expectation Function

Sometimes rates of change of the function at specified design values can be used to obtain parameter starting estimates. For example, the derivative with respect to x of the Michaelis–Menten model at $x = 0$ is θ_1 / θ_2, and so by estimating the rate at $x = 0$ from the ratio of differences of adjacent y values over differences of adjacent x values, and dividing this rate into y_{max}, we can obtain a starting value for θ_2. For Puromycin data, we obtain $\theta_2 = 207/(61/0.02) = 0.068$.

Similarly, derivatives at special values of x, such as limits or points of inflection, can be used. For example, for the double exponential model

$$f = \theta_1 e^{-\theta_2 x} + \theta_3 e^{-\theta_4 x}$$

assuming $\theta_2 > \theta_4$, the function behaves like a simple exponential $\theta_3 e^{-\theta_4 x}$ for large x and like $\theta_3 + \theta_1 e^{-\theta_2 x}$ for small x. Thus, the rate of change at small x provides an estimate of θ_2, and at large x an estimate of θ_4.

3.3.3 Transforming the Expectation Function

Transformations of the expectation function can often be used to obtain starting values. For instance, for the Michaelis–Menten model with a linear or quadratic denominator, simply taking the reciprocal of the function produces a model which can be rewritten as a linear model. Linear least squares can be used on the reciprocal data to estimate the linear parameters, which can then be used to obtain starting values for $\boldsymbol{\theta}$. The model from Example Isomerization 1,

$$f(\mathbf{x}, \boldsymbol{\theta}) = \frac{\theta_1 \theta_3 (x_2 - x_3/1.632)}{1 + \theta_2 x_1 + \theta_3 x_2 + \theta_4 x_3}$$

is also transformably linear, since

$$\frac{x_2 - x_3/1.632}{f(\mathbf{x}, \boldsymbol{\theta})} = \frac{1}{\theta_1 \theta_3} + \frac{\theta_2}{\theta_1 \theta_3} x_1 + \frac{1}{\theta_1} x_2 + \frac{\theta_4}{\theta_1 \theta_3} x_3$$

A linear regression (with a constant term) of $(x_2 - x_3/1.632)/y$ on x_1, x_2, and x_3 would yield starting values

$$\theta_1^0 = \frac{1}{\hat{\beta}_2} \qquad \theta_2^0 = \frac{\hat{\beta}_1}{\hat{\beta}_0} \qquad \theta_3^0 = \frac{\hat{\beta}_2}{\hat{\beta}_0} \qquad \theta_4^0 = \frac{\hat{\beta}_3}{\hat{\beta}_0}$$

For the model $f(\mathbf{x}, \boldsymbol{\theta}) = \exp[-\theta_1 x_1 \exp(-\theta_2/x_2)]$, used in a chemical kinetics example (Bard, 1974, p. 124), taking logarithms twice gives

$$\ln \ln f = \ln x_1 + \ln(-\theta_1) - \frac{\theta_2}{x_2}$$

and one could again use linear least squares to obtain starting values.

Graphical transformations are also very effective. Plotting f versus x on semilog paper or plotting $\ln f$ versus x on regular graph paper often reveals the true nature of the data or enables one to see when one portion of the model is dominant, and hence where one can measure a rate and associate it with a particular parameter.

For example, the double exponential model

$$f(x, \boldsymbol{\theta}) = \theta_1 e^{-\theta_2 x} + \theta_3 e^{-\theta_4 x}$$

with $\theta_2 > \theta_4$ is approximately $\ln f = \ln \theta_3 - \theta_4 x$ at large x, which gives a straight line on a semilog plot. A simple fit can then be made by eye to obtain values for θ_3 and θ_4. These values can then be used to calculate values of $\theta_3 e^{-\theta_4 x}$ at all values of x, and hence residuals $\tilde{y} = y - \theta_3 e^{-\theta_4 x}$ can be derived. Plotting $\tilde{y}$ versus x on semilog paper then enables one to estimate θ_1 and θ_2. This process, known as *peeling*, can be used when the expectation function is a sum of several exponentials.

Example: Sulfisoxazole 1

To demonstrate the technique of peeling, we consider sulfisoxazole data given in Kaplan et al. (1972) and described in Appendix 1, Section A1.7. In this experiment, sulfisoxazole was administered to a subject intravenously, blood samples were taken at specified times, and the concentration of sulfisoxazole in the plasma was measured. The data are plotted in Figure 3.1.

Plotting the sulfisoxazole concentration on a log scale versus x as in Figure 3.2a reveals monotonic decay with straight line behavior for large x,

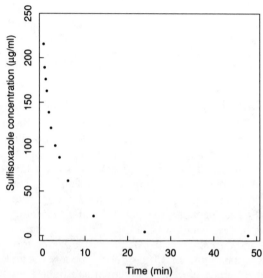

Figure 3.1 Plot of sulfisoxazole concentration in plasma versus time.

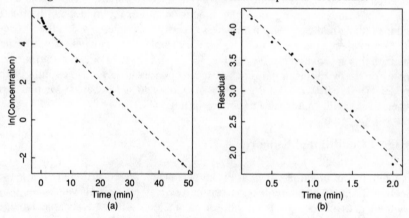

Figure 3.2 Curve peeling using the Sulfisoxazole data. In part *a* we show the data, plotted on a log scale, together with a straight line fit (dashed line) to the last six points. In part *b* we show, on a log scale, the residuals for the first six data points from the straight line fit in part *a*. The dashed line is the fitted line through these (log) residuals.

which suggests a model of the form

$$f(x, \boldsymbol{\theta}) = \theta_1 e^{-\theta_2 x} + \theta_3 e^{-\theta_4 x}$$

with all positive parameters. Fitting a straight line to the last six (log) data values gives an intercept of 5.05 and a slope of -0.153, so that the starting values are $\theta_3^0 = e^{5.05} = 156$ and $\theta_4^0 = 0.153$. Calculating the residuals

$$\tilde{y}_n = y_n - 156\, e^{-0.153\, x_n}$$

and plotting $\ln \tilde{y}$ versus x for the first six data values, as in Figure 3.2b, again reveals straight line behavior. Fitting a straight line to these (log) residuals gives an intercept of 4.55 and a slope of -1.31, so that the starting values are $\theta_1^0 = e^{4.55} = 95$ and $\theta_2 = 1.31$. ∎

3.3.4 Reducing Dimensions

Peeling is an example of the general technique of reducing dimensions in order to obtain starting values. In this technique one estimates parameters successively, each estimated parameter making it easier to estimate the remaining ones. As another example of reducing parameter dimensions, consider the model $f = \theta_1 + \theta_2 e^{-\theta_3 x}$, where θ_3 is positive. Then the limiting value of the response when $x \to \infty$ is θ_1 and the value at $x = 0$ is $\theta_1 + \theta_2$. Depending on whether the data is increasing or decreasing, we can use $y_{\max}$ or $y_{\min}$ to get the starting value θ_1^0, and then use the difference $y(0) - \theta_1^0$ to get θ_2^0. We perform a linear regression (without a constant term) of $\ln[(y - \theta_1^0)/\theta_2^0]$ on x to obtain θ_3^0. Alternatively, once θ_1^0 and θ_2^0 are determined, we could substitute these values into the function and evaluate $(1/x)\ln[(y - \theta_1^0)/\theta_2^0]$ at selected values of x to obtain θ_3^0.

Sometimes we can reduce the dimensionality of the model and indirectly reduce the number of parameters. For example, with the model $f(\mathbf{x},\boldsymbol{\theta}) = \exp[-\theta_1 x_1 \exp(-\theta_2/x_2)]$, if there are some very large values of x_2, then the model is approximately $f(x_1,\boldsymbol{\theta}) = e^{-\theta_1 x_1}$, so it is easy to obtain a starting estimate for θ_1 by taking logarithms of the responses at large x_2. Similarly the model $f(\mathbf{x},\boldsymbol{\theta}) = \theta_1 \theta_2 x_1/(1 + \theta_2 x_1 + \theta_3 x_2)$ reduces to a Michaelis–Menten type when x_2 is small, so it is easy to obtain starting values.

3.3.5 Conditional Linearity

In many model functions, several of the parameters are conditionally linear (see Section 2.1) and linear regression can be used to get starting values for these parameters conditional on the nonlinear parameters. Alternatively, special algorithms which exploit the conditional linearity, described in Section 3.5.5, can be used. These algorithms only require starting estimates for the nonlinear parameters. As an example of conditional linearity, in

$$f(x,\boldsymbol{\theta}) = \theta_1 + \theta_2 e^{-\theta_3 x}$$

both θ_1 and θ_2 are conditionally linear, so it is possible to use linear least squares to estimate θ_1^0 and θ_2^0 once an estimate for θ_3^0 has been obtained. A detailed example involving conditionally linear parameters is given in Section 3.6.

3.4   Parameter Transformations

As will be shown in Chapters 6 and 7, transforming the parameters in a nonlinear regression model can produce a much better linear approximation. This has the beneficial effects of making approximate inference regions better and speeding convergence to the least squares value. Parameter transformations can also be used to enforce constraints on the values of the parameters.

Note that transformations of parameters are very different from transformations of the responses. Transformations of the response distort the response space and create a new expectation surface, thereby affecting the disturbances and the validity of the assumptions on the disturbances. In contrast, transformations of the parameters merely relabel points in the parameter space and on the existing expectation surface. Consequently they do not affect the assumptions about the deterministic or the stochastic parts of the model, although they do affect the validity of the linear approximation and inferences based on it.

The use of parameter transformations to improve validity of the linear approximation is discussed in Chapter 7; here we focus on transformations to impose constraints on parameters and to improve convergence.

3.4.1   Constrained Parameters

The parameters in most nonlinear models are restricted to regions which make sense scientifically. For example, in the Michaelis–Menten model and in the isomerization model, all the parameters must be positive, and in exponential models, the parameters in the exponent usually must be positive.

It is often possible to ignore the restrictions when fitting the model and simply examine the converged parameter estimates to see if they satisfy the constraints. If the model fits the data well, the parameter estimates should be in a meaningful range. Sometimes, though, it may be dangerous to allow the parameter estimates to go into proscribed regions during the iterations because the parameter values may begin to oscillate wildly or cause numerical overflows. In these situations, one should impose the constraints throughout the estimation process.

General techniques for optimizing functions whose parameters are constrained, called *nonlinear programming*, are beyond the scope of this book. See, for example, Gill, Murray, and Wright (1981) or Bard (1974) for details. Fortunately, the types of constraints that are applied to the parameters of a nonlinear regression model are usually simple enough to be handled by parameter transformations. For example, if θ_p must be positive, we reparametrize to $\phi_p = \ln \theta_p$, so throughout the iterations the value of $\theta_p = e^{\phi_p}$ remains positive.

An *interval* constraint on a parameter, say

$$a \leq \theta \leq b$$

can be enforced by a logistic transformation of the form

$$\theta = a + \frac{b-a}{1+e^{-\phi}}$$

while an *order* constraint on parameters $\theta_j, \ldots, \theta_k$, say

$$a \leq \theta_j \leq \theta_{j+1} \leq \cdots \leq \theta_k \leq b$$

can be enforced by a transformation given in Jupp (1978).

The order constraint can be used to ensure a unique optimum in a model with exchangeable parameters. As an example of such a model, consider the double exponential model

$$f(x,\boldsymbol{\theta}) = \theta_1 e^{-\theta_2 x} + \theta_3 e^{-\theta_4 x} \qquad 0 \leq \theta_2, \theta_4$$

where the pairs of parameters (θ_1, θ_2) and (θ_3, θ_4) are *exchangeable*—that is, exchanging the parameter pair (θ_1, θ_2) with the pair (θ_3, θ_4) will not alter the values of the expected responses. Exchangeable parameters can create nasty optimization problems because the linear approximation cannot account for that kind of symmetry.

In this example, we remove the exchangeability by requiring

$$0 \leq \theta_2 \leq \theta_4$$

and enforce this with the transformation

$$\theta_2 = e^{\phi_2}$$

$$\theta_4 = e^{\phi_2}(1 + e^{\phi_4})$$

Since θ_1 and θ_3 are conditionally linear parameters, their optimal values are uniquely determined when θ_2 and θ_4 are distinct. Thus we only need to keep θ_2 and θ_4 ordered to eliminate the exchangeability.

3.4.2 Facilitating Convergence

Parameter transformations can facilitate convergence because they prevent the parameters from venturing into proscribed regions. Transformations can also improve convergence by making the parameter lines behave more uniformly on the expectation surface so that the Gauss increment is more accurate. Joint variable–parameter transformations can also be used to improve the estimation situation by improving conditioning of the derivative matrix **V**. Frequently this is done by *centering* or *scaling* the data. For example, the simple model $f(x,\boldsymbol{\theta}) = \theta_1 e^{-\theta_2 x}$ has derivatives

$$\frac{\partial f}{\partial \theta_1} = e^{-\theta_2 x}$$

$$\frac{\partial f}{\partial \theta_2} = -x\theta_1 e^{-\theta_2 x}$$

and the derivative vectors tend to be collinear when the values of x are all positive. Rewriting the model as

$$f(x,\boldsymbol{\theta}) = \theta_1 e^{-\theta_2(x - x_0 + x_0)}$$

and reparametrizing with

$$\phi_1 = \theta_1 e^{-\theta_2 x_0}$$

$$\phi_2 = \theta_2$$

gives $f(x,\boldsymbol{\phi}) = \phi_1 e^{-\phi_2(x - x_0)}$, and now the derivatives with respect to $\boldsymbol{\phi}$ will be more nearly orthogonal. A useful choice is $x_0 = \bar{x}$.

Scaling the variables and the parameters can also improve conditioning by making the derivative matrix have column vectors which are more nearly equal in length.

Other transformations can be useful, depending on the context of the problem. For example, in chemical kinetics it is often useful to revise the model so that reciprocal absolute temperature is used rather than temperature T. Combining this with centering would then modify a term involving temperature to the form $1/T - 1/T_0$.

The effect of parameter transformations on parameter effects nonlinearities and the adequacy of linear approximation inference regions is discussed in Chapter 7.

3.5 Other Iterative Techniques

The Gauss–Newton iterative algorithm for nonlinear least squares, described in Section 2.2.1, is a simple, useful method for finding $\hat{\boldsymbol{\theta}}$. Some modifications to this method, as well as alternative methods, have been suggested—primarily to deal with ill-conditioning of the derivative matrix $\mathbf{V}$ and to avoid having to code and specify the derivatives.

3.5.1 A Newton–Raphson Method

The Gauss–Newton method for estimating nonlinear parameters can be considered as a special case of the more general Newton–Raphson method (Bard, 1974) which uses a local quadratic approximation to the objective function. Near $\boldsymbol{\theta}^0$, we approximate

$$S(\boldsymbol{\theta}) \approx S(\boldsymbol{\theta}^0) + \boldsymbol{\omega}^T(\boldsymbol{\theta} - \boldsymbol{\theta}^0) + (\boldsymbol{\theta} - \boldsymbol{\theta}^0)^T \frac{\boldsymbol{\Omega}}{2}(\boldsymbol{\theta} - \boldsymbol{\theta}^0)$$

where

$$\boldsymbol{\omega} = \frac{\partial S}{\partial \boldsymbol{\theta}}$$

is the *gradient* of $S(\boldsymbol{\theta})$ evaluated at $\boldsymbol{\theta}^0$ and

$$\Omega = \frac{\partial^2 S}{\partial\theta\,\partial\theta^T}$$

is the *Hessian* of $S(\theta)$ evaluated at θ^0. The approximating sum of squares function will have a stationary point when its gradient is zero—that is, when

$$\omega + \Omega(\theta - \theta^0) = 0$$

and this stationary point will be a minimum if Ω is positive definite (all its eigenvalues positive). If Ω is positive definite, the Newton–Raphson step is

$$\delta^0 = -\Omega^{-1}\omega$$

For the function

$$S(\theta) = (y-\eta)^T(y-\eta)$$

the gradient is

$$\omega = -2V^T(y - \eta)$$

and the Hessian is

$$\Omega = 2V^T V - 2\frac{\partial V^T}{\partial\theta^T}(y - \eta)$$

where V is the derivative matrix. The Gauss–Newton increment is therefore equivalent to the Newton–Raphson increment with the second derivative term $\partial V^T/\partial\theta^T$ set to zero.

Dennis, Gay, and Welsch (1981) describe a nonlinear least squares routine which develops a quasi-Newton approximation (Dennis and Schnabel, 1983) to the second term in the Hessian. This extends the Gauss–Newton algorithm and makes it closer to the Newton–Raphson algorithm, which has the advantage that the approximating Hessian should be closer to the actual Hessian than the single term $V^T V$ used in the Gauss–Newton algorithm. However, the term $V^T V$ is necessarily positive definite (or at least positive semidefinite), since the eigenvalues of $V^T V$ are the squares of the singular values of V. Adding another term on to this to form an approximating Hessian can destroy the positive definiteness, in which case the Newton–Raphson algorithm must be modified to restore positive definiteness in the Hessian.

3.5.2 The Levenberg–Marquardt Compromise

A condition that can cause erratic behavior of Gauss–Newton iterations is singularity of the derivative matrix V caused by collinearity of the columns. When V is nearly singular, δ can be very large, causing the parameters to go into undesirable regions of the parameter space.

One solution to the problem of near-singularity is to perform the calculations for the increment in a numerically stable way, which is why we recommend using the QR decomposition rather than the normal equations. We also recommend using double precision or extended precision arithmetic for the calculations, where feasible, and using joint variable–parameter transformations as discussed in Section 3.4.

Another general method for dealing with near-singularity is to modify the Gauss–Newton increment to

$$\delta(k) = (V^T V + kI)^{-1} V^T (y - \eta) \tag{3.1}$$

as suggested in Levenberg (1944), or to

$$\delta(k) = (V^T V + kD)^{-1} V^T (y - \eta) \tag{3.2}$$

as suggested in Marquardt (1963), where k is a conditioning factor and D is a diagonal matrix with entries equal to the diagonal elements of $V^T V$. This is called the *Levenberg–Marquardt compromise* because the direction of $\delta(k)$ is intermediate between the direction of the Gauss–Newton increment ($k \to 0$) and the direction of *steepest descent* $V^T(y - \eta) / \| V^T(y - \eta) \|$ ($k \to \infty$).

Note that Levenberg recommends inflating the diagonal of $V^T V$ by an additive factor, while Marquardt recommends inflating the diagonal by a multiplicative factor $1 + k$. Marquardt's method produces an increment which is invariant under scaling transformations of the parameters, so that if the scale for one component of the parameter vector is doubled, the increment calculated, and the corresponding component of the increment halved, the result will be the same as calculating the increment in the original scale. In Levenberg's method, this is not true. Box and Kanemasu (1984) showed, however, that if one requires invariance of the increment under linear transformations of the parameter space, the resulting increment is the Gauss–Newton increment with a step factor.

The Levenberg–Marquardt compromise is more difficult to implement than the Gauss–Newton algorithm, since one must decide how to manipulate both the conditioning factor k and the step factor λ; nevertheless it is implemented in many nonlinear least squares programs. Although we presented the increment in terms of the inverse of an augmented $V^T V$ matrix, the actual calculations for the increment should be done using a QR decomposition of V and applying updates from a diagonal matrix using the Givens rotations (Dongarra et al., 1979, Chapter 10; Golub and Pereyra, 1973), since the Levenberg increment (3.1) is the least squares solution to the system with derivative matrix

$$\begin{bmatrix} V \\ \sqrt{k}\, I \end{bmatrix}$$

and response vector

$$\begin{bmatrix} y - \eta \\ 0 \end{bmatrix}$$

For the Marquardt increment (3.2), the derivative matrix is changed to

$$\begin{bmatrix} \mathbf{V} \\ \sqrt{k}\,\mathbf{D}^{1/2} \end{bmatrix}$$

3.5.3 Numerical Derivatives

We have assumed that implementations of the algorithms we have described use analytic derivatives with respect to the parameters. Obtaining these derivatives and coding them is usually the most tedious and error-prone stage in a nonlinear analysis.

As a general rule we recommend using analytic derivatives for accuracy, although it is convenient to use programs which use numerical derivatives from finite differences. Such convenience is not obtained without cost, however, because numerical derivatives can be inaccurate and they usually increase the computing time necessary to obtain convergence. Furthermore, if second derivatives are required to investigate the effect of nonlinearity on inferences, the numerical second derivatives evaluated from numerical first derivatives can be very inaccurate. Other problems with numerical derivatives involve the choice of step size to determine the finite differences, and whether to use central or forward differences.

With forward differences, for the pth parameter we evaluate the model function using the current values of all the parameters except for the pth, which is incremented to $\theta_p(1 + \varepsilon)$. Dividing the differences between the function values by the fractional amount $\varepsilon\theta_p$ gives an approximate derivative. This requires $1 + P$ evaluations of the expected response vector at each iteration. Using central differences would require evaluation of the model function at $\theta_p(1 \pm \varepsilon)$ in addition to the central value, so the total number of evaluations would be $1 + 2P$. Dennis and Schnabel (1983) recommend setting ε equal to the square root of the relative machine precision (that is, the square root of the smallest number which, when added to 1.0 in the floating point arithmetic of the computer, produces a number greater than 1.0).

3.5.4 Derivative-Free Methods

There are derivative-free methods which do not simply use numerical approximations to derivatives. Ralston and Jennrich (1978) introduced one such routine, DUD (Doesn't Use Derivatives), which is based on using a secant plane approximation to the expectation surface rather than a tangent plane approximation.

To use DUD, one must provide starting values θ^0. The program then automatically produces a further set of P parameter vectors by displacing each parameter in turn by 10%. These parameter vectors are then used to calculate expectation vectors $\eta_1, \eta_2, \ldots$, giving a secant plane which matches the expectation surface at $P + 1$ points. A set of linear coordinates is generated on the secant plane, and the projection of **y** onto the secant plane is made and mapped into the parameter plane. This information is used to calculate a new **θ** vector, say **θ′**, for which $\eta(\theta')$ is closer to **y** than any of the other parameter vectors. The parameter vector **θ** corresponding to the η which is farthest from **y** is then replaced by **θ′**, and the process continued until convergence is achieved.

Example: Rumford 6

DUD can be illustrated very effectively using a two-observation example such as in Example Rumford 2. To simplify arithmetic and to provide a better scale for the figure, we provide the necessary two ($=P+1$) starting values rather than using the automatic 10% displacement. The two starting values are chosen to be $\theta^1 = 0.02$ and $\theta^2 = 0.10$. Figure 3.3 shows the expectation surface $\eta(\theta)$ together with the secant line l through the points $\eta(\theta^1)$ and $\eta(\theta^2)$. We now introduce a linear scale parameter α on θ such that $\theta = \theta^1 + T\alpha$, where $T = (\theta^2 - \theta^1)$ and so $\alpha = 0$ at θ^1 and $\alpha = 1$ at θ^2. We also impose a linear scale on l such that $l(\alpha) = \eta(\theta^1) + H\alpha$, where $H = \eta(\theta^2) - \eta(\theta^1)$. The linear coordinate system is also shown in Figure 3.3.

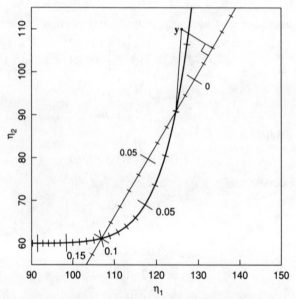

Figure 3.3 A geometric interpretation of the calculation of the DUD increment using the 2-case Rumford data. A portion of the expectation surface (heavy solid line) is shown in the response space together with the observed response **y**. Also shown is the projection of $\mathbf{y} - \eta(0.02)$ onto the secant plane joining $\eta(0.02)$ and $\eta(0.10)$ (solid line). The tick marks indicate true positions on the expectation surface and linear approximation positions on the secant plane.

For this example, $T = \theta^2 - \theta^1 = 0.08$, $\theta = \theta^1 + T\alpha$, so

$$\alpha = \frac{\theta - \theta^1}{T}$$

$$\mathbf{H} = \begin{bmatrix} 60 + 70\, e^{-4\,(0.1)} \\ 60 + 70\, e^{-41\,(0.1)} \end{bmatrix} - \begin{bmatrix} 60 + 70\, e^{-4\,(0.02)} \\ 60 + 70\, e^{-41\,(0.02)} \end{bmatrix}$$

$$= \begin{bmatrix} 106.92 \\ 61.16 \end{bmatrix} - \begin{bmatrix} 124.62 \\ 90.83 \end{bmatrix}$$

$$= \begin{bmatrix} -17.70 \\ -29.67 \end{bmatrix}$$

and

$$\mathbf{l} = \eta(\theta^1) + \mathbf{H}\alpha$$

$$= \begin{bmatrix} 124.62 \\ 90.83 \end{bmatrix} + \begin{bmatrix} -17.70 \\ -29.67 \end{bmatrix} \alpha$$

We now use linear least squares to project the residual vector

$$\mathbf{y} - \mathbf{l}(0) = \begin{bmatrix} 126 \\ 110 \end{bmatrix} - \begin{bmatrix} 124.62 \\ 90.83 \end{bmatrix}$$

$$= \begin{bmatrix} 1.38 \\ 19.17 \end{bmatrix}$$

onto $\mathbf{l}$ to obtain

$$\hat{\alpha} = (\mathbf{H}^T\mathbf{H})^{-1}\mathbf{H}^T(\mathbf{y} - \mathbf{l}(0))$$

For this example

$$\hat{\alpha} = -0.49$$

so new value of θ is

$$\theta_{new} = 0.02 + T(-0.49)$$

$$= 0.02 + 0.08(-0.49)$$

$$= -0.019$$

Evaluating the sum of squares at this point reveals that this new point is farther from $\mathbf{y}$ than either of the two starting points, and so a step factor λ is introduced to search along the increment vector to determine a better point. Incorporating λ as

$$\theta_{trial} = \theta_{new}\lambda + \theta_{old}(1 - \lambda)$$

gives, for this example,

$$\theta_{trial} = (-0.019)\lambda + 0.02(1 - \lambda)$$

and the minimum occurs at $\lambda = 0.5$ with $\theta_{trial} = 0.0005$. The point $\theta^2 = 0.10$ is then replaced by $\theta^3 = 0.0005$ and the process is repeated using the pair (θ^1, θ^3). ∎

In the general case of P parameters, at the ith iteration we use the values of $\eta(\theta)$ at $\theta_1^i, \theta_2^i, \ldots, \theta_{P+1}^i$ to determine the secant plane as the P-dimensional plane which passes through $\eta(\theta_p^i)$, $p = 1, \ldots, P+1$. For convenience, we assume that θ_{P+1}^i corresponds to the point closest to y; we then determine the $P \times P$ matrix T by setting its pth column equal to $\theta_p^i - \theta_{P+1}^i$, and the $N \times P$ matrix H by setting its pth column equal to $\eta(\theta_p^i) - \eta(\theta_{P+1}^i)$. Then, formally,

$$\hat{\alpha} = (H^T H)^{-1} H^T [y - \eta(\theta_{P+1}^i)]$$

$$\theta_{new} = \theta_{P+1}^i + T\hat{\alpha}$$

and

$$\theta_{trial} = \theta_{new}\lambda + \theta_{P+1}^i (1 - \lambda)$$

Note that Ralston and Jennrich (1978) allow the step factor to be negative, by choosing λ from a sequence of values $1, 1/2, -1/4, 1/8, -1/16, \ldots$. At convergence the linear approximation parameter covariance matrix is given by $s^2 T(H^T H)^{-1} T^T$, where s^2 is the usual variance estimate. Note that the matrix T may be ill conditioned by the time convergence is achieved and so the linear approximation standard errors and correlations may not be reliable.

3.5.5 Removing Conditionally Linear Parameters

One way of simplifying a nonlinear regression problem is to eliminate conditionally linear parameters. As mentioned in Sections 2.1 and 3.3.5, the optimal values of the conditionally linear parameters, for fixed values of the nonlinear parameters, can be determined by linear least squares. If we partition the parameter vector θ into the conditionally linear parameters β of dimension P_1 and the nonlinear parameters ϕ of dimension P_2 with $P = P_1 + P_2$, the expected responses can be written

$$\eta(\beta, \phi) = A(\phi)\beta$$

where the $N \times P_1$ matrix A depends only on the nonlinear parameters. For any value of ϕ, the conditional estimate of β is

$$\hat{\beta}(\phi) = A^+(\phi) y$$

where $A^+ = (A^T A)^{-1} A^T$ is the pseudoinverse of A. The associated expected responses are

$$\hat{\eta}(\phi) = A(\phi)A^+(\phi)\,y$$

Golub and Pereyra (1973) formulated a Gauss–Newton algorithm to minimize the reduced sum of squares function

$$S_2(\phi) = \| \, y - A(\phi)\hat{\beta}(\phi) \, \|^2$$

that depends only on the nonlinear parameters. In particular, they give the derivative of $A^+(\phi)$ with respect to ϕ, which is the key ingredient in the algorithm. The expression for this derivative is used in Chapter 4, where we present a Gauss–Newton algorithm for multiresponse parameter estimation.

One difficulty with using projection over the conditionally linear parameters is that additional information about the parameters must be given by the user. The user must specify which parameters are conditionally linear as well as specifying the derivatives of the entries of A with respect to ϕ. This often results in more difficulty than simply ignoring the conditional linearity. There are some structured problems, however—such as spline regression with knot positions allowed to vary, as described in Jupp (1978)—where the division between conditionally linear and nonlinear parameters is inherent in the specification of the problem, so the Golub–Pereyra method can be used to advantage. These methods are discussed further in Kaufman (1975) and Bates and Lindstrom (1986).

3.6   Obtaining Convergence

Obtaining convergence is sometimes difficult. If you are having trouble, check the following:

Is the expectation function correctly specified?
Is the expectation function correctly coded?
Are the derivatives correctly specified?
Are the derivatives correctly coded?
Are the data entered correctly?
Are all the observations reasonable?
Is the response variable correctly identified?
Do the starting values have the correct values?
Do the starting values correspond to the correct parameters?

If the answer to all these questions is yes, look carefully at the output from the optimization program. Most good programs can produce detailed output on each iteration to help find out what is wrong. Check to see that the initial sum of squares, $S(\theta^0)$, is smaller than the sum of squares of the responses. If not, then the fitted function is worse than no function and, in spite of your checks, you probably have an incorrect expectation function, or incorrect data, or incorrect starting values. You may even be trying to fit an x variable rather than the response y.

Look at the parameter values. Do the starting values have the correct magnitudes? Correct signs? And are they assigned to the correct parameters?

Next, look at the parameter increments. Are they all of roughly the same magnitude relative to the parameters? Does the increment, when added to the parameter vector, place the parameter vector in a bad region in the parameter space? For example, are any necessarily positive parameters driven negative? Do any of the parameters become unreasonably large or small? If so, could there be an error in the derivative functions? Try using numerical derivatives at a few design points to check the analytic derivatives. Would different starting values for some of the parameters help? Is there a transformation of the parameters which could help?

Sometimes convergence is not achieved because the model has too many parameters. Look at the parameter values to see whether any of them are being driven to extreme values corresponding to a simpler model function. Also look at combinations of the parameter increments to see, for example, if pairs of them tend to move together, suggesting collinearity or possibly overparametrization. If there is a suspicion of overparametrization, try simplifying the expectation function, even temporarily—it may be that a simpler model will produce better parameter estimates, so that eventually the full model can be fitted.

Check to see that there are enough data in all regions of the design space so that valid parameter estimates can be obtained. For example, when fitting a transition type model in which there is, say, linear behavior to the left of a point and different linear behavior to the right (Bacon and Watts, 1971; Hinkley, 1969; Watts and Bacon, 1974), it is often the case that there are lots of data values to define the behavior away from the join point, but not many near the join point. In this situation, the parameter which describes the sharpness of transition will be poorly estimated, and so convergence may be slow.

When dealing with a comprehensive model which involves combining data from several experiments, it is generally good practice to fit each data set with a possibly simpler restricted model, and gradually extend the model by incorporating more data sets and parameters. An example of this is given in Ziegel (1985). Conversely, a large data set which has several reasonably distinct operating regions can be blocked into small subsets on that basis, so that a reduced model can be fitted to each subset and the results used to provide starting estimates for a model for the full data set, as illustrated below.

Example: Lubricant 1

To illustrate the process of getting starting values and obtaining convergence for a complicated nonlinear model function, we consider data on the kinematic viscosity of a lubricant as a function of temperature (x_1) and pressure (x_2). The data, discussed in Linssen (1975), are reproduced in Appendix 1, Section A1.8, and plotted in Figure 3.4. The model function is

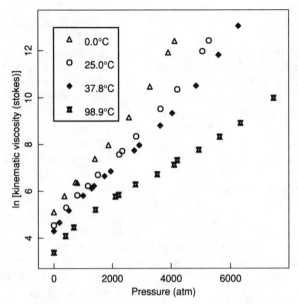

Figure 3.4 Plot of the logarithm of the kinematic viscosity of a lubricant versus pressure for four different temperatures.

$$f(\mathbf{x},\boldsymbol{\theta}) = \frac{\theta_1}{\theta_2 + x_1} + \theta_3 x_2 + \theta_4 x_2^2 + \theta_5 x_2^3$$

$$+ (\theta_6 + \theta_7 x_2^2) x_2 \exp\left[\frac{-x_1}{\theta_8 + \theta_9 x_2^2}\right]$$

(3.3)

To begin, we note that six of the nine parameters are conditionally linear, which is most helpful. Also, to improve conditioning, as discussed in Section 3.4.1, we scale the pressure data x_2 by dividing by 1000 and avoid confusion by writing $w_2 = x_2/1000$.

To obtain a starting estimate for θ_2, we use the data for $w_2 = 0.001$ and assume that for this low value of scaled pressure, the model is a function of x_1 only. Taking reciprocals and using linear least squares as described in Section 3.3.3 gives $\theta_1^0 = 983$ and $\theta_2^0 = 192$.

Now we exploit the conditional linearity in the model because we can use linear least squares to obtain starting estimates for the remaining parameters once we have reasonable estimates for θ_8 and θ_9. Thus we concentrate on getting estimates for only these two. We simplify the situation even more by assuming that when w_2 is small, the model function is essentially linear in w_2, so that

$$f(\mathbf{x}, \boldsymbol{\theta}) \approx \frac{\theta_1}{\theta_2 + x_1} + \theta_3 w_2 + \theta_6 w_2 \, e^{-x_1/\theta_8}$$

That is, we can ignore the terms involving θ_4, θ_5, θ_7, and θ_9. By examining the plot, we see that the data for each temperature follow quite straight lines for $w_2 < 2$, so we choose this for the range. Also, for fixed values of x_1, the leading term and the exponential term are constant and we may rearrange the model as

$$y' = \theta_3 w_2 + \theta_6 w_2 \, g$$

$$= w_2 \beta$$

where

$$y' = y - \frac{983}{192 + x_1}$$

$$g = e^{-x_1/\theta_8}$$

and

$$\beta = \theta_3 + \theta_6 g$$

Regressing y' on w_2 for each of the four temperatures 0, 25, 37.8, 98.9 gives β values of 1.57, 1.49, 1.39, 1.37. We now use the β values and the relation $g = e^{-x_1/\theta_8}$ to obtain estimates for θ_3 and θ_6 by noting that when $x_1 = 0$ we have $g = 1$, so $\beta = \theta_3 + \theta_6$, and when $x_1 \to \infty$, $\beta = \theta_3$. We therefore estimate the sum of the two parameters as 1.57 (the value of β at $x_1 = 0$), and assuming that the lower asymptote has almost been reached at the highest temperature, we choose θ_3 to be 1.35, which is a bit smaller than 1.37 (the value of β at $x_1 = 98.9$). The value for θ_6 is then estimated as $1.57 - 1.35 = 0.22$. Finally, since $\beta = \theta_3 + \theta_6 g$, so $(\beta - \theta_3)/\theta_6 = g$, we regressed

$$\ln\left[\frac{\beta - 1.35}{0.22}\right]$$

on x_1 to give $\theta_8 = 35.5$.

Using these parameter estimates for θ_2 and θ_8, we performed a nonlinear regression on the data for small w_2 values to get more refined estimates, $\theta_2 = 202$ and $\theta_8 = 35.90$. We then used these estimates for θ_2 and θ_8, and the data for all w_2 values, to estimate all the parameters with $\theta_9 = 0$. The new values were $\theta_2 = 209$ and $\theta_8 = 47.55$. Finally, we used these values plus the starting value $\theta_9 = 0$ to converge on the full model. The final parameter estimates were

$$\hat{\boldsymbol{\theta}} = (1053, 206.1, 1.464, -0.259, 0.0224, 0.398, 0.09354, 56.97, -0.463)^{\mathrm{T}}$$

with a residual sum of squares of 0.08996. ∎

3.7   Assessing the Fit and Modifying the Model

In any nonlinear analysis, it is necessary to assess the fit of the model to the data and to assess the appropriateness of the assumptions about the disturbances. To do so, we use the same techniques as in linear regression, namely sensibleness of parameter values, comparison of mean squares and extra sums of squares, and plots of residuals. If there are any inadequacies in the model, or if any of the assumptions do not seem to be appropriate, then the model must be modified and the analysis continued until a satisfactory result is obtained.

In nonlinear estimation, it is possible to converge to parameter values which are obviously, or perhaps suspiciously, wrong. This is because we may have converged to a local minimum, or got stalled because of some awkward behavior of the expectation surface. Assessment of any fitted model should therefore begin with a careful consideration of the parameter estimates and whether they make sense scientifically. If the parameters do not make sense, check to see that the correct starting values were used. Also check to see that the program did not simply terminate due to lack of progress or too many iterations, but that convergence was actually achieved. One should also scan the iteration progress information to see if convergence occurred smoothly. Some programs have special facilities for fixing some parameters while allowing others to vary, and others have poor convergence criteria. It is incumbent on the user to understand fully the program being used and to appreciate its idiosyncrasies. "Caveat emptor" is as true for nonlinear estimation packages as it is for anything else in life.

If the program has proceeded smoothly to an apparently legitimate convergence point, but the parameters are not reasonable, check the expectation function and its coding, the derivatives and their codings, the starting values, and the data, as in Section 3.6. Is the response variable correctly specified? Are the residuals well behaved?

If these checks are satisfactory but the parameter vector is not, try a fairly different starting vector. If you then converge to the same point, it may be that the data are trying to tell you that the expectation function is not appropriate. At this stage it may well be helpful to discuss things with the researcher or a colleague; as often happens, in the course of such a discussion you may discover a simple, "obvious" error.

When convergence to reasonable values has been reached, check the parameter approximate standard errors and approximate t ratios [calculated as (parameter estimate) / (approximate standard error)]. If a t ratio is not significant, consider deleting that parameter from the expectation function and refitting the model, as discussed more fully in Section 3.10.

Generally, the simpler the model the better (Ockham's razor: see quotation, p.1).

Also check the parameter approximate correlation matrix to see whether any parameters are excessively highly correlated, since high correlations may indicate overparametrization (a model which is too complicated for the data set).

Exactly what constitutes a "high" correlation is somewhat dependent on the type of data and model being considered. In general, correlations above 0.99 in absolute value should be investigated. Try simplifying the expectation function in a scientifically sensible way or transforming the variables and parameters to reduce collinearities (Section 3.4). For further discussion on simplifying models, see Section 3.8. Further information on variability of parameter estimates and nonlinear dependencies between parameter estimates can be obtained using the techniques of Chapter 6.

When a simple, adequate expectation function has been found, a plot of the fitted values overlaid with the observed responses is an excellent way to assess the fit. Plots of the residuals versus the fitted values and the control variables are also powerful aids. The residuals should also be plotted against other, possibly lurking factors to help detect model inadequacies. For further discussion, see Draper and Smith (1981), Joiner (1981), or Cook and Weisberg (1983). Particular attention should be paid to whether the residuals have a uniform spread, since any nonsystematic behavior is suggestive of nonconstant variance. If there is nonconstant variance, consider transforming the data to induce constant variance, and transforming the model function to maintain the integrity of the model, possibly using the approach in Carroll and Ruppert (1984) to optimize the transformation parameter, or try using weighted least squares.

Nonrandom behavior of the residuals, as evidenced by plots of the residuals against the regressor variables or other variables, tends to indicate lack of adequacy of the expectation function. In such cases, try expanding the model in a scientifically sensible way to eliminate the nonrandom behavior. For example, add "incremental" parameters to account for differences between subjects or days, or between groups of subjects or days, as discussed in Section 3.10. When dealing with sums of exponentials, perhaps add a constant term to allow for decay to a nonzero asymptote.

Probability plots of the residuals should be made to verify the normal assumption about the disturbances. If there is pronounced lack of normality, try to decide whether it is due to a small number of outliers or whether it is due to inadequacy of the expectation function. For obvious outliers, check that the data have been correctly recorded and correctly entered into the computer. If they have been correctly entered, discuss with the experimenter the propriety of deleting them. Perhaps there are good nonstatistical reasons for removing them—for example, a contaminated sample. If you are considering such editing, it may be helpful to present the experimenter with information concerning the influence of the possible outliers, such as parameter estimates, standard deviations, fitted values, and residual mean squares with and without the suspicious data points.

If the residuals are clearly nonnormal, consider transforming the data and the model (Carroll and Ruppert, 1984) or changing the criterion from least squares to a "robust" estimation criterion (Huber, 1981). Note, however, that the use of criteria other than least squares will usually require special software.

Assessment of adequacy of the expectation function is easier if there are replications, because it will have been possible to check for, or transform to, stable variance before fitting the model. Replications also allow one to test for lack of fit of the model by comparing the ratio of the lack of fit mean square with the replication mean square with the appropriate F distribution value, as discussed in Sections 1.3.2, 3.10, and 3.12.

3.8   Correlated Residuals

Whenever time or distance is involved as a factor in a regression analysis, it is prudent to check the assumption of independent disturbances. Correlation of the disturbances can be detected from a *time series* plot of the residuals versus time (or order of the experiments) or from a *lag* plot of the residual on the nth case versus the residual on the $(n-1)$th case. Tendencies for the residuals to stay positive or negative in runs on the time series plot, or nonrandom scatter of the residuals when plotted on the lag plot, can reveal nonindependence or correlation of the disturbances.

Example: Chloride 1
Sredni (1970) analyzed data on chloride ion transport through blood cell walls. The data, derived from Sredni's thesis, are listed in Appendix 1, Section A1.9, and plotted in Figure 3.5. The observation y_n gives the chloride concentration (in percent) at time x_n (in minutes).

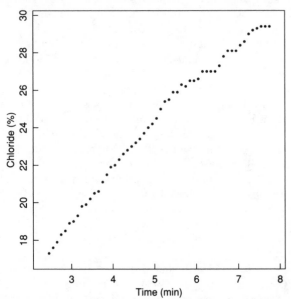

Figure 3.5   Plot of chloride concentration versus time for the chloride transport data.

The model function

$$f(x_n, \boldsymbol{\theta}) = \theta_1 (1 - \theta_2 e^{-\theta_3 x_n})$$

was derived from the theory of ion transport, where θ_1 represents the final percentage concentration of chlorine, θ_3 is a rate constant, and θ_2 accounts for the unknown initial and final concentrations of the chlorine and the unknown initial reaction time. As usual, it was assumed that the disturbances had zero mean and constant variance and were independent.

An initial estimate for θ_1 was obtained by extrapolating the data to large time, giving $\theta_1^0 = 35$. Dividing y_n by θ_1^0 and linearizing the equation by rearranging terms and taking logarithms allowed us to estimate the remaining parameters by linear regression, to give $\boldsymbol{\theta}^0 = (35, 0.91, 0.22)^T$. Convergence was obtained to $\hat{\boldsymbol{\theta}} = (39.09, 0.828, 0.159)^T$ with a residual sum of squares of 1.88. A time series plot of the residuals, shown in Figure 3.6a, shows runs in the residuals. Similarly, the lag plot shown in Figure 3.6b, shows positive correlation. We are thus alerted to the possibility that the disturbances are not independent, or that there is some deficiency in the form of the expectation function. ■

When the disturbances are not independent, the model for the observations must be altered to account for dependence. Common forms for dependence, or *autocorrelation*, of disturbances are *moving average* or *autoregressive* models of variable order (Box and Jenkins, 1976). Simple examples of such forms are a moving average process of order 1 where

$$Z_n = \varepsilon_n - \omega_1 \varepsilon_{n-1}$$

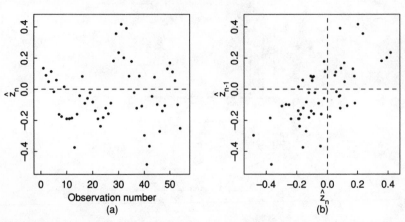

Figure 3.6 Plots of the residuals $\hat{z}$ from the original nonlinear least squares fit to the chloride data. The residuals are plotted as a time series in part a and as a lag plot in part b.

or an autoregressive process of order 1 where

$$Z_n = \varepsilon_n + \phi_1 Z_{n-1}$$

and the ε_n, $n = 1, 2, \ldots, N$, are independent random disturbances with zero mean and constant variance, or more simply, *white noise*.

In regression situations, when the data are equally spaced in time, it is relatively easy to determine an appropriate form for the dependence of the disturbances by calculating and plotting the *residual autocorrelation function*,

$$r_k = \sum_{n=k+1}^{N} \frac{\hat{z}_n \hat{z}_{n-k}}{Ns^2} \qquad k = 1, 2, \ldots$$

versus the lag k. In the definition of r_k, s^2 is the variance estimate, and the residuals are assumed to have zero average. The residual autocorrelation function is usually calculated out to $k \approx N/5$. If the residual autocorrelation function is consistently within the range $\pm 2/\sqrt{N}$ after lag 2 or 3, then the model may be identified as a moving average process of order 1 or 2. If the residual autocorrelation function tends to decay gradually to zero, then the process may be identified as an autoregressive process. Alternatively, to determine the order of the autoregressive process, it may be necessary to calculate the *partial autocorrelation function* (Box and Jenkins, 1976). For regression situations where time is not the only factor, or the most important factor, first order autoregressive processes are often adequate.

Example: Chloride 2

The residual autocorrelation function for the chloride data was calculated

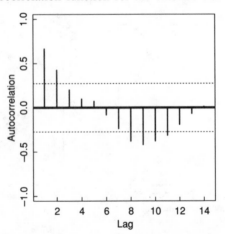

Figure 3.7 Autocorrelation function of the residuals from the original nonlinear least squares fit to the chloride data. The dotted lines enclose the interval in which approximately 95% of the correlations would be expected to lie if the true correlations were 0.

and plotted as in Figure 3.7. The correlation estimates decay towards zero, falling within the limits $\pm 2/\sqrt{N}$ (shown as dotted horizontal lines) quite quickly. On the basis of this plot, it was decided that a first order autoregressive process would adequately model the dependence in the residuals.

The model to be fitted is now of the form $Y_n = f(x_n, \theta) + Z_n$, where $Z_n = \varepsilon_n + \phi Z_{n-1}$. To estimate the parameters θ and ϕ, we reduce the problem to an ordinary nonlinear least squares problem by subtracting ϕ times the equation for Y_{n-1} from Y_n, as

$$Y_n - \phi Y_{n-1} = f(x_n, \theta) - \phi f(x_{n-1}, \theta) + Z_n - \phi Z_{n-1}$$

or

$$Y_n = \phi Y_{n-1} + f(x_n, \theta) - \phi f(x_{n-1}, \theta) + \varepsilon_n$$

Starting values for θ were taken from $\hat{\theta}$ above, and the starting value for ϕ was taken as the lag one correlation estimate, $r_1 = 0.67$. Convergence was obtained to $(\theta^T, \phi) = (37.58, 0.849, 0.178, 0.69)$ with a residual sum of squares of 0.98. The residuals $\hat{\varepsilon}$ from this fit are well behaved, as shown in Figure 3.8 and the residual autocorrelation function, shown in Figure 3.9, was uniformly small. ■

In general, as in the above example, the main effect of accounting for dependence is to reduce the residual variance and reduce the correlation in the residuals: the model parameter estimate $\hat{\theta}$ does not change much. However, the model parameters are better estimated because they have smaller standard errors and because the method of least squares has been applied correctly, since the assumptions are satisfied. For a more complicated application of this technique,

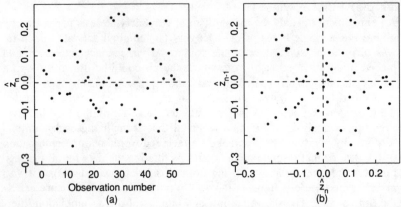

Figure 3.8 Plots of the residuals $\hat{z}$ from the nonlinear least squares fit to the chloride data using $\phi = 0.69$. The residuals are plotted as a time series in part a and as a lag plot in part b.

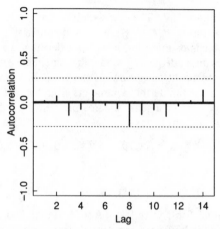

Figure 3.9   Autocorrelation function of the residuals from the nonlinear least squares fit to the chloride data using $\phi = 0.69$. The dotted lines enclose the interval in which approximately 95% of the correlations would be expected to lie if the true correlations were 0.

see Watts and Bacon (1974).

3.9   Accumulated Data

In some studies, when it is impractical to measure instantaneous concentrations, *accumulated* responses are recorded.

Example: Ethyl acrylate 1
An experiment to study the metabolism of ethyl acrylate was performed by giving rats a single bolus of radioactively tagged ethyl acrylate. Each rat was given a measured dose of the compound via stomach intubation and placed in an enclosed cage from which the air could be drawn through a bubble chamber. The exhaled air was bubbled through the chamber, and at a specified time the bubble chamber was replaced by a fresh one, so that the measured response was the accumulated CO_2 during the time interval. Preliminary analysis of the data revealed that normalizing each animal's response by dividing by the actual dose received would permit combination of the data so that a single model could be fitted to the data for all the rats. Furthermore, the variability in the normalized data was such that it was necessary to take logarithms of the data to produce constant variance across the time points. The starting points and lengths of the accumulation intervals and the averages for the nine rats, normalized by actual dose, are given in Appendix 1, Section A1.10 (Watts, deBethizy, and Stiratelli, 1986), and the cumulative CO_2 data are plotted in Figure 3.10.   ∎

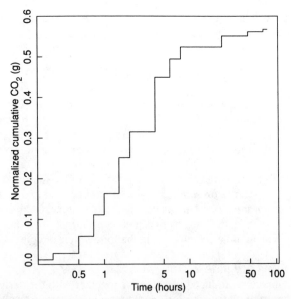

Figure 3.10 Plot of cumulative exhaled CO_2 amounts versus collection interval end point for the ethyl acrylate data.

Two methods for the analysis of such data were given in Renwick (1982). The first method uses peeling of the "approximate concentration" data obtained by dividing the accumulated amount by the accumulation time interval. The second method uses the cumulative total, extrapolated to infinite time, and then peeling of the differences [*extrapolated – (cumulative total)*]. This is called the "sigma–minus" method.

We do not recommend either of these methods, and specifically decry use of the sigma–minus method because it is so sensitive to variations in the extrapolated value. It can be shown, for example, that small percentage changes in the extrapolated value, say less than 2%, can cause changes in the rate constants in excess of 100%. Furthermore, both methods are based on peeling, which requires excessive subjective judgement. Instead of the abovementioned methods, we recommend direct analysis of the accumulated data using integrated responses as described below. In addition to avoiding the disadvantages of the other methods, this method has the advantage that it provides measures of precision of the estimates in the form of parameter approximate standard errors and correlations.

3.9.1   Estimating the Parameters by Direct Integration

Suppose that the theoretical response to the input stimulus at time t is $f(t, \boldsymbol{\theta})$. Then the accumulated output in the interval t_{n-1} to t_n is

$$F_n = \int_{t_{n-1}}^{t_n} f(t, \boldsymbol{\theta}) \, dt$$

We therefore use the integrated function values F_n and the observed accumulated data pairs (y_n, t_n) to estimate the parameters. We rewrite the model in terms of the factors $x_{1n} = t_{n-1}$, the start of the interval, and $x_{2n} = t_n - t_{n-1}$, the length of the interval, so the model for the amount accumulated in an interval is $F(\mathbf{x}_n, \boldsymbol{\theta})$, where $\mathbf{x}_n = (x_{1n}, x_{2n})^{\mathrm{T}}$.

To determine a tentative form for $f(t, \boldsymbol{\theta})$, we plot the approximate rates y_n / x_{2n} versus $x_{1n} + x_{2n}/2$ on semilog paper and use peeling to obtain *starting* estimates for the parameters. The final estimation is done using nonlinear least squares. Note that if the variance is not constant, it may be necessary to transform the data and the function, as in the following example.

Example: Ethyl acrylate 2

The CO_2 data are reproduced in Table 3.1 together with the derived quantities (interval midpoint $x_{1n} + x_{2n}/2$ and approximate rate y_n / x_{2n}) which are plotted in Figure 3.11. We can see from the figure that an appropriate model for the data involves three exponentials (two to account for the peak, and another to account for the change in slope of the decay from the peak). Because the radioactivity prior to injection must be zero, the concentration at $t = 0$ must be zero. A plausible model for the concentration at time t is therefore

$$f(t, \boldsymbol{\theta}) = -(\theta_4 + \theta_5)e^{-\theta_1 t} + \theta_4 e^{-\theta_2 t} + \theta_5 e^{-\theta_3 t}$$

An appropriate model for the accumulated data in the collection interval starting at t_{n-1} is then

$$F_n = -\frac{\theta_4 + \theta_5}{\theta_1}(e^{-\theta_1 t_{n-1}} - e^{-\theta_1 t_n})$$

$$+ \frac{\theta_4}{\theta_2}(e^{-\theta_2 t_{n-1}} - e^{-\theta_2 t_n}) + \frac{\theta_5}{\theta_3}(e^{-\theta_3 t_{n-1}} - e^{-\theta_3 t_n})$$

or

$$F(\mathbf{x}, \boldsymbol{\theta}) = -\frac{\theta_4 + \theta_5}{\theta_1}e^{-\theta_1 x_1}(1 - e^{-\theta_1 x_2})$$

$$+ \frac{\theta_4}{\theta_2}e^{-\theta_2 x_1}(1 - e^{-\theta_2 x_2}) + \frac{\theta_5}{\theta_3}e^{-\theta_3 x_1}(1 - e^{-\theta_3 x_2})$$

Because of the nonconstant variance, the logarithms of F were fitted to the

Table 3.1 Collection intervals and averages of normalized exhaled CO_2 for the ethyl acrylate data together with the derived quantities: interval midpoint and approximate rate

Collection Interval (hr)			Derived Quantities	
Start x_1	Length x_2	CO_2 (g)	Interval Midpoint	Approx. Rate
0.0	0.25	0.01563	0.125	0.0625
0.25	0.25	0.04190	0.375	0.1676
0.5	0.25	0.05328	0.625	0.2131
0.75	0.25	0.05226	0.875	0.2090
1.0	0.5	0.08850	1.25	0.1770
1.5	0.5	0.06340	1.75	0.1268
2.0	2.0	0.13419	3.0	0.0671
4.0	2.0	0.04502	5.0	0.0225
6.0	2.0	0.02942	7.0	0.0147
8.0	16.0	0.02716	16.0	0.0017
24.0	24.0	0.01037	36.0	0.0004
48.0	24.0	0.00602	60.0	0.0003

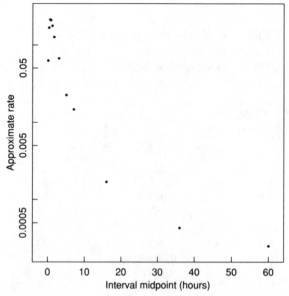

Figure 3.11 Approximate CO_2 exhalation rate versus collection interval midpoint for the ethyl acrylate data.

logarithms of the data. The results of this analysis together with the starting estimates are presented in Table 3.2.

   In an analysis of the logarithmic data for the individual rats, due attention was paid to the behavior of the residuals. The triple rate constant model fitted the data very well. ■

Table 3.2 Parameter summary for the 3-exponential model fitted to the ethyl acrylate data.

		Nonlinear Least Squares	
Parameter	Start	Estimate	Approx. Std. Err.
θ_1	4.461	3.025	0.752
θ_2	0.571	0.481	0.038
θ_3	0.0434	0.0258	0.0096
θ_4	0.355	0.310	0.049
θ_5	0.0034	0.0011	0.0005

Example: Saccharin 1

As a second example of treating accumulated data, we analyze the saccharin data in Renwick (1982). In this experiment, the measured response was the amount of saccharin accumulated in the urine of a rat after receiving a single bolus of saccharin. The data are recorded in Appendix 1, Section A1.11, and plotted in Figure 3.12.

The function involved only two rate constants, and the response was modeled as

$$f(t, \boldsymbol{\theta}) = \theta_3 e^{-\theta_1 t} + \theta_4 e^{-\theta_2 t}$$

so

$$F(\mathbf{x}, \boldsymbol{\theta}) = \frac{\theta_3}{\theta_1} e^{-\theta_1 x_1} (1 - e^{-\theta_1 x_2}) + \frac{\theta_4}{\theta_2} e^{-\theta_2 x_1} (1 - e^{-\theta_2 x_2})$$

As in the ethyl acrylate example, the integrated model was fitted to the logarithms of the accumulated data to stabilize variance.

The curve peeling and the sigma–minus method results from Renwick (1982) are given in columns 2 and 3 of Table 3.3, and the results using the direct integration method are given in column 4. Note the considerable differences between the results based on peeling and those obtained by nonlinear least squares. Note too, that the peeling and sigma–minus

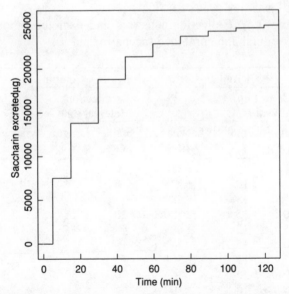

Figure 3.12 Plot of cumulative excreted amount versus collection interval end point for the saccharin data.

Table 3.3 Parameter summary for the saccharin data, comparing estimates obtained using the sigma–minus method, using the approximate rate method, and using nonlinear least squares to fit the integrated response function.

			Estimate by Nonlinear Least Squares	
Parameter	Peeling[a]	Sigma–Minus[a]	Value	Approx. Std. Err.
θ_1	0.0710	0.0833	0.122	0.031
θ_2	0.0234	0.0255	0.0279	0.003
θ_3	830	932	1345	249
θ_4	270	314	402	98

[a] From Renwick (1982).

methods do not provide parameter standard errors.

There were two very large residuals from the nonlinear least squares fit, at $x_1 = 5$ and $x_1 = 105$. A second analysis was done by simply combining the observations at $x_1 = 5$ and $x_1 = 15$ and at $x_1 = 90$ and $x_1 = 105$, as shown in Table 3.4. The residuals from this fit were very well behaved,

Table 3.4 Collection intervals and excreted amounts for original and combined saccharin data.

Original			Combined		
Collection Interval (hr)			Collection Interval (hr)		
Start x_1	Length x_2	Saccharin (μg)	Start x_1	Length x_2	Saccharin (μg)
0	5	7518	0	5	7518
5	10	6275	5	25	11264
15	15	4989			
30	15	2580	30	15	2580
45	15	1485	45	15	1485
60	15	861	60	15	861
75	15	561	75	15	561
90	15	363	90	30	663
105	15	300			

and the residual variance was reduced to 0.0071 from 0.0158. The parameter estimates (standard errors in parentheses) were $\theta_1 = 0.154(0.035)$, $\theta_2 = 0.030(0.002)$, $\theta_3 = 1506(233)$, and $\theta_4 = 472(70)$. ∎

3.10 Comparing Models

In some situations there may be more than one function which could be used as a model. For example, in fitting a double exponential model,

$$f(x, \boldsymbol{\theta}) = \theta_1 e^{-\theta_2 x} + \theta_3 e^{-\theta_4 x}$$

θ_4 could be 0, in which case the model reduces to

$$f(x, \boldsymbol{\theta}) = \theta_1 e^{-\theta_2 x} + \theta_3$$

or θ_3 could be 0, in which case the model reduces to

$$f(x, \boldsymbol{\theta}) = \theta_1 e^{-\theta_2 x}$$

In this situation of *nested* models, we would be interested in finding the simplest model which adequately fits the data.

In other situations, we might compare *non-nested* models—for example, model 1

$$f(x, \boldsymbol{\theta}) = \theta_1 (1 - e^{-\theta_2 x})$$

versus model 2

$$f(x, \boldsymbol{\theta}) = \frac{\theta_1 x}{\theta_2 + x}$$

both of which start at $f = 0$ when $x = 0$ and approach the asymptote θ_1 as $x \to \infty$. In these situations, one model may give a superior fit to the data, and we would like to select that model.

3.10.1 Nested Models

To decide which is the simplest nested model to fit a data set adequately, we proceed as in the linear case and use a likelihood ratio test (Draper and Smith, 1981). Because of the spherical normal assumption, this leads to an assessment of the extra sum of squares due to the extra parameters involved in going from the partial to the full model.

Letting S denote the sum of squares, ν the degrees of freedom, and P the number of parameters, with subscripts f and p for the *full* and *partial* models and a subscript e for *extra*, the calculations can be summarized as in Table 3.5. To complete the analysis, we compare the ratio s_e^2 / s_f^2 to $F(\nu_e, \nu_f; \alpha)$ and accept the partial model if the calculated mean square ratio is lower than the table value. Otherwise, we retain the extra terms and use the full model. Illustrations of the

Table 3.5   Extra sum of squares analysis for nested models.

Source	Sum of Squares	Degrees of Freedom	Mean Square	F Ratio
Extra parameters	$S_e = S_p - S_f$	$v_e = P_f - P_p$	$s_e^2 = S_e / v_e$	s_e^2 / s_f^2
Full model	S_f	$v_f = N - P_f$	$s_f^2 = S_f / v_f$	
Partial model	S_p	$N - P_p$		

use of the extra sum of squares analysis are given below in Example Puromycin 10 and in Section 3.11.

Note that for linear least squares, the extra sum of squares analysis is exact because the data vector y is being projected onto linear subspaces of the response space to determine S_p and S_f. Mathematically, the partial model expectation plane is a linear subspace of the full model expectation plane. Residual vectors can then be decomposed into orthogonal components and, from the fact that the full model residual vector has a squared length which is distributed as a $\sigma^2 \chi^2$ random variable with $N - P$ degrees of freedom, it follows that the squared lengths of the components are also distributed as $\sigma^2 \chi^2$ random variables with degrees of freedom equal to the dimensions of the linear subspaces.

For nonlinear models, as we might expect, the analysis is only approximate because the calculated mean square ratio will not have an exact F distribution. However, the distribution of the mean square ratio is only affected by intrinsic nonlinearity and not by parameter effects nonlinearity, and, as shown in Chapter 7, the intrinsic nonlinearity is generally small. When the partial model is inadequate, the effect of intrinsic nonlinearity on the analysis can be large but the partial model will be rejected anyway: it is only when the fitted values are very close that the form of the distribution is critical. In these cases, the intrinsic nonlinearity will usually have a small effect because the expected responses being compared are close together on the expectation surface.

3.10.2   Incremental Parameters and Indicator Variables

Many nested models can be parametrized in terms of incremental parameters. An *incremental parameter* accounts for a change in a parameter between blocks of cases and is associated with an indicator variable. An advantage of using incremental parameters is that a preliminary evaluation of the need for the full model can be made directly from the regression output without having to do additional computation. The use of incremental parameters is most easily described by means of an example.

Example: Puromycin 10

In the Puromycin experiment, two blocks of experiments were run. In one the enzyme was treated with puromycin (Table A1.3a), and in the other the same enzyme was untreated (Table A1.3b). It was hypothesized that the Puromycin should affect the maximum velocity parameter θ_1, but not the half-velocity parameter θ_2. The two data sets are plotted in Figure 3.13.

To determine if the θ_2 parameter is unchanged, we use an extra sum of squares analysis, which requires fitting a full and a partial model. The full model corresponds to completely different sets of parameters for the treated data and the untreated data, while the partial model corresponds to different θ_1 parameters but the same θ_2 parameter. To combine the full and partial models, we introduce the *indicator variable*

$$x_2 = \begin{cases} 0 & \text{untreated} \\ 1 & \text{treated} \end{cases}$$

and let x_1 be the substrate concentration. The combined model is then written

$$f(\mathbf{x}, \boldsymbol{\theta}) = \frac{(\theta_1 + \phi_1 x_2) x_1}{(\theta_2 + \phi_2 x_2) + x_1} \tag{3.4}$$

where θ_1 is the maximum velocity for the untreated enzyme, ϕ_1 is the in-

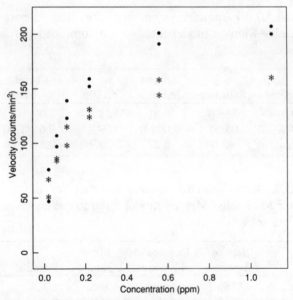

Figure 3.13 Plot of enzyme velocity data versus substrate concentration. The data for the enzyme treated (not treated) with Puromycin are shown as ● (∗).

cremental maximum velocity due to the treatment, θ_2 is the (possibly common) "half-velocity" point, and ϕ_2 is the change in the half-velocity due to the treatment. Since we expect ϕ_1 to be nonzero, we are interested in testing whether ϕ_2 could be zero.

The model (3.4) was fitted and the results of this fit are shown in Table 3.6. It appears that ϕ_2 could be zero, since it has a small t ratio, and so we fit the partial model (3.4) with $\phi_2 = 0$. The results of this fit are given in Table 3.7 and the extra sum of squares analysis is presented in Table 3.8. In this well-designed experiment, which includes replications, it is also

Table 3.6 Parameter summary for the 4-parameter Michaelis–Menten model fitted to the combined Puromycin data set.

Parameter	Estimate	Approx. Std. Err.	t Ratio	Correlation Matrix			
θ_1	160.3	6.90	23.2	1.00			
θ_2	0.0477	0.00828	5.8	0.77	1.00		
ϕ_1	52.4	9.55	5.5	−0.72	−0.56	1.00	
ϕ_2	0.0164	0.0114	1.4	−0.56	−0.72	0.77	1.00

Table 3.7 Parameter summary for the 3-parameter Michaelis–Menten model fitted to the combined Puromycin data set.

Parameter	Estimate	Approx. Std. Err.	t Ratio	Correlation Matrix		
θ_1	166.6	5.81	28.7	1.00		
θ_2	0.058	0.00591	9.8	0.61	1.00	
ϕ_1	42.0	6.27	6.7	−0.54	0.06	1.00

Table 3.8 Extra sum of squares analysis for the 3- and 4-parameter Michaelis–Menten model fitted to the combined Puromycin data set.

Source	Sum of Squares	Degrees of Freedom	Mean Square	F Ratio	p Value
Extra	186	1	186.	1.7	0.21
4-parameter	2055	19	108.2		
3-parameter	2241	20			

possible to analyze for lack of fit of the partial model as shown in Table 3.9. These summary calculations, together with plots of the residuals (not shown), suggest that a model which has a common half-velocity parameter and a higher asymptotic velocity for the treated enzyme is adequate. ∎

In the above example, the t ratios for the incremental parameters permit reliable inferences to be made concerning changes from one block to another. We recommend, however, that the extra sum of squares analysis always be used, since it is unaffected by parameter effects nonlinearity (see Chapter 7) and is therefore more exact than the t test in the nonlinear case. We only use the t ratios to suggest which incremental parameters might be zero and should be investigated further: the actual decision on whether to retain a parameter should be based on an extra sum of squares analysis or a profile t analysis (see Chapter 6).

In summary, incremental parameters provide a direct and simple procedure for determining whether changes in parameters occur between different blocks. Clearly, incremental parameters can also be used to advantage in linear least squares to determine changes in parameters between blocks, since then the t tests are exact. Even for linear least squares, however, we recommend fitting the reduced model and using the extra sum of squares analysis to make any final decisions concerning inclusion or deletion of parameters, so as to avoid problems with multicollinearity and inflation of variances. Incremental parameters can also be used when there are more than two blocks by introducing additional indicator variables or, possibly, by rewriting the parameters as functions of other variables as in Section 3.11.

3.10.3 Non-nested Models

When trying to decide which of several *non-nested* models is best, the first approach should be to the researcher. That is, if there are scientific reasons for preferring one model over the others, strong weight should be given to the researcher's reasons because the primary aim of data analysis is to explain or account for the behavior of the data, not simply to get the best fit.

Table 3.9 Lack of fit analysis for the 3-parameter Michaelis–Menten model fitted to the combined Puromycin data set.

Source	Sum of Squares	Degrees of Freedom	Mean Square	F Ratio	p Value
Lack of fit	1144	9	127.3	1.3	0.35
Replication	1097	11	99.7		
Residuals	2241	20			

If the researcher cannot provide convincing reasons for choosing one model over others, then statistical analyses can be used, the most important of which is probably an analysis of the residuals. Generally the model with the smallest residual mean square and the most random-looking residuals should be chosen. The residuals should be plotted versus the predicted values, the control variables, time order, and any other (possibly lurking) variables; see Section 3.7.

3.11 Parameters as Functions of Other Variables

In many situations, the parameters in a mechanistic model will depend on other variables. For example, in chemical kinetic studies, we may have data from several experiments in which the operating conditions have been varied, and it may be thought that the rate constants should depend in some systematic way on the operating conditions. We would then like to fit a model which incorporates the dependence of the *kinetic parameters* θ on some *process variables*, say $\mathbf{w}$, and some *process parameters*, $\phi = (\phi_1, \ldots, \phi_L)^T$. That is, $\theta = \theta(\mathbf{w}, \phi)$. The expectation function is then $f(\mathbf{x}, \theta) = f(\mathbf{x}, \theta(\mathbf{w}, \phi))$.

To estimate the parameters in such an extended model, we could express the function in terms of the regular variables $\mathbf{x}$, the process variables $\mathbf{w}$, and the process parameters ϕ, determine the derivatives with respect to ϕ, and then use a Gauss–Newton algorithm to converge to $\hat{\phi}$. It is more efficient, however, to build on what we already have and proceed as follows:

(1) At each level of $\mathbf{w}$, estimate the kinetic parameters θ in the regular model.

(2) Plot the parameter estimates $\hat{\theta}_p$ versus $\mathbf{w}$ to determine a plausible form for the relationship of $\hat{\theta}_p$ to $\mathbf{w}$ and to obtain starting estimates for the process parameters ϕ.

(3) Use the chain rule for derivatives to determine the derivatives with respect to ϕ, exploiting the existing derivatives with respect to θ, as

$$\frac{\partial \eta_n}{\partial \phi_l} = \sum_{p=1}^{P} \frac{\partial \eta_n}{\partial \theta_p} \frac{\partial \theta_p}{\partial \phi_l}$$

for $l = 1, 2, \ldots, L$, where L is the total number of process parameters.

An application of this method is described in Section 5.5.

Example: Puromycin 11

Suppose in the research on Puromycin (Example Puromycin 10) there were, say, four treatment levels of Puromycin instead of just two (treated and untreated). We could then proceed by incorporating three indicator variables to account for changes in the parameters due to different treatments. However, if the Puromycin treatments consist of different doses, it might be possible to write

$$f(x,\boldsymbol{\theta}) = \frac{\theta_1(w)x}{\theta_2(w)+x}$$

where a possible form of θ_1 and θ_2 is

$$\theta_1 = \phi_{10} + \phi_{11}\,w$$

$$\theta_2 = \phi_{20} + \phi_{21}\,w$$

In this example, the (regular) variable is x, the substrate concentration, and the process variable is w, the Puromycin concentration.

Now suppose that at Puromycin concentration w_1 we get estimates $\hat{\theta}_{11}$ and $\hat{\theta}_{21}$, at concentration w_2, we get estimates $\hat{\theta}_{12}$ and $\hat{\theta}_{22}$, and so on, and that a plot of $\hat{\theta}_2$ versus w looks essentially flat, which suggests $\theta_2 = \text{constant}$. Then we would choose $\phi_{20} = \hat{\theta}_2$. Suppose further that the plot of $\hat{\theta}_1$ versus w reveals a straight line relationship, $\theta_1 = \phi_{10} + \phi_{11}w$. We could then use linear regression of $\hat{\theta}_1$ on w to get starting estimates for ϕ_{10} and ϕ_{11}.

The model to be fitted to the combined data vector would be

$$f(x,w,\boldsymbol{\phi}) = \frac{\theta_1(w)x}{\theta_2(w)+x}$$

$$= \frac{(\phi_{10}+\phi_{11}w)x}{\phi_{20}+x} \qquad \blacksquare$$

3.12 Presenting the Results

As in all statistical analyses, the results from a nonlinear regression analysis should be presented clearly and succinctly. This is usually done most effectively by considering the needs and abilities of the prospective audience. The report should always include a summary of the main findings and conclusions.

The summary should include a statement of the final model, the parameter estimates and their standard errors, and an interpretation of the model and the parameters in the context of the original problem.

In the main body of the report, it is useful to state the original problem and possibly a derivation of the general form of mechanistic model proposed. Plots of the data should be given, and any preliminary analyses should be discussed, particularly if they involved transformation of the data or the expectation function. A listing of the data should always be included (perhaps in an appendix), but otherwise plots should be used for effective communication.

The initial model should be presented with a brief description of the steps taken to reduce or extend it, if necessary referring to detailed analyses in appendices. The final model, together with parameter estimates and their approximate standard errors and correlation matrix should be stated, along with a plot of the data, the fitted expectation function, and an approximate confidence band for the expectation function. Pairwise plots of the parameter inference region, and possibly profile t plots, as described in Chapter 6, should be given. Of great importance is an interpretation of the expectation function and the parameter values relative to the original problem, and especially any new findings, such as the need for additional variables in the model or the non-necessity of any variables or parameters.

Finally, conclusions and recommendations should be made, especially concerning possible future experiments or development of the research.

For further tips on report writing, see Ehrenberg (1981), Ehrenberg (1982), and Watts (1981). The preparation and presentation of graphical material is covered in Tufte (1983), Cleveland (1984, 1985), and Chambers et al. (1983).

3.13   Nitrite Utilization: A Case Study

To illustrate the techniques presented in this chapter, we present an analysis of data on the utilization of nitrite in bush beans as a function of light intensity (Elliott and Peirson, 1986). Portions of primary leaves from three 16-day-old bean plants were subjected to eight levels of light intensity ($\mu E/m^2 s$), and the nitrite utilization (nmol/g hr) was measured. The experiment was repeated on a different day, resulting in the data listed in Appendix 1, Section A1.12.

The experimenters did not have a theoretical mechanism to explain the behavior, but they thought that nitrite utilization should be zero at zero light intensity, and should tend to an asymptote as light intensity increased.

3.13.1   Preliminary Analysis

From a plot of the data (Figure 3.14) it can be seen that there was a difference in the nitrite utilization between experiments on the two days, particularly at higher light intensities. There is also a tendency for the response to drop at high light intensity. Note too that, even though the response ranges from 200 to 20 000 nmol/g hr, the variance is effectively constant; there is no need to transform to stabilize variance. To verify the apparent stable variance, we performed a two way analysis of variance using indicator variables for days and for light intensities, with the results shown in Tables 3.10 and 3.11.

For our purposes the most useful information from the two way analysis of variance is the replication sum of squares and mean square, which can be used for testing lack of fit. We note, however, that the lack of a significant day×intensity interaction suggests that some of the model parameters may be equal for the two days, although the significant day effect tends to corroborate the observed difference between the heights of the maxima on the two days. A plot of the replication standard deviations versus the replication averages, shown

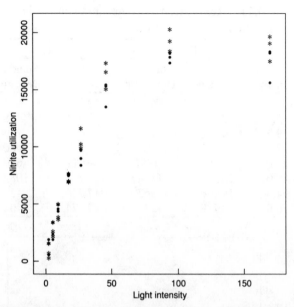

Figure 3.14 Plot of nitrite utilization by bean plants versus light intensity for day 1 (*) and day 2 (•).

Table 3.10 Two way analysis of variance for the nitrite utilization data.

Source	Sum of Squares (10^6)	Degrees of Freedom	Mean Square (10^6)	F Ratio	p Value
Days	4.23	1	4.23	6.1	0.02
Intensity	2040	7	291.5	420.	0.00
Days × intensity	10.07	7	1.44	2.1	0.08
Replication	22.21	32	0.694		

Table 3.11   Replication averages and standard deviations for the nitrite utilization data.

| | Day 1 | | Day 2 | |
Intensity	Average	Standard Deviation	Average	Standard Deviation
2.2	826	652	1 327	694
5.5	2 702	623	2 541	758
9.6	4 136	719	4 619	296
17.5	7 175	401	7 554	86
27.0	10 567	908	9 019	650
46.0	16 302	1154	14 753	1082
94.0	19 296	963	17 786	430
170.0	18 719	1117	17 374	1408

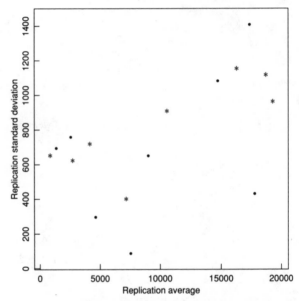

Figure 3.15   Replication standard deviations plotted versus replication averages for the nitrite utilization data. Day 1 data are shown as * and day 2 data as •.

in Figure 3.15, verified our earlier assessment that the variance is stable since there is no systematic relation, and so we proceed to model fitting.

Note that the analysis of variance is used here only as a screening tool. It is not intended as a final analysis of these data, since the underlying additive linear model assumed in an analysis of variance is not appropriate.

3.13.2 Model Selection

Because the researchers did not have a model in mind, it was necessary to select one on the basis of the behavior of the data. The Michaelis–Menten model

$$f(x, \boldsymbol{\theta}) = \frac{\theta_1 x}{\theta_2 + x}$$

and the simple exponential rise model

$$f(x, \boldsymbol{\theta}) = \theta_1 (1 - e^{-\theta_2 x})$$

were selected because they met the researcher's beliefs that nitrite utilization was zero at zero light intensity and tended to an asymptote as the light intensity increased. To simplify the description, we give details for the Michaelis–Menten model analysis, and only present summaries for the exponential rise model.

Since there are 24 observations for each day from this well-designed experiment, it would be reasonable to fit a separate model for each day. We would like to think, however, that the same parameter values, or at least some of the same parameter values, would be valid for both days, and so we proceed to fit a model for day 1 with incremental parameters for day 2. That is, we write

$$f(x, \boldsymbol{\theta}) = \frac{(\theta_1 + \phi_1 x_2) x_1}{(\theta_2 + \phi_2 x_2) + x_1}$$

where x_1 is the light intensity and x_2 is an indicator variable

$$x_2 = \begin{cases} 0 & \text{day 1} \\ 1 & \text{day 2} \end{cases}$$

as described in Section 3.10.

3.13.3 Starting Values

Since the maximum value on day 1 is about 20 000, and on day 2 is about 18 000, we choose $\theta_1^0 = 25\,000$ and $\phi_1^0 = -3000$. The response reaches about 12 500 at a light intensity of about 34 for day 1 and 35 for day 2, which gives $\theta_2^0 = 34$ and $\phi_2^0 = 1$.

3.13.4 Assessing the Fit

Convergence was achieved at the values shown in Table 3.12.

It appears from the t ratios that both the incremental parameters could be estimates of zero, and so a common model could be fitted. However, if we do a lack of fit analysis on this model as in Table 3.13, we see that this four-parameter model is not adequate. (The same conclusion was reached for the ex-

Table 3.12 Parameter summary for the 4-parameter Michaelis–Menten model fitted to the nitrite utilization data.

Parameter	Estimate	Standard Error	t Ratio	Correlation Matrix			
θ_1	24 743	1241	19.9	1.00			
θ_2	35.27	4.66	7.6	0.88	1.00		
ϕ_1	−2329	1720	−1.4	−0.72	−0.64	1.00	
ϕ_2	−2.174	6.63	−0.3	−0.62	−0.70	0.88	1.00

Table 3.13 Lack of fit analysis for the 4-parameter Michaelis–Menten model fitted to the nitrite utilization data.

Source	Sum of Squares (10^6)	Degrees of Freedom	Mean Square (10^6)	F Ratio	p Value
Lack of fit	64.30	12	5.36	7.72	0.00
Replications	22.21	32	0.694		
Residuals	86.51	44			

ponential rise model, in this case with a lack of fit ratio of 3.2, corresponding to a p value of 0.00.)

A plot of the residuals versus light intensity, as in Figure 3.16, reveals nonrandom behavior, with negative residuals at small and large intensities and positive ones in the middle. The model must therefore be modified to allow the nitrite utilization to drop with increasing light intensity, rather than leveling off as suggested by the researchers.

3.13.5   Modifying the Model

To alter the Michaelis–Menten expectation function to rise to a peak and then fall, we added a quadratic term to the denominator to produce the quadratic Michaelis–Menten model,

$$f(x,\boldsymbol{\theta}) = \frac{\theta_1 x}{\theta_2 + x + \theta_3 x^2}$$

which, with incremental parameters and an indicator variable for the different days, becomes

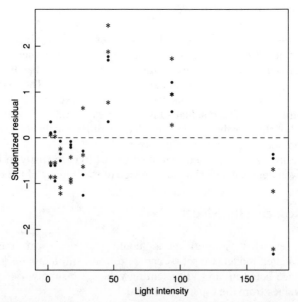

Figure 3.16 Studentized residuals from the 4-parameter Michaelis–Menten model plotted versus light intensity. Day 1 data are shown as * and day 2 data as •.

$$f(\mathbf{x}, \boldsymbol{\theta}) = \frac{(\theta_1 + \phi_1 x_2)x_1}{(\theta_2 + \phi_2 x_2) + x_1 + (\theta_3 + \phi_3 x_2)x_1^2}$$

(For the exponential rise model, we replaced the unit term by an exponential to produce the exponential difference model,

$$f = \theta_1(e^{-\theta_3 x} - e^{-\theta_2 x})$$

This model, augmented with increment parameters and an indicator variable, was also used to fit the data.)

Starting values for the parameters were obtained by taking reciprocals of the function and the data and using linear least squares for the quadratic Michaelis–Menten model. Taking reciprocals worked for the day 2 data, giving $\boldsymbol{\theta} = (107\,411, 234, 0.024)^T$, but gave some negative values for the day 1 data. We therefore used the day 2 starting values with slight perturbations to get starting values for the 6-parameter model of $\boldsymbol{\theta}^0 = (110\,000, 234, 0.024)^T$ and $\boldsymbol{\phi}^0 = (-10\,000, 23, 0.002)^T$. (For the exponential difference model, we guessed that the two rate constants might be in the ratio 1:5 and used the estimate for θ_2 to give $\theta_3 = 0.006$. We then estimated θ_1 by evaluating

$$\theta_1 = \frac{y}{e^{-0.006x} - e^{-0.030x}}$$

for several x values. This gave $\theta_1^0 = 37\,000$ for the day 1 data and 35 000 for the day 2 data, from which we got $\phi_1^0 = -2000$.)

3.13.6   Assessing the Fit

Quick convergence was achieved to the parameter estimates given in Table 3.14 for the quadratic Michaelis–Menten model. All the incremental parameters have nonsignificant approximate t ratios, which suggests that the parameters could be zero, and so a simpler model may be adequate. The extremely high parameter approximate correlations also lead one to suspect that the model may be overparametrized. The residual sum of squares (32.02×10^6 on 42 df) is only about a third of that for the previous model. (Similar conclusions were reached for the 6-parameter exponential difference model.)

The residuals for this model, plotted versus light intensity in Figure 3.17, are clearly well behaved and give no evidence of inadequacy of the model.

3.13.7   Reducing the Model

To determine what simplifications could be made in the quadratic Michaelis–Menten model, we set ϕ_2 and ϕ_3 to zero, still retaining ϕ_1 to account for a difference between days. For starting values, we simply used the relevant converged values from the 6-parameter model.

3.13.8   Assessing the Fit

The results for the 4-parameter quadratic model are given in Table 3.15. The extra sum of squares analysis for the 4-parameter versus the 6-parameter quadratic model, shown in Table 3.16, does not show a significant degradation of the fit with elimination of ϕ_2 and ϕ_3. The residuals, when plotted versus light intensity as in Figure 3.18, attest to the adequacy of the model. Furthermore, a lack of fit analysis, shown in Table 3.17, suggests that the model is adequate.

Table 3.14 Parameter summary for the 6-parameter quadratic Michaelis–Menten model fitted to the nitrite utilization data.

Parameter	Estimate	Standard Error	t Ratio	Correlation Matrix				
θ_1	89 846	37 583	2.4	1.00				
θ_2	186.7	90.1	2.1	1.00	1.00			
θ_3	0.01626	0.00922	1.8	1.00	0.99	1.00		
ϕ_1	−38 956	40 020	−1.0	−0.94	−0.94	−0.94	1.00	
ϕ_2	−83.23	96.8	−0.9	−0.93	−0.93	−0.92	1.00	1.00
ϕ_3	−0.00846	0.0993	−0.9	−0.93	−0.92	−0.93	1.00	0.99

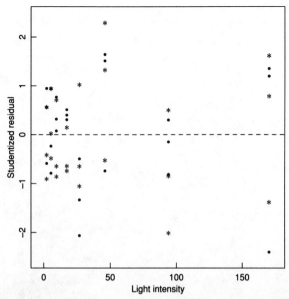

Figure 3.17 Studentized residuals from the 6-parameter quadratic Michaelis–Menten model plotted versus light intensity. Day 1 data are shown as * and day 2 data as •.

Table 3.15 Parameter summary for the 4-parameter quadratic Michaelis–Menten model fitted to the nitrite utilization data.

Parameter	Estimate	Standard Error	t Ratio	Correlation Matrix			
θ_1	70 096	16 443	4.3	1.00			
θ_2	139.4	39.3	3.6	1.00	1.00		
θ_3	0.01144	0.00404	2.8	0.99	0.99	1.00	
ϕ_1	−5381	1915	−2.8	−0.69	−0.66	−0.66	1.00

Table 3.16   Extra sum of squares analysis for the 6-parameter versus the 4-parameter quadratic Michaelis–Menten model fitted to the nitrite utilization data.

Source	Sum of Squares (10^6)	Degrees of Freedom	Mean Square (10^6)	F Ratio	p Value
Extra	0.82	2	0.41	0.54	0.59
6-parameter	32.02	42	0.762		
4-parameter	32.84	44	0.746		

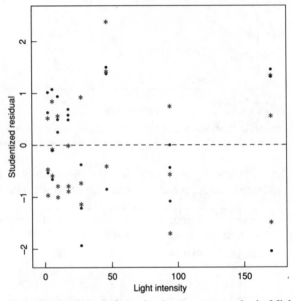

Figure 3.18   Studentized residuals from the 4-parameter quadratic Michaelis–Menten model plotted versus light intensity. Day 1 data are shown as * and day 2 data as ●.

Table 3.17   Lack of fit analysis for the 4-parameter quadratic Michaelis–Menten model fitted to the nitrite utilization data.

Source	Sum of Squares (10^6)	Degrees of Freedom	Mean Square (10^6)	F Ratio	p Value
Lack of fit	10.63	12	0.886	1.28	0.28
Replications	22.21	32	0.694		
Residuals	32.84	44	0.746		

Note that the parameter ϕ_1 is now apparently significantly different from 0, with an approximate t ratio of -2.8, confirming our earlier suspicion that there was a difference between days. This parameter was not significantly different from 0 in the 6-parameter model, which is further evidence for the 6-parameter model being overparametrized and hence the parameter approximate standard errors being artificially inflated, causing nonsignificant t ratios.

The parameter approximate correlation matrix for the quadratic Michaelis–Menten 4-parameter model shown in Table 3.15 reveals that several of the correlations are very large. This is not unusual in nonlinear regression, and is induced by a combination of the form of the expectation function and the design used. For example, for a Michaelis–Menten model, no matter how good the design is, it is impossible to obtain zero correlation between the parameters because it is impossible to force the derivatives to be orthogonal. To see this, we note that the first column of the derivative matrix, v_1, has elements $x/(\theta_2 + x)$, and the second column, v_2, has elements $-\theta_1 x/(\theta_2 + x)^2$. All the elements in v_1 are positive and all the elements in v_2 are negative, and so the two vectors v_1 and $-v_2$ will always tend to point in the same direction in the response space. Consequently, they will tend to be collinear.

As a final check on the model, the 3-parameter Michaelis–Menten model

$$f = \frac{(\theta_1 + \phi_1 x_2) x_1}{\theta_2 + x_1}$$

could be fitted and compared with the 4-parameter quadratic Michaelis–Menten model using an extra sum of squares analysis to further substantiate the necessity for the parameter θ_3. This was not done because the residuals for the original 3-parameter Michaelis–Menten model were so badly behaved.

(Similar results and conclusions were reached for the exponential difference model: that is, a 4-parameter model with common exponential parameters and scale factor, plus an incremental parameter for day 2, was found to give an adequate fit. Summary information on the fit is given in Table 3.18, and comparison with the 6-parameter model in Table 3.19. The lack of fit analysis is given in Table 3.20. In this case, the lack of fit ratio was 1.46, still not significant, but slightly larger than for the quadratic Michaelis–Menten model.)

Table 3.18 Parameter summary for the 4-parameter exponential difference model fitted to the nitrite utilization data.

Parameter	Estimate	Standard Error	t Ratio	Correlation Matrix			
θ_1	35 115	8940	3.9	1.00			
θ_2	0.01845	0.00317	5.8	−0.99	1.00		
θ_3	0.00325	0.00120	2.7	0.99	−0.97	1.00	
ϕ_1	−2686	1006	−2.7	−0.71	0.67	−0.68	1.00

Table 3.19 Extra sum of squares analysis for the 6-parameter versus the 4-parameter exponential difference model fitted to the nitrite utilization data.

Source	Sum of Squares (10^6)	Degrees of Freedom	Mean Square (10^6)	F Ratio	p Value
Extra	0.37	2	0.19	0.23	0.80
6-parameter	33.97	42	0.809		
4-parameter	34.34	44	0.780		

Table 3.20 Lack of fit analysis for the 4-parameter exponential difference model fitted to the nitrite utilization data.

Source	Sum of Squares (10^6)	Degrees of Freedom	Mean Square (10^6)	F Ratio	p Value
Lack of fit	12.13	12	1.011	1.46	0.19
Replications	22.21	32	0.694		
Residuals	34.34	44	0.780		

3.13.9 Comparing the Models

To compare the nested models we have used incremental parameters and the extra sum of squares principal, but they can not be used to compare the quadratic Michaelis–Menten and the exponential difference models. Our first approach was to the researchers, asking them whether one model was preferred on scientific grounds. In this case, the researchers had no preference, and so we simply presented them with the results for both models. Because the lack of fit ratio and the residual mean squares were smaller, we had a slight preference for the Michaelis–Menten model. In Figure 3.19 we show the nitrite utilization data together with the fitted curve and the approximate 95% confidence bands for the 4-parameter quadratic Michaelis–Menten model.

3.13.10   Reporting the Results

A brief report was prepared for Professors Elliott and Peirson, along the lines of Section 3.12. The major finding of interest was the need for a model which rose to a peak rather than to an asymptote. This was not expected, at least at such a low light level. As part of our report, we recommended additional experiments be run, especially at higher light intensities, in order to verify the need for a model which rises to a peak rather than approaching an asymptote, and to help discriminate between the two competing models. It was further suggested that future experiments involve fewer levels at low light intensity to reduce effort.

3.14   Experimental Design

So far we have concentrated more on the analysis of data than on the design of experiments to produce good data, although we believe that good experimental

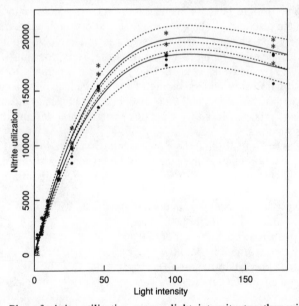

Figure 3.19 Plot of nitrite utilization versus light intensity together with the fitted curves (solid lines) and the 95% approximate inference bands (dotted). Data for day 1 are shown as * and for day 2 as ●.

design is vital to scientific progress. The reason for the prime importance of experimental design is that *the information content of the data is established when the experiment is performed*, and no amount of sensitive data analysis can recover information which is not present in the data.

One reason for our emphasizing analysis rather than design is that we usually have to deal with data that have been obtained without the benefit of good statistical design. Another reason is that, while good experimental design is extremely valuable, it is necessary to know how to analyze data in order to appreciate what "good experimental design" is.

3.14.1   General Considerations

Experimentation is fundamental to scientific learning, which we may characterize as *reducing ignorance*. At any stage of research, we are in a position of having data, and of being able to explain part of that data, and as the research proceeds, we are able to account for, or explain, more of the data. For example, a chemical engineer trying to learn about how a particular product is produced would know very little initially about the factors and the chemical reactions involved. As she proceeds, planning and running experiments under various conditions, she would endeavor to find out, at each stage, what the important factors are, and how they affect the response. Initially, she would be involved in empirical "screening designs" to try to isolate those factors which are most influential in affecting the response, probably using *factorial* or *fractional factorial* designs (Box, Hunter, and Hunter, 1978). If she was interested in optimizing some characteristic, she might then proceed to *response surface* designs (Box, Hunter, and Hunter, 1978; Box and Draper, 1987). Later on, perhaps to fine tune the product or to gain better understanding of the mechanisms involved, she would move from empirical models and their associated strategies to mechanistic (usually nonlinear) models. It is this aspect of experimental design which we consider in this section.

We assume initially that the experimenter has a well-defined *form* for the expectation function relating the factors to the response, and that the objectives of the experiments are to provide the necessary and adequate information to:

(1)   estimate the parameters of interest in the model with
      accuracy (i.e. small bias),
      precision (i.e. small variance), and
(2)   verify the assumptions about
      the expectation function,
      the disturbance model.

As was the case for estimation, it is helpful first to discuss the linear situation. Accordingly, in the following section we present a brief review of experimental design for linear expectation functions. For a more comprehensive presentation, see Box, Hunter, and Hunter (1978), Davies (1956), and Cochran and Cox (1957); and for general considerations on the planning of experiments, Box and Draper (1959) and Draper and Smith (1981). A thorough review of optimal designs is given in St. John and Draper (1975), Cochran (1973), and Steinberg and Hunter (1984). Hamilton and Watts (1985) discussed designs using second order derivatives, and the geometry of experimental designs was discussed in Silvey and Titterington (1973).

Before considering the more technical details of experimental design, we offer some comments which help ensure attainment of the general objectives (1) and (2) above.

With regard to providing accurate and precise estimates of the parameters, it is helpful to recognize that an experimental design involves choosing the values of the factors for a selected number of experimental cases (or runs). It is therefore important that the number of cases be large enough to ensure attainment of the specific objectives of the experiment. For example, if an expectation function involves five parameters, there will have to be at least five distinct experimental conditions. It is equally important to limit the number of experiments done at any one time. That is, one should not construct an extremely large design and then proceed slavishly to follow that design to its completion. Due account should be taken of what is learned at each stage of the experiment, and this information should be exploited in the design of the next stage. The number of experiments which should be run in a *block* will depend on the number of factors and the type of experiment being run, of course, but blocks of size 10 to 20 are usually informative and manageable.

The choices of the factor settings should be such that they are in useful and appropriate ranges of the factors. That is, the factors should be located near sensible values which will permit use of the parameter estimates in future investigations, and the levels of each factor should be spread out enough so that the effect of each factor will be revealed in spite of the inherent variability of the response.

With regard to verifying the assumptions about the expectation function, it is important to provide *replications* to enable testing for lack of fit or inadequacy of the expectation function. It is also important, when possible, to *randomize* the order of the experiments, to ensure that the expectation function is appropriate. (If there are unsuspected factors operating, randomizing will tend to cause their effects to appear as increased variability rather than as incorrect parameter estimates, as discussed in Section 1.3.)

With regard to verifying the assumptions about the disturbance model, replications are again important. As discussed in Section 1.3, replications enable one to test for constancy of variance and to determine a variance stabilizing transformation if the variance is deemed not constant. Randomizing will also tend to ensure that all of the assumptions concerning the disturbances will be appropriate, as discussed in Section 1.3. Once again, we see the importance and power of randomizing.

In summary, *statistical analysis* is concerned with the efficient extraction and presentation of the information embodied in a data set, while *statistical experimental design* is concerned first with ensuring that the important necessary information is embodied in a data set, and second with making the extraction and presentation of that information easy.

3.14.2 The Determinant Criterion

Consider the linear model (1.1)

$$Y = X\beta + Z$$

with the usual assumptions (1.2) and (1.3) about the disturbances Z,

$$E[Z] = 0$$

$$\text{Var}[Z] = \sigma^2 I$$

For a linear regression model, a row of the derivative matrix X depends only on the choice of the K design variables, where the design variables determine such characteristics as when the run is taken, at what pressure, at what temperature, etc. An individual entry in the derivative matrix is calculated from the values of the design variables. For any choice of the design variables generating a derivative matrix X, the parameters β will have a joint inference region whose volume is proportional to $|X^T X|^{-1/2}$. Thus, a logical choice of design criterion is to choose the design points so that the volume of the joint inference region is minimized (Wald, 1943). Since the power $-1/2$ is inconsequential, Wald proposed maximizing the determinant $D = |X^T X|$, and designs which satisfy this criterion are called *D-optimal* designs. The criterion is referred to as the *determinant criterion*.

From a geometric point of view, the determinant criterion implies that we should choose the columns of X so that each vector is as long as possible ($\| x_p \|^2$ is as large as possible, $p = 1, 2, \ldots, P$), and try to make the vectors orthogonal ($x_p^T x_q = 0$, $p \neq q$). The former ensures that the expectation plane will be well supported in the response space, and that the parameter lines will be widely spaced on the expectation plane. Consequently the disturbances, whose variance is beyond our control, will have small effect, thereby producing a joint region in the parameter space with small volume. The latter ensures that the parameter estimates associated with the factors will not be correlated. That is, changes in the response will be correctly associated with changes in the appropriate causative factor, and not attributed to other factors.

The two requirements of long length and orthogonality of the derivative vectors ensure that a disk on the expectation plane will map to a small ellipse in standard position on the parameter plane.

The determinant criterion was applied to nonlinear expectation functions by Box and Lucas (1959) who used, in place of the X matrix, the derivative matrix V^0 evaluated at some initial parameter estimates θ^0. That is, in nonlinear design, the D-optimal criterion is modified to maximize

$$D = |\mathbf{V}^{0\,\mathrm{T}}\mathbf{V}^0| \tag{3.5}$$

The design of an experiment depends on the stage at which the researcher is in an investigation. When only the form of the model is known, but not the parameter values, as could be the case in enzyme kinetics or in biochemical oxygen demand studies, the researcher would be concerned with choosing the values of the factors to produce good parameter estimates. These are called "starting designs." Later on in an investigation, the researcher might wish to design an experiment to improve the precision of estimates of some or all of the parameters, exploiting data already obtained. Such designs are called "sequential designs," and, when special interest is attached to a subset of the parameters, "subset designs."

3.14.3 Starting Designs

Box and Lucas (1959) proposed starting designs consisting of P points for a P-parameter model, and therefore simplified the criterion (3.5) to that of maximizing $|\mathbf{V}^0|$. Geometrically, the determinant criterion ensures that the expectation surface is such that large regions on the tangent plane at $\eta(\theta^0)$ map to small regions in the parameter space. When more than P points are to be chosen, the D-optimal design usually results in replications of P distinct design points (Box, 1968), and these design points are those that would be chosen as D-optimal with $N = P$. We therefore consider starting designs as having only P runs.

Example: Puromycin.12
To illustrate the choice of a starting design, we consider the case of enzyme kinetics, which are assumed to follow a Michaelis–Menten model. We assume that the maximum allowable substrate concentration is specified as $x_{\max}$, and that initial estimates of the parameters θ^0 are given.

The derivatives of the expectation function, evaluated at the initial parameter estimates θ^0, are

$$\frac{x}{\theta_2^0 + x} \qquad \frac{-\theta_1^0 x}{(\theta_2^0 + x)^2}$$

and so the determinant to be maximized is

$$
| \mathbf{V}^0 | = \begin{vmatrix} \dfrac{x_1}{\theta_2^0 + x_1} & \dfrac{-\theta_1^0 x_1}{(\theta_2^0 + x_1)^2} \\[3mm] \dfrac{x_2}{\theta_2^0 + x_2} & \dfrac{-\theta_1^0 x_2}{(\theta_2^0 + x_2)^2} \end{vmatrix}
$$

$$
= \frac{\theta_1^0 x_1 x_2 \, | x_1 - x_2 |}{(\theta_2^0 + x_1)^2 (\theta_2^0 + x_2)^2}
$$

The modulus of this determinant is maximized when

$$
x_1 = x_{\max} \quad \text{and} \quad x_2 = \frac{\theta_2^0}{1 + 2(\theta_2^0 / x_{\max})} \approx \theta_2^0
$$

The determinant criterion therefore places the design points so as to tie down the asymptote (θ_1) by performing one experiment at the maximum concentration, and to tie down the half-concentration by performing the other experiment near the assumed half-concentration.

It is instructive to compare the D-optimal design with the dilution design used by Treloar (1974). The dilution design used $x_{\max} = 1.1$ and five dilutions by approximately one-half, with duplications, giving a total of 12 runs. With the same number of runs, the D-optimal design would consist of 6 replications at $x_{\max}$ and 6 replications at $x_2 = \theta_2^0 / [1 + 2(\theta_2^0 / x_{\max})]$. We take $\theta_2^0 = 0.1$ as a reasonable starting estimate, and so the design is $x_1 = 1.1$, $x_2 = 0.085$. In Figure 3.20 we plot the linear approximation 95% confidence region for the dilution design and data together with the linear approximation confidence region for the D-optimal design assuming that both designs gave the same parameter estimates and residual variance. We see that the D-optimal design does indeed give a smaller joint confidence region and smaller confidence intervals. In addition, the correlation between the parameters is lower. However, the gain in precision from using the D-optimal design would have to be balanced against any loss of information about lack of fit.

Note that the design does not depend on the conditionally linear parameter θ_1, which is true in general for conditionally linear parameters, as shown in Section 3.14.6. ∎

The determinant criterion provides an objective basis for determining P-point designs for P-parameter models, but the design strategy should not be applied blindly. The criterion was derived on the basis that the expectation function is *known*, and provides only P design points to estimate the P parameters. Replications at these P design points are useful because they provide informa-

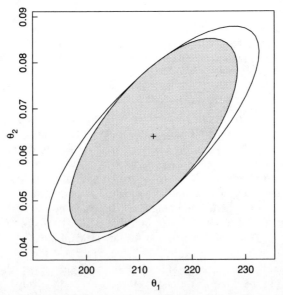

Figure 3.20   Comparison of 95% approximate inference regions for two designs for the Puromycin data. The larger region results from the dilution design used, and the shaded region results from a D-optimal design.

tion concerning constancy of variance, but they cannot provide information about lack of fit. It might be useful, therefore, to perform additional experiments at other design points in order to detect lack of fit. In light of these considerations, the dilution design strategy is eminently sensible, especially given its high level of performance as demonstrated in the above example.

3.14.4   Sequential Designs

In many situations, some experiments will already have been done to check if the equipment is functioning properly, or to screen possible models, as described in Box and Hunter (1965). In other situations, it may be possible to perform and analyze the result from a single experiment quite rapidly. In these situations, it is possible to obtain even better parameter estimates by designing the experiments sequentially; that is, an experimental run is designed, the data are collected and analyzed, and the design for the next run is obtained by maximizing $|\mathbf{V}_1^T\mathbf{V}_1|$ with respect to the design variables, $\mathbf{x}_{N+1}$, where

$$\mathbf{V}_1 = \begin{bmatrix} \mathbf{V}_0 \\ \mathbf{v}_{N+1} \end{bmatrix}$$

and $\mathbf{v}_{N+1}$ is the gradient vector $\partial f/\partial\boldsymbol{\theta}^T$ evaluated at the least squares estimates from the N runs already made.

Example: Isomerization 3

To illustrate sequential design, we consider the model and data set from Example Isomerization 1. The correlations between the parameters are very high, and the linear approximation confidence regions include negative values for the equilibrium constants. We would therefore like to design experiments to provide better precision in the parameter estimates.

The design points are determined by the values of the partial pressure of hydrogen, x_1, the partial pressure of n-pentane, x_2, and the partial pressure of isopentane, x_3. In the previous runs these variables have ranged from about 100 to 400 for x_1, 75 to 350 for x_2, and 30 to 150 for x_3, so we use these limits to define a reasonable region within which to design further runs. We begin by evaluating the sequential D-optimal design criterion at the original design points and at sequential design points at the corners of the region. This gives the values in Table 3.21. The combination which optimizes the D-optimal criterion is low x_1 (100), high x_2 (350), and low x_3 (30). Examination of nearby values confirms that the corner is a local optimum, and since a coarse grid search of the design region did not reveal any optima in the interior, we choose this corner as the design point for the next run. ■

Table 3.21 Sequential D-optimal design criteria for the isomerization model, evaluated at the corners of the design region.

Factor			Criterion
			D
x_1	x_2	x_3	10^6
100	100	30	4.63
400	100	30	1.95
100	350	30	9.44
400	350	30	3.99
100	100	150	1.82
400	100	150	1.82
100	350	150	3.98
400	350	150	2.42

3.14.5 Subset Designs

When only a subset of the parameters $\boldsymbol{\theta}$ is of interest, the design criterion is modified as suggested in Box (1971) and Hill and Hunter (1974). We assume that the parameters have been ordered so the first P_1 parameters are the nuisance parameters and the trailing P_2 parameters are the parameters of interest, and we partition the vector $\boldsymbol{\theta}^T$ as $(\boldsymbol{\theta}_1^T \mid \boldsymbol{\theta}_2^T)$, and the matrix $\mathbf{V}^0$ as $[\mathbf{V}_1^0 \mid \mathbf{V}_2^0]$. Then the variance–covariance matrix of the P_2 parameters is proportional to $\mathbf{D}_{2,2}$, where

$$\mathbf{D} = (\mathbf{V}^{0\,T}\mathbf{V}^0)^{-1}$$

$$= \begin{bmatrix} \mathbf{V}_1^{0\,T}\mathbf{V}_1^0 & \mathbf{V}_1^{0\,T}\mathbf{V}_2^0 \\ \mathbf{V}_2^{0\,T}\mathbf{V}_1^0 & \mathbf{V}_2^{0\,T}\mathbf{V}_2^0 \end{bmatrix}^{-1}$$

$$= \begin{bmatrix} \mathbf{D}_{1,1} & \mathbf{D}_{1,2} \\ \mathbf{D}_{1,2}^T & \mathbf{D}_{2,2} \end{bmatrix}$$

and so the D-optimal criterion is changed to minimization of

$$D_S = |\,\mathbf{D}_{2,2}\,|$$

which is equivalent to maximizing

$$\frac{|\,\mathbf{V}^{0T}\mathbf{V}^0\,|}{|\,\mathbf{V}_1^{0T}\mathbf{V}_1^0\,|}$$

Example: Isomerization 4

To illustrate subset design, we consider the model, data set, and design region from Example Isomerization 3, and treat the situation in which we wish to improve the estimates of θ_2, θ_3, and θ_4. Evaluation of D_S at the corners of the same region gives the results in Table 3.22, which produce similar conclusions and the same design point as in Example Isomerization 3. ■

3.14.6 Conditionally Linear Models

It is awkward to have to specify initial estimates of the parameters $\boldsymbol{\theta}$ before an experimental design can be obtained, since, after all, the purpose of the experiment is to determine parameter estimates. In Examples Puromycin 12 and Isomerization 3, we saw that the D-optimal design was not affected by the value of a conditionally linear parameter. For most models with conditionally linear parameters, the locations of the D-optimal design points do not depend on the conditionally linear parameters (Hill, 1980; Khuri, 1984), so the design problem

Table 3.22 Sequential D-optimal subset design criteria for the isomerization
model, evaluated at the corners of the
design region.

Factor			Criterion D_S 10^6
x_1	x_2	x_3	
100	100	30	8.77
400	100	30	3.90
100	350	30	13.11
400	350	30	7.08
100	100	150	3.69
400	100	150	3.68
100	350	150	7.39
400	350	150	4.70

is simpler.

The easiest type of conditionally linear model to demonstrate this for is
that with only one conditionally linear parameter, so the function can be written

$$f(\mathbf{x}, \boldsymbol{\theta}) = \theta_1 \, g(\mathbf{x}, \boldsymbol{\theta}_{-1})$$

for some function g where $\boldsymbol{\theta}_{-1} = (\theta_2, \dots, \theta_P)^{\mathrm{T}}$. This includes the
Michaelis–Menten, BOD, and isomerization models. The gradient of the model
function can then be written

$$\frac{\partial f}{\partial \boldsymbol{\theta}^{\mathrm{T}}} = \left[g(\mathbf{x}, \boldsymbol{\theta}_{-1}), \frac{\partial g}{\partial \boldsymbol{\theta}_{-1}^{\mathrm{T}}} \right] \begin{bmatrix} 1 & \mathbf{0} \\ \mathbf{0} & \theta_1 \mathbf{I} \end{bmatrix} \tag{3.6}$$

which isolates the dependence of θ_1 from any dependence upon $\mathbf{x}$. Using (3.6),
the derivative matrix $\mathbf{V}$ can be written

$$\mathbf{V} = \mathbf{H}(\mathbf{x}, \boldsymbol{\theta}_{-1}) \, \mathbf{B}(\theta_1) \tag{3.7}$$

where

$$\mathbf{B}(\theta_1) = \begin{bmatrix} 1 & \mathbf{0} \\ \mathbf{0} & \theta_1 \mathbf{I} \end{bmatrix}$$

is $P \times P$, so the D-optimal criterion is

$$|\mathbf{V}^{\mathrm{T}} \mathbf{V}| = |\mathbf{B}^{\mathrm{T}} \mathbf{H}^{\mathrm{T}} \mathbf{H} \mathbf{B}|$$

$$= |\mathbf{B}|^2 \, |\mathbf{H}^{\mathrm{T}} \mathbf{H}|$$

and, again, the dependence of θ_1 is isolated from $\mathbf{x}$. Therefore, the design does not depend upon θ_1.

In general, for conditionally linear models of the form

$$f(\mathbf{x},\boldsymbol{\theta}) = \theta_1 g_1(\mathbf{x},\boldsymbol{\theta}_{-L}) + \cdots + \theta_L g_L(\mathbf{x},\boldsymbol{\theta}_{-L})$$

where $\boldsymbol{\theta}_{-L} = (\theta_{L+1}, \ldots, \theta_P)^T$, the D-optimal design will not depend on the conditionally linear parameters $(\theta_1, \ldots, \theta_L)^T$ if $\mathbf{V}$ can be factored as in (3.7), provided $\mathbf{B}$ is square. The condition that the matrix $\mathbf{B}$ is square was not explicitly stated in Hill (1980), nor was it emphasized in Khuri (1984), where it was shown that conditionally linear parameters will usually affect subset designs. This occurs because, for subset designs, the design criterion involves the *ratio* of determinants of components of $\mathbf{V}$, and so the simple factorization above usually does not occur even if $\mathbf{B}$ is square. Khuri (1984) gives conditions under which the conditionally linear parameters do not affect designs for subsets of parameters.

In the common situation where each component of $\boldsymbol{\theta}_{-L}$ enters into only one of the functions g_i, $i = 1, \ldots, L$, the derivatives can be factored as in (3.7). For example, D-optimal designs for the sum of exponentials model

$$f(x,\boldsymbol{\theta}) = \theta_1 e^{-\theta_2 x} + \theta_3 e^{-\theta_4 x} + \cdots + \theta_{P-1} e^{-\theta_P x}$$

do not depend on the conditionally linear parameters.

3.14.7   Other Design Criteria

Precise parameter estimation is not the only objective used for experimental design. Methods have been proposed for constructing designs for discriminating between possible model functions (Box and Hill, 1974) and for balancing the objectives of model discrimination and precise parameter estimation (Hill, Hunter, and Wichern, 1968). The review article (Steinberg and Hunter, 1984) describes many of these criteria. We also list several of the references for different experimental design criteria for single response and multiresponse nonlinear models in the bibliography.

Exercises

3.1 Use the data from Appendix 4, Section A4.2 to fit the logistic model

$$f(x, \boldsymbol{\theta}) = \theta_1 + \frac{\theta_2}{1 + e^{-\theta_4(x - \theta_3)}}$$

(a) Plot the data versus $x = \log_{10}$ (NIF concentration). Note that you will have to make a decision about how to incorporate the zero concentration data. You may want to incorporate the actual NTD concentrations also.

(b) Give graphical interpretations of the parameters in the model, and use the plot to obtain starting values for each data set.

(c) Use the starting values in a nonlinear least squares routine to find the least squares estimates for the parameters for each data set.

(d) Use incremental parameters and indicator variables to fit all of the data sets together.

(e) Simplify the model by letting some of the parameters be common to all of the data sets. Use extra sum of squares analyses to determine a simple adequate model.

(f) Write a short report about this analysis and your findings.

3.2 Use the data from Appendix 1, Section A1.14 to determine an appropriate sum of exponentials model.

(a) Plot the data on semilog paper and use the plot to determine the number of exponential terms to fit to the data.

(b) Use curve peeling to determine starting estimates for the parameters.

(c) Use the starting estimates from part (b) to fit the postulated model from part (a).

3.3 (a) Use the plot from Problem 2.6 and sketch in the curve of steepest descent from the point θ^0. Hint: The direction of steepest descent is perpendicular to the contours.

(b) Is the direction of the Gauss–Newton increment close to the initial direction of steepest descent?

(c) Calculate and plot the Levenberg increment using a conditioning factor of $k = 4$.

(d) Calculate and plot the Marquardt increment using a conditioning factor of $k = 4$.

(e) Comment on the relative directions of the Gauss–Newton, Levenberg and Marquardt increment vectors.

3.4 Use the data from Appendix 4, Section A4.3 to determine an appropriate model and to estimate the parameters.

(a) Plot the concentration versus time on semilog paper, and use the plot to determine the number of exponential terms necessary to fit the data.

(b) Use the plot and the method of curve peeling to determine starting values for the parameters.

(c) Use a nonlinear estimation routine to estimate the parameters.

3.5 Use a nonlinear estimation routine and the data and model from Appendix 4, Section A4.4 to estimate the parameters. Take note of the number of iterations required and any difficulties you encounter in each attempt.

(a) Use any approach you think is appropriate to obtain starting values for the parameters in the model.

(b) Use your starting values in a nonlinear estimation routine to estimate the parameters. If you achieve convergence, examine the parameter approximate correlation matrix, and comment on the conditioning of the model.

(c) Reparametrize the model by centering the factor $1/x_3$, and use the equivalent starting values from part (a) to estimate the parameters. If you achieve convergence, examine the parameter approximate correlation matrix, and comment on the conditioning of the model. What effect does this reparametrization have on the number of iterations to convergence?

(d) Reparametrize the model in part (a) using $\theta_1 = e^{\phi_1}$ and $\theta_2 = e^{\phi_2}$ and the equivalent starting values from part (a) to estimate the parameters. If you achieve convergence, examine the parameter approximate correlation matrix, and comment on the conditioning of the model. What effect does this reparametrization have on the number of iterations to convergence?

(e) Reparametrize the model in part (b) using the same parametrization as in part (c) and the equivalent starting values from part (a) to estimate the parameters. If you achieve convergence, examine the parameter approximate correlation matrix, and comment on the conditioning of the model. What effect does this reparametrization have on the number of iterations to convergence?

3.6 Use a nonlinear estimation routine and the data and model from Appendix 4, Section A4.5 to estimate the parameters. Take note of the number of iterations required and any difficulties you encounter in each attempt.

(a) Use any approach you think is appropriate to obtain starting values for the parameters in the model.

(b) Use your starting values in a nonlinear estimation routine to estimate the parameters. If you achieve convergence, examine the parameter approximate correlation matrix, and comment on the conditioning of the model.

(c) Reparametrize the model in part (a) using $\theta_2 e^{-\theta_3 x} = e^{-\theta_3(x - \phi_2)}$. If you achieve convergence, examine the parameter approximate correlation matrix, and comment on the conditioning of the model. What effect does this reparametrization have on the number of iterations to convergence?

3.7 (a) Show that the theoretical D-optimal starting design for the logistic model of Problem 3.1 consists of $\mathbf{x} = (-\infty,\ \theta_3 - 1.044/\theta_4,\ \theta_3 + 1.044/\theta_4,\ +\infty)^T$.

(b) Interpret the choice of the design points graphically by plotting the logistic function versus x and plotting the location of the design points on the x-axis.

(c) Plot the derivatives with respect to the parameters versus x and use these plots to help interpret the choice of the design points.

CHAPTER 4.

Multiresponse Parameter Estimation

"Better is the enemy of the good."

– Voltaire

In some experimental situations it is possible to measure more than one response for each case. In the analysis of such experiments, information from all the measured responses can be combined to provide more precise parameter estimation and to determine more realistic models. The information must be combined so as to reflect reasonable assumptions on the behavior of the disturbance terms in the measurements.

A determinant parameter estimation criterion for multiresponse data was derived by Box and Draper (1965) under the assumptions that the disturbance terms in different cases are uncorrelated but the disturbance terms for different responses in the same case have a fixed, unknown variance–covariance matrix. In this chapter, we discuss this criterion and present a generalization of the Gauss–Newton method to optimize it. We also describe a convergence criterion for this optimization method, and discuss modifications which should be made to the method when there are singularities in the data or residual matrix.

4.1 The Multiresponse Model

We assume there are M responses measured on each of N experimental runs and that the models for the M responses depend on a total of P parameters, $\boldsymbol{\theta}$, and write

$$Y_{nm} = f_m(\mathbf{x}_n, \boldsymbol{\theta}) + Z_{nm} \quad n = 1, \dots, N \quad m = 1, \dots, M \quad (4.1)$$

where Y_{nm} is the random variable associated with the measured value of the mth response for the nth case, f_m is the model function for the mth response depending on some or all of the experimental settings $\mathbf{x}_n$ and on some or all of the parameters θ, and Z_{nm} is the disturbance term.

Example: α-Pinene 2

Box et al. (1973) reported a multiresponse analysis of some α-pinene data originally analyzed by Fuguitt and Hawkins (1947). In the experiment, α-pinene, a component of turpentine, was purified and heated to produce by-products. Two sets of measurements were made, at temperatures of 189.5 and 204.5°C. In each experiment, the relative concentrations of α-pinene and three by-products were measured at each of eight times. The relative concentration of a fourth by-product was imputed from the other concentrations. In this example, there are $M = 5$ responses and $N = 8$ cases. The data for 189.5°C are listed in Appendix 1, Section A1.6, and plotted in Figure 4.1. ∎

Example: s-PMMA 1

The behavior of the complex dielectric coefficient of a polymer can be used to help understand the molecular structure of the polymer. Physically, a disk of the polymer is inserted between the two metal electrodes of the dielectric cell which forms one arm of a four armed electrical bridge. The bridge is powered by an oscillating voltage whose frequency (f, in hertz) can be changed over a wide range (say 5 to 500 000 Hz), and bridge balance is achieved using capacitance and conductance standards. The com-

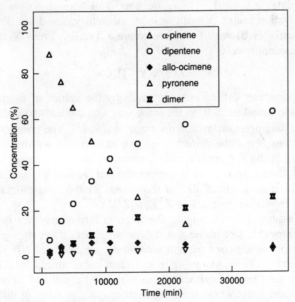

Figure 4.1 Plot of the concentrations of α-pinene and its by-products versus time at 189.5°C.

plex dielectric constant is then calculated using changes from the standards relative to the cell dielectric constant. Measurements are made by simultaneously adjusting the capacitance (real) and the conductance (imaginary) arms of the bridge when it is excited at a specific frequency and temperature.

The complex dielectric constant is written $\varepsilon^* = \varepsilon' - i\varepsilon''$, where ε' is the real component, ε'' is the imaginary component, and i denotes $\sqrt{-1}$. Havriliak and Negami (1967) analyzed the dielectric relaxation data for 21 polymers, and proposed a general model of the form

$$\varepsilon^* = \varepsilon_\infty + \frac{\varepsilon_0 - \varepsilon_\infty}{\left[1 + (i2\pi f/f_0)^\alpha\right]^\beta}$$

In Figure 4.2a and b we plot the imaginary component y_{imag} and the real component y_{real}, versus frequency for syndiotactic poly(methylmethacrylate) (s-PMMA) at 86.7°F, and, as recommended in Cole and Cole (1941), in Figure 4.2c we plot these components in the complex plane. In this example, there are $M = 2$ responses, $N = 23$ cases, and $P = 5$ parameters. The data are listed in Appendix 1, Section A1.13. ∎

As with uniresponse parameter estimation discussed in the previous chapters, in the analysis of experimental data we assume that the N experimental design variables x_n, $n = 1, \ldots, N$, are fixed and known, so we can form the $N \times M$ observation matrix Y with (n,m)th element y_{nm} and the $N \times M$ expected response matrix $H(\theta)$ with (n,m)th element $f_m(x_n, \theta)$. From Y and $H(\theta)$, we create the residual matrix

$$Z(\theta) = Y - H(\theta) \tag{4.2}$$

The parameter estimates $\hat{\theta}$ are given by the values of θ which optimize some criterion based on $Z(\theta)$ in the same way that the least squares estimates in uniresponse parameter estimation minimize $\| z(\theta) \|^2$. The criterion will depend on assumptions about the disturbance. For example, if we make the stringent assumption that the Z_{nm} are normally distributed and independent with the same variance σ^2, then least squares is appropriate and we find $\hat{\theta}$ which minimizes the sum of squared residuals of all NM responses. That is, the estimation criterion would be to minimize the *trace* of $Z^T Z$, $\text{tr}(Z^T Z)$.

The assumptions leading to the trace criterion may not be realistic. It could be reasonable to assume that the variances of different measurements on the same response are constant, but not that the variances of different responses are equal. Furthermore, assuming independent disturbances for different measurements in the same experimental run may not be justified. For example, in chemical experiments where the concentrations of a number of different chemical species are measured from the same sample, if only the relative concentrations can be determined, different measurements on the same sample may be correlated. Similarly, for dielectric determinations, errors in the frequency set-

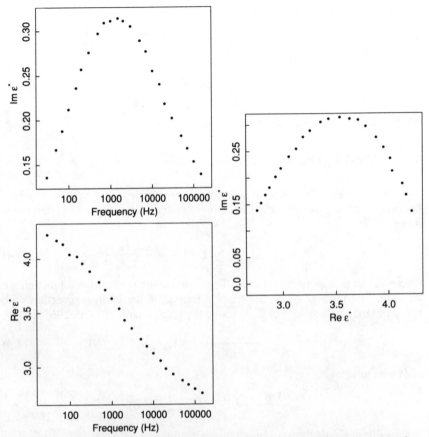

Figure 4.2 Plots of the real and imaginary components of the dielectric constant ε^* (dimensionless) versus frequency (on a logarithmic scale) and in the complex plane for the s-PMMA dielectric data.

tings can induce errors in both components.

Following Box and Draper (1965), the model used to describe the disturbance term is a normal distribution with

$$E[Z_{nm}] = 0$$

and

$$E[Z_{nm}Z_{ri}] = \begin{cases} \{\Sigma\}_{mi} & n = r \\ 0 & n \neq r \end{cases}$$

where Σ is a fixed $M \times M$ covariance matrix. That is, we assume that measurements from different experiments are independent but measurements from the same experiment are correlated. The joint probability density function for the N observations, conditional on all the unknown parameters, is then

$$
\begin{aligned}
p(\mathbf{Y} \mid \boldsymbol{\theta}, \boldsymbol{\Sigma}) &\propto |\boldsymbol{\Sigma}|^{-N/2} \exp\left[-\frac{\text{tr}[(\mathbf{Y}-\mathbf{H})\boldsymbol{\Sigma}^{-1}(\mathbf{Y}-\mathbf{H})^{\text{T}}]}{2} \right] \\
&= |\boldsymbol{\Sigma}^{-1}|^{N/2} \exp\left[-\frac{\text{tr}(\mathbf{Z}\boldsymbol{\Sigma}^{-1}\mathbf{Z}^{\text{T}})}{2} \right]
\end{aligned}
\tag{4.3}
$$

where the vertical bars denote a determinant.

4.1.1 The Determinant Criterion

A parameter estimation criterion under these assumptions can be derived using a likelihood or Bayesian argument. The loglikelihood function for the parameters $\boldsymbol{\theta}$ and $\boldsymbol{\Sigma}^{-1}$ is

$$
L(\boldsymbol{\theta}, \boldsymbol{\Sigma}^{-1}) = k + \frac{N}{2}\ln|\boldsymbol{\Sigma}^{-1}| - \frac{\text{tr}(\mathbf{Z}\boldsymbol{\Sigma}^{-1}\mathbf{Z}^{\text{T}})}{2}
\tag{4.4}
$$

where k is an unimportant constant. To maximize the loglikelihood function we write the last term as $\text{tr}(\mathbf{Z}^{\text{T}}\mathbf{Z}\boldsymbol{\Sigma}^{-1})$ and differentiate the entire expression with respect to the elements σ^{mi} of $\boldsymbol{\Sigma}^{-1}$. Using the result (Bard, 1974, p. 296)

$$
\frac{\partial \ln|\boldsymbol{\Sigma}^{-1}|}{\partial \sigma^{mi}} = \{\boldsymbol{\Sigma}\}_{mi}
\tag{4.5}
$$

allows us to write

$$
\frac{\partial L(\boldsymbol{\theta}, \boldsymbol{\Sigma}^{-1})}{\partial \sigma^{mi}} = \frac{N}{2}\{\boldsymbol{\Sigma}\}_{mi} - \frac{1}{2}\{\mathbf{Z}^{\text{T}}\mathbf{Z}\}_{mi}
$$

Setting this derivative to zero provides the conditional estimates

$$
\{\hat{\boldsymbol{\Sigma}}(\boldsymbol{\theta})\}_{mi} = \frac{\{\mathbf{Z}^{\text{T}}\mathbf{Z}\}_{mi}}{N}
$$

or

$$
\hat{\boldsymbol{\Sigma}}(\boldsymbol{\theta}) = \frac{\mathbf{Z}^{\text{T}}\mathbf{Z}}{N}
$$

which, when substituted into (4.4), gives the conditional loglikelihood function

$$
L(\boldsymbol{\theta}, \hat{\boldsymbol{\Sigma}}(\boldsymbol{\theta})) = k' - \frac{N}{2}\ln|\mathbf{Z}^{\text{T}}\mathbf{Z}|
\tag{4.6}
$$

The maximum likelihood estimates are then obtained by minimizing $|\mathbf{Z}^{\text{T}}\mathbf{Z}|$ with respect to $\boldsymbol{\theta}$.

A Bayesian argument was used by Box and Draper (1965) to derive the marginal posterior density for $\boldsymbol{\theta}$ by integrating over the unknown variances and covariances after incorporating an noninformative prior of the form

$$p(\Sigma, \theta) \propto |\Sigma|^{-(M+1)/2}$$

The marginal posterior density is then

$$p(\theta|Y) \propto |Z^T Z|^{-N/2} \tag{4.7}$$

and so the posterior density is maximized when the determinant is minimized. Thus, the likelihood and Bayesian approaches lead to the same criterion.

As pointed out in Box and Tiao (1973), (4.6) and (4.7) are remarkably general results, since they do not depend on whether the expectation functions are linear or nonlinear, whether the parameters are common to more than one response, or whether the design variables are common to more than one response. Furthermore, a scale change on any of the responses will not affect the estimates, and linear combinations of the responses can be used in place of the original responses.

Geometrically, $|Z^T Z|$ corresponds to the square of the volume of the M-dimensional parallelepiped spanned by the residual vectors, z_m, $m = 1, \ldots, M$, in the N-dimensional case space. Minimizing the determinant corresponds to minimizing the volume enclosed by the residual vectors.

4.1.2   Inferences for Multiresponse Estimation

To draw inferences about parameters in multiresponse estimation, we use the Bayesian formulation and assume that $|Z^T Z|$ can be adequately represented by a quadratic Taylor series near $\hat{\theta}$ to give an approximate marginal posterior density function. From (4.7),

$$p(\theta|Y) \propto \left[1 + (\theta - \hat{\theta})^T \frac{\Omega}{2|\hat{Z}^T \hat{Z}|}(\theta - \hat{\theta}) \right]^{-N/2} \tag{4.8}$$

where Ω is the Hessian of the determinant evaluated at $\hat{\theta}$. This approximation has the form of a P-variate Student's T density with location parameter $\hat{\theta}$, degrees of freedom $N - P$, scale factor

$$s^2 = |\hat{Z}^T \hat{Z}|/(N-P) \tag{4.9}$$

and covariance matrix $2s^2 \Omega^{-1}$ (Box and Tiao, 1973). An approximate $1 - \alpha$ HPD region for the parameters is given by

$$(\theta - \hat{\theta})^T \frac{\Omega}{2}(\theta - \hat{\theta}) \le P s^2 F(P, N-P; \alpha) \tag{4.10}$$

so that the square of the volume in the parameter space enclosed by the joint region is proportional to the determinant of the Hessian.

Because we are approximating $|Z^T Z|$, the approximations (4.8) and (4.10) may be very poor: additional research needs to be done to assess the adequacy of these approximations even for cases where the model functions are linear. More accurate HPD regions can be written as either

$$\frac{(|\mathbf{Z}^T\mathbf{Z}| - |\hat{\mathbf{Z}}^T\hat{\mathbf{Z}}|)/P}{s^2} < F(P, N-P; \alpha) \tag{4.11}$$

or

$$\ln[p(\hat{\boldsymbol{\theta}}|\mathbf{Y})] - \ln[p(\boldsymbol{\theta}|\mathbf{Y})] < \frac{1}{2}\chi^2(P;\alpha) \tag{4.12}$$

(Box and Tiao, 1973), where $\chi^2(P;\alpha)$ is the upper α percentile of the χ^2 distribution with P degrees of freedom. Such regions would have to be determined numerically and displayed in contour plots, and therefore suffer from the disadvantages inherent in exact confidence and likelihood regions for uniresponse models, as discussed in Chapter 6. Nevertheless, the methods of Chapter 6 (profile t and profile trace plots) can be used for multiresponse problems.

An approximate $1 - \alpha$ HPD interval for the parameter θ_p is given by

$$\hat{\theta}_p \pm t(N-P; \alpha/2) s \sqrt{2\{\boldsymbol{\Omega}^{-1}\}_{pp}} \tag{4.13}$$

and an approximate $1 - \alpha$ HPD band for the mth expectation function $f_m(\mathbf{x}, \boldsymbol{\theta})$ is

$$f_m(\mathbf{x}, \hat{\boldsymbol{\theta}}) \pm s \sqrt{2 \mathbf{v}_m^T \boldsymbol{\Omega}^{-1} \mathbf{v}_m} \sqrt{P F(P, N-P; \alpha)}$$

where $\mathbf{v}_m$ is the gradient of f_m with respect to $\boldsymbol{\theta}$ evaluated at $\mathbf{x}$ and $\hat{\boldsymbol{\theta}}$.

4.1.3   Dimensional Considerations in Multiresponse Estimation

Note that the determinant criterion implies two important constraints on the number of observations, N, the number of responses, M, and the number of parameters, P.

First, M can not exceed N, since otherwise the determinant is identically zero. To see this, note that the rank of the $N \times M$ matrix $\mathbf{Z}$ cannot exceed the minimum of (N, M), and when $N < M$ the rank of the $M \times M$ matrix $\mathbf{Z}^T\mathbf{Z}$ is less than M and hence the determinant is identically zero. Another way of seeing this is to recall from the geometric interpretation that $|\mathbf{Z}^T\mathbf{Z}|$ gives the square of the volume, in the N-dimensional case space, enclosed by the residual vectors (columns of $\mathbf{Z}$). If the case dimension N does not at least equal the response dimension M, then the volume is zero. For example, the volume of a rectangle is zero.

Second, in general P must be less than N, since otherwise the criterion can be made zero by fitting any one response perfectly, or even by fitting a linear combination of the responses perfectly. That is, if there is an M-vector $\mathbf{v}$ such that $\mathbf{Z}(\boldsymbol{\theta})\mathbf{v} = \mathbf{0}$ for some $\boldsymbol{\theta}$, then the determinant will be zero at that value of $\boldsymbol{\theta}$ regardless of how well the remaining responses have been fitted.

The reasoning leading to the constraint $N > P$ provides justification for the use of $N - P$ for the residual degrees of freedom proposed above. It would seem that with NM data values there should be $NM - P$ degrees of freedom for the residuals, as suggested in Bard (1974), but in fact, near the optimum the value of the determinant is controlled by the linear combination of responses corresponding to the smallest singular value of Z, and this vector has dimension N. The vector corresponding to this singular value therefore has $N - P$ degrees of freedom.

In summary, the number of cases, N, should exceed the maximum of M and P to ensure a successful analysis.

A great advantage in using multiresponse data is the increased precision of parameter estimates relative to those obtained from uniresponse data. However, we cannot attribute this increased precision to additional denominator degrees of freedom when multiple responses are used. The increased precision is due to the combination of different types of information from the responses.

One difficulty with the use of multiresponse data is that all problems become nonlinear optimization problems. That is, even if the expectation functions are linear in the parameters, iterative methods must be used to obtain the estimates which minimize the determinant criterion. The problem of obtaining the best estimates is also more difficult than in the uniresponse nonlinear case, since the Hessian need not be positive definite. Further discussion on these aspects of optimizing the determinant is given in Section 4.2.3.

Another difficulty with multiresponse estimation is that inference regions for the parameters based on (4.10) or (4.13) are only approximate, even when all the expectation functions are linear in the parameters. The accuracy of these approximations is questionable. On the other hand, inference regions from multiresponse estimation are usually much smaller than those from uniresponse estimation, and so approximate multiresponse regions may in fact be better than approximate uniresponse regions for nonlinear models.

In spite of the difficulties, multiresponse estimation is a valuable technique and should be used whenever multiresponse data are available. The reduction in size of the parameter inference regions, together with the extra ability to discriminate between rival models, is well worth any additional effort required.

4.2 A Generalized Gauss–Newton Method

One advantage of least squares as a criterion is that specialized methods can be used to exploit properties of the criterion and to provide standard optimization algorithms. In this section, we describe a Gauss–Newton method for minimizing the determinant criterion.

To evaluate the determinant, following Bates and Watts (1987), we take a QR decomposition of $Z(\theta)$,

$$Z(\theta) = QR = Q_1 R_1$$

Then, since

$$|\mathbf{Z}(\boldsymbol{\theta})^\mathrm{T}\mathbf{Z}(\boldsymbol{\theta})| = |\mathbf{R}_1^\mathrm{T}\mathbf{R}_1|$$

$$= |\mathbf{R}_1|^2$$

$$= \prod_{m=1}^{M} \{\mathbf{R}_1\}_{mm}^2$$

we have an easy way to evaluate the determinant criterion for any $\boldsymbol{\theta}$.

4.2.1 The Gradient and Hessian of the Determinant

The decomposition of $\mathbf{Z}(\boldsymbol{\theta})$ as $\mathbf{Q}_1\mathbf{R}_1$ is also helpful in evaluating the gradient and Hessian of the determinant criterion. To simplify notation we omit the dependence on $\boldsymbol{\theta}$ and use a subscript enclosed in parentheses to denote differentiation, as

$$\frac{\partial \mathbf{Z}}{\partial \theta_p} = \mathbf{Z}_{(p)}$$

Using the result (1.1.34) from Fedorov (1972), we have

$$\frac{\partial |\mathbf{Z}^\mathrm{T}\mathbf{Z}|}{\partial \theta_p} = |\mathbf{Z}^\mathrm{T}\mathbf{Z}|\, \mathrm{tr}\left[(\mathbf{Z}^\mathrm{T}\mathbf{Z})^{-1} \frac{\partial(\mathbf{Z}^\mathrm{T}\mathbf{Z})}{\partial \theta_p} \right] \tag{4.14}$$

with

$$\frac{\partial(\mathbf{Z}^\mathrm{T}\mathbf{Z})}{\partial \theta_p} = \mathbf{Z}^\mathrm{T}\mathbf{Z}_{(p)} + \mathbf{Z}_{(p)}^\mathrm{T}\mathbf{Z} \tag{4.15}$$

so the gradient $\boldsymbol{\omega} = \partial |\mathbf{Z}^\mathrm{T}\mathbf{Z}| / \partial \boldsymbol{\theta}^\mathrm{T}$ has components

$$\{\boldsymbol{\omega}\}_p = 2|\mathbf{Z}^\mathrm{T}\mathbf{Z}|\, \mathrm{tr}[(\mathbf{Z}^\mathrm{T}\mathbf{Z})^{-1}\mathbf{Z}^\mathrm{T}\mathbf{Z}_{(p)}]$$

$$= 2|\mathbf{Z}^\mathrm{T}\mathbf{Z}|\, \mathrm{tr}[\mathbf{R}_1^{-1}\mathbf{R}_1^{-\mathrm{T}}\mathbf{R}_1^\mathrm{T}\mathbf{Q}_1^\mathrm{T}\mathbf{Z}_{(p)}]$$

$$= 2|\mathbf{Z}^\mathrm{T}\mathbf{Z}|\, \mathrm{tr}[\mathbf{R}_1^{-1}\mathbf{Q}_1^\mathrm{T}\mathbf{Z}_{(p)}] \tag{4.16}$$

$$= 2|\mathbf{Z}^\mathrm{T}\mathbf{Z}|\, \mathrm{tr}[\mathbf{Z}^+\mathbf{Z}_{(p)}]$$

where $\mathbf{Z}^+ = \mathbf{R}_1^{-1}\mathbf{Q}_1^\mathrm{T}$ is the pseudoinverse of $\mathbf{Z}$.

To obtain the second derivative or Hessian terms, we write

$$g = \ln|\mathbf{Z}^\mathrm{T}\mathbf{Z}|$$

so that

$$|\mathbf{Z}^\mathrm{T}\mathbf{Z}| = e^g \tag{4.17}$$

and

$$g_{(p)} = 2\,\mathrm{tr}[\mathbf{Z}^+\mathbf{Z}_{(p)}] \tag{4.18}$$

and then use the expressions for the derivative of the pseudoinverse (Golub and Pereyra, 1973) to obtain

$$g_{(pq)} = 2\{-\text{tr}[\mathbf{Z}^+\mathbf{Z}_{(p)}\mathbf{Z}^+\mathbf{Z}_{(q)}] + \text{tr}[\mathbf{Z}^+(\mathbf{Z}^+)^{\text{T}}\mathbf{Z}_{(p)}^{\text{T}}(\mathbf{I}-\mathbf{Z}\mathbf{Z}^+)\mathbf{Z}_{(q)}]$$
$$+ \text{tr}[\mathbf{Z}^+\mathbf{Z}_{(pq)}]\} \tag{4.19}$$

From (4.17), a second derivative term for $|\mathbf{Z}^{\text{T}}\mathbf{Z}|$ is then

$$\frac{\partial^2 |\mathbf{Z}^{\text{T}}\mathbf{Z}|}{\partial\theta_p\partial\theta_q} = |\mathbf{Z}^{\text{T}}\mathbf{Z}|[g_{(p)}g_{(q)} + g_{(pq)}] \tag{4.20}$$

Alternative expressions for the gradient and Hessian of $|\mathbf{Z}^{\text{T}}\mathbf{Z}|$ are obtained by expanding (4.16) as

$$\{\boldsymbol{\omega}\}_p = |\mathbf{Z}^{\text{T}}\mathbf{Z}|\,\text{tr}[(\mathbf{Z}^{\text{T}}\mathbf{Z})^{-1}(\mathbf{Z}^{\text{T}}\mathbf{Z}_{(p)} + \mathbf{Z}_{(p)}^{\text{T}}\mathbf{Z})]$$
$$= |\mathbf{Z}^{\text{T}}\mathbf{Z}|\,\text{tr}[\mathbf{U}_p] \tag{4.21}$$

where $\mathbf{U}_p = (\mathbf{Z}^{\text{T}}\mathbf{Z})^{-1}(\mathbf{Z}^{\text{T}}\mathbf{Z}_{(p)} + \mathbf{Z}_{(p)}^{\text{T}}\mathbf{Z})$. Differentiating (4.21) with respect to θ_q gives

$$\frac{\partial^2 |\mathbf{Z}^{\text{T}}\mathbf{Z}|}{\partial\theta_q\partial\theta_p} = \{\boldsymbol{\omega}\}_q\text{tr}[\mathbf{U}_p] + |\mathbf{Z}^{\text{T}}\mathbf{Z}|\{-\text{tr}[\mathbf{U}_q\mathbf{U}_p] + \text{tr}[(\mathbf{Z}^{\text{T}}\mathbf{Z})^{-1}(\mathbf{Z}_{(q)}^{\text{T}}\mathbf{Z}_{(p)} + \mathbf{Z}_{(p)}^{\text{T}}\mathbf{Z}_{(q)})]$$

$$+ \text{tr}[(\mathbf{Z}^{\text{T}}\mathbf{Z})^{-1}(\mathbf{Z}^{\text{T}}\mathbf{Z}_{(pq)} + \mathbf{Z}_{(pq)}^{\text{T}}\mathbf{Z})]\}$$

$$\tag{4.22}$$

$$= |\mathbf{Z}^{\text{T}}\mathbf{Z}|\{\text{tr}[\mathbf{U}_q]\text{tr}[\mathbf{U}_p] - \text{tr}[\mathbf{U}_q\mathbf{U}_p] + \text{tr}[(\mathbf{Z}^{\text{T}}\mathbf{Z})^{-1}(\mathbf{Z}_{(q)}^{\text{T}}\mathbf{Z}_{(p)} + \mathbf{Z}_{(p)}^{\text{T}}\mathbf{Z}_{(q)})]$$

$$+ \text{tr}[(\mathbf{Z}^{\text{T}}\mathbf{Z})^{-1}(\mathbf{Z}^{\text{T}}\mathbf{Z}_{(pq)} + \mathbf{Z}_{(pq)}^{\text{T}}\mathbf{Z})]\}$$

4.2.2   An Approximate Hessian

The last term in the expression for $g_{(pq)}$ requires second derivatives of the model functions. We prefer to avoid calculating second derivatives, especially since the Hessian matrix is being used primarily to determine an increment, and so we make the same assumption as in the Gauss–Newton method for nonlinear least squares. That is, we assume that the model functions can be locally approximated by linear functions and set $\mathbf{Z}_{(pq)}$ to zero. The *approximate Hessian* matrix $\boldsymbol{\Omega}$ is therefore calculated with entries

$$\{\boldsymbol{\Omega}\}_{pq} = 4|\mathbf{Z}^{\text{T}}\mathbf{Z}|\,\text{tr}[\mathbf{Z}^+\mathbf{Z}_{(p)}]\,\text{tr}[\mathbf{Z}^+\mathbf{Z}_{(q)}]$$
$$+ 2|\mathbf{Z}^{\text{T}}\mathbf{Z}|\{-\text{tr}[\mathbf{Z}^+\mathbf{Z}_{(p)}\mathbf{Z}^+\mathbf{Z}_{(q)}] + \text{tr}[\mathbf{Z}^+(\mathbf{Z}^+)^{\text{T}}\mathbf{Z}_{(p)}^{\text{T}}(\mathbf{I}-\mathbf{Z}\mathbf{Z}^+)\mathbf{Z}_{(q)}]\} \tag{4.23}$$

These can be collected into $\boldsymbol{\Omega}$ and used with the gradient vector $\boldsymbol{\omega}$ to form the increment $\boldsymbol{\delta} = -\boldsymbol{\Omega}^{-1}\boldsymbol{\omega}$ in a Newton–Raphson iterative scheme to optimize $|\mathbf{Z}^{\text{T}}\mathbf{Z}|$. Since only first derivatives of the model functions are used, this is a generalization of the Gauss–Newton method for nonlinear least squares.

Some rearrangement of the terms in (4.16) and (4.19) can be used to simplify the calculations of $\boldsymbol{\omega}$ and $\boldsymbol{\Omega}$ (Bates and Watts, 1984). In particular, we can use the relationship $\text{tr}(\mathbf{AB}) = \text{tr}(\mathbf{BA})$ to change (4.16) to

$$\{\boldsymbol{\omega}\}_p = 2\,|\mathbf{Z}^T\mathbf{Z}|\,\text{tr}[\mathbf{Q}_1^T\mathbf{Z}_{(p)}\mathbf{R}_1^{-1}]$$

$$= 2\,|\mathbf{Z}^T\mathbf{Z}|\,\sum_{m=1}^{M} g_{p,mm}$$

where $g_{p,mm}$ is the (m,m)th element of the $N\times M$ matrix

$$\mathbf{G}_p = \mathbf{Q}^T\mathbf{Z}_{(p)}\mathbf{R}_1^{-1} \qquad (4.24)$$

This does not change the gradient calculation substantially, but now (4.23) can be rewritten to give

$$\{\boldsymbol{\Omega}\}_{pq} = 4\,|\mathbf{Z}^T\mathbf{Z}|\,\sum_{m=1}^{M} g_{p,mm}\,\sum_{m=1}^{M} g_{q,mm}$$

$$+ 2\,|\mathbf{Z}^T\mathbf{Z}|\,\{-\text{tr}[\mathbf{Q}_1^T\mathbf{Z}_{(p)}\mathbf{R}_1^{-1}\mathbf{Q}_1^T\mathbf{Z}_{(q)}\mathbf{R}_1^{-1}]$$

$$+ \text{tr}[\mathbf{R}_1^{-1}\mathbf{Q}_1^T\mathbf{Q}_1\mathbf{R}_1^{-T}\mathbf{Z}_{(p)}^T\mathbf{Q}_2\mathbf{Q}_2^T\mathbf{Z}_{(q)}]\}$$

$$= 4\,|\mathbf{Z}^T\mathbf{Z}|\,\sum_{m=1}^{M} g_{p,mm}\,\sum_{m=1}^{M} g_{q,mm} \qquad (4.25)$$

$$+ 2\,|\mathbf{Z}^T\mathbf{Z}|\left[-\sum_{m=1}^{M}\sum_{i=1}^{M} g_{p,mi}g_{q,im} + \text{tr}[(\mathbf{Q}_2^T\mathbf{Z}_{(p)}\mathbf{R}_1^{-1})^T(\mathbf{Q}_2^T\mathbf{Z}_{(q)}\mathbf{R}_1^{-1})]\right]$$

$$= 4\,|\mathbf{Z}^T\mathbf{Z}|\,\sum_{m=1}^{M} g_{p,mm}\,\sum_{m=1}^{M} g_{q,mm}$$

$$+ 2\,|\mathbf{Z}^T\mathbf{Z}|\left[-\sum_{m=1}^{M}\sum_{i=1}^{M} g_{p,mi}g_{q,im} + \sum_{m=M+1}^{N}\sum_{i=1}^{M} g_{p,mi}g_{q,mi}\right]$$

Equation (4.25) permits very efficient evaluation of $\boldsymbol{\Omega}$, because once the QR decomposition of $\mathbf{Z}$ is done and the matrices $\mathbf{G}_p$, $p = 1, \ldots, P$, are formed, it is only necessary to collect a few inner products. As discussed in Appendix 2, although $\mathbf{Q}^T$ occurs as a factor in (4.24), the matrix $\mathbf{Q}$ is not explicitly formed; instead, a product such as $\mathbf{Q}^T\mathbf{Z}_{(p)}$ is formed by applying Householder transformations to $\mathbf{Z}_{(p)}$.

4.2.3   Calculations for Each Iteration

At each iteration, the current value of the parameter vector, $\boldsymbol{\theta}^0$, is used to evaluate $|\mathbf{Z}^T\mathbf{Z}|$, the gradient $\boldsymbol{\omega}$, and the approximate Hessian $\boldsymbol{\Omega}$. If $\boldsymbol{\Omega}$ is positive definite, the increment is calculated by solving

$$\Omega \delta^0 = -\omega \qquad (4.26)$$

for δ^0 and setting

$$\theta^1 = \theta^0 + \lambda \delta^0$$

where λ is a step size factor chosen to ensure that $|Z(\theta^1)^T Z(\theta^1)| < |Z(\theta^0)^T Z(\theta^0)|$. The solution to (4.26) is accomplished most efficiently by taking a Cholesky decomposition of Ω (Dongarra et al., 1979, Chapter 8) as

$$\Omega = C^T C \qquad (4.27)$$

where C is $P \times P$ and upper triangular.

Unlike the Gauss–Newton method for nonlinear least squares, the generalized Gauss–Newton method for multiresponse data need not result in a positive definite Ω. One of the situations in which negative eigenvalues of the Hessian can occur is when there are multiple minima for the determinant criterion, such as in the case study of Section 5.5.

When Ω is not positive definite, the quadratic approximation to $|Z^T Z|$ does not have a minimum and C cannot be calculated. As in Section 3.5, we restore positive definiteness to the Hessian by inflating the diagonal and modifying the increment to be the solution of

$$(\Omega + k I)\delta^0 = -\omega$$

where k is large enough to make $\Omega + kI$ positive definite. Such a k can be calculated by determining the eigenvalues of Ω and setting k to twice the magnitude of the most negative eigenvalue, or by using a modified Cholesky decomposition (Dennis and Schnabel, 1983).

4.2.4   A Multiresponse Convergence Criterion

To decide whether we have convergence at a particular parameter vector θ^0, we reason as in Section 2.2.3 and compare the magnitude of the increment at that point with the statistical variability in the estimates. The statistical variability is accounted for in the elliptical regions of (4.10), and so we take a linear transformation of the parameters to make the regions spherical. With such a transformation, the length of the increment from θ^0 is simply $\| C\delta \|$, where C is the Cholesky factor from (4.27), and the region is simply a disk with radius proportional to $s \sqrt{P \, F(P, N-P; \alpha)}$. The convergence criterion is then (Bates and Watts, 1987)

$$\frac{\| C\delta \|^2 / P}{2s^2} < \epsilon^2$$

where ϵ is the tolerance level and s^2 is the scale factor (4.9). When the criterion is small, it indicates that the requested increment is negligible relative to the statistical variability. The value of ϵ can be set at 0.001, reasoning as in Section

2.2.3.
Pseudocode for multiresponse parameter estimation is presented in Appendix 3, Section A3.3.

4.3   Practical Considerations

As in uniresponse estimation, care should be taken in selecting the model and obtaining starting estimates for the parameters. After convergence, residuals for all the responses should be examined using plots as described in Chapter 3. However, multiresponse modeling involves additional practical considerations, as discussed below.

4.3.1   Obtaining Starting Values

The techniques for obtaining starting estimates for uniresponse models described in Chapter 3 can be used for multiresponse models by applying the procedures to each response and then combining the estimates to give starting values for the complete parameter vector. Graphical analyses can be especially helpful, as illustrated in the following example.

Example: s-PMMA 2
Starting estimates for the parameters in the expectation function for the complex dielectric coefficient can be obtained from graphical considerations, following Havriliak and Negami (1967). They showed that the real and imaginary components can be written

$$\varepsilon' = \varepsilon_\infty + (\varepsilon_0 - \varepsilon_\infty) R^{-\beta} \cos \beta \phi$$

$$\varepsilon'' = (\varepsilon_0 - \varepsilon_\infty) R^{-\beta} \sin \beta \phi$$

where

$$R^2 = \left[1 + (2\pi f/f_0)^\alpha \cos(\pi\alpha/2) \right]^2 + \left[(2\pi f/f_0)^\alpha \sin(\pi\alpha/2) \right]^2$$

and

$$\phi = \arctan \left[\frac{(2\pi f/f_0)^\alpha \sin(\pi\alpha/2)}{1 + (2\pi f/f_0)^\alpha \cos(\pi\alpha/2)} \right]$$

The parameters ε_0 and ε_∞ are the limiting low and high frequency intercepts of the locus with the real axis, when the function is plotted in the complex plane. Furthermore, the limiting angle the high frequency locus makes with the real axis is $\psi_L = \pi\alpha\beta/2$, and the angle bisector of ψ_L from $(\varepsilon_\infty, 0)$ intersects the locus at the frequency $\tilde{f}$ for which $2\pi\tilde{f}/f_0 = 1$. And finally, α is related to ψ_L through

$$\psi_L = -\pi\alpha \; \frac{\ln\left[\dfrac{\tilde{R}}{\varepsilon_0 - \varepsilon_\infty}\right]}{\ln\left[2 + 2\cos(\pi\alpha/2)\right]}$$

where $\tilde{R}$ is the length of the line from $(\varepsilon_\infty, 0)$ to $\varepsilon^*(\tilde{f})$.

To obtain starting values for the s-PMMA data, we plotted the data in the complex plane, as in Figure 4.2c, but this time we made the scales of the real and imaginary parts equal so that angles and distances would be correct. We extrapolated the right hand portion of the curve to the real axis to give the starting value $\varepsilon_0^0 = 4.40$, and extrapolated the left hand portion to the real axis to give the starting value $\varepsilon_\infty^0 = 2.36$. Next, we measured the angle of the left hand extrapolation line to the real axis to give the limiting angle estimate $\psi_L = 19°$. The bisector of this angle intercepts the data between the points corresponding to 200 and 300 Hz, so we took the value of $(\ln f_0)^0 = \ln[2\pi(250)] = 7.36$. The length $\tilde{R}$ was measured to be 1.6, and using this value together with that of the limiting angle, we solved for $\alpha^0 = 0.53$ and, finally, $\beta^0 = 0.40$. ■

4.3.1.1 Starting Estimates for Multiresponse Models Described by Systems of Linear Differential Equations

For multiresponse models described by systems of differential equations, such as in Example α-Pinene 1 or α-Pinene 2, one can exploit the relation between the rates and the responses to develop a simple procedure for determining starting values (Bates and Watts, 1985; Varah, 1982). The general approach is to derive estimates for the rates and then solve the simpler linear or nonlinear set of equations rather than using numerical integration to solve the differential equations. In Varah (1982), cubic spline fits were made to the data and rates were obtained by differentiating the spline fits. A cruder approach is to use simple differences to obtain rate estimates, as was used in Example Ethyl acrylate 2, and illustrated below for multiresponse data.

Example: α-Pinene 3

A linear kinetic model was proposed in Box et al. (1973) for the α-pinene data, of the form

$$\frac{d\gamma_1}{dt} = -(\theta_1 + \theta_2)\gamma_1$$

$$\frac{d\gamma_2}{dt} = \theta_1\gamma_1$$

$$\frac{d\gamma_3}{dt} = \theta_2\gamma_1 - (\theta_3 + \theta_4)\gamma_3 + \theta_5\gamma_5$$

$$\frac{d\gamma_4}{dt} = \theta_3\gamma_3$$

$$\frac{d\gamma_5}{dt} = \theta_4\gamma_3 - \theta_5\gamma_5$$

The explicit solution to this set of linear differential equations was given in Box et al. (1973), and involves long complicated expressions.

An alternative form is the matrix equation

$$
\begin{bmatrix} \dot{\gamma}_1 \\ \dot{\gamma}_2 \\ \dot{\gamma}_3 \\ \dot{\gamma}_4 \\ \dot{\gamma}_5 \end{bmatrix}
=
\begin{bmatrix}
-\theta_1-\theta_2 & 0 & 0 & 0 & 0 \\
\theta_1 & 0 & 0 & 0 & 0 \\
\theta_2 & 0 & -\theta_3-\theta_4 & 0 & \theta_5 \\
0 & 0 & \theta_3 & 0 & 0 \\
0 & 0 & \theta_4 & 0 & -\theta_5
\end{bmatrix}
\begin{bmatrix} \gamma_1 \\ \gamma_2 \\ \gamma_3 \\ \gamma_4 \\ \gamma_5 \end{bmatrix}
$$

or

$$\dot{\gamma} = A\gamma$$

where A is the system transfer matrix, and a dot denotes differentiation with respect to time. Further discussion of linear differential equation models is given in Chapter 5.

To derive an expression useful for obtaining starting values, we rewrite the matrix equation as

$$
\begin{bmatrix} \dot{\gamma}_1 \\ \dot{\gamma}_2 \\ \dot{\gamma}_3 \\ \dot{\gamma}_4 \\ \dot{\gamma}_5 \end{bmatrix}
=
\begin{bmatrix}
-\theta_1\gamma_1-\theta_2\gamma_1 \\
\theta_1\gamma_1 \\
\theta_2\gamma_1-\theta_3\gamma_3-\theta_4\gamma_3+\theta_5\gamma_5 \\
\theta_3\gamma_3 \\
\theta_4\gamma_3-\theta_5\gamma_5
\end{bmatrix}
= X(t)\theta
$$

where

$$
X(t) =
\begin{bmatrix}
-\gamma_1 & -\gamma_1 & 0 & 0 & 0 \\
\gamma_1 & 0 & 0 & 0 & 0 \\
0 & \gamma_1 & -\gamma_3 & -\gamma_3 & \gamma_5 \\
0 & 0 & \gamma_3 & 0 & 0 \\
0 & 0 & 0 & \gamma_3 & -\gamma_5
\end{bmatrix}
$$

At any time t, therefore, if we have estimates for the rates and the concentrations, we could estimate θ by linear regression of γ on X. Collecting the estimated rates for each time into a vector gives the "response" vector for the linear regression. Similarly, we calculate $X(t)$ matrices for each time, using the average concentrations, and stack them to form the X

matrix.

For example, the estimated rates at $t = 1230$ are

$$(-9.47, 5.93, 1.87, 0.33, 1.43)^T \times 10^{-3}$$

and the average concentrations, inserted into the appropriate matrix, are

$$\begin{bmatrix} -94.2 & -94.2 & 0 & 0 & 0 \\ 94.2 & 0 & 0 & 0 & 0 \\ 0 & 94.2 & -1.15 & -1.15 & 0.88 \\ 0 & 0 & 1.15 & 0 & 0 \\ 0 & 0 & 0 & 1.15 & -0.88 \end{bmatrix}$$

Finally, we stack the vectors from each time to form a single vector, stack the matrices to form a single matrix, and then perform a simple linear regression with no intercept term to get the starting estimates. The starting values so obtained are

$$\theta^0 = (5.84, 2.65, 1.63, 27.77, 4.61)^T \times 10^{-5}$$

Because the parameters are rate constants, which are necessarily positive, we fit the model in the parameters $\phi_p = \ln \theta_p$ (see Section 3.4.1). ■

When some of the responses are not measured, it is still possible to use approximate rates provided other information, such as a mass balance, is substituted. In addition to providing starting values, the approximate rate method provides useful information on the estimation situation, and can even be used for parameter estimation (Varah, 1982), although, when estimating parameters, one should ensure that the implicit assumptions on the distribution of the noise terms are reasonable.

4.3.2 Assessing the Fit

As in any statistical analysis, it is extremely important to assess the fit. Generally, the best type of assessment involves plotting the residuals for all responses versus the design variables, versus each other, and versus the fitted responses, plus overlay plots of the data and the fitted responses. These plots are especially important in that they can reveal whether the program has converged to a spurious optimum due to dependencies in the data or in the residuals.

Example: s-PMMA 3

Convergence output for the s-PMMA data is given in Table 4.1. The residuals for the real and imaginary components are plotted versus frequency in Figure 4.3. The imaginary residuals are quite well behaved, but the real residuals are grouped and have a strong trend with frequency.

As discussed in Havriliak and Watts (1987), this behavior can be explained by considering the way in which the frequencies are set in an ex-

Table 4.1   Parameter summary for the s-PMMA data.

Parameter	Estimate	Approx. Std.Error	Approximate Correlation Matrix				
ε_0	4.320	0.011	1.00				
ε_∞	2.522	0.018	0.75	1.00			
$\ln f_0$	7.956	0.084	0.46	0.74	1.00		
α	0.531	0.010	−0.57	−0.71	−0.93	1.00	
β	0.554	0.030	0.53	0.84	0.95	−0.95	1.00

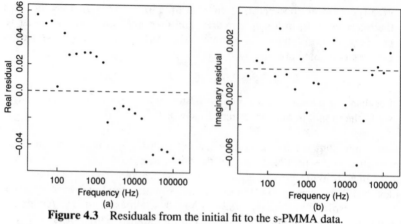

Figure 4.3   Residuals from the initial fit to the s-PMMA data.

periment. When the frequency of an oscillator is made to cover an extremely large range (in this example, from 30 to 150 000 Hz), it is done by manipulating two dials, a *units* dial which covers a range of, say, 2 to 20, and a *decade* dial which changes the frequency by multiples of 10. Thus, to set the frequency to 150 Hz, the operator would set the units dial to 15 and the decade dial to ×10; and to set the frequency to 30 000 Hz, the operator would set the units dial to 3 and the decade dial to ×10 000. In this experiment, the capacitance of the polymer sample was apparently large enough to affect the frequency of the oscillator, so that the actual frequency delivered was not that indicated on the dials. At high frequencies the fitted values were too large, and at low frequencies the fitted values were too small, suggesting that the indicated frequencies were below the actual, with the discrepancy (indicated − actual) increasing with each decade increase.

A decade correction was therefore made to the indicated frequencies so that when the decade was increased, the frequency was multiplied by $10 \times K$. Assuming the first decade was correct, the second decade would have actual frequencies of $K \times$ the indicated values, the third decade $K^2 \times$ the indicated values, and so on. Rather than incorporate the decade factor

K as a parameter in the model, we performed a search by selecting values for K, modifying the indicated frequencies, fitting the model and examining the residuals, and choosing that value of K which gave the best behaved residuals. For this data set, a decade correction of $K = 1.25$ was found.

The convergence output for the decade-corrected data is given in Table 4.2. The major changes were a reduction in the determinant and in the variance estimate of the real residuals by a factor of about 10. The residuals for the real and imaginary components are plotted versus frequency in Figure 4.4, from which it can be seen that the imaginary residuals are very well behaved, with perhaps two or three outliers. The real residuals are much better behaved now, with no trend. There is, however, one obvious outlier and one other possible outlier. Plotting the imaginary residuals versus the real residuals more clearly discloses two outliers. Since the residuals are bad in both the real and imaginary components, we simply delete these two cases. If only one residual were bad, we could treat the observation which gave rise to the bad residual as missing, and proceed as in Section 4.4.

Analysis of the decade-corrected and edited data set produced the results in Table 4.3. Removing the two unusual cases reduced the parameter and variable variances, but the parameter estimates were not materially affected. The residuals from this fit are very well behaved, as can be seen from Figure 4.5.

We also analyzed the data by estimating K rather than obtaining it from a search. The optimum value was $\hat{K} = 1.24$; the other parameter estimates and their approximate standard errors changed slightly. ∎

Example: α-Pinene 4
The starting values in Example α-Pinene 2 were used together with the techniques described in Chapter 5 for obtaining the expectation function and derivatives, and convergence was obtained for the five response data set as shown in Table 4.4. In Figure 4.6 we show a plot of the data and the fitted responses. The fitted curves do not follow the data very well, sug-

Table 4.2 Parameter summary for the decade-corrected s-PMMA data.

Parameter	Estimate	Approx. Std.Error	Approximate Correlation Matrix				
ε_0	4.400	0.007	1.00				
ε_∞	2.447	0.013	0.58	1.00			
$\ln f_0$	8.228	0.091	0.68	0.84	1.00		
α	0.486	0.008	−0.86	−0.68	−0.91	1.00	
β	0.571	0.026	0.76	0.85	0.99	−0.95	1.00

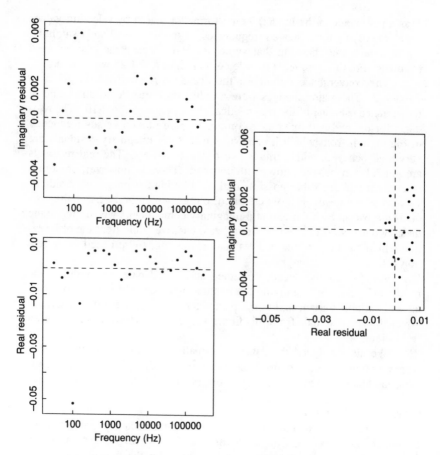

Figure 4.4   Residuals from the fit to the decade-corrected s-PMMA data.

Table 4.3   Parameter summary for the decade-corrected and edited s-PMMA data.

Parameter	Estimate	Approx. Std.Error	Approximate Correlation Matrix				
ε_0	4.398	0.006	1.00				
ε_∞	2.451	0.010	0.53	1.00			
$\ln f_0$	8.245	0.074	0.63	0.91	1.00		
α	0.487	0.007	−0.86	−0.75	−0.90	1.00	
β	0.571	0.021	0.74	0.91	0.98	−0.95	1.00

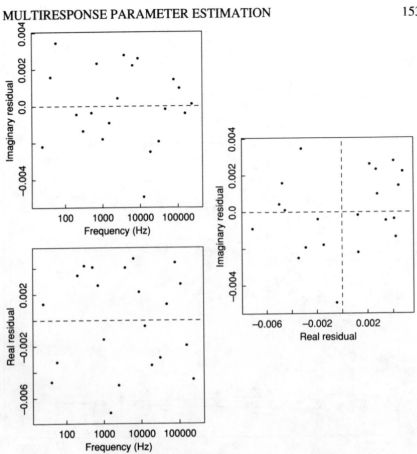

Figure 4.5 Residuals from the fit to the decade-corrected and edited s-PMMA data.

Table 4.4 Parameter summary for the α-pinene data using five responses.

Parameter		θ			Logarithm Scale				
From	To	(10^{-5})	φ	Std.Error			Correlation		
1	2	3.74	−10.19	0.085	1.00				
1	3	1.95	−10.85	0.073	0.84	1.00			
3	4	1.65	−11.01	0.104	−0.20	−0.41	1.00		
3	5	27.01	−8.217	0.128	0.00	−0.00	0.85	1.00	
5	3	2.61	−10.55	0.195	0.68	0.78	−0.01	0.40	1.00

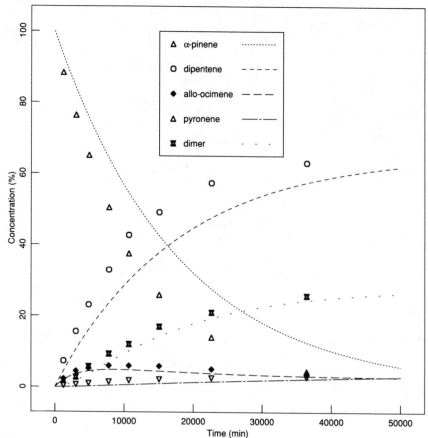

Figure 4.6 Observed values and the predicted curves obtained by fitting five responses to the α-pinene data

gesting that convergence to a spurious optimum has occurred. As will be shown in the next section, this has occurred because there are dependencies in the data. ∎

4.3.3 Dependencies Among Responses

Convergence to a spurious optimum due to dependencies in the response data is an important problem which can easily arise in multiresponse estimation, but which can not happen in uniresponse estimation. Data dependencies can occur, for example, because the responses are constrained through mass balances or because one or more responses are not measured but are imputed from other measured responses. If dependencies occur in the data or in the expected responses, then the estimation procedure must be modified so as to avoid convergence to spurious optima (Box et al., 1973; McLean et al., 1979).

To detect dependencies in a multiresponse data set, Box et al. (1973) used an eigenvalue analysis of the inner product of the centered data matrix, $(Y - \bar{Y})^T (Y - \bar{Y})$, where $\bar{Y}$ is the matrix of response averages obtained by replacing each column of Y by the average of the column. They then compared the eigenvalues with an estimate of the roundoff sum of squares, $(N - 1)u^2/12$, where u is the rounding unit of the data. Any eigenvalues which were of the same magnitude as the roundoff sum of squares were assumed to be associated with linear dependencies in the data.

This approach can reveal singularities due to conditions that cause a linear combination of the responses from all cases to be a constant (for example, a mass balance), but, as described in McLean et al. (1979), analysis of the centered *data* matrix can fail to detect singularities in the *residual* matrix, and hence one may still be trying to converge with a "defective" data set. As was also pointed out by these authors, in certain circumstances linear dependencies among the data need not cause singularities in the residual matrix $Z(\theta)$, so removal of singularities detected through analysis of the centered data matrix can cause unnecessary loss of precision in the parameter estimates. Therefore, it is necessary to search for singularities in both the centered data matrix and the residual matrix.

As an example where there can be singularities in Z but no singularities in $Y - \bar{Y}$, following McLean et al. (1979), we consider a chemical reaction in which two responses are measured. The two responses are normalized so that the total for the nth case is γ_n^0, the initial concentration of the first chemical. Unless the initial concentrations are all the same, the matrix $Y - \bar{Y}$ will not be singular. However, if the reaction follows first order kinetics so that $f_{n1} = \gamma_n^0 e^{-\theta t_n}$ and $f_{n2} = \gamma_n^0 (1 - e^{-\theta t_n})$, then the residual matrix Z with nth row

$$(z_{n1}, z_{n2}) = (y_{n1} - f_{n1}, y_{n2} - f_{n2})$$

involves the linear dependency $z_{n1} + z_{n2} = 0$ for all n, and the residual matrix is singular. It would be futile, therefore, to try to estimate the parameter θ using a multiresponse estimation criterion.

As an example where there can be singularities in $Y - \bar{Y}$ but no singularities in Z, suppose that in the example above, the two responses are obtained from chromatograph area fractions, so the measurement for y_{n1} is

$$y_{n1} = a_1 + b_1 \left[\frac{\text{area}_{n1}}{\text{area}_{n1} + \text{area}_{n2}} \right]$$

and that for y_{n2} is

$$y_{n2} = a_2 + b_2 \left[\frac{\text{area}_{n2}}{\text{area}_{n1} + \text{area}_{n2}} \right]$$

where a_1, b_1, a_2, and b_2 are calibration constants. Then a linear dependency will exist in the data of the form $b_2 y_{n1} + b_1 y_{n2} = \text{constant}$ for all n, and so $Y - \bar{Y}$

will be singular. However, unless for every case

$$\gamma_n^0 \left[b_1 + (b_2 - b_1)e^{-\theta t_n} \right] = a_2 b_1 + a_1 b_2 + b_1 b_2$$

the residual matrix will not be singular because of the linear dependence in the data.

Singularities in $\mathbf{Y} - \overline{\mathbf{Y}}$ and in $\mathbf{Z}$ can be detected by performing an eigenvalue–eigenvector decomposition of the inner product, as proposed by Box et al. (1973), but we prefer to arrange the rounding units in the columns of $\mathbf{Y}$ to be approximately equal and then take singular value decompositions of $\mathbf{Y} - \overline{\mathbf{Y}}$ and $\mathbf{Z}$ (Dongarra et al., 1979, Chapter 11). As explained there, singular values on the order of the rounding unit indicate singularity and should prompt the analyst to search for dependencies in the data.

A singular value decomposition of the centered data matrix, and of the residual matrix using the initial parameter values, should be done at the beginning of the analysis so as to avoid unnecessary calculations caused by dealing with a defective data set which involves linear dependencies. If small singular values are obtained, the corresponding singular vectors should be examined to reveal what is causing the dependencies. If the dependency can be explained (e.g., a mass balance, or a response has been imputed from other measured responses) and the offending responses identified, they should be removed and a multiresponse analysis performed on the reduced data set. If a dependency can not be explained, then the multiresponse analysis should be modified to take account of the dependency as described in Section 4.3.4. The residual matrix at the converged parameter values should also be analyzed for singular values so as to detect possible dependencies in the residuals. Further comments on detecting and eliminating linear dependencies are given in McLean et al. (1979).

Example: s-PMMA 4

For the decade-corrected and edited s-PMMA data, the singular values of the centered data matrix are 0.278 and 2.161, and since the rounding units in the data are both 0.001, neither of these singular values is small enough to suggest a linear dependency. The singular values of the residual matrix at the converged values are 0.009 and 0.017 and neither of these is small enough to cause concern. ■

Example: α-Pinene 5

The centered data matrix for the α-pinene data, has the singular value decomposition

Singular value	0.04	0.13	1.10	5.08	98.30
	−0.17	0.48	−0.30	0.06	−0.81
	−0.21	0.49	−0.61	−0.22	0.54
Singular vectors	−0.16	0.43	0.64	−0.61	0.01
	0.93	0.36	−0.01	0.00	0.02
	−0.19	0.46	0.36	0.76	0.23

which clearly indicates dependencies in the data because the two small singular values are of the same magnitude as the rounding unit in the data (0.1, see Appendix 1, Section A1.6).

The residual matrix at the starting estimates has the singular value decomposition

Singular value	0.06	0.14	0.46	1.63	42.70
	0.34	−0.30	−0.28	0.26	0.81
	0.39	−0.26	−0.39	0.55	−0.57
Singular vectors	0.60	−0.27	0.75	−0.08	−0.07
	−0.50	−0.86	0.08	−0.05	−0.06
	0.36	−0.20	−0.45	−0.79	−0.12

which also reveals two dependencies.

As noted by Box et al. (1973), from careful reading of the paper by Fuguitt and Hawkins (1947), the response y_4 was not in fact measured, but was imputed as 3% of the amount of converted y_1, i.e., $y_4 = 0.03(100 - y_1)$. The first singular vector of the centered data matrix reflects this dependency and so the imputed data for y_4 should not be used in estimation. The second singular vector, consisting of almost equal entries, reflects a mass balance dependency, i.e., the data must sum to 100%. This occurs because the system is a conservative one, as can easily be seen, since all the columns of the system matrix A sum to zero. The singular vectors of the residual matrix do not reflect these dependencies, so that while the singular value decomposition of Z does suggest that there are dependencies, it does not reveal their nature.

Because there are two small singular values, suggesting two linear dependencies in the data, only three responses should be retained for parameter estimation. ■

When linear dependencies are found, the problem of choosing an appropriate subset of the responses must be addressed. One approach is to retain those responses which the researcher thinks are most reliable. It may not be possible to select the responses on this basis, however, and so we follow Box et al. (1973) and use a linear combination of the responses instead. In either situation, it would be helpful to have a procedure for estimating parameters in the presence of dependencies. Accordingly, in the following section we describe a procedure for estimating parameters in the presence of linear dependencies.

4.3.4   Linear Combinations of Responses

Suppose there are d linear dependencies, and there are no missing values in the data matrix. To deal with linear dependencies, we generate an $N \times (M - d)$ reduced residual matrix $\mathbf{ZB}$ by combining the d linear dependency vectors into an $M \times d$ dependency matrix $\mathbf{D}$, performing a QR decomposition on $\mathbf{D}$, and letting the rotation matrix $\mathbf{B}$ be the $M - d$ columns of $\mathbf{Q}$ which are orthogonal to the dependency vectors.

Example: α-Pinene 6

For the α-pinene data, we have decided that response 4 should not be used in estimation, and that there is a mass balance relation in the data. The dependency matrix is therefore

$$\mathbf{D} = \begin{bmatrix} 0 & 1 \\ 0 & 1 \\ 0 & 1 \\ 1 & 1 \\ 0 & 1 \end{bmatrix}$$

Performing a QR decomposition produces $\mathbf{B}$ as the last three columns of $\mathbf{Q}$. Again, as discussed in Appendix 2, although $\mathbf{Q}$ is required to obtain $\mathbf{B}$, $\mathbf{Q}$ is not explicitly formed; a product such as $\mathbf{Z}_{(p)}\mathbf{B}$ is formed by applying Householder transformations to $\mathbf{Z}_{(p)}^{T}$, retaining the last $M - d$ rows to give $(\mathbf{Z}_{(p)}\mathbf{B})^{T}$, and then transposing the result. ∎

To minimize $|(\mathbf{ZB})^{T}(\mathbf{ZB})|$ using the generalized Gauss–Newton method of Section 4.2, we need $(\mathbf{ZB})_{(p)}$. This is easily obtained because $\mathbf{B}$ is independent of $\boldsymbol{\theta}$, and so

$$(\mathbf{ZB})_{(p)} = \mathbf{Z}_{(p)}\mathbf{B}$$

Thus, the terms in the determinant, the gradient and the approximate Hessian for the reduced data set can be calculated by simply using $\mathbf{Z}$ and $\mathbf{Z}_{(p)}, p = 1, \ldots, P$.

Example: α-Pinene 7

Using the starting values from Example α-Pinene 4 and three (rotated) responses, we obtained the results in Table 4.5.

The overlay plot of the data and fitted curves in Figure 4.7 gives no evidence of inadequacy of the fitted model. However, the residuals, shown in Figure 4.8, are not well behaved, with a large negative residual for response 3 and a trend and a large positive residual for response 2. There is also a preponderance of negative residuals. Also the approximate confidence limits on ϕ_3 are very wide, suggesting that it is badly estimated and that θ_3 could be zero. We temporarily ignore the defective residuals, and try to see if a simpler model would be adequate. ∎

Table 4.5 Parameter summary for the α-pinene data using three rotated responses.

Parameter		θ	Logarithm Scale						
From	To	(10^{-5})	ϕ	Std.Error	Correlation				
1	2	5.94	−9.731	0.021	1.00				
1	3	2.86	−10.47	0.042	−0.20	1.00			
3	4	0.453	−12.31	3.92	−0.37	0.91	1.00		
3	5	31.12	−8.072	0.124	−0.22	0.51	0.45	1.00	
5	3	5.79	−9.757	0.21	0.10	0.16	0.16	0.78	1.00

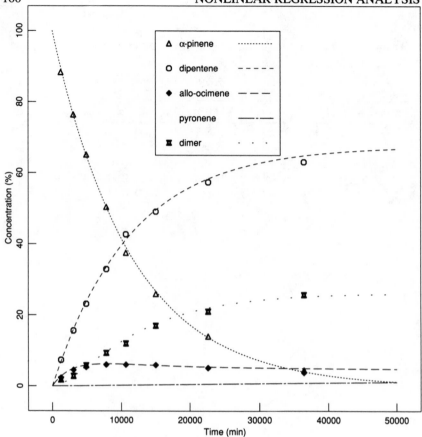

Figure 4.7   Observed values and the predicted curves obtained by fitting three rotated responses to the α-pinene data.

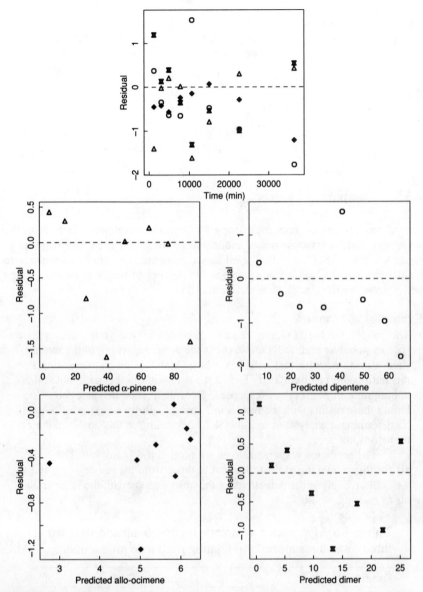

Figure 4.8   Residuals from the three rotated response fit to the α-pinene data plotted versus time and versus predicted response.

Linear combinations of responses can be used to check for consistency of information by analyzing subsets of the responses, as suggested in Box and Draper (1965). We simply let **B** be the matrix derived from an identity matrix by deleting columns corresponding to the unused responses.

Example: α-Pinene 8

Suppose we wished to estimate the parameters using only the responses y_1, y_2, and y_5. Then we would use as the rotation matrix

$$
\mathbf{B} = \begin{bmatrix} 1 & 0 & 0 \\ 0 & 1 & 0 \\ 0 & 0 & 0 \\ 0 & 0 & 0 \\ 0 & 0 & 1 \end{bmatrix}
$$

■

4.3.5   Comparing Models

Nested models can be compared using an "extra determinant" analysis in the same way that uniresponse nested models were compared using an extra sum of squares analysis (Section 3.10). That is, we compare the ratio of the change in the determinant divided by the change in the degrees of freedom with the scaled determinant for the complete model as in (4.11).

Example: α-Pinene 9

The model for the α-pinene reaction includes a path from species 3 to species 4, but as seen in Example α-Pinene 6, the logarithm of the rate constant associated with that path has a large standard error, suggesting that this path could be eliminated. Fitting the data without this path, but still retaining only three (rotated) responses, gives the results in Table 4.6. Combining these results with the results in Table 4.5 allows us to perform an extra determinant analysis as in Table 4.7. According to this analysis, the extra path is not necessary.

The predicted response curves are plotted in Figure 4.9. The residuals for this model are almost identical to those from the previous fit, and so we could reanalyze the data, treating the observations with the large residuals as missing.   ■

Table 4.6   Parameter summary for the α-pinene data using three rotated responses, eliminating pyronene production.

Parameter		θ	Logarithm Scale		
From	To	(10^{-5})	φ	Std.Error	Correlation
1	2	5.94	−9.73	0.018	1.00
1	3	2.82	−11.28	0.016	0.44 1.00
3	5	30.75	−8.09	0.093	−0.07 0.26 1.00
5	3	5.72	−9.77	0.182	0.16 0.05 0.81 1.00

Table 4.7 Extra determinant analysis of the 4-parameter model versus the 5-parameter model for the α-pinene data.

Source	Determinant	Degrees of Freedom	Mean Det.	F Ratio	p Value
Extra	0.60	1	0.60	0.06	0.822
Full model	28.39	3	9.46		
partial model	28.99	4			

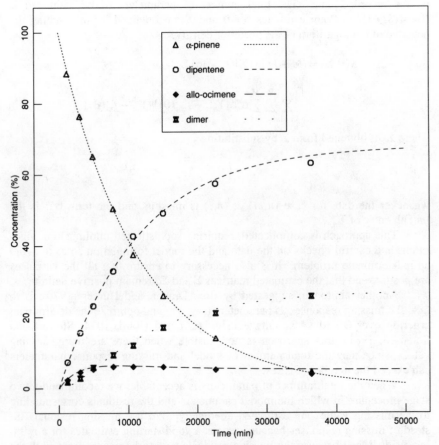

Figure 4.9 Observed values and the predicted curves obtained by fitting three rotated responses to the α-pinene data, eliminating pyronene production.

4.4 Missing Data

Missing data are a source of difficulty in statistics. In uniresponse linear or non-linear regression analysis, if the value of a predictor variable is missing, or if the response itself is missing, the residual cannot be calculated and the only course is to delete the case. In multiresponse estimation, however, it is possible to have all the predictor variables recorded and some, but not all, of the responses recorded. In such situations, it is still possible to use the recorded response values even though there are incomplete data for that case.

Stewart and Sorensen (1981) gave a Bayesian approach for multiresponse data with missing values based on the posterior density for θ and Σ conditional on the recorded data. The total number of parameters to be estimated is $P + M(M+1)/2$. Point estimates for θ and Σ are obtained by minimizing the negative of the logarithm of the posterior density,

$$S(\theta,\Sigma) = (M+1)\ln|\Sigma| + \sum_{n=1}^{N}\ln|\Sigma_n|$$
$$+ \sum_{n=1}^{N}\sum_{m=1}^{M}\sum_{i=1}^{M}\sigma_n^{mi}\{Y_{nm} - f_{nm}(\theta)\}\{Y_{ni} - f_{ni}(\theta)\}$$

where Σ_n is obtained from Σ by substituting

$$\delta_{mi} = \begin{cases} 1 & m = i \\ 0 & m \neq i \end{cases}$$

whenever the data for case (n,m) or (n,i) is missing, and the term σ_n^{mi} is the (m,i)th entry of Σ_n^{-1}.

This approach is complicated, requiring sophisticated minimization algorithms and careful checks on the data and the model formulation so as to avoid an indeterminate problem. It is also necessary to ensure that all the variances are positive and that the estimated matrices Σ and Σ_n remain positive definite

Another approach, suggested by Box, Draper, and Hunter (1970), is to treat the missing responses as parameters (say, y^*) and optimize the determinant criterion over θ and y^* simultaneously. As noted (Bard, 1974; Stewart and Sorensen, 1981), this approach is not feasible when there are many missing values, since then the total number of model and missing response parameters can exceed the number of cases.

When the total number of parameters is acceptable, we recommend a two stage procedure in which the model parameters and the residuals corresponding to the missing values are estimated alternately. We use missing residuals instead of missing responses because zero is a good starting estimates for a missing residual, and because the missing residuals tend to be uncorrelated with the model parameters. In the first stage, the missing residuals are fixed and the model parameters are estimated using a generalized Gauss–Newton algorithm. The algorithm must be modified because after each function evaluation, the entries in $Z(\theta)$ corresponding to missing data must be replaced by their current values. Also, the corresponding entries in $Z_{(p)}$ must be replaced by zeros, since those residuals do not depend on the model parameters.

In the second stage, θ is held fixed and the determinant is minimized with respect to the missing residuals. The generalized Gauss–Newton method can also be used here, since the derivatives of Z with respect to a missing residual consist of zeros everywhere except for a one in the location of the missing residual.

Example: s-PMMA 5

Recall from Example s-PMMA 3 that the residuals at 100 and 150 Hz were anomalous, and so we deleted those cases. We now illustrate the two stage approach for fitting multiresponse data with missing observations by treating the y_{real} values as missing and the y_{imag} values as good.

We begin with initial estimates $\theta = (4.40, 2.45, 8.25, 0.49, 0.57)^T$ and set the missing residuals, $\{Z\}_{4,1}$ and $\{Z\}_{5,1}$, to zero. Converging on the parameters gives $\theta = (4.41, 2.45, 8.24, 0.48, 0.57)^T$ with a determinant of 4.500×10^{-8}. We now fix θ and optimize the determinant with respect to $\{Z\}_{4,1}$ and $\{Z\}_{5,1}$. This gives estimates 0.00248 and 0.00270 and a determinant of 4.373×10^{-8}.

Fixing these residuals and optimizing with respect to θ produces minor changes in θ (e.g., $\ln f_0$ changes from 8.237 to 8.252). Optimizing the residuals again gives estimates 0.00252 and 0.00277 and a determinant of 4.371×10^{-8}. In the next stage, the values of the parameters do not change, so convergence is achieved. ■

Example: α-Pinene 10

As discussed in Examples α-Pinene 7 and α-Pinene 9, the residuals exhibited trends with respect to the fitted value for response 2 and response 4, and unequal distributions of the residuals with respect to sign. There were also two possible outliers, $\hat{z}_{5,2}$ and $\hat{z}_{8,3}$. To see if the trends or unequal distributions could be caused by these outliers, we reanalyzed the data using the 4-parameter model and treating the corresponding observations as missing. A summary of the results is given in Table 4.8. The main effect is that $\ln \theta_4$ changes by 0.317, which corresponds to a factor of 1.37 for θ_4. The residuals, not shown, were very similar to those from the fit to the complete data set, plotted in Figure 4.8, so the imbalance in signs and the trends do not appear to be caused by the two residuals we characterized as outliers. We therefore interpret the nonrandom behavior of the residuals as indicating a fundamental inadequacy in the form of the model. This finding is in accord with that of Stewart and Sorensen (1981), who analyzed the complete data set reported by Fuguitt and Hawkins (1945, 1947). The model proposed by Stewart and Sorensen (1981) consisted of the set of nonlinear differential equations presented in Example α-pinene 1 of Chapter 3. ■

Table 4.8   Summary of the effects of treating two observations as missing in the α-pinene data.

	Data Set			
	Complete		Incomplete	
Quantity	Estimate	Std. Err.	Estimate	Std. Err.
$\ln \theta_1$	−9.729	0.018	−9.740	0.013
$\ln \theta_2$	−10.478	0.016	−10.475	0.019
$\ln \theta_3$	−8.087	0.093	−8.229	0.105
$\ln \theta_4$	−9.769	0.183	−10.086	0.265
$\hat{z}_{5,2}$	1.528		−0.562	0.138
$\hat{z}_{8,3}$	−1.214		−1.804	0.381
Determinant	28.99		24.44	

Exercises

4.1 Write a computer routine in a language of your choice to calculate the determinant, the gradient of the determinant, and the approximate Hessian of the determinant, for a multiresponse estimation routine. If necessary, use the pseudocode in Appendix 3, Section A3.3 for guidance.

4.2 Use the data for responses 1 and 2 in the α-pinene data set, Appendix 4, Section A4.6, to fit the multiresponse model

$$
\boldsymbol{\gamma}(t) = \begin{bmatrix} e^{-(\theta_1+\theta_2)t} \\ \dfrac{\theta_1}{\theta_1+\theta_2}\left[1-e^{-(\theta_1+\theta_2)t}\right] \end{bmatrix}
$$

Assume the initial concentration of α-pinene (response 1) is 100% and of dipentene (response 2) is 0%.

(a) Use the approximate rate procedure of Section 4.3.1 to obtain starting estimates for the parameters.

(b) Use a nonlinear estimation routine to obtain the parameter estimates. Replace the missing value for response 1 at time 16 020 by 0 to obtain the parameter estimates.

(c) Use the procedure in Section 4.4 to estimate the parameters and the missing value.

4.3 Perform a singular value decomposition of the centered data matrix for the data from Appendix 4, Section A4.7, to determine if there are any linear dependencies in the data.

4.4 For the data and model of Problem 4.2, the parameter estimates and summary statistics from part (b) are as follows:

		Logarithm Scale			
			Std.	Correlation	
Parameter	Estimate	$\ln \theta$	Error	Matrix	
θ_1	0.000221	-8.417	0.0085	1.00	
θ_2	0.000139	-8.881	0.0059	0.69	1.00

(a) Calculate joint and marginal 95% inference regions for the parameters using equations (4.9) and (4.12).

(b) Use a grid of values of $\ln \theta_1$ from -8.46 to -8.38 in steps 0.005 and $\ln \theta_2$ from -8.904 to -8.854 in steps of 0.002, and calculate the determinant at each point. Join points of equal value to delineate contours.

(c) Plot the joint 95% inference region from part (a) on the contour plot in part (b). Is the linear approximation region accurate in this case?

4.5 Use the data and model from Appendix 4, Section A4.7 to fit a multiresponse model. Reduce the model to a simple form by eliminating parameters which could be zero. Your analysis to Problem 4.3 should have alerted you to the fact that there was a dependency in the data. In fact, the water component y_6 was imputed from a mass balance equation, and so this response should not be used in fitting the model. Because of this, it is convenient to estimate the parameters θ_6 and β_6 from the parameter constraint equations.

CHAPTER 5.

Models Defined by Systems of Differential Equations

"The universe is like a safe to which there is a combination, but the combination is locked up in the safe."

— *Peter de Vries*

An important special class of nonlinear models is that in which the responses are described by a linear system of ordinary differential equations. These models are used in chemical kinetics (Froment and Bischoff, 1979) and in pharmacokinetics (Godfrey, 1983), where they are called *compartment* models. Because they are used in so many areas, it is worthwhile to have special techniques to make their analysis easier. Accordingly, in this chapter we present efficient methods for estimating parameters in compartment models and for developing and testing competing models. Techniques for dealing with systems of nonlinear differential equations are discussed in Bard (1974) and Caracotsios and Stewart (1985).

5.1   Compartment Models and System Diagrams

A common use of compartment models is in pharmacokinetics, where the exchange of materials in biological systems is studied. A system is divided into compartments, and it is assumed that the rates of flow of drugs between compartments follow first order kinetics, so that the rate of transfer to a receiving, or *sink*, compartment is proportional to the concentration in the supplying, or *source*, compartment. The transfer coefficients, which are assumed constant with respect to time, are called *rate constants*.

Example: Tetracycline 1

As an example of a compartment model, we consider data on the concentration of tetracycline hydrochloride in serum. A tetracycline compound was administered to a subject orally, and the concentration of tetracycline hydrochloride in the serum was measured over a period of 16 hours (Wagner, 1967). The data are recorded in Appendix 1, Section A1.14, and plotted in Figure 5.1.

The biological system can be modeled by a gut compartment into which the chemical is introduced, a blood compartment which absorbs the chemical from the gut, and an elimination path. Assuming first order kinetics, the concentrations $(\gamma_1(t), \gamma_2(t))^T$ of tetracycline hydrochloride in the two compartments can be described by the following pair of differential equations:

$$\frac{d\gamma_1(t)}{dt} = \dot{\gamma}_1 = -\theta_1 \gamma_1(t)$$

$$\frac{d\gamma_2(t)}{dt} = \dot{\gamma}_2 = \theta_1 \gamma_1(t) - \theta_2 \gamma_2(t)$$

(5.1)

where the dot denotes differentiation with respect to time.

The system can be represented graphically as a compartment or system diagram as in Figure 5.2. ∎

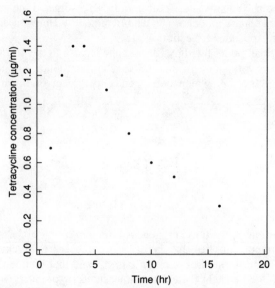

Figure 5.1 Plot of tetracycline concentration versus time.

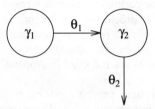

Figure 5.2   A compartment or system diagram for the tetracycline model.

Chemical reactions can also be described by linear systems of first order differential equations. In this context, the chemical species of the reaction constitute the compartments, the original species being termed "parents," and the product species "daughters."

Example: Oil shale 1
As a chemical example, we consider the pyrolysis of oil shale described by Ziegel and Gorman (1980). Oil shale contains organic material which is organically bonded to the structure of the rock. To extract oil from the rock, heat is applied so the technique is called pyrolysis.

During pyrolysis, the benzene organic material, called kerogen, decomposes to oil and bitumen, and there are unmeasured by-products of insoluble organic residues and light gases. Ziegel and Gorman, using data obtained from Hubbard and Robinson (1950), estimated the rate constants in several candidate models. The data obtained by Hubbard and Robinson are listed in Appendix 1, Section A1.15.

The final model fitted by Ziegel and Gorman to the 400°C data using multiresponse estimation techniques can be represented by the system diagram in Figure 5.3, which corresponds to the set of linear differential equations,

$$\frac{d\gamma_1}{dt} = -(\theta_1 + \theta_4)\gamma_1$$

$$\frac{d\gamma_2}{dt} = \theta_1\gamma_1 - (\theta_2 + \theta_3)\gamma_2 \qquad (5.2)$$

$$\frac{d\gamma_3}{dt} = \theta_4\gamma_1 + \theta_2\gamma_2$$

In this equation, γ_1 denotes kerogen, γ_2 bitumen, and γ_3 oil.

The model implies that kerogen decomposes to bitumen with rate constant θ_1 and to oil with rate constant θ_4, and that bitumen decomposes to oil with rate constant θ_2 and to unmeasured by-products with rate constant θ_3. ■

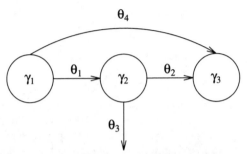

Figure 5.3 System diagram for the oil shale pyrolysis model.

In the general compartment model consisting of K compartments, we write the concentrations at time t as $\pmb{\gamma}(t) = (\gamma_1(t), \ldots, \gamma_K(t))^{\mathrm{T}}$. Assuming first order kinetics with rate constants $\theta_1, \theta_2, \ldots, \theta_P$, the concentrations obey the linear system of differential equations

$$\frac{d\pmb{\gamma}}{dt} = \dot{\pmb{\gamma}}(t) = \mathbf{A}\pmb{\gamma}(t) + \pmb{\iota}(t) \tag{5.3}$$

where $\mathbf{A}$ is the $K \times K$ system *transfer matrix* containing the rate constants and $\pmb{\iota}(t)$ is a vector function representing input to the system.

Although more complicated inputs may be used (Bates, Wolf, and Watts, 1985), in this book we consider only two input functions. One is a continuous infusion of material or *step input* into the system,

$$\pmb{\iota}(t) = \begin{cases} \pmb{\iota} & t \geq 0 \\ \mathbf{0} & t < 0 \end{cases}$$

where $\pmb{\iota}$ is a constant vector. The other is a bolus or instantaneous injection, and although it can be considered as an impulse or Dirac δ-function input, it is simpler to consider it as determining a vector of initial conditions $\pmb{\gamma}(0) = \pmb{\gamma}_0$.

Example: Tetracycline 2

For the tetracycline example, the input is a bolus in the gut, and the transfer matrix $\mathbf{A}$ can be readily obtained by inspection of the differential equations (5.1) or from the system diagram (Figure 5.2), as

$$\mathbf{A} = \begin{bmatrix} -\theta_1 & 0 \\ \theta_1 & -\theta_2 \end{bmatrix}$$

The initial concentration of tetracycline hydrochloride in the gut is unknown, but the concentration in the serum is assumed to be zero, so we incorporate another parameter θ_3 and write $\pmb{\gamma}_0 = (\theta_3, 0)^{\mathrm{T}}$. ∎

Example: Oil shale 2

For the model (5.2) suggested by Ziegel and Gorman (1980),

$$
\mathbf{A} = \begin{bmatrix} -\theta_1-\theta_4 & 0 & 0 \\ \theta_1 & -\theta_2-\theta_3 & 0 \\ \theta_4 & \theta_2 & 0 \end{bmatrix}
$$

The recorded measurements for bitumen and oil are percentages of the initial amount of kerogen, so we take $\gamma_0 = (100, 0, 0)^T$. Ziegel and Gorman (1980) found it necessary to incorporate a fifth parameter in the model to account for the unknown dead time before the reaction began. ∎

5.2   Estimating Parameters in Compartment Models

Several methods can be used to estimate parameters in compartment models. The most obvious is to obtain the analytic solution to the system of differential equations and then use the expectation function corresponding to the compartment for which data are available in a standard nonlinear estimation program. A second approach is to use a standard nonlinear estimation program, but calculate the function by solving the equations using numerical integration. A third approach (Anderson, 1983) is to recognize that the responses $\gamma_1, \gamma_2, \ldots, \gamma_K$ generally consist of weighted sums of exponential functions of time, with the exponents related to the system rate constants θ. One can then fit a general sum of exponentials model and derive estimates for the rate constants and other parameters. This is not efficient, especially when the fitting is done using the process of *peeling* (see Sections 3.3 and 3.9). A fourth and superior *matrix exponential* approach, proposed by Jennrich and Bright (1976), generates the solution to the system of equations by calculating values for the model function $\gamma(t)$ and its derivatives directly, given values of θ, t, and $\iota(t)$.

The matrix exponential approach is superior to the analytic solution approach because it avoids the difficult and sometimes impossible task of deriving explicit expressions for the model function and its derivatives. In addition, it is possible to obtain the derivatives with respect to the parameters in the same way as the expectation function itself. It is superior to the numerical integration approach because it is faster and more accurate. And finally, it is superior to the sum of exponentials approach because it avoids having to solve for the rate constants in terms of the exponent and weight coefficients, and because the correct number of parameters is incorporated directly into the model.

In the matrix exponential approach, if only one compartment is observed, the expectation function $f(t, \theta)$ is simply the appropriate element of the vector $\gamma(t)$, and, as discussed in Section 4.3.4, the function and its derivatives can be obtained from the general solution by multiplying the expected response matrix $\mathbf{H}$, and the derivative of the expected response matrix with respect to the parameters, by a $K \times 1$ vector which is 0 except for a 1 in the appropriate row. For example, for the tetracycline data, the concentration of tetracycline hydrochloride in the serum is measured, and so $\eta = \gamma_2$; this response is therefore used in estimating θ_1 and θ_2, and the expected response matrix is multiplied by the vector $(0, 1)^T$. In the oil shale example, oil and bitumen concentrations are available, and so the multiresponse expectation matrix $H = (\gamma_2, \gamma_3)$ can be used to estimate the system parameters using the methods discussed in Chapter 4. In this case, the expected responses and their derivatives with respect to the parameters will be multiplied by the 3×2 rotation matrix B, which consists of a row of zeros stacked above a 2×2 identity matrix.

5.2.1 Solving Systems of Linear Differential Equations

The general solution to (5.3) can be written

$$\gamma(t) = e^{At}\gamma_0 + e^{At} * \iota(t) \tag{5.4}$$

where the matrix exponential e^{At} represents the convergent power series

$$e^{At} = I + \frac{At}{1!} + \frac{(At)^2}{2!} + \cdots \tag{5.5}$$

and the $*$ denotes convolution,

$$e^{At} * \iota(t) = \int_0^t e^{A(t-u)}\iota(u)\, du \tag{5.6}$$

The vector function is integrated componentwise.

Suppose A is *diagonalizable*, so there is a nonsingular matrix of eigenvectors, U, and a diagonal matrix of eigenvalues, $\Lambda = \text{diag}(\lambda_1, \ldots, \lambda_K)$, such that

$$A = U\Lambda U^{-1}$$

Then

$$e^{At} = Ue^{\Lambda t}U^{-1}$$

with

$$e^{\Lambda t} = \text{diag}(e^{\lambda_1 t}, \ldots, e^{\lambda_K t})$$

General computational methods for evaluating the convolution integral are given in Appendix 5, and pseudocode is given in Appendix 3.

To develop the matrix exponential solution, we consider the special situation in which A is diagonalizable and the input is a bolus, so the system (5.3) can be written

$$\dot{\gamma} = A\gamma \qquad t > 0$$
$$\gamma(0) = \gamma_0 \tag{5.7}$$

Then (5.7) becomes

$$\dot{\boldsymbol{\gamma}} = \mathbf{A}\boldsymbol{\gamma}$$
$$= \mathbf{U}\boldsymbol{\Lambda}\mathbf{U}^{-1}\boldsymbol{\gamma}$$

Premultiplying both sides of the equation by $\mathbf{U}^{-1}$, and letting $\boldsymbol{\xi} = \mathbf{U}^{-1}\boldsymbol{\gamma}$, gives

$$\dot{\boldsymbol{\xi}} = \boldsymbol{\Lambda}\boldsymbol{\xi}$$

which is a set of independent first order differential equations

$$\dot{\xi}_k = \lambda_k \xi_k \qquad k = 1, 2, \ldots, K$$

with solutions

$$\xi_k(t) = e^{\lambda_k t} \xi_k(0)$$

where $\xi_k(0)$ is the kth element of $\mathbf{U}^{-1}\boldsymbol{\gamma}_0$. Reverting to $\boldsymbol{\gamma} = \mathbf{U}\boldsymbol{\xi}$ gives

$$\boldsymbol{\gamma}(t) = \mathbf{U}e^{\Lambda t}\mathbf{U}^{-1}\boldsymbol{\gamma}_0 = e^{\mathbf{A}t}\boldsymbol{\gamma}_0 \tag{5.8}$$

Thus, for a bolus or impulse input, the convolution integral (5.6) reduces to (5.8).

Example: Tetracycline 3

For the tetracycline example, $\boldsymbol{\gamma}_0 = (\theta_3, 0)^{\mathrm{T}}$, and

$$\mathbf{A} = \begin{bmatrix} -\theta_1 & 0 \\ \theta_1 & -\theta_2 \end{bmatrix} \tag{5.9}$$

For this simple system, we can calculate eigenvalues and eigenvectors of the transfer matrix (5.9) and use these to obtain explicit analytic expressions for the responses. Thus,

$$\boldsymbol{\Lambda} = \begin{bmatrix} -\theta_1 & 0 \\ 0 & -\theta_2 \end{bmatrix}$$

and

$$\mathbf{U} = \begin{bmatrix} 1 & 0 \\ \dfrac{\theta_1}{\theta_2 - \theta_1} & -\theta_1 \end{bmatrix}$$

so

$$\mathbf{U}^{-1} = \begin{bmatrix} 1 & 0 \\ \dfrac{1}{\theta_2 - \theta_1} & -\dfrac{1}{\theta_1} \end{bmatrix}$$

and, using (5.8), the responses are

$$\gamma = \begin{bmatrix} \theta_3 e^{-\theta_1 t} \\ \dfrac{\theta_3 \theta_1 (e^{-\theta_1 t} - e^{-\theta_2 t})}{\theta_2 - \theta_1} \end{bmatrix} \qquad \blacksquare$$

5.2.1.1 Dead Time

For the oil shale data, it was noted that the system does not respond immediately to the input, so a "dead time," t_0, must be incorporated into the model. We then modify (5.3) to

$$\dot{\gamma}(\tau) = A\gamma(\tau) + \iota(\tau)$$

$$\gamma(0) = \gamma_0 \qquad (5.10)$$

where $\tau = (t - t_0)_+$, that is,

$$\tau = \begin{cases} t - t_0 & t > t_0 \\ 0 & t \le t_0 \end{cases}$$

where t_0 can be known or unknown. The general solution is then

$$\gamma(\tau) = \begin{cases} \gamma_0 & \tau \le 0 \\ e^{A\tau}\gamma_0 + e^{A\tau} * \iota(\tau) & \tau > 0 \end{cases} \qquad (5.11)$$

Example: Tetracycline 4

The tetracycline data also shows evidence of dead time in the system. Fitting the model (5.1) gives the parameter estimates in Table 5.1. A plot of the data and the fitted response versus time, in Figure 5.4, shows a poor fit, since the fitted curve is too squat.

Allowing for dead time with a fourth parameter produces the estimates in Table 5.2 and the fitted curve plotted in Figure 5.5. This fit is better, especially for small time values. An extra sum of squares analysis, as in Table 5.3, confirms the need for dead time in the model. $\blacksquare$

Table 5.1 Parameter summary for the tetracycline model without dead time.

Parameter	Value	$\ln \theta$	Logarithm Scale Std. Error	Correlation Matrix
θ_1	0.1830	−1.698	0.244	1.00
θ_2	0.4345	−0.8335	0.272	−0.96 1.00
$\gamma_1(0)$	5.996	1.791	0.318	−0.98 0.99 1.00

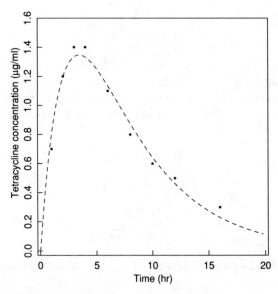

Figure 5.4 Plot of the tetracycline data and the fitted response curve for the model without dead time.

Table 5.2 Parameter summary for the tetracycline model with dead time.

| | | | Logarithm Scale | | |
Parameter	Value	$\ln \theta$	Std. Error	Correlation Matrix	
θ_1	0.1488	−1.905	0.097	1.00	
θ_2	0.7158	−0.3343	0.176	−0.86 1.00	
$\gamma_1(0)$	10.10	2.312	0.198	−0.92 0.99 1.00	
t_0	0.4123		0.095	−0.54 0.81 0.77 1.00	

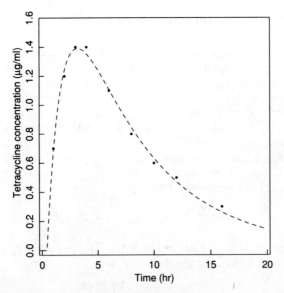

Figure 5.5 Plot of the tetracycline data and the fitted response curve for the model with dead time.

Table 5.3 Extra sum of squares analysis for dead time in the tetracycline model.

Source	Sum of Squares	Degrees of Freedom	Mean Square	F Ratio	p Value
Extra	0.02560	1	0.02560	12.736	0.016
4-parameter	0.01005	5	0.00201		
3-parameter	0.03565	6			

5.2.1.2 Cessation of Infusion

With continuous infusion there is sometimes another critical time, t_f, when the infusion is stopped. In pharmacokinetic studies, the period $0 < t \leq t_f$ is called the *on-infusion* stage, and the period $t > t_f$ is called the *off-infusion* stage. If there are measurements in the off-infusion stage, the model function during off-infusion, say $\gamma_{\text{off}}(t)$, is evaluated by using the on-infusion model function evaluated at t_f, as the initial condition vector in a new system with $\iota = 0$. Thus, assuming the initial conditions are zero, for the on-infusion stage we have

$$\gamma_{\text{on}}(t) = e^{At} * \iota(t) \qquad t \leq t_f$$

and for the off-infusion stage we have

$$\gamma_{\text{off}}(t) = e^{A(t - t_f)} \gamma_{\text{on}}(t_f) \qquad t > t_f$$

5.2.2   Derivatives of the Expectation Function

To estimate the parameters using a Gauss–Newton procedure, we must evaluate the derivatives with respect to the parameters. As shown by Jennrich and Bright (1976), a great advantage of systems of linear differential equations is that these derivatives can be evaluated in the same manner as the model function itself. They differentiated the general solution (5.11) directly to get the gradient terms, but in Bates and Watts (1985), we exploited the interchangability of differentiation with respect to time and with respect to a parameter to generate another set of linear system of differential equations which can be solved directly.

As in Chapter 4, we use a subscript in parentheses to denote differentiation with respect to a parameter and write, for example,

$$\frac{\partial \gamma(\tau)}{\partial \theta_p} = \gamma_{(p)} \qquad p = 1, 2, \ldots, P$$

If only τ depends on θ_p, the derivative of $\gamma(\tau)$ with respect to θ_p can be evaluated directly from (5.10) using the chain rule, so

$$\gamma_{(p)}(\tau) = \tau_{(p)}[A\gamma(\tau) + \iota] \tag{5.12}$$

When A, γ_0, or ι, but not τ, depends on θ_p, we get the derivative $\gamma_{(p)}(\tau)$ by differentiating (5.10) with respect to θ_p to obtain

$$\dot{\gamma}_{(p)}(\tau) = A\gamma_{(p)}(\tau) + A_{(p)}\gamma(\tau) + \iota_{(p)}$$

This is simply another linear system of differential equations with driving function $A_{(p)}\gamma(\tau) + \iota_{(p)}$, for which the solution is

$$\begin{aligned} \gamma_{(p)}(\tau) &= e^{A\tau}\gamma_{(p)}(0) + e^{A\tau} * [A_{(p)}\gamma(\tau) + \iota_{(p)}] \\ &= e^{A\tau}\gamma_{(p)}(0) + e^{A\tau} * \iota_{(p)} + e^{A\tau} * A_{(p)}e^{A\tau}\gamma_0 + e^{A\tau} * A_{(p)}e^{A\tau} * \iota \end{aligned} \tag{5.13}$$

To get a general expression for θ_p determining any of τ, A, γ_0, and ι, we combine (5.13) and (5.12) to give the expression

$$\gamma_{(p)}(\tau) = e^{A\tau}\gamma_{(p)}(0) + e^{A\tau} * [A_{(p)}\gamma(\tau) + \iota_{(p)}] + \tau_{(p)}[A\gamma(\tau) + \iota] \tag{5.14}$$

which is true for an impulse or step input.

It is easy to evaluate $A_{(p)}$, $\gamma_{(p)}(0) = \partial\gamma_0/\partial\theta_p$, $\iota_{(p)}$, and $\tau_{(p)}$, since the elements of the derivatives are always -1, $+1$, or 0.

Note that the method can be extended to higher order derivatives: in particular, the derivative with respect to θ_p and θ_q is

$$\gamma_{(pq)}(\tau) = e^{A\tau} * (A_{(p)}\gamma_{(q)}(\tau)) + e^{A\tau} * (A_{(q)}\gamma_{(p)}(\tau)) \tag{5.15}$$

since the elements of $A_{(pq)}$, $\gamma_{(pq)}(0)$, $\iota_{(pq)}$, and $\tau_{(pq)}$ are all 0.

Example: Tetracycline 5

For the tetracycline example with delay time, we have $\tau = (t - \theta_4)_+$, $\gamma_0 = (\theta_3, 0)^T$ and

$$A = \begin{bmatrix} -\theta_1 & 0 \\ \theta_1 & -\theta_2 \end{bmatrix}$$

so that

$$A_{(1)} = \begin{bmatrix} -1 & 0 \\ 1 & 0 \end{bmatrix}, \quad A_{(2)} = \begin{bmatrix} 0 & 0 \\ 0 & -1 \end{bmatrix}, \quad A_{(3)} = A_{(4)} = \begin{bmatrix} 0 & 0 \\ 0 & 0 \end{bmatrix}$$

$$\gamma_{(1)}(0) = \gamma_{(2)}(0) = \gamma_{(4)}(0) = \begin{bmatrix} 0 \\ 0 \end{bmatrix}, \quad \gamma_{(3)}(0) = \begin{bmatrix} 1 \\ 0 \end{bmatrix}$$

$$\tau_{(1)} = \tau_{(2)} = \tau_{(3)} = 0, \quad \tau_{(4)} = \begin{cases} -1 & \tau \geq 0 \\ 0 & \tau < 0 \end{cases}$$

and all second derivatives of these quantities are zero. ∎

The functions $\gamma_{(p)}(\tau)$, $p = 1, \ldots, P$, are called the *sensitivity functions* of the system (Caracotsios and Stewart, 1985) and can be evaluated for any τ and θ using (5.14) and the results of Appendix 5. Pseudocode for fitting compartment models is given in Appendix 3.

5.3 Practical Considerations

In this section we discuss some practical considerations related to fitting compartment models.

5.3.1 Parameter Transformations

A property of compartment models is that the rate constants, initial concentrations, and infusion rates must be positive. As discussed in Section 3.4, an effective way to ensure positive values is to use logarithms of the parameters in the model. This also enables linear approximation inference intervals for some important derived quantities to be obtained easily.

For example, the *half-life*, $t_{1/2}$, associated with the rate constant θ is $\ln 2 / \theta \approx 0.693 / \theta$. Then

$$\ln t_{1/2} = \ln \ln 2 - \ln \theta$$

$$\approx -0.367 - \ln \theta$$

and the width of a linear approximation inference interval for $\ln t_{1/2}$ is the same as the width of the interval for $\ln\theta$.

Another derived quantity of interest in pharmacological studies is the *volume of distribution* in a compartment. With a bolus injection, the dose, say D, in the initial compartment is known, but the concentration γ_0 is estimated. These are related by

$$\gamma_0 = \frac{D}{V_i}$$

where V_i is the volume of distribution for the injection compartment. Again, the logarithms of γ_0 and V_i are linearly related, $\ln V_i = \ln D - \ln\gamma_0$, and linear approximation confidence intervals on the logarithms have the same width.

A third derived quantity of interest in pharmacological studies is the *area under the curve* (AUC). For many simple compartment models this is equal to the initial concentration in the injection compartment, say $\gamma_1(0)$, divided by the elimination rate, say θ_1, so $\text{AUC} = \gamma_1(0)/\theta_1$. Again, $\ln\text{AUC}$ is linearly related to $\ln\gamma_1(0)$ and $\ln\theta_1$, so linear approximation confidence intervals for $\ln\text{AUC}$ are easily calculated.

In chemical kinetics, sometimes data are collected under different experimental conditions, and the analyst would like to combine the data in order to fit a more general model, as discussed in Section 3.11 and demonstrated in Section 5.5. In these cases, it is often assumed that the rate constants depend on the absolute temperature T according to an Arrhenius relation ($\theta \propto e^{-k/T}$) multiplied by products of pressures P_i raised to powers. For these models, the logarithms of the rate constants are linear functions of $1/T$ and $\ln P_i$, which provides another rationale for using logarithms.

An apparent disadvantage of using logarithms is that we cannot use linear approximation inference intervals to indicate whether a parameter could be zero, because they will never contain points corresponding to zero. However, a logarithm which is tending to a large negative value suggests that the parameter might be zero, and by using the matrix exponential method it is straightforward to eliminate that path or term in the compartment model, and then compare the reduced model with the original model using an extra sum of squares analysis. Besides, as explained in Section 3.10, the extra sum of squares test is more valid than the approximate t test for nonlinear regression.

5.3.2   Identifiability

A problem in fitting compartment models *when only one response is observed* is that some configurations result in exchangable parameters. This can cause problems in estimation, as mentioned in Section 3.4.1, because discrete sets of parameters give the same predicted responses. The parameters in such models are said to be *locally* identifiable rather than *globally* (uniquely) identifiable (Godfrey, 1983). For example, in the system of Figure 5.6 with $\gamma_0 = (1, 0, 0)^T$, the same $\gamma_3(t)$ curve results for the parameter pair (a, b) as for (b, a), so when only the third compartment is measured, the parameters θ_1 and θ_2 are exchangable.

A worse problem, though, is *unidentifiable* models, where continuous *sets* of parameters give the same predictions. For example, the system of Figure 5.7 produces the same $\gamma_1(t)$ curve for any set of parameters which satisfy

$$\theta_1 + \theta_2 = a$$

$$\theta_3 + \theta_4 = b$$

$$\theta_1\theta_3 + \theta_1\theta_4 + \theta_2\theta_4 = c$$

Thus continuous subspaces of the parameter space give the same predictions, so there are no unique parameter estimates for this system if only γ_1 is observed. However, if either θ_1 or θ_4 is zero, the system is identifiable.

A straightforward way to check the local identifiability of a compartment model with only one observed response is to fix a set of design times and generate the parameter derivative matrices at a number of different parameter values. If the matrices are all computationally singular, the model can be assumed to be unidentifiable. Note that we must use several parameter values, since a particular derivative matrix could be computationally singular due to an unfortunate choice of parameter values.

The ambiguity of compartment models when only one compartment is observed provides motivation for multiresponse experiments. The additional information not only provides better estimates of the parameters, but permits better discrimination between competing models.

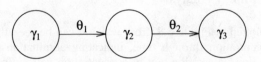

Figure 5.6 A system which has exchangable parameters when only γ_3 is observed.

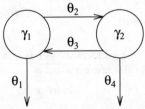

Figure 5.7 A system which is unidentifiable when only γ_1 is observed.

5.3.3   Starting Values

Obtaining starting values for compartment models can be difficult in the uniresponse case. Peeling (see Section 3.3) can be used, but an alternative procedure is to start with a simple model, such as a 1-compartment model, and extend it.

A plot of the data can be used to estimate the initial concentration and the single rate constant, and a plot of the residuals can then reveal how the model should be extended. The parameter estimates from the 1-compartment model can then be used to derive estimates for the rate constants in the new model. The model is extended as necessary, gradually adding compartments and paths, and using parameter estimates from the current model to obtain starting estimates for the next.

5.4   Lipoproteins: A Case Study

The ease with which compartment models can be fitted using the matrix exponential approach enables an analyst to try many different models on the same data set, and so engage in highly effective model development. To demonstrate this process, we consider the lipoprotein data in Table 23.1 of Anderson (1983), reproduced in Appendix 1, Section A1.16. The single response is the percentage concentration of a tracer in the serum of a baboon given a bolus injection at time 0. It is assumed that there is an initial concentration of 100% in compartment 1 and zero in all other compartments.

5.4.1   Preliminary Analysis

The data are plotted in Figure 5.8, from which it can be seen that there is a decrease in concentration through time, indicating elimination from the serum compartment. From a semilog plot of concentration versus time, it is apparent that there are at least 2 compartments, but to begin developing a model we fit a 1-compartment elimination model, as shown in Figure 5.9.

5.4.2   One Compartment

We see from the plot that the concentration has reached 46% by time 0.5 day, and so the starting value for the rate constant is

$$\theta = \frac{-\ln 0.46}{0.5}$$

$$\approx 1.55$$

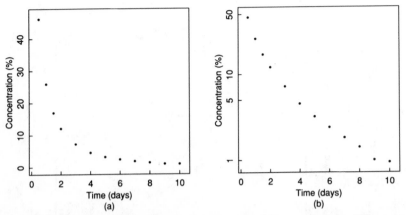

Figure 5.8 Plot of the lipoprotein concentration versus time, on a linear scale in part *a*, and on a logarithmic scale in part *b*.

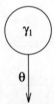

Figure 5.9 A 1-compartment elimination model.

Convergence to $\hat{\theta} = 1.31$ was achieved with a residual sum of squares of 133 on 11 degrees of freedom.

5.4.3 Two Compartments

The residuals, plotted against time in Figure 5.10, have a noticeable pattern, suggesting that the model initially underestimates and then overestimates the concentration. This pattern is consistent with the presence of another compartment with a system diagram as in Figure 5.11, possibly with θ_2 and θ_3 equal. It is easy to fit such a 2-parameter model first and use the estimates to provide starting values for a 3-parameter model.

To get starting estimates for the 2-parameter model, we let $\theta_1 + \theta_2 = 1.31$ from the 1-compartment model fit, and try $\theta^0 = (1.0, 0.31)^T$. Convergence was obtained to $\hat{\theta} = (0.992, 0.663)^T$ with a residual sum of squares of 2.65 on 10 degrees of freedom. Allowing θ_2 and θ_3 to differ, we used starting estimates $\theta^0 = (0.99, 0.67, 0.65)^T$, which yielded $\hat{\theta} = (1.022, 0.662, 0.820)^T$ with a residual sum of squares of 1.26 on 9 degrees of freedom.

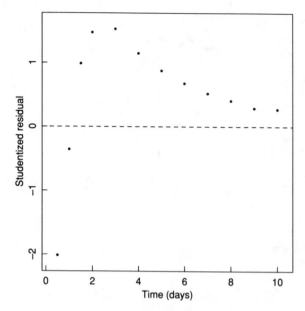

Figure 5.10   Residuals from a 1-compartment model fitted to the lipoprotein data.

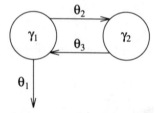

Figure 5.11   A 2-compartment open model.

5.4.4   Three Compartments

The residuals from the 3-parameter model, plotted in Figure 5.12, still display a pattern, so we continue to extend the model. We can extend it in a number of different ways: if the experimenter was uncertain how the concentrations were normalized to produce $\gamma_1(0) = 100$, we could introduce a parameter to represent this initial value, or we could introduce a delay time into the model, or (as seems more appropriate in this case) we could introduce another compartment. Even when introducing a third compartment, however, we must decide how to do so. The simplest extensions are the *catenary* system (in which the compartments are chained together), and the *mamillary* system (in which each "daughter" compartment communicates only with the central "mother" compartment.) A catenary system is shown in Figure 5.13, and a mamillary system is shown in

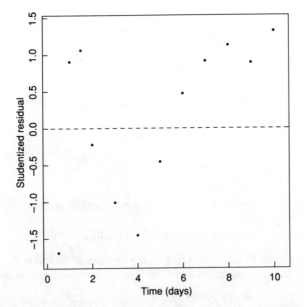

Figure 5.12   Residuals from a 2-compartment model fitted to the lipoprotein data.

Figure 5.14.

To fit these systems, we could use 5, 4, or 3 parameters by assuming some of the parameters equal. We chose to fit the 5-parameter models and examine the fits to determine a simple adequate model.

For the catenary model we added two parameters with values smaller than, and distinct from, the current parameter estimates to produce the starting estimates

$$\boldsymbol{\theta}^0 = (1.00, 0.66, 0.82, 0.5, 0.2)^{\mathrm{T}}$$

from which we converged to

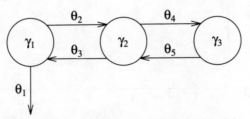

Figure 5.13   A 3-compartment catenary model.

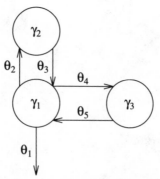

Figure 5.14   A 3-compartment mamillary model.

$$\hat{\boldsymbol{\theta}} = (0.990, 0.762, 1.015, 0.240, 0.352)^{\mathrm{T}}$$

with a residual sum of squares of 0.043 on 7 degrees of freedom.
Using the same starting values, the mamillary model converged to

$$\hat{\boldsymbol{\theta}} = (0.990, 0.532, 1.340, 0.231, 0.267)^{\mathrm{T}}$$

with the same residual sum of squares as the catenary model. The residuals (for both models) are shown in Figure 5.15, and are well behaved.

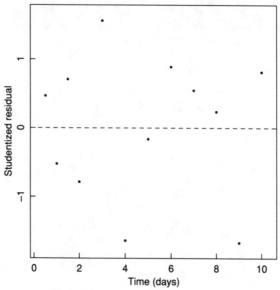

Figure 5.15   Residuals from a 3-compartment model fitted to the lipoprotein data.

It is not an accident that the same residuals and the same sum of squares occur for these two models, since they are equivalent when compartment 1 is the only one measured. Thus, for this data set, the model is not identifiable. Writing ϕ for the parameters of the catenary model and θ for the mamillary model parameters, the equivalence is given by

$$\phi_1 = \theta_1$$

$$\phi_2 = \theta_2 + \theta_4$$

$$\phi_3 + \phi_4 + \phi_5 = \theta_3 + \theta_5$$

$$\phi_3 \phi_5 = \theta_3 \theta_5$$

$$\phi_2 \phi_4 + \phi_2 \phi_5 = \theta_2 \theta_5 + \theta_3 \theta_4$$

5.4.5 Three Compartments, Common Parameters

The extra sum of squares due to extending the model from two to three compartments was highly significant [an extra sum of squares ratio of 97 to be compared with an $F(2,7)$ distribution]. We now try to simplify the model by letting some parameters be equal. We take starting values from the 5-parameter fits using the average of the pair of rate constants with the smallest difference relative to the standard error of the difference, so that, for both models, we equate θ_4 and θ_5. For the catenary model, we converged to $\hat{\theta} = (0.967, 0.778, 0.948, 0.224)^T$ with a residual sum of squares of 0.062, and for the mamillary model, to $\hat{\theta} = (0.978, 0.558, 1.27, 0.213)^T$ with a residual sum of squares of 0.050. The parameter estimates and approximate standard errors strongly suggest that none of the other parameters are equal, and so we do not reduce the models further.

Normal plots and plots of the residuals versus time and versus the fitted response (not shown) did not show inadequacy of the 4-parameter models. The judgement of which model to use must then be based on extra sum of squares analyses and the opinion of the experimenter as to which model is better. Extra sum of squares analyses for the nested models are shown in Table 5.4.

5.4.6 Conclusions

The conclusion of this analysis is that the data can be adequately fitted by a 3-compartment model in either the catenary or mamillary configuration. For five rate constants, the two models are equivalent: for four rate constants, slightly better results are obtained with the mamillary configuration. Whether or not equal rate constants is physically sensible must be decided by the experimenter on the basis of theory or on the basis of further experimental results.

Table 5.4   Extra sum of squares analyses for compartment models fitted to the lipoprotein data. The models with 4 parameters are the 3-compartment catenary (model 1) and the 3-compartment mamillary (model 2), each with two of the rate constants contrained to be equal. The 5-parameter 3-compartment model is model 3.

Source	Sum of Squares (10^{-6})	Degrees of Freedom	Mean Square (10^{-7})	F Ratio	p Value
Extra	1.857	1	18.57	3.0	0.13
Model 3	4.339	7	6.20		
Model 1	6.196	8			
Extra	0.682	1	6.82	1.1	0.33
Model 3	4.339	7	6.20		
Model 2	5.021	8			

5.5   Oil Shale: A Case Study

As an example of multiresponse parameter estimation using compartment models, we return to the oil shale data obtained by Hubbard and Robinson (1950). This case study also demonstrates the use of process parameters to model kinetic parameters (see Section 3.11).

5.5.1   Preliminary Analysis

In Figure 5.16 we plot the two measured responses, oil and bitumen, versus time for the six temperatures. One thing to note from these plots is that kerogen decomposition occurs more rapidly with increased temperature; at 673 K there is a substantial fraction of bitumen after 100 minutes, but at 773 K there is only a small fraction after 10 minutes. This strongly suggests that the rate constants depend on temperature.

A common form of rate constant dependence upon temperature is the Arrhenius relation

$$k_i(T) = k_{i,0}\, e^{-E_i/RT} \tag{5.16}$$

where $k_i(T)$ is the rate constant at temperature T, $k_{i,0}$ is the preexponential term, E_i is the activation energy for the reaction, R is the universal gas constant of 1.987 cal/g-mole K, and T is the temperature in kelvins.

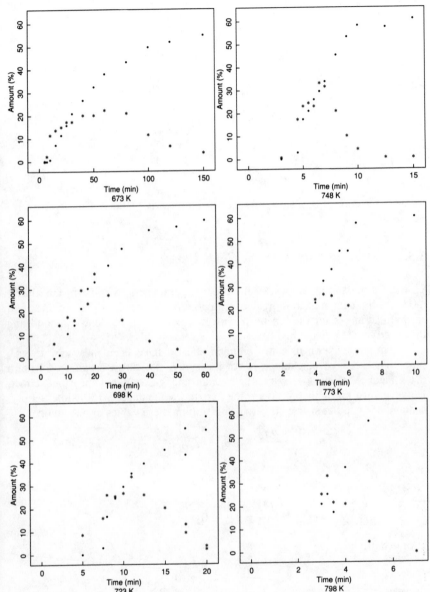

Figure 5.16   Plot of oil (•) and bitumen (∗) amounts versus time for six temperatures for the oil shale pyrolysis data.

Estimating the activation energies and the preexponential terms usually results in highly correlated estimates, since the range of the observed temperatures is small relative to the mean temperature. To reduce the correlations, we center the temperatures about an intermediate temperature, T_0, as discussed in Section 3.4.2, and write (5.16) as

$$k_i(T) = k_i(T_0) \exp\left[-\frac{E_i}{R}\left(\frac{1}{T} - \frac{1}{T_0}\right)\right]$$

Then

$$\ln k_i(T) = \ln k_i(T_0) - \frac{E_i}{R}\left(\frac{1}{T} - \frac{1}{T_0}\right) \tag{5.17}$$

$$= \phi_i - \frac{E_i}{R}\left(\frac{1}{T} - \frac{1}{T_0}\right)$$

so the logarithms of the rate constants depend linearly on the scaled inverse temperature.

5.5.2 Starting Values for the 673 K Data

To determine starting values for the process parameters, we first fit the kinetic model to the data at each individual temperature. This means that we must find starting estimates for the kinetic parameters, which can be done by modifying the approximate rate method described in Section 4.3.1.

For these data sets, only bitumen and oil have been measured at each time. The kerogen percentage is not measured, nor can it be inferred from a mass balance, since the by-products, coke and gas, are not measured either. However, we know that at time 0 the kerogen percentage is 100 while the percentage of the other species is zero. Substituting these values into the model

$$\frac{d\gamma_1}{dt} = -(\theta_1 + \theta_4)\gamma_1$$

$$\frac{d\gamma_2}{dt} = \theta_1\gamma_1 - (\theta_2 + \theta_3)\gamma_2$$

$$\frac{d\gamma_3}{dt} = \theta_4\gamma_1 + \theta_2\gamma_2$$

at time 0 produces

$$\frac{d\gamma_2(0)}{dt} = \theta_1\gamma_1(0)$$

$$= 100\,\theta_1$$

and

$$\frac{d\gamma_3(0)}{dt} = 100\,\theta_4$$

and we can use approximate rates from early observations of γ_2 and γ_3 to obtain starting estimates θ_1^0 and θ_4^0. From these, we can infer a percentage of kerogen as

$$\gamma_1(t) \approx 100\,e^{-(\theta_1^0 + \theta_4^0)t}$$

and use the approximate rate method of Section 4.3.1 to obtain starting estimates θ_2^0 and θ_3^0.

The plot of the 673 K data in Figure 5.16 reveals evidence of dead time in the reactions, as described in Ziegel and Gorman (1980). We therefore use the first two nonzero observations of γ_2 and γ_3 to calculate θ_1^0 and θ_4^0 as

$$\theta_1^0 = \frac{1}{\gamma_1(0)} \left. \frac{d\gamma_2}{dt} \right|_0$$

$$= \frac{1}{100} \frac{11.5 - 2.2}{3}$$

$$= 0.031$$

and

$$\theta_4^0 = \frac{1}{100} \frac{7.2 - 0.7}{5}$$

$$= 0.013$$

A starting estimate of the dead time, $t_0^0 = 6$ minutes, is read from Figure 5.16. Using these values in the approximate rate procedure produces starting estimates of 0.0131 for θ_2^0 and 0.0286 for θ_3^0.

5.5.3 Fitting the Individual Temperature Data

The generalized Gauss–Newton algorithm converged to the parameter estimates shown in Table 5.5 with a determinant value of 428.

The converged values for the 673 K data can be used as starting estimates for the 698 K data, except for the dead time which we estimate from Figure 5.16 to be 5 minutes. Convergence was obtained to the results shown in Table 5.6.

To obtain starting estimates for the kinetic parameters at the other temperatures, we assume that an Arrhenius relation holds and fit linear models to the logarithms of the rate constants as a function of scaled inverse temperature. Extrapolations of these linear fits are used to get starting estimates for the kinetic parameters at the next temperature. Since the dead time decreases with in-

Table 5.5 Parameter summary for the oil shale data at 673 K.

Parameter	Value	ln θ	Std. Error	Correlation Matrix				
θ_1	0.0172	−4.064	0.1219	1.00				
θ_2	0.00891	−4.721	0.2524	0.85	1.00			
θ_3	0.0200	−3.912	0.1117	0.30	0.64	1.00		
θ_4	0.0105	−4.557	0.0645	−0.71	−0.89	−0.36	1.00	
t_0	7.772		0.5263	−0.07	−0.34	−0.09	0.64	1.00

Table 5.6 Parameter summary for the oil shale data at 698 K.

Parameter	Value	ln θ	Std. Error	Correlation Matrix				
θ_1	0.0784	−2.546	0.1648	1.00				
θ_2	0.0473	−3.051	0.2270	0.46	1.00			
θ_3	0.0510	−2.975	0.1560	0.02	0.75	1.00		
θ_4	0.0249	−3.694	0.2290	−0.48	−0.91	−0.47	1.00	
t_0	6.247		0.5065	−0.09	−0.53	−0.17	0.76	1.00

creasing temperature, we also regress t_0 on scaled inverse temperature and extrapolate to get starting estimates.

Care must be taken when fitting the 723 K data because there are two optima for the determinant criterion, as shown in Table 5.7. A plot of the data and

Table 5.7 Parameter summary for the oil shale data at 723 K, showing two optima.

Parameter	Optimum 1	Optimum 2
θ_1	0.2637	0.1596
θ_2	0.08496	0.1512
θ_3	0.1587	0.1020
θ_4	0.1248	0.02706
t_0	6.775	4.526
Determinant	28 309	53 422

the two sets of fitted curves, as in Figure 5.17, reveals that a tradeoff is being made: the oil concentration is best fitted with a dead time 6.8 minutes, while the bitumen concentration is best fitted with a dead time of 4.5 minutes. The optimum with the larger dead time has a smaller determinant, but from the plots and from consideration of the data at other temperatures, it appears that the predictions with the smaller dead time are better.

Individual fits were made to the data at the remaining temperatures and are recorded in Table 5.8.

5.5.4   Starting Estimates for the Process Parameters

To get starting estimates for the process parameters in the Arrhenius relation, we introduced the negative scaled inverse temperature variable

$$T_{inv} = \frac{-1000}{1.987}\left[\frac{1}{T} - \frac{1}{723}\right]$$

which centers about the middle temperature 723 K and includes a factor of 1000 to convert the units of the activation energy from cal/g-mole to the more convenient kcal/g-mole. The negative sign is used so that increasing T increases

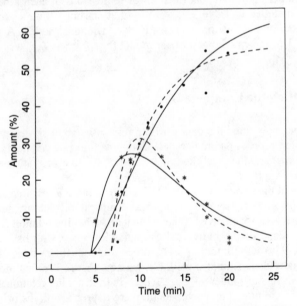

Figure 5.17   Plot of oil (•) and bitumen (*) amounts versus time for the temperatures for the oil shale data at 723 K. The fitted curves for a dead time of 4.5 minutes are shown as solid lines, and the fitted curves for a dead time of 6.8 minutes are shown as dashed lines.

Table 5.8　Parameter summary for the oil shale data at all temperatures together with the scaled inverse temperature variable and the parameters from a linear regression of each kinetic parameter on scaled inverse temperature.

Temperature (K)	$\ln \theta_1$	$\ln \theta_2$	$\ln \theta_3$	$\ln \theta_4$	t_0	T_{inv}
673	−4.064	−4.720	−3.912	−4.557	7.771	−0.0517
698	−2.546	−3.051	−2.975	−3.694	6.247	−0.0249
723	−1.835	−1.889	−2.283	−3.610	4.526	0.0000
748	−0.801	−1.252	−1.264	−2.082	4.082	0.0233
773	−0.447	−0.853	−0.803	−1.623	2.938	0.0450
798	0.287	−0.120	−0.297	−0.998	2.849	0.0654
Intercept:	−1.907	−2.335	−2.221	−3.056	5.146	
Slope:	35.73	37.27	31.37	31.09	−43.14	

T_{inv}.

The slopes and intercepts from linear regressions of each kinetic parameter on T_{inv}, included in Table 5.8, were used as starting estimates for the scaled preexponential and activation energies in the Arrhenius model. A plot of dead time versus T_{inv} indicated that a linear model for t_0 versus T_{inv} was also reasonable.

5.5.5　Fitting the Complete Data Set

We simultaneously fitted the data for both responses at all six temperatures to a model with ten process parameters, consisting of four rate constants (i.e., preexponential terms) and the dead time t_0 at 723 K, plus four activation energies and the slope of t_0 versus T_{inv}.

The final parameter summary is given in Table 5.9. Estimates of each of the kinetic parameters from the individual temperature data are plotted versus T_{inv} in Figure 5.18 together with the estimated Arrhenius relation from the process model. Each of the individual estimates is shown with bars representing approximate 95% HPD intervals. The process model for t_0 does not appear to follow the individual estimates well, but we note that t_0 is much more precisely determined at higher values of T_{inv}, where the Arrhenius relation fits the data well. Plots of the fitted curves versus time are overlaid with the original data in Figure 5.19. For low temperatures and early times, the model does not fit well.

Table 5.9 Parameter summary for the complete oil shale data set.

	Est.	Approx. Std. Error	Approximate Correlation Matrix									
ϕ_1	-1.920	0.079	1.00									
ϕ_2	-2.277	0.127	0.38	1.00								
ϕ_3	-2.195	0.076	0.52	0.09	1.00							
ϕ_4	-3.024	0.164	-0.02	-0.84	0.25	1.00						
t_0	4.406	0.227	0.50	-0.15	0.44	0.52	1.00					
E_1	38.14	1.956	0.08	-0.12	0.03	0.19	0.19	1.00				
E_2	34.25	3.303	-0.06	-0.17	-0.02	0.07	0.00	0.54	1.00			
E_3	34.41	1.848	0.01	-0.07	-0.16	0.10	0.14	0.45	0.30	1.00		
E_4	36.13	3.864	0.18	0.02	0.10	0.16	0.21	-0.25	-0.84	0.01	1.00	
β	-24.67	3.311	-0.43	0.13	-0.39	-0.45	-0.96	-0.08	-0.01	-0.07	-0.12	

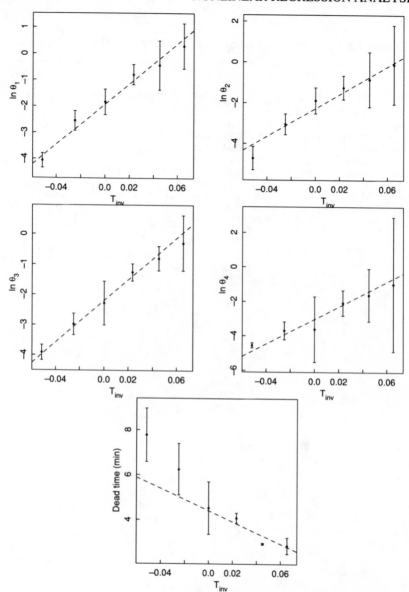

Figure 5.18 Plots of kinetic parameter estimates and Arrhenius model fits for the oil shale data. The kinetic parameter estimates and their approximate 95% inference intervals are shown as solid lines. The Arrhenius model fits are shown as dashed lines.

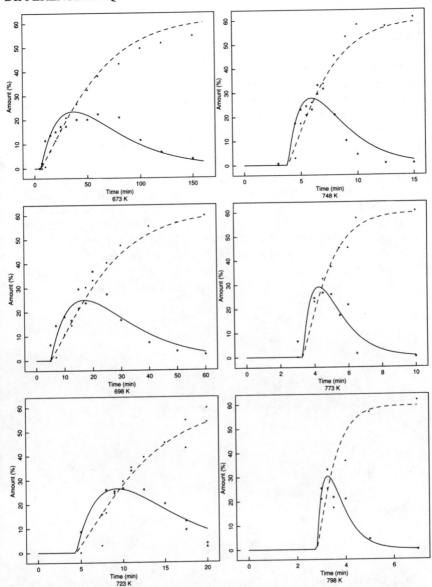

Figure 5.19 Plot of oil (•) and bitumen (*) amounts versus time for six temperatures for the oil shale pyrolysis data together with the fitted curves. The fitted curves for oil are shown as dashed lines, and those for bitumen as solid lines.

5.5.6   Conclusions

We have fitted the process model to the multiresponse data over a range of temperatures. The fitted parameters have reasonable values, and the assumptions on the disturbances do not appear inappropriate. However, the assumed kinetic model does have deficiencies, and so we should consult experts on chemical kinetics to try to formulate a better model. One obvious change in the model is to allow for different dead times for bitumen and for oil, with $t_0^{oil} > t_0^{bitumen}$.

Exercises

5.1 (a) Write a computer routine in a language of your choice to solve systems of linear differential equations, using the pseudocode of Appendix 3, Section A3.4. Assume that the transfer matrix $\mathbf{A}$ is diagonalizable.

   (b) Extend the subroutine to evaluate derivatives of the expectation functions with respect to the parameters for bolus and step inputs.

5.2 (a) Show that the system matrix $\mathbf{A}$ for the chemical reaction with system diagram

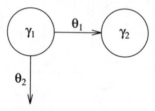

has eigenvalues $(-(\theta_1 + \theta_2), 0)^T$ and eigenvectors

$$\mathbf{U} = \begin{bmatrix} \theta_1 + \theta_2 & 0 \\ -\theta_1 & 1 \end{bmatrix}$$

with

$$\mathbf{U}^{-1} = \begin{bmatrix} \dfrac{1}{\theta_1 + \theta_2} & 0 \\ \dfrac{\theta_1}{\theta_1 + \theta_2} & 1 \end{bmatrix}$$

   (b) Use the results from part (a) to show that the response at time t to an initial concentration of 100% in response 1 and 0% concentration in response 2 is

$$\boldsymbol{\gamma}(t) = \begin{bmatrix} e^{-(\theta_1 + \theta_2)t} \\ \dfrac{\theta_1}{\theta_1 + \theta_2} \left[1 - e^{-(\theta_1 + \theta_2)t} \right] \end{bmatrix}$$

5.3 Use the data from Appendix 4, Section A4.8 to fit a compartment model.

5.4 (a) Use the results from Example Tetracycline 5 to derive the derivatives of the model function with respect to the parameters.

   (b) Verify that the derivatives in part (a) are correct by differentiating the explicit solutions for the functions given in Example Tetracycline 3.

5.5 Use a multiresponse parameter estimation criterion to fit the model from Example α-pinene 2, to the α-pinene data at 204.5°C given in Appendix 4, Section A4.6.

   (a) Use the method of Section 4.3 to determine starting values.

   (b) Use an extra determinant analysis to decide whether the path from allo-ocimene to pyronene is necessary.

CHAPTER 6.

Graphical Summaries of Nonlinear Inference Regions

*"What can we know? or what
can we discern,
When error chokes the windows
of the mind?"*

– Sir John Davies

So far we have assumed that linear approximations provide adequate summaries of the inferential results of a nonlinear analysis. Unfortunately, in many nonlinear analyses they will be woefully inadequate. In this chapter we present improved graphical methods for summarizing the inferential results of a nonlinear analysis, and in Chapter 7 methods for assessing the severity of the nonlinearity in an estimation situation.

6.1 Likelihood Regions

6.1.1 Joint Parameter Likelihood Regions

The spherical normal assumption for the disturbance Z in the model (2.2) dictates that statistical inference using the likelihood approach is closely linked to the geometry of the expectation surface in the response space. For linear and nonlinear models with the spherical normal assumption, a likelihood contour consists of all values of θ for which $\eta(\theta)$ is a fixed distance from y, that is, all θ for which $S(\theta)$ equals a constant. To associate a "confidence" level with a contour, by analogy with the linear model (1.39), we let the nominal $1-\alpha$ joint likelihood region be all values of θ such that

$$S(\boldsymbol{\theta}) \leq S(\hat{\boldsymbol{\theta}}) \left[1 + \frac{P}{N-P} F(P, N-P; \alpha) \right] \qquad (6.1)$$

As with the linear model, this is the intersection of the expectation surface with a sphere centered at **y**. Now, however, the surface is not planar and there is no easy way to map the points on the expectation surface back to the parameter space even if we could determine those points on the intersection.

When $P = 2$, we can determine a likelihood contour in $\boldsymbol{\theta}$ by standard contouring methods, that is, by evaluating $S(\boldsymbol{\theta})$ for a grid of $\boldsymbol{\theta}$ values and approximating the contour by straight line segments in the grid.

Example: Puromycin 13

Figure 6.1 shows nominal 80 and 95% likelihood contours for the Puromycin parameters. The contours are nearly elliptical and concentric, and the least squares estimate $\hat{\boldsymbol{\theta}}$ is well centered in the region. The linear approximation ellipses, shown as dashed lines, provide quite good approximate regions. ∎

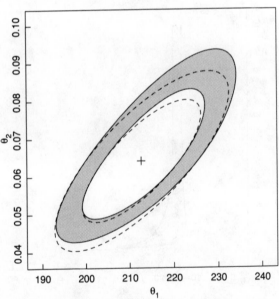

Figure 6.1 Nominal 80 and 95% likelihood contours for the Puromycin parameters. The dashed lines are the linear approximation ellipses, and the least squares estimate is indicated by +.

Example: BOD 7

Figure 6.2 shows nominal 80 and 95% likelihood contours for the BOD
parameters, together with the linear approximation ellipses. These contours are not at all elliptical; in fact, the contours are more like hyperbolas,
extending to ∞ in the positive θ_2 direction. The linear approximation ellipses are completely inadequate.

The occurrence of hyperbolic contours can be explained by looking
at the data and the behavior of the model function, $f = \theta_1(1 - e^{-\theta_2 x})$. From
Figure 6.3, where we plot the data and the estimated model function, we
see that the data are very scattered and consequently the fitted model is not
well determined.

Analyzing the model function, as $\theta_2 \to \infty$, the model reduces to
$f = \theta_1$, and becomes insensitive to changes in θ_2. For large θ_2, therefore,
the conditional estimate of θ_1 is $\bar{y}$. Setting $\theta = (\bar{y}, \infty)^T$, which corresponds
to fitting the data by the horizontal line in Figure 6.3, produces a sum of
squares of 107.2. Since the data are so noisy, this fit is not significantly
worse than the best fit of the nonlinear model, having an F ratio of

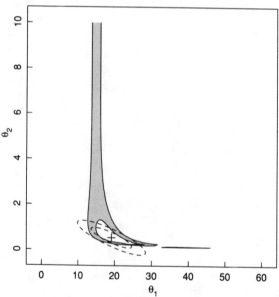

Figure 6.2 Nominal 80 and 95% likelihood contours for the BOD parameters. The
dashed lines are the linear approximation ellipses, and the least squares estimate is indicated by +.

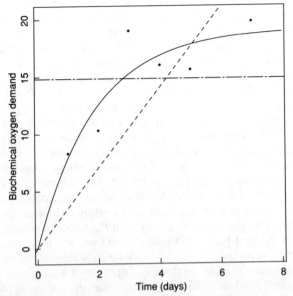

Figure 6.3 Estimated response curves for the BOD data. The solid line is the least squares response curve. The dashed line is the limiting curve as $\theta_2 \to 0$ and the dot-dashed line is the limiting curve as $\theta_2 \to \infty$.

$$\frac{[S((\bar{y},\infty)^T) - S(\hat{\theta})]/P}{S(\hat{\theta})/(N-P)} = \frac{(107.21 - 25.99)/2}{25.99/4}$$

$$= 6.25$$

and a probability level of 94%. Thus, any likelihood contours at a nominal level greater than 94% will be open.

As $\theta_2 \to 0$, the model function reduces to

$$f(x,\theta) = \theta_1\theta_2 x$$

which gives a straight line through the origin with slope 3.52, as shown in Figure 6.3. Since the residual sum of squares for this straight line is 135.82, corresponding to an F ratio of 8.45 and a probability level of 96%, the likelihood contour will be open on the right for any nominal level greater than 96%.

For this example, then, the large scatter in the data and the form of the model function combine to produce hyperbolic-like contours which, for large enough confidence level, will be open. Consequently, the likelihood regions are not well approximated by linear approximation regions. ■

Determining the shape of badly distorted contours like those in Figure 6.2 can take several tries. We evaluated an initial grid of likelihood values and found that the contour went beyond the grid, so we changed the limits and reevaluated the grid, repeating the procedure until we obtained a satisfactory plot. The contours in Figure 6.2 illustrate another deficiency of standard contouring methods. The nominal 95% contour appears to have two disjoint pieces—the main body and a thin region centered near $\theta = (40, 0)^T$. In fact, this contour should be one continuous curve, and the two pieces are an artifact of the way that the curve is traced by a computer program. Contouring programs typically have difficulty with long, thin segments of contours.

This discussion has focused on 2-parameter models, but nonlinear models with many more parameters occur and, unfortunately, standard contouring methods are not easily extended beyond $P = 2$. One approach for multiparameter models is to try to evaluate the likelihood on a P-dimensional grid. This can be expensive, since the amount of computing effort and the amount of storage required for the grid grows exponentially with P. Also, the analyst must choose the bounds of the grid before evaluating a contour, and these bounds may not encompass the entire contour, or they may be so wide that the resolution over the region of interest is poor. In this case, the analyst would have to guess at a new set of bounds and reevaluate the contour, thereby adding to the expense of the process. Even when the grid is evaluated, approximation of the contour and display of the approximation in many dimensions is difficult.

One way of avoiding multidimensional grids is to evaluate the sum of squares function on a series of 2-dimensional grids corresponding to each pair of parameters. This requires one grid for the (θ_1, θ_2) pair, one grid for the (θ_1, θ_3) pair, and so on, for a total of $P(P-1)/2$ grids. Contours on the 2-dimensional grids can be easily calculated and displayed, and from these contours the analyst can gain insight into the multidimensional shape of the likelihood region. However, it is not clear which likelihood or sum of squares to evaluate at each point in these 2-dimensional grids. Two choices are to evaluate the *conditional likelihood* function by varying a pair of parameters while holding the others fixed at their least squares estimates, or to evaluate the 2-dimensional *profile likelihood* function by finding the minimum sum of squares over all the other coordinates for each point on the grid.

Both these approaches have disadvantages. On the one hand, the conditional likelihood function does not always present a comprehensive view of the likelihood contour, since it only shows selected cross-sections of the contour, and the global behavior of the contour can be quite different from the sectional behavior. On the other hand, evaluating the profile likelihood requires solving a $(P-2)$-dimensional nonlinear least squares problem for each of the points on the $P(P-1)/2$ grids, which could be computationally expensive. To mitigate these difficulties, we propose making profile t plots and profile pair sketches as described in the next section.

6.1.2   Profile t Plots, Profile Traces, and Profile Pair Sketches

To develop marginal likelihood intervals for nonlinear model parameters, we begin by relating a linear model interval to the sum of squares function. For a linear model, a $1 - \alpha$ marginal interval for β_p can be written in terms of the studentized parameter

$$\frac{\beta_p - \hat{\beta}_p}{\text{se}(\hat{\beta}_p)} = \delta(\beta_p)$$

as

$$-t(N-P;\alpha/2) \le \delta(\beta_p) \le t(N-P;\alpha/2)$$

But the studentized parameter can also be written

$$\frac{\beta_p - \hat{\beta}_p}{\text{se}(\hat{\beta}_p)} = \text{sign}(\beta_p - \hat{\beta}_p)\sqrt{\tilde{S}(\beta_p) - S(\hat{\boldsymbol{\beta}})}/s \tag{6.2}$$

where

$$\tilde{S}(\beta_p) = \min_{\boldsymbol{\beta}_{-p}} S((\beta_p, \boldsymbol{\beta}_{-p}^{\text{T}})^{\text{T}}) = S((\beta_p, \tilde{\boldsymbol{\beta}}_{-p}^{\text{T}})^{\text{T}}) \tag{6.3}$$

is the profile sum of squares function and $\tilde{\boldsymbol{\beta}}_{-p} = (\tilde{\beta}_1, \ldots, \tilde{\beta}_{p-1}, \tilde{\beta}_{p+1}, \ldots, \tilde{\beta}_P)^{\text{T}}$ is the least squares estimate of $\boldsymbol{\beta}_{-p}$ conditional on β_p. The notation $(\beta_p, \tilde{\boldsymbol{\beta}}_{-p}^{\text{T}})^{\text{T}}$ indicates the vector with elements $(\tilde{\beta}_1, \ldots, \tilde{\beta}_{p-1}, \beta_p, \tilde{\beta}_{p+1}, \ldots, \tilde{\beta}_P)$. (The derivation of (6.2) is assigned as Problem 6.2.)

For a nonlinear model, we define the *profile t* function, $\tau(\theta_p)$, as

$$\tau(\theta_p) = \text{sign}(\theta_p - \hat{\theta}_p)\sqrt{\tilde{S}(\theta_p) - S(\hat{\boldsymbol{\theta}})}/s \tag{6.4}$$

using the same notation. By analogy with the linear model, we define a nominal $1 - \alpha$ likelihood interval for θ_p as the set of all θ_p for which

$$-t(N-P;\alpha/2) \le \tau(\theta_p) \le t(N-P;\alpha/2)$$

The profile t function is similar to the χ statistic used by Bliss and James (1966).

Plots of the profile t function provide exact likelihood intervals for individual parameters and, in addition, reveal how nonlinear the estimation situation is. To see this, suppose the model were linear. Then a plot of $\tau(\theta_p)$ versus θ_p would be a straight line. In particular, as seen from (6.2), a plot of $\tau(\theta_p)$ versus the studentized parameter, $\delta(\theta_p) = (\theta_p - \hat{\theta}_p)/\text{se}(\hat{\theta}_p)$, would be a straight line through the origin with unit slope. For a nonlinear model, a plot of $\tau(\theta_p)$ versus $\delta(\theta_p)$ will be curved, the amount of curvature giving information about the nonlinearity of the model.

Example: Puromycin 14

To make the profile t plot for θ_1 for the Puromycin data, we let $\delta(\theta_1) =$ 0.2, 0.4, . . . , and for each value we converged on θ_2. This gave a series of values for θ_1, $\tilde{\theta}_2(\theta_1)$, and $\tau(\theta_1)$. Repeating the process to the left of the estimate gave the necessary data to plot $\tau(\theta_1)$ versus θ_1 as in Figure 6.4a.

In this figure, we have included a straight line with slope 1 (dashed), corresponding to the linear case, and axes in scales of δ and nominal confidence level, which make it easy to read off likelihood intervals. The nominal 99% likelihood interval for θ_1 is [191.1, 236.7], which is well approximated by the (symmetric) linear approximation interval [190.7, 234.7]. The profile t plot is only slightly curved, suggesting that the nonlinearity is slight.

The profile t plot for θ_2 is shown in Figure 6.4b, from which we see that the likelihood intervals are slightly skewed to the right. The nominal 99% likelihood interval for θ_2 is [0.0408, 0.0972], which is well approximated by the linear approximation interval, [0.0379, 0.0903]. The nonlinearity for θ_2 is somewhat worse than that for θ_1, but it is still small. ∎

Example: BOD 8

Profile t plots for the BOD parameters are given in Figure 6.5a and b. The plots are badly curved and tend to asymptotes, indicating severe nonlinearity. The likelihood intervals are skewed and do not close on the right for levels above 98%. These observations are in accord with those made from the contour plot in Figure 6.2. The nominal 95% likelihood intervals are [14.05, 37.77] for θ_1 and [0.132, 1.77] for θ_2, which are very different from the linear approximation intervals, [12.2, 26.1] and

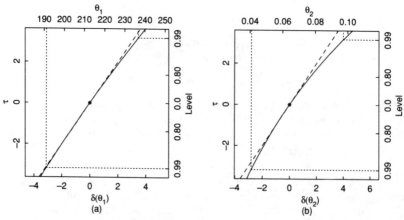

Figure 6.4 Profile t plot for θ_1 (part a) and θ_2 (part b) for the Puromycin data. The curve (solid) is the profile t, and the line (dashed) is the linear approximation. Dotted lines show the construction of a 99% marginal likelihood interval.

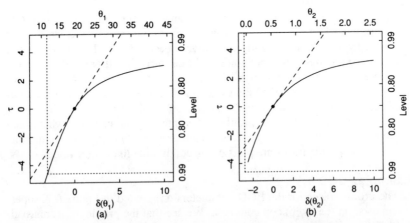

Figure 6.5 Profile t plot for θ_1 (part a) and θ_2 (part b) for the BOD data. The curve (solid) is the profile t, and the line (dashed) is the linear approximation. Dotted lines show the construction of a 99% marginal likelihood interval which extends to $+\infty$ in both cases, and is undefined on the left for θ_2.

[−0.033, 1.095]. ■

6.1.2.1 Profile Traces

Another useful plot is the likelihood *profile trace* obtained by plotting the components of the conditional maximum $\tilde{\boldsymbol{\theta}}_{-p}$ as a function of θ_p. For example, after evaluating the profile likelihood for θ_1, we can plot $\tilde{\theta}_2$ versus θ_1, $\tilde{\theta}_3$ versus θ_1, and so on, up to $\tilde{\theta}_P$ versus θ_1. Next, we evaluate the profile likelihood for θ_2 and plot $\tilde{\theta}_1$ versus θ_2, $\tilde{\theta}_3$ versus θ_2, and so on, up to $\tilde{\theta}_P$ versus θ_2. We continue to work through the parameters θ_3 to θ_P, calculating the conditional minima of the other parameters, and plotting the profile traces. Finally, we combine the plots of $\tilde{\theta}_q$ versus θ_p and $\tilde{\theta}_p$ versus θ_q, to generate the pairwise profile traces. As before, it is convenient to do the calculations using studentized parameters.

Plots of the profile traces provide useful information on how the parameters interact. For a linear model with studentized parameters, the profile traces on a plot of $\delta(\theta_q)$ versus $\delta(\theta_p)$ consist of straight lines intersecting at $(0, 0)$ with slopes of $\{C\}_{pq}$ for the trace of $\tilde{\delta}(\theta_q)$ on $\delta(\theta_p)$ and $1/\{C\}_{pq}$ for the trace of $\tilde{\delta}(\theta_p)$ on $\delta(\theta_q)$, where C is the parameter correlation matrix. If the correlation between the parameters is zero, the angle between the profile traces is 90°.

For nonlinear models, the profile traces will be curved, the curving of the lines providing information on how the parameter estimates affect one another and on the shape of the projection of the likelihood contours onto the (θ_p, θ_q) plane. If the contours are long and thin, the profile traces will be close together; if the contours are fat, the profile traces will tend to be perpendicular; and if the contours are nearly elliptical, the profile traces will be straight.

Example: Puromycin 15

The profile traces for the Puromycin parameters are plotted in Figure 6.6, superimposed on the likelihood contours from Figure 6.1. We see that the profile traces are only slightly curved and, because they do not intersect at too sharp an angle, the contours should be fairly fat ellipses. Because the profile traces are quite straight, linear approximation regions should give good approximations to the joint likelihood regions. Inspection of the actual contours reveals that this is the case.

We also see that the profile traces intersect the contours where they are parallel to the coordinate axes, which graphically demonstrates that the likelihood profile traces are plots of the conditional likelihood values. ■

Example: BOD 9

The profile traces for the BOD parameters are plotted in Figure 6.7, superimposed on the likelihood contours. We see that the profile traces are badly curved, intersect at a sharp angle, and are coincident over a long range, indicating that the contours are long, tapering, and markedly nonelliptical. It is clear that the model–data set combination is highly nonlinear, and that linear approximation inference regions will be unsatisfactory, as was noted in Example BOD 7. The plots of the contours bear this out. ■

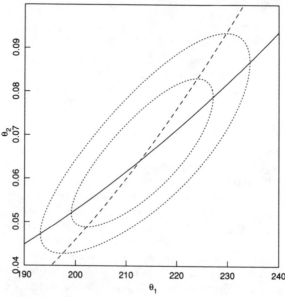

Figure 6.6 Likelihood profile traces for the Puromycin parameters, showing $\tilde{\theta}_2$ on θ_1 (solid) and $\tilde{\theta}_1$ on θ_2 (dashed). Nominal 80 and 95% likelihood contours (dotted) have been added to show that the solid lines intersect the contours at the vertical tangents to the contours and the dashed lines intersect the contours at the horizontal tangents.

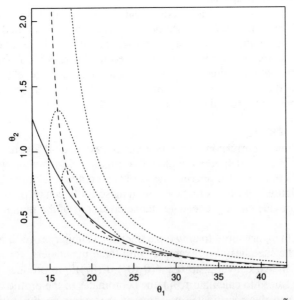

Figure 6.7 Likelihood profile traces for the BOD parameters, showing $\tilde{\theta}_2$ on θ_1 (solid) and $\tilde{\theta}_1$ on θ_2 (dashed). Nominal 50, 80, and 95% likelihood contours (dotted) have been added to show that the profile traces intersect the contours at the vertical or horizontal tangents to the contours.

6.1.2.2 Profile Pair Sketches

As stated earlier, it is not generally feasible to determine and plot likelihood contours for models with several parameters. However, we can use the profile sums of squares and the profile traces to create very accurate approximations to the 2-dimensional projections of the likelihood region and thus get a visual indication of the extent of the region and the nonlinear dependence of parameter estimates upon each other. To determine the projections of the 95% contour on the (θ_1, θ_2) plane, for example, we use the profile sum of squares for θ_1 to find where the contour intersects the trace of $\tilde{\theta}_2$ on θ_1. This gives two points on the contour. In addition, we know that the tangent to the contour must be vertical at these points, since they represent the bounds of the contour in the θ_1 direction. Similarly, from the profile sum of squares for θ_2 and from the trace of $\tilde{\theta}_2$ on θ_1, we determine two more points on the contour and we know that the contour will have horizontal tangents at these points.

By using all of this information—the profile t plots, the points on the contour, the directions of the tangent to the contour at these points, and the fact that the contour is bounded by the parameter values at these points—we can create a very accurate interpolation of a contour using the methods described in Appendix 6. We call these interpolated curves *profile pair sketches*.

Example: Puromycin 16

The coordinates on the traces corresponding to nominal 50, 80, 95, and 99% confidence levels for the Puromycin parameters are plotted in Figure 6.8a together with the contour sketches based on those points. The sketches and the exact contours are plotted in Figure 6.8b, from which it can be seen that the sketches are extremely accurate at all levels. This is in contrast to the linear approximation ellipses, shown in Figure 6.1, which deviate noticeably from the true contours. ∎

Example: BOD 10

The coordinates corresponding to nominal 50, 80, and 90% confidence levels for the BOD parameters are plotted in Figure 6.9a together with the interpolated contours. Comparing the sketched contours with the exact contours in Figure 6.9b shows that even with these badly behaved contours, the sketches provide entirely adequate characterizations of the joint region. ∎

When there are more than two parameters, a similar procedure is followed to generate the sketches. For example, with three parameters, for each of a set of values of θ_1 we converge to $\tilde{\boldsymbol{\theta}}_{-1} = (\tilde{\theta}_2(\theta_1), \tilde{\theta}_3(\theta_1))^T$, to produce $\tilde{S}(\theta_1)$. This information is used to calculate $\tau(\theta_1)$, the coordinates of the profile traces $\tilde{\theta}_2(\theta_1)$ and $\tilde{\theta}_3(\theta_1)$, and the coordinates of some of the points on the joint likelihood contour for (θ_1, θ_2) and for (θ_1, θ_3). Next, we choose a set of values for θ_2 and converge to $\tilde{\boldsymbol{\theta}}_{-2} = (\tilde{\theta}_1(\theta_2), \tilde{\theta}_3(\theta_2))^T$, this time producing $\tau(\theta_2)$, the coordinates of the profile traces $\tilde{\theta}_1(\theta_2)$ and $\tilde{\theta}_3(\theta_2)$, and the coordinates of some of the points on the joint likelihood contour for (θ_1, θ_2) and for (θ_2, θ_3). Then a range of values

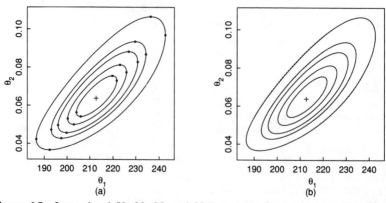

Figure 6.8 Interpolated 50, 80, 95, and 99% contours for the Puromycin parameters. Shown in part *a* are the interpolated contours with the points on the profile traces used to construct them, and in part *b*, the interpolated contours overlaid with the exact contours (dotted lines). On this scale, the exact contours cannot be distinguished from the interpolated contours.

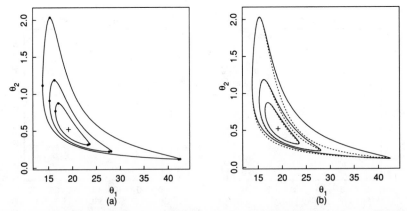

Figure 6.9   Interpolated 50, 80, and 90% contours for the BOD parameters. Shown in part a are the interpolated contours with the points on the profile traces used to construct them, and in part b, the interpolated contours overlaid with the exact contours (dotted lines).

of θ_3 is chosen and we converge to $\tilde{\boldsymbol{\theta}}_{-3} = (\tilde{\theta}_1(\theta_3), \tilde{\theta}_2(\theta_3))$, this time producing $\tau(\theta_3)$, the coordinates of the profile traces $\tilde{\theta}_1(\theta_3)$ and $\tilde{\theta}_2(\theta_3)$, and the coordinates of some of the points on the joint likelihood contour for (θ_1, θ_3) and for (θ_2, θ_3). We then plot the interpolated contours for each pair of parameters. If the profile traces are fairly straight and distinct in both the original and the τ coordinates, the contour will be fairly elliptical and the sketches will be very accurate. If the traces are curved in the original coordinates and tend to be coincident in the τ coordinates over an appreciable range, then the contours will be decidedly nonelliptical in the original coordinates and the sketches may not be accurate.

Example: Isomerization 5

Profile t plots for the isomerization data are shown in Figure 6.10, from which it can be seen that the parameters are very poorly determined. There is no upper bound on the likelihood intervals for the equilibrium constants even for nominal levels of 50%, so that effectively the only information about these parameters is that they are positive. Profile traces for some of the parameters, plotted in Figure 6.11, enable us to see why the equilibrium constants are so poorly determined.

The profile traces of θ_1 versus θ_3, shown in Figure 6.11a, look like a pair of sharply curved hyperbolas. These can be explained by noting that θ_1 appears only with θ_3 in the form of a product, and so values for which $\theta_1\theta_3 = $ constant will produce similar residual sums of squares, and therefore, hyperbolic traces.

The traces of the equilibrium constant θ_3 versus θ_2 shown in Figure 6.11b (and those for θ_4 versus θ_3, not shown) consist of a pair of coincident straight lines through the origin. This allows us to see why there is no

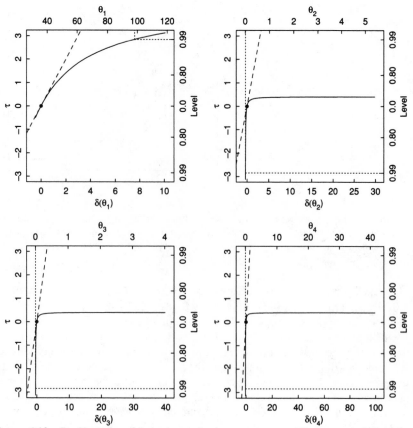

Figure 6.10 Profile t plots for the isomerization parameters. The curve (solid) is the profile t, and the line (dashed) is the linear approximation. Dotted lines show the construction of a 99% likelihood interval, which extends to $+\infty$ in three cases and which is not defined on the left for θ_1.

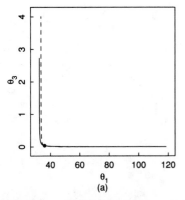 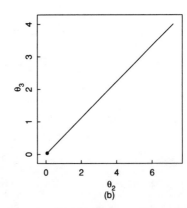

θ₁
(a)

θ₂
(b)

Figure 6.11 Profile traces for θ_1 versus θ_3 (part *a*) and θ_2 versus θ_3 (part *b*) in the isomerization data model. The traces of $\tilde{\theta}_3$ on θ_2 and $\tilde{\theta}_2$ on θ_3 are coincident.

upper bound on the likelihood intervals for the equilibrium constants. When the denominator in

$$f(\mathbf{x}, \boldsymbol{\theta}) = \frac{\theta_1\theta_3(x_2 - x_3/1.632)}{1 + \theta_2 x_1 + \theta_3 x_2 + \theta_4 x_3}$$

is substantially greater than one, the model is approximately

$$f(\mathbf{x}, \boldsymbol{\theta}) \approx \frac{\theta_1\theta_3(x_2 - x_3/1.632)}{\theta_2 x_1 + \theta_3 x_2 + \theta_4 x_3}$$

and scaling θ_2, θ_3, and θ_4 by the same factor without changing θ_1 produces essentially the same predictions and residual sums of squares.

We have not bothered to plot profile pair sketches, because of the extremely bad behavior of the profile t plots and the profile traces. This behavior reveals that very little information has been gained so far. Additional experiments would have to be performed so that meaningful parameter estimates with reasonable inference regions could be obtained.

Box and Hill (1974) presented a different analysis of these data by writing the model

$$f(\mathbf{x}, \boldsymbol{\beta}) = \frac{x_2 - x_3/1.632}{\beta_1 + \beta_2 x_1 + \beta_3 x_2 + \beta_4 x_3} \tag{6.5}$$

using an obvious reparametrization. (This form of reparametrization has been recommended by Ratkowsky (1985) for use with models consisting of ratios of polynomials.) This gave the estimates $\hat{\boldsymbol{\beta}} = (0.739, 0.0523, 0.0278, 0.123)^T$. The profile t plots shown in Figure 6.12 are much better behaved than those for the $\boldsymbol{\theta}$ parameters, producing almost perfectly symmetric likelihood regions. The profile traces (not shown) are also straight, and the

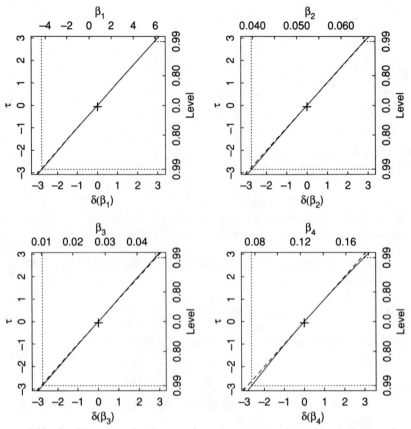

Figure 6.12 Profile t plots for the transformed parameters in the isomerization data model. The solid lines are the profile t curves, and the dashed lines are the linear approximation. Dotted lines show the construction of 99% marginal likelihood intervals.

profile pair sketches are remarkably elliptical, so that individual and joint linear approximation regions and summaries are extremely accurate for the β parameters. We note that the likelihood interval for β_1 included negative values even for moderate confidence levels. Since this parameter only has physical meaning when it is positive, we are still alerted to the fact that the data set is of limited value. ∎

6.1.3 Comments

Using profile t plots, profile traces, and profile pair sketches to summarize the inferential results of a nonlinear analysis has much to recommend it. The computations for the profile t and profile traces are very efficient because we start from the least squares estimates of the previous calculation, and because the problem is always of reduced dimension $P-1$. Also, at each value of the parameter of interest, we simultaneously generate the profile t value and the converged values of the vector $\tilde{\theta}_{-p}$, which also provides most of the data necessary for sketching the profile pairs. Profile t functions can also be used to determine exact likelihood intervals and bands for the expectation function. For all these calculations, only minor modifications to standard nonlinear regression software are necessary. Pseudocode for generating profile t plots and profile traces is given in Appendix 3.

The approach also provides important detailed information about the estimation situation. In addition to providing exact likelihood intervals for each parameter, the profile t plots reveal how nonlinear each parameter is. This can help guide the analyst towards nonlinear reparametrizations to be used for future data sets with the same model function. Such reparametrizations could be used to provide accurate linear approximation marginal and joint parameter regions, and so obviate the need for plots. A reparametrization could also be used to accelerate convergence. (For example, we recommend using the reparametrization suggested by Ratkowsky (1985) during estimation, since it simplifies the determination of starting values for the parameters and accelerates convergence. However, we recommend that the estimates and likelihood intervals be reported in terms of the original parameters, since these are physically meaningful to chemists and chemical engineers. If a reparametrization can be determined which has all the attributes of near linearity, assured convergence, and meaningfulness to the researcher, then of course, that should be used.)

Note that for univariate reparametrizations in which, say, ϕ_p is a function only of θ_p, the profile t plot (and associated profile traces) for ϕ_p can be obtained directly from the profile t plot (and associated profile traces) for θ_p: there is no need to reparametrize the model function or reestimate the parameters. This, of course, is a consequence of invariance of the likelihood function.

The profile t function can be used to determine likelihood intervals for the expectation function at any point x_0 by reparametrizing the model function so that a new parameter, say ϕ_1, is the response at x_0. The remaining parameters can be chosen as $\phi_p = \theta_p$, $p = 2, \ldots, P$, and derivatives of the expectation function with respect to the new parameters can be determined simply by using the chain rule. To determine a likelihood interval for the response at a particular point we find the values of ϕ_1 such that $\tau(\phi_1) = \pm t(N-P; \alpha/2)$, and to determine a likelihood band for the fitted response function at any x, we find the values of ϕ_1 such that $\tau(\phi_1) = \pm F(P, N-P; \alpha)$.

The profile traces and the profile pair sketches provide important information on the pairwise behavior of the parameters, which can also be used in the search for effective reparametrizations. Perhaps more importantly, however, the plots collectively provide insights into the experimental situation, so that steps can be taken to design experiments which will generate better data. For example, for the BOD data, future experiments should include more replications at each sampling time in order to reduce the scatter in the data, and some observations should be taken at about 36 hours (instead of just 24 and 48) to provide vital information about the rate constant θ_2. Similarly, for the isomerization data, more informative data must be obtained about the converted parameter θ_1. Nonlinear design techniques using the subset design criterion (Section 3.14) would be useful here.

6.2 Bayes Regions

Inferences about nonlinear models using the Bayesian approach involve the same difficulties as the likelihood approach, with the additional complexity of choosing a prior density for the parameters.

6.2.1 Choice of Bayes Prior on the Parameters

In the Bayesian analysis of a linear regression model, described in Section 1.1.4, a prior density

$$p(\boldsymbol{\beta}, \sigma) \propto \sigma^{-1}$$

is often used. This does not correspond to an actual probability density, since the integral of this density over the parameter σ or $\boldsymbol{\beta}$ is infinite, but the use of such "uninformative" or "improper" priors can be justified because the posterior density obtained by multiplying the prior by the likelihood function *is* a proper density. That is, the posterior density has a finite integral over all possible parameter values and can be normalized so that the integral is unity. This follows because, for linear models, whenever $\| \boldsymbol{\beta} \| \to \infty$, $\| \boldsymbol{\eta}(\boldsymbol{\beta}) \| \to \infty$, and since $\mathbf{y}$ is fixed, this means that $\| \mathbf{z} \| \to \infty$, so $l(\boldsymbol{\beta}, \sigma | \mathbf{y}) \to 0$. [Technically, more is required for the finite integral: we must have $l(\boldsymbol{\beta}, \sigma | \mathbf{y})$ going to zero "quickly," which it does.]

An uninformative prior can usually be considered to be the limit of proper priors that are more and more diffuse (for example, a limit of multivariate normal priors on $\boldsymbol{\beta}$ with variance–covariance matrices consisting of a fixed matrix multiplied by a factor that approaches infinity). In this limiting process, quantities calculated from the posterior densities, such as highest posterior density (HPD) regions, approach finite limits smoothly. However, for nonlinear models it is not always true that locally uniform priors produce proper posterior densities. Nonlinear models frequently have asymptotes, so $\| \boldsymbol{\theta} \| \to \infty$ does not imply that $\| \boldsymbol{\eta}(\boldsymbol{\theta}) \| \to \infty$ or $l(\boldsymbol{\theta}, \sigma | \mathbf{y}) \to 0$. [For example, as $\boldsymbol{\theta} \to \infty$ the Rumford model approaches a finite limit, the point $(60, \ldots, 60)^T$.] This means that when an improper prior on the parameters is used, the posterior density will also be improper. Even if one regards the uninformative prior as being the limit of a sequence of proper prior densities, the situation is not improved because the properties of the posterior density do not approach a finite limit satisfactorily. For example, if one were to apply a uniform prior density on θ for the Rumford model over the interval $0 \le \theta < k$ and let k approach infinity while calculating a

95% HPD interval for each value of k, the right hand end points of the HPD intervals would go to infinity.

Consideration of the Rumford example enables us to see how to avoid obtaining improper posterior densities: instead of putting a locally uniform prior on the parameter space, we should put a locally uniform prior *on the expectation surface* to represent an uninformative prior (Bates, 1978). For linear models, a locally uniform prior in the parameter space produces a locally uniform prior on the expectation plane, so this prior is consistent with standard practice for the linear model. For a nonlinear model, the uninformative prior on $\boldsymbol{\theta}$ is proportional to the Jacobian of the mapping to the expectation plane, so we set

$$p(\boldsymbol{\theta}) \propto \frac{dA}{d\boldsymbol{\theta}}$$

$$= |\mathbf{V}^T\mathbf{V}|^{1/2}$$

where dA represents an element of area on the expectation surface.

For the Rumford example, the expectation surface is finite, so a uniform prior density over the expectation surface will be a proper prior density and hence the posterior density will be a proper density. When the expectation surface has infinite extent, so the uninformative prior is not a proper density, the likelihood will force the posterior density to be proper because the surface extends to infinity. (Mathematically it is possible to get surfaces of infinite extent which are restricted to a finite region in the response space, but such pathological cases would not occur as expectation surfaces.)

We could also justify a locally uniform prior on the expectation surface by arguing that prior ignorance about the responses corresponds to a locally uniform prior on the sample space for the responses. This induces a locally uniform prior over the expectation surface as the prior for the model parameters $\boldsymbol{\theta}$. Note that this choice makes the prior *independent of the parametrization* used in the model function, since the Jacobian for the transformation cancels out.

Example: Puromycin 17

Contours of the prior density $p(\boldsymbol{\theta})$ for the model and design of the Puromycin data are shown in Figure 6.13. The prior density has been scaled so that it attains a maximum value of 1 over a region which covers the area of appreciable likelihood for these data. This prior gives greater weight to smaller θ_2 values, but the changes in the weights are small. For these data, the likelihood (whose contours were shown in Figure 6.1) will clearly dominate the prior in determining the posterior density, and so the contours of the posterior density look almost identical to the contours of the likelihood function. (The maximum and minimum value of the prior density over this region have a ratio of about 10, while the maximum and minimum likelihood values have a ratio of about 10^{195}.) ∎

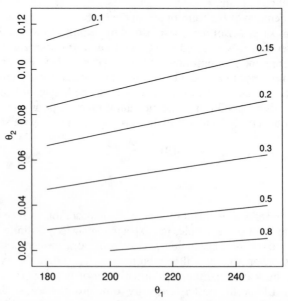

Figure 6.13   Contours of relative prior density for the parameters in the Puromycin data model.   The prior density has been scaled so it attains a maximum of 1 over the region shown.

Example: BOD 11

Contours of prior density for the model and design of the BOD data are shown in Figure 6.14. As before, the prior density has been scaled so that it has a maximum of 1 over the region which includes most of the area of appreciable likelihood. In this example, we cannot include all the parameter values with appreciable likelihood, since that region is unbounded, as demonstrated in Example BOD 7. The prior varies considerably over the region, reaching zero for $\theta_2 = 0$. The prior is very small for large values of θ_2, which correspond to the region of the expectation surface where the parameter curves are approaching a limit as described in Example BOD 7. The very small prior values discount the parameter values in that area. ■

To complete the prior density, we must specify the joint prior for θ and σ. Following Box and Tiao (1973), we choose independent priors for θ and σ with $p(\sigma) \propto \sigma^{-1}$, so the joint prior density is

$$p(\theta,\sigma) \propto p(\theta)p(\sigma)$$
$$= |V^TV|^{1/2}\, \sigma^{-1}$$

(6.6)

It is noteworthy that the prior density does not depend on the parametrization, but it is equally noteworthy that the prior depends on the design used by

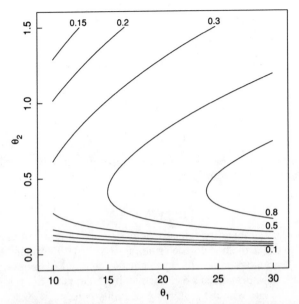

Figure 6.14 Contours of relative prior density for the parameters in the BOD data model. The prior density has been scaled so it attains a maximum of 1 over the region shown.

the experimenter. This makes good sense, since no scientific experiment is done in the complete absence of knowledge, and the prior subtly expresses the current knowledge of the experimenter through the design.

To illustrate, suppose one wished to measure BOD of a river, and the model function $f = \theta_1(1 - e^{-\theta_2 x})$ was considered appropriate. The BOD, and consequently the parameters, would depend on the season of the year, the latitude of the river, the rate of flow of the river, the number and types of sources of pollution along the river, the type of river bed, and so on. For fast-flowing northern mountain rivers with no immediate pollution sources, the rate constant θ_2 would likely be very small, and so samples taken from the river should be analyzed at rather long intervals and over a long time, say every three days for three weeks. For a sluggish meandering river in an industrial area, on the other hand, the rate constant θ_2 would likely be large, and so the samples should be analyzed at shorter intervals and over a shorter time, say every twelve hours for five days. These considerations clearly affect the design and, in turn, the prior on the parameters.

6.2.2 Joint HPD Regions

After choosing a prior density, we form the posterior density by multiplying the prior by the likelihood function. Thus the posterior density, $p(\boldsymbol{\theta}, \sigma \,|\, \mathbf{y})$, becomes

$$p(\boldsymbol{\theta},\sigma\,|\,\mathbf{y}) \propto |\,\mathbf{V}^T\mathbf{V}\,|^{1/2}\,\sigma^{-(N+1)}\exp\!\left[-\frac{S(\boldsymbol{\theta})}{2\sigma^2}\right]$$

where $S(\boldsymbol{\theta})$ is the residual sum of squares at $\boldsymbol{\theta}$. As shown in Box and Tiao (1973), the marginal posterior density of $\boldsymbol{\theta}$ is obtained by integrating the joint posterior over the nuisance parameter σ to yield

$$p(\boldsymbol{\theta}\,|\,\mathbf{y}) = \int_0^\infty p(\boldsymbol{\theta},\sigma\,|\,\mathbf{y})\,d\sigma$$
$$\propto |\,\mathbf{V}^T\mathbf{V}\,|^{1/2}\,[S(\boldsymbol{\theta})]^{-N/2} \tag{6.7}$$

An HPD region will be bounded by a contour of this posterior density function, or equivalently, by a contour of

$$\frac{S(\boldsymbol{\theta})}{|\,\mathbf{V}^T\mathbf{V}\,|^{1/N}}$$

To assign a probability value to the region, we must determine the level of contour. The exact method for determining a $1-\alpha$ HPD region is to integrate (6.7) over all possible values of $\boldsymbol{\theta}$, obtain the constant of proportionality, and then integrate the normalized posterior within contours of the posterior density until we find the one with the required probability content.

All the integrations in this exact procedure make it too computationally intensive for general use, but fortunately there is a convenient approximation to the probability content of a contour. For any expectation surface, a set of *geodesic* parameters exists, say $\boldsymbol{\phi}$, for which the prior density will be approximately constant near $\hat{\boldsymbol{\phi}}$. That is,

$$|\,\mathbf{V}_\phi^T\mathbf{V}_\phi\,| \approx \text{constant} \tag{6.8}$$

where

$$\mathbf{V}_\phi = \frac{d\boldsymbol{\eta}}{d\boldsymbol{\phi}^T}$$

If the expectation surface is perfectly flat or, more generally, if it has zero Gaussian curvature everywhere (O'Neill, 1966), (6.8) is an equality.

Besides having a locally uniform prior density, the $\boldsymbol{\phi}$ parameters also have an easily expressed likelihood function, since when the expectation surface is reasonably flat over the region of nonnegligible likelihood, the sum of squares function $S_\phi(\boldsymbol{\phi})$ is quadratic in $\boldsymbol{\phi}$. That is,

$$p_\phi(\boldsymbol{\phi}\,|\,\mathbf{y}) \propto [S_\phi(\boldsymbol{\phi})]^{-N/2}$$
$$\approx \left[S_\phi(\hat{\boldsymbol{\phi}}) + \tfrac{1}{2}(\boldsymbol{\phi}-\hat{\boldsymbol{\phi}})^T \left.\frac{\partial^2 S_\phi}{\partial\boldsymbol{\phi}\partial\boldsymbol{\phi}^T}\right|_{\hat{\boldsymbol{\phi}}}(\boldsymbol{\phi}-\hat{\boldsymbol{\phi}})\right]^{-N/2}$$

which is in the form of a multivariate T density (Box and Tiao, 1973). Thus, an approximate $1-\alpha$ HPD region consists of all values of $\boldsymbol{\phi}$ enclosed by the contour $S_\phi(\phi)$ determined by

$$\frac{[S_\phi(\phi) - S_\phi(\hat{\phi})]/P}{S_\phi(\hat{\phi})/(N-P)} \leq F(P, N-P; \alpha)$$

In terms of θ, the HPD region becomes a contour in $S(\theta)/|V^T V|^{1/N}$, and so the approximate $1 - \alpha$ HPD region in θ is bounded by the contour

$$\frac{S(\theta)}{|V^T V|^{1/N}} = \frac{S(\hat{\theta})}{|\hat{V}^T \hat{V}|^{1/N}} \left[1 + \frac{P}{N-P} F(P, N-P; \alpha)\right]$$

Computationally, it is more convenient to determine contours of $|V^T V|^{1/N}/S(\theta)$, since sometimes $|V^T V| = 0$ on the boundary of the parameter region, as in Example BOD 11.

Example: Puromycin 18

The approximate 80 and 95% HPD regions for the Puromycin parameters are shown in Figure 6.15, together with the corresponding likelihood regions (dotted lines). The HPD contours are very similar to the likelihood contours but are slightly more symmetric about the least squares estimate, since large values of θ_2 are given less weight. ■

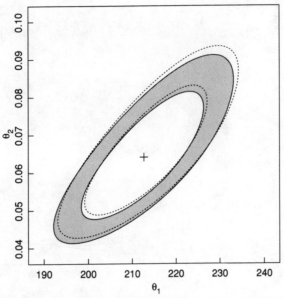

Figure 6.15 Nominal 80 and 95% HPD regions (solid lines) and the corresponding likelihood regions (dotted) for the Puromycin parameters.

Example: BOD 12

The approximate 80 and 95% HPD regions for the BOD parameters are shown in Figure 6.16 together with portions of the corresponding likelihood regions (dotted lines). The HPD contours are closed in the θ_2 direction, unlike the corresponding likelihood contours, but they are still decidedly nonelliptical. ∎

Sketches could be made of the pairwise projections of HPD regions using the same approach as for likelihood regions. Instead of minimizing the conditional sum of squares, however, we determine the posterior profile traces by minimizing $S(\boldsymbol{\theta})/|\mathbf{V}^T\mathbf{V}|^{1/N}$. Minimizing this is much more difficult than minimizing the profile sum of squares, but fortunately the *locus* of the minima, say $\boldsymbol{\theta}^*_{-p}(\theta_p)$ (i.e., the posterior profile trace) will be essentially the same as $\tilde{\boldsymbol{\theta}}_{-p}(\theta_p)$ (the likelihood trace) because the term $|\mathbf{V}^T\mathbf{V}|^{1/N}$ will usually vary more slowly than the term $S(\boldsymbol{\theta})$. It is therefore easy to evaluate the posterior density along the likelihood trace and so generate sketches of the projections of HPD regions using the methods of Appendix 6.

In theory, Bayesian marginal inferences are straightforward: the posterior density is simply integrated over the nuisance parameters, as in eliminating σ. If θ_1 is the single parameter of interest and $\boldsymbol{\theta}_{-1}$ represents the nuisance parameters, the marginal density for θ_1 is

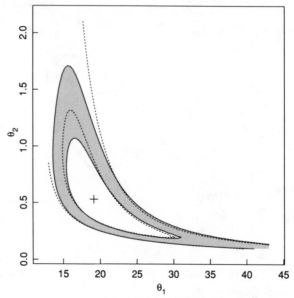

Figure 6.16   80 and 95% HPD regions (solid lines) and the corresponding likelihood regions (dotted) for the BOD parameters.

$$p_{\theta_1}(\theta_1) \propto \int p_\theta(\theta_1, \theta_{-1}^T) \, d\theta_{-1}$$

This method of eliminating components of θ would generally require a prohibitive amount of numerical integration, so approximations based on the density conditional on the parameter of interest are used. A first approximation is to use the analogue of the profile likelihood,

$$\int p_\theta(\theta_1, \theta_{-1}^T) \, d\theta_{-1} \propto p_\theta(\theta_1, \theta_{-1}^*(\theta_1))$$

where $\theta_{-1}^*(\theta_1)$ is the value which maximizes $p_\theta(\theta_1, \theta_{-1})$ over θ_{-1} for that value of θ_1. That is, the marginal density for θ_1 is assumed to be proportional to the maximum value of the conditional density on θ_1. To obtain more accurate intervals, a quadratic approximation could be used in which the integral of the joint density is replaced by the product of its maximum value and a measure of its spread at the maximum, as discussed in Tierney and Kadane (1986).

6.3 Exact Sampling Theory Confidence Regions

Sampling theory methods for linear regression can be extended to provide joint confidence regions for parameters in nonlinear regression models. We only do this for completeness, however, because *we do not recommend the approach*.

The method involves hypotheses of the form

$$H_0 : \quad \theta = \theta_0$$

versus

$$H_A : \quad \theta \neq \theta_0$$

where, as in the linear model, the test is based on the relative lengths of tangential and orthogonal components of the residual vector $z_0 = y - \eta(\theta_0)$. For linear models, the tangent plane is independent of θ and the length of the orthogonal component of the residual vector is fixed. For nonlinear models, however, the tangent plane changes with the value of θ and so does the length of the orthogonal component.

Even with a nonlinear model, this test provides a locally most powerful, unbiased test of the hypothesis, and under the assumptions on the model, the confidence region

$$\frac{\| Q_1^T(\theta) z(\theta) \|^2 / P}{\| Q_2^T(\theta) z(\theta) \|^2 / (N-P)} \leq F(P, N-P; \alpha) \tag{6.9}$$

is an exact $1 - \alpha$ confidence region. In (6.9), $Q_1(\theta)$ and $Q_2(\theta)$ are the orthogonal parts of the QR decomposition of $V(\theta)$, the derivative matrix evaluated at θ. When there is an independent variance estimate s_r^2 with v_r degrees of freedom, an alternative form of the confidence region is

$$\| Q_1^T(\theta)z(\theta) \|^2 \leq Ps_r^2 \, F(P, v_r; \alpha)$$

Example: Puromycin 19

Figure 6.17 shows portions of the 80, 95, and 99% exact confidence regions for the Puromycin parameters. The 80% region is quite elliptical and nicely centered about the least squares estimate $\hat{\theta}$, but the 95 and 99% regions are very badly behaved, neither region appearing to close.

Comparing Figure 6.17 with Figures 6.1 and 6.15, we see that the confidence regions are larger and less well behaved than the corresponding likelihood or HPD regions. The fact that the confidence regions do not close for moderate confidence levels for this well-behaved example is particularly damaging testimony against using exact confidence regions. ∎

Example: BOD 13

The 80 and 95% exact confidence regions for the BOD data set are shown in Figure 6.18. Again, the contours at moderate confidence levels are open and are very badly behaved relative to the likelihood and HPD contours. The "shoulders" on the contours near $\theta_2 = 1.4$ are not an artifact of the contouring program, but appear to be a genuine feature of the contours. ∎

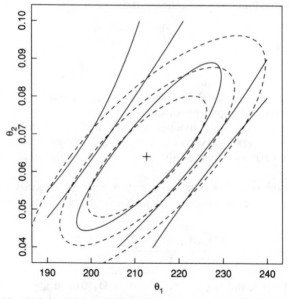

Figure 6.17 Nominal 80, 95, and 99% confidence regions (solid lines) and the linear approximation ellipses (dashed) for the Puromycin parameters.

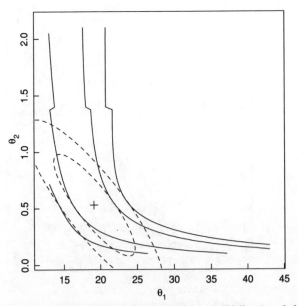

Figure 6.18 Nominal 80 and 95% confidence regions (solid lines) and the linear approximation ellipses (dashed) for the BOD parameters.

As pointed out in Beale (1960), sampling theory confidence regions have undesirable properties because they are determined by values of a ratio in which both the numerator and the denominator vary with θ. The ratio in (6.9) can be small because the tangential component is small or because the orthogonal component is large. When the expectation surface bends, the ratio often falls below the critical value for points which are very far away from the least squares values because the tangent plane has tilted.

Example: Rumford 7

It is instructive to examine exact confidence regions in more detail geometrically. For the 2-case Rumford example, a 50% confidence region for the parameter θ is defined as the set of all parameter values θ for which the F ratio does not exceed $F(1,1;0.50) = 1.0$. That is, a point θ^0 is included in the 50% confidence region if the angle that the residual vector makes with the tangent line exceeds 45°. For this example, the region will include values close to the least squares point $\hat{\theta} = 0.00832$, and will also include values close to 0.1. Figure 6.19 illustrates the situation for $\theta^0 = 0.1$, for which the angle between the residual vector and the tangent line is about 54°. (The shaded region enclosed by the 45° lines indicates the exclusion region for residual vectors at $\theta = 0.1$.)

In fact, plotting the F ratio versus θ, as in Figure 6.20, shows that the F ratio decreases to a minimum around $\hat{\theta}$, goes through a maximum,

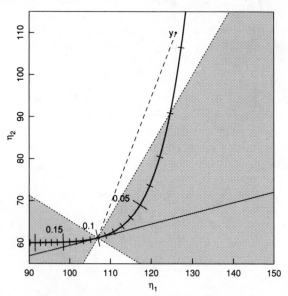

Figure 6.19   Test to determine if $\theta = 0.1$ should be included in a 50% confidence set for the 2-case Rumford data. The heavy solid line is the expectation curve; the light solid line is the tangent at $\boldsymbol{\eta}(0.1)$. The dotted lines at 45° to the tangent delimit the exclusion region (shaded) for residual vectors at $\theta = 0.1$. Since the residual vector (dashed line) forms an angle of more than 45° to the tangent, $\theta = 0.1$ is included in the 50% confidence set.

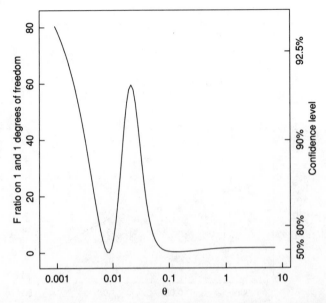

Figure 6.20   Plot of the F ratio versus θ for the 2-case Rumford example.

reaches another minimum near 0.1, and then remains small as $\theta \to \infty$. Some confidence intervals (actually "confidence sets") derived in this way are given in Table 6.1.

It may seem unreasonable to calculate confidence intervals for a 2-case data set, because there is only one degree of freedom for residuals. But the same behavior occurs with the full data set. The F ratios, plotted in Figure 6.21, have a minimum at $\hat{\theta}$ (= 0.00942), reach a maximum, and decrease again as $\theta \to \infty$, which produces confidence sets as in Table 6.2.
■

We see that even for a simple 1-parameter model, exact confidence regions can consist of disjoint portions which include parameter values whose residual vectors are much longer than the residual vector at $\hat{\theta}$. Moreover, even without producing confidence regions in disjoint portions, the method is subject

Table 6.1   Confidence sets for the 2-case Rumford example.

Confidence Level (%)	Set		
50	[0.0076, 0.0091]	and	[0.0813, 0.3869]
80	[0.0058, 0.0111]	and	[0.0475, ∞]
90	[0.0032, 0.0154]	and	[0.0302, ∞]
95	[0, ∞]		

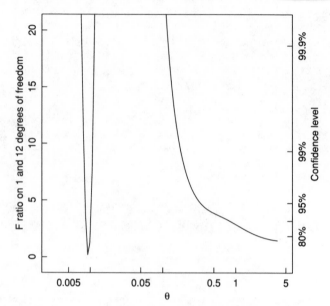

Figure 6.21   Plot of the F ratio versus θ for the Rumford data.

Table 6.2   Confidence sets for the Rumford data.

Confidence Level (%)	Set
50	[0.0092, 0.0094]
80	[0.0089, 0.0100] and [2.0947, ∞]
90	[0.0087, 0.0101] and [0.8224, ∞]
95	[0.0085, 0.0103] and [0.3261, ∞]

to enclosing clearly inappropriate parameter values in the confidence sets.

Marginal inferences are difficult to formulate using sampling theory because the method for constructing joint or marginal confidence regions for the parameters in a linear model does not generalize to nonlinear models except when conditional linearity can be exploited (Hamilton, 1986). As described in Section 1.2.3 for linear models, the method involves decomposing the residual vector for a representative point on the subplane defined by $\beta_2 = c$ into three components: one *orthogonal to* the expectation plane, one *in* the expectation plane and *orthogonal to* the subplane, and one *parallel to* the subplane. For a nonlinear model, both the expectation surface and the subsurface generated by a constraint such as $\theta_2 = c$ are nonlinear, and there is no general decomposition giving three orthogonal components. In theory, marginal confidence regions could be computed, but a reference distribution would have to be computed for each model, each data set, and each parameter value, and so there would be no straightforward way to obtain marginal confidence regions using standard (F or *t*) distributions.

The only instance where the approach from linear models can be used is when there are conditionally linear parameters. If the model reduces to a linear model when a subset of the parameters is held fixed, then exact marginal confidence regions for the nonlinear parameters can be calculated. For example, the model

$$f(x, \boldsymbol{\theta}) = \theta_1 + \theta_2 e^{\theta_3 x}$$

reduces to a linear model when θ_3 is held fixed. Thus confidence intervals for θ_3 can be determined using a *t* distribution, as described in Halperin (1963) and Williams (1962).

6.4 Comparison of the Likelihood, Bayes, and Sampling Theory Approaches

Four methods for summarizing joint and marginal inference regions have been given. In Chapter 2 we discussed linear approximations, and in this chapter we presented profile *t* and profile pair plots, Bayes joint and marginal HPD procedures, and sampling theory procedures. The linear approximation methods are the easiest to use, and most nonlinear regression programs produce the linear approximation standard errors for the parameters and the approximate correlation matrix for the parameters in addition to the parameter estimates. The major disadvantage of linear approximations is that the validity of the approximation over the region of interest is not known. This approximation involves both the *planar* assumption and the *uniform coordinate* assumption, one or both of which could be invalid—as shown in the next chapter, it is usually the uniform coordinate assumption.

The other approaches to inference produce joint regions defined by contours. Determining and displaying exact contours is generally too expensive when $P > 2$, but displaying profile *t* plots, profile traces, and profile pair sketches is eminently practical. This approach requires a minor amount of extra computation over the linear approximation approach but provides valuable information on the behavior of the marginal and joint regions. Fortunately, the calculations only require slight modifications of standard nonlinear programs. The confidence level associated with likelihood regions is not well defined, but in contrast to the linear approximation intervals, the likelihood regions require only the planar assumption.

Similarly, examination of the approximate marginal and joint HPD regions provides much more information than does the linear approximation. The Bayes prior moderates the tendency of likelihood contours to open as the model function approaches an asymptote, making the Bayes intervals more satisfactory. The probability associated with the HPD intervals is based on an approximation to the expectation surface that, like the likelihood approach, only requires probability content or level of a region than the likelihood approach.

It is noteworthy that the prior density does not depend on the parametrization, but it is equally noteworthy that the prior depends on the design used by the experimenter. As demonstrated in Section 6.2.1, however, this makes good sense, since no scientific experiment is done in the complete absence of knowledge, and the prior expresses the current knowledge of the experimenter through the design.

The sampling theory approach, which uses the ratio of lengths of components of the residual vector rather than the total length of the residual vector to determine the region, can result in regions which include inappropriate parameter values. In addition, the difficulty of defining marginal regions for a general case makes this approach completely unsuitable.

To summarize, when a nonlinear regression is performed, we recommend producing the linear approximation standard errors and correlations, and profile t plots, profile traces, and profile pair sketches for either the likelihood function or the Bayesian posterior density.

Exercises

6.1 Write a computer routine in a language of your choice to generate profile t and profile trace plots. Use the nonlinear subroutine from Problem 2.1.

6.2 Use Lagrange multipliers to show analytically that the profile t value for a parameter in a linear model can be written as in equation (6.2).

6.3 (a) Use the data and model from Appendix 4, Section A4.1 to make profile t and profile trace plots for the parameters. Does this model–data set–parametrization combination suffer from bad nonlinearity?

     (b) Use the profile t plots to determine nominal 50, 75, and 95% intervals for the parameters.

     (c) Plot the points on the profile traces corresponding to the 50, 75, and 95% nominal confidence level in the (θ_1, θ_2) plane. Using the information concerning the tangents of the contours at these points, sketch the joint regions.

     (d) Compare your sketch with the exact sum of squares contours from Problem 2.6. Comment on the accuracy of the sketch.

6.4 Use the data from Appendix 4, Section A4.3 and the model fitted in Problem 3.4 to make profile t and profile trace plots for the parameters.

6.5 Use the data and model from Appendix 4, Section A4.4 to make profile t and profile trace plots for the parameters.

     (a) Use the model with the factor $1/x_3$ centered.

     (b) Reparametrize the model using $\theta_1 = e^{\phi_1}$ and $\theta_2 = e^{\phi_2}$, and plot the profile t values. Is is necessary to recalculate the t values or the trace values?

6.6 (a) Use the data and model from Appendix 4, Section A4.5 to make profile

t and profile trace plots for the parameters.

(b) Reparametrize the model in part (a) using $\theta_2\, e^{-\theta_3 x} = e^{-\phi_3(x - \phi_2)}$. Is it necessary to recalculate the t values or the trace values? Which ones?

(c) Comment on the effects of this transformation on the profile t plots and on the profile trace plots.

6.7 (a) Calculate and plot contours of the Bayesian prior density for the exponential rise model of Example BOD 11 but using the design with $\mathbf{x} = (2, 10)^T$. (This is the optimal experimental design for this model, assuming that the true parameter value is $\theta_2 = 0.5$ and that $x_{max} = 10$.) Use the same region for $\boldsymbol{\theta}$ as was used in Figure 6.14.

(b) Compare this prior with the prior shown in Figure 6.14.

(c) Calculate and plot contours for the prior corresponding to n replications of the optimal design, where $n = 2, 4, 8$. Comment on the effect of increasing the number of replications.

CHAPTER 7.

Curvature Measures of Nonlinearity

"The great tragedy of Science: the slaying of a beautiful hypothesis by an ugly fact."

— *Thomas Huxley*

In Chapter 2 we presented linear approximation inference intervals and regions for parameters in nonlinear regression models, and in Chapter 6 we discussed improved methods for summarizing inferences about the parameters. An important assumption used in the development of these methods is that the expectation surface is flat (the planar assumption), so that the tangent plane provides an accurate approximation. In this chapter, we develop relative curvature measures of the nonlinearity of an estimation situation, and discuss how they can be used to indicate the adequacy of the linear approximation in a particular case. We then apply the curvature measures to 67 real data set–model combinations to gain some idea of how serious the two kinds of nonlinearity are in practice. Finally, we discuss more direct assessment of intrinsic nonlinearity to provide practical justification for assuming planarity.

As discussed in Section 2.5, linear approximation inference regions can be obtained from a first order Taylor series approximation to the expectation function evaluated at $\hat{\boldsymbol{\theta}}$. The $1 - \alpha$ region is

$$(\boldsymbol{\theta} - \hat{\boldsymbol{\theta}})^{\mathrm{T}} \hat{\mathbf{V}}^{\mathrm{T}} \hat{\mathbf{V}} (\boldsymbol{\theta} - \hat{\boldsymbol{\theta}}) \leq Ps^2 F(P, N-P; \alpha) \tag{7.1}$$

where $\hat{\mathbf{V}}$ is the derivative matrix evaluated at $\hat{\boldsymbol{\theta}}$.

Geometrically, the linear approximation inference region (7.1) assumes that, over the region of interest, the mapping of $\boldsymbol{\theta}$ to $\boldsymbol{\eta}(\boldsymbol{\theta})$ is

$$\hat{\boldsymbol{\eta}} + \hat{\mathbf{V}}(\boldsymbol{\theta} - \hat{\boldsymbol{\theta}})$$

This approximation, as pointed out by Beale (1960) and as discussed in Section 2.5, will be good only if the expectation surface is sufficiently flat to be replaced by the tangent plane, and if straight, parallel equispaced lines in the parameter space map into nearly straight, parallel equispaced lines on the expectation sur-

232

face. In that event, we can assume that the expectation surface inference region is a sphere of radius $\sqrt{Ps^2 F(P, N-P; \alpha)}$ on the tangent plane and that the mapping of the tangent plane to the parameter space is linear.

To determine how planar the expectation surface is, and how uniform the parameter lines are on the tangent plane, we use second derivatives of the expectation function to derive *curvature measures* of *intrinsic* and *parameter effects nonlinearity*. The curvatures can also be used to investigate reparametrizations of expectation functions so as to obtain models which have more valid linear approximation parameter inference regions.

7.1 Velocity and Acceleration Vectors

A fundamental feature of linear models is that second and higher order derivatives of the expectation function with respect to the parameters are zero. It is logical, therefore, to attempt to measure the nonlinearity of a model by investigating second order derivatives of the expectation function (Bates, 1978; Bates and Watts, 1980; Beale, 1960). For clarity, we introduce a dot notation to distinguish between first and second derivatives. Thus for a nonlinear model $\eta(\theta)$, the $N \times P$ derivative matrix is written as $\dot{V}$ with elements

$$\{\dot{V}\}_{np} = \frac{\partial f(x_n, \theta)}{\partial \theta_p} \tag{7.2}$$

and the $N \times P \times P$ second derivative array is written as $\ddot{V}$ with elements

$$\{\ddot{V}\}_{npq} = \frac{\partial^2 f(x_n, \theta)}{\partial \theta_p \, \partial \theta_q} \tag{7.3}$$

In (7.2) and (7.3), n runs from 1 to N while p and q run from 1 to P. In matrix notation,

$$\dot{V} = \frac{\partial \eta}{\partial \theta^T}$$

where each row of $\dot{V}$ is the gradient of one coordinate of $\eta(\theta)$ with respect to θ. Alternatively, we may regard $\dot{V}$ as consisting of vectors $\dot{v}_p, p = 1, 2, \ldots, P$.

Also,

$$\ddot{V} = \frac{\partial^2 \eta}{\partial \theta \, \partial \theta^T}$$

where each face $\ddot{V}_n$ of $\ddot{V}$ is a complete $P \times P$ second derivative matrix, or Hessian, of one element of $\eta(\theta)$ with respect to θ. As above, we may regard the Hessian array as consisting of vectors $\ddot{v}_{pq}, p, q = 1, 2, \ldots, P$.

The vectors $\dot{v}$ are, of course, the tangent vectors, and they are also called *velocity* vectors, since they give the rate of change of η with respect to each parameter. Accordingly, the vectors $\ddot{v}$ are called *acceleration* vectors, since

$$\ddot{v}_{pq} = \frac{\partial^2 p}{\partial \theta_q}$$

Example: Puromycin 21

For the Michaelis–Menten expectation function

$$f(x, \boldsymbol{\theta}) = \frac{\theta_1 x}{\theta_2 + x}$$

the elements in $\dot{\mathbf{V}}$ are

$$\{\dot{\mathbf{V}}\}_{n1} = \frac{x_n}{\theta_2 + x_n}$$

$$\{\dot{\mathbf{V}}\}_{n2} = \frac{-\theta_1 x_n}{(\theta_2 + x_n)^2}$$

Evaluating these functions at each x_n value for a particular parameter pair $\boldsymbol{\theta}$ produces the matrix $\dot{\mathbf{V}}$.

The elements in $\ddot{\mathbf{V}}$ can also be evaluated, as

$$\{\ddot{\mathbf{V}}\}_{n11} = 0$$

$$\{\ddot{\mathbf{V}}\}_{n12} = \frac{-x_n}{(\theta_2 + x_n)^2}$$

$$\{\ddot{\mathbf{V}}\}_{n21} = \{\ddot{\mathbf{V}}\}_{n12}$$

$$\{\ddot{\mathbf{V}}\}_{n22} = \frac{2\theta_1 x_n}{(\theta_2 + x_n)^3}$$

For the Puromycin data, the concentrations and the velocity and acceleration vectors at $\hat{\boldsymbol{\theta}}$ are given in Table 7.1. ∎

7.1.1 Tangential and Normal Accelerations

The acceleration vectors can be decomposed into components *in* and *orthogonal to* the tangent plane. Because there are only $P(P+1)/2$ distinct acceleration vectors, the acceleration vectors will span a subspace of maximum dimension $P(P+1)/2$ in the response space, so the maximum dimension of the combined tangent and acceleration spaces is $P(P+3)/2$ (Hamilton, 1980). In many cases the combined dimension is only slightly larger than P, say $P + P'$.

Table 7.1 Velocity and acceleration vectors for the Puromycin data evaluated at $\hat{\theta} = (212.7, 0.0641)^T$.

Conc.	Velocity		Acceleration		
	$\dot{v}_1$	$\dot{v}_2$	$\ddot{v}_{11}$	$\ddot{v}_{12}$	$\ddot{v}_{22}$
0.02	0.237812	−601.458	0	−2.82773	14 303.4
0.02	0.237812	−601.458	0	−2.82773	14 303.4
0.06	0.483481	−828.658	0	−3.89590	13 354.7
0.06	0.483481	−828.658	0	−3.89590	13 354.7
0.11	0.631821	−771.903	0	−3.62907	8 867.4
0.11	0.631821	−771.903	0	−3.62907	8 867.4
0.22	0.774375	−579.759	0	−2.72571	4 081.4
0.22	0.774375	−579.759	0	−2.72571	4 081.4
0.56	0.897292	−305.807	0	−1.43774	980.0
0.56	0.897292	−305.807	0	−1.43774	980.0
1.10	0.944936	−172.655	0	−0.81173	296.6
1.10	0.944936	−172.655	0	−0.81173	296.6

Example: Puromycin 22

For the Michaelis–Menten model, $\ddot{v}_{11} \equiv 0$ because θ_1 is a conditionally linear parameter. This conditional linearity causes the acceleration vector $\ddot{v}_{12} = \ddot{v}_{21}$ to be a simple multiple of $\dot{v}_2$, so that the only acceleration vector which is not in the tangent plane is $\ddot{v}_{22}$. The tangent space has dimension 2, the acceleration space has dimension 2, and the combined tangent and acceleration spaces have dimension 3.

In Figure 7.1 we show the projection of the tangent vectors and the acceleration vectors into the combined tangent and acceleration space for the Puromycin data. To provide a clearer figure, we have scaled the response by dividing by 100 and scaled the concentrations by multiplying by 10. Note that only the vector $\ddot{v}_{22}$ has a component outside the tangent plane, and that this component is small. ∎

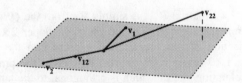

Figure 7.1 Projection of the scaled velocity and acceleration vectors for the Puromycin data at $\hat{\theta} = (212.7, 0.0641)^T$ in the 3-dimensional space spanned by these vectors. The tangent plane is shaded.

vectors into a matrix $\mathbf{W}$ and combining them with the tangent vectors in $\dot{\mathbf{V}}$ to give

$$\mathbf{D} = (\dot{\mathbf{V}}, \ddot{\mathbf{W}}) \tag{7.4}$$

We then perform a QR decomposition on $\mathbf{D}$, as $\mathbf{D} = (\mathbf{Q}_1 \,|\, \mathbf{Q}'_1 \,|\, \mathbf{Q}_2)\mathbf{R}$, and multiply the array $\ddot{\mathbf{V}}$ by $(\mathbf{Q}_1 \,|\, \mathbf{Q}'_1)^T$ to give

$$\ddot{\mathbf{A}} = [(\mathbf{Q}_1 \,|\, \mathbf{Q}'_1)^T][\ddot{\mathbf{V}}] \tag{7.5}$$

where $\mathbf{Q}_1$ is the first P columns of $\mathbf{Q}$ and $\mathbf{Q}'_1$ is the next P' columns of $\mathbf{Q}$. This provides a compact $(P + P') \times P \times P$ *acceleration array* $\ddot{\mathbf{A}}$ with P faces in the tangent space and P' faces in the acceleration space. (The square bracket notation indicates that the summation is over the numerator index: that is, the element in the nth face, pth row, and qth column of the product $\mathbf{A} = [\mathbf{B}][\mathbf{C}]$, where $\mathbf{B}$ is an $N_1 \times N_2$ matrix and $\mathbf{C}$ is an $N_2 \times N_3 \times N_4$ array, is

$$\{\mathbf{A}\}_{npq} = \sum_{i=1}^{N_2} \{\mathbf{B}\}_{ni} \{\mathbf{C}\}_{ipq}$$

and $\mathbf{A}$ is an $N_1 \times N_3 \times N_4$ array.)

Example: Puromycin 23

To illustrate these calculations, we use the velocity and acceleration vectors from Example Puromycin 21, Table 7.1, to form the matrix $\mathbf{D}$. Performing a QR decomposition on $\mathbf{D}$ gives

$$\mathbf{R}_1 = [(\mathbf{Q}_1 \,|\, \mathbf{Q}'_1)^T][\mathbf{D}] = \begin{bmatrix} \mathbf{R}_{11} & \mathbf{R}_{12} \\ \mathbf{0} & \mathbf{R}_{22} \end{bmatrix}$$

$$= \begin{bmatrix} -2.44 & 1568.7 & 0 & 7.378 & -16185.7 \\ 0 & 1320.3 & 0 & 6.210 & -25030.4 \\ 0 & 0 & 0 & 0 & 8369.1 \end{bmatrix}$$

The left upper 2×2 matrix, $\mathbf{R}_{11}$, is simply $\hat{\mathbf{R}}_1$ from the QR decomposition of $\dot{\mathbf{V}}$ (cf. Example Puromycin 7), and the right upper 2×3 matrix, $\mathbf{R}_{12}$, gives the projection of the acceleration vectors into the tangent plane, $[\mathbf{Q}_1^T][\ddot{\mathbf{W}}]$. The 1×3 lower right matrix, $\mathbf{R}_{22}$, gives the projection of that part of the acceleration vector which is orthogonal to the tangent space but in the space spanned by the acceleration vectors, $[\mathbf{Q}'_1^T][\ddot{\mathbf{W}}]$. In this example, this extra space has dimension $P' = 1$.

Reforming the elements of $\mathbf{R}_{12}$ and $\mathbf{R}_{22}$ into a $3 \times 2 \times 2$ acceleration array $\ddot{\mathbf{A}}$ gives

$$\ddot{A} = \begin{bmatrix} 0 & 7.378 \\ 7.378 & -16185.7 \end{bmatrix} \begin{bmatrix} 0 & 6.210 \\ 6.210 & -25030.4 \end{bmatrix} \begin{bmatrix} 0 & 0 \\ 0 & 8369.1 \end{bmatrix}$$

These are the values which, when scaled as in Example Puromycin 22, were used to generate Figure 7.1. ■

The extent to which the acceleration vectors lie outside the tangent plane measures how much the expectation surface deviates from a plane, and hence measures the nonplanarity of the expectation surface. We call this nonplanarity *intrinsic nonlinearity* because, as discussed in Chapter 2, it does not depend on the parametrization chosen for the expectation function, but only on the design and the expression for the expectation function. The projections of the acceleration vectors in the tangent plane necessarily depend on the parametrization, and measure the nonuniformity of the parameter lines on the tangent plane. This nonuniformity is called *parameter effects nonlinearity* or, more simply, *parameter effects*.

Because the elements in the array $\ddot{A}$ provide information on the parameter effects and intrinsic nonlinearities, we write the first P faces of $\ddot{A}$ as A^{θ}, to denote the parameter effects acceleration array, and the last P' faces as A^{ι}, to denote the intrinsic acceleration array.

Example: Rumford 8

In Figure 7.2a we show the expectation surface (curve) $\eta(\theta)$ for the Rumford model with the design $x = (4, 41)^T$ and the parametrization

$$f = 60 + 70\, e^{-x\theta}$$

The marks on the expectation curve correspond to

$$\theta = 0.01, 0.02, \ldots, 0.08, 0.1, 0.2, \ldots, 0.9, 1.0$$

and as pointed out in Chapter 2, equally spaced values of θ map to unequally spaced values on η. This is a manifestation of the parameter effects nonlinearity, while the curving of the line is a manifestation of intrinsic nonlinearity.

In Figure 7.2b we show the expectation surface $\eta(\phi)$ for the Rumford model with the same design and the reparametrization $\phi = \log_{10}\theta$,

$$f = 60 + 70 \exp(-x\, 10^{\phi})$$

The marks on the expectation curve correspond to the values

$$\phi = -2.0, -1.9, -1.8, \ldots, -0.1, 0$$

so that the same range of θ is covered. Note that the expectation curves are identical, and that the only change is a relabeling of the points on the curve. It is because the curve does not change with the parametrization that we call the nonlinearity *intrinsic*. Note, too, that points which are equally spaced in the ϕ space still map to unequally spaced points on the expecta-

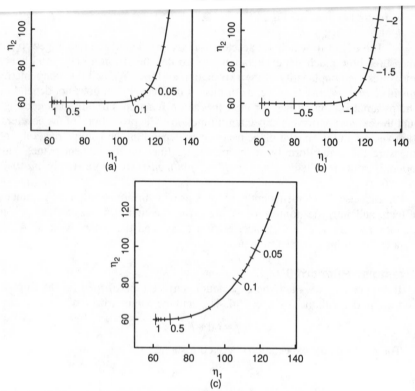

Figure 7.2 Plot of the expectation surface (curve) for the 2-case Rumford example. In part *a*, the design is $(4,41)^T$ and the parameter is the original parameter θ. In part *b*, the same design is used but the parameter is $\phi = \log_{10}\theta$. In part *c*, the original parameter θ is used, but the design is changed to $(4,12)^T$.

tion curve, but the nonuniformity in the spacing on η is not as severe as it was for the θ parametrization. The ϕ parametrization is therefore said to have smaller parameter effects nonlinearity.

In Figure 7.2*c* we show the expectation surface $\eta(\theta)$ for the Rumford model with the θ parametrization and the design $\mathbf{x} = (4, 12)^T$. The main feature to notice is that the expectation surface is different from that in Figure 7.2*a* and *b* because the design has been changed. ∎

Reparametrizing a model not only affects the mapping of the parameter lines to the expectation surface but also the tangent and acceleration vectors, and consequently the parameter effects nonlinearity.

Example: Rumford 9

Shown in Figure 7.3 are the expectation surface and the acceleration and the tangent vectors at a point on the surface. As in Example Puromycin 22, we have scaled the parameters and the design variable to provide a clearer figure. The design variable is scaled by 0.1, and the parameter θ by 10. In this scaling, the point is $\theta = 1.0$ ($\phi = 0.0$) for the $(0.4, 4.1)^T$ design, corresponding to $\theta = 0.1$ ($\phi = -1.0$) for the $(4, 41)^T$ design in the original scaling.

Note that the tangent vectors are in the same direction, as they must be for them both to be tangent to the same curve. The *lengths* of the tangent vectors are very different, however, and the acceleration vectors are different not only in length, but also in orientation. Both these differences are due to the reparametrization, and so we see some of the effects of parameter nonlinearity. ■

7.1.2   The Acceleration in an Arbitrary Direction

The velocity and acceleration vectors only provide information about the expectation surface corresponding to changes along the parameter axes in the parameter space. To measure the velocity and acceleration near $\hat{\theta}$ in an arbitrary direction $\mathbf{u}$ in the parameter space, we introduce a distance parameter b and let

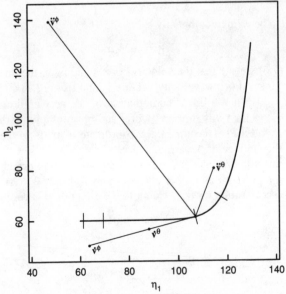

Figure 7.3   Scaled velocity and acceleration vectors at $\theta = 1$ for the 2-case Rumford example using the parameter θ and the parameter $\phi = \log_{10}\theta$.

tote which is less than τ_{max}, so we impose a condition on the maximum number of values k_{max} to be calculated on either side of $\hat{\theta}_p$, say $k_{max} = 30$. A nominal step size of $se(\hat{\theta}_p)/step$ with $step = 8$ is used to start the process, but thereafter the step size is determined from the slope of the curve τ versus t, with limits to prevent the step size from becoming too large.

Pseudocode for the calculation is:

```
for p = 1, . . . , P {
    Δ = -se(θ̂_p)/step
    t = 0
    repeat {
        invslope = 1
        for k = 1, . . . , k_max {
            t = t + invslope
            minimize S(θ) with θ_p = θ̂_p + Δ × t obtaining S̃(θ_p) and θ̃_-p
            invslope = abs [ τ × s²  /  se × zᵀv_p ]
            record τ(θ_p) = sign(Δ) × √S̃ - Ŝ / s, θ, and invslope
            invslope = min(4, max(invslope, 1/16))
            if (abs(τ) > τ_max) break loop
        }
        Δ = -Δ
        if (Δ < 0) break loop
    }
}
```

Minimizing $S(\boldsymbol{\theta})$ with $\theta_p = \hat{\theta}_p + \Delta \times k$ is done with a few simple modifications to the Gauss–Newton code. In addition to evaluating the residuals and derivatives we remove the pth column of the derivatives, then solve for the increment $\boldsymbol{\delta}_{-p}$ and form $\boldsymbol{\delta}$ from $\boldsymbol{\delta}_{-p}$ with zero in the pth position. Note that $\tilde{\boldsymbol{\theta}}_{-p}$ is used as the starting value for the next iteration.

A3.5.2 Profile Pair Plots

In producing the profile pair plots, we first generate a vector of τ values, $\boldsymbol{\tau}_p, p = 1, \dots, P$, of length n_p for each parameter, and the corresponding $n_p \times P$ matrix $\mathbf{M}_p$ of parameter values. Each of these matrices is transformed to the τ scale in the following steps:

```
for p = 1, 2, . . . , P {
    store s_{θ→τ,p}, the interpolating spline for the pth
        column of M_p as a function of τ_p.
    store s_{τ→θ,p}, the interpolating spline for τ_p
        as a function of the pth column of M_p
    for q = 1, 2, . . . , P and q ≠ p {
        g_pq = s_{θ→τ,p}(pth column of M_q)
```

To interpolate the projection of the contours $S(\theta) = S^i$, $i = 1, \ldots, m$, into the (θ_p, θ_q) plane, we convert the levels to the τ scale as

$$k^i = \sqrt{S^i - S(\hat{\theta})}\,/s$$

and determine the angles for the points on the traces as described in Appendix 6. These four angle pairs are

$$\mathbf{p}_1 = (0, s_{t \to g, pq}(+k^i))$$

$$\mathbf{p}_2 = (\pi, s_{t \to g, pq}(-k^i))$$

$$\mathbf{p}_3 = (s_{t \to g, qp}(+k^i), 0)$$

$$\mathbf{p}_4 = (s_{t \to g, qp}(-k^i), \pi)$$

We convert these angles to an average angle and a phase difference by

```
for j = 1, . . . ,4{
    a_j = ({p_j}_1 + {p_j}_2)/2
    d_j = {p_j}_1 - {p_j}_2
    if (d_j < 0) {
        replace d_j by -d_j
        replace a_j by -a_j
    }
}
```

and for d_j as a function of a_j, determine $sp_{a \to d, pqi}$, an interpolating spline with period 2π. A sequence of K points (usually K is between 50 and 100) on the interpolating contour is evaluated using

```
for k = 1, . . . ,K {
    a = (k - 1) × 2π/(K - 1) - π
    d = sp_{a→d,pqi}(a)
    τ_p = cos(a + d/2)
    τ_q = cos(a - d/2)
    θ_p = s_{τ→θ,p}(τ_p)
    θ_q = s_{τ→θ,q}(τ_q)
}
```

and plotted.

APPENDIX 4.

Data Sets Used in Problems

A4.1 BOD Data Set 2

Data on biochemical oxygen demand (BOD) were obtained by Marske (1967) as described in Appendix 1, Section A1.3. A second set of data is reported in Table A4.1.

A model was derived based on exponential decay with a fixed rate constant as

$$f(x, \boldsymbol{\theta}) = \theta_1 (1 - e^{\theta_2 x})$$

where f is predicted biochemical oxygen demand and x is time.

Table A4.1 Biochemical oxygen demand versus time.

Time (days)	Biochemical Oxygen Demand (mg/l)	Time (days)	Biochemical Oxygen Demand (mg/l)
1	0.47	5	1.60
2	0.74	7	1.84
3	1.17	9	2.19
4	1.42	11	2.17

........ation ~5×10⁻¹⁰ in the presence of different concentrations of NIF, which are given in Table A4.2 as $x = \log_{10}$(NIF concentration), except for the rows with (0), for which the actual concentration was 0. The NIF has greater binding ability and so displaces the NTD. Counts on radioactive material were obtained to determine how much material was bound under different conditions. When the NIF concentration is 0, all of the radioactive NTD is bound to the sites, and so a large count is recorded: as the NIF concentration increases, it displaces NTD and so lower counts are recorded. Although the nominal NTD concentration was 5×10^{-10}, the actual concentrations were 4.76, 5.11, 4.78, and 5.02×10^{-10} respectively, for the four tissue samples.

The proposed model is

$$f(x, \boldsymbol{\theta}) = \theta_1 + \frac{\theta_2}{1 + \exp[-\theta_4(x - \theta_3)]}$$

where f is the predicted total count and x is $\log_{10}$(NIF concentration).

A4.3   Saccharin Data Set 2

Data on the concentration of saccharin in plasma were reported in Renwick (1982) and are reproduced in Table A4.3.

A4.4   Steady State Adsorption

Data on the disappearance of o-xylene as a function of oxygen concentration, inlet o-xylene concentration, and temperature, were obtained by Juusola (1971) and were further analyzed by Pritchard (1972). The data are reproduced in Table A4.4.

The postulated model is a steady state adsorption model written

$$f(\mathbf{x}, \boldsymbol{\theta}) = \frac{f_1 f_2}{f_1 + 2.2788 f_2}$$

$$f_1 = \theta_1 x_1 e^{-\theta_3/x_3}$$

$$f_2 = \theta_2 x_2 e^{-\theta_4/x_3}$$

Table A4.6 Relative concentrations of products versus time for thermal isomerization of α-pinene at 204.5°C.

Time (min)	α-Pinene (%)	Dipentene (%)	Alloocimene (%)	Pyronene (%)	Dimer (%)
440	85.9	8.2	4.1	0.4	0.6
825	74.3	15.6	6.8	0.8	1.6
1200	65.1	21.5	7.7	1.0	3.4
1500	58.6	25.5	8.4	1.2	5.0
2040	48.1	31.9	8.5	1.6	8.2
3060	32.1	42.0	8.2	2.0	13.5
6060	11.2	54.7	6.9	2.7	21.9
16020		61.3	5.0	3.0	27.8

A4.7 Coal Liquefaction

Data on coal liquefaction were analyzed in Lythgoe (1986). The reaction conditions and inlet (x) and outlet (y) data are presented in Tables A4.7a, b, and c. The model formulated by Lythgoe can be represented as

$$y_1 = x_1 + \theta_1 x_8 - \phi_1 t$$

$$y_2 = x_2 + \theta_2 x_8 + \alpha_2 \phi_1 t - \phi_2 t$$

$$y_3 = x_3 + \theta_3 x_8 + \beta_3 \phi_2 t$$

$$y_4 = x_4 + \theta_4 x_8 + \beta_4 \phi_2 t$$

$$y_5 = x_5 + \theta_5 x_8 + \beta_5 \phi_2 t$$

$$y_6 = x_6 + \theta_6 x_8 + \beta_6 \phi_2 t$$

$$y_7 = x_7 + \theta_7 x_8 + \alpha_7 \phi_1 t + \beta_7 \phi_2 t$$

where

$$\phi_1 = \gamma_1 P [1 + (F/100)] e^{-\gamma_2/T}$$

$$\phi_2 = \gamma_3 [1 + (F/100)] T R_{feed} \, e^{-\gamma_4/T}$$

Table A4.7a   Reaction conditions for autoclave runs.

Run No.	Time (min)	Temp (K)	Pressure (MPa)	Fe_2O_3 (wt% maf)[a]	TR_{feed} (wt% maf)[a]
52	25	713.7	16.028	2.608	66.341
53	25	713.7	16.304	2.609	66.340
54	25	713.7	16.166	2.611	66.341
55	25	713.7	16.166	2.607	66.339
56	25	713.7	13.960	2.597	66.358
57	25	713.7	13.822	2.607	66.373
58	25	705.4	13.684	2.611	66.395
59	40	705.4	13.546	2.612	66.380
60	25	705.4	13.063	2.640	85.878
61	25	705.4	13.063	2.639	77.927
64	25	705.4	13.684	2.609	83.915
65	25	705.4	16.235	2.511	56.633
77	25	705.4	13.684	2.593	66.358
78	70	697.0	13.270	2.589	66.359
79	90	688.7	13.270	2.599	66.346
80	70	697.0	13.339	2.599	66.351
81	25	697.0	13.339	2.597	66.358
82	55	697.0	12.926	2.599	66.351
86	55	697.0	15.270	1.688	48.740
91	55	697.0	18.717	0.000	46.306
92	55	697.0	17.338	1.723	46.440
94	55	697.0	14.442	1.650	24.786
95	55	697.0	17.338	2.611	66.332

[a] wt% maf is $100 \times$ (mass of material/mass of moisture-ash-free coal).

Table A4.7b   Inlet compositions for autoclave runs (weight %).

Run No.	Unconv. Coal x_1	Thermal Resid. x_2	C_4–822K Dist. x_3	C_1–C_3 Gases x_4	Byproduct Gases x_5	Water x_6	Hydrogen x_7	Coal In x_8
52	0.015	22.308	41.013	0.180	0.008	0.820	2.029	33.627
53	0.015	22.306	41.009	0.180	0.007	0.820	2.040	33.623
54	0.015	22.316	41.027	0.184	0.016	0.820	1.984	33.638
55	0.015	22.308	41.013	0.180	0.008	0.820	2.030	33.627
56	0.015	22.384	41.133	0.180	0.009	0.821	1.726	33.731
57	0.015	22.381	41.130	0.180	0.008	0.822	1.746	33.719
58	0.015	22.390	41.134	0.180	0.007	0.823	1.730	33.722
59	0.015	22.388	41.142	0.180	0.007	0.823	1.717	33.728
60	0.015	28.726	35.106	0.181	0.009	0.819	1.694	33.450
61	0.015	26.043	37.783	0.185	0.017	0.818	1.719	33.419
64	0.012	23.684	45.926	0.151	0.006	0.688	1.310	28.223
65	0.014	18.764	43.472	0.173	0.011	2.812	1.622	33.132
77	0.015	22.423	41.217	0.000	0.000	0.822	1.733	33.790
78	0.015	22.388	41.147	0.184	0.019	0.820	1.689	33.738
79	0.015	22.389	41.166	0.179	0.007	0.822	1.676	33.747
80	0.015	22.416	41.207	0.000	0.000	0.823	1.757	33.783
81	0.015	22.418	41.209	0.000	0.000	0.822	1.753	33.783
82	0.015	22.387	41.154	0.180	0.009	0.822	1.693	33.740
86	0.000	17.879	41.423	0.000	0.000	2.137	1.880	36.682
91	0.000	16.896	39.141	0.000	0.000	4.805	2.670	36.489
92	0.000	16.879	39.110	0.000	0.000	4.998	2.669	36.345
94	0.000	9.017	51.088	0.000	0.000	1.570	1.946	36.380
95	0.018	20.634	37.928	0.000	0.000	7.618	2.696	31.106

Table A4.7c Outlet compositions for autoclave runs (weight %).

Run No.	Unconv. Coal y_1	Thermal Resid. y_2	C_4–822K Dist. y_3	C_1–C_3 Gases y_4	Byproduct Gases y_5	Water y_6	Hydrogen y_7
52	1.702	35.197	53.884	1.729	1.985	4.010	1.491
53	1.777	34.870	54.317	1.715	1.830	4.020	1.470
54	1.390	36.224	52.909	1.902	2.063	4.027	1.485
55	1.674	36.295	52.692	1.842	2.006	4.017	1.474
56	2.392	35.439	52.698	2.046	2.146	3.986	1.294
57	1.909	34.650	53.758	1.972	2.067	4.401	1.242
58	2.694	36.093	53.323	1.442	1.935	3.234	1.279
59	1.843	33.549	55.452	1.816	2.041	4.151	1.148
60	2.998	42.572	46.972	1.404	1.620	3.199	1.235
61	2.793	40.889	48.832	1.461	1.744	3.051	1.229
64	2.103	34.867	56.440	1.182	1.619	2.759	1.030
65	2.455	36.858	48.818	1.567	3.015	5.909	1.380
77	2.276	38.326	50.961	1.424	1.797	3.870	1.346
78	1.500	36.885	52.210	2.225	2.099	3.990	1.091
79	1.699	35.716	53.325	1.854	2.289	4.032	1.084
80	1.679	36.764	52.093	2.017	2.183	4.085	1.178
81	3.138	38.821	50.516	0.927	1.710	3.532	1.356
82	1.615	36.610	52.378	1.744	2.137	4.403	1.113
86	2.177	39.042	46.474	1.904	3.339	5.737	1.327
91	4.423	35.829	44.133	1.989	3.558	7.811	2.258
92	1.672	35.249	47.062	1.882	3.356	8.813	1.967
94	2.347	29.585	55.937	1.832	3.231	5.660	1.410
95	1.226	31.952	50.266	1.856	2.203	10.507	1.989

subject to the conditions

$$\theta_1 + \cdots + \theta_7 = 1$$

$$\alpha_2 + \alpha_7 = 1$$

$$\beta_3 + \cdots + \beta_7 = 1$$

In the model, the reaction condition variables are time, t; temperature, T; pressure, P; Fe_2O_3 concentration in the inlet feed, F; and thermal residual in the inlet feed, TR_{feed}. The inlet and outlet compositions are unconverted coal, (x_1, y_1); thermal residual, (x_2, y_2); C_4–822K distillate, (x_3, y_3); C_1–C_3 gases, (x_4, y_4); byproduct gases, (x_5, y_5); water, (x_6, y_6); hydrogen, (x_7, y_7); and coal in, x_8. Note that hydrogen is consumed and so the parameters θ_7, α_7, and β_7 are negative.

A4.8 Haloperidol

Data on plasma concentrations of Haloperidol were reported in Wagner (1975, pp. 60–63) and are reproduced in Table A4.8.

Table A4.8 Haloperidol concentration versus time.

Time (hr)	Haloperidol Conc. (ng/ml)	Time (hr)	Haloperidol Conc. (ng/ml)
0.17	2.99	4.00	0.945
0.33	4.82	6.00	0.679
0.67	2.86	8.00	0.619
1.00	2.23	12.00	0.462
1.50	1.65	24.00	0.336
2.00	1.33	48.00	0.178
3.00	1.05	72.00	0.084

From "Use of Computers in Pharmacokinetics," by J.G. Wagner, in *Journal of Clinical Pharmacology and Therapeutics*, 1967, **8**, 201. Reprinted with permission of the publisher.

APPENDIX 5.

Evaluating Matrix Exponentials and Convolutions

In Sections 5.1 and 5.2 we showed how to obtain response functions for systems of linear differential equations and how to find derivatives of the response functions with respect to the parameters. In this appendix, we present efficient methods for evaluating the functions, given a parameter vector θ, and N cases at observation times $t_1, t_2, \ldots, t_N$.

Expressions for the model function and derivatives of a compartment model have been given in terms of the matrix e^{At} and convolutions with this matrix. In practice, it is recommended (Moler and Van Loan, 1978) that the eigenvalues and eigenvectors of A be used when evaluating e^{At} at a number of different t values. It may seem computationally intensive to determine the eigenvalues of A for each value of θ at which γ is to be evaluated, but this is not so, because the dimension K of A is usually small and A is usually sparse. This sparsity can be exploited to isolate some eigenvalues without the need for iterative calculations, as in Example Tetracycline 2, where the eigenvalues are already isolated on the diagonal of A. Routines such as BALANC from EISPACK (Smith et al., 1976) isolate such eigenvalues by means of row and column interchanges, when possible.

The methods for computing the matrix exponential and the convolutions depend on whether A can be diagonalized and whether all the eigenvalues are real. A matrix A can be diagonalized if there is an invertible matrix U such that

$$A = U\Lambda U^{-1}$$

with Λ diagonal. The elements on the diagonal of Λ are the eigenvalues and the columns of U are the (right) eigenvectors of A. Diagonalization is not always possible; for instance, if we set $\theta_1 = \theta_2$ in Example Tetracycline 2, then there is no invertible matrix U which will diagonalize A. Because of roundoff in calculations, however, an eigenvector routine will usually return a matrix U, even for nondiagonalizable matrices, but U will be badly conditioned. The condition of the returned U can be checked using routines from LINPACK (Dongarra et al., 1979) to determine if A is diagonalizable. Alternatively, the modification suggested in Moler and Van Loan (1978) for the EISPACK routines ORTHES, ORTRAN, and HQR2 (Smith et al., 1976) can be used to compute the QR decomposition of U directly and the condition of R evaluated using LINPACK routines.

In Section A5.1 we present methods for when A is diagonalizable, in Section A5.2 for when A is nondiagonalizable, and in Section A5.3 for when A has complex eigenvalues.

A5.1   Diagonalizable A

When A can be diagonalized by a well-conditioned matrix U, calculations of the matrix exponential and matrix convolutions can be transformed into scalar calculations, because all power series expressions will have internal products $U^{-1}U$ which cancel and the powers of Λ will be diagonal with the appropriate power of the λ_i on the diagonal. Thus,

$$A^k = (U\Lambda U^{-1}) \cdots (U\Lambda U^{-1})(U\Lambda U^{-1}) = U\Lambda^k U^{-1} \qquad (A5.1)$$

and so (5.6) becomes

$$e^{At} = Ue^{\Lambda t}U^{-1}$$

where $e^{\Lambda t}$ is diagonal with entries $e^{\lambda_i t}$ on the diagonal.

Because there will be factors U and U^{-1} in many of the expressions we need, it is convenient to take a linear transformation of coordinates for γ and write

$$\xi(t) = U^{-1}\gamma(t)$$

$$\xi_0 = U^{-1}\gamma_0$$

$$\kappa = U^{-1}\iota$$

Similarly, for the derivatives we write

$$\xi_{(p)}(t) = U^{-1}\gamma_{(p)}(t)$$

$$\kappa_{(p)} = U^{-1}\iota_{(p)}$$

$$C_{(p)} = U^{-1}A_{(p)}U$$

(The notation $\xi_{(p)}$ and $\kappa_{(p)}$ is convenient, but not strictly correct, since, for example, $\xi_{(p)}$ is not the partial derivative of $U^{-1}\gamma(t)$ with respect to θ_p.)

Substituting $A = U\Lambda U^{-1}$ into (5.11) and (5.13) and premultiplying both sides of the equations by U^{-1} gives

$$\xi(t) = e^{\Lambda t}\xi_0 + (e^{\Lambda t} * I)\kappa$$

and

$$\xi_{(p)}(t) = e^{\Lambda t}\xi_{(p)}(0) + (e^{\Lambda t} * C_{(p)}e^{\Lambda t})\xi_0 + (e^{\Lambda t} * I)\kappa_{(p)} + (e^{\Lambda t} * C_{(p)}e^{\Lambda t} * I)\kappa$$

where $e^{\Lambda t}$ is evaluated as above. The matrix $e^{\Lambda t} * I$ is also a diagonal matrix with diagonal elements

$$\{e^{\mathbf{A}t} * \mathbf{I}\}_{ii} = e^{\lambda_i t} * 1$$

$$= \begin{cases} \dfrac{e^{\lambda_i t} - 1}{\lambda_i} & \lambda_i \neq 0 \\[2ex] t & \lambda_i = 0 \end{cases}$$

Since the matrices $e^{\mathbf{A}t} * \mathbf{C}_{(p)} e^{\mathbf{A}t}$ and $e^{\mathbf{A}t} * \mathbf{C}_{(p)} e^{\mathbf{A}t} * \mathbf{I}$ are not diagonal, we must evaluate each element. But these elements can be expressed in terms of scalar convolutions as

$$\{e^{\mathbf{A}t} * \mathbf{C}_{(p)} e^{\mathbf{A}t}\}_{ij} = \{\mathbf{C}_{(p)}\}_{ij} \, e^{\lambda_i t} * e^{\lambda_j t}$$

and

$$\{e^{\mathbf{A}t} * \mathbf{C}_{(p)} e^{\mathbf{A}t} * \mathbf{I}\}_{ij} = \{\mathbf{C}_{(p)}\}_{ij} \, e^{\lambda_i t} * e^{\lambda_j t} * 1$$

To evaluate the scalar convolutions we use the fact that $f * g = g * f$ to arrange that $\lambda_i \leq \lambda_j$. We also note from the form of $\mathbf{A}$ that $\lambda_i \leq 0$ and $\lambda_j \leq 0$. Then

$$e^{\lambda_i t} * e^{\lambda_j t} = e^{\lambda_j t}(e^{(\lambda_i t - \lambda_j t)} * 1) = \begin{cases} \dfrac{e^{\lambda_i t} - e^{\lambda_j t}}{\lambda_i - \lambda_j} & \lambda_i < \lambda_j \\[2ex] t e^{\lambda_i t} & \lambda_i = \lambda_j \end{cases}$$

and

$$e^{\lambda_i t} * e^{\lambda_j t} * 1 = \begin{cases} 1 * 1 * 1 & \lambda_i = \lambda_j = 0 \\[1.5ex] e^{\lambda_i t} * 1 * 1 & \lambda_i < \lambda_j = 0 \\[1.5ex] e^{\lambda_i t}(e^{-\lambda_i t} * 1 * 1) & \lambda_i = \lambda_j < 0 \\[1.5ex] e^{\lambda_i t} * \dfrac{e^{\lambda_j t} - 1}{\lambda_j} & \lambda_i < \lambda_j < 0 \end{cases}$$

$$= \begin{cases} \dfrac{t^2}{2} & \lambda_i = \lambda_j = 0 \\[2ex] \dfrac{e^{\lambda_i t} - (1 + \lambda_i t)}{\lambda_i^2} & \lambda_i < \lambda_j = 0 \\[2ex] \dfrac{1 - e^{\lambda_i t}(1 - \lambda_i t)}{\lambda_i^2} & \lambda_i = \lambda_j < 0 \\[2ex] \dfrac{1}{\lambda_i \lambda_j}\left[1 + \dfrac{\lambda_j e^{\lambda_i t} - \lambda_i e^{\lambda_j t}}{\lambda_i - \lambda_j}\right] & \lambda_i < \lambda_j < 0 \end{cases}$$

In practice, the condition $\lambda_i = \lambda_j$ is determined by comparing $|(\lambda_i - \lambda_j)t_{max}|$ with the relative machine precision, where t_{max} is the maximum value of t for which the system is to be evaluated. If this difference is less than the relative machine precision, then the form for equality is used.

A5.2 Nondiagonalizable A

When **A** cannot be diagonalized, a method given by Bavely and Stewart (1979) is used to reduce **A** to block-diagonal form as

$$A = UBU^{-1}$$

where **B** is formed from r triangular blocks $\mathbf{B}_i$ of size K_i, $i = 1, \ldots, r$, on the diagonal, and in each block the diagonal elements are almost equal. We express each $\mathbf{B}_i$ as

$$\mathbf{B}_i = d_i\mathbf{I} + \mathbf{E}_i$$

where d_i is the average of the diagonal elements of $\mathbf{B}_i$, **I** is the identity matrix of size K_i, and $\mathbf{E}_i$ is the remainder. Since $\mathbf{E}_i$ is triangular with small entries on the diagonal, the K_ith power of $\mathbf{E}_i$ will be approximately zero.

These blocks are gathered into $K \times K$ matrices **D** and **E** to give

$$B = D + E$$

where **D** is blockwise a multiple of the identity matrix, and

$$E^J \approx 0$$

where J is the maximum of the K_i, $i = 1, \ldots, r$. Since **D** is blockwise a multiple of the identity matrix, it commutes with **E**; then

$$DE = ED$$

and so

$$e^{\mathbf{B}t} = e^{(\mathbf{D}+\mathbf{E})t} = e^{\mathbf{D}t}e^{\mathbf{E}t} = e^{\mathbf{E}t}e^{\mathbf{D}t}$$

(It is not generally true for matrices that the exponential of a sum is the product of the exponentials.)

Since **D** is diagonal, $e^{\mathbf{D}t}$ is also diagonal with diagonal elements of the form $e^{d_i t}$ along the ith block. The other term is evaluated by

$$e^{\mathbf{E}t} = \mathbf{I} + \mathbf{E}t + \frac{\mathbf{E}^2 t^2}{2!} + \cdots + \frac{\mathbf{E}^J t^J}{J!}$$

and the convolutions can be evaluated for each term in the series. For example,

$$e^{\mathbf{B}t} * \mathbf{I} = e^{\mathbf{D}t}(\mathbf{I} + \mathbf{E}t + \frac{\mathbf{E}^2 t^2}{2!} + \cdots + \frac{\mathbf{E}^J t^J}{J!}) * \mathbf{I}$$

$$= e^{\mathbf{D}t} * \mathbf{I} + \mathbf{E}t\, e^{\mathbf{D}t} * \mathbf{I} + \cdots + \frac{\mathbf{E}^J t^J e^{\mathbf{D}t} * \mathbf{I}}{J!}$$

The basic scalar convolution

$$t^k e^{-at} * 1 = \frac{k![1 - e^{-at}(1 + at + \cdots + a^k t^k / k!)]}{a^k}$$

is used to evaluate this matrix convolution with similar expressions for the other matrix convolutions such as

$$e^{\mathbf{B}t} * \mathbf{C}_{(p)} e^{\mathbf{B}t} * \mathbf{I}$$

A5.3   Complex Eigenvalues

In most simple compartment models, the eigenvalues will be real and the methods of the previous sections can be used. In fact, all the eigenvalues must be real whenever the greatest length of a cycle in the model is less than 3, where a cycle is a chain of distinct compartments in which there is transfer of material from the first to the second and so on until the last one, which transfers back to the first. The mammillary and catenary models described in Section 5.4 only have cycles of length 2.

A cycle of length 3 can be easily generated, for example, as in Figure A5.1, and this system could have complex eigenvalues. Complex eigenvalues and their corresponding eigenvectors always occur in conjugate pairs, so the values of the model function and its derivatives are real and can be calculated without having to resort to complex arithmetic. The basic method with real arithmetic is first to reduce **A** to a quasitriangular matrix and then to a quasidiagonal matrix. The quasitriangular matrix is triangular except for disjoint blocks of order 2 on the diagonal, where each block corresponds to a pair of complex conjugate eigenvalues. This reduction is accomplished using the QR method with implicit shifts as implemented in the subroutine HQR2 from EISPACK (Smith et al.,

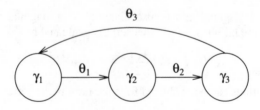

Figure A5.1   Cycle of length 3.

1976) or HQR3 (Stewart, 1976) and results in an orthogonal matrix $\mathbf{Q}$ such that

$$\mathbf{C} = \mathbf{Q}^T \mathbf{A} \mathbf{Q}$$

is quasitriangular. Any 2×2 block on the diagonal of $\mathbf{C}$ is of the form

$$\begin{bmatrix} a & b \\ c & d \end{bmatrix}$$

with $(a - d)^2 + 4bc < 0$.

When the quasitriangular matrix $\mathbf{C}$ is produced, an attempt can be made to produce a quasidiagonal form using the method in Bavely and Stewart (1979) based on the subroutine SHRSLV (Bartels and Stewart, 1972). That is, a matrix $\mathbf{R}$ is calculated such that

$$\mathbf{D} = \mathbf{R}^{-1} \mathbf{C} \mathbf{R}$$

is diagonal except for 2×2 blocks on the diagonal corresponding to each complex conjugate pair. The matrix $\mathbf{R}$ is upper triangular with ones on the diagonal, and the blocks on the diagonal of $\mathbf{D}$ are the same as the corresponding blocks of $\mathbf{C}$. If all the eigenvalues are real, the matrices $\mathbf{Q}$ and $\mathbf{R}$ produced in this manner are the QR decomposition of a matrix of eigenvectors of $\mathbf{A}$.

If the matrix $\mathbf{A}$ has complex eigenvalues and is also nondiagonalizable, the matrix $\mathbf{R}$ cannot be calculated (or, in practice, will be very badly conditioned). In this case, the methods of this section must be combined with those of Section A5.2. Fortunately, nondiagonalizable matrices with complex eigenvalues occur very rarely, and so we do not give the explicit forms, as they are very complicated.

Assuming that a well-conditioned $\mathbf{R}$ can be calculated so

$$\mathbf{A} = \mathbf{Q} \mathbf{R} \mathbf{D} \mathbf{R}^{-1} \mathbf{Q}^T$$

we form

$$\boldsymbol{\xi}(t) = \mathbf{R}^{-1} \mathbf{Q}^T \boldsymbol{\gamma}(t)$$

$$\boldsymbol{\xi}_0 = \mathbf{R}^{-1} \mathbf{Q}^T \boldsymbol{\gamma}_0$$

$$\boldsymbol{\kappa} = \mathbf{R}^{-1} \mathbf{Q}^T \boldsymbol{\iota}$$

$$\boldsymbol{\xi}_{(p)}(t) = \mathbf{R}^{-1} \mathbf{Q}^T \boldsymbol{\gamma}_{(p)}(t)$$

$$\boldsymbol{\kappa}_{(p)} = \mathbf{R}^{-1} \mathbf{Q}^T \boldsymbol{\iota}_{(p)}$$

and

$$\mathbf{C}_{(p)} = \mathbf{R}^{-1} \mathbf{Q}^T \mathbf{A}_{(p)} \mathbf{Q} \mathbf{R}$$

as in Section A5.1. Evaluation of the model function and derivatives is then reduced to evaluating $e^{\mathbf{D}t}$ and convolutions such as $e^{\mathbf{D}t} * \mathbf{I}$ and $e^{\mathbf{D}t} * \mathbf{C}_{(p)} e^{\mathbf{D}t}$.

Both $e^{\mathbf{D}t}$ and $(e^{\mathbf{D}t} * \mathbf{I})$ are quasidiagonal with 2×2 blocks in the same positions as $\mathbf{D}$, so we only need to consider what the results for each 2×2 block are, as 1×1 diagonal blocks were considered in Section A5.2. Each 2×2 block will have the form

$$\mathbf{D}_i = \begin{bmatrix} a & b \\ c & d \end{bmatrix}$$

with $(a - d)^2 + 4bc < 0$. We calculate the quantities

$$\zeta = \frac{a + d}{2}$$

$$\delta = \frac{a - d}{2}$$

$$\rho = \sqrt{-\delta^2 - bc}$$

and the matrix

$$\mathbf{F}_i = \begin{bmatrix} \dfrac{\delta}{\rho} & \dfrac{b}{\rho} \\ \dfrac{c}{\rho} & \dfrac{-\delta}{\rho} \end{bmatrix}$$

to give

$$e^{\mathbf{D}_i t} = e^{\zeta t}[(\cos \rho t)\mathbf{I} + (\sin \rho t)\mathbf{F}_i]$$

and

$$e^{\mathbf{D}_i t} * \mathbf{I} = \mu\{[\cos \phi - e^{\zeta t}\cos(\rho t + \phi)]\mathbf{I} + [\sin \phi - e^{\zeta t}\sin(\rho t + \phi)]\mathbf{F}_i\}$$

where

$$\mu = (\zeta^2 + \rho^2)^{-1/2}$$

and

$$\phi = \tan^{-1}(-\rho/\zeta)$$

The phase angle ϕ is always in the first quadrant because ζ will be negative for a compartment model. That is, $0 < \phi \leq \pi/2$.

APPENDIX 6.

Interpolating Profile Pair Contours

To interpolate the (p,q) projection of a likelihood contour from points on the profile traces, we first transform from θ_p, θ_q to τ_p, τ_q coordinates using cubic splines. This transforms the likelihood surface so that, in the τ coordinates, the surface is nearly a paraboloid with elliptical contours, and it is easy to interpolate points on these near-ellipses.

Example: Puromycin 28

The profile traces for the Puromycin parameters, shown in Figure 6.7, are plotted in the τ coordinates in Figure A6.1, from which it can be seen that

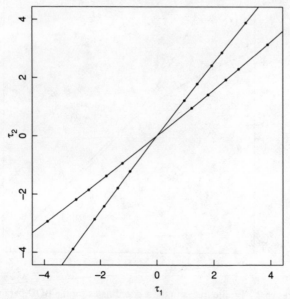

Figure A6.1   Profile traces in the τ coordinates for the Puromycin parameters.

323

the profile traces are very nearly straight lines through the origin. Because
the traces are straight, the contours will be nearly elliptical, and so the the
likelihood surface is quite parabolic in these coordinates. The contours in
the θ coordinates will also be quite elliptical, because the profile t plots
(Figure 6.4) are quite straight. This implies that the likelihood surface in
the θ coordinates is also quite parabolic.   ■

Example: BOD 17

The profile traces for the BOD parameters, shown in Figure 6.8, are plotted
in the τ coordinates in Figure A6.2. The profile traces for the BOD parameters are curved and tend to a common asymptote in the lower right quadrant. For this example, the likelihood surface is not close to being an elliptical paraboloid, even in the τ coordinates, and therefore we should not
expect to produce very accurate contour interpolations.   ■

To interpolate a particular contour, we scale the τ coordinates by dividing
by $\sqrt{P\, F(P, N - P; \alpha)}$ so that a nominal $1 - \alpha$ joint likelihood contour in the scaled
τ coordinates is bounded by the square $-1 \le \tau_p$, $\tau_q \le 1$.

If the contour were a ellipse, it could be represented in the scaled coordinates in the parametric form

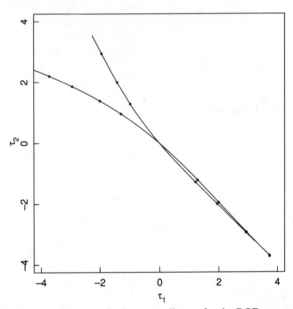

Figure A6.2   Profile traces in the τ coordinates for the BOD parameters.

$$\tau_p = \cos(a + d/2)$$
$$\tau_q = \cos(a - d/2)$$
$$(A6.1)$$

where the angle a goes from $-\pi$ to π and the phase d is a constant. When the contour is not elliptical, the phase angle will vary. Therefore, to interpolate a contour given a set of points $(\tau_{p,r}, \tau_{q,r})$, $r = 1, \ldots, 4$, we could calculate the arccosines $s_{p,r} = \arccos \tau_{p,r}$ and $s_{q,r} = \arccos \tau_{q,r}$, form the averages and differences, and interpolate the differences as a function of the average. Finally we could transform back to τ_p and τ_q using (A6.1).

Example: Puromycin 29

The scaled τ coordinates for the points on the nominal 95% contour for the Puromycin parameters, derived from the profile traces, are given in Table A6.1 together with the arccosines and the averages and differences of the arccosines. Since this contour is nearly elliptical, the phase d should be almost constant and the angle a should extend over the range $-\pi$ to π. However, from the table we see that the differences of the arccosines vary in sign and the averages of the arccosines all lie between 0 and π. ∎

Even for an ellipse, the differences of the arccosines will vary in sign and the averages of the arccosines will lie between 0 and π because the arccosine transformation only yields values in the range 0 to π. To obtain suitable values for a and d we note that, since $\cos(-x) = \cos x$, (A6.1) will yield the same τ_p and τ_q if the sign of the average *and* the sign of the difference is reversed. We therefore reverse the sign of any negative difference and its corresponding average to give a and d values suitable for interpolation with a periodic spline.

Example: Puromycin 30

The angle a and phase d for the points on the 95% contour for the Puromycin parameters are given in Table A6.1 and plotted in Figure A6.3a. Also shown is the interpolated phase, which is relatively constant, varying from

Table A6.1 Calculating the angle and phase for the Puromycin 95% contour.

Scaled		Arccosine				Angle	Phase
τ_1	τ_2	1	2	Avg.	Diff.	a	d
1.000	0.801	0.000	0.641	0.321	-0.641	-0.321	0.641
0.795	1.000	0.651	0.000	0.326	0.651	0.326	0.651
-1.000	-0.762	3.142	2.437	2.789	0.704	2.789	0.704
-0.769	-1.000	2.448	3.142	2.795	-0.693	-2.795	0.693

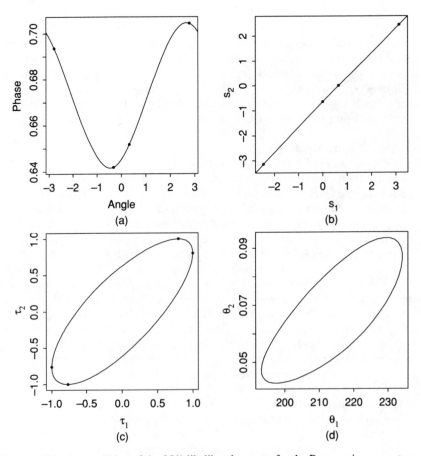

Figure A6.3   Interpolation of the 95% likelihood contour for the Puromycin parameters. The phases (•) corresponding to the points on the profile traces are shown in part a together with the interpolated curve, and the corresponding points (•) and interpolated values $a+d/2$ and $a-d/2$ are shown in part b. The points on the traces (•) and the interpolated contour are shown in the τ coordinates in part c, and in the θ coordinates in part d.

$0.64 < d < 0.71$. This implies that a plot of $a - d/2$ versus $a + d/2$ will be very close to a straight line, as demonstrated in Figure A6.3b. The relatively constant phase also implies that the contour is nearly elliptical in the (τ_1, τ_2) coordinates, as shown in Figure A6.3c. Finally, because the profile t plots for the Puromycin parameters are quite straight, the near ellipse in the τ coordinates maps to a nearly elliptical contour in the θ coordinates, as shown in Figure A6.3d.   ■

Example: BOD 18

In Figure A6.4a we plot the phase d versus the angle a for the 90% contour for the BOD parameters, together with the interpolated curve. For this example, the phase is more variable so that a plot of $a-d/2$ versus $a+d/2$ will not be very straight, as is demonstrated in Figure A6.4b. This also implies that the contour will not be an ellipse in the (τ_1,τ_2) coordinates, which is demonstrated in Figure A6.4c. Finally, because the profile t plots for the BOD parameters are badly curved, the elongated ellipse in the τ coordinates maps to a tapered curved contour in the θ coordinates, as shown in

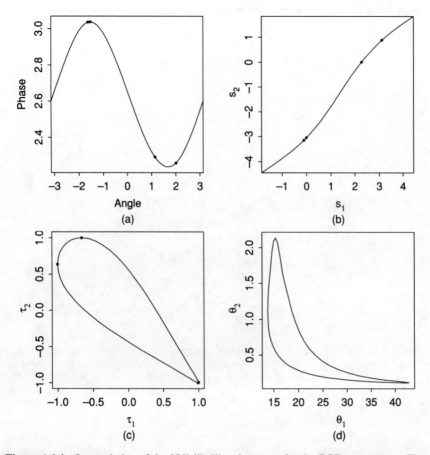

Figure A6.4 Interpolation of the 90% likelihood contour for the BOD parameters. The phases (•) corresponding to the points on the profile traces are shown in part a together with the interpolated curve, and the corresponding points (•) and interpolated values $a+d/2$ and $a-d/2$ are shown in part b. The points on the traces (•) and the interpolated contour are shown in the τ coordinates in part c, and in the θ coordinates in part d.

Figure A6.4d. This relatively poor performance was predicted from inspection of the profile trace plots; nevertheless, we find it rather remarkable that interpolated contours based on only four points can be so accurate. ∎

In the above example it is clear from the profile t and profile trace plots that the true contours are badly behaved, and so interpolations based on only four intersection points of a contour with the traces will not be accurate. To generate more accurate contour plots, additional points on the contour must be calculated and used in the interpolation process. A procedure for adding points to generate accurate contour sketches based on traces is being developed.

APPENDIX 7.

Key to Data Sets

The model functions for the data sets in Section 7.3.2 are:

Model A: Michaelis–Menten model,

$$f(x,\boldsymbol{\theta}) = \frac{\theta_1 x}{\theta_2 + x}$$

Model B:

$$f(x,\boldsymbol{\theta}) = \theta_1 \left[1 - \exp(-\theta_2 x)\right]$$

Model C:

$$f(x,\boldsymbol{\theta}) = \theta_1 + (0.49 - \theta_1) \exp[-\theta_2(x-8)]$$

Model D:

$$f(\mathbf{x},\boldsymbol{\theta}) = \exp\left\{-\theta_1 x_1 \exp\left[-\theta_2\left(\frac{1}{x_2} - \frac{1}{620}\right)\right]\right\}$$

Model E:

$$f(x,\boldsymbol{\theta}) = \theta_1 x^{\theta_2}$$

Model F: Asymptotic regression model,

$$f(x,\boldsymbol{\theta}) = \theta_1 + \theta_2 \exp(\theta_3 x)$$

Model G: Logistic model,

$$f(x,\boldsymbol{\theta}) = \frac{\theta_1}{1 + \theta_2 \exp(\theta_3 x)}$$

Model H: Gompertz growth model,

$$f(x,\boldsymbol{\theta}) = \theta_1 \exp[-\exp(\theta_2 - \theta_3 x)]$$

Model I:

$$f(x,\boldsymbol{\theta}) = \theta_1 \left[1 - \theta_2 \exp(-\theta_3 x)\right]$$

Model J: Log logistic growth model,

$$f(x,\boldsymbol{\theta}) = \theta_1 - \ln[1 + \theta_2 \exp(-\theta_3 x)]$$

Model K:

$$f(x,\boldsymbol{\theta}) = \theta_1 + \theta_2 / x^{\theta_3}$$

Model L:

$$f(x,\boldsymbol{\theta}) = \ln[\theta_1 \exp(-\theta_2 x) + (1 - \theta_1) \exp(-\theta_3 x)]$$

Model M:

$$f(\mathbf{x},\boldsymbol{\theta}) = \frac{\theta_1 \theta_3 (x_2 - x_3 / 1.632)}{1 + \theta_2 x_1 + \theta_3 x_2 + \theta_4 x_3}$$

Model N: Steady state adsorption model,

$$f(\mathbf{x},\boldsymbol{\theta}) = \frac{\theta_1 x_1 \exp(-\theta_3 x_{\text{inv}}) \theta_2 x_2 \exp(-\theta_4 x_{\text{inv}})}{\theta_1 x_1 \exp(-\theta_3 x_{\text{inv}}) + 2.28 \theta_2 x_2 \exp(-\theta_4 x_{\text{inv}})}$$

where

$$x_{\text{inv}} = \frac{1}{x_3 + 273} - \frac{1}{558}$$

Model O: Morgan–Mercer–Florin growth model,

$$f(x,\boldsymbol{\theta}) = \frac{\theta_2 \theta_3 + \theta_1 x^{\theta_4}}{\theta_3 + x^{\theta_4}}$$

Model P: Richards growth model,

$$f(x,\boldsymbol{\theta}) = \frac{\theta_1}{[1 + \theta_2 \exp(-\theta_3 x)]^{1/\theta_4}}$$

Model Q:

$$f(x,\boldsymbol{\theta}) = \theta_1 + \theta_2 \exp(-\theta_4 x) + \theta_3 \exp(-\theta_5 x)$$

Model R:

$$f(x,\boldsymbol{\theta}) = \frac{x \exp\left[\dfrac{\theta_1 - \theta_2 / x}{R}\right]}{1 + \exp\left[\dfrac{\theta_3 - \theta_4 / x}{R}\right] + \exp\left[\dfrac{\theta_5 - \theta_6 / x}{R}\right]}$$

where

$$R = 1.98$$

Model S:

$$f(\mathbf{x}, \boldsymbol{\theta}) = \frac{\theta_1}{\theta_2 + x_1} + \theta_3 x_2 + \theta_4 x_2^2 + \theta_5 x_2^3 + (\theta_6 + \theta_7 x_2^2) \, x_2 \exp\left[\frac{-x_1}{\theta_8 + \theta_9 x_2^2} \right]$$

References for the data sets are given in Table A7.1. Some of these data sets were used in the examples and exercises. The correspondence between the data set number and the section of Appendix 1 or Appendix 4 is given in Table A7.2.

Table A7.1   References for data sets in Section 7.3.2.

Data Set	Reference
1	Michaelis and Menten (1913)
2	Treloar (1974)
3	Treloar (1974)
4	Draper and Smith (1981), p. 522, problem L, set 1
5	Draper and Smith (1981), p. 522, problem L, set 2
6	Draper and Smith (1981), p. 522, problem L, set 3
7	Draper and Smith (1981), p. 522, problem L, set 4
8	Draper and Smith (1981), p. 522, problem L, set 5
9	Draper and Smith (1981), p. 522, problem L, set 6
10	Draper and Smith (1981), p. 522, problem L, set 7
11	Draper and Smith (1981), p. 522, problem L, set 8
12	Draper and Smith (1981), p. 522, problem L, set 9
13	Draper and Smith (1981), p. 476
14	Draper and Smith (1981), p. 519, problem H
15	Draper and Smith (1981), p. 519, problem M
16	Ratkowsky (1983), p. 88, set 1
17	Ratkowsky (1983), p. 88, set 2
18	Gregory (1956)
19	Heyes and Brown (1956)
20	Ratkowsky (1983), Appendix 5.A, set 1
21	Ratkowsky (1983), Appendix 5.A, set 2
22	Ratkowsky (1979), barley yields
23	Pimentel-Gomes (1953)
24	Draper and Smith (1981), p. 524, problem N, set 1
25	Draper and Smith (1981), p. 524, problem N, set 2
26	Draper and Smith (1981), p. 524, problem N, set 3
27	Draper and Smith (1981), p. 524, problem N, set 4
28	Draper and Smith (1981), p. 524, problem N, set 5
29	Draper and Smith (1981), p. 524, problem P, tensile strength
30	Draper and Smith (1981), p. 524, problem P, yield strength
31	Dierburg and Ewel (1982)
32	Carr (1960)
33	Pritchard (1972), model 1
34	Pritchard (1972), model 2
35	Osborne (1971)
36	Miller (1983)
37	Linssen (1975)

Table A7.2 Correspondence of data set numbers to sections of Appendix 1 or Appendix 4.

Data Set	Section.
2	A1.3, Table A1.3b
3	A1.3, Table A1.3a
5	A4.1
11	A1.4
19	A4.5
32	A1.5
33	A4.4
37	A1.8

References

Abdollah, Shirin (1986), *The Effect of Doxorubicin on the Specific Binding of [^{3}H] Nitrendipine to Rat Heart Microsomes.* Master's Thesis, Queen's University at Kingston.

Anderson, David H. (1983), *Compartmental Modeling and Tracer Kinetics.* Springer Verlag.

Ansley, Craig F. (1985), "Quick proofs of some regression theorems via the QR algorithm." *American Statistician,* **39**(1), 55–59.

Armstrong, P. W., D. G. Watts, D. C. Hamilton, M. A. Chiong, and J. O. Parker (1979), "Quantification of myocardial infarction: Template model for serial creatine kinase analysis." *Circulation,* **60**(4), 856–865.

Bache, C. A., J. W. Serum, W. D. Youngs, and D. J. Lisk (1972), "Polychlorinated biphenyl residues: Accumulation in Cayuga Lake trout with age." *Science,* **117**, 1192–1193.

Bacon, D. W., and D. G. Watts (1971), "Estimating the transition between two intersecting straight lines." *Biometrika,* **58**, 525–534.

Bard, Y. (1974), *Nonlinear Parameter Estimation.* New York: Academic Press.

Bartels, R. H., and G. W. Stewart (1972), "Algorithm 432, the solution of the matrix equation AX − XB = C." *Communications of the Association for Computing Machinery,* **15**(9), 820–826.

Bates, Douglas M. (1978), *Curvature Measures of Nonlinearity.* Ph.D. Thesis, Queen's University at Kingston.

Bates, D. M., D. C. Hamilton, and D. G. Watts (1983), "Calculation of intrinsic and parameter-effects curvatures for nonlinear regression models." *Communications in Statistics—Simulation and Computation,* **12**, 469–477.

Bates, Douglas M., and Mary J. Lindstrom (1986), "Nonlinear least squares with conditionally linear parameters," in *Proceedings of the Statistical Computing Section.* New York: American Statistical Association.

Bates, D. M., and D. G. Watts (1980), "Relative curvature measures of nonlinearity (with discussion)." *Journal of the Royal Statistical Society, Ser. B,* **42**(1), 1–25.

Bates, D. M., and D. G. Watts (1981a), "Parameter transformations for improved approximate confidence regions in nonlinear least squares." *Annals of Statistics,* **9**(6), 1152–1167.

Bates, D. M., and D. G. Watts (1981b), "A relative offset orthogonality convergence criterion for nonlinear least squares." *Technometrics,* **23**(2), 179–183.

Bates, D. M., and D. G. Watts (1984), "A multi-response Gauss–Newton algorithm." *Communications in Statistics—Simulation and Computation,* **13**(5), 705–715.

Bates, Douglas M., and Donald G. Watts (1985), "Multiresponse estimation with special application to systems of linear differential equations (with discussion)." *Technometrics,* **27**(4), 329–360.

Bates, Douglas M., and Donald G. Watts (1987), "A generalized Gauss–Newton procedure for multi-response parameter estimation." *SIAM Journal of Scientific and Statistical Computing*, 7(1), 49–55.

Bates, Douglas M., Dennis A. Wolf, and Donald G. Watts (1985), "Nonlinear least squares and first-order kinetics," in David Allen, Ed., *Proceedings of Computer Science and Statistics: Seventeenth Symposium on the Interface*. New York: North-Holland.

Bavely, Connice A., and G. W. Stewart (1979), "An algorithm for computing reducing subspaces by block diagonalization." *SIAM Journal of Numerical Analysis*, 16(2), 359–367.

Beale, E. M. L. (1960), "Confidence regions in nonlinear estimation (with discussion)." *Journal of the Royal Statistical Society, Ser. B*, 22, 41–88.

Becker, Richard A., John M. Chambers, and Allan R. Wilks (1988), *The New S Language: A Programming Environment For Data Analysis and Graphics*. Belmont, Calif.: Wadsworth.

Belsley, D. A., E. Kuh, and R. E. Welsch (1980), *Regression Diagnostics—Identifying Influential Data and Sources of Variation*. New York: Wiley.

Bliss, C. I., and A. T. James (1966), "Fitting the rectangular hyperbola." *Biometrics*, 22, 573–602.

Box, G. E. P. (1960), "Fitting empirical data." *Annals of the New York Academy of Sciences*, 86, 792–816.

Box, G. E. P., and G. A. Coutie (1956), "Applications of digital computers in the exploration of functional relationships." *Proceedings of the IEEE*, 103B (Supplement no. 1), 100–107.

Box, George E. P., and David R. Cox (1964), "An analysis of transformations." *Journal of the Royal Statistical Society, Ser. B*, 26, 211–252.

Box, G. E. P., and N. R. Draper (1959), "A basis for the selection of a response surface design." *Journal of the American Statistical Association*, 54, 622–653.

Box, G. E. P., and N. R. Draper (1965), "The Bayesian estimation of common parameters from several responses." *Biometrika*, 52, 355–365.

Box, George E. P., and Norman R. Draper (1987), *Empirical Model-Building and Response Surfaces*. New York: Wiley.

Box, G. E. P., and W. J. Hill (1974), "Correcting inhomogeneity of variance with power transformation weighting." *Technometrics*, 16, 385–389.

Box, G. E. P., and W. G. Hunter (1965), "Sequential design of experiments for nonlinear models" in *IBM Scientific Computer Symposium in Statistics*, pp. 113–137.

Box, G. E. P., W. G. Hunter, and J. S. Hunter (1978), *Statistics for Experimenters*. New York: Wiley.

Box, G. E. P., W. G. Hunter, J. F. MacGregor, and J. Erjavec (1973), "Some problems associated with the analysis of multiresponse models." *Technometrics*, 15(1), 33–51.

Box, George E. P., and Gwilym M. Jenkins (1976), *Time Series Analysis: Forecasting and Control* (revised edition). San Francisco: Holden-Day.

Box, George E. P., and Hiromitsu Kanemasu (1984), "Constrained nonlinear least squares," in Klaus Hinkelmann, Ed., *Contributions to Experimental Design, Linear Models, and Genetic Statistics: Essays in Honor of Oscar Kempthorne*. New York: Marcel Dekker.

Box, G. E. P., and H. L. Lucas (1959), "Design of experiments in non-linear situations." *Biometrika*, 46, 77–90.

Box, G. E. P., and G. C. Tiao (1973), *Bayesian Inference in Statistical Analysis*. Reading, Mass.: Addison-Wesley.

Box, George E. P., and Paul W. Tidwell (1962), "Transformations of the independent variables." *Technometrics*, **4**, 531–550.

Box, M. J. (1968), "The occurence of replications in optimal designs of experiments to estimate parameters in nonlinear models." *Journal of the Royal Statistical Society, Ser. B*, **30**, 290–302.

Box, M. J. (1971), "An experimental design criterion for precise parameter estimation of a subset of the parameters in a nonlinear model." *Biometrika*, **58**, 149–153.

Box, M. J., N. R. Draper, and W. G. Hunter (1970), "Missing values in multi-response nonlinear data fitting." *Technometrics*, **12**, 613–620.

Caracotsios, M., and W. E. Stewart (1985), "Sensitivity analysis of initial value problems with mixed ODE's and algebraic equations." *Computers and Chemical Engineering*, **9**(4), 359–365.

Carr, N. L. (1960), "Kinetics of catalytic isomerization of *n*-pentane." *Industrial and Engineering Chemistry*, **52**, 391–396.

Carroll, Raymond J., and David Ruppert (1984), "Power transformation when fitting theoretical models to data." *Journal of the American Statistical Association*, **79**(386), 321–328.

Chambers, J. M. (1977), *Computational Methods for Data Analysis*. New York: Wiley.

Chambers, John M., William S. Cleveland, Beat Kleiner, and Paul A. Tukey (1983), *Graphical Methods for Data Analysis*. Belmont, Calif.: Wadsworth.

Cleveland, William S. (1984), "Graphs in scientific publications." *American Statistician*, **38**(4), 261–269.

Cleveland, William S. (1985), *Elements of Graphing Data*. Belmont, Calif.: Wadsworth.

Cochran, W. G. (1973), "Experiments for nonlinear functions." *Journal of the American Statistical Association*, **68**, 771–778.

Cochran, W. G., and G. M. Cox (1957), *Experimental Designs*. New York: Wiley.

Cole, K. S., and R. H. Cole (1941), "Dispersion and absorption in dielectrics I: Alternating current characteristics." *Journal of Physical Chemistry*, **9**, 341–351.

Conte, Samuel D., and Carl de Boor (1980), *Elementary Numerical Analysis, an Algorithmic Approach* (third edition). New York: McGraw-Hill.

Cook, R. D., and S. Weisberg (1982), *Residuals and Influence in Regression*. London: Chapman and Hall.

Cook, R. D., and S. Weisberg (1983), "Diagnostics for heteroscedasticity in regression." *Biometrika*, **70**(1), 1–10.

Daniel, C., and F. S. Wood (1980), *Fitting Equations to Data* (second edition). New York: Wiley.

Davies, O. L., Ed. (1956), *The Design and Analysis of Industrial Experiments* (second edition). Edinburgh: Oliver and Boyd.

Dennis, Jr., J. E., D. M. Gay, and R. E. Welsch (1981), "An adaptive nonlinear least-squares algorithm." *ACM Transactions on Mathematical Software*, **7**, 348–368.

Dennis, Jr., J. E., and Robert B. Schnabel (1983), *Numerical Methods for Unconstrained Optimization and Nonlinear Equations*. Englewood Cliffs, N. J.: Prentice Hall.

Dierburg, F., and K. C. Ewel (1982), "The effects of treated sewage effluent on decomposition and organic matter accumulation in cypress domes," in K. C. Ewel and H. T. Odum, Eds., *Cypress Domes*. Florida University Press.

Dongarra, J. J., J. R. Bunch, C. B. Moler, and G. W. Stewart (1979), *Linpack Users' Guide*. Philadelphia: SIAM.

Draper, N. R., and H. Smith (1981), *Applied Regression Analysis* (second edition). New York: Wiley.

Edlefsen, Lee E., and Samuel D. Jones (1986), *GAUSS™ Programming Language Manual*. Kent, Wash.: Aptech Systems Inc..

Ehrenberg, A. S. C. (1981), "The problem of numeracy." *American Statistician*, **35**(2),

67–71.

Ehrenberg, A. S. C. (1982), "Writing technical reports or papers." *American Statistician*, **36**(4), 326–329.

Elliot, J. R., and D. R. Pierson (1986), Private communication.

Fedorov, V. V. (1972), *Theory of Optimal Experiments*. New York: Academic Press. (Translated by W. J. Studden and E. M. Klimko.)

Fisher, R. A. (1935), *Design of Experiments*. London: Oliver and Boyd.

Froment, Gilbert F., and Kenneth B. Bischoff (1979), *Chemical Reactor Analysis and Design*. New York: Wiley.

Fuguitt, R. E., and J. E. Hawkins (1945), "The liquid-phase thermal isomerization of α-pinene." *Journal of the American Chemical Society*, **67**, 242–245.

Fuguitt, R. E., and J. E. Hawkins (1947), "Rate of the thermal isomerization of α-pinene in the liquid phase." *Journal of the American Chemical Society*, **69**, 319–322.

Gill, P. E., W. Murray, and M. H. Wright (1981), *Practical Optimization*. New York: Academic Press.

Godfrey, Keith (1983), *Compartmental Models and Their Application*. New York: Academic Press.

Golub, G. H., and V. Pereyra (1973), "The differentiation of pseudo-inverses and non-linear least squares problems whose variables separate." *Journal of SIAM*, **10**, 413–432.

Gregory, F. G. (1956), "General aspects of leaf growth," in F. L. Milthorpe, Ed., *The Growth of Leaves*. London: Butterworth.

Halperin, M. (1963), "Confidence interval estimation in nonlinear regression." *Journal of the Royal Statistical Society, Ser. B*, **25**, 330–333.

Hamilton, D. C. (1980), *Experimental Design for Nonlinear Regression Models*. Ph.D. Thesis, Queen's University at Kingston.

Hamilton, D. C. (1986), "Confidence regions for parameter subsets in nonlinear regression." *Biometrika*, **73**(1), 57–64.

Hamilton, David C., and Donald G. Watts (1985), "A quadratic design criterion for precise estimation in nonlinear regression models." *Technometrics*, **27**(3), 241–250.

Hamilton, D. C., D. G. Watts, and D. M. Bates (1982), "Accounting for intrinsic nonlinearity in nonlinear regression parameter inference regions." *Annals of Statistics*, **10**(2), 386–393.

Hartley, H. O. (1961), "The modified Gauss–Newton method for the fitting of non-linear regression functions by least squares." *Technometrics*, **3**, 269–280.

Havriliak, Stephen Jr., and S. Negami (1967), "A complex plane representation of dielectric and mechanical relaxation processes in some polymers." *Polymer*, **8**, 161–205.

Havriliak, Stephen Jr., and Donald G. Watts (1987), "Estimating dielectric constants: A complex multiresponse problem," in C. Mallows, Ed., *Data, Design, and Analysis*. New York: Wiley.

Heyes, J. K., and R. Brown (1956), "Growth and cellular differentiation," in F. L. Milthorpe, Ed., *The Growth of Leaves*. London: Butterworth.

Hill, P. D. H. (1980), "D-optimal designs for partially nonlinear regression models." *Technometrics*, **22**(2), 275–276.

Hill, W. J., and W. G. Hunter (1974), "Design of experiments for subsets of the parameters." *Technometrics*, **16**, 425–434.

Hill, W. J., W. G. Hunter, and D. W. Wichern (1968), "A joint design criterion for the dual problem of model discrimination and parameter estimation." *Technometrics*, **10**, 145–160.

Himmelblau, D. M. (1972), "A uniform evaluation of unconstrained optimization techniques," in F. A. Lootsma, Ed., *Numerical Methods for Nonlinear Optimization*.

London: Academic Press.

Hinkley, D. V. (1969), "Inference about the intersection in two-phase regression." *Biometrika*, **56**, 495–504.

Hocking, R. R. (1983), "Developments in linear regression methodology: 1959–1982 (with discussion)." *Technometrics*, **25**(3), 219–249.

Hougen, O. A., and K. M. Watson (1947), *Chemical Reaction Principles*. New York: Wiley.

Householder, A. S. (1958), "Unitary triangularization of a nonsymmetric matrix." *Journal of the Association for Computing Machinery*, **5**, 339–342.

Hubbard, A. B., and W. E. Robinson (1950), "A thermal decomposition study of colorado oil shale." U.S. Bureau of Mines, Rept. Invest. No. 4744.

Huber, P. J. (1981), *Robust Statistics*. New York: Wiley.

Jennrich, R. I., and P. B. Bright (1976), "Fitting systems of linear differential equations using computer generated exact derivatives (with discussion)." *Technometrics*, **18**(4), 385–399.

Jennrich, R. I., and P. F. Sampson (1968), "An application of stepwise regression to nonlinear estimation." *Technometrics*, **10**(1), 63–72.

Joiner, B. L. (1981), "Lurking variables: Some examples." *American Statistician*, **35**, 227–233.

Jupp, David L. B. (1978), "Approximation to data by splines with free knots." *SIAM Journal of Numerical Analysis*, **15**(2), 328–343.

Juusola, J. A. (1971), *A Kinetic Mechanism for the Vapor-phase Oxidation of o-Xylene over a Vanadium Oxide Catalyst*. Ph. D. thesis, Queen's University at Kingston.

Kaplan, Stanley A., Robert E. Weinfeld, Charles W. Abruzzo, and Margaret Lewis (1972), "Pharmacokinetic profile of sulfisoxazole following intravenous, intramuscular, and oral administration to man." *Journal of Pharmaceutical Sciences*, **61**, 773–778.

Kaufman, Linda (1975), "A variable projection method for solving separable nonlinear least squares problems." *BIT*, **15**, 49–57.

Kennedy, Jr., W. J., and J. E. Gentle (1980), *Statistical Computing*. New York: Marcel Dekker.

Khuri, A. I. (1984), "A note on D-optimal designs for partially nonlinear regression models." *Technometrics*, **26**(1), 59–61.

Lawton, W. H., E. A. Sylvestre, and M. S. Maggio (1972), "Self modeling nonlinear regression." *Technometrics*, **14**(3), 513–532.

Levenberg, K. (1944), "A method for the solution of certain nonlinear problems in least squares." *Quarterly of Applied Mathematics*, **2**, 164–168.

Linssen, H. N. (1975), "Nonlinearity measures: a case study." *Statistica Neerlandica*, **29**, 93–99.

Lythgoe, Steven C. (1986), *A model for the Thermal Dissolver of the Wilsonville Direct Coal Liquefaction Process*. Master's Thesis, Queen's University at Kingston.

Marquardt, D. W. (1963), "An algorithm for the estimation of non-linear parameters." *Journal of SIAM*, **11**, 431–441.

Marske, Donald (1967), *Biochemical Oxygen Demand Data Interpretation Using Sum of Squares Surface*. M.S. Thesis, University of Wisconsin—Madison.

McLean, D. D., D. J. Pritchard, D. W. Bacon, and J. Downie (1979), "Singularities in multiresponse modelling." *Technometrics*, **21**(3), 291–298.

Michaelis, L., and M. L. Menten (1913), "Kinetik der Invertinwirkung." *Biochemische Zeitschrift*, **49**, 333.

Miller, Allan (1983), "BMD P3R – A warning." CSIRO–DMS Newsletter, Sydney, Australia: CSIRO.

Moler, Cleve, and Charles Van Loan (1978), "Nineteen dubious ways to compute the exponential of a matrix." *SIAM Review*, **20**(4), 801–836.

Montgomery, Douglas C., and Elizabeth A. Peck (1982), *Introduction to Linear Regression Analysis*. New York: Wiley.

O'Neill, Barrett (1966), *Elementary Differential Geometry*. New York: Academic Press.

Osborne, M. R. (1971), "Some aspects of non-linear least squares calculations," in F. A. Lootsma, Ed., *Numerical Methods for Non-linear Optimization*. New York: Academic Press.

Pimentel-Gomes, F. (1953), "The use of Mitscherlich's regression law in the analysis of experiments with fertilizers." *Biometrics*, **9**, 498–516.

Pritchard, Douglas (1972), *Statistical Design and Analysis Using Experimental Kinetic Data*. Master's Thesis, Queen's University.

Ralston, M. L., and R. I. Jennrich (1978), "DUD, a derivative-free algorithm for nonlinear least squares." *Technometrics*, **20**, 7–14.

Ratkowsky, David A. (1979), "Choosing the 'best' parameterization of the asymptotic regression model." Technical Report, CSIRO Division of Mathematics and Statistics, Tasmania.

Ratkowsky, D. A. (1983), *Nonlinear Regression Modelling: A Unified Practical Approach*. New York: Marcel Dekker.

Ratkowsky, D. A. (1985), "A statistically suitable general formulation for modelling catalytic chemical reactions." *Chemical Engineering Science*, **40**(9), 1623–1628.

Renwick, A. G. (1982), "Pharmacokinetics in toxicology," in A. Wallace Hayes, Ed., *Principles and Methods of Toxicology*. New York: Raven Press, pp. 659–710.

Roller, Duane (1950), *The Early Development of the Concepts of Temperature and Heat: The Rise and Decline of the Caloric Theory*. Cambridge, Mass.: Harvard University Press.

SAS Institute Inc. (1985), *SAS User's Guide: Statistics, Version 5 Edition*. Cary, N.C.: SAS Institute Inc..

SAS Institute Inc. (1985), *SAS/IML™ User's Guide, Version 5 Edition,*. Cary, N.C.: SAS Institute Inc..

Seber, G. A. (1977), *Linear Regression Analysis*. New York: Wiley.

Silvey, S. D., and D. M. Titterington (1973), "A geometric approach to optimal design theory." *Biometrika*, **60**, 21–32.

Smith, B. T., J. M. Boyle, J. J. Dongarra, B. S. Garbow, Y. Ikebe, V. C. Klema, and C. B. Moler (1976), *Matrix Eigensystem Routines—EISPACK Guide*. Springer Verlag.

Sredni, J. (1970), *Problems of Design, Estimation, and Lack of Fit in Model Building*. Ph.D. Thesis, University of Wisconsin—Madison.

St. John, R. C., and N. R. Draper (1975), "D-optimality for regression designs: a review." *Technometrics*, **17**, 15–23.

Steinberg, David M., and William G. Hunter (1984), "Experimental design: review and comment (with discussion)." *Technometrics*, **26**(2), 71–130.

Stewart, G. W. (1973), *Introduction to Matrix Computations*. New York: Academic Press.

Stewart, G. W. (1976), "HQR3 and EXCHNG: Fortran subroutines for calculating the eigenvalues of a real upper Hessenberg matrix." *ACM Transactions on Mathematical Software*, **2**(3), 275–280. (Algorithm 506.)

Stewart, W. E., and J. P. Sorensen (1981), "Bayesian estimation of common parameters from multiresponse data with missing observations." *Technometrics*, **23**, 131–141.

Tierney, Luke, and Joseph B. Kadane (1986), "Accurate approximations for posterior moments and densities." *Journal of the American Statistical Association*, **81**(393), 82–86.

Treloar, M. A. (1974), *Effects of Puromycin on Galactosyltransferase of Golgi Membranes*. Master's Thesis, University of Toronto.

Tufte, Edward R. (1983), *The Visual Display of Quantitative Information*. Cheshire, Conn.: Graphics Press.

Varah, J. M. (1982), "A spline least squares method for numerical parameter estimation in differential equations." *SIAM Journal of Scientific and Statistical Computing*, **3**(1), 28–46.

Wagner, J. G. (1967), "Use of computers in pharmacokinetics." *Clinical Pharmacology and Therapeutics*, **8**, 201.

Wagner, John G. (1975), *Fundamentals of Clincal Pharmacokinetics*. Hamilton, Illinois: Drug Intelligence Publications.

Wald, A. (1943), "On the efficient design of statistical investigations." *Annals of Mathematical Statistics*, **14**, 134–140.

Watts, Donald G. (1981), "A task-analysis approach to designing a regression analysis course." *American Statistician*, **35**(2), 77–84.

Watts, D. G., and D. W. Bacon (1974), "Using a hyperbola as a transition model to fit two-regimen straight-line data." *Technometrics*, **16**, 369–373.

Watts, Donald G., Donald deBethizy, and Robert G. Stiratelli (1986), "Toxicity of Ethyl Acrylate." Technical Report, Rohm and Haas Co., Spring House, Pa.

Williams, E. J. (1962), "Exact fiducial limits in nonlinear estimation." *Journal of the Royal Statistical Society, Ser. B*, **24**, 125–139.

Ziegel, E. R., and J. W. Gorman (1980), "Kinetic modelling with multiresponse data." *Technometrics*, **22**(2), 139–151.

Ziegel, Eric R. (1985), "Discussion of the paper by Bates and Watts." *Technometrics*, **27**(4), 352–357.

Bibliography

BOOKS

Bard, Y. (1974), *Nonlinear Parameter Estimation.* New York: Academic Press.

Beck, J. V., and K. J. Arnold (1977), *Parameter Estimation in Engineering and Science.* New York: Wiley.

Box, George E. P., and Norman R. Draper (1987), *Empirical Model-Building and Response Surfaces.* New York: Wiley.

Box, G. E. P., W. G. Hunter, and J. S. Hunter (1978), *Statistics for Experimenters.* New York: Wiley.

Box, G. E. P., and G. C. Tiao (1973), *Bayesian Inference in Statistical Analysis.* Reading, Mass.: Addison-Wesley.

Chambers, J. M. (1977), *Computational Methods for Data Analysis.* New York: Wiley.

Daniel, C., and F. S. Wood (1980), *Fitting Equations to Data* (second edition). New York: Wiley.

Dennis, Jr., J. E., and Robert B. Schnabel (1983), *Numerical Methods for Unconstrained Optimization and Nonlinear Equations.* Englewood Cliffs, N.J.: Prentice-Hall.

Dixon, W. J., M. B. Brown, L. Engleman, J. W. Frane, M. A. Hill, R. I. Jennrich, and J. D. Toporek (1983), *BMDP Statistical Software.* Berkeley, Calif.: University of California Press.

Draper, N. R., and H. Smith (1981), *Applied Regression Analysis* (second edition). New York: Wiley.

Gallant, A. Ronald (1987), *Nonlinear Statistical Models.* New York: Wiley.

Kennedy, Jr., W. J., and J. E. Gentle (1980), *Statistical Computing.* New York: Marcel Dekker.

Myers, R. H. (1986), *Classical and Modern Regression with Applications.* Boston: Duxbury.

Nash, John C., and Mary Walker-Smith (1987), *Nonlinear Parameter Estimation: An Integrated System in Basic.* New York: Marcel Dekker.

Neter, J., W. Wasserman, and M. H. Kutner (1983), *Applied Linear Regression Models.* Homewood, Ill.: Irwin.

Ratkowsky, D. A. (1983), *Nonlinear Regression Modelling: A Unified Practical Approach.* New York: Marcel Dekker.

SAS Institute Inc. (1985), *SAS User's Guide: Statistics, Version 5 Edition.* Cary, N.C.: SAS Institute Inc..

Snedecor, George W., and William G. Cochran (1980), *Statistical Methods* (seventh edition). Ames, Iowa: Iowa State University Press.

343

GENERAL ARTICLES

Box, G. E. P. (1960), "Fitting empirical data." *Annals of the New York Academy of Sciences*, **86**, 792–816.

Box, G. E. P., and W. G. Hunter (1962), "A useful method of model building." *Technometrics*, **4**, 301–318.

Box, G. E. P., and W. G. Hunter (1965), "The experimental study of physical mechanisms." *Technometrics*, **7**, 23–42.

Gallant, A. R. (1975), "Nonlinear regression." *American Statistician*, **29**(2), 73–81.

Motulsky, H. J., and L. A. Ransanas (1987), "Fitting curves to data using nonlinear regression: a practical and nonmathematical review." *FASEB Journal*, **1**, 365–374.

Watts, D. G. (1981), "An Introduction to Nonlinear Least Squares," in L. Endrenyi, Ed., *Kinetic Data Analysis—Design and Analysis of Enzyme and Pharmacokinetic Experiments*. New York: Plenum, pp. 1–24.

NONLINEAR LEAST SQUARES—THEORY

Allen, D. M. (1983), "Parameter estimation for nonlinear models with emphasis on compartmental models." *Biometrics*, **39**(3), 629–637.

Bates, D. M., and D. G. Watts (1980), "Relative curvature measures of nonlinearity (with discussion)." *Journal of the Royal Statistical Society, Ser. B*, **42**(1), 1–25.

Bates, D. M., and D. G. Watts (1981), "Parameter transformations for improved approximate confidence regions in nonlinear least squares." *Annals of Statistics*, **9**(6), 1152–1167.

Beal, S. L. (1982), "Reader response: Bayesian analysis of nonlinear models." *Biometrics*, **38**(4), 1089–1092.

Beale, E. M. L. (1960), "Confidence regions in nonlinear estimation (with discussion)." *Journal of the Royal Statistical Society, Ser. B*, **22**, 41–88.

Berkey, C. S. (1982), "Bayesian approach for a nonlinear growth model." *Biometrics*, **38**(4), 953–961.

Clarke, G. P. Y. (1980), "Moments of the least squares estimators in a nonlinear regression model." *Journal of the Royal Statistical Society, Ser. B*, **42**(2), 227–237.

Clarke, G. P. Y. (1987), "Approximate confidence limits for a parameter function in nonlinear regression." *Journal of the American Statistical Association*, **82**(397), 221–230.

Cook, R. D., and C. L. Tsai (1985), "Residuals in nonlinear regression." *Biometrika*, **72**(1), 23–29.

Cook, R. Dennis, and Jeffrey A. Witmer (1985), "A note on parameter-effects curvature." *Journal of the American Statistical Association*, **80**(392), 872–878.

Currie, D. (1982), "Estimating Michaelis–Menten parameters: Bias, variance, and experimental design." *Biometrics*, **38**(4), 907–919.

DiCiccio, T. J. (1984), "On parameter transformations and interval estimation." *Biometrika*, **71**(3), 477–485.

Donaldson, Janet R., and Robert B. Schnabel (1987), "Computational experiences with confidence regions and confidence intervals for nonlinear least squares." *Technometrics*, **29**(1), 67–82.

Gallant, A. R. (1975), "The power of the likelihood ratio test of location in nonlinear regression models." *Journal of the American Statistical Association*, **70**(349), 198–203.

Gallant, A. R. (1975), "Testing a subset of the parameters of a nonlinear regression model." *Journal of the American Statistical Association*, **70**(352), 927–932.

Gallant, A. R. (1977), "Testing a nonlinear regression specification; a nonregular case."

Journal of the American Statistical Association, **72**(359), 523–529.

Guttman, I., and D. A. Meeter (1965), "On Beale's measure of nonlinearity." *Technometrics*, **7**, 623–637.

Halperin, M. (1963), "Confidence interval estimation in nonlinear regression." *Journal of the Royal Statistical Society, Ser. B*, **25**, 330–333.

Hamilton, D. (1986), "Confidence regions for parameter subsets in nonlinear regression." *Biometrika*, **73**(1), 57–64.

Hamilton, D. C., D. G. Watts, and D. M. Bates (1982), "Accounting for intrinsic nonlinearity in nonlinear regression parameter inference regions." *Annals of Statistics*, **10**(2), 386–393.

Hartley, H. O. (1964), "Exact confidence regions for the parameters in nonlinear regression laws." *Biometrika*, **51**, 347–353.

Hougaard, P. (1982), "Parameterizations of non-linear models." *Journal of the Royal Statistical Society, Ser. B*, **44**(2), 244–252.

Hougaard, P. (1985), "The appropriateness of the asymptotic distribution in a nonlinear regression model in relation to curvature." *Journal of the Royal Statistical Society, Ser. B*, **47**(1), 103–114.

Jennrich, R. I. (1969), "Asymptotic properties of nonlinear least squares estimation." *Annals of Mathematical Statistics*, **40**, 633–643.

Kass, Robert E. (1984), "Canonical parameterizations and zero parameter-effects curvature." *Journal of the Royal Statistical Society, Ser. B*, **46**, 86–92.

Katz, D., S. P. Azen, and A. Schumitzky (1981), "Bayesian approach to the analysis of nonlinear models: Implementation and evaluation." *Biometrics*, **37**, 137–142.

Linssen, H. N. (1975), "Nonlinearity measures: A case study." *Statistica Neerlandica*, **29**, 93–99.

Moolgavkar, Suresh H., Edward D. Lustbader, and David J. Venzon (1984), "A geometric approach to nonlinear regression diagnostics with application to matched case-control studies." *Annals of Statistics*, **12**(3), 816–826.

Peduzzi, P. N., R. J. Hardy, and T. R. Holford (1980), "A stepwise variable selection procedure for nonlinear regression models." *Biometrics*, **36**, 511–516. (See also **37**, 595–596.)

Racine-Poon, A. (1985), "A Bayesian approach to nonlinear random effects models." *Biometrics*, **41**(4), 1015–1023.

Ross, G. J. S. (1970), "The efficient use of function minimization in non-linear maximum-likelihood estimation." *Applied Statistics*, **19**, 205–221.

Ross, G. J. S. (1978), "Exact and approximate confidence regions for functions of parameters in non-linear models," in L. Corstein, and J. Hermans, Eds., *COMPSTAT 78, Third Symposium on Computation*. Vienna: Physica-Verlag.

Schwetlick, Hubert, and Volker Tiller (1985), "Numerical methods for estimating parameters in nonlinear models with errors in the variables." *Technometrics*, **27**(1), 17–24.

Wilks, S. S., and J. F. Daly (1939), "An optimum property of confidence regions associated with the likelihood function." *Annals of Mathematical Statistics*, **10**, 225–239.

Williams, E. J. (1962), "Exact fiducial limits in nonlinear estimation." *Journal of the Royal Statistical Society, Ser. B*, **24**, 125–139.

Wolter, K. M., and W. A. Fuller (1982), "Estimation of nonlinear errors-in-variables models." *Annals of Statistics*, **10**(2), 539–548.

Wu, C. F. (1981), "Asymptotic theory of nonlinear least squares estimation." *Annals of Statistics*, **9**, 501–513.

NONLINEAR LEAST SQUARES—COMPUTING

Barham, R. H., and W. Drane (1972), "An algorithm for least squares estimation of nonlinear parameters when some of the parameters are linear." *Technometrics*, **14**, 757–766.

Bates, Douglas M., and Mary J. Lindstrom (1986), "Nonlinear least squares with conditionally linear parameters," in *Proceedings of the Statistical Computing Section*. New York: American Statistical Association.

Bates, D. M., and D. G. Watts (1981), "A relative offset orthogonality convergence criterion for nonlinear least squares." *Technometrics*, **23**(2), 179–183.

Chambers, J. M. (1973), "Fitting nonlinear models: Numerical techniques." *Biometrika*, **60**, 1–13.

Dennis Jr., J. E., D. M. Gay, and R. E. Welsch (1981), "An adaptive nonlinear least-squares algorithm." *ACM Transactions on Mathematical Software*, **7**, 348–368.

Golub, G. H., and V. Pereyra (1973), "The differentiation of pseudo-inverses and nonlinear least squares problems whose variables separate." *J. SIAM*, **10**, 413–432.

Guttman, I., V. Pereyra, and H. D. Scolnik (1973), "Least squares estimation for a class of non-linear models." *Technometrics*, **15**(2), 209–218.

Hartley, H. O. (1961), "The modified Gauss–Newton method for the fitting of non-linear regression functions by least squares." *Technometrics*, **3**, 269–280.

Harville, D. A. (1973), "Fitting partially linear models by weighted least squares." *Technometrics*, **15**(3), 509–515.

Hiebert, K. L. (1981), "An evaluation of mathematical software that solves the nonlinear least squares problem." *ACM Transactions on Mathematical Software*, **7**(1), 1–16.

Jennrich, R. I., and P. B. Bright (1976), "Fitting systems of linear differential equations using computer generated exact derivatives (with discussion)." *Technometrics*, **18**(4), 385–399.

Jennrich, R. I., and P. F. Sampson (1968), "An application of stepwise regression to nonlinear estimation." *Technometrics*, **10**(1), 63–72.

Lawton, W. H., and E. A. Sylvestre (1971), "Elimination of linear parameters in nonlinear regression." *Technometrics*, **13**, 461–467.

Levenberg, K. (1944), "A method for the solution of certain nonlinear problems in least squares." *Quarterly of Applied Mathematics*, **2**, 164–168.

Marquardt, D. W. (1963), "An algorithm for the estimation of non-linear parameters." *J. SIAM*, **11**, 431–441.

Marquardt, D. W. (1970), "Generalized inverses, ridge regression, biased linear estimation, and nonlinear estimation." *Technometrics*, **12**, 591.

Meyer, R. R., and P. M. Roth (1972), "Modified damped least squares." *Journal of the Institute of Mathematics and Its Applications*, **9**, 218.

Pedersen, P. V. (1977), "Curve fitting and modeling in pharmacokinetics and some practical experiences with NONLIN and a new program FUNFIT." *Journal of Pharmacokinetics and Biopharmaceutics*, **5**, 513.

Pedersen, P. V. (1978), "Curve fitting and modeling in pharmacokinetics: A reply from the author." *Journal of Pharmacokinetics and Biopharmaceutics*, **6**, 447.

Peduzzi, P. N., R. J. Hardy, and T. R. Holford (1980), "A stepwise variable selection procedure for nonlinear regression models." *Biometrics*, **36**, 511–516. (See also **37**, 595–596.)

Ralston, M. L., and R. I. Jennrich (1978), "DUD, a derivative-free algorithm for nonlinear least squares." *Technometrics*, **20**, 7–14.

SELF-MODELING

Armstrong, P. W., D. G. Watts, D. C. Hamilton, M. A. Chiong, and J. O. Parker (1979), "Quantification of myocardial infarction: Template model for serial creatine kinase analysis." *Circulation*, **60**(4), 856–865.

Graham, B. V. (1976), "Wavelength discrimination derived from color naming." *Vision Research*, **16**, 559–562.

Guardabasso, V., P. J. Munson, and D. Rodbard (1988), "A versatile method for simultaneous analysis of families of curves." *FASEB Journal*, **2**, 209–215.

Guardabasso, V., D. Rodbard, and P. J. Munson (1987), "A model-free approach to estimation of relative potency in dose-response curve analysis." *American Journal of Physiology*, **252**, E357–E364.

Lawton, W. H., E. A. Sylvestre, and M. S. Maggio (1972), "Self modeling nonlinear regression." *Technometrics*, **14**(3), 513–532.

Levine, H. D., A. L. Rosen, R. DeWoskin, and G. S. Moss (1977), "Application of self-modeling nonlinear regression to ventricular pressure data." *Computers in Biomedical Research*, **10**, 363–372.

Reeves, R. L., R. S. Kain, M. S. Maggio, E. A. Sylvestre, and W. H. Lawton (1973), "Analysis of the visual spectrum of methyl orange in solvents and in hydrophobic binding sites." *Canadian Journal of Chemistry*, **96**, 628–635.

Reeves, R. L., M. S. Maggio, and L. F. Costa (1974), "Importance of solvent cohesion and structure in solvent effects on binding site probes." *Journal of the American Chemical Society*, **96**, 5971–5925.

SPECIAL MODEL FORMS

Allen, D. M. (1983), "Parameter estimation for nonlinear models with emphasis on compartmental models." *Biometrics*, **39**(3), 629–637.

Bates, Douglas M., Dennis A. Wolf, and Donald G. Watts (1985), "Nonlinear least squares and first-order kinetics," in David Allen, Ed., *Proceedings of Computer Science and Statistics: Seventeenth Symposium on the Interface*. New York: North-Holland.

Bliss, C. I., and A. T. James (1966), "Fitting the rectangular hyperbola." *Biometrics*, **22**, 573–602.

Currie, D. (1982), "Estimating Michaelis–Menten parameters: Bias, variance, and experimental design." *Biometrics*, **38**(4), 907–919.

Jennrich, R. I., and P. B. Bright (1976), "Fitting systems of linear differential equations using computer generated exact derivatives (with discussion)." *Technometrics*, **18**(4), 385–399.

Kittrell, J. R. (1970), "Mathematical modelling of chemical reactions." *Advances in Chemical Engineering*, **8**, 97–183.

Kittrell, J. R., W. G. Hunter, and C. C. Watson (1965), "Nonlinear least squares analysis of catalytic rate models." *American Institute of Chemical Engineers Journal*, **11**, 1051–1057.

Mezaki, R., N. R. Draper, and R. A. Johnson (1973), "On the violation of assumptions in nonlinear least squares by interchange of response and predictor variables." *Industrial and Engineering Chemistry Fundamentals*, **12**, 251–254.

Mezaki, R., and J. R. Kittrell (1968), "Nonlinear least squares for model screening." *American Institute of Chemical Engineers Journal*, **14**, 513.

Peterson, T. I., and L. Lapidus (1966), "Nonlinear estimation analysis of the kinetics of catalytic ethanol dehydrogenation." *Chemical Engineering Science*, **21**, 655–664.

Reilly, P. M., and H. Patino-Leal (1981), "A Bayesian study of the errors-in-variables model." *Technometrics*, **23**, 221–231.

MULTIRESPONSE MODELS

Bates, D. M., and D. G. Watts (1984), "A multi-response Gauss–Newton algorithm." *Communications in Statistics—Simulation and Computation*, **13**(5), 705–715.

Bates, Douglas M., and Donald G. Watts (1985), "Multiresponse estimation with special application to systems of linear differential equations (with discussion)." *Technometrics*, **27**(4), 329–360.

Bates, Douglas M., and Donald G. Watts (1987), "A generalized Gauss–Newton procedure for multi-response parameter estimation." *SIAM Journal of Scientific and Statistical Computing*, **7**(1), 49–55.

Box, G. E. P., and N. R. Draper (1965), "The Bayesian estimation of common parameters from several responses." *Biometrika*, **52**, 355–365.

Box, G. E. P., W. G. Hunter, J. F. MacGregor, and J. Erjavec (1973), "Some problems associated with the analysis of multiresponse models." *Technometrics*, **15**(1), 33–51.

Box, M. J., and N. R. Draper (1972), "Estimation and design criteria for multiresponse nonlinear models with non-homogeneous variance." *Applied Statistics*, **21**, 13–24.

Box, M. J., N. R. Draper, and W. G. Hunter (1970), "Missing values in multi-response nonlinear data fitting." *Technometrics*, **12**, 613–620.

Draper, N. R., H. Kanemasu, and R. Mezaki (1969), "Estimating rate constants." *Industrial and Engineering Chemistry Fundamentals*, **8**, 423–427.

Hunter, W. G. (1967), "Estimation of unknown constants from multi-response data." *Industrial and Engineering Chemistry Fundamentals*, **8**, 423–427.

McLean, D. D., D. J. Pritchard, D. W. Bacon, and J. Downie (1979), "Singularities in multiresponse modelling." *Technometrics*, **21**(3), 291–298.

Mezaki, R., and J. B. Butt (1968), "Estimation of rate constants from multiresponse kinetic data." *Industrial and Engineering Chemistry Fundamentals*, **7**, 120–125.

Stewart, W. E., and J. P. Sorensen (1981), "Bayesian estimation of common parameters from multiresponse data with missing observations." *Technometrics*, **23**, 131–141.

Ziegel, E. R., and J. W. Gorman (1980), "Kinetic modelling with multiresponse data." *Technometrics*, **22**(2), 139–151.

EXPERIMENTAL DESIGN—PRECISE PARAMETER ESTIMATION

Atkinson, A. C., and W. G. Hunter (1968), "The design of experiments for parameter estimation." *Technometrics*, **10**(2), 271–289.

Bates, Douglas M. (1983), "The derivative of $|X'X|$ and its uses." *Technometrics*, **25**(4), 373–376.

Box, George E. P. (1984), "The importance of practice in the development of statistics." *Technometrics*, **26**(1), 1–8.

Box, G. E. P., and H. L. Lucas (1959), "Design of experiments in non-linear situations." *Biometrika*, **46**, 77–90.

Box, M. J. (1968), "The occurrence of replications in optimal designs of experiments to estimate parameters in nonlinear models." *Journal of the Royal Statistical Society, Ser. B*, **30**, 290–302.

Box, M. J. (1968), "The use of designed experiments in nonlinear model building," in Donald G. Watts, Ed., *The Future of Statistics*. New York: Academic Press, pp. 241–257.

Box, M. J. (1970), "Some experiences with a nonlinear experimental design criterion." *Technometrics*, **12**(3), 569–589.

Box, M.J. (1971), "An experimental design criterion for precise parameter estimation of a subset of the parameters in a nonlinear model." *Biometrika*, **58**, 149–153.

Box, M. J. (1971), "Simplified experimental design." *Technometrics*, **13**(1), 19–31.

Box, M. J., and N. R. Draper (1971), "Factorial designs, the |X'X| criterion, and some related matters." *Technometrics*, **13**, 731–742.

Chernoff, H. (1953), "Locally optimal designs in estimating parameters." *Annals of Mathematical Statistics*, **24**, 586–602.

Cochran, W. G. (1973), "Experiments for nonlinear functions." *Journal of the American Statistical Association*, **68**, 771–778.

Cox, D. R. (1984), "Design of experiments and regression." *Journal of the Royal Statistical Society, Ser. A*, **147**(2), 306–315.

Currie, D. (1982), "Estimating Michaelis–Menten parameters: Bias, variance, and experimental design." *Biometrics*, **38**(4), 907–919.

Draper, N. R., and W. G. Hunter (1967), "The use of prior distributions in the design of experiments for parameter estimation in nonlinear estimation." *Biometrika*, **54**, 147–153.

Evans, J. W. (1979), "Computer augmentation of experimental designs to maximize |X'X|." *Technometrics*, **21**(3), 321–330.

Graham, R. J., and F. D. Stevenson (1972), "Kinetics of chlorination of niobium oxychloride by phosgene in a tube flow reactor. Application of sequential experimental design." *Industrial and Engineering Chemistry Process Design and Development*, **11**, 160–164.

Hahn, Gerald J. (1984), "Experimental design in the complex world." *Technometrics*, **26**(1), 19–31.

Hamilton, David C., and Donald G. Watts (1985), "A quadratic design criterion for precise estimation in nonlinear regression models." *Technometrics*, **27**(3), 241–250.

Herzberg, A. M., and D. R. Cox (1969), "Recent work on the design of experiments: A bibliography and a review." *Journal of the Royal Statistical Society, Ser. B*, **31**, 29–67.

Hill, P. D. H. (1980), "D-optimal designs for partially nonlinear regression models." *Technometrics*, **22**(2), 275–276.

Hill, W. J., and W. G. Hunter (1974), "Design of experiments for subsets of the parameters." *Technometrics*, **16**, 425–434.

Hill, W. J., W. G. Hunter, and D. W. Wichern (1968), "A joint design criterion for the dual problem of model discrimination and parameter estimation." *Technometrics*, **10**, 145–160.

Hunter, W. G., and A. C. Atkinson (1966), "Statistical designs for pilot plant and laboratory experiments." *Chemical Engineering*, **73**, 159–164.

Hunter, W. G., W. J. Hill, and T. L. Henson (1969), "Designing experiments for precise estimation of all or some of the constants in a mechanistic model." *Canadian Journal of Chemical Engineering*, **47**, 76–80.

Hunter, W. G., J. R. Kittrell, and R. Mezaki (1967), "Experimental strategies for mechanistic models." *Transactions of the Institute of Chemical Engineers*, **45**, T146-T152.

Juusola, J. A., D. W. Bacon, and J. Downie (1972), "Sequential statistical design stategy in an experimental kinetic study." *Canadian Journal of Chemical Engineering*, **50**,

796–801.

Katz, D., and D. Z. D'Argenio (1983), "Experimental design for estimating integrals by numerical quadrature." *Biometrics*, **39**(3), 621–628.

Khuri, A. I. (1984), "A note on D-optimal designs for partially nonlinear regression models." *Technometrics*, **26**(1), 59–61.

Kittrell, J. R., W. G. Hunter, and C. C. Watson (1966), "Obtaining precise parameter estimates for nonlinear catalytic rates." *American Institute of Chemical Engineers Journal*, **12**, 5–10.

Pritchard, D. J., and D. W. Bacon (1977), "Accounting for heteroscedasticity in experimental design." *Technometrics*, **19**(2), 109–115.

Reilly, P. M., R. Bajramovic, G. E. Blau, D. R. Branson, and M. W. Sauerhoff (1977), "Guidelines for the optimal design of experiments to estimate parameters in first order kinetic models." *Canadian Journal of Chemical Engineering*, **55**, 614–622.

St. John, R. C., and N. R. Draper (1975), "D-optimality for regression designs: a review." *Technometrics*, **17**, 15–23.

Steinberg, David M., and William G. Hunter (1984), "Experimental design: Review and comment (with discussion)." *Technometrics*, **26**(2), 71–130.

EXPERIMENTAL DESIGN—MODEL DISCRIMINATION

Atkinson, A. C. (1981), "A comparison of two criteria for the design of experiments for discriminating between models." *Technometrics*, **23**, 301–305.

Atkinson, A. C., and D. R. Cox (1974), "Planning experiments for discriminating between models (with discussion)." *Journal of the Royal Statistical Society, Ser. B*, **36**, 321–348.

Atkinson, A. C., and V. V. Fedorov (1975), "The design of experiments for discriminating between two rival models." *Biometrika*, **62**(1), 57–70.

Atkinson, A. C., and V. V. Fedorov (1975), "Optimal design: Experiments for discriminating between several models." *Biometrika*, **62**(2), 289–304.

Box, G. E. P., and W. J. Hill (1967), "Discrimination among mechanistic models." *Technometrics*, **9**(1), 57–71.

Froment, G. F., and R. Mezaki (1970), "Sequential discrimination and estimation procedures for rate modeling in heterogeneous catalysis." *Chemical Engineering Science*, **25**, 293–301.

Hill, P. D. H. (1978), "A review of experimental design procedures for regression model discrimination." *Technometrics*, **20**(1), 15–21.

Hill, W. J., and W. G. Hunter (1969), "A note on designs for model discrimination: Variance unknown case." *Technometrics*, **11**, 396–400.

Hill, W. J., W. G. Hunter, and D. W. Wichern (1968), "A joint design criterion for the dual problem of model discrimination and parameter estimation." *Technometrics*, **10**, 145–160.

Hunter, W. G., and A. M. Reiner (1965), "Designs for discriminating between two rival models." *Technometrics*, **7**, 307–323.

Kittrell, J. R., and R. Mezaki (1967), "Discrimination among rival Hougen–Watson models through intrinsic parameters." *American Institute of Chemical Engineers Journal*, **13**(2), 389–392.

Moeter, D., W. Pirie, and W. Blot (1970), "A comparison of two model discrimination criteria." *Technometrics*, **12**, 457–470.

Pritchard, D. J., and D. W. Bacon (1974), "Potential pitfalls in model discrimination." *Canadian Journal of Chemical Engineering*, **52**, 103–109.

Reilly, P. M. (1970), "Statistical methods in model discrimination." *Canadian Journal of Chemical Engineering*, **48**, 168–173.

EXPERIMENTAL DESIGN — MULTIRESPONSE MODELS

Box, M. J., and N. R. Draper (1972), "Estimation and design criteria for multiresponse nonlinear models with non-homogeneous variance." *Applied Statistics*, **21**, 13–24.
Draper, N. R., and W. G. Hunter (1966), "Design of experiments for parameter estimation in multiresponse situations." *Biometrika*, **53**, 525–553.
Draper, N. R., and W. G. Hunter (1967), "The use of prior distributions in the design of experiments for parameter estimation in nonlinear situations: Multi-response case." *Biometrika*, **54**, 662–665.

HETEROSCEDASTICITY

Box, G. E. P., and W. J. Hill (1974), "Correcting inhomogeneity of variance with power transformation weighting." *Technometrics*, **16**, 385–389.
Box, M. J., and N. R. Draper (1972), "Estimation and design criteria for multiresponse nonlinear models with non-homogeneous variance." *Applied Statistics*, **21**, 13–24.
Carroll, Raymond J., and David Ruppert (1984), "Power transformation when fitting theoretical models to data." *Journal of the American Statistical Association*, **79**(386), 321–328.
Pritchard, D. J., and D. W. Bacon (1977), "Accounting for heteroscedasticity in experimental design." *Technometrics*, **19**(2), 109–115.
Pritchard, D. J., J. Downie, and D. W. Bacon (1977), "Further considerations of heteroscedasticity in fitting kinetic models." *Technometrics*, **19**(3), 227–236.

DIAGNOSTIC PARAMETERS

Box, G. E. P., and W. G. Hunter (1962), "A useful method of model building." *Technometrics*, **4**, 301–318.
Hunter, W. G., and R. Mezaki (1964), "A model building technique for chemical engineering kinetics." *American Institute of Chemical Engineers Journal*, **10**, 315–322.
Kittrell, J. R., W. G. Hunter, and R. Mezaki (1966), "The use of diagnostic parameters for kinetic model building." *American Institute of Chemical Engineers Journal*, **12**(5), 1014–1017.

APPLICATIONS

Bacon, D. W. (1970), "Making the most of a one-shot experiment." *Industrial and Engineering Chemistry*, **62**(7), 27–34.
Behnken, D. W. (1964), "Estimation of copolymer reactivity ratios: an example of nonlinear estimation." *Journal of Polymer Science Part A*, **2**, 645–668.
Bliss, C. I., and A. T. James (1966), "Fitting the rectangular hyperbola." *Biometrics*, **22**, 573–602.
Boag, I. F., D. W. Bacon, and J. Downie (1975), "Analysis of the reaction network for the vanadium-catalyzed oxidation of ortho-xylene." *Journal of Catalysis*, **38**, 375–384.

Currie, D. (1982), "Estimating Michaelis–Menten parameters: Bias, variance, and experimental design." *Biometrics*, **38**(4), 907–919.

Draper, N. R., H. Kanemasu, and R. Mezaki (1969), "Estimating rate constants." *Industrial and Engineering Chemistry Fundamentals*, **8**, 423–427.

Fisher, R. A. (1939), "The sampling distribution of some statistics obtained from nonlinear equations." *Annals of Eugenics*, **9**, 238–249.

Froment, G. F., and R. Mezaki (1970), "Sequential discrimination and estimation procedures for rate modeling in heterogeneous catalysis." *Chemical Engineering Science*, **25**, 293–301.

Gallant, A. R., and A. Holly (1980), "Statistical inference in an implicit, nonlinear, simultaneous equation model in the context of maximum likelihood estimation." *Econometrica*, **48**, 697–720.

Graham, R. J., and F. D. Stevenson (1972), "Kinetics of chlorination of niobium oxychloride by phosgene in a tube flow reactor. Application of sequential experimental design." *Industrial and Engineering Chemistry Process Design and Development*, **11**, 160–164.

Hoffman, T., and P. M. Reilly (1979), "Transferring information from one experiment to another." *Canadian Journal of Chemical Engineering*, **57**, 367–374.

Hsiang, T., and P. M. Reilly (1971), "A practical method of discriminating among mechanistic models." *Canadian Journal of Chemical Engineering*, **49**, 865–871.

Hunter, W. G. (1967), "Estimation of unknown constants from multi-response data." *Industrial and Engineering Chemistry Fundamentals*, **8**, 423–427.

Hunter, W. G., and A. C. Atkinson (1966), "Statistical designs for pilot plant and laboratory experiments." *Chemical Engineering*, **73**, 159–164.

Hunter, W. G., W. J. Hill, and T. L. Henson (1969), "Designing experiments for precise estimation of all or some of the constants in a mechanistic model." *Canadian Journal of Chemical Engineering*, **47**, 76–80.

Hunter, W. G., J. R. Kittrell, and R. Mezaki (1967), "Experimental strategies for mechanistic models." *Transactions of the Institute of Chemical Engineers*, **45**, T146-T152.

Hunter, W. G., and R. Mezaki (1964), "A model building technique for chemical engineering kinetics." *American Institute of Chemical Engineers Journal*, **10**, 315–322.

Johnson, R. A., N. A. Standal, and R. Mezaki (1968), "Weighted linear plots for discrimination of nonlinear rate models." *Industrial and Engineering Chemistry Fundamentals*, **7**, 181.

Juusola, J. A., D. W. Bacon, and J. Downie (1972), "Sequential statistical design stategy in an experimental kinetic study." *Canadian Journal of Chemical Engineering*, **50**, 796–801.

Kittrell, J. R. (1970), "Mathematical modelling of chemical reactions." *Advances in Chemical Engineering*, **8**, 97–183.

Kittrell, J. R., W. G. Hunter, and R. Mezaki (1966), "The use of diagnostic parameters for kinetic model building." *American Institute of Chemical Engineers Journal*, **12**(5), 1014–1017.

Kittrell, J. R., W. G. Hunter, and C. C. Watson (1965), "Nonlinear least squares analysis of catalytic rate models." *American Institute of Chemical Engineers Journal*, **11**, 1051–1057.

Kittrell, J. R., W. G. Hunter, and C. C. Watson (1966), "Obtaining precise parameter estimates for nonlinear catalytic rates." *American Institute of Chemical Engineers Journal*, **12**, 5–10.

Kittrell, J. R., and R. Mezaki (1967), "Discrimination among rival Hougen-Watson models through intrinsic parameters." *American Institute of Chemical Engineers*

Journal, **13**(2), 389–392.

Kittrell, J. R., R. Mezaki, and C. C. Watson (1965), "Estimation of parameters for nonlinear least squares analysis." *Industrial and Engineering Chemistry*, **57**(12), 18–27.

Kittrell, J. R., R. Mezaki, and C. C. Watson (1966), "Precise determination of reaction orders." *Industrial and Engineering Chemistry*, **58**(5), 50–59.

Kittrell, J. R., R. Mezaki, and C. C. Watson (1966), "Model-building techniques for heterogeneous kinetics." *British Chemical Engineering*, **11**(1), 15–19.

McLean, D. D., D. W. Bacon, and J. Downie (1980), "Statistical identification of a reaction network using an integral plug flow reactor." *Canadian Journal of Chemical Engineering*, **58**, 608–619.

Mezaki, R., and J. B. Butt (1968), "Estimation of rate constants from multiresponse kinetic data." *Industrial and Engineering Chemistry Fundamentals*, **7**, 120–125.

Mezaki, R., N. R. Draper, and R. A. Johnson (1973), "On the violation of assumptions in nonlinear least squares by interchange of response and predictor variables." *Industrial and Engineering Chemistry Fundamentals*, **12**, 251–254.

Mezaki, R., and J. R. Kittrell (1966), "Discrimination between rival models through nonintrinsic parameters." *Canadian Journal of Chemical Engineering*, **44**, 285.

Mezaki, R., and J. R. Kittrell (1967), "Parametric sensitivity in fitting nonlinear kinetic models." *Industrial and Engineering Chemistry*, **59**(5), 63–69.

Mezaki, R., and J. R. Kittrell (1968), "Nonlinear least squares for model screening." *American Institute of Chemical Engineers Journal*, **14**, 513.

Mezaki, R., J. R. Kittrell, and W. J. Hill (1967), "An analysis of kinetic power function models." *Industrial and Engineering Chemistry*, **59**(1), 93–95.

Peterson, T. I., and L. Lapidus (1966), "Nonlinear estimation analysis of the kinetics of catalytic ethanol dehydrogenation." *Chemical Engineering Science*, **21**, 655–664.

Podolski, W. F., and Y. G. Kim (1974), "Modelling the water-gas shift reaction." *Industrial and Engineering Chemistry Process Design and Development*, **13**, 415–421.

Pritchard, D. J., and D. W. Bacon (1974), "Potential pitfalls in model discrimination." *Canadian Journal of Chemical Engineering*, **52**, 103–109.

Pritchard, D. J., and D. W. Bacon (1975), "Statistical assessment of chemical kinetic models." *Chemical Engineering Science*, **30**, 567–574.

Pritchard, D. J., D. D. McLean, D. W. Bacon, and J. Downie (1980), "Testing the assumption of surface homogeneity in modelling catalytic reactions." *Journal of Catalysis*, **61**, 430–434.

Reilly, P. M. (1970), "Statistical methods in model discrimination." *Canadian Journal of Chemical Engineering*, **48**, 168–173.

Reilly, P. M., R. Bajramovic, G. E. Blau, D. R. Branson, and M. W. Sauerhoff (1977), "Guidelines for the optimal design of experiments to estimate parameters in first order kinetic models." *Canadian Journal of Chemical Engineering*, **55**, 614–622.

Reilly, P. M., and G. E. Blau (1974), "The use of statistical methods to build mathematical models of chemical reacting systems." *Canadian Journal of Chemical Engineering*, **52**, 289–299.

Sutton, T. L., and J. F. MacGregor (1977), "The analysis and design of vapour-liquid equilibrium experiments." *Canadian Journal of Chemical Engineering*, **55**, 602–608.

Author Index

Subject Index